J2EE Applications and BEA WebLogic Server

MICHAEL GIRDLEY
ROB WOOLLEN
SANDRA L. EMERSON

PH
PTR

Prentice Hall PTR, Upper Saddle River, NJ   07458
www.phptr.com

Editorial/Production Supervision: *Kathleen M. Caren*
Acquisitions Editor: *Greg Doench*
Editorial Assistant: *Brandt Kenna*
Marketing Manager: *Debby van Dijk*
Manufacturing Manager: *Alexis R. Heydt*
Cover Design: *Talar Agasyan*
Cover Design Direction: *Jerry Votta*
Art Director: *Gail Cocker-Bogusz*

Printed in the United States of America

10 9 8 7 6 5 4 3 2 1

ISBN 0-13-091111-9

Pearson Education LTD.
Pearson Education Australia PTY, Limited
Pearson Education Singapore, Pte. Ltd.
Pearson Education North Asia, Ltd.
Pearson Education Canada, Ltd.
Pearson Educación Mexico, S.A. de C.V.
Pearson Education—Japan
Pearson Education Malaysia, Pte. Ltd.
Pearson Education, Upper Saddle River, New Jersey

Contents

Foreword . . . . **xix**

Preface . . . .**xxiii**

1   Introduction **1**

What Is BEA WebLogic Server?   *1*

WebLogic Server Overview   *2*

    The Container-Component Model   *3*

    WebLogic Server Strengths: Component Support and Scalability   *4*

How to Use this Book   *5*

    Road Map   *6*

    Chapter Summaries   *7*

System Requirements   *9*

    Supported Platforms   *9*

    Software on the CD-ROM   *9*

    Versions Supported   *10*

    Conventions   *10*

2   Overview of J2EE Technologies **12**

WebLogic Server and J2EE   *13*

J2EE Technologies Covered in this Book   *13*

Presentation Logic   *14*

    Java Servlets   *14*

    JavaServer Pages (JSPs)   *15*

    WebLogic Server JavaBeans and Tag Libraries   *16*

Database and Transaction Support   16

Java Database Connectivity (JDBC)   16

Java Transaction API (JTA) Support   17

Object Registry and Remote Method Invocation (RMI)   18

Java Naming and Directory Interface (JNDI)   18

Remote Method Invocation (RMI)   18

Enterprise JavaBeans (EJBs)   19

WebLogic Server Entity EJBs   19

WebLogic Server Session EJBs   20

WebLogic Server Message-Driven Beans   21

Java Message Service (JMS)   21

JavaMail   22

Security   22

WebLogic Server's Distributed Deployment Support   22

About WebAuction   23

WebAuction Application Technology Requirements   23

3   Building Presentation Logic with WebLogic Server Servlets . . . 26

Introducing WebLogic Server Servlets   28

WebLogic Server Servlets Handle HTTP Requests   28

Generic Servlets   29

How Servlets Are Used   29

WebLogic Server JavaServer Pages (JSPs)   29

Servlets or JSPs?   30

Developing Servlets   31

Anatomy of a Servlet   31

A Basic Servlet   32

About the Packaging and Deployment Process   41

About Web Applications (.war Files)   41

The Lifecycle of a Servlet   42

Handling Basic Servlet Requests   44

Generating the Servlet Response   49

Using Default Methods to Handle Web Forms   51

Servlets and Web Sessions   60

    Conventional Methods for Session Tracking Are Difficult   60

    The Servlet Specification to the Rescue   61

    The Scope of a Session   64

    Sessions and Servlets Example   66

    Baking Your Own Cookies   71

    Dealing with Users   72

    Creating a Cookie   72

    URL Rewriting   74

    Custom Cookies for Personalization   76

    Long-Term CookieServlet Example   78

The Web Application Package   84

    About Web Applications   84

    Web Application Overview   85

    Web Archive Organization   85

Using Servlets with WebLogic Server Clustering   101

    Persisting Session Information   101

    Session Protection Performance Implications   102

    Choosing the Right Level of Protection   103

    Special Considerations for In-Memory Replication   103

Best Practices for Servlets   104

    Be Smart About Session State   104

    Don't Close/Terminate the Response Stream   104

    Always Activate URL Rewriting   105

    Session Objects Are Not Appropriate for Long-Term Data   105

    Keep Scalability in Mind   105

4   Using WebLogic Server JavaServer Pages. 106

About WebLogic Server JSPs   107

    Why JSP?   108

    Integrating Java Code with JSP   108

JSP Basics   110

    Anatomy of a JSP   111

A Basic JSP Example   111

Running the Basic JSP Example in WebLogic Server   112

The Lifecycle of a JSP   113

Initialization   114

Loading and Instantiation   114

End of Service   115

JSP Page Elements   115

JSP Directives   115

Page Directives   116

Implicit Objects and Scripting Elements   122

Actions   129

Using Java Beans with JSPs   134

JSP Tags for Using Beans   135

Building a JavaBean into a JSP   136

Using JavaBean Properties   148

Custom Tag Libraries   152

Using Custom Tag Libraries in JSP   153

Error Pages, Comments, and Deployment Descriptors   159

JSP Error Page   159

JSP Comments   160

JSP Deployment Descriptor Options   160

Using Servlets and JSPs Together: Model View Controller   161

MVC Components   161

MVC in Web Applications   162

MVC Applicability   162

Best Practices for Debugging and Developing JSPs   163

Create Scripts to Take Advantage of Automatic Deployment   163

Base Your Development on Templates   163

Be Careful About Capitalization and Spacing   163

Turn on the Debugging Messages Using the Console   164

Best Practices for JSPs   164

Keep in Mind that JSPs Are Just Specialized Servlets   164

Encapsulate Complex Data and Logic in JavaBeans and
Custom Tag Libraries   164

Always Activate and Use URL Rewriting   164

Use JSP Error Pages   165

JSPs in the WebAuction Application   165

browseitems.jsp   165

ItemBean JavaBean   167

Browsing the WebAuction Code   170

5   Using Databases and Transactions with JDBC and JTA 172

WebLogic Server JDBC   173

Why JDBC?   174

JDBC Drivers   174

Using JDBC to Read Data   180

Using JDBC to Update the Database   198

Transactions   205

Using the JTA Driver   208

WebLogic Server Multi-Database Transaction Services: JTA, XA, and
2PC   208

Complete WebLogic Server JTA Example   212

WebLogic Server and Distributed Transactions   218

Distributed Transactions and Standards   219

Using XA-Compliant Resources and JTA   219

Transaction Isolation Levels   220

Prepared Statements   222

Error Handling and SQL Warnings   224

Handling SQLException Errors   224

Handling SQL Warnings   225

Metadata   226

Using Metadata   226

Advanced Features   228

BLOBs and CLOBs   228

Best Practices for JDBC   231

Make Your Queries as Smart as Possible *231*

Tune the Database *231*

Put Initialization Code in init() *232*

Get Your JDBC Connection from a TxDataSource or the JTS Driver *232*

Use Batch Updates *232*

Do In-Place Updates Where Possible *232*

Use the Appropriate Method to Get a JDBC Connection Object *233*

Release the JDBC Resources Appropriately *233*

Use Autocommit Appropriately *233*

Don't Hang onto JDBC Connections *233*

Work in the Database If You Can *234*

Commit or Roll Back Your Transactions as Soon as Possible *234*

Set Your Pool Size Appropriately *234*

Do Not Have Your Transactions Span User Input *235*

JDBC and Transactions in the WebAuction Application *235*

6   Remote Method Invocation and Distributed Naming 236

Remote Method Invocation *237*

Using the Remote Interface *238*

The RMI Programming Model *239*

Serialization *240*

The Serializable Interface *240*

The Remote Interface *241*

Hand-Coding Serialization *242*

Using RMI in Distributed Applications *243*

Handling the Unreliable Network *244*

Performance Implications of Cross-Network Method Calls *245*

WebLogic RMI Optimizations *246*

JNDI: Java's Naming Service *246*

Using JNDI *247*

JNDI, Security, and Identity *250*

JNDI and Clustering *250*

Replicated Naming Service *251*

Understanding Conflicts in the JNDI tree   252

Clustered JNDI with Replicated Bindings   253

Clustered JNDI with Nonreplicated Bindings   253

JNDI Best Practices   254

Local Caching   254

Using JNDI Effectively to Increase Performance   254

Minimizing Frequency of Updates   255

Conclusion   256

7   Enterprise Messaging with the Java Message Service (JMS) . . . 258

Benefits of JMS   259

Interprocess Communication   260

JMS Fundamentals   261

Connection Factories   261

Sample JMS Queue Producer/Consumer   263

Configuring JMS   263

Sample JMS Queue Producer/Consumer   265

Running the Queue Example   268

Sample JMS Topic Producer/Consumer   270

Message Producer   270

Synchronous Message Consumer   271

Asynchronous Message Consumer   271

Running the Topic Example   272

JMS Messages   274

JMS Header   275

Message Properties   278

Message Types   278

JMS Message Types   278

Reusing Message Objects   279

JMS Delivery Modes   279

Synchronous vs. Asynchronous Receivers   280

Message Selectors   282

Durable JMS Subscriptions   282

Using Temporary Destinations   *284*

Message Acknowledgment   *285*

Which Acknowledgment Mode Is Right for Your Application?   *286*

JMS and Transactions   *287*

Using Transacted Sessions   *287*

Using JTA Transactions with JMS   *288*

Clustering JMS   *289*

Exception Listeners   *291*

Using Multicast JMS   *292*

Configuration Changes for Multicast JMS   *293*

Using Multicast JMS Sessions   *294*

JMS Best Practices   *295*

Avoid Unneeded Features   *295*

Selection Performance Costs   *295*

Using Asynchronous Message Consumers Where Possible   *296*

Prefer JTA Transactions to Transacted Sessions   *296*

JMS Transactions and Error Handling   *297*

Conclusion   *298*

8   Using Session Enterprise JavaBeans **300**

Enterprise JavaBeans Overview   *301*

Basics of EJBs   *301*

Session Beans   *302*

Entity Beans   *302*

Message-Driven Beans   *303*

Stateless Session EJB Example: HelloWorld   *303*

Building the EJB Jar File   *307*

Writing a Simple EJB Client   *309*

The EJB Container   *310*

Stateless Session EJBs   *312*

Stateless Programming Model   *313*

Stateless Session Bean Clustering   *315*

Using Member Variables with Stateless Session Beans   *317*

Stateful Session EJBs   *318*

    The Stateful Programming Model   *318*

    Stateful Session EJB Lifecycle   *319*

    Stateful Session EJBs and Clustering   *322*

    Stateful Session Beans and Concurrency   *325*

Using Transactions with Session Beans   *326*

    Container-Managed Transactions   *327*

    Bean-Managed Transactions   *330*

EJB Security   *331*

    Assigning Security Roles in the EJB Deployment Descriptors   *331*

    Using Programmatic Security with EJBs   *333*

EJB Environment   *335*

    Declaring Environment Variables   *335*

EJB References   *336*

    Declaring EJB References   *337*

Resource Manager References   *338*

    Declaring Resource Manager References   *338*

    Resource Reference Advantages   *339*

Handles   *340*

    HomeHandles   *341*

Cars Example   *342*

    Running the Example   *343*

Best Practices   *354*

    Coding Business Interfaces   *354*

    Tips for Transactions   *356*

    When Not to Use Stateful Session Beans   *359*

    Best Practices for EJB Security   *360*

Conclusion   *361*

9   Entity EJBs **362**

Rationale for Entity EJBs   *363*

Entity Bean Basics   *364*

    Entity Bean Components   *364*

Activation and Passivation   *367*

Home Methods and Business Methods   *367*

CMP Entity Bean Example   *367*

Container-Managed Fields   *368*

Student CMP Example   *369*

CMP   *374*

ejbCreate   *374*

ejbRemove   *374*

ejbLoad   *374*

ejbStore   *374*

Finders   *375*

ejbPostCreate   *375*

Container-Managed Entity Bean Lifecycle   *375*

Anonymous Instances   *375*

Identified Instances   *376*

Reading and Writing the Database   *376*

Introduction to CMRs   *377*

Unidirectional and Bidirectional Relationships   *377*

CMR Example   *378*

Creating the Database Tables   *384*

Mapping CMP Entity Beans to the Database   *384*

Running the Example   *386*

Writing EJB-QL for CMP Finders   *389*

CMR Programming Restrictions   *392*

BMP Entity Beans   *393*

Writing the Student BMP Entity EJB   *394*

Writing the BMP Bean Class   *395*

Best Practices for BMP Entity EJBs   *408*

Advanced Topics for Writing Entity EJBs   *408*

How to Write a Primary Key Class   *408*

Implementing hashCode   *410*

Implementing equals   *410*

Entity Bean Inheritance and Polymorphism   *411*

    Inheritance Restrictions   *411*

    Design Patterns for Inheritance and Polymorphism   *412*

Entity Beans and Locking   *415*

    Database Concurrency   *415*

    EJB Container Concurrency   *415*

    Choosing a Database Concurrency Strategy   *416*

    Optimizing Data Access Calls   *417*

    Optimizing CMP Entity Beans   *419*

Using Read-Only Entity Beans   *420*

    Designing Read-Mostly Entity Beans   *421*

Session Beans as a Wrapper for Entity Beans   *422*

Using Java Beans as Value Objects   *423*

BMP vs. CMP   *424*

    CMP Design Advantages   *425*

    CMP Performance Advantages   *425*

    Combining CMP and BMP   *426*

    Stateless Session Beans vs. Entity EJBs   *427*

Conclusion   *428*

10   Using Message-Driven EJBs 430

Message-Driven EJB Basics   *432*

    Message-Driven EJB Lifecycle   *432*

Message-Driven EJB Example   *433*

    MessagePrinterBean Class   *433*

    Writing Deployment Descriptors for Message-Driven EJBs   *434*

Message-Driven Beans and Concurrency   *438*

    Parallel Message Dispatch   *438*

    Setting max-beans-in-freepool for
       Message-Driven EJBs   *439*

    Message Ordering   *439*

Specifying a JMS Connection Factory   *439*

Using Transactions with Message-Driven Beans   *440*

Required Transaction Attribute   *440*

NotSupported Transaction Attribute   *440*

Bean-Managed Transactions   *441*

Error Handling with the Required Transaction Attribute   *441*

Message Acknowledgment   *442*

New Customer Example   *443*

Building and Running the Example   *447*

Message-Driven EJB Advantages   *448*

Using JTA Transactions with an Asynchronous Consumer   *448*

Parallel Message Processing   *448*

Simple and Standards-Based   *449*

Conclusion   *449*

11   Interfacing with Internet Mail Using WebLogic Server JavaMail 450

About Email   *451*

About Simple Mail Transport Protocol (SMTP)   *452*

Mail Retrieval Protocols (POP3, IMAP)   *452*

About JavaMail   *452*

The Session Class   *453*

The Message Class   *453*

The Transport Class   *456*

Mapping to Internet Addresses   *456*

Using JavaMail to Send Simple Email   *457*

Deploying MailSender.jsp   *460*

Adding Email Capability to the WebAuction Application   *463*

Where to Find More Information on JavaMail and Internet Mail   *464*

JavaMail Best Practices   *464*

Using JavaMail to Confirm Email Addresses   *464*

12   Developing Security with WebLogic Server JNDI and JAAS . . 466

Security Technology Overview   *468*

Users and Groups   *468*

Roles and Principals   *468*

J2EE Security Programming Models   *469*

Authentication   *469*

Secure Sockets Layer (SSL)   *472*

Authorization   *472*

WebLogic Server Security Realms   *473*

Creating Secure Web Applications   *474*

Declarative Security in Web Applications   *475*

Developing Form-Based Authentication   *476*

Programming to the Caching Realm in Web Applications   *493*

The Realm API   *494*

Getting an Instance of the Realm   *494*

Adding and Retrieving Users in the Realm   *494*

Adding a User to a Group   *495*

Adding and Removing Groups   *495*

NewUser.jsp Example   *495*

Deploying a Realm API Authentication Example Using the RDBMS
Realm   *499*

Developing Browser-Based Authentication   *506*

Specifying Deployment Descriptor Web Authorization Methods   *506*

Programmatic Security in Web Applications   *509*

Programmatic Security API   *509*

Programmatic Security Example   *510*

Developing Secure Application Clients   *511*

Why Two Security Services?   *511*

WebLogic Server JAAS Authentication   *512*

Using JAAS for Application Client Security   *512*

Writing JAAS Authentication Code   *512*

Using WebLogic Server JAAS Authentication   *513*

JAAS-Secured Application Client: Implementation Notes   *515*

Using WebLogic Server JNDI for Application Client Security   *517*

WebLogic Server JNDI-Based Authentication   *518*

Example: Secure Application Client Using EJB   *520*

weblogic-ejb-jar.xml   *522*

SecureBean.java   *522*

Deploying the Secured EJB Client   *524*

About WebLogic SSL   *526*

Symmetric Key Encryption   *526*

Digital Certificates   *527*

Certificate Authorities   *528*

Notes on SSL Encryption   *529*

WebLogic Server SSL Usage Scenarios   *530*

Web Clients: Using SSL Security   *531*

SSL Security Example   *531*

Application Clients: Using SSL Security   *536*

WebLogic Server Security Best Practices   *537*

Putting It All Together   *538*

Securing the WebAuction Application   *540*

13   Designing the Production Deployment **542**

Designing for Deployment   *544*

WebLogic Deployment Scenarios: Case Studies   *544*

Types of Client Software   *545*

Web Deployments: A Standard Configuration   *545*

Web Deployment Scenario #1: Commercial Web Server   *546*

Scenario #2: Using WebLogic Server as the Web Server   *547*

Using a DMZ and Firewalls in a Web Deployment   *548*

Firewalls   *549*

Integrating Web Deployments with Data Stores   *550*

Using WebLogic Server Clustering in a Web Deployment   *550*

Configuring Hardware for a Clustered Web Deployment   *551*

Clustering on a Multi-CPU Server   *553*

Hardware Specifics for Clustering   *554*

Web Application Deployment Details   *558*

Co-located Front- and Back-End Services   *558*

Web Services in the DMZ; EJB Outside   *559*

Using WebLogic Server as the Web Server   *559*

Application Deployments   *560*

Typical Application Deployment Architecture   *560*

Security Considerations in an Application Deployment   *561*

Recommended Application Deployment Architecture   *562*

Mixed Deployments   *562*

Simple Mixed Deployment Architectures   *562*

Using WebLogic Server Clustering in a Mixed Deployment   *563*

Security Considerations in a Mixed Deployment   *563*

Recommended Mixed Deployment Architecture   *564*

Application Deployment Process   *565*

Infrastructure Components in Application Deployment   *565*

Stages in Application Deployment   *567*

Best Practices for Deploying WebLogic Server   *571*

Design for Security   *571*

Test and Stage Your Application   *572*

Don't Get Too Creative   *572*

Minimize the Number of Moving Parts   *573*

14   The WebAuction Application **574**

Application Architecture and Design: WebAuction   *575*

WebAuction Design Goals   *576*

WebAuction Subsystems   *576*

WebAuction Interfaces   *577*

Separating the Web and Business Logic Tiers   *578*

Accessing Server-Side Business Logic from JSP Pages   *578*

JavaBeans in the Presentation Layer   *579*

The Tag Library-to-Business Logic Interface   *579*

Utility Methods   *581*

WebAuction Security   *582*

Authenticating Users   *583*

Creating New User Accounts   *584*

Business Logic Design   *585*

WebAuction Stateless Session Bean   *586*

Transaction Flow   *587*

Entity Bean Relationships   *588*

Changes Required for a Production Application   *588*

Limiting Query Results   *589*

Unique ID Generation   *589*

Internationalizing WebAuction   *590*

Database Tuning   *590*

Assembling the Application Components: WebAuction   *591*

About Enterprise Archives   *591*

Enterprise Archive Organization   *591*

Writing application.xml   *592*

Packaging the Enterprise Archive (.ear)   *593*

Quick Deployment of the WebAuction Application   *596*

Deploying the WebAuction Application: In Detail   *599*

Deploying the WebAuction on Another Database   *621*

Testing the WebAuction Application   *624*

Functional Testing   *625*

Stress and Performance Testing   *631*

Understanding ExecuteThreads   *639*

15   Capacity Planning for the WebLogic Server 648

Analysis of Capacity Planning   *649*

Factors Affecting Capacity   *650*

Methodology and Metrics for Capacity Planning   *651*

Setting Capacity Goals   *652*

Server Hardware Capacity Planning   *653*

A Baseline Capacity Profile   *655*

LAN Infrastructure Capacity Planning   *658*

External Connectivity Capacity Planning   *659*

Capacity Planning Best Practices   *663*

Index 665

Foreword

Something significant takes place in the software industry every time we see a paradigm shift in the way software is put forward. From mainframes to minis to PCs to client-server to Internet to wireless, *the fault line continues to shift underneath our feet*. As a professional software engineer/consultant, your gross value in the industry as well as the impact of your work shifts along this fault line. In the last few years, nothing has affected your work more powerfully than the significant paradigm shift that is taking place with Internet solutions: applications that use the Internet as the foundation, as the community, as the fabric.

As a technologist reading this book, you are witnessing the convergence of several elements that, *as an ensemble*, have previously eluded the software industry. These elements are:

- The broad adoption of standards in software design and its underlying infrastructure

- The opportunity for software systems to both reduce operating costs and offer enormous strategic business advantages via the Web

- The promise of platform independence and "open" solutions through the emergence of Java and UNIX

The institution of broad standards for software design and its underlying infrastructure have long eluded the software industry, although such criteria have been commonplace in the hardware industry for decades. For software, many narrow standards have existed for various aspects of software development, such as SQL, CORBA, and UML.

The convergence of J2EE, Web, and modeling standards now gives us a set of mature design standards from which to build entire new systems. These J2EE and Web standards—EJB, JMS, JNDI, JDBC, HTTP, XML, and so forth—are now sufficiently mature, and carry tremendous mind share in the developer community. This book provides guiding lights for navigating these new standards, and tips on the best angles from which to leverage *your* Internet applications.

That Internet systems can offer a competitive and strategic advantage has become abundantly clear. Following the mad rush of dot-com speculators, you now find yourself ready to approach the "generation real" stage of Internet solutions! The strategic advantage of Internet and wireless solutions stems in large part from Metcalf's Law of Connectivity: *The value of a network is a function of the number of nodes connected to that network; value increases in proportion to the square of the number of nodes.*

Given the number of users that likely will use your new Internet solution, you will do well to build in fault-resistance and performance. WebLogic Server provides you with the robustness and scalability necessary for your Internet project, no matter what its scope. The most widely used and proven infrastructure platform for Internet applications, WebLogic Server's functionality comes with a wide array of tuning dials and knobs, giving *you* the ultimate power. The examples and expert tips in this book give you the tools to use this power effectively.

Platform independence is a much-used expression that simultaneously implies too little and too much. As a software developer, your goal is to deploy your solution on the most common array of hardware types, operating systems, and databases without rebuilding or recompiling. You want to be able to share your code—in any form, shape, or consistency—with others in the vast community that is J2EE, Web, UNIX, Linux, and OpenSource.

Chances are infinitely greater today that someone else will be able to make use of a software system created by you. This has little to do with object-oriented design or the creation of relatively small reusable classes. Neither of these, in practice, has become a catalyst for code reusability. In today's deployment environment, *reusable services* really set the stage for software reuse. Using the J2EE standard and this book, you will gain valuable insight on creating systems that are flexible, malleable, and inherently ready for use as a Web service. In fact, the authors stress that WebLogic Server's design and usage model focuses on *providing services to the applications deployed within it*.

Part of the secret to providing lasting value, particularly given the intense networking effect of the Web, is to put forward your software systems as services using open standards. Think of your software as providing a Web service: This is part of its intrinsic value when deployed. A commerce site showing order status information is cool; one that also allows programmatic access to the information via open standards (such as UDDI/WSDL/SOAP) is likely more valuable. Don't merely think about an FTP site for downloads; think of Napster! Harness the power of an online community using software services. Instead of creating software tools, create online services that leverage the Internet. *Create your own networking effect*.

Truly open and accessible online services have only begun to emerge. Wireless devices, voice applications, and Internet-connected systems that are not primarily browse-oriented also are strong catalysts for open and accessible Internet services. As you design your Web system, imagine that it is also serving devices that are *not* browsing the Web, *not* using Internet Explorer. Within a few years, Web-connected devices (cell phones and hand-helds) will outnumber Windows devices. Applications prepared to serve these open and accessible Internet clients will be able to take advantage of the enormous networking effect they create.

This book and the WebLogic Server product will give you the necessary edge to achieve your goals as a software developer. You will become successful more rapidly in tracking to the emerging paradigm. Regardless of your specific J2EE project goals, I am confident that Michael and Rob, through this book, will guide you well.

George Kassabgi
VP Engineering, WebLogic Server
BEA Systems
San Francisco, December 2000

Preface

Introducing BEA WebLogic Application Servers

J2EE Applications and BEA WebLogic Server addresses the need for a practical, state-of-the art book on developing enterprise applications with the market-leading BEA WebLogic® Java application servers. The BEA WebLogic family of application servers includes BEA WebLogic Server, BEA WebLogic Enterprise, BEA WebLogic Commerce Server, and BEA WebLogic Personalization Server. This book focuses on BEA WebLogic Server™.

BEA WebLogic Server (*WebLogic Server*) is a widely used Java application server for constructing multi-tier, secure, large-scale, distributed Web applications for e-commerce and other high-volume applications. Distributed applications require sophisticated, fast, fault-tolerant networked communication among application tiers and components. In a client-server application, client programs send requests and receive responses from a server system. With the advent of middleware and the Web revolution, many enterprise sites have moved from client-server application environments to *n*-tier—usually, 3- or 4-tier—architectures. In multi-level architectures, efficient network connectivity is paramount.

In a multi-tier application, WebLogic Server provides the framework for developing and deploying *server-side business logic*, and supports a distributed programming model that hides the complexity of distributed programming from the application writer. The programming model provided by J2EE and the WebLogic Server extensions provides some level of transparency, so that writing a distributed application is similar to writing a local application. Although the programmer must still be concerned about error handling and efficiency, WebLogic Server's implementation of the J2EE services provides an excellent development and execution environment for an enterprise-level distributed application.

An application server such as BEA WebLogic Server handles server-side business logic and the administration of a multi-client, distributed application that uses a variety of clients and servers. Giving the responsibility for business logic and traffic control to an application server has the following benefits:

- Efficiency: Web browser and application clients can share the same business logic, rather than having to deploy business rules with each instance of a client.
- Performance: Locating server-side business logic with or near resource-intensive modules such as data stores can improve performance.
- Manageability: System administration and security issues are easier to address when business logic is centralized in an application server.

History of BEA's WebLogic Server Division

WebLogic, Inc. was founded in 1995—when Java, still a "think tank" project of Sun Microsystems, was code-named "Oak." In 1998, WebLogic merged with BEA Systems, Inc., a major vendor of transaction monitors and other tools for creating and managing enterprise-scale distributed systems. The BEA WebLogic Server product is a part of the BEA E-Business Platform.

From the beginning, the WebLogic Server developers determined to use only Java, and to focus on server-side technologies: server support and middleware management of multi-tier applications. Using off-the-shelf Java development tools (and general-purpose text-editing tools such as emacs), the WebLogic Server developers implemented APIs for each new Java standard feature that Sun specified. As a result, WebLogic Server has not only kept current with Java standards development but has also had the capability to influence emerging Java standards.

BEA WebLogic Server was an early implementer of each emerging Java Enterprise standard, including Enterprise JavaBeans (EJB), Remote Method Invocation (RMI), servlets, the Java Naming and Directory Interface (JNDI), and Java Database Connectivity (JDBC) for Oracle, Informix, Sybase, and Microsoft SQL Server. Each of these technologies is explained and illustrated in the chapters that follow.

In July 2000, the BEA Systems family of application servers successfully completed Sun Microsystems Java 2 Enterprise Edition (J2EE) certification, becoming the first independent company to achieve official J2EE certification.

BEA WebLogic Server has won several industry awards, including:

- Best Java Application Server (*JavaPro*, June 2000)
- Product Excellence and Productivity Award (*Software Development Magazine*, March 2000)
- *Java World* Reader's Choice Award for best e-commerce application server, 1999
- *Infoworld's* Product of the Year, 1999
- *Java Developers Journal* Editor's Choice Award in 1998 and 1999

Why We Wrote this Book

BEA WebLogic Server has a growing installed base that has been supported by training classes and extensive documentation, but there has been no comprehensive, practical coverage of full-scale application development on the WebLogic Server platform. This step-by-step book explains where to start, and how to put all the pieces together. Planning for deployment and selecting the technologies that you'll use for each tier of the application is as important as laying down code.

Target Audience

J2EE Applications and BEA WebLogic Server is targeted at intermediate to professional-level Java programmers developing applications for the BEA WebLogic Server platform, the market leader among application servers. This book focuses on best practices for developing enterprise applications using the WebLogic Server APIs. The WebAuction application, a complete sample e-commerce application, is explained and developed as an example in Chapter 14. An accompanying CD-ROM includes all software and code needed to implement the sample application in your own environment.

After reading this book, Java developers will possess the skills and knowledge required to develop scalable and robust applications on the WebLogic platform. This book is targeted at programmers who know basic Java on at least an intermediate level and would like to learn WebLogic Server. We assume that readers know about standard Java programming concepts such as exceptions and threads. However, we do not assume that readers know much about J2EE or application servers.

Brief Overview of the Book

J2EE Applications and BEA WebLogic Server contains both a descriptive narrative and examples for each major J2EE API, and a sample application that concludes the book. Using a step-by-step approach, the book introduces each major J2EE API and uses it to build a component of the WebAuction application, which supports an online auction site.

Building the WebAuction application gives users the opportunity to explore significant areas of building a distributed Enterprise Java application, including:

- Overview of J2EE technologies (Chapter 2)
- Building presentation logic with servlets or Java Server Pages (JSPs); (Chapters 3 and 4)
- Establishing database connectivity and using transactions (Chapter 5)
- Using Remote Method Invocation, and the Naming and Directory Interface (Chapter 6)

- Using a message-oriented middleware layer to coordinate all the components and operations in your multi-tier, distributed WebAuction application (Chapter 7)

- Creating Enterprise Java Beans (Chapters 8–10)

- Integrating Internet mail (Chapter 11)

- Adding security (Chapter 12)

- Designing a distributed deployment (Chapter 13)

- Building and deploying the completed application (Chapter 14)

- Performing a capacity-planning exercise to assess the performance of the deployed application (Chapter 15)

Chapter 1 presents a detailed overview of the book, with a roadmap and chapter summaries. Chapter 1 also lists system requirements and conventions. Chapter 2 surveys the J2EE technologies that are described in depth, with examples, in Chapters 3–12.

About the Authors

Michael Girdley is the Senior Product Manager for the BEA WebLogic Server, a role in which he acts as marketing liaison to over 200 engineers. An experienced application developer in Java, HTML, C, and C++, Michael is a co-author of *Web Programming with Java* (Sams-net Publishing, 1996) and *Java Unleashed, Second Edition* (Sams-net Publishing, 1997). Michael holds a bachelor's degree in computer science with honors from Lafayette College.

Rob Woollen is a Senior Software Engineer at BEA Systems. He is currently the lead developer for the WebLogic Server EJB Container. Before joining BEA, Rob worked on UNIX kernel networking for Hewlett-Packard. Rob holds a bachelor's degree in computer science from Princeton University.

Sandra L. Emerson is a technical writer and consultant with 20 years' experience in the software industry. She is a co-author of four computer trade books: *The Business Guide to the UNIX System* (Addison-Wesley); *Database for the IBM PC* (Addison-Wesley); *Troff Typesetting for UNIX Systems* (Prentice-Hall); and *The Practical SQL Handbook* (Addison-Wesley, Fourth Edition, 2001).

Acknowledgments

The authors would like to thank the following editors and reviewers for their insightful comments on the manuscript and their prompt responses to our questions.

Without their energy and effort, it would not have been possible to create a world-class book on J2EE and BEA WebLogic Server.

Greg Doench, our acquisitions editor

Kathleen Caren, production editor

Jessica McCarty, copyeditor

Robert Lynch, technical reviewer

From BEA Systems:

The following people from BEA Systems (listed in no particular order) volunteered their personal time to review our chapters:

Joe Weinstein, WebLogic JDBC Engineer

Sam Pullara, WebLogic XML Engineer and Thought Leader

Don Ferguson, WebLogic Engineering Manager

Steve Maxwell, BEA Field Readiness

Robert Patrick, BEA Principal Consultant (our other official technical reviewer)

Jeff McDaniel, BEA Principal Consultant

Paul Bauerschmidt, BEA Security Engineer

Nicholas D'Attoma, WebLogic Engineering Manager

Andrew Sliwkowski, WebLogic Quality Assurance Engineer

Thorick Chow, WebLogic EJB Engineer

Seth White, WebLogic EJB Engineer

Matt Shinn, WebLogic EJB Engineer

Cedric Beust, WebLogic EJB Engineer

Keng Woei Tan, WebLogic EJB Engineer

Carole Yang, WebLogic EJB Engineer

Adrian Chan, WebLogic Engineering Director

Tom Barnes, WebLogic JMS Engineer

Zach, WebLogic JMS Architect

John Greene, WebLogic Technical Support Manager

Belinda M. Leung, WebLogic Quality Assurance Engineer

Mark Spotswood, WebLogic Servlet/JSP Engineer

Ruslan Bilorusets, WebLogic Servlet/JSP Engineer

Reto Kramer, WebLogic Core Server Engineer

(Apologies to anyone we omitted from this list.)

The following people from BEA Systems gave "the little bit extra" to make this book possible:

John Kiger, BEA Director of Product Marketing, who sponsored the effort inside of BEA.

Dee Elling, WebLogic Documentation Manager, who first approached us with the book idea.

Katherine Barnhisel, BEA Director of Developer Programs, who has worked diligently to get us the appropriate software for our CD.

And finally, we give special thanks to two individuals who astounded us with the amount of energy they placed in reviewing and improving our work:

George Kassabgi, Vice President of Engineering for BEA WebLogic Server. George is the first person outside of the authors to have read this book from cover to cover. From day one, George provided incredible input both at a micro and macro level. Without him, it is unlikely that some of the cooler features of the book, including comprehensive step-by-step examples and many of the WebLogic-specific best practices would have been included. George also contributed the foreword to the book. George, thank you very much—we owe you.

Taraka Siva Rama Prasad Peddada, WebLogic Clustering Engineer. Prasad took more pride in our book than it sometimes seemed that we did. He toiled intensely over poorly written chapters, helping us to shape them to meet his high standards. Without Prasad, this book would not have been possible. Taraka, you are the man.

Michael Girdley
Robert Woollen
Sandra Emerson

Acknowledgments—Michael Girdley

It's the Sunday after Thanksgiving, 2000, at 11:36 PM. I haven't showered in four days. My wrists hurt and I am wrestling with WebLogic Server 6 Beta 1 and our book. I woke up at 9 AM and have been sitting at the computer since. Over the course of that weekend and many other days, I will put in some 12 and 18 hour days while my friends are out frolicking in the snow or at the beach or in the mountains or anywhere but inside.

Looking back over the past year, writing this book has been one of the best experiences of my life and undoubtedly one of the worst. Completing hundreds of pages of technical text on the world's leading application server is rewarding. I have learned more about our product than I could have imagined. On the other hand, working 70 hours a week is not a healthy way to live. For those of you considering writing a technical book, be sure to quit your fifty-hour-a-week job first.

Without the support of many people and organizations, I do not believe that any of this would be possible:

My parents, who I now realize dedicated their lives to make their children's lives happy, rich and well-balanced.

My grandparents, Dorothy Williams, Harvey Haskel Girdley and Mary Girdley.

Shandelle Wertz, who did a lot of sleeping while I was writing.

Robert Woollen, who kept us technically sane.

Sandra Emerson, who made our writing good.

Mike McHugh, who has taught me by example many of the secrets to success.

George Kassabgi, who has mentored tirelessly and taught me how and when "to take the bridge."

Dragon Systems NaturallySpeaking Version 4.0 & 5.0 dictation software.

Bob Pasker, Paul Ambrose, Ian King, Laura Cerrutti, Kurt Zimmerman, Hunter Kelly, Will Robb, Rob Schafer, Myriam Lanau, Luke Girdley, Karyn Girdley, Dean Kuehnen.

Michael Girdley
San Francisco, 4/5/01
http://www.girdley.com/
http://learnweblogic.com/

Acknowledgments—Sandy Emerson

I could never have finished buffing and polishing this book without the patience and support of my best friend and partner in life, Mary L. Hackney.

Thanks to my co-authors for supplying both the brains and brawn of this book. It's been a pleasure to prod and preen it into its present form.

Thanks also to Dee Elling, my long-time friend and colleague, who's become a publications manager with the vision to realize that documentation goes beyond users' manuals.

Acknowledgments—Rob Woollen

Although there are only three names on the cover, this book is the product of many people's work.

I'd like to dedicate this book to my parents. I can't thank you enough for a lifetime of love and support.

To my sister Michelle—most of my success came from imitating you, and you've always been there for me when it counts. Merci.

Finally, I want to thank everyone who made the WebLogic Server such an incredible product. From everyone at 235 Montgomery to BEA employees and customers around the world, we've developed not only a server but also a community.

INTRODUCTION

In this chapter:

- WebLogic Server Overview
- How to Use this Book: Roadmap and Chapter Summaries
- System Requirements and Conventions

What Is BEA WebLogic Server?

BEA WebLogic Server is a Java™ application server that supports enterprise-level, multi-tier, fully distributed Web applications. WebLogic Server is widely recognized as the market leader and *de facto* industry standard for developing and deploying Java e-commerce applications. BEA WebLogic Server:

- Maintains and manages application logic and business rules for a variety of clients, including Web browsers, applets, and application clients.

- Supports software clustering of WebLogic Servers for running both Web and Enterprise JavaBeans (EJB) services to ensure reliability, scalability, and high performance.

- Provides the application services necessary for building a robust, scalable, Web-based application.

- Provides a current and complete implementation of the protocols of Sun Microsystems' Java 2 Platform Enterprise Edition (J2EE).

With its emphasis on maximizing efficient use of system resources such as client and database connections, BEA WebLogic Server can support e-commerce applications for millions of users and hundreds of thousands of requests per hour.

This chapter and the next introduce many acronyms that are part of the J2EE suite of technologies. If this thicket of acronyms does not make much sense at this point, don't worry. The remaining chapters in this book cover each technology in detail.

WebLogic Server Overview

Figure 1-1 shows a typical multi-tier WebLogic Server configuration. Clients include Web browsers and application clients. The WebLogic Server tier is usually a *cluster* of cooperating WebLogic Servers.

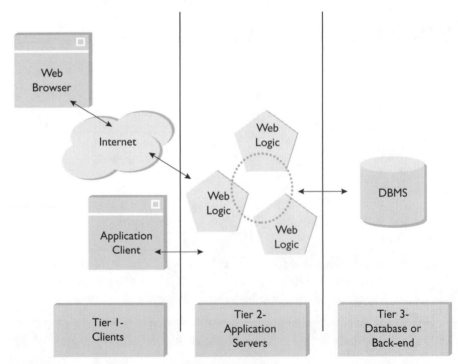

Figure 1-1 Typical BEA WebLogic Server Configuration

The pentagon is the WebLogic Server container, a complex concept encompassing a wide variety of services and facilities.

The Container-Component Model

The WebLogic Server platform (in Java parlance) can be thought of as a *container* that provides services to *components* of user applications. Components such as EJBs, JavaServer Pages (JSPs), and servlets reside in the WebLogic Server container and take advantage of the services provided by it.

In Figure 1-2, the WebLogic Server container (the large pentagon) encloses various J2EE services. Interconnections of services are depicted with lines and arrows. WebLogic Server management (via the WebLogic Server console) and security are shown as layers external to the container.

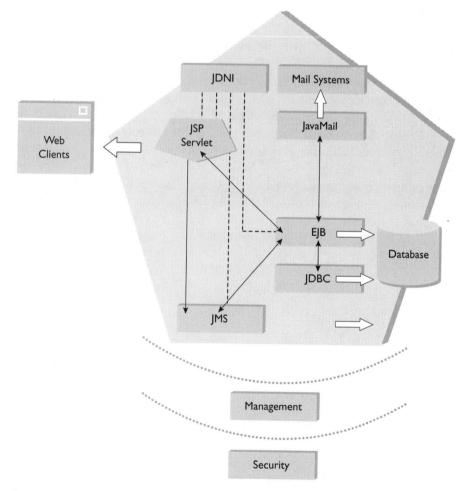

Figure 1-2 A Snapshot of the WebLogic Server Container

WebLogic Server Strengths: Component Support and Scalability

WebLogic Server's implementation of the J2EE server-based programming strategy centers on EJBs, which are at the heart of most enterprise-level Web applications. EJBs integrate data management, session management, and business logic, and coordinate among all the tiers of the application. For example, you use entity beans to represent data from the database. You use session beans to implement business logic that is either too complex or too sensitive to be managed with presentation logic, and you use message-driven beans to set up asynchronous data processing.

Within the WebLogic Server container, components are given connection and communications services, transactional support for multi-user operations, and the capability to replicate, or cluster, to provide better performance and scalability.

To the container and component framework, WebLogic Server added several important mechanisms for *clustering* to ensure high availability and scalability of distributed applications. A BEA WebLogic Server cluster is a group of WebLogic Servers that coordinate their actions to provide scalable, highly available services in a transparent manner. WebLogic Servers in a cluster can run on a heterogeneous mix of hardware and operating platforms: They interoperate through their Java-based, platform-independent APIs.

WebLogic Server clustering technologies transparently support replication, load balancing, and failover for both Web page generation (presentation logic) and EJB components (business logic).

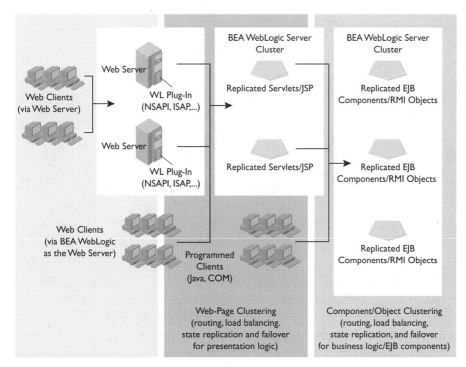

Figure 1-3 Clustering

How to Use this Book

J2EE Applications and BEA WebLogic Server contains 15 chapters, each of which covers one phase of developing Web-based applications using J2EE and WebLogic Server. Each chapter is organized around a particular Java Enterprise technology that you use to create a component of the *WebAuction* application, an online auction site that functions as the core example set for this book. The discussion of EJBs, which are the major players in J2EE application development, spans three chapters.

Each chapter notes where an application module fits in an overall application design; how to plan for efficient implementation; the specifics of the example implementation; and recommendations for "best practices" that can guide the implementation of a similar component at your site.

The Enterprise Java APIs and associated APIs that are part of the J2EE specification are discussed in this book in the approximate order in which a developer might use them. However, each technology is described and illustrated without dependencies on material covered in any other chapter.

Road Map

Whether you're an experienced Java developer or a novice, we assume that you're just getting started with developing applications for an application server. Because individual application development styles differ, each chapter is self-contained. You can read the chapters in the order that best suits your development style. The sequence of chapters moves generally from the simpler technologies to the more complex technologies: For example, the EJB and Java Message Service (JMS) chapters (Chapters 7–10) build on concepts learned in the Remote Method Invocation (RMI)/Java Naming and Directory Interface (JNDI) and Java Database Connectivity (JDBC) chapters (Chapters 5 and 6).

After getting a basic idea of the concepts and best practices for each technology, the developer can begin to design some of the major modules, such as the EJBs for the server-side logic, or the JSPs for the user interface.

In narrative form, the chapters follow this sequence:

First, the developer can *prototype the user interface*, coding the server-side presentation logic in servlets (Chapter 3) or JSPs (Chapter 4).

When the basic outline of the application behavior is known, the developer can *plan for database connectivity* with JDBC and transactions (Chapter 5).

As application modules emerge, the developer sets up the central registry for object and method names, and the framework for RMI (Chapter 6).

In order to ensure efficient performance when executing an application over a cluster of WebLogic Servers, the developer uses the JMS protocol to *set up the middleware-oriented messaging layer* to sequence and manage correct object behaviors (Chapter 7).

To ensure application component independence and to take maximum advantage of the WebLogic Server container's services, the developer *codes the EJBs*, which are at the heart of the application's functionality (Chapters 8–10).

To include email functionality, the developer *connects the application to Internet mail* using the JavaMail protocol (Chapter 11). It is also necessary to *design and code the appropriate levels of security* (Chapter 12), which can be done with a combination of WebLogic Server features and J2EE security functions.

After unit testing, the developer *plans for deployment* of the completed application, surveying the hardware and software elements that need to interoperate when an application is deployed (Chapter 13). After the deployment design, methodology, and tools have been surveyed, the developer *compiles, tests, and deploys* the completed application (Chapter 14).

As appropriate to compare performance of this application to a previous version or to stated performance goals, the developer uses a *capacity planning* guide to assess the capacity of the production application and the deployment environment (Chapter 15).

Chapter Summaries

For your reference, here are the chapter summaries:

Chapter 1, *Introduction*, summarizes the features and benefits of the BEA WebLogic Server, and gives an overview of the book and its stylistic conventions.

Chapter 2, *Overview of J2EE Technologies*, surveys the major J2EE technologies to provide an orientation to the rest of the book.

Chapter 3, *Building Presentation Logic with WebLogic Server Servlets*, covers the construction of a user interface module with a servlet. Although servlets are not used in the WebAuction application, prototyping the behavior of the user interface is discussed as the logical way to begin the WebAuction application and to capture expected functionality.

Chapter 4, *Using WebLogic Server JavaServer Pages*, continues the construction of the user interface using JSP scripts. JSPs are used for all of the WebAuction application's interactions with users. This chapter illustrates best practices for coding JSPs with several example JSP scripts.

Chapter 5, *Using Databases and Transactions with JDBC and JTA*, details how to connect to a data store and how to use transaction management with databases or other legacy data stores.

Chapter 6, *Remote Method Invocation and Distributed Naming*, discusses RMI and how to configure calls to RMI clients, including application clients and EJBs. It also discusses setting up the central registry of object names and locations with the JNDI.

Chapter 7, *Enterprise Messaging with the Java Message Service (JMS)*, covers the fundamentals of JMS, describing and illustrating both point-to-point and publish-and-subscribe messaging. Topics include how JMS works in a WebLogic Server cluster, JMS exception handling, and best practices for using JMS in WebLogic Server applications.

Chapter 8, *Using Session Enterprise JavaBeans,* gives an overview of the very important EJB technology, which is the main mechanism for capturing business logic and managing interactions with data stores. This chapter covers stateless and stateful session beans, which provide services to clients. Like other J2EE objects, EJBs reside in the WebLogic Server container.

Chapter 9, *Entity EJBs,* describes how entity EJBs interact with data stores. EJBs provide several mechanisms for making data persistent in the context of the application. The WebLogic Server container handles security and transactioning for data managed by entity beans.

Chapter 10, *Using Message-Driven EJBs,* describes message-driven EJBs, which are the integration between EJB and the JMS. Like other EJB types, message-driven EJBs live within an EJB container and benefit from EJB container services such as transactions, security, and concurrency control. Message-driven EJBs do not interface directly with clients: They set a listener that receives messages from the interaction of the JMS provider with the EJB container.

Chapter 11, *Interfacing with Internet Mail Using WebLogic Server Java-Mail,* discusses Internet mail (email) protocols, including the Simple Mail Transport Protocol (SMTP) and the POP3 and IMAP mail retrieval protocols. This chapter details the JavaMail API and shows how to add email capability to the WebAuction application.

Chapter 12, *Developing Security with WebLogic Server JNDI and JAAS,* surveys security technologies and shows you how to incorporate WebLogic Server security realms and Java Authentication and Authorization Service (JAAS) into your WebLogic Server applications. This chapter includes abundant details on how to create secure application clients and Web clients for WebLogic Server.

Chapter 13, *Designing the Production Deployment,* discusses scenarios for deployment of the production application. This chapter emphasizes the importance of planning ahead for deployment. Your deployment design choices are determined by the installation environments of servers and clients, and by the anticipated levels of use of the application. This chapter describes:

- Typical WebLogic Server deployment scenarios
- Sample deployment configurations for each scenario
- Best practices for deploying WebLogic Server in the enterprise

Chapter 14, *Packaging, Deploying, and Testing the WebAuction Application,* discusses the architecture of the WebAuction application and how the various J2EE technologies were selected and employed. The chapter details how to package application components into an enterprise archive (.ear) file, and how to build and deploy the WebAuction application, step by step. The chapter concludes with a section on strategies for functional and performance testing of the completed application.

Chapter 15, *Capacity Planning for the WebLogic Server*, describes and illustrates a methodology and metrics for assessing the total capacity (user load, response times) of the WebAuction application. It includes:

- Methodology and metrics for capacity planning
- Examples that compare WebAuction to a hypothetical application, WebTrade
- Capacity planning best practices

System Requirements

This book and accompanying CD-ROM can be used standalone as a learning tool. A public Web site is also available at *www.learnweblogic.com*.

Complete documentation for BEA WebLogic Server and other BEA products is available at *http://e-docs.bea.com*.

Supported Platforms

Supported platforms for BEA WebLogic Server include (among others) Windows 2000, Windows NT, and UNIX systems. For a complete list of supported platforms, refer to the BEA WebLogic Server data sheet at *www.bea.com/products/weblogic/server/datasheet.shtml*.

Software on the CD-ROM

The WebLogic Server and the other software necessary to develop the sample application are included on the CD that accompanies this book. The CD includes:

- WebLogic Server 6.0 evaluation copy
- EJB 2.0 upgrade
- WebLogic Server Console
- Administrative tools and utilities
- Example code and build scripts for each chapter

- Source code for the WebAuction application
- WebAuction application data, JSPs, EJBs, build scripts, and so forth

Developers can use the Cloudscape all-Java relational database (included as part of the WebLogic Server product suite), for prototyping. WebLogic Server supports many other commercial databases, including those from Oracle, Sybase, Informix, and IBM (DB2).

Versions Supported

Versions of BEA WebLogic Server tested for this book include:

- WebLogic Server 6.0, Service Pack 1
- Check the BEA Web site at *www.bea.com* for news on the latest supported versions of J2EE technologies.

Conventions

This book uses the following typographic conventions:

Italics	Glossary terms
	Emphasis
	Names of files, scripts, directory paths, URLs
	Chapter names, book titles, and other proper names
	Web addresses
`Courier`	Names of Java programming elements, including:
	Object names, method names, classnames, variable names
	Code, in general
Boldface	Default values
	Emphasis
Bars	Best Practice, Note

OVERVIEW OF J2EE TECHNOLOGIES

In this chapter:

- Overview of BEA WebLogic Server's support for the Sun Microsystems Java 2 Enterprise Edition (J2EE) platform

- Brief description of WebLogic Server's distributed deployment support

- The WebAuction sample application's use of J2EE technologies

Chapter 2

WebLogic Server and J2EE

Sun Microsystems' J2EE framework was unveiled at the Java One conference in 1997. J2EE defines the standard for developing and deploying enterprise-level Web applications. With J2EE, the developer-friendly Java language and tools are extended for use in complex, multi-tier e-commerce and enterprise-level applications. J2EE provides broad support for the *component* model of development, providing tools and services for business logic in modular, reusable, platform-independent components.

J2EE Technologies Covered in this Book

J2EE Applications and BEA WebLogic Server covers the following J2EE technologies, all of which have been implemented in WebLogic Server according to the specifications certified by Sun. The following table is a brief summary of the J2EE technologies we cover in this book:

J2EE Service	*Purpose*
WebLogic Servlets	**Presentation Logic**
WebLogic JavaServer Pages (JSP)	**Presentation Logic**
WebLogic Java Database Connectivity (JDBC)	**Access to Data Repositories**
WebLogic Java Transaction API (JTA)	**Transaction Management**
WebLogic Java Naming and Directory Interface (JNDI)	**Central Registry for Object Names**
WebLogic Remote Method Invocation (RMI)	**Distributed Execution of RMI Objects**
WebLogic Enterprise JavaBeans (EJB)	**Implementing Business Logic**
WebLogic Java Message Service (JMS)	**Coordinating Distributed Execution**

Presentation Logic

Presentation logic is the server-side code in a WebLogic Server application that determines the client-side response to a specific request. For example, your presentation logic can be as simple as "report the time of day when a request is received." Coding server-side presentation logic can be done using Java servlets, JSPs, JavaBeans, and tag libraries.

Java Servlets

The Java servlet is a server-side technology that accepts HTTP requests from a Web browser and returns HTTP responses. Servlets, which can be multi-threaded, have performance advantages over CGI for coding presentation logic for a Web client. Because servlets are written in Java, they are portable from one platform to another. Servlets are an enterprise Java standard for the development of presentation logic.

WebLogic Server servlets act on the *request-response model*. Requests come into the servlet engine. The WebLogic server then executes the appropriate servlet and returns a response to the client.

The most commonly used servlet type is the HTTP servlet designed to fill HTTP protocol (Web) requests. WebLogic Server supports *only* HTTP servlets.

HTTP servlets provide the following core features:

- `HttpRequest` objects capture request details from requests submitted via Web page forms, including data availability, protocol types, security levels, and so forth.

- `HttpSession` objects specific to each user handle user session information in the server. The servlet developer can add and remove information about the user during execution of the servlet.

- `HttpResponse` objects capture response details. The servlet developer can output everything that is sent back to the client making the request. The servlet engine handles the rest.

Chapter 3 discusses how to integrate and build servlets for your application.

JavaServer Pages (JSPs)

The JSP technology gives developers a simple, HTML-like interface for creating servlets. JSPs can contain HTML code, Java code, and code modules called JavaBeans. The JSP technology provides the same functionality as servlets, but the development interface is easier to use. When a JSP page is requested for the first time, the application server compiles that page into a servlet. This servlet is then executed to serve further requests. In this way, the servlet engine and the JSP engine are intimately tied together.

The benefit of JSP pages is their simplicity: They look like typical HTML pages. In fact, you can edit JSP pages in a standard Web composition tool such as Macromedia Dreamweaver.

Chapter 4 describes and illustrates the technical details for using JSPs in a WebLogic Server application.

WebLogic Server JavaBeans and Tag Libraries

JavaBeans (which are different from EJBs) are Java components (classes) that developers use in WebLogic Server applications to encapsulate data, either for display or for actions against the database. Developers create class-files with a number of methods, which are typically used to get and set values.

JSP pages have special tags for including JavaBeans and automatically populating them with values. The JSP page calls methods on those JavaBeans to help create its HTML output.

Tag libraries supply custom HTML-like tags for use in JSP pages. Tag libraries abstract Java code into tags that can be easily manipulated by Web editors and designers. To build a tag library, a developer creates classfiles and a file called a Tag Library Descriptor that lists the available tags from the tag library.

JavaBeans and tag libraries manage the data and Java code that interacts with the data sources available via JDBC and EJB. As we cover in subsequent chapters, JavaBeans and tag libraries perform a valuable service by enabling Web application developers to keep explicit Java code out of JSP pages and servlets. This modularization minimizes the chance of accidental damage to the JSP page during an HTML editing session, and permits presentation logic to be changed independent of the JSP page. Chapter 4 contains more information on the techniques and development of JavaBeans and tag libraries.

Database and Transaction Support

Database and transaction support is provided (behind the scenes) by JDBC and the JTA. The high-level interface to database use is provided by EJB.

Java Database Connectivity (JDBC)

JDBC is the Java standard for database connectivity. The JDBC specification provides everything needed to connect to databases from a standard set of Java APIs. Vendors supply JDBC "drivers" that map this standard set of Java APIs to the specifics of the underlying database.

WebLogic Server provides a number of JDBC drivers for different databases. You can, however, use almost any JDBC driver for a WebLogic Server–supported database, even drivers from vendors other than BEA Systems. WebLogic Server supports JDBC drivers for Oracle, MS SQL Server, Sybase, Informix, DB2, and Cloudscape.

Note that JDBC is the bridge that connects WebLogic Server with the database, from a programming standpoint. This functionality is transparent to the programmer: It's provided by EJB. The developer does not program JDBC directly, except in special cases.

The typical WebLogic Server application relies on a database for key e-commerce application functionality such as transaction support, support for concurrent data access, and data integrity features. Relational databases support a common declarative language for access called Structured Query Language (SQL). WebLogic Server's JDBC and SQL are covered in Chapter 5. Chapter 5 also discusses transactions.

WebLogic Server JDBC provides the following functionality:

- *APIs for operations that modify the database.* These operations include SQL updates and administrative commands.
- *APIs for operations that read from the database by making SQL queries to the database.* These queries return `ResultSet` Java objects, which return results of JDBC database queries. These objects enable J2EE developers to programmatically access (via standard APIs) the values returned by a given SQL query.
- *Support for basic transactions.* JDBC provides an "automatic commit" of simple SQL statements. So, a simple single method call can pass a SQL statement directly to the database, and changes are automatically committed to the database.
- *Support for complex transactions.* WebLogic Server provides a service called JTA, which provides the capability to begin transactions and propagate them across multiple J2EE services and WebLogic Server.

Java Transaction API (JTA) Support

JTA gives Web application developers access to the transaction functions in database systems, or any legacy data store. Transactions coordinate single-database and multi-database operations to ensure that all data resources remain accurate and consistent, and that operations against the database are repeatable and durable. Transaction management is essential for enterprise-level e-commerce applications, which need to be Web-based and fault-tolerant.

JTA defines a high-level transaction management specification for resource managers for distributed applications. WebLogic Server transaction services provide connectivity and support for database transaction functionality, most notably the two-phase commit (2PC) engine used to manage multi-database transactions.

Object Registry and Remote Method Invocation (RMI)

JNDI and RMI support naming services and remote method execution.

Java Naming and Directory Interface (JNDI)

JNDI is the Java standard for the "central registry" of naming and directory services. JNDI manages references to the core components needed to build distributed applications. When a developer builds an application that accesses a remote object, JNDI provides the application with a way to locate that object. The JNDI technology is the interface to naming and directory services, and acts as a central registry for named application and data objects. The JNDI services help assure the proper level of uniqueness in the names of application components, and help prevent, diagnose, and treat naming conflicts that might arise.

WebLogic Server implements JNDI as part of its platform. Application developers can store, modify, and remove references to Java components and resources in the WebLogic Server JNDI implementation. In the case of WebLogic Server clustering, JNDI is also used as the shared naming service across the entire cluster.

The usage pattern of JNDI is relatively simple. Application developers do an initial lookup to find the object that they require in the WebLogic Server deployment. WebLogic Server services will return everything the application needs to access that object.

JNDI and the complete interfaces to build a WebLogic Server application that uses JNDI are covered in Chapter 6.

Remote Method Invocation (RMI)

RMI is the Java standard that a Java application uses to make a method call on a remote Java object. RMI enables remote objects to "virtually" appear as if they are local to the application. RMI provides the framework for your distributed application and its remote clients to interact with remote methods and services. The remote host to allow calling by RMI exports the methods of remote objects. Objects can be located across the network or perhaps across your WebLogic Server cluster, on another WebLogic Server implementation.

Chapter 6 covers the steps required to use RMI in your application.

Enterprise JavaBeans (EJBs)

EJB is the enterprise Java standard for building server-side business logic in Java. Whereas presentation logic automatically handles the type and format of information to be displayed to clients, business logic is used for operations such as funds transfers, product orders, and so forth. Developers build EJBs that take advantage of services provided by the WebLogic Server container.

This container provides services including transaction support and security, and handles concurrency issues. All of these services are required for scalable, secure, and robust electronic commerce applications.

WebLogic Server's EJB container provides everything needed for developers to build business logic such as funds transfers, employee record management, or other functionalities.

There are four basic types of EJBs:

- Entity
- Message-driven
- Stateful session
- Stateless session

WebLogic Server Entity EJBs

Entity EJBs (*entity beans*) are the enterprise Java standard for representing data. They are standard Java language objects that reside in the WebLogic Server container.

In most cases, entity beans represent data from a database, although they also can represent data stored in other locations. In WebLogic Server deployments, beans represent data stored in a relational database, such as Oracle, IBM's DB2, Informix, and so forth.

Objects such as entity beans need to be mapped to the relational structure of a relational database management system (DBMS). WebLogic Server includes *object-relational mapping technology*, and also permits plug-ins that implement other mapping mechanisms.

The EJB specification defines an API for developers to create, deploy, and manage cross-platform, component-based enterprise applications. The EJB component model supports three types of components:

- Session beans, which capture business rules and methods that persist for the duration of a session
- Entity beans, which encapsulate specific data items from a database
- Message-driven beans, which integrate EJBs with the Java Message Service (JMS)

WebLogic Server makes activities such as managing transactions, concurrency issues, security, and other functionality automatic because the WebLogic Server container provides these services. When programming EJBs, developers do not have to worry about all of the low-level plumbing issues: The container takes care of that.

Chapter 10 covers the technical implementation details surrounding entity beans.

WebLogic Server Session EJBs

The enterprise Java standards specify two types of session beans: *stateless* and *stateful*. *Stateless beans* receive requests via RMI but do not keep any data associated with the client they are serving internally. *Stateful beans*, on the other hand, keep data specific to the client they are serving. From a developer's perspective, these two types of session beans are similar in construction. However, the way that the WebLogic Server container treats them is very different.

WebLogic Server session beans handle requests that arrive via RMI. Typically, they provide services to other Java objects. This is in contrast to servlets and JSPs, which are focused primarily on responding to requests from Web clients such as Web browsers (whose requests arrive via HTTP).

The objects that initiate requests to session beans can be any arbitrary object that is able to access the appropriate RMI client classes. In the case of WebLogic Server deployments, these Java objects are typically application clients. However, it is also possible for servlets and JSPs to be RMI clients to session beans. Use session beans to implement business logic on the server side for your application clients, servlets, or JSPs.

Session beans are covered in Chapter 8.

WebLogic Server Message-Driven Beans

With Version 2.0, the EJB specification added a completely new type of EJB and the option to use an entirely new execution paradigm in enterprise Java applications. In both entity beans and session beans, a synchronous programming model is used. Clients make requests to the EJB and wait for work to be completed on their behalf. Using message-driven beans (MDBs), the EJB is not attached to a client. Instead, it is attached to a message queue or topic defined in the JMS, as described later. When a message arrives, a method on the EJB is executed.

MDBs introduce an *asynchronous* processing paradigm to enterprise Java applications. Tasks can be queued and made available for processing when resources are available.

Use message-driven beans when your application requires asynchronous processing for tasks such as sending email responses or tabulating the winners of this month's lottery. MDBs are discussed in Chapter 10.

Java Message Service (JMS)

The JMS specification provides developers with a standard Java API for enterprise messaging services such as reliable queuing, publish and subscribe communication, and various aspects of push/pull technologies. JMS is the enterprise Java standard for messaging. It enables applications and components in Java to send and receive messages. WebLogic Server provides a complete implementation of the JMS standard.

There are several paradigms for messaging in JMS, including:

- Queue model
- Topic-based, publish-subscribe system

The queue model enables JMS clients to push messages onto a JMS queue. Clients can then retrieve these messages. The topic-based model enables publishers to send messages to registered subscribers of the JMS topic.

WebLogic Server adds a number of features in its implementation of the JMS specification that are allowed by the specification but are not part of Sun's reference implementation:

- *Implementation of a guaranteed messaging service.* This messaging service uses the database or a file storage mechanism in order to make sure that messages are durable (able to persist when either the server or the client goes down).
- *Message filtering.* The WebLogic Server JMS implementation enables you to designate rules to filter the distribution of messages.

Chapter 7 discusses the technical details for using JMS.

JavaMail

The JavaMail API provides classes that support a simple email and messaging service, as well as connections to any standard email system. The JavaMail interface provides a standard, object-oriented protocol for connecting to many different types of email systems. Chapter 11 covers JavaMail.

Security

The J2EE security model is still evolving. The Java Authentication and Authorization Service (JAAS) provides the framework for authenticating clients and authorizing differential access to application resources. Security technologies are discussed in Chapter 12.

WebLogic Server's Distributed Deployment Support

In addition to J2EE technologies, WebLogic Server provides several important APIs and extensions to J2EE APIs that help provide reliable, scalable performance for a distributed application. The WebLogic Server clustering technology permits interconnection of several WebLogic Server instances (one per CPU) on a LAN, so that the WebLogic Servers in a cluster can distribute workload and provide fault-tolerance as application demands increase.

Scenarios for distributed deployment are discussed in Chapter 13. Chapter 14 describes the mechanics of packaging, building, and deploying a moderately complex sample application called WebAuction.

About WebAuction

Given the array of technologies supported by the J2EE platform, how is a developer to choose among them to create an application such as WebAuction?

The first task, of course, is to create a functional specification that describes exactly what the application is supposed to do.

For WebAuction, we started with the mental model of a "web auction" site similar to existing auction sites on the Internet. Functionally, the WebAuction application supports:

- Secure user registration
- Email validation of user's login credentials
- Browsing, for both registered and unregistered users
- Browsing by category for auction items (with some minor searching functionality)
- Placing bids
- Email confirmation of bids
- Viewing open bids

The J2EE services introduced in this chapter are discussed in subsequent chapters in detail. A more detailed description of the WebAuction application architecture appears in Chapter 14.

WebAuction Application Technology Requirements

Based on the functional specification, the WebAuction technology requirements include services for:

- *Storing data in a database.* User account information should be stored persistently, in a database, on disk. In the event of a power failure, we do not want to lose any user information.

- *Handling concurrency issues*. Concurrency becomes an issue when multiple threads of execution try to access the same resource at the same time. For example, users might try to bid on a given item simultaneously. The developer should enclose data access operations in transactions, which can help prevent or resolve concurrency issues. Both the database and the WebLogic Server container provide support for transactions.

- *Handling user sessions*. Because the WebAuction application needs to handle many concurrent users, session information must be maintained for each user. A session begins when the user attempts to log in. The application must determine that a user is valid before allowing that user to access the auction area. If the user is not a registered user, logic should exist to point the user to a "create user account" page.

- *Representing database data*. The WebAuction application's data is stored in a relational database. However, the application uses that data in the context of the object-oriented Java environment. The technology requirements therefore include mechanisms to represent relational data in a way that is consistent with the J2EE environment.

- *Updating data from the Web interface*. In the WebAuction application, users can update their personal inventory and data on items for auction. Technology must support updating the database from a Web form.

- *Querying data*. Many features of WebAuction require searching and querying data. For example, one feature requires that users be able to browse auction items by category, such as "all the books available for auction."

- *Securing user information*. It must be possible to protect user information and accounts so that other users cannot access them. It must be impossible to access another user's information inside of the WebAuction application, and for someone to view the auction information that belongs to a given user while it is in transit to that user. In order to secure user information, the WebAuction application must take advantage of the security services of WebLogic Server.

We now begin the first of the detailed chapters on J2EE technologies, with a discussion of servlets.

BUILDING PRESENTATION LOGIC WITH WEBLOGIC SERVER SERVLETS

In this chapter:

- Building presentation logic
- The pros and cons of servlets and JSPs
- The details for building servlets in WebLogic Server
- Samples of servlets built for WebLogic Server
- Best practices for deploying servlets on WebLogic Server

Chapter 3

Presentation logic is the code that dynamically generates display elements and programmatically decides what content is displayed to the user. For example, presentation logic could enable the application to decide what sort of book to suggest to a visitor to your electronic bookstore. Or, presentation logic might adjust the color of HTML pages on your Web site based on a user's specific preferences.

In the WebAuction application, presentation logic is used to dynamically generate the interface for the users of the application. Example tasks handled by presentation logic include:

- Determining if a visitor needs to register
- Providing an interface for a new user to register
- Displaying available auction items, based on a user's query
- Displaying a user's inventory of auction items

WebLogic Server supports two mechanisms for creating *presentation logic* in applications: *servlets* and JavaServer Pages (*JSPs*). The WebLogic Server container executes servlets and JSPs, as specified in the Java 2 Enterprise Edition (J2EE) standards.

In practice, Web applications (including WebAuction) primarily use JSP pages for their presentation logic. In some cases, such as when you use the Model View Controller (MVC) paradigm described in Chapter 4, servlets and JSP pages work together in Web applications. As we shall see, JSP pages are simply servlets implemented in a different way; they derive virtually all their functionality from servlet technology. To understand JSP pages and how to implement them, you need to understand servlets. WebLogic Server 6.0 supports the J2EE servlet specification Version 2.2, and JSP Version 1.1.

In this chapter, we cover servlets so that you'll understand the underlying mechanisms of dynamic HTTP generation. The next chapter deals with JSPs, which are much easier to use.

Introducing WebLogic Server Servlets

Servlets are server-side Java code designed to respond to requests. Servlets act, by default, in a stateless request-response paradigm. Requests are typically generated in a Web browser, but other clients such as Java applications and Visual Basic clients also make requests. Requests are usually specified in HTTP, the hypertext transfer protocol that is the basic protocol for the World Wide Web.

WebLogic Server Servlets Handle HTTP Requests

After receiving an HTTP request, WebLogic Server determines which servlet should be executed to fulfill the request. The servlet selection is typically determined by the Web's *uniform resource locator* (URL) that specifies the location of the requested resource, its type, and its protocol. For example, *http://www.learnweblogic.com/picture.gif* is a URL that specifies an HTTP request to the host *http://www.learnweblogic.com* for a resource named *picture.gif*.

The WebLogic Server container then executes the appropriate servlet and provides services to that servlet. Services include user authentication, parallel execution, memory management, access control, and so forth.

Your code typically takes the form of handling a *request object* that represents the details of the request. Using the information contained in this request object, the servlet code you write generates a response that you place into a separate *response object*. The container then translates this response object into an HTTP response to the requester.

Generic Servlets

Servlets can be *generic servlets*, which do not specify what kind of protocol should be used to service requests. Generic servlets are not often used today. *HTTP servlets*, a specialized version of servlets to handle HTTP requests, are more common. WebLogic Server supports only HTTP servlets.

The servlet API specifies a number of methods that are called during the servlet's lifetime. Otherwise, the source code looks like any other Java class. Details on building servlets and best practices for servlets are covered later in this chapter.

How Servlets Are Used

Using HTTP servlets to generate Web pages has become virtually the only use of servlets by Java developers building J2EE applications.

Unfortunately, building Web pages with servlets is very tedious. Every piece of content or formatting tag that you would like to put into your Web page must be explicitly specified using a line such as:

```
out.println("<h1>My tag and text </h1>");
```

In this code, the object `out` is an output stream that is written to the client and obtained from the request object. This stream is an abstraction of the underlying TCP/IP socket connection to the client. The method `println` accepts a string value and includes that into the output stream.

WebLogic Server JavaServer Pages (JSPs)

JSPs evolved to help solve some of the issues of creating dynamic Web pages with servlets. JSPs, also a part of the J2EE standards, enable the quick and efficient building of dynamic and personalized Web content.

When a WebLogic Server client issues an HTTP request, the WebLogic Server JSP container executes the appropriate JSP page, and then sends the response back to the requester.

Sound familiar? At base, JSPs are simply a more efficient way of building servlets. But instead of the assembly-language-like coding style required for creating servlets, JSPs are encoded just like a Web page but with special embedded tags and Java code. When the WebLogic Server container grabs a

JSP page to service requests, it first compiles and translates that JSP page into a servlet. This servlet then exists to service further requests.

Chapter 4, *Using WebLogic Server JavaServer Pages*, contains more detail on how to build JSPs and the best practices for doing so.

Servlets or JSPs?

A typical application architecture for WebLogic Server can include both servlets and JSPs. The question of when to use JSPs instead of servlets, and/ or both together, is an easy one. However, there are some basic guidelines that you can use to help you decide which technology is appropriate for your given task.

Use JSPs if:

- You are building HTML pages that are not trivial (having more than a few lines and with advanced features such as tables and so forth).
- You have one development group doing the interface design (Web pages) while another is building the Java code.
- Your HTML code changes much more frequently than the presentation logic specified by Java code.

Use servlets if:

- You are planning to service clients other than Web browsers, such as application clients. Even in this case, it is often useful to prototype in JSP.
- You have a complex user interaction model, which includes complicated Web pages that are highly customized.

Use both JSPs *and* servlets if:

- You have application requirements indicating both the previously stated scenarios for JSP pages and servlets.
- You are using the MVC model (described in Chapter 4). In this model, you have servlets handling input from clients and directing requests to the appropriate JSP page to generate the HTML.

This chapter covers everything you need to know about developing servlets. Chapter 4 covers JSP development.

Even though JSP is the predominant paradigm for building J2EE application presentation logic, it is necessary to understand how servlets work in order to fully understand and make use of the power of the JSP model. Learning the servlet paradigm will allow you to take advantage of the power of JSPs.

Developing Servlets

Developing servlets is remarkably easy. The next sections cover:

- The anatomy of a servlet
- Session tracking
- Cookies and URL rewriting
- Security and WebLogic Server servlets

Anatomy of a Servlet

The servlet classes that you build must extend the class `javax.servlet.http.HttpServlet`. This class is one of the standard classes available as part of the Java extensions. For your convenience, these Java extensions are included as part of the WebLogic Server package.

A servlet instantiated by the WebLogic Server container begins by calling the `init()` method in your servlet class. This method must take as a parameter an instance of the `ServletConfig` class that contains information about the configuration of the servlet generated by the container.

When developing a servlet, you begin by extending the `HttpServlet` class, which provides implementations of all these methods, including the `service()` method. In this way, you are not required to re-implement every single method, but only those you'll need to change from the default behavior.

To implement a servlet, you override one of a number of different methods included from the default `HttpServlet` object provided. The focal method is called the `service()` method. It is called every time a request is made for your servlet.

There are two parameters accepted by the service method: an instance of the `Javax.servlet.http.HttpServletRequest` class and an instance of the `Javax.servlet.http.HttpServletResponse` class. The container uses the HTTP `ServletRequest` object request to pass the contents of the HTTP request to your servlet. The `Javax.serv-`

`let.http.HttpServletResponse` object directs your HTTP response to the requester.

The default implementation of the `service()` method dispatches calls to other, more specialized methods based on the request type. You can override this default behavior. The specialized methods exist to handle different types of user input, such as Web forms. These other, more specialized methods for handling different types of requests into servlets are discussed later in this chapter.

A Basic Servlet

No programming book would be complete without at least one "Hello World" demonstration. Let's look at a basic Hello World servlet.

First, we need to import the requisite classes into our servlet. For convenience, we grab everything in the `javax.servlet`, `javax.servlet.http`, and `java.io` packages by adding the following to the top of our servlet classfile, which we are calling *HelloServlet.java*:

```
import javax.servlet.*;
import javax.servlet.http.*;
import java.io.*;

// Next, we define our class:
public class HelloServlet extends HttpServlet {

    // And finally, we define our two methods:
    // The Service Methods to Handle HTTP Requests and Responses
    public void service(HttpServletRequest requ,
                HttpServletResponse resp)
      throws IOException
    {
      // Now Set the Response Content Type
      resp.setContentType("text/html");
      // Now obtain a PrintWriter stream to write to.
      PrintWriter out = resp.getWriter();


      // Now Print Out Our Text
      out.println("<html><head><title>" +
                "Hello World!</title></head>" +
                "Hello World!</h1></body></html>");
    }

    // The INIT Method Called by the Container Before the
    // First Call to the Service Method.
```

```
public void init(ServletConfig config)
  throws ServletException
{
  // Must call super.init to parse init arguments
  super.init(config);
  // ...
}
} // HelloServlet
```

Let's take a closer look at what went on in this example. The most important method that we implemented was the `service()` method, which takes two of the request and response objects as parameters. The request object encapsulates all the details and parameters of the HTTP request. In the case of this example, there is no information that the servlet cares about other than the fact that the request was made. Later in this chapter, we examine how to receive information from clients through this object and handle the requests appropriately.

WebLogic Server immediately begins creating a response for the client in the response object, which includes the HTTP response header. In order to create the body of the response for the client, we call the `out` method on the response object to grab a `PrintWriter` stream. We then use the standard `print` methods to write text to the stream.

Note that we did not close by calling the `flush()` method on the output stream. This allows WebLogic Server to try and keep open the socket with the client using a feature of HTTP 1.1 called *Keep-Alive*. Using this functionality allows WebLogic Server to be more efficient by reusing sockets whenever possible.

Keep-Alive is a key component of the HTTP 1.1 protocol. It helps Web servers be more efficient by minimizing the number of times that a socket is created to service a given client. To explain: Each Web page has multiple components on it that are actually downloaded separately and put together by the Web browser.

These components might include not only the HTML page itself, but also images, sounds, and so forth.
In the early days of the Web, the HTTP protocol required that the client and Web server mutually establish a socket for every one of these requests. With the advent of HTTP 1.1, it is possible to have the Web server maintain a single socket to the client for all that client's requests in a given period of time.

> *Keep-Alive can work if all the following conditions are met:*
> *1. The client specifies that it can do Keep-Alive by including either an "accept Keep-Alive" message in its request or specifies that it supports HTTP 1.1. Every commercial Web browser supports HTTP 1.1.*
> *2. WebLogic Server is able to determine the content length when it writes the response. This implies that the application code does not call* `flush()` *or improperly set the wrong content length in the response.*
> *3. The client does not break the socket, and there is no interruption in the connection between the client and the server.*

Because the creation, removal, and establishment of sockets are very expensive to a server, Keep-Alive enhances scalability. You should do everything possible to encourage WebLogic Server to use Keep-Alive: Therefore, do not close streams at the end of your servlets. And, do not exceed the buffer size. If you know the content length, set it to get past this restriction. Setting the content length is discussed later in this chapter.

What happens to all the sockets? Of course, clients and servers must close sockets connecting them; otherwise, you end up with empty sockets consuming resources. There are several ways to close a socket if:

- The socket is removed by network failure
- The client breaks the connection
- A timeout limit is reached

WebLogic Server enables you to specify the number of seconds that Keep-Alive is maintained. The default value is 30 seconds. The socket timeout interval can be modified on a per-server basis, using the WebLogic Server console.

You should increase the timeout value if you have users who spend very large amounts of time interacting with your Web application and repeatedly make requests at very short intervals.

The next step is to compile the servlet using your favorite Java compiler, package it up as a Web application, and then deploy it.

Deploying the Basic Servlet in WebLogic Server

In order to deploy the basic servlet, use an example deployment process that applies to every example in this chapter. The deployment process has four steps:

1. Set up the development environment.
2. Copy and unpack the example.
3. Build and deploy the example.
4. View the example.

First, find the example code for the basic servlet on the CD accompanying this book. It is located in the Web archive file named *HelloServlet.war*, which is located in the subdirectory */examples/ch3*.

Step 1: Setting Up the Development Environment

Create a new, empty directory on your local hard disk. For this example, the directory *c:\dev10* will be used. You can do this either using the Windows 2000 Explorer or through the DOS command-line shell. To access a command-line shell, type the letters "cmd" into the dialog box displayed when you click on Run on the Windows Start menu.

Then, set your environment variables correctly so that you can access the WebLogic Server Java services in WebLogic Server, such as the included Java compiler:

```
c:\bea\wlserver6.0\config\mydomain\setEnv.cmd
```

The preceding path may differ if you have installed WebLogic Server on a different drive. In Figure 3–1, WebLogic Server is installed on the C: drive.

Figure 3–1 Setting the Environment

Next, change to the new directory that you just created. You can do this using the cd command (see Figure 3–2).

Figure 3-2 Changing to the Example Directory

Step 2: Copying and Unpacking the Example

You should now copy over the example code from the CD-ROM into this directory. If your CD-ROM drive is the E: drive, you could use the following command:

```
copy E:\examples\ch3\HelloServlet.war c:\dev10\
```

Double check that the file has arrived correctly by doing a directory listing using the `dir` command (see Figure 3–3).

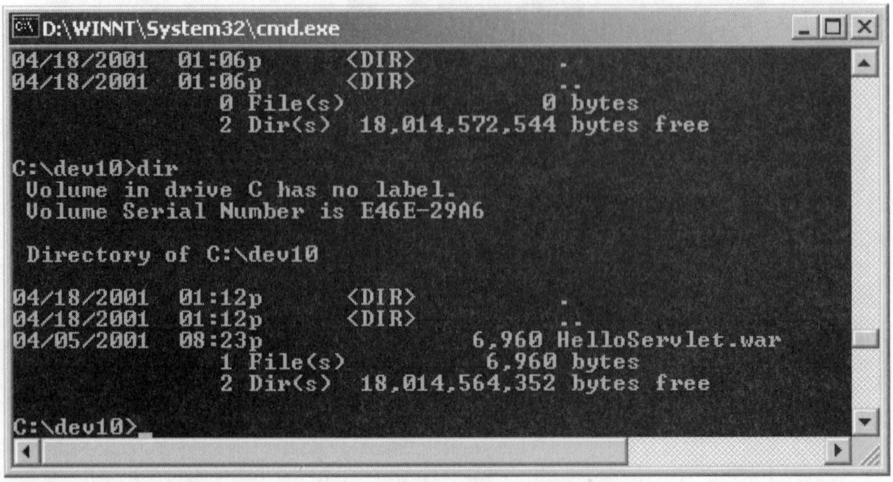

Figure 3-3 Checking that the Web Archive Has Arrived

Unpack the package using the `jar` utility that is included as part of WebLogic Server. This utility is used to package and unpackage application components. To extract all the components from the *.war* file, type the following into the command line:

```
"jar xvf *.war"
```

You should see something like Figure 3–4.

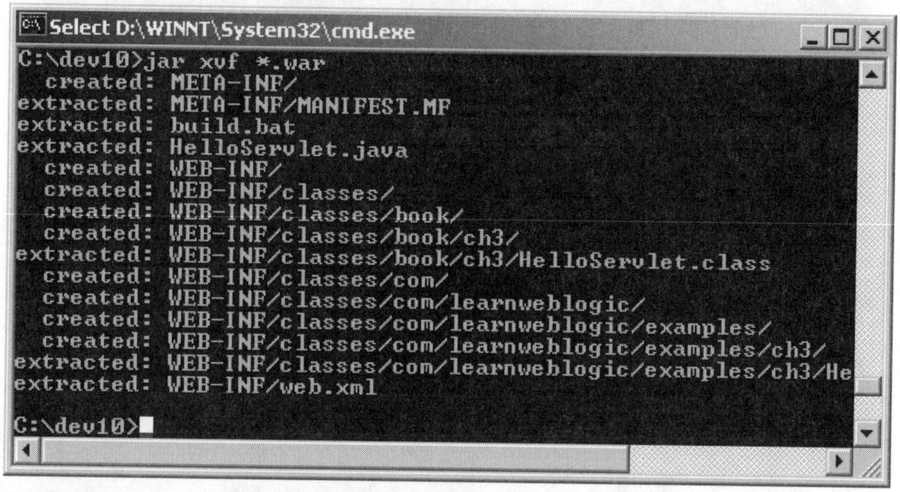

Figure 3–4   Unpacking the Example Package

The `jar` tool is very powerful and used throughout J2EE applications. Virtually all the components of J2EE applications are packaged and unpackaged using `jar`.
To see all the things `jar` can do and to display all the available options, type "jar" by itself into the command line.

The `jar` utility creates packages in the Zip file format. This means that you can use a standard utility, such as WinZip (http://www.winzip.com), to view the contents of any J2EE application package.

Step 3: Building and Deploying the Example

A compile script for the example is included with this package. This script only works for Microsoft Windows, but can be easily tailored to work for other platforms. Remember to edit the build script to point to the proper location of your WebLogic Server deployment if you did not install WebLogic Server on the C: drive.

Type "build" and press Enter. The compilation, packaging, and deployment of the application should take place automatically (see Figure 3–5).

```
D:\WINNT\System32\cmd.exe

C:\dev10>build

C:\dev10>set DEPLOY_DIR=c:\bea\wlserver6.0\config\mydomain\a

C:\dev10>del c:\bea\wlserver6.0\config\mydomain\applications

C:\dev10>javac -d WEB-INF\classes *.java

C:\dev10>jar cvf c:\bea\wlserver6.0\config\mydomain\applicat
r *
added manifest
adding: build.bat(in = 179) (out= 136)(deflated 24%)
adding: HelloServlet.java(in = 1050) (out= 525)(deflated 50%
adding: HelloServlet.war(in = 4141) (out= 2670)(deflated 35%
ignoring entry META-INF/
ignoring entry META-INF/MANIFEST.MF
adding: WEB-INF/(in = 0) (out= 0)(stored 0%)
adding: WEB-INF/classes/(in = 0) (out= 0)(stored 0%)
adding: WEB-INF/classes/book/(in = 0) (out= 0)(stored 0%)
adding: WEB-INF/classes/book/ch3/(in = 0) (out= 0)(stored 0%
adding: WEB-INF/classes/book/ch3/HelloServlet.class(in = 899
d 43%)
adding: WEB-INF/classes/com/(in = 0) (out= 0)(stored 0%)
adding: WEB-INF/classes/com/learnweblogic/(in = 0) (out= 0)(
adding: WEB-INF/classes/com/learnweblogic/examples/(in = 0)
adding: WEB-INF/classes/com/learnweblogic/examples/ch3/(in =
0%)
adding: WEB-INF/classes/com/learnweblogic/examples/ch3/Hello
21) (out= 525)(deflated 42%)
adding: WEB-INF/web.xml(in = 685) (out= 309)(deflated 54%)

C:\dev10>
```

Figure 3–5 Compiling the Servlet with the Build Script

The build script takes advantage of a feature of WebLogic Server called *directory deployments* of applications. If you copy an application component into the *applications* directory of your WebLogic Server installation, the application code is automatically recognized and made available for deployment. If that application component is already deployed, the new and updated version is distributed to all instances of WebLogic Server that have it deployed.

You can view deployed applications in the WebLogic Server console at *http://127.0.0.1:7001/console/* (see Figure 3–6).

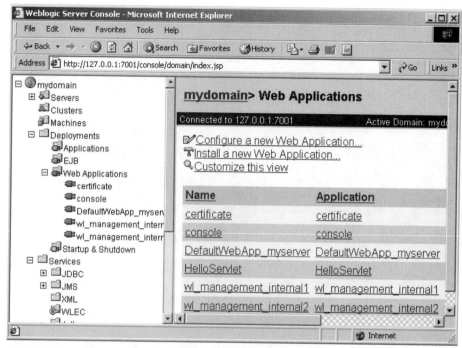

Figure 3–6   Viewing Deployed Applications in the WebLogic Server Console

Step 4: Viewing the Example

To view the example, point a Web browser to *http://127.0.0.1:7001/HelloS-ervlet/*. Don't forget to include the "/" at the end of the URL.

You should see something like Figure 3–7.

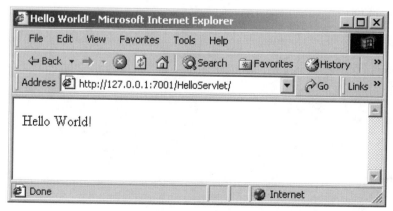

Figure 3–7   Output of the Hello World Servlet

If you do not see anything, be sure to check out the execution window for your Examples Server. The servlet in this example is designed to print out any problems to the console window for review.

If you receive an error that you cannot locate the server, or the connection is refused, then you likely need to turn off your HTTP proxy settings inside the Web browser (see Figure 3–8).

Figure 3–8 Connection Failed Error

About the Packaging and Deployment Process

The *build.bat* script included with this example performs four steps. First, it sets an environment variable for the deployment directory that you plan to use to install your WebLogic Server application components:

```
set DEPLOY_DIR=C:\bea\wlserver6.0\config\mydomain\applications
```

Next, this script removes any packages that you might have previously built:

```
del %DEPLOY_DIR%\HelloServlet.war
```

This action effectively undeploys the component from WebLogic Server, because WebLogic Server watches the applications directory. If anything changes in the applications directory for a server instance, WebLogic Server recognizes that and makes the appropriate changes to its deployed application components. We take advantage of this feature to deploy and undeploy applications from a running WebLogic Server instance. In production situations, it is recommended that you use the WebLogic Server console to deploy application components.

Next, the script calls the Java compiler, `javac`, which is included with WebLogic Server:

```
javac -d WEB-INF\classes *.java
```

This compiles all the Java files into the directory *WEB-INF\classes*. This is required by the J2EE definition of a Web application, which is discussed in a moment.

Finally, the `jar` utility mentioned previously is used to create a new application package:

```
jar cvf %DEPLOY_DIR%\HelloServlet.war *
```

The parameters `cvf` tell `jar` that we are creating an archive, with `jar` displaying verbose output, and that we are specifying the files to be included. The second parameter on the command line, `%DEPLOY_DIR%\HelloServlet.war`, tells `jar` to output the file to a *war* located in our deployment directory with the name *HelloServlet.war*. The third parameter, a wild card specified by `*`, tells `jar` to include every file in the current directory and those below it into the package.

About Web Applications (.war Files)

A Web application archive encapsulates a Web application, including servlets, JSP pages, static HTML pages, and supporting Java code. These files can be deployed on any application server that supports the appropriate J2EE standards.

Web application files use the Zip file format, the *de facto* standard for compressing and bundling multiple files into a single unit. Web applications also include information about how each application component should be deployed, including security information and mappings to URLs. The J2EE standards also define a directory structure for the Web application packages.

The WEB-INF Directory

Each Web application includes a directory called *WEB-INF*. This directory, unlike the rest of the components in the *.war* file, is not made directly available to client browsers. Instead, it contains the deployment information in the form of XML files called *deployment descriptors*. XML, the emerging industry standard for encapsulating data in a common format, is used extensively in J2EE applications. WebLogic Server builds many services around XML. More information on XML is available in the WebLogic Server documentation at *http://www.weblogic.com/docs60/xml/index.html*.

The Java code used in the Web application is placed in a directory under *WEB-INF* as *WEB-INF/classes*. The *web.xml* file contains mappings to tell the application server how to deploy those classes for given requests.

Application Deployment Descriptors

The deployment descriptors tell the J2EE application server how to deploy the components inside the Web application. There are two deployment descriptors. The first, *web.xml*, defines deployment information that is standard on every application server. The second, *weblogic.xml*, is application-server specific and encapsulates deployment information that is only relevant to the application server being used.

In the Hello World servlet, a simple deployment descriptor is included under the name *web.xml* in the *WEB-INF* directory. This deployment descriptor is discussed in detail later in this chapter.

The Lifecycle of a Servlet

The lifecycle of a servlet is relatively simple. Although much of the lifecycle is automatically handled, understanding how servlets behave in the context of WebLogic Server helps you understand best practices for development.

Loading and Instantiation

WebLogic Server is responsible for loading and instantiating servlets. In this case, *instantiating* means creating one or more instances of a servlet.

Initialization

WebLogic Server then calls the init() method of your servlet. This method initializes your servlet to handle subsequent requests, such as database connections or initialization of per-instance local variables.

Each servlet instance created can have per-instance local variables. Unless you're prepared to deal with per-instance local variables in a multi-user distribution, don't use per-instance local variables. You can use local variables within servlet methods, but not on a per-servlet instance basis.

Request Handling

WebLogic Server encapsulates the details of an incoming request into an instance of the javax.servlet.HttpServletRequest object. WebLogic Server then automatically calls an appropriate method in the servlet to handle this request. In the generic case, this generates calls to the service() method of the servlet. In other cases, such as handling POSTs and GETs, other methods are called.

There are two options when building servlets: multi-threaded and single-threaded. Single-threaded servlets implement the SingleThreadModel interface in their class declaration. This model means that only one request can be served at a time by your servlet class, even though WebLogic Server starts multiple threads of execution. Single-threading limits scalability, so it is not appropriate for Web sites where thousands of requests are handled per second.

WebLogic Server creates a pool of servlets if you implement SingleThreadModel. However, this pool is currently statically defined to be of size 5.

End of Service

WebLogic Server removes a servlet instance from active duty by calling the Destroy() method in response to a command from the WebLogic Server console, or when WebLogic Server is shut down.

End of service is different than undeployment of a servlet from a WebLogic Server. *Undeployment* is when the administrator of WebLogic Server removes a servlet from service. In the end-of-service section of the servlet lifecycle, the WebLogic Server container removes a servlet instance whenever the servlet engine deems necessary.

Handling Basic Servlet Requests

The servlet gains access to the `request` object when it is passed as a parameter to the appropriate method handling the request. In the generic case for a request, the `service ()` method of the servlet handles the request:

```
// The Service Method to Handle HTTP Requests and Responses
public void service(HttpServletRequest requ,
                    HttpServletResponse resp)
       throws IOException
{
.
.
.
```

In this example, an instance of the `javax.servlet.HttpServletRequest` object is available through the variable name `requ` inside the scope of that method.

Accessing Data in the Servlet Request Object

The `javax.servlet.HttpServletRequest` object supports a number of methods for accessing data regarding a given request. Request object methods include:

- `public String getMethod()`—Returns the name of the HTTP method with which this request was made, for example, GET, POST, or PUT. Unless the Web browser is instructed otherwise, all requests are GETs of information.
- `public String getAuthType()`—Returns a string containing the name of the authentication scheme used to protect the servlet, for example, BASIC or SSL, or null if the servlet was not protected.
- `public String getRequestURL()`—Returns the part of this request's URL from the protocol name up to the query string in the first line of the HTTP request. For example, this would return *http://learnWeblogic.com/index.jsp* for the HTTP request of GET *http://learnWeblogic.com/index.jsp* HTTP/1.0.

- `public String getProtocol()`—Returns a string containing the name and version of the protocol the request uses in the form protocol/majorVersion.minorVersion, for example, HTTP/1.1.
- `public String getServletPath()`—Returns a string containing the part of this request's URL that calls the servlet. This includes either the servlet name or a path to the servlet, but does not include any extra path information or a query string.
- `public String getPathInfo()`—Returns a string containing any extra path information associated with the URL the client sent when it made the request.
- `public String getPathTranslated()`—Returns a string representing any extra path information after the servlet name but before the query string, and translates it to a real path.
- `public String getQueryString()`—Returns the query string that is contained in the request URL after the path. This method returns null if the URL does not have a query string.
- `public int getContentLength()`—Returns an integer representing the length, in bytes, of the request body in the input stream, or −1 if the length is not known. This is only useful when PUT or POST HTTP requests are made.
- `public String getContentType()`—Returns the MIME type of the body of the request, or null if the type is not known.
- `public String getServerName()`—Returns the host name of the server that received the request.
- `public int getServerPort()`—Returns the port number on which this request was received. Typically, this is the port on which WebLogic Server is listening.
- `public String getRemoteAddr()`—Returns the Internet Protocol (IP) address of the client that sent the request.
- `public String getRemoteHost()`—Returns the fully qualified name of the client that sent the request, or the IP address of the client if the name cannot be determined.
- `public String getRemoteUser()`—Returns the login of the user making this request if the user has been authenticated, or null if the user has not been authenticated. Whether the user

name is sent with each subsequent request depends on the browser and type of authentication.

- `public String getScheme()`—Returns the name of the scheme used to make this request, for example, http, https, or ftp.

A complete list of request methods is available in the JavaDoc for the HttpServletRequest object. You can find this packaged with WebLogic Server, or online at http://java.sun.com/j2ee/j2sdkee/techdocs/api/index.html.

The following code illustrates the process of obtaining the `request` object and using multiple methods to determine information about the request. First, define a servlet class:

```
public class viewRequestServlet extends HttpServlet {
```

When you create a servlet, be sure to define it as a public class so that WebLogic Server (or any other application server) can access your class. Application servers can display lack-of-access errors that are very difficult to diagnose.

As with any other servlet discussed so far, the only work to be done is in the `service()` method of the servlet. WebLogic Server generates an instance of the `HttpServletRequest` object that encapsulates the details surrounding the servlet requests. This object is specific to this request and is passed as a parameter along with the response object.

```
public void service(HttpServletRequest req, HttpServletResponse res)
            throws ServletException, IOException
        {
```

Set the appropriate return content type, and begin to compose the HTML page:

```
    res.setContentType("text/html");
    PrintWriter    out = res.getWriter();

    out.println("<html>");
    out.println("<head><title>viewRequest Servlet</title></head>");
    out.println("<body>");
```

The `HttpUtils.getRequestURL(javax.servlet.http.HttpServletRequest)` method, which is available in the `HttpUtils` package, can be used to acquire an instance of a string representing the URL with a request scheme and complete host:

```
out.println("<h1>Requested URL:</h1>");
out.println("<pre>");
out.println(HttpUtils.getRequestURL(req).toString());
out.println("</pre>");
```

Next, call a sampling of the available methods for the `HttpServletRe-quest` object and print out the results for each:

```
        out.println("<h1>HttpServletRequest information:</
h1><pre>");

    // Returns the Request Method.  For Example, PUT or GET.
    out.println("<br>Request method " + req.getMethod());

    // Returns Request Scheme.  Likely "HTTP 1.1"
    out.println("<br>Request scheme " + req.getScheme());

    // The protocol type for the request.  Likely HTTP.
    out.println("<br>Request protocol " + req.getProtocol());

    // A subset of the complete URL.
    out.println("<br>Request URL " + req.getRequestURI());

    // Info on the path to the servlet.
    out.println("<br>Servlet path "     +   req.getServlet-
Path());
    out.println("<br>Path info "        +   req.getPathInfo());
    out.println("<br>Path translated "  +req.getPathTrans-
lated());
    out.println("<br>Query string "     +   req.getQue-
ryString());

    // Info on the Request Content
    out.println("<br>Content length "   + req.getCon-
tentLength());
    out.println("<br>Content type "     +   req.getContent-
Type());

    // Local Server Details.
    out.println("<br>Server name "      +   req.getServerName());
    out.println("<br>Server port "      +   req.getServerPort());

    // Remote Host and User Information
    out.println("<br>Remote user "      +   req.getRemoteUser());
    out.println("<br>Remote address "   +   req.getRemoteAddr());
    out.println("<br>Remote host "      +   req.getRemoteHost());
```

Finally, close off the HTML page:

```
    out.println("</body></html>");
    }
}
```

The output from an execution of this servlet might look like Figure 3–9.

Figure 3–9 Output from Servlet Execution

Deploying the viewRequestServlet in WebLogic Server

The `viewRequestServlet` is part of the *viewRequestServlet.war* package, which can be found on the CD accompanying this book in the directory *examples\ch3*. It can be compiled, packaged, and deployed using the process previously described for the Hello World example. Be sure to create a separate directory for building and deploying each servlet.

Generating the Servlet Response

As you have seen, the HTTP response that your servlet generates is handled by the instance of the `HttpServletResponse` object passed to your servlet via the `service()` method. Methods standard to this `HttpServletResponse` object enable you to format the response you send to clients.

Getting an Output Stream

First, we'll use the response object, the `HttpServletResponse` object, to get a stream to write your output to the client:

```
// Now obtain a PrintWriter stream to write to.
PrintWriter out = resp.getWriter();
```

Setting the Response Content Type

You must define the type of content (the **MIME** type) that you send to the client. In most cases, you'll use WebLogic Server to send out HTML as in the following:

```
// Now Set the Response Content Type
resp.setContentType("text/html");
```

You can then print to that stream:

```
// Now Print Out the Text
out.println("<html><head><title>" +
            "Hello World!</title></head>" +
            "Hello World!</h1></body></html>");
```

Note that in no case have we explicitly closed/flushed the output stream. This is intentional. As noted previously, WebLogic Server is very efficient at buffering the responses that it sends back to clients. In addition, WebLogic Server supports the notion of HTTP 1.1 Keep-Alive. Using this optimization,

WebLogic Server tries to keep open sockets for as long as possible. This saves greatly in terms of the overhead required to create and destroy sockets.

Other Useful Response Methods

There are a number of other useful methods to use when generating responses:

- `public void sendError(int status) throws IOException;`
- `public void sendError(int status, String message) throws IOException;`

These methods allow you to send an error message to the client. To send a status of 808 with a message of `"invalid state acquired"`, use the following code:

```
public void service(HttpServletRequest req, HttpServletResponse res)
        throws ServletException, IOException
 {
res.sendError(808, "invalid state acquired");
 }
```

- `public void sendRedirect(String location) throws IOException;`—Allows you to redirect the request to a different URL. To redirect the client to *http://www.bea.com,* include the following code in your servlet:

```
public void service(HttpServletRequest req, HttpServletResponse res)
        throws ServletException, IOException
 {
res.sendRedirect(http://www.bea.com/)
 }
```

- `public void setDateHeader(String headername, long date);`—Sets a response header with the given name and date value. The date is specified in terms of milliseconds since the epoch. If the header has already been set, the new value overwrites the previous one. The `containsHeader` method can be used to test for the presence of a header before setting its value.

- `public boolean containsHeader(String name);`—Used to test for the presence of a header before setting its value.

- `public void setHeader(String headername, String value);`—Sets a response header with the given name and value. If the header has already been set, the new value overwrites the previous one. If the header value has already been flushed, then this method and all other methods dealing with the header are ignored.

- `public void addHeader(String headername, String value);`—Adds a response header with the given name and value. This method allows response headers to have multiple values.

- `public void addIntHeader(String headername, int value);`—Adds a response header with the given name and integer value. This method allows response headers to have multiple values.

- `public void setIntHeader(String headername, int value);`—Sets a response header with the given name and integer value. If the header has already been set, the new value overwrites the previous one.

Using Default Methods to Handle Web Forms

In the previous examples, we built servlets that *override* default methods such as `service()`.

Overriding the default methods is not always required. If it is not overwritten, the default `service()` method automatically dispatches requests to the appropriate method, based on the request type. There are a number of other useful default methods. For example, the servlet specification defines methods for handling different types of HTTP requests. These methods take the form of "do<request type>", where the type of HTTP request the method handles replaces <request type>.

Servlet default methods that deal with HTTP interactions (GETs and POSTs) are `doGet()` and `doPost()`, respectively. The next section discusses the mechanics behind Web forms and the use of these methods.

About GETs

A GET request instructs the Web server to return a given resource to the client. A sample GET might look like the following:

```
GET http://www.bea.com/pictures/nickd/index.html HTTP/1.1
```

The Web server receives this GET, parses it, and responds with the appropriate resource via the protocol specified, version 1.1 of HTTP.

About POSTs

POSTs are the mechanism for transferring data from the Web browser to the servlet. POSTs are most often used to transfer data (user name, password, bid amount, etc.) from Web forms.

The parameters to POSTs consist of name/value pairs. Each field in the form is given a name. When the user completes that field in the form, the name is initialized with the value the user entered. Once the request is completed (when the user presses the Submit button), the name/value pairs are encapsulated in the HTTP request sent to the Web server, and eventually handed off to the servlet specified in the form.

> Note: At best, this section is a simplification of the HTTP protocol as it relates to POSTs and GETs in a WebLogic Server application. For a more detailed look into the HTTP protocol, the specification is located at a number of sites on the Internet. One reliable mirror is located at ftp://ftp.isi.edu/in-notes/rfc2616.txt.
> The complete listing of these standards can be located at the World Wide Web Consortium (W3C) Web site at http://www.W3C.org.
> Other methods that are part of the servlet specification for `HttpServlet` include:
> • doPut, for HTTP PUT requests.
> • doDelete, for HTTP DELETE requests.
> More information on each of these methods, which are not commonly used, can be found in the API documentation for servlets. Currently, this API documentation is located on the JavaSoft Web site at http://java.sun.com/products/servlet/2.2/javadoc/index.html.

POSTs on the Form Side

The first step in building a Web form is to code the HTML. The following is a very basic HTML page for a Web form:

```
<html>
<body bgcolor=#FFFFFF>
<h1>
My Form!
</h1>

<p>
<font face="Helvetica">
<form method="post" action="formServlet">
  <table border="0" bgcolor=#eeeeee align=center cellspacing=10>
    <tr>
      <td>Username:</td>
      <td>
        <input type="TEXT" name="username">
      </td>
    </tr>
    <tr>
      <td>Your age:</td>
      <td>
        <input type="TEXT" name="age">
      </td>
    </tr>
  </table>
  <p>
  <center>
    <input type="SUBMIT" name="submit" value="Submit">
  </center>
</form>
</font>
</body>
</html>
```

In a Web browser, this page might look like the Web input form in Figure 3–10.

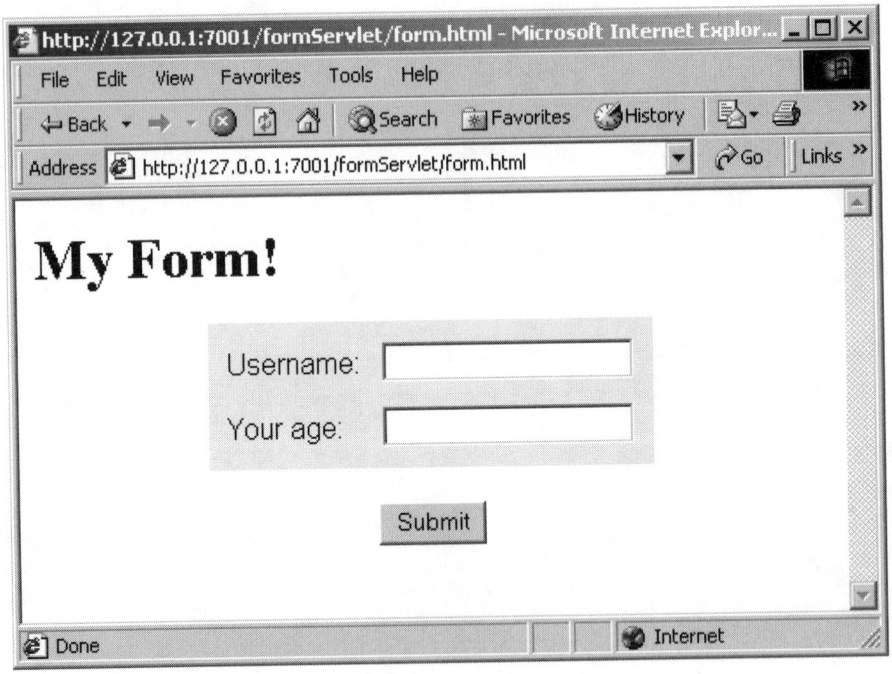

Figure 3-10 Web Input Form

The form has two fields, Username and Your Age. When the user completes the form and presses Submit, a POST of the data is sent to WebLogic Server. WebLogic Server encapsulates that request in an instance of the HttpServletRequest object.

The next step is to write a method called doPost() into the servlet that handles the POST. As specified by the HTML form, the servlet that handles the POST is called formServlet.

POSTs on the Servlet Side

When a POST is received, WebLogic Server calls the doPost() method in the servlet. The method signature looks like the following:

```
public void doPost(HttpServletRequest req, HttpServletResponse
res)
        throws IOException, ServletException
```

This is very similar to the service() method and is used in much the same way. The first step is to create an Enumeration of all the names of the parameters specified in the request using the getParameterNames() method available as part of the HttpServletRequest object:

```
Enumeration ParamNames = req.getParameterNames();
```

Then, that Enumeration can be traversed to look at each individual name/value pair:

```
while(ParamNames.hasMoreElements()){

    // Get the next name.
    String ParamString = (String)ParamNames.nextElement();

    // Print out the current name's value:
    pw.println("<b>" + ParamString + ":</b> " +
            req.getParameterValues(ParamString)[0]);
    pw.println("<P>");

}
}
```

The `getParameterValues()` method returns an array of string objects containing the values of the given request name, or null if the parameter does not exist. This method is useful in situations in which a given parameter is POSTed with more than one value for a given name. In this simple case, we only need to look at the first value in the array at index 0.

All name/value pairs are encoded as strings. So, for example, if you are attempting to receive a dollar amount or a phone number, the return type out of the `getParameterValues` method always will be a string, which you must be sure to parse appropriately.

You can also access each parameter value directly by explicitly asking for it by name:

```
req.getParameter("name");
```

This returns the value of a request parameter called `"name"` as a String, or null if the parameter does not exist. You should only use this method when you are sure the parameter has only one value. If the parameter might have more than one value, you would use `getParameterValues(java.lang.String`. A complete `doPost()` method for this form is included later in this section.

Note: Handling secure logins is slightly different from standard Web forms. Forms for secure logins are covered in Chapter 4, Using WebLogic Server JavaServer Pages.

Handling GETs and POSTs Together

Servlets can handle both GET and POST inside a single class. You can treat the `doGet` and `doPost` methods just as you treated the `service()` method in previous examples.

A simple servlet with a `doGet` method might look like the following:

```
// Import Classes and Declare Servlet Class
import java.io.*;
import java.util.*;

import javax.servlet.*;
import javax.servlet.http.*;

public class viewRequestServlet extends HttpServlet {

    // Define Method to Handle GETs
    public void doGet(HttpServletRequest req, HttpServletResponse
res)
            throws ServletException, IOException
    {

        /* Set the appropriate return content type,
           and compose the HTML page: */
        res.setContentType("text/html");
        PrintWriterout = res.getWriter();

        out.println("<html>");
        out.println("<head><title>doGet Servlet</title></head>");
        out.println("<body></body></html>");
    }
}
```

The output of the servlet should be a simple HTML page with no content.

Extending the Servlet

We can now put together a single servlet to handle both the initial GET from a user and the subsequent POST. This simply involves creating a servlet with both the `doGet()` and `doPost()` methods. First, we need to import the necessary classes and declare our servlet class:

```
package com.learnweblogic.examples.ch3;

import java.io.*;
import java.util.*;
import javax.servlet.*;
```

```
import javax.servlet.http.*;

public class formServlet extends HttpServlet{

   /*  The doGet method handles the initial invocation of
       the servlet.  The default service() method recognizes
       that it has received a GET and calls this method
       appropriately. It responds with a form that uses
       the POST method to submit data.
   */
   public void doGet(HttpServletRequest req, HttpServletResponse
res)
     throws IOException, ServletException
   {
     res.setContentType("text/html");
     res.setHeader("Pragma", "no-cache");

     PrintWriter   out = res.getWriter();

     out.println("<html>");
     out.println("<body bgcolor=#FFFFFF>");
     out.println("<h1>");
     out.println("My Form!");
     out.println("</h1>");
     out.println("<font face=Helvetica>");
     out.println("<form method=post action=FormServlet>");
     out.println("<table border=0 bgcolor=#eeeeee cellspac-
ing=10>");
     out.println("<tr>");
     out.println("<td>Username:</td>");
     out.println("<td>");
     out.println("<input type=TEXT name=username>");
     out.println("</td>");
     out.println("</tr>");
     out.println("<tr>");
     out.println("<td>Your age:</td>");
     out.println("<td>");
     out.println("<input type=TEXT name=age>");
     out.println("</td>");
     out.println("</tr>");
     out.println("</table>");
     out.println("<p>");
     out.println("<center>");
     out.println("<input type=SUBMIT name=submit value=Submit>");
     out.println("</center>");
     out.println("</form>");
     out.println("</font>");
     out.println("</body>");
```

```
     out.println("</html>");
   }

   /* Finally, include a separate doPost() method to be called
      when the user responds by clicking on the submit button: */

   /*
     Responds to the "POST" query from the
     original form supplied by the doGet() method.
   */
   public void doPost(HttpServletRequest req, HttpServletResponse
res)
      throws IOException, ServletException
   {

     // Set the content type of the response.
     res.setContentType("text/html");
     res.setHeader("Pragma", "no-cache");

     PrintWriter pw = res.getWriter();

     pw.println("<HTML><HEAD><TITLE>Form Completed</TITLE></
HEAD>");
     pw.println("<BODY>The information you have" +
       " submitted is as follows:");
     pw.println("<P>");

     // Loop through all the name/value pairs.
     Enumeration ParamNames = req.getParameterNames();

     // Loop through all the name/value pairs.
     while(ParamNames.hasMoreElements()) {

       // Get the next name.
       String ParamString = (String)ParamNames.nextElement();

       // Print out the current name's value:
       pw.println("<b>" + ParamString + ":</b> " +
         req.getParameterValues(ParamString)[0]);
       pw.println("<P>");
     }
     pw.println("</BODY></HTML>");
   }
}
```

Figure 3–11 shows what the first screen for the user might look like.

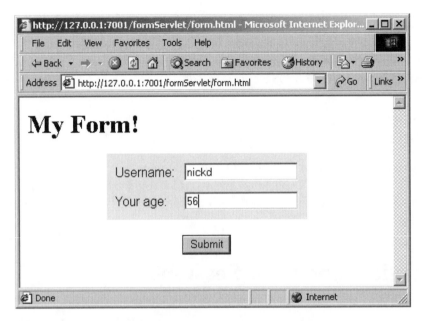

Figure 3-11   The User's First Screen

The completed form after the POST is shown in Figure 3-12.

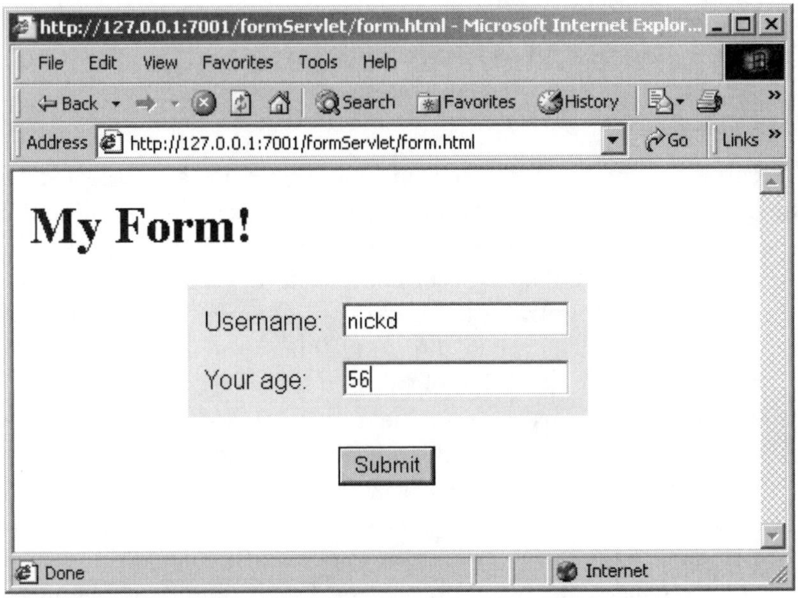

Figure 3-12   After the POST

Why is the input type defined in the HTML page posted as one of the HTML POST parameters? This is to support pages that may have multiple different submit buttons, each with a different name and value. Your servlet can look at the value of the submit parameter to see which button was pressed and handle the POST appropriately.

Deploying the Form Servlet in WebLogic Server

Use the code included on the CD accompanying this book to deploy the form servlet. The Web application archive is located in the file */examples/ch3/ formServlet.war*. Use the process described for the Hello Servlet example as your guide.

Servlets and Web Sessions

The Hypertext Transfer Protocol (HTTP) is by design a *stateless* protocol. However, an effective Web application requires that a series of requests from a particular client be grouped together. The notion of grouping multiple requests from a single client is typically referred to as a *Web session*.

Conventional Methods for Session Tracking Are Difficult

In the early days of the Web, few mechanisms were available for session tracking. The earliest of these was hidden form fields in pages. Later, this was supplanted by the use of *cookies* and *URL rewriting*. Cookies are defined text objects that can be placed in the user's offline store, via their browser. Subsequent requests to a site retrieve the cookie, which serves the session information. URL rewriting does much the same thing except it adds the session information to the extended URL of subsequent requests.

These early mechanisms were not ideal. Hidden fields are hard to manage. As for cookies, many users rejected them because they considered cookies to be a violation of their privacy. URL rewriting displays a messy URL to the user. In each case, you are storing user session information on the *client*, where it is subject to attack. (Malicious hackers can change the data in the cookies to wreak havoc in your Web system.) Finally, shipping volumes of client data over the wire can slow down even the fastest Web servers.

The Servlet Specification to the Rescue

A major advantage of the servlet specification over other dynamic content generation technologies is its support for session tracking that keeps the user information on the *server*. Via the server, cookies can be stored in a database and made persistent. By design, URL rewriting persists only during an active HTTP session.

The servlet object that tracks a user's state is called `javax.servlet.http.HttpSession`, which is available as part of the `HttpServletRequest` object. This mechanism enables session information to be automatically handled by WebLogic Server. Developers don't need to deal with the details of tracking sessions.

Session Identification

Every session is given a unique, randomly generated session identification number. The servlet engine uses this number to track sessions. WebLogic Server automatically handles the assignment of session ID numbers and transparently places session information in the client browser. This information is a placeholder to match the browser to the `HttpSession` object that is automatically created for each user session. In addition, as of Version 5.1 and above, WebLogic Server supports the capability to configure the length of the session ID.

Technically, WebLogic Server automatically creates temporary cookies for each browser session with a very long number, the *session identifier*, each time a session is created. WebLogic Server places these temporary cookies in the client browser. This cookie is sent along with each subsequent request that the browser makes. WebLogic Server automatically maps the session identifier to the `HttpSession` object it is tracking for that user. When the servlet is invoked to handle the request, WebLogic Server locates the appropriate `HttpSession` and automatically hands that off to the servlet.

If a browser has disabled cookies, WebLogic Server automatically attempts to use URL rewriting, which involves adding information usually kept in the cookie to the end of the URL string.

For most standard Web browser clients, the default length of session IDs is acceptable. In other cases, such as for wireless (WAP) devices, shorter session IDs are required. Where possible, the best practice is to use the longest session ID possible to ensure security. The longer the session ID, the more difficult it is for attackers to randomly guess numbers that might be valid session IDs and masquerade as a valid user.

Accessing the Session Object

The session object exists during the lifetime of the session and is available for each new request by the same client. A reference to the `HttpSession` object can be obtained from the `HttpServletRequest` object using the `HttpServletRequest.getSession()` method like this:

```
HttpSession session = request.getSession (false);
```

This method takes a Boolean. If the value is true, a new session object is created if one does not already exist. If the value is false, the server does *not* create a new session object. For reasons that become apparent later, you typically want to set a value of `false` when you call this method.

What to Put in Your Session

There are a number of things you could store in a session object, including:

- Virtual shopping carts to hold the items that a user is currently interested in purchasing.
- A history of what a resources user has looked at during the current session. For example, if you are building an e-commerce site, you'll want to see what pages the user has visited during the session, to help decide what other things to show him or her.

There also are things that you would *not* want to store in a session object, including long-term data, such as a user record or profile.

Recognizing New Sessions

Use the `isNew()` method of the `HttpSession` object to determine if you are accessing a new session. For example, you can use this method to force users to log in each time they begin a new session, which prevents them from bypassing your security mechanisms.

After you acquire the session object, check to see if it is null (that is, its value has not already been set). If it is not null, then you can continue using the session. If it is null, you simply redirect the client browser to the login page for your Web application:

```
HttpSession session = request.getSession (false);

If (session==null) {
// We  Send a Redirect
responseObj.sendRedirect("http://www.blahblah.com/login");

}
```

What NOT to Do

On the other hand, do *not* do something like this:

```
// An Example of What Not to Do:
HttpSession session = request.getSession (true);
// Check to See If the Session Is New
If (session.isNew()) {
// We  Send a Redirect
responseObj.sendRedirect("http://www.blahblah.com/login");
}
```

In this code, we ask for the session object as usual. However, because we set the parameter value equal to *true* in the `getSession` method, *a new session is created if one does not already exist*. Unfortunately, this leaves a security hole: Someone could create a large number of session objects, which could eat up memory on your server for as long as he or she wanted to make requests.

> *Check for new sessions in your servlets to ensure that someone is not trying to "work around" your security measures by not logging in.*

Storing and Accessing Session Data

Session data is stored in the session object (`HttpSession`) via name/value pairs. With each name, which is a string value, the `HttpSession` object stores a value. This value can be any Java type.

> *Store user information such as shopping carts in a session object for your servlets.*

The servlet specification defines four methods that you can use to access the values in the `HttpSession` object. These are:

- `public Object getAttribute (String name)`—Returns the object bound with the specified name in this session, or null if no object is bound under the name.

- `public void setAttribute (String name, Object attribute)` —Binds an object to this session using the name specified.

- `public Enumeration getAttributeNames ()`—Returns an Enumeration of string objects containing the names of all the objects bound to this session.

- `public void removeAttribute(String name)`—Removes the object bound with the specified name from this session.

The Scope of a Session

In WebLogic Server, a session begins when a user first accesses the site and a servlet instructs that a new session be created. WebLogic Server creates the HTTP session object and attaches cookies to the browser for the duration of the browser session. The browser session is a single continuous period of time in which the Web browser is active on the client. If the user shuts down the Web browser, these particular cookies disappear. While the particular HTTP session object is stored in WebLogic Server until a timeout is reached, the removal of the cookie from the browser means that the HTTP session object for that browser is no longer accessible.

The timeout interval for sessions is specified in the WebLogic Server configuration. If there is no request to WebLogic Server for the duration of the timeout interval, WebLogic Server automatically invalidates and removes the HTTP session. If a user returns to WebLogic Server after the session has been closed, that user has to log in again, and any information that you have kept in the HTTP session object is gone.

It is also possible to declare the session to end in your servlets, as we see in this next section.

HttpSession objects themselves should not be considered to be available outside the scope of the request. Therefore, you should not pass references to the session objects that you receive in your session () method. If you want to use those values elsewhere, you should make a clone () of them first.

Note that this refers to the HttpSession objects themselves and not the attributes that you bind into it. Attributes are available outside of the scope of the session.

Invalidating a Session

Invalidate a session when a user performs some specific action, such as logging out. Use the `invalidate()` method of the `HttpSession` object, like this:

```
// Create the Session Object
HttpSession session = request.getSession (false);
// Invalidate the Session
session.invalidate();
```

The HTTP session is cleared and invalid for further use. The next time the user visits your servlet, a new session object is created.

When users want to log out, do so by invalidating their session.

Sessions, Inactivity, and Time

The `HttpSession` object supports other useful methods:

- `public long getCreationTime();`—Returns a long integer that represents when the session was created. To print the creation time of the object:

```
HttpSession session = request.getSession (true);
// Get the Creation Time and Print it
system.out.println(session.getCreationTime());
```

- `public String getId();`—Returns a long integer of the ID number that WebLogic Server has associated with the session. To print the ID number of the servlet session:

```
HttpSession session = request.getSession (true);
// Get the Creation Time and Print it
system.out.println(session.getID());
```

- `public long getLastAccessedTime();`—Returns a long integer that represents the last time the session object was accessed.
- `public int getMaxInactiveInterval();`—Returns an integer that represents the number of seconds that the session can be inactive before it is automatically removed by WebLogic Server.

- `public void setMaxInactiveInterval(int interval);`—Sets the number of seconds that the session can be inactive before the session is invalidated.

Sessions consume resources in WebLogic Server. For that reason, set your inactive intervals to be as short as possible.

Sessions and Servlets Example

Building servlets to use sessions is relatively simple. As an example, let's build a servlet that counts the number of times you have visited a given page. To do so, insert a counter object into the session object for the user. Each time the user revisits the page, we update and increment the counter object.

First, import the necessary classes and declare your class name:

```java
import java.io.*;
import java.util.Enumeration;
import javax.servlet.*;
import javax.servlet.http.*;

public class SessionServlet extends HttpServlet {

    /*
        Next, create a method to handle the
        GET request for your servlet:
    */

public void doGet (HttpServletRequest req, HttpServletResponse res)
        throws ServletException, IOException
    {
    /*
        Get the session object
    */
    HttpSession session = req.getSession(true);

    /* set content type and other
        response header fields first */
    res.setContentType("text/html");

    /*
        then write the data of the response
    */
    PrintWriter out = res.getWriter();
```

```
    out.println("<HEAD><TITLE> " + "SessionServlet Output " +
                "</TITLE></HEAD><BODY>");
    out.println("<h1> SessionServlet Output </h1>");

    /*
       Retrieve the count value from the session
    */
Integer ival = (Integer)
session.getAttribute("sessiontest.counter");

    /*
       If the counter is not currently contained in the session,
       one needs to be created:
    */

    if (ival==null) {
      ival = new Integer(1);
    } else {
      ival = new Integer(ival.intValue() + 1);
    }

    session.setAttribute("sessiontest.counter", ival);

    /*
       And print out how many times the user has hit the
       current page:
    */
    out.println("You have hit this page <b>" + ival +
    "</b> times.<p>");
    out.println("Click <a href=" + res.encodeURL("session") +
                ">here</a>");
    out.println(" to ensure that session tracking is working even
" +
                "if cookies aren't supported.<br>");
    out.println("<p>");

    /*
       Finally, demonstrate some of the more common methods in the
       HttpSession object surrounding sessions:
    */
    out.println("<h3>Request and Session Data:</h3>");
    out.println("Session ID in Request: " +
                req.getRequestedSessionId());
    out.println("<br>Session ID in Request from Cookie: " +
                req.isRequestedSessionIdFromCookie());
    out.println("<br>Session ID in Request from URL: " +
                req.isRequestedSessionIdFromURL());
```

```
    out.println("<br>Valid Session ID: " +
                req.isRequestedSessionIdValid());
    out.println("<h3>Session Data:</h3>");
    out.println("New Session: " + session.isNew());
    out.println("<br>Session ID: " + session.getId());
    out.println("<br>Creation Time: " + session.getCreation-
Time());
    out.println("<br>Last Accessed Time: " +
                session.getLastAccessedTime());

    out.println("</BODY>");
  }
}
```

The output of this servlet looks something like Figure 3–13.

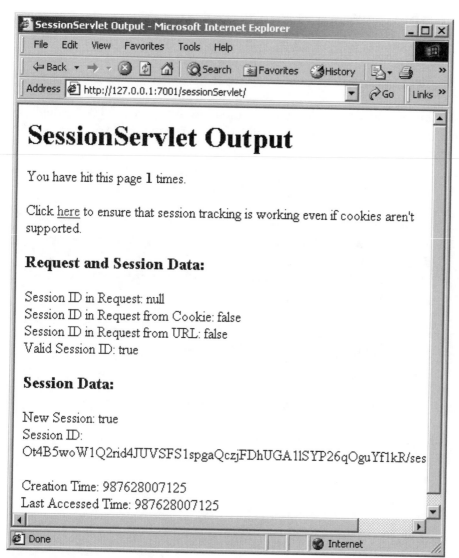

Figure 3–13 Servlet Output

If you click refresh to visit this page multiple times, you'll see that the counter increments each time by incrementing the HTTP session object. If you restart the Web browser, the counter restarts at 1 because the previous session has been removed from WebLogic Server.

Deploying the Session Servlet in WebLogic Server

In order to deploy the session servlet, you can use the code included on the CD accompanying this book. It is located in the file named *sessionServlet.war*, which is located in the subdirectory */examples/ch3*. It is deployed using the same process used for the Hello servlet example and every other application sample.

The Servlet API enables you to specify that the objects you place in the HTTP session can be notified when they are added to or removed from the session object. This is an advanced technique, which is not discussed in detail in this book. However, you can learn more about session notification from the servlet API documentation, at
http://java.sun.com/products/servlet/2.2/javadoc/javax/servlet/http/
HttpSessionBindingListener.html.

To specify the objects that you want to be notified when they are removed from or added to a session, implement this interface, including the two methods:

```
public void valueBound(HttpSessionBindingEvent event)
public void valueUnBound(HttpSessionBindingEvent event)
```
Your class definition may look like this:

```
import javax.servlet.http;

public class myObjectInSession implements
HttpSessionBindingListener  {
```

These methods on the object are called when the object is bound and unbound into the `HttpSession` *object. The single parameter is an instance of* `HttpSessionBindingEvent`, *which includes information about the event that has happened. More information on this class is available at*

http://java.sun.com/products/servlet/2.2/javadoc/javax/servlet/http/
HttpSessionBindingEvent.html.

Baking Your Own Cookies

While WebLogic Server uses cookies for its internal mechanisms, it also enables developers to *create their own cookies* either in conjunction with servlet sessions or alone. Cookies are very useful for storing long-term identities for users. For example, you might want users to be recognized when they return to the bookstore so they do not have to log in every time. To facilitate this, place a cookie on the user's Web browser using the APIs provided in the servlet engine. (This assumes that the user permits cookies to be attached to his or her Web browser.)

A cookie contains the following data:

- Name
- A single value
- Optional attributes such as a comment, path and domain qualifiers, a maximum age, and a version number

---

Cookies can store information over a long period of time. However, this does not mean that they are appropriate for storing sensitive data. For long-term storage of sensitive data, the best practice is to use a database. Using WebLogic Server to access a database via the J2EE standards is covered in Chapter 5, Using Databases and Transactions with JDBC and JTA.

Cookies vs. Servlet Sessions

Servlet sessions have a limitation in that they are only active for a short period of time. Typically, servlet sessions only last as long as the lifetime of the browser session, or a (shorter) defined period of time. Once the Web browser is exited or the session "times out," WebLogic Server automatically disposes of the HttpSession object.

When you want your Web application automatically to recognize a given user without requiring him or her to log back in, use a cookie.

Here are other examples of when to use servlets and when to use cookies. Problems best solved with a servlet session:

- Tracking a user shopping cart
- Caching data such as account balances that the user might look up more than once during a session

- Storing references or addresses of resources on which you are relying

Problems best solved with a cookie:

- "Remembering users" over a long period of time

Dealing with Users

Web applications typically attempt to personalize content. In the WebAuction application, when a given user logs in, only that user's auction items are displayed. Similarly, an online bookstore might use a recommendation engine to recommend books according to your personal tastes, when you visit the site.

How to Track Users

For the most part, WebLogic Server handles users and logins automatically. Security on components is handled by configuring the Web application deployment descriptor. WebLogic Server has its own security store, and supports connections to external security stores. WebLogic Server automatically maps users of your Web application to known security stores. When a user visits your site, WebLogic Server handles authentication and permissions for you. Chapter 12 contains a complete example of coding and configuring user login and tracking for a Web-based application.

Creating a Cookie

The process of creating a cookie is very simple. First, you need to create the cookie object by creating an instance of the cookie class, which is part of the servlet package. The constructor for a cookie class takes two parameters: a name for the cookie and a value. This value is the information that you want to store, such as the user's name or any arbitrary string value. To create a cookie, put the following in your servlet:

```
Cookie myCookie = new Cookie(" Cookie name ", "63");
```

Then, add your cookie to the HTTP response:

```
response.addCookie(myCookie);
```

Note that the values stored in cookies can only be strings. Therefore, you should text-encode all data that you store in a cookie. Once you add a cookie to your response object, WebLogic Server automatically places it in the client browser, which stores it on the local computer disk.

Getting Cookies

When WebLogic Server invokes a servlet, the cookies sent by the browser are included in the `HttpServletRequest` object that is passed as a parameter to your service method. These are stored as an array of cookie objects. To access them, use the following code:

```
Cookie[] cookies = request.getCookies();
```

Once you have the cookie objects, you can search for your specific cookie. You can use the `getname()` method to look at each cookie's name:

```
// Assign the Name of the First
// Cookie in The Array to String foo
String foo = Cookies[0].getname();
```

Note that you can use more than one cookie. The typical browser supports 20 cookies for each Web server, 300 cookies total, and may limit cookie size to 4KB each.

Useful Methods for Dealing with Cookies

There are a number of other methods that you can use with cookies:

- `public void setComment(String comment);` and `public String getComment();`—Can be used to set the comment field in your cookie. This is very useful for occasions when individuals are browsing their cookie store on their Web browser. To set the comment field in a cookie named `myCookie`, place the following code in your servlet:

```
// Set the Comment Field in Cookie myCookiemyCookie.setComment("gumby999");
```

- `public void setMaxAge(int expiry);` and `public int getMaxAge();`—Set and get the number of seconds before the cookie expires. A value of negative one (−1) means that the cookie expires when the Web browser exits. To make your cookies last indefinitely, set the value as high as possible:

```
// Set the cookie myCookie to last indefinitely
myCookie.setMaxAge(Integer.MAX_VALUE);
```

- `public String getValue()` and `public void setValue(String newValue)`—Enable you to *access* the value stored in the cookie and *set* the value stored in the cookie, respectively.
- `public void setSecure(boolean);` and `public boolean getSecure();`—Enable you to set the security settings for the cookie. The following code requires that the cookie be sent only over a secure channel such as SSL:

```
// Require That the Cookie myCookie
// Only Be Sent over Secure Channels
myCookie.setSecure(true);
```

URL Rewriting

What if a client does not accept cookies? URL rewriting is a way of dealing with clients *who do not accept cookies*. URL rewriting works by adding a session ID to the end of the URL returned to clients in your response method. It can be used in place of cookies by your application. URL rewriting only lasts for the scope of the session.

Using URL rewriting is also important when using Web frames and redirects. Depending on timing or the type of request, the cookie may not be sent with subsequent requests from the browser. If you notice that your Web site mysteriously loses contact with the user sessions when frames are being used, you should attempt to enable URL rewriting to solve the problem.

WebLogic Server uses URL rewriting at the beginning of every session to ascertain whether the client supports cookies. If the client browser does support cookies, then WebLogic Server automatically uses cookies. If not, WebLogic Server can be configured to use URL rewriting.

To enable URL rewriting in WebLogic Server, set the `"URLRewritingEnabled"` attribute in `<session-descriptor>` to `true` in the WebLogic Server–specific deployment descriptor, *weblogic.xml*. (The default value for this attribute is `true`.)

```
<session-descriptor>
  <session-param>
    <param-name>
      URLRewritingEnabled
    </param-name>
    <param-value>
      true
    </param-value>
  </session-param>
```

```
</session-descriptor>
```

Using URL Rewriting in Applications

URL rewriting requires a method in the servlet response object to encode the URL. This method takes two forms:

- `public String encodeURL(String url);`—Includes the logic required to encode the session information in the returned URL. WebLogic Server automatically determines whether the session ID needs to be encoded in the URL. If the browser supports cookies, or session tracking is turned off, URL encoding is unnecessary. To encode the URL, add the following code to your servlet:

```
// Add the Session Information Via URL Encoding
myHttpServletResponse.encodeURL(thisURL);
```

- `public String encodeRedirectURL(String url);`—Performs the same task as the previous method, except it is specially geared to redirects in the response object. For redirection you should have the following in your servlet:

```
// Sending a Redirect with URL Encoded session ID
myHttpServletResponse.sendRedirect
        (myHttpServletResponse.encodeRedirectUrl(anotherURL));
```

So, if your original URL was:

```
<a href="foo.jsp">bar</a>
```

You would use the `HttpServletResponse.encodeURL()` method, on that URL:

```
        out.println("<a href=\""
    + response.encodeURL("<a href=\"foo.jsp\">")
    + "\">bar</a>");
```

Note that all servlets in an application must use URL rewriting for this to work properly.

Testing URL Rewriting

Once you get URL rewriting engaged, the clients that you point at your server see a difference. In fact, you see something like this:

```
http://www.shinn.com/index.html;jsessionid=1234
```

The Session ID number is encoded at the end of the URL for each page.

Servlet/JSP developers should always use the URL encoding methods when embedding URLs in their HTML so that WebLogic Server can properly take advantage of URL rewriting if the client's browser does not accept cookies.

Custom Cookies for Personalization

Applications that remember users over long periods of time and across browser sessions *set their own cookie* (different from the cookies used by WebLogic Server) after the user logs in to the site. In subsequent contact with the server that set the cookie, the browser piggybacks that cookie onto the request. The application can check to see whether that cookie exists and log in the user automatically, without requiring a user name and password for authentication.

This kind of behavior is common in many e-commerce sites. For example, Amazon.com remembers users by a cookie stored in the browser. When you return to their site, you do not need to log in again.

The first step in implementing a custom login cookie is to add the mechanism to set and look for the cookie in your pages. The following is a trivial doGet method that indicates how to look for a cookie showing that the user does not need to log in:

```
public void doGet(HttpServletRequest req, HttpServletResponse
res)
    throws IOException
{

    boolean cookieFound = false;
    Cookie thisCookie = null;

    /*
      Ask for the session object associated with the request.
      Because we are passing a parameter of false, a new
      session is not automatically created.
    */
    HttpSession session = req.getSession (false);

    // If we were unable to find a new session...
    if (session==null) {

        // Try to retrieve the cookie from the request.
        Cookie[] cookies = req.getCookies();

        /*
            Look through all the cookies and see if the
```

```
cookie with the login info is there.
   */
   for(int i=0; i < cookies.length; i++) {
       thisCookie = cookies[i];
       if (thisCookie.getName().equals("LoginCookie")) {
         cookieFound = true;
         break;
       }
   }

   /*
     If we found the cookie, then we know who this is because
     the value of the cookie is the username of this user.  We
     first create a new session.  Next, we refresh
     the cookie stored in the browser.
   */
   if (cookieFound) {

       // Create a new session for this user.
       HttpSession session = req.getSession (true);

       /*
           If you are assigning a user name to each user, then
         you'll likely want to update that value in the session
           that you just created.
       */
       session.setAttribute("username", this-
Cookie.getValue());

       // Set this cookie so that it will live indefinitely.
       thisCookie.setMaxAge(Integer.MAX_VALUE);

       // Add the cookie to the response
       res.addCookie(thisCookie);
   } else {
       /*
         If we were unable to find a session and we were unable
         to find a cookie for this user, then we redirect
         to our login page.
       */
responseObj.sendRedirect("http://www.blahblah.com/login");
       }
   }

   // Continue with the business of the servlet here...

}
```

Long-Term CookieServlet Example

In this example, we use the preceding code to create two servlets. The first servlet, `CookieServlet`, checks to see if your browser has a cookie stored named "LoginCookie". If you do not have this cookie, you are redirected to another servlet. This second servlet, `putCookieServlet`, creates a new "LoginCookie" and places it in your browser. When you visit the `CookieServlet` again, it recognizes that you have the appropriate cookie and allows you to access the site.

putCookieServlet.java

This servlet takes a request, creates a new cookie, places that in the user browser, and replies to the HTML page. This HTML page reports that the cookie has been implanted in the browser:

```java
package com.learnweblogic.examples.ch3;

import java.io.*;
import java.util.Enumeration;
import javax.servlet.*;
import javax.servlet.http.*;

public class putCookieServlet extends HttpServlet {

  public void doGet(HttpServletRequest req, HttpServletResponse res)
    throws IOException
  {

    // Create a new cookie object:
    Cookie thisCookie = new Cookie("LoginCookie", "Michael");

    // Set this cookie so that it will live indefinitely.
    thisCookie.setMaxAge(Integer.MAX_VALUE);

    // Add the cookie to the response
    res.addCookie(thisCookie);

    /*
      Set the appropriate return content type, and begin to compose
      the HTML page:
    */
    res.setContentType("text/html");
    PrintWriterout = res.getWriter();

    out.println("<html>");
```

```
        out.println("<head><title>putCookieServlet</title></head>");
                out.println("<body>");

        out.println("A cookie has been added to your browser." +
          "Now go back and visit the CookieServlet.");

        out.println("</body></html>");


    }

}
```

CookieServlet.java

This servlet takes a request and checks to see if a user has the appropriate cookie in the browser. If not, the user is automatically redirected to the put-CookieServlet, which is contained in the same Web application. If the user has the correct cookie, then a welcome message is displayed:

```
package com.learnweblogic.examples.ch3;

import java.io.*;
import java.util.Enumeration;
import javax.servlet.*;
import javax.servlet.http.*;

public class cookieServlet extends HttpServlet {

  public void doGet(HttpServletRequest req, HttpServletResponse res)
    throws IOException
  {

    boolean cookieFound = false;
    Cookie thisCookie = null;

    /*
      Ask for the session object associated with the request.
      Because we are passing a parameter of false, a new
      session is not automatically created.
    */
    HttpSession session = req.getSession (false);

    // If we were unable to find a new session...
    if (session==null) {
```

```
// Try to retrieve the cookie from the request.
Cookie[] cookies = req.getCookies();

/*
   Look through all the cookies and see if the
   cookie with the login info is there.
*/
for(int i=0; i < cookies.length; i++) {
  thisCookie = cookies[i];
  if (thisCookie.getName().equals("LoginCookie")) {
    cookieFound = true;
    break;
  }
}

/*
   If we found the cookie, then we know who this is because
   the value of the cookie is the username of this user.  We
   first create a new session.  Next, we refresh
   the cookie stored in the browser.
*/
if (cookieFound == true) {

  // Create a new session for this user.
  session = req.getSession (true);

  /*
     If you assign a user name to each user,
     update that value in the session
     that you just created.
  */
  session.setAttribute("username", thisCookie.getValue());

  // Set this cookie so that it lives indefinitely.
  thisCookie.setMaxAge(Integer.MAX_VALUE);

  // Add the cookie to the response
  res.addCookie(thisCookie);

  /*
  Set the appropriate return content type, and begin to compose
   the HTML page:
  */
  res.setContentType("text/html");
  PrintWriter     out = res.getWriter();

  out.println("<html>");
  out.println("<head><title>CookieServlet</title></head>");
```

```
        out.println("<body>");

    out.println("You had visited us before at the put cookie servlet!"
        + "Welcome!");

    out.println("</body></html>");

} else {
    /*
        If we were unable to find a session or
        a cookie for this user, then we redirect
        to our login page.
    */
    res.sendRedirect(
        " /cookieServlet/putCookieServlet");

    }
}

// Continue the servlet here...

}
}
```

Notice that the servlet uses the `sendRedirect()` method on the HTTP response object to instruct the browser to redirect to another URL. In this case, the redirect automatically goes to the servlet that installs the cookie on the browser, `putCookieServlet`.

In a real-world situation, you want your application to recognize new users and automatically log them in to WebLogic Server. In Chapter 12, *Developing Security with WebLogic Server JNDI and JAAS*, we further discuss how to have your application log in an existing user.

Deploying the CookieServlet in WebLogic Server

To deploy the cookie servlet, use the code included on the CD accompanying this book, in */code/ch3/cookieServlet.war*.

Step 0: Installing the CookieServlet Application

Follow the steps used in previous examples to build and deploy the application code. Be sure to create a new directory for your work.

Step 1: Modifying Browser Settings

To view the cookie servlet, modify your Web browser to enable you to see better what happens with cookies. If you are using Netscape Navigator Version 4, locate the Preferences option in the Edit menu. Choose the Advanced option in the left-hand panel. You see a screen such as the one in Figure 3–14.

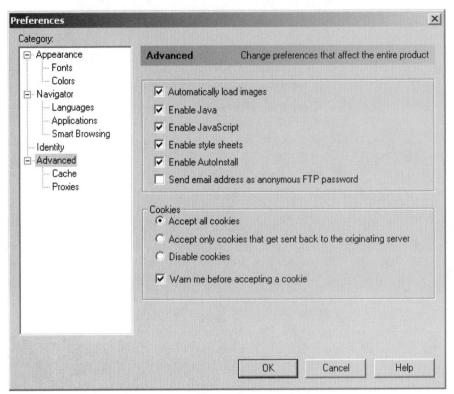

Figure 3–14   Netscape Navigator's Preferences Dialog

Select the option to warn you before accepting cookies. This enables you to see any cookies that WebLogic Server intends to put into your browser. Microsoft Internet Explorer requires that you modify the settings and set your Internet security configuration for the browser. If you decide not to modify your browser settings, you won't see the details of the cookie placement—but the example still works.

Step 2: Visiting the CookieServlet

Visit the CookieServlet by pointing your Web browser at the deployment location for your WebLogic Server instance. If you have deployed on your local machine, at port 7001 (the default), you can view the example at *http:// 127.0.0.1:7001/cookieServlet/cookieServlet*.

You should be immediately redirected to the putCookieServlet (see Figure 3–15), which tells you the following:

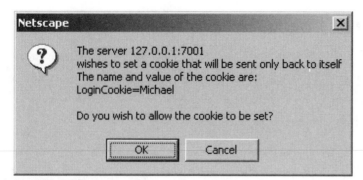

Figure 3–15 Response from putCookieServlet

Click OK. You should see the cookie servlet display (see Figure 3–16).

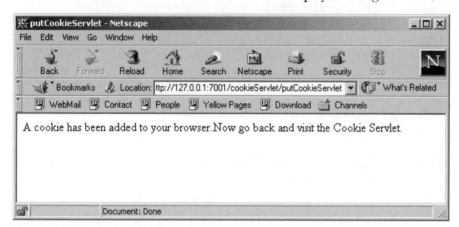

Figure 3–16 CookieServlet Display

Step 3: Revisiting the CookieServlet

Visit the CookieServlet again, with the same Web browser, at *http:// 127.0.0.1:7001/cookieServlet/putCookieServlet*.

You should see the cookie servlet shown in Figure 3–17.

Figure 3-17 Revisiting the CookieServlet

The CookieServlet recognizes that you now have the correct cookie in your Web browser and welcomes you.

The Web Application Package

So far, we've talked about servlets as distinct objects. In what we've seen, the only thing binding them together is the notion of a shared HttpSession object. As you might guess, it is desirable to package servlets (and other Web resources) into a single package. We might want to do this so that we can host multiple applications on a single WebLogic Server, update a group of resources wholesale, or easily refer to a group of multiple resources under a single name.

About Web Applications

As of the servlet specification Version 2.2, a new feature was added to J2EE: the *Web Application*. A Web application is a collection of servlets, HTML pages, classes, and other resources that can be bundled and run on multiple containers from multiple vendors.

By its nature, a Web application is rooted at a specific path within WebLogic Server. For example, a Web application could be located at http://www.bea.com/mywebapp. All requests that start with this prefix are handled by the Web application designated for that path. Web applications are typically bundled together to form a Web Archive (*WAR*) and are designated by a .war suffix in the filename.

The next section discusses how to build Web applications. It also covers the mechanics of how to package the Web archive, write the appropriate deployment descriptors, set up WebLogic Server to use a Web archive, and other topics.

Web Application Overview

A Web application can include:

- Servlets
- JSPs
- Utility classes
- Static documents (HTML, images, sounds, etc.)
- Client-side applets, beans, and classes
- Descriptive meta information that ties all the preceding elements together

Of these items, *the last is the most important*. Typically, the descriptive meta information (documents that describe other documents in the Web application) resides in *XML encoded files*. The XML files describe how the elements combine to make a single application.

Web Archive Organization

Web archives have a hierarchical organization. The root of the archive maps to the root of the application path, for example, http://www.bea.com/mywebapp. Other components reside in particular directories in the Web archive. To illustrate, let's say that we have the following components in our Web archive:

```
/index.html
/howto.jsp
/feedback.jsp
/images/banner.gif
/images/jumping.gif
```

Top-level files such as *index.html* map to http://www.bea.com/mywebapp/index.html. The image jumping.gif maps to http://www.bea.com/mywebapp/images/jumping.gif.

Servlet classes, supporting classes, and meta documents are included in the *WEB-INF* directory. In a typical Web application, this might look like the following:

```
/WEB-INF/web.xml   ← The main meta document
/WEB-INF/lib/jspbean.jar   ← Supporting classes for JSPs
/WEB-INF/classes/com/mycorp/servlets/MyServlet.class   ← Servlet
classes
/WEB-INF/classes/com/mycorp/util/MyUtils.class   ← Utility classes
```

The components stored in the */WEB-INF* directory of the archive are not directly visible to the client. They are never sent to the Web browser. Instead, they are used by the Web application either to directly service clients or as infrastructure to service clients. The *web.xml* deployment descriptor ties all these components together for WebLogic Server.

Building a .war File

There are four steps to build a *.war* file out of the items in the directory structure previously described.

Step 0: Creating a Directory Structure

Create a working directory for your Web application. This discussion uses the directory *C:\dev13*; however, you can use whatever directory you like. Open a command shell and change to that directory. Copy the CookieServlet example code fragments from their location on the CD into your new directory. You should see something like Figure 3–18 after you have created your directory structure.

```
D:\WINNT\System32\cmd.exe                                    _ □ ×

C:\dev13>dir
 Volume in drive C has no label.
 Volume Serial Number is E46E-29A6

 Directory of C:\dev13

04/18/2001  02:46p       <DIR>          .
04/18/2001  02:46p       <DIR>          ..
03/13/2001  01:05p                181  build.bat
03/13/2001  01:05p              2,852  cookieServlet.java
04/18/2001  02:46p       <DIR>          META-INF
03/13/2001  01:05p              1,049  putCookieServlet.java
04/18/2001  02:46p       <DIR>          WEB-INF
               3 File(s)          4,082 bytes
               4 Dir(s)  18,003,537,920 bytes free

C:\dev13>_
```

Figure 3–18   Directory Listing for Building the CookieServlet Package

Step 1: Setting Your Environment

You can use the environment scripts included with WebLogic Server as we have in the previous examples. Depending upon the location of your WebLogic Server installation, choose the *setEnv.cmd* script, located in the *mydomain* directory:

```
c:\bea\wlserver6.0\config\mydomain\setEnv.cmd
```

You should see something like Figure 3–19.

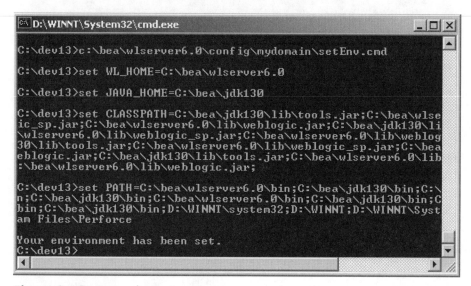

Figure 3-19 Setting the Environment

Step 2: Running the Jar Utility

To run the `jar` utility, simply type "jar" at the command line with the options to instruct the utility to create a new file:

```
jar cvf cookieServlet.war *
```

The "c" option tells the jar utility to create a new file. The "v" option says that we would like for jar to work in a verbose mode, which means that it outputs details about everything that it does. And finally, the "f" option tells `jar` that we specify the files for it to use. The third and fourth entries in the command line tell `jar` the name of the package to create and the files to include. The asterisk (*) is a wild card that instructs `jar` to include all the files in this directory, and all subdirectories.

After typing the preceding into the command line, you should see something like Figure 3–20.

```
D:\WINNT\System32\cmd.exe                                       _ □ ×
C:\dev13>jar cvf cookieServlet.war *
added manifest
adding: build.bat(in = 181) (out= 136)(deflated 24%)
adding: cookieServlet.java(in = 2852) (out= 1146)(deflated 59%
ignoring entry META-INF/
ignoring entry META-INF/MANIFEST.MF
adding: putCookieServlet.java(in = 1049) (out= 521)(deflated 5
adding: WEB-INF/(in = 0) (out= 0)(stored 0%)
adding: WEB-INF/classes/(in = 0) (out= 0)(stored 0%)
adding: WEB-INF/classes/book/(in = 0) (out= 0)(stored 0%)
adding: WEB-INF/classes/book/ch3/(in = 0) (out= 0)(stored 0%)
adding: WEB-INF/classes/book/ch3/cookieServlet.class(in = 1673
ted 43%)
adding: WEB-INF/classes/book/ch3/putCookieServlet.class(in = 1
flated 42%)
adding: WEB-INF/classes/com/(in = 0) (out= 0)(stored 0%)
adding: WEB-INF/classes/com/learnweblogic/(in = 0) (out= 0)(st
adding: WEB-INF/classes/com/learnweblogic/examples/(in = 0) (o
adding: WEB-INF/classes/com/learnweblogic/examples/ch3/(in = 0
0%)
adding: WEB-INF/classes/com/learnweblogic/examples/ch3/session
 2820) (out= 1393)(deflated 50%)
adding: WEB-INF/web.xml(in = 884) (out= 285)(deflated 67%)

C:\dev13>
```

Figure 3-20   Creating the Archive

You now have a new *war* file that can be deployed in WebLogic Server. Note that if you look at the build script (*build.bat*) included with all the examples, these steps are automatically done for you.

You can view the contents of the war file in any compression utility that supports the Zip file format. For example, the *war* file can be loaded into WinZip (*http://www.winzip.com*). See Figure 3–21.

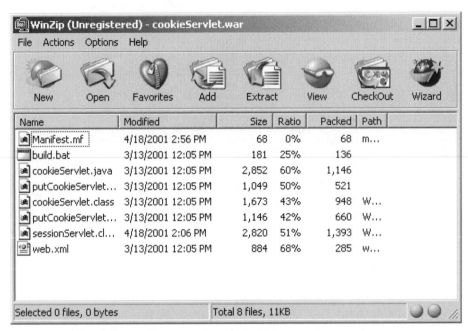

Figure 3–21   Looking at the .war File with the WinZip Utility

The directory called *meta-inf* is automatically created for you. It includes information about the package itself.

IMPORTANT: Note also that this Web archive includes both the build script and the source code in the application. In a real-world application, you probably would not want to make the source code to your application available to anyone visiting your site. For that reason, do not put it in your Web archive file unless you wish to make it available to users of your application.

web.xml

WebLogic Server needs to know information about the Web application, such as what components compose the Web application, where they are located, what type they are, and so forth. As defined by the servlet standard, this information about Web applications is included in multiple meta documents, which are also known as *deployment descriptors*.

In the case of WebLogic Server, there are two different deployment descriptors for Web applications. The first is a *generic deployment descriptor* named *web.xml*, which is placed in the */WEB-INF/* directory in the Web application *jar* file. The second is a WebLogic Server–specific deployment descriptor called *weblogic.xml*. This deployment descriptor is used to define external resources that are WebLogic Server–specific, such as such as Data-Sources, EJBs, or a Security realm.

In order to create *web.xml* files and to understand how they work for Web applications, it is best to learn by example. In this section, we show three examples of *web.xml* files, and discuss what they configure. These files are available on the CD accompanying this book.

Sample1-web.xml

This sample *web.xml* is very simple. It is the deployment descriptor for the first Hello World servlet.

```
<!DOCTYPE web-app PUBLIC "-//Sun Microsystems, Inc.//DTD Web
Application 2.2//EN" "http://java.sun.com/j2ee/dtds/web-
app_2_2.dtd">

<web-app>

  <context-param>
    <param-name>weblogic.jsp.compileCommand</param-name>
    <param-value>javac</param-value>
  </context-param>

  <servlet>
    <servlet-name>HelloServlet</servlet-name>
    <servlet-class>book.ch3.HelloServlet</servlet-class>
  </servlet>

  <welcome-file-list>
    <welcome-file>/HelloServlet</welcome-file>
  </welcome-file-list>

  <servlet-mapping>
    <servlet-name>HelloServlet</servlet-name>
    <url-pattern>/</url-pattern>
  </servlet-mapping>

</web-app>
```

If you are familiar with HTML, this format should look very familiar. The first entry defines the document type to be an XML document. The document type description (DTD) tells WebLogic Server what format is being used for the deployment descriptor XML. Note also that this tag includes an external URL. WebLogic Server does not use this external URL, but relies upon a local copy. This enables WebLogic Server to work with XML, even when not connected to the Internet.

The second tag, `<web-app>`, signifies a Web application.

The first tag inside the Web application tag specifies the Java compiler to be used in building this application. This second tag specifies an included server class. The third, `<welcome-file-list>`, specifies what servlet should be activated by default when someone accesses the Web application. So, if someone visits *http://127.0.0.1:7001/*, the Hello Servlet is activated. Note that the Web application is deployed at the URL:

```
http://<server name>/<Web application archive name>/
```

So, a Web application archive named "foo.war" is automatically deployed at:

```
URL: http://<server name>/foo/
```

The last entry specifies the URL pattern to which the Hello Servlet should map. In this case, we've specified that it should map to any URL pattern for the application. In a real-world application, you specify the full path for the servlet URL.

Sample2-web.xml

This sample *web.xml* includes a number of other options. Comments about each component are included.

```
<!DOCTYPE web-app PUBLIC "-//Sun Microsystems, Inc.//DTD Web
Application 2.2//EN" "http://java.sun.com/j2ee/dtds/web-
app_2_2.dtd">

<web-app>
```

The `<display-name>` tag signifies the name used when the application is displayed in something like the WebLogic Server console:

```
<display-name>A Simple Application</display-name>
```

The `<context-param>` tag specifies a parameter to be included in the `ServletContext`, which is a topic covered in the next section. In this case, the `ServletContext` now includes a parameter named `Webmaster`, with the value of the email address of the `Webmaster`:

```
<context-param>
    <param-name>Webmaster</param-name>
    <param-value>webmaster@mycorp.com</param-value>
</context-param>
```

The following specifies a servlet with the name `catalog`. It specifies the class to be used, `com.mycorp.CatalogServlet` and some initial parameters for the servlet. These are also located in the `ServletContext` for the servlet:

```
<servlet>
    <servlet-name>catalog</servlet-name>
    <servlet-class>com.mycorp.CatalogServlet</servlet-class>

    <init-param>
        <param-name>catalog</param-name>
        <param-value>Spring</param-value>
    </init-param>
</servlet>
```

The following maps the catalog servlet to a URL pattern. WebLogic Server receives requests for any URL beginning with `catalog/`.

```
<servlet-mapping>
    <servlet-name>catalog</servlet-name>
    <url-pattern>/catalog/*</url-pattern>
</servlet-mapping>
```

The following specifies the default timeout for HTTP session objects—in this case, 30 seconds:

```
<session-config>
    <session-timeout>30</session-timeout>
</session-config>
```

The following specifies a mime type extension to be used. If a file with the .pdf suffix extension is sent, WebLogic Server affixes the mime type as follows:

```
<mime-mapping>
    <extension>pdf</extension>
    <mime-type>application/pdf</mime-type>
</mime-mapping>
```

The next specifies the file to be used as a welcome file to the Web application. If someone accesses the Web application without specifying a file (such as *http://www.girdley.com/myApp/*), WebLogic Server attempts to display the *welcome* file. The files are chosen in order, with highest precedent on the file listed first:

```
<welcome-file-list>
    <welcome-file>index.jsp</welcome-file>
    <welcome-file>index.html</welcome-file>
    <welcome-file>index.htm</welcome-file>
</welcome-file-list>
```

The following specifies the page to be used in the event of a 404 (File Not Found) HTTP Error:

```
<error-page>
    <error-code>404</error-code>
    <location>/404.html</location>
</error-page>
```

The following concludes the definition of the Web application:

```
</web-app>
```

Note that you can set the error page for any number of `http://error` codes. The complete list of all possible `http://error` codes is in the HTTP specification, available on the Internet at *ftp://ftp.isi.edu/in-notes/ rfc2616.txt*.

You also can map an error page to an exception type. To do this, instead of listing an error code, list the fully qualified name of your Java exception type:

```
<error-page>
<exception-type>
      com.learnweblogic.exceptiontype
</exception-type>
<location>/error.html</location>
</error-page>
```

The complete *Sample2-web.xml* listed here is located on the CD accompanying this book in the *code\ch3* directory:

```
<!DOCTYPE web-app PUBLIC "-//Sun Microsystems, Inc.//DTD Web Application
2.2//EN" "http://java.sun.com/j2ee/dtds/web-app_2_2.dtd">

<web-app>

    <display-name>A Simple Application</display-name>

    <context-param>
        <param-name>Webmaster</param-name>
      <param-value>webmaster@mycorp.com</param-value>
    </context-param>

    <servlet>
        <servlet-name>catalog</servlet-name>
      <servlet-class>com.mycorp.CatalogServlet</servlet-class>

        <init-param>
            <param-name>catalog</param-name>
            <param-value>Spring</param-value>
        </init-param>
    </servlet>
```

```
<servlet-mapping>
    <servlet-name>catalog</servlet-name>
  <url-pattern>/catalog/*</url-pattern>
</servlet-mapping>

<session-config>
    <session-timeout>30</session-timeout>
</session-config>

<mime-mapping>
    <extension>pdf</extension>
  <mime-type>application/pdf</mime-type>
</mime-mapping>

<welcome-file-list>
    <welcome-file>index.jsp</welcome-file>
    <welcome-file>index.html</welcome-file>
    <welcome-file>index.htm</welcome-file>
</welcome-file-list>

<error-page>
    <error-code>404</error-code>
    <location>/404.html</location>
</error-page>
```

```
</web-app>
```

Other web.xml Options

Many of the other options specifically support security, EJB, or JSP. We will cover these other web.xml options in subsequent chapters.

For your reference, here are some other important options that can be included in a web.xml file, with examples of each.

Icon Element

The icon element contains a small-icon and a large-icon element, which specify the location of a small and a large image used to represent the Web application in a GUI tool. At a minimum, tools must accept GIF and JPEG format images. The small-icon element contains the location of a file containing a small (16×16 pixel) icon image. The large-icon element contains the location of a file containing a large (32×32 pixel) icon image.

```
<icon>
<small-icon>filename</small-icon>
<large-icon>filename</large-icon>
```

```
</icon>
```

Display-Name Element

The display-name element contains a short name that is intended to be displayed by GUI tools.

```
<display-name>name</display-name>
```

Description Element

The description element provides descriptive text about the parent element.

```
<description>name</description>
```

The ServletContext

A Web application needs a way to tie all its components together programmatically. For example, as part of a Web application, a servlet should be able to define elements that other servlets can use. To solve this problem, the ServletContext is available as part of the specification. It is a variable specific to a given Web application that is used to define how a given servlet looks at the rest of the Web application. ServletContext also includes information on where external resources are located in which the servlet can rely.

Some of the things that the servlet can do with the ServletContext include:

- Log events.
- Obtain URL references to resources such as images, multimedia, or a temporary working directory.
- Set and store attributes that other servlets in the context can use. Examples of these attributes include objects such as JavaBeans (covered in Chapter 4, *Using WebLogic Server JavaServer Pages*); cached results from database queries (covered in Chapter 5, *Using Databases and Transactions with JDBC and JTA*); and any other object that should be shared by all the servlet resources for any user who visits the application.

Getting the ServletContext

The process of acquiring the ServletContext is very straightforward. The following simple servlet demonstrates this:

```
import java.io.*;
import java.util.*;
```

```
import javax.servlet.*;
import javax.servlet.http.*;

public class ContextServlet extends HttpServlet {

    public void doGet(HttpServletRequest req, HttpServletResponse res)
        throws IOException
    {

        // Locate Our Servlet Context
        ServletContext sc = getServletConfig().getServletContext();

        // Use the Context here.

    }
}
```

Setting and Getting Attributes

The `ServletContext` object offers you the ability to set and retrieve attributes. The attributes can be Java objects. After they are set in the `ServletContext`, attributes are then available to any other servlet that is part of the same Web application. Attributes are useful any time you want to track a resource and share it among multiple servlets.

> Context attributes exist locally to the instance of WebLogic Server in which they are created. This prevents the `ServletContext` from being used as a distributed shared memory store. In later sections, we describe how to share data among multiple servers in the distributed computing environment that WebLogic Server provides.

The following simple servlet shows how to acquire the `ServletContext` object, add an attribute, retrieve an attribute, and retrieve an Enumeration of all the attributes available in the `ServletContext`:

```
import java.io.*;
import java.util.*;
import javax.servlet.*;
import javax.servlet.http.*;

public class ContextServlet extends HttpServlet {

    public void doGet(HttpServletRequest req, HttpServletResponse res)
        throws IOException
```

```
{
    // Locate Our Servlet Context
    ServletContext sc = getServletConfig().getServletContext();

    /*
       Set an attribute named "attrib1" that contains
       a value of "my value":
    */
    sc.setAttribute("attrib1", "my value");

    /*
       Get an Enumeration of all the attributes
       currently active in our ServletContext.
    */
    Enumeration myAttributes = sc.getAttributeNames();

    /*
       Remove attribute named "attrib1".
    */
    sc.removeAttribute("attrib1");

    }
}
```

The above example employed a number of the methods available in `Serv-letContext`. The first declared a new attribute named `"attrib1"` and set its value equal to a string literal of `"my value"`. It is notable that `setAt-tribute()` can incorporate any derivative of `java.lang.Object` (that is, any Java object) as an attribute. You should also note that calling `setAt-tribute()` on an attribute that already exists *updates the value* of that attribute.

After setting the first attribute, we call the `getAttributeNames()` method, which returns a `java.util.Enumeration` of all the names of the attributes available in the `ServletContext`. This is useful if you need to locate an attribute but you're unsure of its name. Finally, we call the `removeAttribute()` method to remove the attribute that we added.

The following summarizes the methods that are available for attributes:

- `public java.lang.Object getAttribute(String name)`—Returns the servlet container attribute with the given name, or null if there is no attribute by that name.
- `public java.util.Enumeration getAttribute Names()`—Returns an enumeration containing the attribute names available within this servlet context.

- `public void removeAttribute(String name)`—
  Removes the attribute with the given name from the servlet
  context.
- `public void setAttribute(String name,
  java.lang.Object object)`—Binds an object to a given
  attribute name in this servlet context.

Using Web Application Resources

Web applications can also include resources that are defined and contained
in its *package*. These resources can be virtually anything that is static content:
text files, images, or other multimedia. They must also be included in the
Web application package itself in order to be accessed by components of the
Web application.

The ability to access resources from your servlets can be very useful. Some
uses include:

- *Dynamically processing and filtering images for a given user.*
  For example, you might want to overlay a user's name on top of
  a standard image, to customize it.
- *Simple queries of text resources or other data stored in the Web
  application.* This is very helpful for rapid prototyping.

Your application locates and accesses resources using the `ServletCon-
text` object. Two methods are useful to locate and access resources:

- `public java.net.URL getResource(String
  path)`—Useful when you wish to understand the complete
  URL of a given Web application resource. You supply a relative
  path to the resource; you are returned the full URL.
- `public java.io.InputStream getResourceAs
  Stream(String path)`—This method returns a reference
  to an `InputStream` whose source is the resource specified by
  `path`.

In both of these methods, the parameter is a relative path to the resource
from the root of the Web application. To illustrate, if you have a resource
contained in your Web application package in a subdirectory named */luke/
images/* and the resource is named *myimage.gif*, the relative path would be */
luke/images/myimage.gif*.

The following locates the full URL for this image and makes it available as an `InputStream`:

```
// Import classes, define servlet, etc. here.

public void doGet(HttpServletRequest req, HttpServletResponse res)
    throws IOException
{

    // Locate Our Servlet Context
    ServletContext sc = getServletConfig().getServletContext();

    // Get the Full URL to Our Image:
    java.net.URL myURL = sc.getResource("/luke/images/myim-
age.gif");

    // Get Our Image As an InputStream:
    java.io.InputStream myIS =
    sc.getResourceAsStream("/luke/images/myimage.gif");
}
```

Note that any resource accessed in this manner is treated as static content. As you'll see later, JSPs are stored as text files and compiled automatically. If you were to try to load a JSP using these methods for resources, you would see the text of the JSP page and not the output of the executed code. If you wish to include the output of another executable component of the Web application such as a JSP or a servlet, you should take advantage of the `RequestDispatcher` *interface discussed in the next section.*

Using the RequestDispatcher

In many cases, a Web application requires that a client be directed to another servlet. One way of doing this is to send a redirect back to the client. However, this is inefficient because it requires the client to make another HTTP request.

The solution for this problem is the servlet `RequestDispatcher` mechanism. This mechanism allows requests to be handled by another Web resource on the server such as a servlet, JSP, or HTML page. This is done in a way that is completely transparent to the user.

There are two ways to use the `RequestDispatcher` functionality: forwarding a request to other resources, or including the output of other resources in your servlet output.

Forwarding to Other Resources

Using the `RequestDispatcher` requires information stored in the `ServletContext` of the servlet. We can use the following to locate the `ServletContext` as mentioned in the previous section:

```
// Locate Our Servlet Context
ServletContext sc = getServletConfig().getServletContext();
```

Next, you'll need to get a handle to the resource that you'll be forwarding to:

```
/*
  Specify the path of the resource we want to get using
  the Servlet context from above.
  */
RequestDispatcher my RequestDispatcher = sc.getRequestDis-
patcher(String path)
```

You can then use the `forward()` method to direct the request to the object of your choice:

```
/*
  Call forward on this request dispatcher using the
  parameters sent to our service method.
  */
myRequestDispatcher.forward(HttpServletRequest myHttpServletRe-
quest ,
HttpServletResponse myHttpServletResponse );
```

The forward functionality of the `RequestDispatcher` may only be called if you have not sent any output to the client. If output exists that has already been placed in a response buffer that has not been committed (i.e., sent to the client), then the buffer must be cleared. If a response has already been sent to the client and the forward functionality is in use, an `Illegal-StateException` will be thrown at runtime. In any servlet that you forward to, you should make sure to explicitly instruct the servlet container to "return" at the end of your method:

```
return;
```

This causes the servlet container to stop processing your code. This action is also helpful when you have a servlet or JSP page that you wish to have stop processing and simply return to the user the response that has been constructed so far in your servlet.

---

*Use the **forward** method to redirect a user to a login page if that user's session is invalid.*

Including Other Resources

It is also useful to include the output of other resources in your responses. For example, if you want to include a standard header that is generated by another servlet or a static HTML file in your servlet output, use the include functionality of the RequestDispatcher.

First, follow the process used above to locate the RequestDispatcher for the object that you want to include. Then, call the include method on that resource:

```
// Call Include on This Request Dispatcher Using the
// Parameters Send to Our Service Method
myRequestDispatcher.include (HttpServletRequest myHttpServletRequest ,
HttpServletResponse myHttpServletResponse );
```

> A best practice is to use this *include* method for programmatic server-side includes. For example, you have a single servlet that responds with a sports score for the entire user base. You can include that servlet in multiple pages.

Using Servlets with WebLogic Server Clustering

Clustering, discussed in Chapter 13, is important functionality that allows for redundancy and task balancing across multiple pieces of independent hardware and/or processes. For a WebLogic Server deployment, it is necessary to design your hardware environment to accommodate clustering. Similarly, you must design your servlets and Web applications to work well in a cluster environment.

Persisting Session Information

It is highly desirable to protect users' session information in the event of hardware or software failure. For example, if you are storing your shopping carts in the user session, it is desirable to have other nodes in the cluster be aware of the session information in order to protect against the loss of information in the event of failure.

You have three options for session information in a WebLogic Server deployment:

- *Do Not Protect Your Session Information*. In the event of a failure, all user session information is lost. This is because the session is only stored in a single WebLogic Server instance.
- *Protect Your Session Information in the Database*. In the event of a failure, all session information is persisted in the database and readily available.
- *Protect Your Session Information with In-Memory Replication*. In this model, a given session is always directed to the same server in a cluster, typically referred to as the primary. The cluster automatically chooses another server to act as a hot backup to the primary server. This is typically referred to as the secondary server. This node is updated across the network by the primary node after every change to the `HttpSession` object. In other words, every time you call the `setAttribute()` or `removeAttribute()` method, WebLogic Server automatically synchronously updates the copy of the `HttpSession` on the secondary server. In the event of a failure of either the primary or secondary, a different server in the cluster automatically takes its place to handle the session; thus, the session data will not be lost.

In each case where session information is persisted, only serializable data can be replicated.

Session Protection Performance Implications

There are performance implications when the different types of session protection are used. To illustrate, a test was run using a single-processor Windows NT box running a cluster of two servers under maximum load:

- In-memory replication is 5.5 (389tps/68tps) times faster than database replication.
- Session-state handling for Web connections results in a 66 percent slowdown over static page serving.
- Remote database operations result in a 68 percent slowdown versus local disk database storage.

As demonstrated in Chapter 15, *Capacity Planning for the WebLogic Server*, the type of session persistence used in an application has an impact upon the hardware required for a given application.

Choosing the Right Level of Protection

Which method of session protection is right for your deployment depends upon your needs. If performance, and not protection of your data, is key, you may choose not to protect your session information. Given that most Web server hardware today has a 99.9 percent up time or better, this is not a bad bet.

For rock-solid protection of session information, *database persistence* is the best choice. You are absolutely guaranteed not to lose your session information, because every change in the session is enacted as a transaction against the database. Unfortunately, database persistence comes at a cost. JDBC storage of session information can reduce performance substantially.

The mechanism that provides the best of both worlds is *in-memory replication*. The likelihood that multiple servers go down simultaneously is very low. Yet, the performance costs are minimal. Benchmarks have shown a reasonable amount of overhead for in-memory replication.

Special Considerations for In-Memory Replication

There are a number of special considerations for using in-memory replication of session state:

- In a single server instance, nonserializable data placed into HTTP sessions works fine. Unfortunately, in-memory replication does not work with nonserializable data. You'll incur many debugging headaches to discover that a portion of the data is not being replicated.
- Large, complex objects bring down the server performance. There is a good amount of overhead for serializing/deserializing the data, in addition to the network costs.
- Don't put hash tables, vectors, and so forth in the session because WebLogic Server cannot detect changes to objects in them. WebLogic Server ends up replicating the whole object, even though you changed just one part.
- It is a good practice to make all custom objects implement the serializable interface.
- Data that doesn't change should be made static so that it is not replicated.

To protect your session information while maintaining high performance, use in-memory replication of servlet session state.

Best Practices for Servlets

There are a number of best practices that can enable your servlet-based applications to be as successful as possible:

Be Smart About Session State

If you are using in-memory replication, or any other mechanism to protect your session state, it is important to be smart about how you treat the session state objects. In order to maximize efficiency, you want to make sure that session information is only updated when needed. Minimizing the changes that are made to the session state minimizes the number of updates either to the database or to the other nodes in the cluster.

WebLogic Server is very smart about what it needs to replicate for in-memory replication. WebLogic Server monitors the session object to see what objects are placed in it. Updates made to the secondary node transmit only the *difference* in the session state. To take advantage of this, you should make session information stored in the session object *as granular as possible*. It is better to store many small objects rather than one large object, such as a hash table. If you change the state of a complex object that is already in the session you must use `setAttribute` again to transmit the change to the secondary.

Finally, do not include information in a session unless it is necessary. If possible, put data in static variables, which are not shared across nodes in the cluster. This is especially applicable for data that does not change across user sessions or over multiple accesses by clients.

Don't Close/Terminate the Response Stream

As mentioned previously, performance is enhanced when WebLogic Server is not required to create and destroy sockets many times to handle a single client session. In normal operation, the notion of Keep-Alive works well. However, it is possible for you as the developer to keep these optimizations from working. In order to avoid this, do not `close()` or `flush()` streams that you send in your `service()` or `do<request type>` methods. Instead, just don't touch them.

Always Activate URL Rewriting

Many Web browsers enable users to disable the acceptance of cookies. For this reason, you should always enable URL rewriting in your servlets, as specified in this chapter. This ensures that you maintain the appropriate compatibility and the highest level of usability for all your users.

Session Objects Are Not Appropriate for Long-Term Data

Session objects are appropriate for transient data that is specific to beginning a user session. You should not expect that session objects are available for very long periods of time. Instead, for information that you expect to store for long periods, your best strategy is to store information about the user in the database. The database is the best resource for storing long-term data.

You may also want to use cookies to store identification for users to make it easier for them to log in. However, you should remember that cookies are not your best resource for permanent storage. More information on how to access the database is included in Chapter 5.

Keep Scalability in Mind

Avoid doing things that inhibit scalability, such as using the *single thread model* for your servlets. If you recall, this model allows only a single thread of execution at a time to execute your servlet. If possible, do not use this model.

USING WEBLOGIC SERVER JAVASERVER PAGES

In this chapter:

- The details for building JSPs in WebLogic Server
- Samples of JSPs built for WebLogic Server
- Techniques for including Java code such as JavaBeans and custom tag libraries
- Best practices for developing and deploying WebLogic Server JSPs
- JSPs in the WebAuction application

Chapter 4

WebLogic Server provides two mechanisms for building presentation logic: servlets and JavaServer Pages (JSPs). Chapter 3 focused on servlets and Web applications; this chapter focuses on how to design and write JSPs for WebLogic Server.

About WebLogic Server JSPs

JSPs provide essentially the same services as the servlet API, but they have a higher level, more user-friendly, HTML-tag-like development interface. JSPs, also a part of the Java 2 Enterprise Edition (J2EE) standards, greatly accelerate the process of creating Web applications that use dynamic and personalized Web content.

Like servlets, JSPs reside in the WebLogic Server container, which instantiates, executes, and provides services to JSP classes called by the JSPs. When a WebLogic Server client sends an HTTP request to a WebLogic Server for a JSP page, the WebLogic Server JSP container executes the appropriate JSP page, provides services to that JSP page, and then sends the response back to the requester. The first time a client requests a JSP page, the JSP container converts the page into compiled Java code (a class very similar to a servlet) that is executed at each subsequent request.

JSPs differ greatly from servlets in how they are developed. JSPs, which are tightly focused toward producing content for Web browsers, look very much like an HTML page with some special tags. As mentioned previously, you can use a WYSIWYG (what you see is what you get) editor such as Macromedia Dreamweaver to edit a JSP page along with its surrounding HTML.

Why JSP?

The JSP standard is a result of the recognition by the enterprise Java community that there are typically two distinct groups working together to create a Web application: the programming team and the Web design team. Programmers build the code that executes business and presentation logic, to perform tasks such as credit card transactions or order processing. The Web design team, on the other hand, builds the HTML pages and associated graphics. Web designers use WYSIWYG tools to design Web pages that are then hosted on the corporate Web server.

These two groups have fundamentally different roles. Programmers do not want the Web development team to touch the Java code. Web developers do not want the programmers to muck around with the graphics and layout. JSP is a technology that cleanly separates the efforts, enabling programmers to develop business and presentation logic, while the Web development team focuses on site composition. The Java classes that implement business and presentation logic are simply called from a standard HTML page, using special tags and syntax.

Finally, building HTML pages with a servlet is a pain. If you remember from our servlet samples from Chapter 3, writing HTML pages with a servlet requires that you encapsulate every line of output in an `out.println()` command. This makes outputting Web pages tedious, at best.

If you have separate programming and Web content teams, take advantage of JSPs to build your Web application's user interface.

Integrating Java Code with JSP

With JSPs, both Java code and standard HTML can appear in the same file. However, it is not desirable to *directly* include the Java code that does the "work" of your application into your JSP files. There are a couple of reasons for this:

- It is desirable to keep Web designers from accidentally spoiling your code with errant keypresses or overaggressive find/replace. An extra semicolon or bracket left in your JSP file could have unexpected consequences.

- It is desirable to modularize your application as much as possible. This makes maintenance easier because you can plug and play components as you update them. Placing too much logic in a JSP page means that you'll need to rule out entire suites of JSP pages every time you want to make a change. Modularizing your code also makes your JSP pages easier to understand when it is time to fix bugs or add features.

JSP supports two different mechanisms for embedding code and using more complicated logic. Both of these mechanisms are described in this chapter. The first mechanism is called *JavaBeans*; the second is called *custom tag libraries*.

Minimize the amount of directly included Java code in your JSP pages by using JavaBeans and custom tag libraries.

JavaBeans and JSP

JavaBeans for JSP are *not the same as* the Enterprise JavaBeans (EJBs) discussed later in this book. JSP JavaBeans are basically special Java classes that you build to capture business logic for methods called from a JSP page. To use JavaBeans, create a generic Java class with methods that include your Java code. You specify the JavaBean to your JSP page with the useBean tag:

```
<jsp:useBean …>
```

More details on using JavaBeans with JSPs appear later in this chapter.

Custom Tag Libraries

Custom tag libraries are a second mechanism for specifying business and presentation logic in JSP pages. Custom tag libraries, introduced in Version 1.1 of the JSP specification, enable you to define your own specific HTML-like tags that can be used by Web developers. We cover custom tag libraries later in this chapter, with examples.

JavaBeans vs. Custom Tag Libraries

Use a JavaBean when:

- You are primarily encapsulating data, rather than business logic.
- You want to modularize your Java code for reuse in something other than JSP.
- You want to minimize the chance of having the Web/HTML designers inadvertently modify your Java code.

Use custom tag libraries when:

- You have relatively simple business logic that you *do* want to make available for use by Web developers. For example, you can create a login module for your Web application that the HTML designers can include in every page requiring a user login.
- You want to do pre- and post-processing of content for tasks such as personalization or content management. Personalization might include special tags that look up a user's information. Content management would enable you to create special tags to load data from your content repository.

In the final analysis, much of what you can do with JavaBeans you can also do with custom tag libraries. Other things being equal, the deciding factor is the preference of the developer.

JSP Basics

This section covers the basics and many of the advanced topics surrounding the development of JSPs for WebLogic Server or any other J2EE platform. Specifically, this section discusses:

- The anatomy of a JSP
- Session tracking
- Cookies and URL rewriting
- Security and WebLogic Server JSPs

Anatomy of a JSP

A JSP is a sequence of HTML interleaved with special tags that the JSP container uses to generate responses to requests. There are three categories of JSP tags. These are:

- *Directives*, which are messages that your page sends the JSP container
- *Scripting elements*, which are variable declarations, Java code to be executed, and expressions
- *Actions*, which are messages to the JSP container that affect how responses are handled by the JSP container

We discuss each of these in detail in this chapter. In addition to directives, scripting elements, and actions, there are a number of *objects* available to the JSP that are provided by WebLogic Server. The JSP developer uses these objects to gain access to things such as the output stream, page context information, and so forth. More information on objects is included in the section on scripting elements, later in this chapter.

A Basic JSP Example

Here's the "Hello World" (hello1.jsp) example implemented in JSP:

```
<!doctype html public "-//w3c/dtd HTML 4.0//en">
<html>
<head>
<title>Hello World</title>
</head>
<body>
<!-- Grab the output stream object and print to it: -->
<%
out.print("<p><b>Hello World!</b>");
%>
</body>
</html>
```

You'll note that calls to Java code, such as the out.print directive to the print method, are simply embedded in the HTML page. This is what makes it a JSP page.

The page has the usual HTML header using the <head> tag, and a body using the <body> tag. Comments use the format: <!-- my comments here -->. Comments do not appear in output but are available to anyone who views the source of the HTML output of the JSP page. Comments are passed as-is to the browser. No evaluation of them is made.

The JSP tag included in this example demonstrates a simple *scripting element*. A scripting element in a JSP page is Java code that the JSP container executes when it responds to the request received.

Note that each tag for JSP-specific elements uses a unique syntax. In almost all cases, these elements are delimited by something like `<%` to specify the beginning of the tag and `%>` to specify the end of the tag, like this:

```
<%
...JSP-specific tag stuff here...
%>
```

The `out` object is one of the standard objects provided by the JSP container. It represents the output stream that contains the data to be sent to the requestor.

Running the Basic JSP Example in WebLogic Server

To deploy the basic JSP example, `hello1.jsp`, first install BEA WebLogic Server 6.0. Start the server using the command specific to your platform. If you are using Microsoft Windows, choose the Start Default Server option from the Start menu.

Once the server is started, do the following:

1. Locate the `hello1.jsp` code on the CD included with this book. It should be located in the directory titled *examples\ch4* under the root directory of the CD.

2. Copy this file from the CD into the default Web server directory under the application directory of your BEA WebLogic Server 6.0 installation. If you are using Microsoft Windows, you can use the Windows Explorer or the command line to copy this file. Depending upon the location of your installation, this directory path should look something like the following:

```
c:\bea\wlserver6.0\config\mydomain\applications\DefaultWebApp_myserver
```

If you use the command line to copy the file, first open a command shell in Windows. Click on the Start menu and choose the Run option. Enter the letters "cmd" into this dialog box and click OK. A command-line window should appear on your screen.

If your CD-ROM is on the E: drive and you installed WebLogic Server on your C: drive, you would type the following to copy the file:

```
copy e:\examples\ch4\hello1.jsp c:\bea\wlserver6.0\config\mydomain\applica-
tions\
DefaultWebApp_myserver\hello1.jsp
```

3. The JSP page is now installed. You can view it by opening a Web browser and viewing the URL *http://127.0.0.1:7001/hello1.jsp*.

Note: If you have an HTTP proxy enabled in your Web browser, as many organizations require, you must disable this in some circumstances.

Figure 4–1 shows the complete output of our JSP.

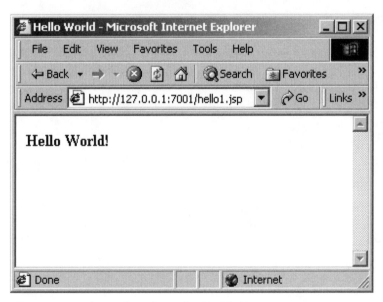

Figure 4–1 Output from the Hello World JSP

The Lifecycle of a JSP

The lifecycle of a JSP is one you should be familiar with from the discussion of servlets in Chapter 3. Because JSPs are compiled into classes very similar to servlets the first time they are requested, their behavior and controls are identical to servlets after the first request. The WebLogic Server JSP container handles the lifecycle automatically.

For all practical purposes, JSPs are compiled into servlets. Technically speaking, JSPs are not compiled into pure servlets. Some slight differences are introduced in the compilation and translation process. However, the JSP developer and deployer never actually deal with the compiled servlet code, and the development model of JSPs follows the servlet paradigm.

Initialization

Before WebLogic Server compiles your JSPs into servlet classes, the code to handle any initialization phase of your JSP lifecycle is automatically created.

Loading and Instantiation

WebLogic Server is responsible for loading and instantiating JSPs. Like all JSP containers, WebLogic Server uses Java class-loading mechanisms to load classes automatically.

Request Handling

The request-handling section of the JSP lifecycle is where real work gets done. Requests come in to the WebLogic Server, which then calls `_jspservice()`, which is analogous to the `service()` method of a servlet. The JSP container automatically creates `_jspservice()` methods. You'll never even realize they are in the development cycle (except when debugging).

There are two options when building JSPs: multi-threaded and single-threaded. Single-threaded JSPs, defined in a property that is specific to each application server or by setting the `isThreadSafe=false` attribute in the page directive, means that only one request can be served at a time by your JSP class, for each instance. WebLogic Server, by default, automatically creates five instances of every servlet for each JSP that uses the single-threaded model. Because multiple threads of execution in WebLogic Server can only execute a single-threaded JSP one at a time, scalability is limited.

You should not use the single-threaded model if you are building a site that handles many concurrent users.

On the other hand, the single-threaded model can make development easier and simpler because you need not worry about handling multiple users at the same time. Use single-threaded only when very few users will access the system concurrently, and scalability is not an important factor.

End of Service

As defined by the JSP specification, the JSP container can remove the JSP from active duty at any time. WebLogic Server commits an end of service for a JSP only on receiving a command from the administration console, or when WebLogic Server itself shuts down.

Most JSP containers, including WebLogic Server, allow you to configure how often your JSP page should be recompiled and reinitialized. In WebLogic Server, this time is configurable through a parameter called `pageCheckSeconds`. *Review your product documentation for more information. After an end of service, the JSP lifecycle starts over again with initialization.*

JSP Page Elements

This section discusses how to use each of the three different JSP page element types:

- Directives
- Scripting elements and implicit objects
- Expressions

JSP Directives

When you construct JSP pages, you can specify certain directives to the JSP container. For example, you can specify an error page that is called if there are problems with your JSP page. Or, you can specify what Java classes you want to include during execution. The way to do this is through a JSP directive.

Directives are specified by tags that use the `<%@` and `%>` characters. An example of a page directive that tells the JSP container to import all the classes in the `java.util` package is:

```
<%@ page import= "java.util.*" %>
```

There are several types of directives for JSP:

- *Page directives*, which are specific to the current page.
- *Include directives*, which specify how to include another file in a JSP.
- *Tag library directives*, which specify how to include and access custom tag libraries. Note that tag libraries enable developers to create custom tags for Web developers to use.

For each of these directives, there are defaults for commonly used values. For example, the default is to have a page be within the scope of an `HttpSession`. In the following sections, **bold text** signifies the default values if the tag is not specified. The default values are very convenient because developers don't have to specify every single directive explicitly.

Page Directives

A page directive tag begins with the characters `<%@ page` and then includes directive types and values in the body of the tag. For example, the following tag is a page directive that tells the JSP container that your JSP page should be activated to work with sessions. As you would expect, sessions for JSP pages are very similar to those for servlets.

```
<%@ page session ="true" %>
```

You can include more than one page directive per page directive tag, like this:

```
<%@ page session ="true"  import="com.girdley.package.*" %>
```

Other useful page directives include:

- `language="language name"` enables you to specify the programming language used in the JSP page. The default value for this directive is "Java." For applications built on WebLogic Server, this tag is not of much use because WebLogic Server only supports the Java language for JSPs. In the future, the JSP standard may allow other languages.
- `extends="package.class"` enables you to specify that your JSP page (and therefore the resulting servlet class) extends another class. For example, if you want to have your JSP extend a base class called `foo.class`, include a page directive like this:

```
<%@ page extends ="foo" %>
```

You also can create a public class that includes "helper" methods to use in all your JSP pages. You could create this class like this:

```
public class myBaseClass {

    public String myHelperMethod() {
         // Do work here...
    }
}
```

Then, if your JSP page included the following directive,

```
<%@ page extends ="myBaseClass" %>
```

this would access the method `myHelperMethod()` from within the Java code in your JSP page. Note that this class must be included in your *classpath* directly, or indirectly by the `include` tag in a Web application. Otherwise, you receive a `ClassNotFoundException` exception.

- `import= " { package. class | package .* } , ... "` enables you to specify that the container should import Java classes into your JSP page. You will then be able to make calls and instantiate classes that should be imported. For example, if you want to use a cryptographic library in your JSP pages, include the following page directive:

```
<%@ page import="com.cryptographic.package.*"%>
```

The following would make one of the utility Java classes, `java.util.Hashtable`, available in your JSP page:

```
<%@ page import="java.util.Hashtable"%>
```

Note: The following packages are implicitly imported, so you don't need to specify them with the import attribute:
```
java.lang.*
javax.servlet.*
javax.servlet.jsp.*
javax.servlet.http.*
```
Some versions of WebLogic Server also (incorrectly) import `java.util*` and `java.io.*`. To be safe, import classes from these packages explicitly.

- `session="true |false"` enables you to specify whether your JSP page *requires* that someone visiting it be involved in an HTTP session. In the servlet programming discussion in Chapter 3, we had to check manually to see if a given session existed. The JSP `session` tag enables you to specify whether a session is required and the container checks automatically for you. We discuss how to access session information later in this chapter. The default value for the session directive is `true`. So, if you do not specify it as `false`, the JSP page automatically requires that a client be part of a session.

- `buffer=" none|` **8KB** `| size KB"` enables you to specify the minimum buffer size for the HTTP response that goes to the client. By default, the response is buffered in 8KB (kilobytes) chunks. You can change the buffer size to suit the needs of your application. If you are returning very large files to the client, you might need to increase the buffer size. In typical Web scenarios, leaving the buffer size at the default value of 8KB is preferable because it allows the Web browser to begin displaying your page before it has been completely downloaded.

- `isThreadSafe="`**true** `|false"` specifies whether the JSP page is *threadsafe*. Setting this value to true means that multiple threads can execute the code in your JSP page at the same time. Setting this value to "false" means that only one thread can execute the code in your JSP page at a time. The default value of this directive is true if it is not explicitly set.

Using a JSP page that is not threadsafe limits scalability because only one thread of execution can run in your JSP page at any given time. For this reason, you should always design your JSP pages to be threadsafe.

- `errorPage=" relativeURL"` enables you to specify a relative path to a JSP page that WebLogic Server uses to handle errors thrown from the current page. For example, to specify that `error.jsp` handle errors that arise in the execution of your JSP page, you include this page directive:

```
<%@ page errorPage="error.jsp"  %>
```

Your JSP pages will encounter errors that cause the WebLogic Server JSP container to throw exceptions. A good architecture for a JSP application includes one or more error-handling JSPs. Use the `errorPage` *directive to specify your error pages.*

- `isErrorPage="true|` **false**`"` enables you to specify that the given JSP page is an error-handling page. As mentioned previously, you want to build JSP pages specifically to handle the errors that arise during execution of your application. This tag indicates for the JSP container that the page being executed is an error page and should be handled differently. Later in this chapter, we cover how to access the error information to handle it appropriately.
- `contentType="`*mimeType* [; charset `=`*characterSet*] enables you to specify the MIME type and character set that be used on output by your JSP page. The default values are **text/html** and **charset=ISO-8859-1** for the character set. Use this tag to define the character set for languages other than English. The following defines that the JSP should display a Kanji (Japanese) character set:

```
<%@ page contentType = "text/html"; charset="SJIS"; %>
```

The following defines that the page should use the default values for English text:

```
<%@ page contentType = "text/html"; charset="ISO-8859-1"; %>
```

WebLogic Server inherits its support for internationalized text and content directly from the Java platform. Therefore, WebLogic Server also supports any content type that is supported by the underlying Java platform. More information on locales and types supported by Java can be located on the Java Web site at *http://java.sun.com/products/jdk/1.2/docs/guide/internet/index. html.*

Page Directives in Use

The following example shows page directives in a simple JSP "hello world" page (`hello2.jsp`).

```
<!doctype html public "-//w3c/dtd HTML 4.0//en">
<html>

<!-- A page directive to import a number of classes.   -->
<%@ page import="javax.naming.*, java.util.*,java.sql.*" %>
```

```
<!-- A page directive that specifies the page to be called if an
exception is thrown.   -->
<%@ page errorPage="error.jsp"  %>


<!--A page directive that specifies that the page is thread safe.
The container allows multiple threads of execution to service JSP
requests at the same time. -->
<%@ page isThreadSafe="true" %>


<!--A page directive that specifies that the page should have a
session associated with it.  If "true", WebLogic Server creates a
session automatically if one does not exist. If "false", and the
JSP page is not part of a session, the implicit session object is
not available and our JSP page throws an error if we try to
access it. -->
<%@ page session ="false" %>


<!-- Standard HTML -->
<head>
<title>Hello World</title>
</head>

<body bgcolor=#FFFFFF>
<font face="Helvetica">


<h2>
<font color=#DB1260>
Hello World
</font>
</h2>

<!--An expression to print hello world to the out object. -->
<%
out.print("<p><b>Hello World!</b>");
%>


</body>
</html>
```

The output of this JSP page might look like Figure 4–2.

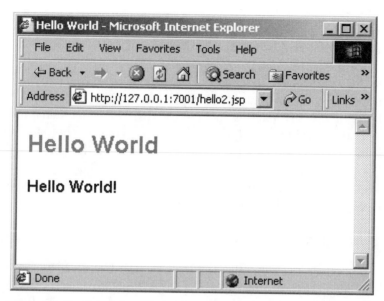

Figure 4-2   Output from the JSP Page Directive

Note that all the white space included in your JSP page outside of the <% .. %> tag is rendered as well.

Include Directives

The `include` directive includes any arbitrary text or JSP page code when the JSP is executed. The `include` directive refers to a file specified by a path relative to the current location of the JSP page. If the included JSP page were in a subdirectory named *mysubdirectory* and was named *foo.jsp*, the relative path would be *my subdirectory/foo.jsp*.

The `include` directive is delimited by the <%@ and %> characters. For example, if you want to instruct WebLogic Server to include the contents of a text file named *todaysweather.txt* in the output of your JSP, use the following code:

```
<%@ include file="todaysweather.txt" %>
```

If the *todaysweather.txt* file is located in a subdirectory named *secret*, specify a relative URL:

```
<%@ include file="secret/todaysweather.txt" %>
```

The `include` directive can also be used to include entire JSP files. WebLogic Server executes JSP files, unlike text files, when their output is included. The following code includes a JSP file named *myresponse.jsp*:

```
<jsp:include page="response.jsp">
```

Remember that JSP files are evaluated from the top down. Output from a given include directive is inserted at that point in the evaluation of the JSP page.

Note that the directive to include a JSP page is different from the directive that includes text documents. If you use the file include to pull in a JSP page, the *source* of the JSP page is included and then recompiled, rather than including the possibly already-compiled page. That is, the `<%@include file="foo.jsp"%>` directive pulls in the text of the included file and compiles it as if it were part of the including file. The `<jsp:include page="foo.jsp">` tag compiles the file as a separate JSP file, and embeds a call to it in the compiled JSP.

Why Include Directives?

Include directives are very powerful in the context of a J2EE Web application. They enable you to modularize your JSP pages, making development and maintenance much simpler. For example, to place a navigation bar into every JSP page, create a single page called `navigation.jsp`. The output of this JSP page would be the navigation bar that you show to every user.

Then, simply add an include directive to every page that you develop for your Web application. The same technique can be extended to page headers and footers as well. Different JSP pages can be added together to create the entire site. And, if you want to change any component of all pages, you simply change the individual `navigation.jsp`, `footer.jsp`, and so forth. The WebAuction site uses this technique for the header and for the navigation bar.

> *Use the include directive to modularize your pages. If you have a site design that includes the reuse of components regularly, such as a navigation bar or a banner across the top of the Web site, consider placing the code to generate those components into separate JSP pages. Then, use the JSP include directive to include that into each one of your pages.*

Implicit Objects and Scripting Elements

While directives are special JSP tags that enable you to give commands to the WebLogic Server JSP container, scripting elements are a way to specify arbitrary Java code for the container to execute. The major convenience of using JSP instead of arbitrary application code is that JSP contains many pre-defined *implicit objects*. This means that you do not need to write code to generate an output stream, instantiate an HTTP response object, and so forth—the container does it all for you.

There are three types of *scripting elements* for use with JSP. These are:

- A *declaration*, which enables you to declare methods, variables, and so forth in a JSP page.
- A *scriptlet*, which is a Java code fragment to be executed when clients request your JSP page.
- An *expression*, which is a Java code expression that is evaluated, converted to a string, and then shipped to the requesting client.

Before discussing the three types of scripting elements in detail, we'll discuss implicit objects.

Implicit Objects

Implicit objects are objects automatically provided to JSPs by the JSP container. For example, user session information: The JSP container provides an implicit object that you can use in your Java code to get and set the user session information. Other objects are available for different tasks. In general, these objects are very similar to the objects available for servlet development.

The following is a summary of the other available objects:

Implicit Object: out

out is a subclass of the standard Java extension class `javax servlet. jsp JspWriter`, which enables you to print information to the requester. Whenever you need to send the results of an operation back to the client browser, use the out object that is provided by the JSP container. The simplest way to do this is to call the `print` method. The following code prints "I play basketball with Nick D." to the requesting client:

```
out.print("I play basketball with Nick D.");
```

The out object has a scope of one page. That means that there is a single instance of the object per JSP page. You can do everything with this out object that you did with the `output` object you used in your servlets in Chapter 3. This includes modifying HTTP headers, specifying URL rewriting, and so forth.

Remember, the out object is buffered in 8KB chunks. But, you can change the value of this buffering using the page directive `buffer` described earlier in this chapter. Regardless of the size of the buffer, at the end of the execution of your JSP, WebLogic Server flushes your output buffer and sends the remaining data in your response back to the client.

Best practice: JSP buffer size should be set to maximize efficiency. A larger buffer allows more content to be written before anything is actually sent, which provides the servlet with more time to set appropriate status codes and headers. A smaller buffer decreases server memory load and allows the client to start receiving data more quickly. Typically, the 8KB buffer works fine for most applications.

If you have a JSP page that is outputting very large files, you may want to increase this buffer size. This improves the efficiency of your WebLogic Server deployment by reducing the number of system calls and network traffic. For example, if you are returning a 512KB HTML page, system calls and network traffic must flush the buffer each time it fills, and return data to the client. By setting the buffer to a higher value, you can substantially improve efficiency. To illustrate, if you use an 8KB buffer with your 512KB file, the buffer will be emptied by the container and sent to the client 512/8= 64 buffer flushes. If you were to increase your buffer size to 32KB, this reduces the number of buffer flushes to 512/32= 16 buffer flushes.

You can use a number of other methods on the `out` object:

- `public abstract void clear()` and `public abstract void clearBuffer ()` enable you to clear the existing buffer for the JSP page. Add the following code if you have data already buffered for output to the client, but decide that you want to clear that buffer:

```
out.clear();
```

The difference between the two methods is that `clear()` throws an exception if data has already been sent to the client when it is called. `clearBuffer()` does not throw an exception if called after data has already been sent to the client.

Best practice: If possible, develop JSPs so that they do not rely on methods to clear the buffer because clearing data from the output buffer is expensive.

- `public abstract void flush()` causes the current output buffer to be cleared and the data to be sent to the client. This method is automatically called by the JSP container, so you should not use it unless your application explicitly requires you to flush the current buffer output. This method might be useful if you set a very large buffer size in order to streamline transfer of large files. Or, use it as a response to an exception, such as a disk exception.

```
out.flush();
```

*Best practice: When the **flush** method described here is called by the application, it forces unnecessary clearing of optimized and work for the server machine, reducing scalability. Wherever possible, allow WebLogic Server to handle flushing buffers automatically. While a number of JSP actions, including those for forwarding to other resources, do **flush ()** the output buffer, WebLogic Server is optimized to work in those circumstances.*

- `public int getBufferSize()` returns the size of the buffer in bytes. This is basically the value set using the `<%@buffer` page directive discussed earlier.
- `public abstract int getRemaining()` returns the size in bytes of the remaining free space in the output buffer.

Implicit Object: request

`request` is a subclass of `javax.servlet.HttpServletRequest` that includes all information provided by the `request` objects. You should use this `request` object to access the parameters and the respective values included in the request. To do this, you should use the same methods that were used to access the servlet `request` object as described in Chapter 3.

To get an Enumeration of the parameter names in this request and assign them to `variable foo`, you would say:

```
Enumeration foo = request.getParameter();
```

To get an Enumeration of all parameter names and values, use the `get-ParameterNames` and `getParameterValues` methods, respectively.

`getParameterNames()` returns an enumeration of string objects containing the names of the parameters contained in this request.

`getParameterValues(java.lang.String   name)` returns an array of string objects containing all values the given request parameter has, or null if the parameter does not exist. For both of these methods, you could use the methods available in the `java.utils.Enumeration` class to access the values. To print every parameter name to the requester, use the `out` implicit object described above:

```
Enumeration foo = request.getParameterNames();
```

```
while (foo.hasMoreElements()) {
out.print (e.nextElement());
}
```

Implicit Object: session

session is an instance of the `javax.servlet.http.HttpSession` class. It represents the current session information for the user session. The same methods are available that were described in Chapter 3 for user sessions. For more information on using servlet sessions, review the section in Chapter 3 titled "Conventional Methods for Session Tracking Are Difficult."

Implicit Object: exception

exception is an instance of `java.lang.Throwable` that encapsulates the error message received if the page you are creating is an error-handling page. Remember, error-handling pages are those that include the page directive `isErrorPage=true`. To access the error messages, you can use a number of available methods:

- public `String getMessage()` and public `String getLocalizedMessage()`, which return the message contained in the `exception` object and a localized version of the message, respectively. Localized messages are those intended for different languages. To print out the message of your exception to your user, you could use the following code in your JSP:

```
out.print("exception: " + exception.getMessage());
```

- public void `printStackTrace()` prints out a complete stack trace of the error. This is very helpful to see where the error originated and how it propagated through the system. By default, this method outputs the stack trace to the standard error output stream, which is logged in the application server log on most platforms. This makes it very difficult to locate the error. Fortunately, WebLogic Server provides an extra service that prints out JSP error directly to the Web browser. This is extremely helpful during debugging.

```
exception.printStackTrace();
```

If you attempt to use these methods in a page that is not an error page, as specified with the page directive `isErrorPage=true`, your page execution will fail. If you've specified an error page for your JSP, the error page is executed.

Best practice: To make debugging your JSP files easier, use the WebLogic Server feature that allows error messages to be displayed in the browser. See the WebLogic Server documentation for more details on how to configure this feature.

Note: The `pageContext`, `application`, and `config` implicit objects are discussed in Chapter 3 in the section titled "The Web Application Package."

Scripting Elements

Scripting elements are segments of Java code that are embedded in the JSP page. Scripting elements are compiled and then executed.

There are three types of scripting elements:

- *Declarations* are scripting elements that declare methods, variables, and so forth in a JSP page. They are used to declare functions and variables to be used during the execution of the page.
- *Scriptlets* are Java code that is executed when the JSP page responds to a request. Scriptlets define the logic for your JSP pages.
- *Expressions* are scripting elements written in Java that the JSP container evaluates when the JSP page is executed. Expressions are used to quickly embed dynamic values into JSP pages.

In the following sections, we'll describe each of the scripting elements and how to use them.

Declarations

Declarations are scripting elements that declare methods, variables, or both in a JSP page. The special tags that designate declarations begin with `<%!` and end with `%>`. So, let's say you want to declare a variable named `foo` and assign the value of 3 to it. You use the following declaration tag:

```
<%! int foo=3;  %>
```

This variable, like all declarations, has a scope limited to the current page. If you declare a variable *myInt* in your JSP page *xyz.jsp*, it can be accessed by any scripting element on your page but is not available by default to any other JSP page. To get around this problem, the JSP and servlet specifications include the notion of a *Web application*. Web applications are discussed later in this chapter in the section titled "Using Servlets and JSPs Together: Model View Controller."

Best practice: Use local methods or variables when you have code or temporary values that need to be used more than once in the execution of a given JSP page.

It also is possible to declare *methods* in your JSP declarations. For example, if you want to create a method named `inc` that increments an integer, you could say:

```
<%!
private int inc(int x) {
return x++;
}
%>
```

The use of internal method declarations should be done with care. For example, you can create member variables that are available to more than just the individual JSP page. If so, it is possible that other JSP pages will attempt to access them at the same time. Developers commonly get into trouble with member functions when they use member variables to supplement the argument list, which creates thread-safety issues. Instead, pass all variables needed in the method argument list so that the method is still thread-safe. Declarations should always be crafted so that they can be accessed in parallel.

Scriptlets

Scriptlets are essentially code fragments that exist in the JSP page and are executed by the container to service client requests. In the current JSP specification, the only language that is available for scriptlets is Java. Scriptlets are designated using the `<%` and `%>` characters.

If you have the variable `foo` and the `inc()` declarations in your JSP page and wish to increment the variable `foo`, use the following code:

```
<%
foo = inc(int foo);
%>
```

As with declarations, scriptlets by default have a scope limited to the current page.

> *Best practice: Use scriptlets as the place to put any arbitrary code you want to run during the execution of your JSP.*

Expressions

Expressions are scripting elements that contain valid expressions in Java. At execution time for the JSP page, the expression is evaluated, converted to a string, and then placed in the implicit object `out`. These expressions can be any valid expression in Java. To designate an expression in your JSP page, use the `<%=` and `%>` characters to signify the beginning and end of your expression, respectively.

For example, to output the value of the variable `foo` as used in the previous sections on scriptlets and declarations, use the following code:

```
<%= foo %>
```

Any valid expression can be placed in a JSP expression tag.

Actions

Actions are special JSP tags for use with implicit objects and other server-side objects, and for use in defining new scripting variables. Actions are defined using XML syntax only. They typically take the form of `<jsp: action name/>`. For example, the following action specifies to the JSP container that you wish to include the output of a JSP page named `mypage.jsp` in the output of your JSP page:

```
<jsp:include page="mypage.jsp" />
```

Why Use Actions?

Use actions for certain types of operations: for example, to include the output of another JSP page in your current JSP page. One instance in which this is helpful is if you have a single JSP page that dynamically generates the copyright information for each page of your Web site. Or, perhaps you would like to make use of the capability to forward a user to another JSP page. Standard action tags enable you to do all these things in only one line of code.

Action Types

Two types of actions are available to JSP developers:

- *Standard actions* are available, by definition, in every JSP container. To use these, you need not import any special classes or libraries.
- *Custom actions* are available to be "plugged-in" through the use of a JSP feature (discussed later) called *tag libraries*.

In this section, we'll discuss how to use each of the standard actions.

Standard Actions

Seven standard actions are required to be included in every JSP 1.1–compliant container. These have varied functions and uses. Let's discuss the first four of the standard actions:

- `<jsp:include>`
- `<jsp:forward>`
- `<jsp:plugin>`
- `<jsp:param>`

We defer discussion of the final three standard actions to a section later in this chapter titled "Using Java Beans with JSPs":

- `<jsp:useBean>`
- `<jsp:setProperty>`
- `<jsp:getProperty>`

<jsp:include>

The `include` standard action provides for the inclusion of static and dynamic resources in the current JSP page. The tag specifies the relative URL of the resource to be included in the following format:

```
<jsp:include page=" copyright.html" />
```

Note that the `include` tag begins with `<jsp:include` and is completed with `/>`.

The `include` tag is able to refer to any piece of content including HTML pages, JSP pages, servlets, and so forth. The only requirement is that the relative URL specified with the page attribute must be a valid resource type for your JSP container/Web server and *also be located in the same application context*.

After the included resource is placed on the output stream by the JSP container, request processing resumes. Note that the page output during the execution of the included pages is buffered and flushed prior to inclusion, just as if the remote client requested the included page. Included pages have access only to the `out` object and cannot set headers. This means that included pages that try to do things like `setCookie()` on the output stream throw exceptions. This is because both the included and forward actions cause the current JSP/servlet output to be flushed by calling the `flush()` method. Once a buffer is flushed, the data written to that buffer cannot be modified, including the HTTP header.

Why two different mechanisms for including resources in JSP pages? So far, this chapter has described the include page directive and the include page action. The difference between the two is when the JSP engine does the include. For the include page directive, the inclusion of the content from the other page is done at compile time. It causes WebLogic to copy the entire JSP page into the generated Java source code to be compiled in the resulting JSP page. For the include page action, the data included happens at runtime. Directives should be used to include other JSP pages, while the include action is most suitable for including static content, such as copyright text.

The JSP `include` functionality is the same as that imposed on users of the Request Dispatcher in servlets.

It is sometimes desirable to include content from other resources, not located inside of the same Web application as a JSP page. To accomplish this inside your JSP pages, create a plain URL connection over a socket to the location of the remote resource. Then, load the resource using an input stream and write it to the implicit output object:

```
URL url = new URL("http://www.nickdattoma.com/nick.gif");
URLConnection connection = url.openConnection();
BufferedInputStream bis = new BufferedInputStream(connec-
tion.getInputStream());
FileOutputStream file =
BufferedOutputStream out = new BufferedOutputStream(new FileOut-
putStream("newnick.gif"));

int i;
i = in.read();

while (i != -1) {
    out.write(i);
    i = in.read();
}
out.flush;
```

You can do this with text documents as well. In WebLogic Server, you can do the same with SSL security. However, instead of opening a standard URL, you open it using HTTPS. More information on SSL in WebLogic applications is included in Chapter 12, *Developing Security with WebLogic Server JNDI and JAAS.*

<jsp:forward>

The `forward` action allows for the dispatch of the current JSP request to another resource. The tag specifies the resource to which the request is forwarded using the `page` attribute. The `forward` tag begins with `<jsp:forward` and is completed with `/>`. For example, the following tag forwards the JSP request to the resource named `foo.jsp`:

```
<jsp: forward page =" foo.jsp" />
```

> The *forward* tag is very useful to redirect misdirected requests. For example, you might want to check that a user still has a valid account. If not, you can forward the user to a page such as *invalidAccount.jsp*, which displays his or her lapsed account information.

When using the JSP `forward` tag, you should use buffered output on the JSP pages. Buffered output is on by default. The buffer is automatically cleared when the forward occurs or when the buffer overflows. If you are using unbuffered pages, any attempt to forward the request after data has been written to the output stream raises an exception.

A JSP forward is different than an HTTP Redirect. With an HTTP Redirect, you send a message back to the Web browser, instructing it to forward to another resource:

```
response.sendRedirect(myNewURL);
```

This causes the new URL to display in the Web browser. It also requires another communication between your server and the client browser. On the other hand, the JSP forward is processed on the server. Your JSP forwards handling of the response to another resource.

Using the JSP forward functionality is almost always preferable to sending HTTP redirects—except when you are processing data and concerned if a user clicks Reload on the Web browser, thus resending the data. In those cases, you should use an HTTP Redirect.

<jsp:param>

When the `forward` or `include` actions are used, the included page or forwarded page sees the original `request` object. The original parameters of the request can be augmented with new parameters, as specified by the `param` tag. The `param` action provides name/value information pairs to other actions.

The format of the `param` tag begins with `<jsp:param` and is completed with `/>`. The following `param` tag specifies a name/value pair of `foo/bar`:

```
<jsp: param name=" foo" value="bar" />
```

The `param` element is used in the `include`, `forward`, and `plugin` actions to provide information to other pages in the form of request parameters. These parameters are additive: Each parameter added in the request takes precedence over existing parameters.

When using this tag in conjunction with other actions, the syntax is as follows:

```
<jsp:forward page=" urlHere"> { <jsp:param .... /> }* </jsp:forward>
```

Note that two new tags were added in this statement syntax: the parameter and the closing tag `</jsp:forward>` for the `forward` action. You can include multiple parameter tags, as indicated by the `*`, previously. The same syntax applies to the `include` and `plugin` actions. An example of using the `include` action with parameters would be:

```
<jsp:include page="copyright.jsp">
{ <jsp: param name=" foo" value="bar" /> }
</jsp:include>
```

<jsp:plugin>

The `plugin` action instructs the client browser to download the Java plug-in for executing a client-side job. The capability to invoke a plug-in helps the application developer overcome compatibility and versioning issues caused by the wide variety of Web browsers. By using this tag, you can be sure that your applet or JavaBean executes on the appropriate JVM. This ensures a better user experience.

> *Due to the wide variety of JVM and browser versions and vendors available on the marketplace today, use the **plugin** tag to get the client browser to download the Java plug-in version that you specify. This helps alleviate compatibility problems for clients.*

The following example shows the JSP plug-in being used for an applet:

```
<jsp:plugin type=applet code="Food.class" codebase="/html" >
<jsp:params>
<jsp:param
name="foo"
value="bar"/>
</jsp:params>
<jsp:fallback>
<p> Unable to load the plug-in. Error!</p>
</jsp:fallback>
</jsp:plugin>
```

The `fallback` component specifies what the JSP page should do in case the plug-in is unable to be downloaded to the client. The following is the complete syntax for the plug-in action:

```
<jsp: plugin type=" bean| applet"
code=" classFileName "
codebase=" classFileDirectoryName "
[ name=" instanceName " ]
[ archive=" URIToArchive, ... " ]
[ align=" bottom |top| middle| left| right" ]
[ height=" displayPixels " ]
[ width=" displayPixels " ]
[ hspace=" leftRightPixels " ]
[ vspace=" topBottomPixels "]
[ jreversion=" JREVersionNumber | 1.1 " ]
[ nspluginurl=" URLToPlugin " ]
[ iepluginurl=" URLToPlugin "] >
[ <jsp: params>
[ <jsp: param
name=" parameterName "
value=" parameterValue " /> ]+
</ jsp: params> ]
[ <jsp: fallback> text message for user </ jsp: fallback> ]
</ jsp: plugin>
```

Use the `plug-in` tag to avoid browser compatibility issues.

Using Java Beans with JSPs

The JSP specification enables you to include *JavaBeans*, which are different from the *Enterprise JavaBeans* discussed later in this book. JavaBeans encapsulate presentation logic or rudimentary business logic in your pages. By encapsulating logic in a JavaBean, you can keep your Web developers from accidentally compromising or corrupting your Java code. JavaBeans help you create more maintainable pages.

Integration of JavaBeans with JSP pages is done through the use of three JSP actions. Let's take a look at each of these tags and how to use them.

JSP Tags for Using Beans

The `<jsp:useBean>` tag enables a JSP developer to specify a JavaBean to be included in the JSP page. This tag tries to instantiate a JavaBean, and gets any parameters that are specified. There are three major parameters that affect the capability of the container to instantiate your JavaBean. These are: the scope of the JavaBean, an ID field that represents the bean's name as it should be referenced in your application, and the class name of the Java-Bean. The following is a simple example of this tag:

```
<jsp:useBean id="mybean" class="com.myco.myapp.mybean"
scope="page">
</jsp:useBean>
```

It is a best practice to use packages for your JavaBeans. If a class is not assigned to a package, then it is not available unless it is explicitly imported into a class that does exist in a package. If you do not specify a package, it is more likely that you can run into errors that are difficult to diagnose.

The following is the complete syntax for this tag:

```
<jsp: useBean
id=" beanInstanceName "
scope=" page |request| session| application"
{ class=" package. class " |
  type=" package. class " |
  beanName=" { package. class | <%= expression %> } "
{/>| > other tags </ jsp: useBean> }
```

There are a number of possible attributes for the `useBean` tag:

- `id`—Represents the bean's name as it should be referenced in your application, and the class name of the JavaBean. This is the name your Java code in the JSP page uses to access the JavaBean instance.
- `class`—Specifies the complete class name representing the JavaBean. It does not include the class extension. For example: `com.myco.myapp.mybean`.

- scope—Specifies the scope in which the JavaBean is available. There are four different possible values:
  - page—The JavaBean is available for the current page. Your JavaBean is discarded upon completion of the current request for your JSP.
  - request—The JavaBean is available from the current page's ServletRequest object. This is useful when you forward or include another JSP page using the page directives described earlier in this chapter. You can use the getAttribute(name) method on the ServletRequest object to locate a reference to the JavaBean in the forward or included pages.
  - Session—The JavaBean is available for the duration of the user session. It is available from the current page's HttpSession object.
  - Application—The JavaBean is available indefinitely and is stored in the current page's ServletContext object as defined for Web applications. To access the JavaBean, use the getAttribute(name) method on the ServletContext object.
- Class—The fully qualified name of the class that defines the implementation of the object. The class name is case sensitive.
- BeanName—The name of a JavaBean.

If you include the useBean tag in your JSP page, the WebLogic Server container automatically creates an instance of that bean. And depending upon the scope of that bean as specified by the tag, it is available to your JSP page or to the entire session. WebLogic Server automatically handles the disposal of the bean.

Building a JavaBean into a JSP

Let's say we have a user name and some data associated with that user name in a remote location such as a database or a text file. This data could be, for example, the user's employee ID and Social Security number.

We first create a JavaBean to get the user ID and other data. Then, we access the data by calling methods in the JavaBean from two JSP pages. The first JSP page has a form for input of the user name. Form results are posted to another JSP page, which handles the form and makes the appropriate calls to the JavaBean.

Creating a JavaBean

First, let's specify the JavaBean that encapsulates the logic required to get the user and the data associated with that user:

```
package com.mypackage;

public class UserDataBean {
```

You must also specify a default constructor. This constructor method is called when the JavaBean object is created:

```
// The default constructor.
public UserDataBean ()
{
}
```

> If we want to put the JavaBean in an HTTP session so that it can take advantage of clustering, the JavaBean must be serializable for all components that are placed into the HTTP session. In this case, the class declaration would look like this:
>
> ```
> public class UserDataBean implements
> Serializable
> ```
>
> Serializability of a class is enabled when the class implements the `java.io.Serializable` interface. It is a key component for `HttpSessions` clustering.

Next, define methods that are called by a JSP page to get the values that we want. The following method takes the user name and returns the user ID number:

```
public int getID()
{
    /*
In the real world, code would go off to another resource such as
a database or an Enterprise JavaBean to locate the ID that goes
with the name provided.  In this case, we simply provide a dummy
ID that is returned no matter what name we receive.
*/
return 7;
}
```

This method takes the user name as a parameter and returns the user Social Security number:

```
public void setID(int ID)
    {
    /*
```

```
In the real world, code would go off to another resource such as
a database or an Enterprise JavaBean to set the ID that goes with
the name we are provided.  In this case, we simply provide a
dummy SSN that is returned no matter what name we receive.
*/
    }
```

The JSP Form Page: form.jsp

A JSP form page can contain a field for users to input a user name. The user name value can then be posted to another JSP page.

```
<!doctype html public "-//w3c/dtd HTML 4.0//en">
<html>
<head>
    <title> Enter User Name</title>
</head>
<body>
```

Next, define a form that posts to the JSP page that uses our JavaBean:

```
<FORM action="beanuser.jsp">
Enter Name: <INPUT type="text" size="30"
name="Name">
 <input type=submit value="Submit">
<FORM>
```

Finally, finish off the HTML page by closing off the HTML tags:

```
</body>
</html>
```

The output of this JSP page might look like Figure 4–3.

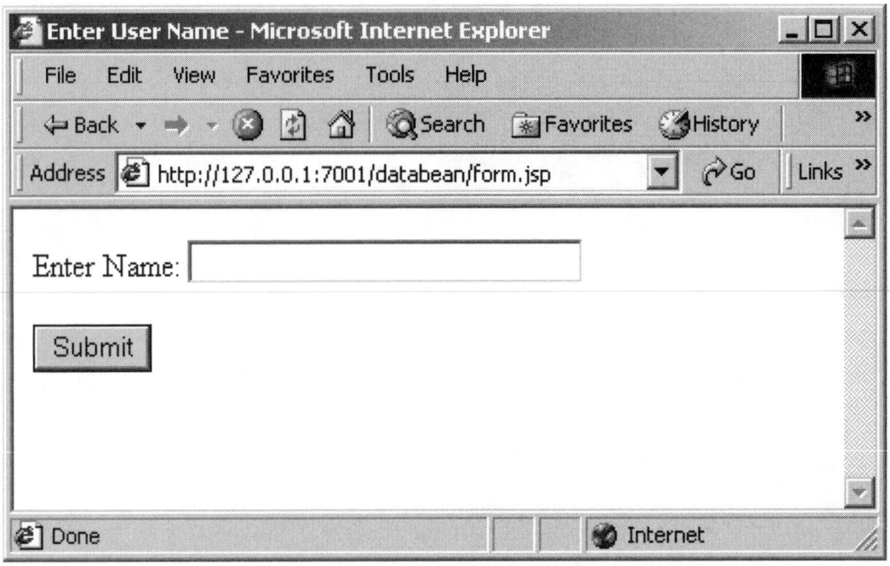

Figure 4–3   Form for Entering User Name

To view the form, copy it into the default Web applications directory, as you did before. The viewer of this page enters a user name and clicks the Submit button. This results in a POST to the page named `beanuser.jsp`.

The beanuser.jsp Page

The `beanuser.jsp` page takes the user name entered in `form.jsp` and uses that to make calls into the `UserDataBean` JavaBean created earlier. Build `beanuser.jsp` using the script provided.

We need to specify the JavaBean. In this case, we set the ID of the bean (the name we use to reference the bean in our JSP page) to be equal to `"OurBean"`. We also set the scope of the JavaBean to be equal to `"page"`, meaning that it persists only for the life of the page. Finally, we specify the Java class to be loaded:

```
<jsp:useBean id="OurBean"
    scope="page"
    class="com.mypackage.UserDataBean"
/>
```

Set the typical HTML header information:

```
<!doctype html public "-//w3c/dtd HTML 4.0//en">
<html>
<head>
```

```
<title>Using Bean</title>
</head>
<body>

<h1>Using Bean</h1>
```

Next, call methods on the JavaBean and print out the results:

```
<%
String userName = request.getParameter( "Name" );
out.print(OurBean.getSSN(userName));
out.print(OurBean.getID(userName));
%>
```

Finally, finish off the HTML page:

```
</body>
</html>
```

When viewing this set of pages, a user first sees the `form.jsp` page in the Web browser (see Figure 4–4).

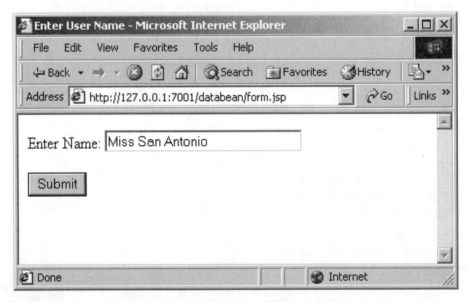

Figure 4–4   The form.jsp Page

After entering the user name, the `beanuser.jsp` page is executed (see Figure 4-5).

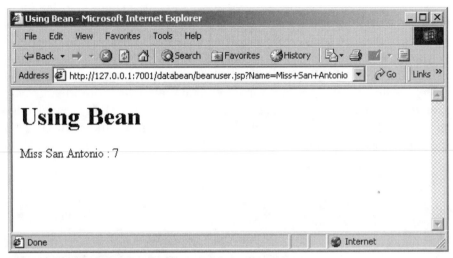

Figure 4–5 Output from the JavaBean

Running the JavaBean Example in WebLogic Server

To deploy the basic JavaBean example, `databean.war`, first be sure that you have installed BEA WebLogic Server 6.0. Start the default server; then do the following:

1. Locate the `databean.war` code on the CD included with this book. It should be located in the directory titled *examples\ch4* under the root directory of the CD.

2. Copy this file from the CD into the applications directory of your BEA WebLogic Server 6.0 installation. If you are using Microsoft Windows, you can use the Windows Explorer or the command line to copy this file. Depending upon the location of your installation, the directory path should look something like the following:

`c:\bea\wlserver6.0\config\mydomain\applications\`

3. The Web application is now installed. You can view it by opening a Web browser and viewing the following URL: *http://127.0.0.1:7001/databean/*.

Note: If you have an HTTP proxy enabled in your Web browser, as many organizations require, you may need to disable it.

WebLogic Server includes the option to show debugging information in the window running it. This can be very useful when trying to determine why your application is not performing as expected. To turn this on, start your WebLogic Server console. Then, click on the navigation panel to the left to locate information for the server for which you want debugging information. Once you find the appropriate server, such as "myserver", information specific to that server should appear on the right side of the Web browser. Click on the Logging tab, set a severity level such as "info", and then click the check box next to the Debug to Stdout option (see Figure 4–6).

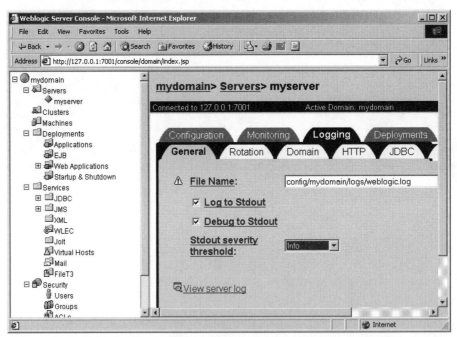

Figure 4–6   Enabling Error Logging to the WebLogic Server Startup Window

The next time your instance of WebLogic Server starts, you are presented with a voluminous amount of information about everything going on (see Figure 4–7).

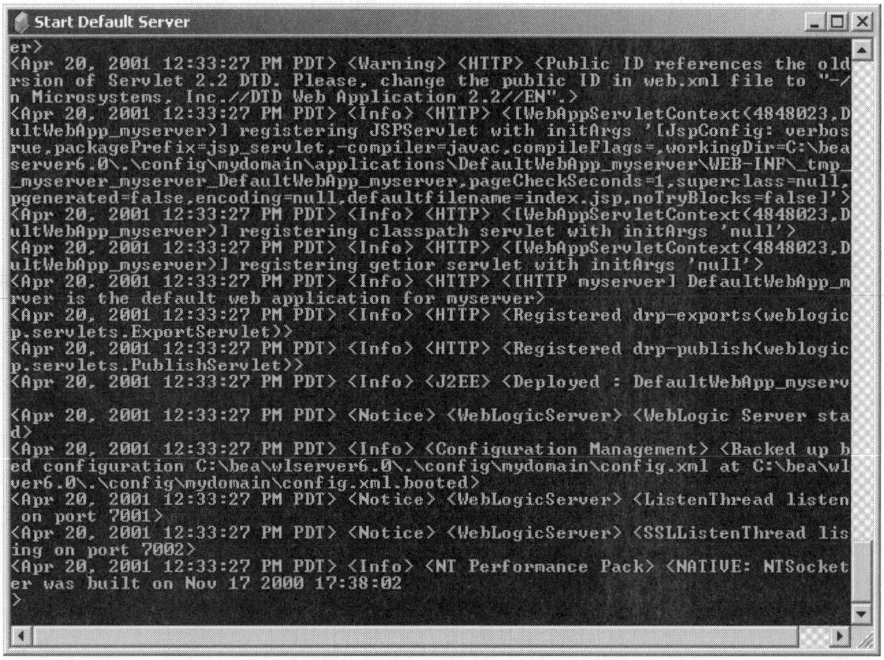

Figure 4–7 Logging Output to the Startup Window

The databean.war Example Components

The *databean.war* is a complete Web application that includes all the necessary components required by the Java specifications. The most notable of
these components is the *WEB-INF/* directory. As mentioned in Chapter 3,
the *WEB-INF* directory holds the configuration and deployment information
for the Web application. Objects such as JavaBeans are also stored in this
directory. These components are not available directly to clients of the Web
application.

Configuration information for the Web application is contained in the
web.xml deployment descriptor file. This includes information for the
WebLogic Server deployment to recognize what components are included in
the Web application and what settings they should have. A comprehensive
description of how to create these deployment descriptor files is included
with the WebLogic Server documentation at

`http://e-docs.bea.com/wls/docs60/programming/webappdeployment.html.`

Similar documentation exists for other JSP engines. Consult your individual product documentation because many application servers slightly differ

from the specification in this area and have added application server–specific extensions.

The JavaBean classes themselves are kept in the *WEB-INF/classes* subdirectory. The application server looks for JavaBean code in this directory.

Building the JavaBean Example in WebLogic Server

To build and deploy the basic JavaBean example, *databean.war*, you can use the included Microsoft Windows build script.

Once the server is started, do the following:

1. Locate the *databean.war* file on the CD included with this book. It should be located in the directory titled *examples\ch4\databean* under the root directory of the CD.
2. Copy this file into an empty directory that you will use for code development on your PC. For this example, we use the directory *c:\dev*.
3. The Web application code is now copied over. We need to unpack it using the `jar` utility included with WebLogic Server. First, make sure that you have your environment set correctly. Start a command shell and run the *setEnv.cmd* script that is included as part of the WebLogic Server installation. In most cases, this is located at:

```
c:\bea\wlserver6.0\config\mydomain\setEnv.cmd
```

This sets the environment so that you can access all WebLogic Server utilities from the command line (see Figure 4–8).

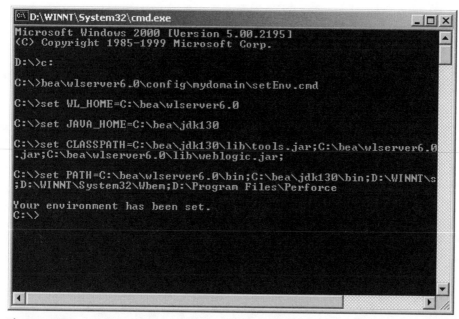

Figure 4–8   Output from Running the setEnv.cmd Script

The screen shot in Figure 4–8 shows WebLogic Server installed on the C: drive. Your installation may be on another drive.

4. Navigate to your development directory (for example, *c:\dev*), and unpack the *war* file with the `jar` command:

```
jar xvf databean.war
```

You should see something that looks like Figure 4–9. Note that unpacking the *.war* file creates the *META-INF* and *WEB-INF* directories, plus any sub-directories:

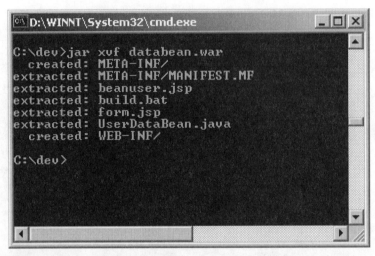

Figure 4–9 Output of the jar Command

5. A batch file (*build.bat*) is included in the *.war* file. This would not have been done in a standard *.war* file because any file in that *.war* file would be available, once the Web application is deployed, to anyone with a Web browser. For the sake of simplicity, all the files are included in this single *.war*.

6. Now, edit *build.bat* with your favorite text editor. You may need to change the first line of the script to point to the location of your WebLogic Server's applications directory.

7. Execute *build.bat* from the command line by typing "build.bat" (see Figure 4–10).

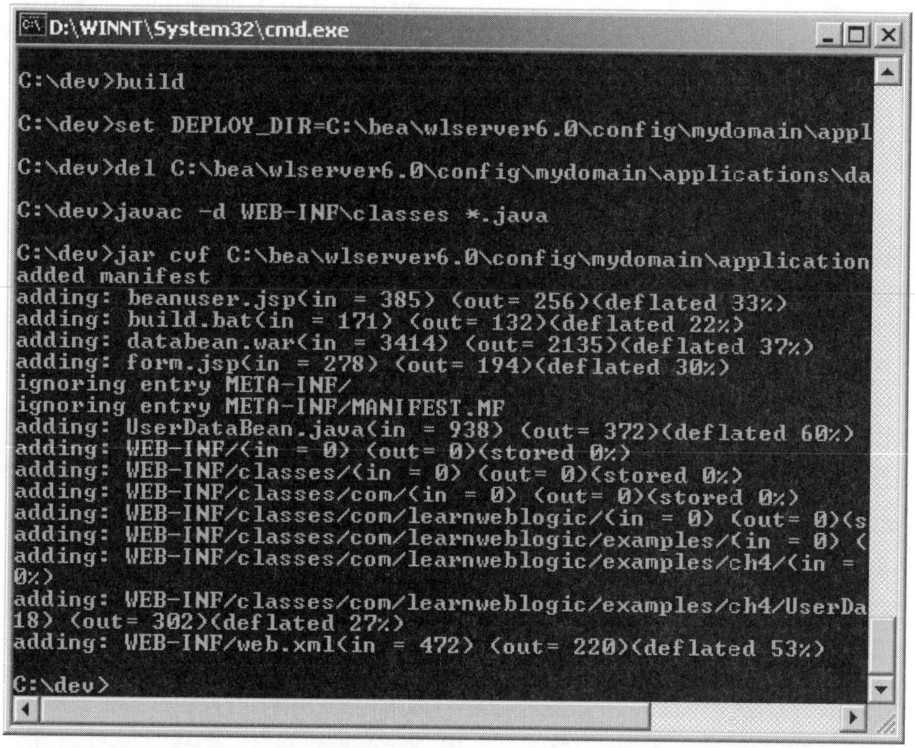

Figure 4-10 Results of Running build.bat

The build script has set the deployment directory (in this case) on the C: drive. Next, it attempts to delete any existing installation of this *.war* file. Then, it compiles any Java classes and places them in the *classes* directory. Finally, it uses the `jar` command to create a final package and places that in the *applications* directory.

In the window running the WebLogic Server, you should see something like this each time you run the script, if you have turned on debugging for the server in the WebLogic Server console:

```
<Nov 24, 2000 11:16:17 AM PST> <Info> <J2EE> <Undeployed :
databean>

<Nov 24, 2000 11:16:17 AM PST> <Info> <J2EE> <Deployed :
databean>
```

This indicates that the component has been deployed or undeployed. To view the deployed component, point your Web browser to *http://127.0.0.1:7001/databean/*.

Note: If you have an HTTP proxy enabled in your Web browser, as many organizations require, you might need to disable this to access your own machine as a Web server.

Using JavaBean Properties

Properties allow for convenient setting and retrieving of parameters in a Java-Bean. They are useful for streamlining the retrieval of values in a JavaBean. One intended benefit of properties lies in the promise of off-the-shelf Java-Beans, which are configured when they are employed in your JSP page. In reality, off-the-shelf JavaBean components have not really proven to be viable in the J2EE marketplace.

How Properties Work

The `<jsp:useBean>` tag lets the JSP developer set properties in a given JavaBean. These tags are actually embedded in the `<jsp:useBean>` tag at instantiation time to pass properties into the JavaBean. A simple example of property setting is as follows:

```
<jsp:useBean id="mybean" class="com.myco.myapp.mybean"
scope="page">
<jsp:setProperty name="mybean" property="gumby" value="999">
</jsp:useBean>
```

This instantiates a bean with ID `"mybean"` with a scope of one page if the bean does not already exist. It also sets a property named `"gumby"` with a value of 999. The full syntax of this tag is as follows:

```
<jsp:setProperty name=" beanName" prop_expr />
prop_expr ::= property="*" |
property=" propertyName"|
property=" propertyName" param=" parameterName"|
property=" propertyName" value=" propertyValue"
propertyValue ::= string
```

It is also possible to have all bean properties transparently populated from the HTTP request parameters. A complete example of this is included later in this chapter.

The <jsp:getProperty> Tag

The `<jsp:getProperty>` tag allows a JSP page to query a JavaBean for a given property. It is the opposite of the `setProperty` tag. `getProperty` puts the value of the property in the JSP's out object for display back to the client.

The following is a simple example using this tag that queries the mybean JavaBean for the value of the property equal to the name gumby :

```
<jsp:getProperty name="mybean" property="gumby" />
```

The full syntax of the tag is:

```
<jsp:getProperty name=" name" property=" propertyName" />
```

The name is the name of the JavaBean, and property is equal to the property name that is to be retrieved. getProperty can be used anywhere in a JSP page.

This tag is very useful because it enables us to replace the following Java expression:

```
<%
out.print(OurBean.getID());
%>
```

with a simpler form:

```
<jsp:getProperty name="OurBean" property="ID" />
```

In the preceding example, the JavaBean named "OurBean" has a property named "ID".

Note that problems in instantiating your bean cause exceptions to be thrown by JSP. You should always specify an error page in your original page declaration as noted earlier in this chapter.

Building a Bean to Use Properties

To build a JavaBean to support properties, first use a JSP to reference the JavaBean:

```
<jsp:useBean id="mybean"
class="com.myco.myapp.mybean" scope="page">
<jsp:setProperty name="mybean" property="gumby" value="999">
</jsp:useBean>
```

Note that this JavaBean has a property named "Gumby" that we set to a value of 999. To support this in our JavaBean we must *add two methods*: a "getter" and a "setter." They look like this:

```
public String getGumby() { };
public void setGumby(String a);
```

The full format of these two methods is:

```
public < PropertyType> get< PropertyName>();
public void set< PropertyName>(< PropertyType> a);
```

First, you have a method that is used to retrieve the value of the property that is defined by simply putting the keyword `get` in front of your property name. Similarly, a method used to set the value of the property inside of the bean is the name of the property prefaced by the word `set`.

The full JavaBean would be:

```
package com.myco.myapp;

public class mybean
{
    private String gumby;

    public void setGumby(String newGumby )
    {
        gumby=newGumby;
    }

    public User getGumby()
    {
        return gumby;
    }
}
```

You can use more complex types for property values, including user-defined classes, and types such as booleans and integers.

Case is significant: Note that `getGumby()` and `setGumby()` access the variable `gumby`, not `Gumby`. Using the wrong case is a common mistake that can result in some very strange errors.

Automatically Populating JavaBean Properties

The most powerful use of JavaBeans is when they are automatically populated with request parameters. To explain, requests contain parameters such as those included in a Web form. Each of these parameters contains a name and a text value. The JavaBean model with JSPs allows for a JSP with the appropriate `get<name>` and `set<name>` methods to be automatically filled.

This is accomplished by using the `<jsp:setProperty name="beanName" property="<property expression>"/>` tag, where `<property expression>` is an expression representing all properties to be set. For example, "`*`" is the regular expression meaning "all

properties." It is not possible to have a regular expression like foo*, meaning all properties whose names begin with the letters foo such as foobu
and foobar.

Suppose we have an HTML page that includes the following form:

```
<FORM action="beanuser2.jsp">
Enter Name: <INPUT type="text" size="30"
name="Name">
 <input type=submit value="Submit">
<FORM>
```

This is the same form that we specified in previous sections in this chapter.
It includes a text field that takes a user name. The field has a size of 30 characters, and the value is stored in the request parameter named "Name".

We can then build the following JavaBean. It includes a private value,
called myName, which is used in the JavaBean to keep the name value. It also
includes two methods, getName and setName, which are used to retrieve
this name value and set the name values, respectively:

```
Package com.mypackage;

public class MyNameBean {

  private String myName;

  /*
    The default constructor.
  */
  public MyNameBean ()
  {

  }

  public String getName()
  {
    /*
      In a real application, code that would do some
      work would be located here.
    */
    return myName;
  }

  public void setName(String InName)
  {
    myName=InName;
  }
```

```
}
```

beanuser2.jsp

The `beanuser2.jsp` page receives the user name entered in `form.jsp`. Unlike the original `beanuser.jsp`, it uses `useBean` to automatically populate the bean parameters.

```
<%@ page import="com.mypackage.*" %>

<jsp:useBean id="myNameBean"
    scope="page"
    class="com.mypackage.UserDataBean"
    property="*"
/>

<!doctype html public "-//w3c/dtd HTML 4.0//en">
<html><head>
<title>Using Bean</title>
</head><body>

<h1>Using Bean</h1>
<jsp:getProperty name="myNameBean" property="Name" />
</body></html>
```

A complete example of automatic population of JavaBeans with submitted form values is included as part of the WebAuction application.

Custom Tag Libraries

Custom tag libraries, added to JSP in Version 1.1, enable developers to encapsulate complex functionality inside of HTML-like tags. Basically, you can write your own action tags. If you remember from earlier in this chapter, actions are JSP tags for using implicit objects and other server-side objects, and for defining new scripting variables. They typically take the form of `<jsp: action name/>`. A Web developer can use these tags from a custom tag library just like any other HTML or JSP tag.

Using Custom Tag Libraries in JSP

Custom tag libraries are designed to hide complexity behind simple JSP tags. The following JSP code (`main.jsp`) demonstrates just how simple they are to use:

```
<%@ taglib uri="tlds/stockPrice.tld" prefix="stock" %>

<!doctype html public "-//w3c/dtd HTML 4.0//en">
<HTML>
<BODY>

<H1>Today's Stock Price</H1>

<stock:stockPrice tickerSymbol="PRAS" /> <p>

<stock:stockPrice tickerSymbol="GIRD" />

</BODY>
</HTML>
```

Figure 4–11 shows this page displayed in a Web browser.

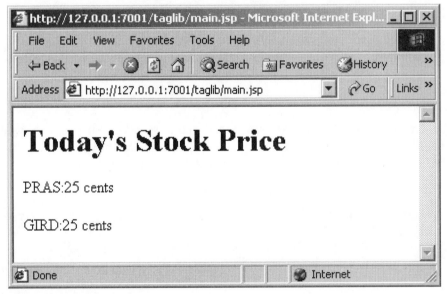

Figure 4–11 Output of a Custom Tag Library

In this case, we've created a page that relies upon a custom tag library to print out the stock price for our fictional company, Prasad Systems, which trades under the symbol PRAS. A second company is shown as well. This is a standard JSP page that includes two special tags. The first is a standard directive that specifies a *tag library descriptor* (TLD):

```
<%@ taglib uri="tlds/stockPrice.tld" prefix="stock" %>
```

This tag specifies that our JSP page uses the TLD file *stockPrice.tld*. A TLD is an *XML* file that contains mappings from the tags in the tag library to the handler classes that are also part of the tag library. The developer also creates these handler classes. The preceding directive specifies that the tag library should handle every tag that begins with the prefix `"stock"`. Note that the preceding path is a relative path. You must specify the TLD relative to the WEB-INF directory in your Web applications directory.

Then we insert a tag that calls the appropriate method to return the current stock price of Prasad Systems:

```
<stock: insert StockPrice tickerSymbol="PRAS" >
```

This tag outputs some HTML that lists the stock price. It also is possible to create a library that returns objects for use inside of the JSP page. This mechanism is used extensively in the WebAuction application.

Building a Custom Tag Library

There are two steps in creating a custom tag library. First, you build a TLD that specifies what tags in the library match to what handlers. Then, you build the handlers themselves—the Java classes that are executed by the JSP container when the appropriate tags are used in JSP pages.

The TLD

As noted, the TLD is an XML-encoded file that specifies what tags are to be handled by the tag handler classes that you write. This file is named with a *.tld* extension. The following demonstrates the format for this file:

```
<? xml version="1.0" ?>    → The version of XML that this is encoded in.

<!DOCTYPE taglib PUBLIC "-//Sun Microsystems, Inc.//DTD JSP Tag
Library 1.1//EN"
"http://java.sun.com/j2ee/dtds/web-jsptaglibrary_1_1.dtd">   →
The document type for this XML document.

<taglib> → A tag saying that we are now starting definition of a
tag library

<tlibversion>1.0</tlibversion> → version of the tag libraries
implemented
<jspversion>1.1</jspversion> → version of JSP being used.
```

```
<tag>
<name>StockPrice</name>

<tagclass>com.learnweblogic.examples.ch4.StockPriceHandler</tag-
class>

<info>A Comment/Descriptor of the Tag</info>

<attribute>   ß A tag saying that we'll now define an attribute

<name>tickerSymbol</name> → The name of the attribute
      <required>true</required>   → Whether attribute is required
      <rtexprvalue>true</rtexprvalue> →Whether attribute can be
expression

</attribute>

</tag>   → To specify that this tag is finished.

</taglib>
```

The *.tld* file is included in the *taglib.war* example on the CD, in the directory named *examples\ch4*. It is a sample TLD that specifies a tag library with a single tag that inserts a stock price based on the stock symbol provided. This single tag, named `StockPrice`, is handled by a class called `com.learnweblogic.examples.ch4.stockHandler`. This handler has one attribute, `tickerSymbol`. Remember, attributes are values sent as parameters when the tag is used.

> The WebLogic Server package includes documentation on every possible field for the TLD. You can find this on the Web at *http://e-docs.bea.com/wls/docs60/taglib/tld.html*.

When developing a tag library, you probably will not write a TLD from scratch. Either use an integrated development environment such as Web-Gain Studio or IBM VisualAge, or modify the TLD that is included in this book and in the WebLogic Server samples.

The Tag Library Handler

Basic tag library handlers are simple to implement. There are four basic requirements:

- *Have your class extend the* `javax.servlet.jsp.tagext.`
  `TagSupport` *class*. This class provides implementations of all

the methods required by the `javax.servlet.jsp.tagext.Tag` interface. The basic APIs you need to implement for the JSP container to call your handler are included for your convenience.

- *Create a* `get<attribute>` *and* `set<attribute>` *method for each tag attribute*. These are the methods that the container requires to pass parameters to your handler.

- *Create a constructor and a destructor for your tag handler*. The constructor is called by the container to instantiate your handler. The *destructor* is defined in a method called `release()` and called at the end of your handler's life in code to release resources.

- *Create methods that do the work and output named* `doStartTag()` *and* `doEndTag()`. These methods are called at the beginning and end of the evaluation of your tag, respectively. They are analogous to the `service()` method in the servlet specification. Each of these returns status codes that tell the JSP container how to evaluate either your custom tag or the entire JSP page.

Tag Library Handler Simplified Lifecycle

The lifecycle for a tag handler is as follows:

1. WebLogic Server instantiates your tag handler by calling your constructor method when it first appears on the JSP page.

2. WebLogic Server takes all attributes and values out of the tag and calls the respective `set<attribute>` method for each that is not already set. When the tag is first used, no attributes are set, so the `set` method is called for everyone.

3. WebLogic Server then calls `doStartTag()` and subsequently calls `doEndTag()` for your handler.

4. WebLogic Server continues processing the JSP page. If your custom tag handler is required again, steps 2 through 4 are repeated with the same instance of your handler.

5. Finally, at the end of the JSP page, the `release()` method is called to dispose of all the resources that you are using. These might be database connections for example, or variables that you have created.

Tag Library Handler Example (StockPriceHandler.java)

Let's implement a handler for the stock price tag that we specified in the previous two sections. First, import the necessary classes:

```
package com.learnweblogic.examples.ch4;
import javax.servlet.jsp.*;
import javax.servlet.jsp.tagext.*;
import java.util.Hashtable;
import java.io.Writer;
```

Next, define the class. Notice that the class extends

```
javax.servlet.jsp.tagext.TagSupport:

public class StockPriceHandler extends TagSupport {

And, define a constructor and a destructor for this tag handler:

public StockPriceHandler() {
super();
    }

/* Called when the container wants to dispose
of the current tag library. */
public void release() {
myTickerSymbol = myOptionSymbol = null;
super.release();
    }
```

Next, define a `get<attribute>` and `set<attribute>` method for each attribute:

```
public void setTickerSymbol (String ts) {
myTickerSymbol=ts;
    }
public String getTickerSymbol () {
return myTickerSymbol;
    }
```

When a tag handler executes, the JSP container first calls the `doStart-Tag()` method, much like the `service()` method of the servlet:

```
public int doStartTag() throws JspException {
/*

You could place any work that you want to have done here.

This method returns a status code.  There are a number of dif-
ferent options for these codes, which are discussed later in this
```

section.   This one instructs WebLogic Server not to evaluate any expressions inside of the body of the tag.

```
At this point, you would insert code to go out and get the
stock price from your source.  Take that value and put it into a
string variable named 'price'.
*/

  String stockPrice=price;

  try {

    JspWriter out = pageContext.getOut();
    out.print(myTickerSymbol + ":" + price);

  } catch (Exception e) {
    e.printStackTrace();
    throw new JspException(e.getMessage());
  }

  return(SKIP_BODY);

}


private String myTickerSymbol;
private String price = "25 cents";

}
```

In this handler, only the start tag method is required because we do not care about evaluating expressions inside of the tag. Otherwise, we would need to implement the end tag method.

All the work gets done within the start tag method. When the method is called, it gets the current output stream, which is the response being prepared for the client requesting the JSP page, and prints out the stock price text into that stream.

Packaging Custom Tag Libraries

If you are packaging a Web application, put your JSP pages and custom tag libraries into the package. First, place your TLD *XML* files into the *META-INF* directory in your jar package. Put the *JSP* files in the appropriate directories in the jar package; then add your compiled tag files into *WEB-INF/classes*. The previous example would have its compiled classes placed in the package under *WEB-INF/classes /com/mypkg*. Then, deploy your Web application as stated in the documentation for your application server.

Running the Tag Library Example in WebLogic Server

The tag library example is included on the CD for this book. It is available in the directory *examples\ch4\taglib.war*. To install and run it, use the same steps that you followed for the JavaBean example in the previous sections.

Error Pages, Comments, and Deployment Descriptors

An earlier section discussed how to include the implicit exception object for JSP pages. This object is provided to a JSP error page, using the following page directive:

```
<%@ page isErrorPage="true" %>
```

You can also provide a specific JSP error page containing your error text.

JSP Error Page

The following is a complete JSP error page similar to the one used in the WebAuction application. The error page accesses the implicit `exception` object and prints out a stack trace of the error:

```
<%@ page isErrorPage="true" %>
<!doctype html public "-//w3c//dtd html 4.0 transitional//en">
<html>
<head>
    <title>WebLogic Server WebAuction Error</title>
</head>
<body text="#000000" bgcolor="#FFFFFF"
 link="#0000EE" vlink="#551A8B" alink="#FF0000">

<P>An error occurred while processing the WebLogic Server WebAuc-
tion:</P>

<%= exception.printStackTrace(); %>
```

```
<P>If this error persists, please contact the site administra-
tor</p>

</body>
</html>
```

JSP Comments

There are two different types of comments in JSP pages. The first enables you to generate comments in the output that is sent to client Web browsers:

```
<!-- comments ... -->
```

These comments are ignored by WebLogic Server. If you want to generate comments that have dynamic data, you can include JSP expressions in the comments code:

```
<!-- comments <%= expression %> more comments ... -->
```

These comments show up in the Web browser. If you would like to generate comments that only stay in the JSP page and are *not* sent to client Web browsers, you can use the following syntax to create a JSP comment:

```
<%-- comments comments ... --%>
```

The body of the comments is ignored completely. Comments are useful for documentation but also to "comment out" some portions of a JSP page. Note that JSP comments do not nest, so you cannot place multiple sets of comments inside of other comments.

JSP Deployment Descriptor Options

It is often desirable to have a Web application be precompiled at deployment time. To do this, add the following to your *weblogic.xml* deployment descriptor:

```
<jsp-descriptor>
 <jsp-param>
        <param-name>
        precompile
        </param-name>
        <param-value>
        TRUE
        </param-value>
 </jsp-param>
</jsp-descriptor>
```

To hide the `.jsp` extension to your JSP pages, you can map them as serv-lets inside your *web.xml* deployment descriptor:

```
<servlet>
  <servlet-name>browse</servlet-name>
  <jsp-file>browseitems.jsp</jsp-file>
</servlet>
```

The URL path `/browse/` would be mapped to resolve `browseitems.jsp`, hiding the fact that you're using JSP pages.

You can find the complete description of the functionality for both types of Web deployment descriptors on the WebLogic Server Web site at *http://e-docs.bea.com/wls/docs60/programming/weblogic_xml.html*.

Using Servlets and JSPs Together: Model View Controller

J2EE includes a notion of the Model View Controller (MVC) pattern. This design pattern shows how multiple components can cooperate inside of the scope of a single J2EE application. In fact, the MVC pattern is not new. Developers using Smalltalk, a language that was one of the early object-oriented languages in computing, invented it. The pattern focuses on decoupling the graphical interface of an application from the code that actually does the work. This pattern turns out to be a very important idea that affects how code is built. MVC applies to other object-oriented languages, including Java.

MVC Components

There are three components in the MVC pattern in a typical J2EE Web application:

- *Model* encapsulates the application data. Typically, the model is the relational database or EJB. But, this can be any component that is used to access the data (or "state"). In MVC, there exists only one model while there are multiple views and controllers.
- *View* renders the interface to the user. Typically, the view is a JSP page. However, it also can be an application GUI as well.
- *Controller* receives user actions and makes changes to the application state (data) accordingly. Typically, this is a servlet in a J2EE Web application.

MVC in Web Applications

A very common case in J2EE Web applications is to use servlets to do the form processing before forwarding control to the JSPs to do the HTML generation. In addition, the servlets interact with the business logic encapsulated in EJBs or elsewhere. Typically, a controller exists for each area of functionality of a Web application. So, a controller might exist for checking the balance in a user's account while another exists for transferring money. A single model might support multiple sets of controllers. For example, a set of controllers might exist for bank employees, while another exists for customers.

For each controller, JSP pages generate the user interface. These JSP pages typically include forms, which POST data to the appropriate servlet. Security and localized content can be applied by creating different JSP pages for each individual view. For example, a set of JSP pages might exist for bank customers in Japan while another set exists for American bank customers viewing U.S. bank accounts. Each JSP page would take the existing money values in an account and display that appropriately for the audience, while sharing the same controller and model.

MVC Applicability

MVC is most applicable as a design pattern when:

- *You are building a Web application that has very complex user interaction models*. For example, it is very difficult to parse the results of HTTP POSTs in the context of a simple JavaBean in a JSP page. Or, if several different forms can post to the same page, or the same form can post to various different pages. The MVC pattern can enable you to avoid having to embed the logic for handling the query parameters in many different places.

- *You are building a Web application that is internationalized with many different views.*

MVC is not applicable in some cases, such as simple applications with simple user interaction models. In any case, MVC can be considered as a design pattern when building your own Web application using servlets and JSPs.

Best Practices for Debugging and Developing JSPs

Debugging and developing JSPs for WebLogic Server is sometimes like performing microsurgery. The smallest details can cause much confusion during the development process. Of course, there are great benefits to success. This section includes best practices for debugging and developing JSPs and related technologies in WebLogic Server.

Create Scripts to Take Advantage of Automatic Deployment

One of the most powerful features of WebLogic Server is the automatic deployment of application components when they are placed into the applications directory of your installation. You can create development scripts that automatically package up (jar up) your code into packages and copy them into the deployment directory. See the example applications and scripts included on the CD.

Base Your Development on Templates

There is no reason to write application components from scratch. Take an application that is close to the application you plan to develop, and modify it to meet your needs. The WebAuction application is designed to be used this way.

Be Careful About Capitalization and Spacing

The advent of J2EE deployment descriptors that are XML-encoded means you need to be careful about capitalization and spacing. Hours can be spent trying to debug an application, only to realize that an errant space or bracket is causing failure. Tools are available to make this easier including J2EE-specific development environments, such as WebGain, and J2EE modes for Emacs and other editors. A free set of JSP-editing modes for Emacs is available from the BEA Developer Center at *http://www.developer.bea.com/*.

Turn on the Debugging Messages Using the Console

As mentioned previously, the WebLogic Server console allows you to enable debugging (verbose) messages to be displayed on the window running WebLogic Server. This can be very helpful to understand when your applications are being deployed correctly and you understand the complete state of WebLogic Server.

Best Practices for JSPs

There are a number of best practices that can enable your JSP-based applications to be as successful as possible:

Keep in Mind that JSPs Are Just Specialized Servlets

Actually, JSPs are a simplification of the servlet paradigm. However, that does not mean that you should not follow the same best practices noted in Chapter 3, *Building Presentation Logic with WebLogic Servlets*. By doing so, you can ensure that JSPs you build have the same level of scalability, reliability, and maintainability as the servlets we built in Chapter 3.

Encapsulate Complex Data and Logic in JavaBeans and Custom Tag Libraries

The goal of your JSP design should be to avoid having sensitive code be visible to your Web designers. In other words, you should take advantage of Java-Beans and custom tag libraries as much as possible.

Always Activate and Use URL Rewriting

Many Web browsers enable users to disable the acceptance of cookies. For this reason, you should always enable URL rewriting in your JSPs as specified in this chapter. This ensures that you maintain appropriate compatibility and the highest level of usability for all your users. Activate URL rewriting as a configuration parameter in WebLogic Server and add URL rewriting code to your JSP pages if you are worried about users who do not accept cookies being able to access your site.

Use JSP Error Pages

You never know when your application code might run into trouble and throw an exception. At the very least, you should always make sure that you handle problems in your application gracefully. To do this, use the errorPage functionality described in this chapter.

JSPs in the WebAuction Application

As discussed in Chapter 2, *Overview of J2EE Technologies*, the WebAuction application includes a suite of JSP pages that handle the user interaction. In this section, we detail one of those JSP pages: browseitems.jsp, and the JavaBean ItemBean that encapsulates the Java code so that it does not appear in the JSP page.

The browseitems.jsp does what its name implies. This JSP page is called when a user wants to look at the current auction items. There are different categories of items up for auction including books, computers, and clothing. When a request comes in to view items of a certain type, the Item-Bean queries the appropriate back end resources (in this case, EJBs), and outputs the data.

browseitems.jsp

To build the browseitems.jsp, begin with the basic HTML page. First, define the document type, HTML header, and body style:

```
<!doctype html public "-//w3c//dtd html 4.0 transitional//en">
<html>
<head>
    <title>WebLogic Server WebAuction: Browse Items</title>
</head>
<body text="#000000" bgcolor="#FFFFFF">
```

The content type for this HTML document is Version 4.0. Subsequent tags specify the HTML document title and set the colors for the body of the HTML document.

Next, we specify that this page is visible only in the context of a session. We also specify an `errorPage` for this JSP:

```
<%@ page session="true" errorPage="error.jsp" %>
```

The page also uses a JavaBean. The following tag directs WebLogic Server to instantiate an instance of `webauction.jsp.ItemBean` and makes that available for the JSP page under the identifier `"itembean"`:

```
<jsp:useBean id="itembean" scope="page"
 class="webauction.jsp.ItemBean" />
```

Next, we define some text and a table for the links for the different categories:

```
<H2>Select a category to browse for Items</H2>

<CENTER>
<table width="100%" bgcolor="#0000ff" fgcolor="#FFFFFF">

<TR>
```

The links contained in this page enable users to browse through the categories of auction items. If a user clicks on one of those links, a parameter is created named `cat`, which is short for category. We create links that pass this parameter automatically when clicked by adding the parameter and value to the URL. For example, a relative URL of `"browseitems.jsp?cat=books"` passes the parameter `cat` with a value of `books`:

```
<TD ALIGN="CENTER"><A
href="browseitems.jsp?cat=books"><H4>Books</H4></A></TD>
<TD ALIGN="CENTER"><A href="browseitems.jsp?cat=cloth-
ing"><H4>Clothing</H4></A></TD>
<TD ALIGN="CENTER"><A href="browseitems.jsp?cat=comput-
ers"><H4>Computers</H4></A></TD>
<TD ALIGN="CENTER"><A href="browseitems.jsp?cat=electron-
ics"><H4>Electronics</H4></A></TD>


</TR>

</table>

</CENTER>
```

When a user chooses to browse a category by clicking on a link, the following scriptlet invokes the JavaBean and deals with it appropriately. First, the category is recognized by looking for it in the request using the `getParam-`

`eter()` method on the implicit object request. If the category exists, a method on the JavaBean is called to request all the items in the category. In addition, the current user's name is located in the `session` object and sent to the JavaBean.

```
<%
  String category = request.getParameter("cat");

  if (category != null) {

    String userName = (String) session.getAttribute("username");
    itembean.outputItemsInCategory(out, category, userName);
  }
%>
```

Finally, the JSP page is finished by adding the appropriate closing HTML tags:

```
</body>
</html>
```

You should note that very little Java code is encapsulated in this JSP page. This is a good thing: It makes the page more maintainable and presents less of your Java code in a form that Web developers can see and change. This JSP page relies on a JavaBean to do the real work, as discussed in the next section.

ItemBean JavaBean

The `ItemBean` JavaBean encapsulates the Java code for accessing the back end resources to locate auction items. It can do two things: locate all items in a given category, and also add a new item to the auction.

In the case of `browseitem.jsp`, the `ItemBean` is used only to view items up for auction. The capability to enter items is coded in different JSP pages. This is a good example of how JavaBeans enable code to be reused among multiple JSP pages in a Web application.

The `ItemBean` also relies on EJBs, which are accessed by standard Java calls. EJBs are described in Chapters 8 through 10.

To build `ItemBean`, first declare the package name and import the necessary classes:

```
package webauction.jsp;

import java.io.Writer;
import java.sql.Date;
import java.util.Calendar;
```

```
import java.util.Collection;
import java.util.Iterator;
```

Next, define the class and the constructor for this JavaBean:

```
public final class ItemBean {

  public ItemBean() {
  }
```

The `enterItem` method (to be added later) enables the user to create a new auction item:

```
    public void enterItem(...)
    throws Exception
  {
/* Here, we will add the code for the method to enter an item
into the auction.
*/
  }
```

The `outputItemsInCategory` method is called by the `browseitems.jsp`. Three parameters are passed to this method including the output writer, the category string, and the current user's name:

```
  public void outputItemsInCategory(Writer out, String category,
    String userName)
  {
   /* This section eventually accesses the WebAuction
      EJB and locates a Collection of all the items in the pro-
vided category.
     */

    Collection items = itemHome.findItemsInCategory(category);

    /* If the Collection is empty, then print an appropriate mes-
sage
     */
    if (items.isEmpty()) {
      out.write("<H2>There is nothing in the "+category+
              " category currently available for bidding.");
    } else {

      out.write("<table border=2 cellspacing=2 cellpadding=2");

      out.write("<TR><TD>Category</TD> "+
        "<TD>Description</TD><TD>Offerred by</TD>"+
        "<TD>Top Bidder</TD>"+
        "<TD>Top Bid Amount</TD><TD>Auction Ends</TD></TR>");
```

```
        Iterator it = items.iterator();

        while (it.hasNext()) {

          Item item = (Item) it.next();

          String topBidString = null;
          String topBidUser = "None";

  /* In future chapters, we'll add code to query the EJB for
     the data on the item up for bid here.
*/
  .

  .

  .


        /* Next, print out data about the item. */
        out.write("<TR>" +
           "<TD>" + item.getCategory() + "</TD>" +
           "<TD>"+ item.getDescription() + "</TD>" +
    "<TD>"+ topBidUser + "</TD>" +
           "<TD>"+topBidString+"</TD>"+
           "<TD>"+item.getAuctionEnd()+"</TD>"+
           "<TD BGCOLOR=\"0x0000FF\"><A href=\"bid.jsp?id="+
item.getId() +
           "\">Bid on this item</A></TD>");

}

        out.write("</TR>");
      }
      out.write("</table>");
    }
  }


}
```

In subsequent chapters, additional functionality is added to `ItemBean`, such as the capability to interact with back end resources. For now, we have a shell that we can fill in with data access code as we continue to develop the WebAuction application.

Browsing the WebAuction Code

The WebAuction application code is contained in its entirety on the CD accompanying this book. Some of the code, such as the EJB access, may not make much sense at this point in the text. However, it would be beneficial for you to take a look at the real WebAuction application at this point, with a focus on the JSP technologies used there.

The WebAuction application is located in the WebAuction directory available from the top-level directory of the CD.

USING DATABASES AND TRANSACTIONS WITH JDBC AND JTA

In this chapter:

- How to build database connectivity in WebLogic Server applications
- Sample database access using JDBC
- Best practices for using JDBC in WebLogic Server
- Using JDBC in transactions
- Sample JTA use
- Prepared statements, metadata, and batch database operations
- Coding database access in the WebAuction application

Chapter 5

This chapter focuses on designing and coding database access for your applications, using WebLogic Server Java Database Connectivity (JDBC) and the Java Transaction API (JTA). JDBC technology provides the basic APIs for connecting your client application to a database and submitting Structured Query Language (SQL) commands to select or modify data. JTA technology and other advanced WebLogic Server/Java 2 Enterprise Edition (J2EE) features support transactions, which provide a safe and structured environment for executing multi-statement or even multi-database operations.

Note: This chapter assumes a basic knowledge of relational databases and SQL. If you need more information on these topics, consult an appropriate resource such as C. J. Date's An Introduction to Database Systems (Addison-Wesley, 1999).

WebLogic Server JDBC

JDBC is the J2EE standard for accessing your application's database resources. The JDBC standard specifies a Java API that enables you to write SQL statements that are then sent to your database.

Why JDBC?

JDBC is one of the oldest enterprise Java specifications: The earliest drafts date back to 1996. JDBC addresses the same problems as the Open Database Connectivity (ODBC) standard developed by Microsoft: to provide a universal set of APIs for accessing any database, using the database-specific driver. Without JDBC or ODBC, developers must use a different set of APIs to access each database: one for Oracle, one for Informix, and so on. With JDBC or ODBC, a single set of APIs can access any database using the drivers specific to that database. Developers are able to write applications to a single set of APIs and then plug and play different database drivers, depending upon what resource type they are accessing. With JDBC, it is possible to migrate an enterprise Java application from one database to another with only marginal pain, because no custom Java APIs are used.

JDBC Drivers

While SQL is generally portable across multiple databases, the actual protocols that those databases use to communicate (and some database-specific features) are not portable. For that reason, the JDBC specification supports products that map the calls in a JDBC-based application to the appropriate calls specific to the database. Such a product is called a *JDBC driver*.

There are JDBC drivers specific to commercial databases such as Oracle, Sybase, and others. When you want to access a database of a specific type, you must acquire the database driver for that database. WebLogic Server supports any JDBC driver that complies with the JDBC specification. This means that you can use any JDBC driver with WebLogic Server—including drivers that are available from other vendors—so long as the driver supports the JDBC standard.

JDBC Driver Types

There are four different types of JDBC drivers. However, most enterprise Java applications use only two of these types. The other two are mentioned here for completeness.

- *Type 1* is a JDBC driver that is commonly called a *JDBC-ODBC bridge*. This was the original implementation of JDBC provided by Sun to enable rapid adoption of the JDBC standard. Basically, calls are mapped from JDBC APIs to ODBC APIs. In this way, a Type 1 driver enabled developers to leverage the existing ODBC drivers on the marketplace when JDBC first became available. In today's practice, Type 1 drivers are very rarely used.

- *Type 2* is a JDBC driver that maps JDBC APIs directly to the proprietary client APIs provided by the database vendor. The WebLogic Server includes a Type 2 driver for Oracle databases. A native code library exists for each of these drivers that includes the platform-specific code that accesses the database-specific client APIs. For Oracle, this is called the Oracle Client Interface (OCI) library. This type of driver is frequently used in enterprise Java applications.

- *Type 3* is a JDBC driver that supports 3-tier JDBC access. In the early days of Java, when applets were very popular, it was common to build an applet that directly accessed the database. However, the security model for applets prohibits applets from accessing data resources from more than one Web server. A Type 3 JDBC driver acts as a *proxy* for database access by the applet or another application. In practice, this type of driver is not used very often.

- *Type 4* is a JDBC driver that is all Java and speaks directly to the database instance. These drivers are intelligent enough to know exactly which underlying protocol the database instance uses. Type 4 drivers are the future of database access in Java and are the drivers most commonly used in practice today. As the efficiency of Java code and Java virtual machines (JVMs) improves, these drivers are becoming markedly more attractive because of their simplicity and ease-of-use.

The Type 1 JDBC-ODBC bridge available from Sun Microsystems is not thread-safe. That is, it is not suitable for use in applications that require concurrent access to the database and database driver. Because of its inherent performance and scalability limitations, this Type 1 driver should not be used in enterprise-level applications. There are other vendor implementations (e.g., NEON Systems, IBM, etc.) of a JDBC-ODBC bridge that are thread-safe and can be used in an enterprise-level application.

WebLogic Server includes a suite of JDBC drivers for databases including Oracle, Informix, Sybase, and Microsoft SQL Server. Other JDBC drivers are available free or for a nominal fee, including a driver for IBM's DB2. A complete list of available JDBC drivers is on the Sun Web site at *http://industry.java.sun.com/products/jdbc/drivers*.

Choosing the Right JDBC Driver

In years past, the decision of what JDBC driver to use was more difficult than it is today. Before the advent of more advanced JVMs with performance equivalent to native code, developers often chose Type 2 drivers for performance reasons, even though Type 4 drivers offer other advantages for coding and maintenance.

For developers writing new applications, the advent of faster JVMs such as that included in Java Development Kit (JDK) 1.3 in the "Hotspot" performance engine, make Type 4 drivers viable for enterprise class applications. Type 4 drivers remove a level of complexity in application development by bypassing the native code interfaces. Less complexity is better because there are fewer components that must work together. When there are fewer components, there is typically less room for conflict and error.

The presence of native code in Type 2 drivers means, in fact, that it is much easier to crash your entire Java application. That is, a bug in the native code portion of the driver could cause the entire process to fail—including your application and WebLogic Server itself. Therefore, Type 4 drivers are preferable because they do not require any porting of native code. With a Type 4 driver, any obscure platform can be supported so long as it has a JVM.

For reasons of equivalent performance and simplicity, Type 4 drivers are a safe bet. On the other hand, Type 2 drivers have the advantage of having been tested over several years. Perhaps the best practice would be to ask your application server vendor what they recommend. In the case of WebLogic Server, viable Type 4 drivers are available for databases such as Sybase, Informix, and Microsoft SQL Server. A Type 2 driver is available for Oracle from WebLogic Server; and Oracle provides a Type 4 driver for free, which is bundled with WebLogic Server.

> The Type 4 driver for Oracle can be found on the Oracle Web site. It is supported (as is any JDBC driver) for WebLogic Server. To download it, go to http://technet.oracle.com/software/tech/java/sqlj_jdbc/software_index.htm.

> Strongly consider a Type 4 JDBC driver for your deployment if ultra-high performance is not a paramount consideration. The all-Java nature of Type 4 drivers provides a level of simplicity not seen in Type 2 drivers. Follow the recommendation of your application server vendor.

Configuring and Installing Your JDBC Driver

Configuring and installing your JDBC driver is beyond the scope of this book, because configuration and installation details depend on the application server platform and JDBC driver that you are using. You should review the documentation for your specific driver or application server in order to install and configure it correctly. For WebLogic Server, the documentation for installing and testing your JDBC driver is located in the section titled *WebLogic Server JDBC Options*, which is available via the Web at *http://www.weblogic.com/docs60/*.

Database Connection Pooling

When WebLogic Server (or any other modern application server) starts, it creates what are called *connection pools* to the database resource. Connection pools contain connections that are kept open to the database resource by the application server. When your application needs to access the database, it grabs a connection from the connection pool and uses it to communicate with the database. Once the work being done with the database for a given user is completed, the database connection is released back to the database connection pool.

Why Connection Pooling?

There are a number of reasons to pool connections to the database:

- *Creating a new connection for every individual client that visits your site is very expensive.* Using connection pools is much more efficient than creating a new database connection for each client, each time.

- *You do not need to hard-code details such as the database management system (DBMS) password in your application.* This is particularly beneficial in the case of J2EE services such as JavaServer Pages (JSPs), which typically store the source code with the application.

- *You can change the database system you are using without changing your application code.*

- *Databases are most effective when the number of incoming connections is limited.* With connection pooling, you can limit the number of connections to your DBMS.

Configuring Connection Pools

In the WebLogic Server, connection pools are specified in the configuration of the server. Configuration parameters for connection pools include:

- Name of connection pool, used to identify which pool is being used by the application
- Number of connections to be made initially
- Maximum size of pool
- Minimum size of pool
- Location/URL for database
- Driver class name
- Driver-specific properties

In WebLogic Server 6.0, database connection configuration is handled through the WebLogic Server console. The console provides a graphic user interface (GUI) and facilitates configuration of database connectivity (see Figure 5–1). This chapter's examples use the Cloudscape database, which is included in the WebLogic Server distribution. Connection pools are also configured through the console (Services-JDBC-Connection Pools).

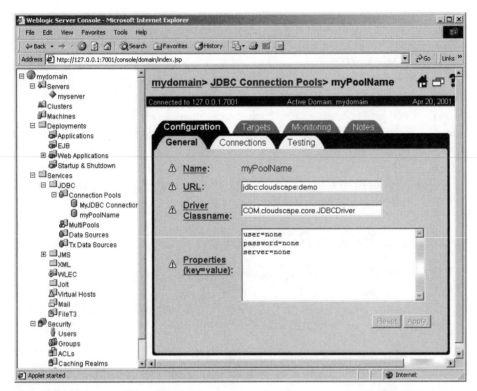

Figure 5–1 Using the WebLogic Server Console to Configure Database Connection Pools

This configuration defines a number of parameters including the driver name, URL value, filename of the driver code, pool capacity, and so forth. Many more configuration parameters are available, as specified in the WebLogic Server documentation.

JDBC URLs

The connection pool configuration information includes a JDBC URL. This URL is a locator for the database resource. All JDBC drivers follow this pattern for the URL:

```
jdbc:driver:databasename
```

Because every database has many possible configuration options, parameters must be provided so that the driver can work for a specific deployment. You set parameters such as your JDBC URL in the configuration file. You also can specify a name for the connection pool that you want to use. Consult your JDBC driver vendor documentation for how to correctly compose your URL in your configuration file.

JDBC DataSource

To simplify the process for acquiring a connection to the database, the JDBC DataSource concept was introduced in the JDBC 2.0 specification. A Data-Source object is a factory for Connection objects. To use a DataSource, you specify a connection pool to provide connections to the DataSource in the WebLogic Server Java Naming and Directory Interface (JNDI) store, which is a registry of user and application variables and values, which are described in detail in Chapter 6. DataSources allow either standard or trans-actional database connections that automatically use the JTA driver.

Using JDBC to Read Data

We discuss two facets of JDBC access: using JDBC to read data stored in the database and using JDBC to update data in the database. While these two processes have many steps in common, there are some substantial differences. Let's look first at JDBC reads and then move on to updates.

Basic Steps for JDBC Reads

There are five basic operations for JDBC reads in your WebLogic Server application. These are:

- Establishing a connection to the database
- Sending a query to the database
- Getting results
- Handling results
- Releasing the connection

Establishing Connections to the Database

Connections to the database are represented by instances of the java.sql.Connection object. Each instance of this object represents an individual database connection. Access connections by calling factory methods on instances of the javax.sql.DataSource class.

To create a new connection to the database, you could use the following code block:

```
Connection myConn = null;

try {
```

```
Context ctx = new InitialContext();

javax.sql.DataSource ds
          = (javax.sql.DataSource)
              ctx.lookup ("examples-dataSource-demoPool");

java.sql.Connection myConn = ds.getConnection();

} catch (SQLException sqle)
{
  // Handle the exception
}
```

This code first locates the WebLogic Server JNDI naming service, which is discussed in detail in Chapter 6. The JNDI naming service is relevant because it is where your code accesses the DataSources. Then, it creates a new instance of the `java.sql.Connection` class and assigns the object returned by `ds.getConnection()` to it. By calling `getConnection` with the appropriate DataSource as defined in the WebLogic Server configuration, we can abstract out our database configuration.

Note that the method described here is the preferred method to gain a connection to the database. There are a number of antiquated methods that are not as efficient and should not be used. For example, *avoid using Driver-Manager*, which is unfortunately often used in many JDBC tutorials:

```
Class.forName("WebLogic.jdbc.pool.Driver").newInstance();

    /* Get a Connection from the Driver from the connection Pool
named demoPool.
    */
    Connection myConn =
      DriverManager.getConnection("jdbc:WebLogic:pool:demoPool",
null);
```

The problem with the DriverManager method is that it is a synchronized class, which means that only one thread of execution can run at a single time. Use the multi-threaded DataSource technique instead.

Sending a Query to the Database

The process of interacting with the database centers on the `java.sql.Statement` class. You first create an instance of this `Statement` class by calling a factory method, `createStatement()`, on the instance of the `Connection` class that was created. This typically looks like this:

```
Statement stmt = myConn.createStatement();
```

This code creates a new instance of the `Statement` object native to our connection.

Executing SQL

You can then use your statement to execute SQL queries against the database. This is accomplished via the `execute()` method. For example, to return all rows from the table named `EMPLOYEE`:

```
stmt.execute("SELECT * FROM EMPLOYEE");
```

You can execute any valid SQL query using the `execute` method. (We cover statements that do not return results, such as the `CREATE` or `UPDATE` commands, later in the section, "Using JDBC to Update the Database.")

To display the results of the query, use the `java.sql.ResultSet` datatype described in the next section.

Result Sets

The `Statement` class includes a method `getResultSetType()`, which returns query results as instances of the `java.sql.ResultSet` class. To get the result set for the previous query, use the following code:

```
ResultSet rs = stmt.getResultSet();
```

This creates an instance of the `ResultSet` class and returns the results of the query. A shortcut, single line method is available for simple queries. This method is within the statement class: `executeQuery(String SQLstring)`. For example,

```
ResultSet rs = stmt.executeQuery("SELECT * FROM EMPLOYEE ");
```

This executes the SQL and returns the resulting data in a single line of code.

Accessing Results

The `ResultSet` (`rs`) is a virtual table of data representing a database result set. For the statement:

```
ResultSet rs = stmt.executeQuery(
"SELECT * FROM EMPLOYEE ");
```

The result set `rs` might display:

```
NAME            LOCATION            ID
Zornoza         Connecticut         1
Prasad          India               2
Shinn           Oregon              3
D'Attoma        New York            4
```

The next step is to access the results of your query. As mentioned previously, the data returned from the query using the `Statement` class is encapsulated in an instance of the `ResultSet` class. Call methods on the `ResultSet` to access the data. These methods follow the format of `get???`, where the `???`s are replaced by a Java type.

`ResultSet` is accessed very much like an Enumeration. A `ResultSet` object keeps a cursor pointing to its current row of data. Initially the cursor is positioned before the first row. The `next()` method moves the cursor to the next row. Because it returns `false` when there are no more rows in the `ResultSet` object, it can be used in a `WHILE` loop to iterate through the result set. The following is an example:

```
while (rs.next()) {
    System.out.println(rs.getString("ID") + " - " +
                       rs.getString("NAME")   + " - " +
                       rs.getString("LOCATION"));
}
```

The output for this might be:

```
1-Zornoza-Connecticut
2-Prasad-India
3-Shinn-Oregon
4-D'Attoma-New York
```

`ResultSet` maps the data from the database to instances of Java objects. A relational-object mapping is required for object-oriented Java programs to be able to use relational data. Usually, results map directly from the SQL types that are defined by the database. Consult your database driver documentation to see how the types that are stored in the database map to Java objects.

Handling Result Sets

There are many more important methods available in the `ResultSet` class. In fact, there are over 100 methods available to handle result sets. This section covers some of the more important of these methods and gives examples of their use.

- `next()` moves the cursor down one row from its current position.
- `getString(int columnIndex)` gets the value of the designated column in the current row of this `ResultSet` object as a string. The following code gets the string in the second column at the row that is currently selected by the cursor and prints out its value:

```
System.out.println(rs.getString(2));
```

- Similarly, `String getString(String columnName)` gets the value of the designated column in the current row of this `ResultSet` object as a string. The following code gets the string in the column named `"ID"` that is currently selected by the cursor and prints out its value:

```
System.out.println(rs.getString("ID"));
```

This `get???()` pattern holds for virtually every other datatype available through JDBC. Examples include `getDecimal()`, `getByteStream()`, and so forth. The complete list is found in the JavaDoc available in your JDK.

- `Void absolute(int row)` moves the cursor to the given row number in this `ResultSet` object. The following code accesses the third row in the result set and prints out its value:

```
rs.absolute(3);
System.out.println(rs.getString("ID") + "-" +
                   rs.getString("NAME")  + "-" +
                   rs.getString("LOCATION"));
```

The output of this code would be:

```
3-Shinn-Oregon
```

- `beforeFirst()` moves the cursor to the beginning of this `ResultSet` object, just before the first row. The following code puts the cursor at the beginning of the rows in the `ResultSet` object and begins a new Enumeration:

```
rs.beforeFirst();
while (rs.next()) {
    System.out.println(rs.getString("ID") + "-" +
                       rs.getString("NAME") + "-" +
                       rs.getString("LOCATION"));
}
```

The output of this code would be:

```
1-Zornoza-Connecticut
2-Prasad-India
3-Shinn-Oregon
4-D'Attoma-New York
```

- `boolean isAfterLast()` indicates whether the cursor is after the last row in this `ResultSet` object.

- `boolean isBeforeFirst()` indicates whether the cursor is before the first row in this `ResultSet` object.
- `boolean isFirst()` indicates whether the cursor is on the first row of this `ResultSet` object.
- `boolean isLast()` indicates whether the cursor is on the last row of this `ResultSet` object.
- `void refreshRow()` refreshes the current row with its most recent value in the database.

Releasing Connections

After you complete a query, you should release your statements and connections. This is done through the `close()` method available on both of those types of objects. For example, given these `Connection`, `ResultSet`, and `Statement` objects:

```
Connection myConn = null;

try {

    /* Create a connection to the WebLogic JNDI Naming Service:
    */
    Context ctx = new InitialContext();

    /* Create a new DataSource by Locating It in the Naming Service:
    */
javax.sql.DataSource ds
        = (javax.sql.DataSource)
            ctx.lookup ("examples-dataSource-demoPool");

    /* Get a new JDBC connection from the DataSource:
    */
myConn = ds.getConnection();

Statement stmt = myConn.createStatement();

ResultSet rs = stmt.executeQuery("SELECT * FROM EMPLOYEE ");
```

We can call the `close()` method on each of these objects to release the resources:

```
    /* Release the ResultSet and Statement.
    */
    rs.close();
    stmt.close();

} catch (Exception E) {
    /*
        Handle exception here.
```

```
*/
System.out.println("Service Error: " + E);
} finally {
  if (rs != null) {
    try { rs.close(); } catch (Exception ignore) {};
  }
  if (stmt != null) {
    try { stmt.close(); } catch (Exception ignore) {};
  }
  if (myConn != null) {
    try { myConn.close(); } catch (Exception ignore) {};
  }
```

This closes the connection and releases the database and JDBC resources immediately instead of waiting for them to be closed automatically. It is important to close and release resources in the correct order: the reverse of the order in which they were opened. First, close the instance of the ResultSet class. Next, close the Statement. This is accomplished, in both cases, by calling the close() method.

In each case, close() is called in a try/catch block. If an exception is raised, it can be handled in the catch { ... } statement. Note that the finally { ...} block includes a single call to close the connection. Make sure that your connection objects are released as soon as possible in order to make the connection immediately available to serve other clients.

Make sure to release objects in the correct order when doing JDBC. Make sure that you close your Connection object in the finally { ... } block of your JDBC access. Do not overload the finally { ... } block by placing more than one close () statement there. For example, if an attempt to close your ResultSet receives an exception, the rest of the finally { ... } block is not executed, including the rest of the close () statements. If one of the close () statements is your Connection object, this unnecessarily ties up a database connection and limits the performance of your application.

The Entire JDBC Read Example

The following is the complete listing of the JDBC Read example covered in this section. It can be located in the file *myJDBCReadServlet.war* in the *examples/ch5* directory on the accompanying CD. Note that the JDBC access is encapsulated in a servlet:

```
package com.learnweblogic.examples.ch5;

import java.io.*;
```

```java
import java.sql.*;
import javax.servlet.http.*;
import javax.naming.Context;
import javax.naming.InitialContext;
import javax.naming.NamingException;
import javax.sql.DataSource;

public class myJDBCReadServlet extends HttpServlet {

  /*
   * This method is called when the servlet is first initialized.
   * Note here that both the initial lookup into the WebLogic Server JNDI
   * naming context and the location of a DataSource object from it
   * are placed here.  This ensures that the operations are only done
   * once instead of every time that the servlet is accessed.  This is
   * very important for efficiency.
   */
  public void init() {

    try {

      /* Create a connection to the WebLogic Server JNDI Naming Service:
       */
      ctx = new InitialContext();

      /* Create a new DataSource by Locating It in the Naming Service:
       */
      ds = (javax.sql.DataSource)
        ctx.lookup ("examples-dataSource-demoPool");

    } catch (Exception E) {
      /*
         Handle exception here.
      */
      System.out.println("Init Error: " + E);
    }
  }


  public void service(HttpServletRequest requ,
    HttpServletResponse resp)
    throws IOException

  {
    Connection myConn = null;

    try {

      PrintWriter out = resp.getWriter();

      out.println("<html>");
      out.println("<head><title>myJDBCReadServlet</title></head>");
      out.println("<body>");

      out.println("<h1>myJDBCReadServlet</h1>");
```

```
     /* Get a new JDBC connection from the DataSource:
      */
     myConn = ds.getConnection();

     /* Create an Instance of the java.sql.Statement class
        and use the factory method called createStatement()
        available in the Connection class to create a new statement.
     */
     stmt = myConn.createStatement();

     /* Use the shortcut method the available in the Statement
        class to execute our query.  We are selecting all rows
        from the EMPLOYEE table.
     */
     rs = stmt.executeQuery("SELECT * FROM EMPLOYEE ");

     /* This enumerates all of the rows in the ResultSet and
        prints out the values at the columns named ID, NAME,
        LOCATION.
     */
     while (rs.next()) {
       out.println(rs.getString("ID") + "- " +
         rs.getString("NAME") + "- " +
         rs.getString("LOCATION") + "<p>");
     }

     /* Release the ResultSet and Statement.
      */
     rs.close();
     stmt.close();

   } catch (Exception E) {
     /*
        Handle exception here.
     */
     System.out.println("Service Error: " + E);
   } finally {
     if (rs != null) {
       try { rs.close(); } catch (Exception ignore) {};
     }
     if (stmt != null) {
       try { stmt.close(); } catch (Exception ignore) {};
     }
     if (myConn != null) {
       try { myConn.close(); } catch (Exception ignore) {};
     }
   }
 }

 /*
  * Local Variables
  */
 Context ctx;
 DataSource ds;
 Statement stmt;
 ResultSet rs;

}
```

> Put code that is meant to be executed only once, at servlet initialization, inside the `init ()` method of your servlet. A common mistake is to cause your servlet to do more work than necessary by putting too much in the `service ()` method. For example, all requests for a JNDI named `InitialContext` (a topic discussed in detail in Chapter 6) should only be done once in the life of the servlet. For this reason, you should only execute this lookup in the `init ()` method. This ensures that the operations are only done once instead of every time the servlet is accessed. This is very important for efficiency.

Running the JDBC Read Example in WebLogic Server

This section describes how to deploy the JDBC Read example using WebLogic Server on Microsoft Windows 2000. All the JDBC examples in this chapter are run using the Examples Server, as opposed to the Default Server (mydomain server) used in previous chapters. The Examples Server is a standard instance of WebLogic Server that is preconfigured for running the examples. The Examples Server also has the demonstration Cloudscape database already installed. Start the Examples Server from the Start menu, under the Examples menu item.

The first step in running the JDBC Read example is to configure Cloudscape, as follows:

Step 1: Navigate to the Correct Directory

To begin, open a command shell and navigate to the *config\examples* subdirectory for the Examples Server. For example:

```
C:\bea\wlserver6.0\config\examples\
```

Step 2: Configure the Environment

To configure your environment to run the tools correctly, run the *setExamplesEnv.cmd* script in the *examples* directory. You should see something like Figure 5–2.

Figure 5-2 Setting the Examples Environment

In the preceding screen shot, WebLogic Server is installed on the C: drive. Your installation location may differ.

Step 3: Run the IJ Utility

The interactive Java (IJ) utility included with Cloudscape gives you a command-line interface for running SQL statements on data in the Cloudscape database. First, change your working directory to the location of the Cloudscape data. If you installed WebLogic Server on your C: drive, this directory would be:

```
c:\bea\wlserver6.0\samples\eval\cloudscape\data
```

To reach it, use the same command shell as previously and type:

```
cd \bea\wlserver6.0\samples\eval\cloudscape\data
```

You should see something like Figure 5-3 if you do a directory listing.

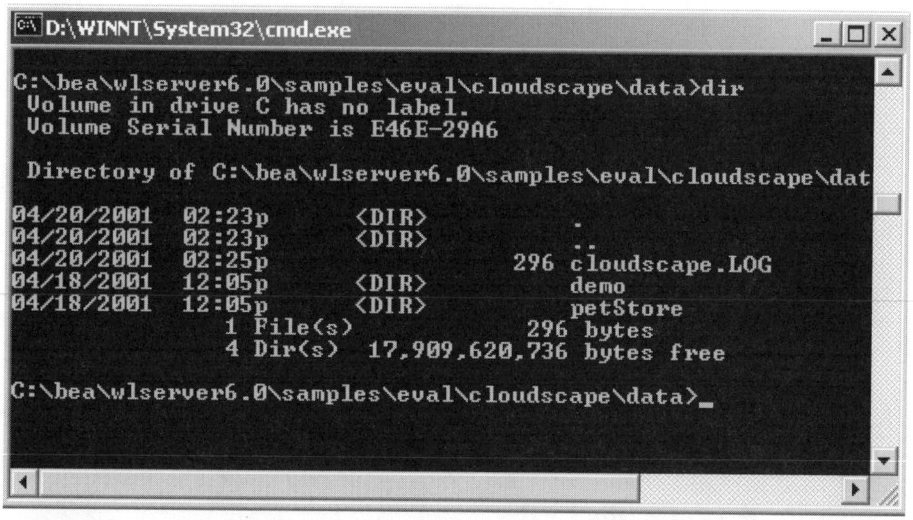

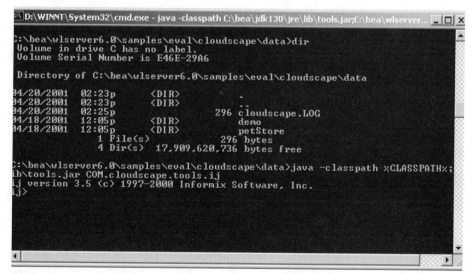

Figure 5–3 Directory Listing of the Cloudscape Data Store

Next, type the following (all on one line) and press Enter to run the IJ utility:

```
java -classpath %CLASSPATH%;..\lib\tools.jar COM.cloud-
scape.tools.ij
```

The –classpath setting launches Cloudscape's IJ utility. After entering
this command, you should see something like Figure 5–4.

Figure 5–4 Launching the IJ Utility

When you see the `ij >` prompt, the Cloudscape IJ tool is ready for use.

Step 4: Create a Database Instance and Employee Table

First, make sure that you do not have an instance of the Examples Server running. If your Examples Server is running, shut it down by closing its startup window, or through the administration console. Cloudscape, unlike other databases, does not allow concurrent access to the same database instance by different JVMs.

To create a database instance, use the CONNECT command:

```
CONNECT 'jdbc:cloudscape:demo;create=true';
```

This instructs Cloudscape to connect to a database instance called `demo`. The `create=true` command instructs Cloudscape to create the database instance if it does not already exist. To check that this action has been successful, use the SHOW command:

```
ij> SHOW CONNECTIONS;
CONNECTION0* -  jdbc:cloudscape:demo;create=true
* = current connection
ij>
```

Congratulations—you have created a database instance. Now create the Employee table that is used by the JDBC Read example. Type the following SQL into the command line of IJ:

```
CREATE TABLE EMPLOYEE(NAME CHAR(25), LOCATION CHAR(20), ID INTE-
GER);
```

You should see the following:

```
ij> CREATE TABLE EMPLOYEE(NAME CHAR(25), LOCATION CHAR(20), ID INTEGER);
0 rows inserted/updated/deleted
ij>
```

Step 5: Populate the Database

To populate the database, type the following SQL and press Enter after each line:

```
INSERT INTO employee VALUES ('SHANDELLE', 'Ohio'   ,6);
INSERT INTO employee VALUES ('JMG', 'Texas'   ,2);
INSERT INTO employee VALUES ('JOE', 'Louisiana'   ,5);
```

It should look something like Figure 5–5 on the screen.

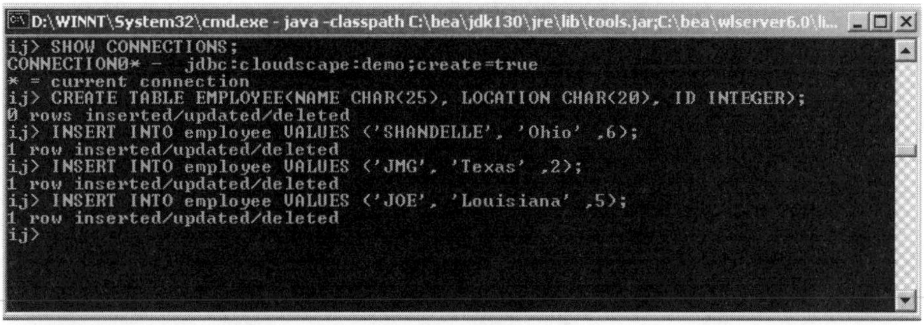

Figure 5–5   Adding Data to the Employee Table

Now exit the IJ utility by pressing Ctrl+C.

Step 6: Launch the WebLogic Examples Server

To see the results of your work, navigate to Start Examples Server on the Windows Start menu. You should see something like Figure 5–6 after a few moments indicating that the server has started successfully.

Figure 5–6   Starting the Examples Server

The Examples Server already has the Cloudscape connection configured. You can view this by starting the WebLogic Server console (click on the Start Default Console option in the Windows Start menu). In the Console window, click on the Connection Pools option under the JDBC menu item (see Figure 5–7).

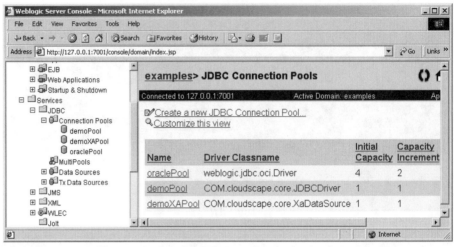

Figure 5–7   Configuring the Database Connection Pools

Three database connection pools are already configured. We will use the pool named `demoPool`. If you click on the demoPool link, you should see the following configuration options for the database connection pool (see Figure 5-8).

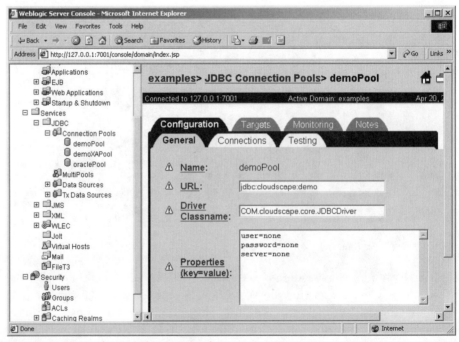

Figure 5–8   Configuring the demoPool

More information on configuring database connection pool parameters is available in the WebLogic Server documentation. The WebLogic Server console offers more information on each setting: Click on the link for the parameter name next to the parameter entry field.

As you can see from the WebLogic Server's configuration, a single database connection pool is created on behalf of a single user. How do WebLogic Server applications implement user- or role-based security, in which only authorized users can access sensitive data? The most common technique is to create a separate connection pool and database account for each individual user role. For example, the Administrator role might log in to the database under the name "admin" and have the ability to access all information across all accounts. Regular users could use another connection pool and have access only to user accounts in a certain group.

In addition, you can programmatically check that a given user has the right to access a given section of the database. However, you would need to program this yourself because WebLogic Server does not provide services in this area. In the Enterprise JavaBeans (EJB) model, security is implemented and supported in a granular form. For applications that demand specific security on a per-user basis, use the EJB model.

Step 6a: Configure a DataSource

DataSources are configured with the WebLogic Server console. Navigate to Services→JDBC→DataSources. Complete the form to map a connection-Pool to a DataSource name (see Figure 5–9).

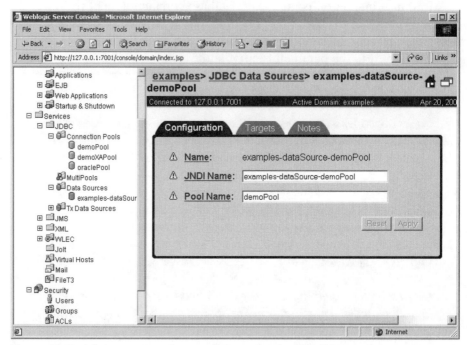

Figure 5–9   Mapping a DataSource Name to the demoPool Connection

The preceding screen shot shows a demonstration DataSource mapped through the demoPool connection to the Cloudscape database. This configuration is used throughout this chapter.

Step 7: Deploy the Example from the CD

To deploy the JDBC Read example from the CD, locate the example code in the *examples\ch5* directory on the CD. Copy all files and subdirectories for this example into a new directory on your local hard disk, such as *c:\dev4*. You can continue to work in the same command-shell window you used earlier.

Change to the new directory, and again execute the environment script for the Examples Server:

```
c:/bea/wlserver6.0/config/examples/setExamplesEnv.cmd
```

To run the `jar` utility, you must also set the default environment:

```
c:/bea/wlserver6.0/config/mydomain/setEnv.cmd
```

Then, use the `jar` utility to extract the code from the package:

```
jar xvf *.war
```

See Figure 5–10.

Figure 5-10   Unpacking the JDBC Read Example

Review the *build.bat* build script and edit it if necessary, to make sure it points to the location of your WebLogic Server deployment.

Type "build" and press Enter. The compilation, packaging, and deployment of the application should happen automatically (see Figure 5–11).

Figure 5-11   Results of Running the Build Script on the JDBC Read Example

Step 8: View the Example

To view the example, point a Web browser to *http://127.0.0.1:7001/myJDB-CReadServlet/*.

You should see something that looks like Figure 5–12.

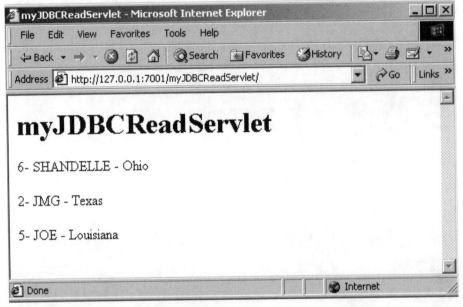

Figure 5-12   Results of the JDBC Read Example

If you do not see anything, be sure to check out the execution window for your Examples Server. The servlet in this example is designed to print out any problems to the console window for review.

Using JDBC to Update the Database

Using JDBC to update the database is actually *simpler* than JDBC reads. There are three basic operations for JDBC updates in your WebLogic Server application. These are:

- Establishing connections to the database
- Executing statements
- Releasing connections

Establishing Connections to the Database

As with database reads, connections for database updates are represented by instances of the `java.sql.Connection` object. We can reuse the previous code for creating database connections:

```
/* Create a connection to the WebLogic Server JNDI Naming Service:
```

```
*/
      Context ctx = new InitialContext();

      /* Create a new DataSource by Locating It in the Naming Ser-
vice:
       */
      javax.sql.DataSource ds
        = (javax.sql.DataSource)
        ctx.lookup ("examples-dataSource-demoPool");

      /* Get a new JDBC connection from the DataSource:
       */
      myConn = ds.getConnection();
```

This code behaves the same way as the JDBC Read example. Using the JDBC DataSource, a connection to the database is created.

Executing Statements

An instance of the `Statement` class is required to execute database updates. To get an instance for use, call the `createStatement()` method available in the `Connection` class. Here's the code:

```
Statement stmt = myConn.createStatement();
```

An instance of the `Statement` class is created for the specific connection to the database that you are using.

Three types of database updates are available in SQL:

- INSERT—To insert rows of data into tables
- UPDATE—To modify data in tables
- DELETE—To remove rows from tables

To use any of these statements via JDBC, insert the SQL string in an `executeUpdate()` method call on the instance of the `Statement` class.

For example, the following inserts a new employee into the Employee table:

```
stmt.executeUpdate ("INSERT INTO employee VALUES ('JOE', 'Louisiana'  ,5)");
```

If the original data in the database looked like the following:

```
NAME            LOCATION           ID
Zornoza         Connecticut        1
Prasad          India              2
Shinn           Oregon             3
D'Attoma        New York           4
```

The updated data in the table named EMPLOYEE would be:

```
NAME            LOCATION           ID
```

```
Zornoza          Connecticut      1
Prasad           India            2
Shinn            Oregon           3
D'Attoma         New York         4
JOE              Louisiana        5
```

Releasing Connections

After updating the data in the database, release the connections and objects by running the close() method on each of these objects:

```
stmt.close();
myConn.close();
```

The Entire JDBC Update Example

The following is the complete listing of the JDBC Update (myJDBCUpdateServlet) covered in this section:

```
package com.learnweblogic.examples.ch5;

import java.io.*;
import java.sql.*;
import javax.servlet.http.*;
import javax.naming.Context;
import javax.naming.InitialContext;
import javax.naming.NamingException;
import javax.sql.DataSource;

public class myJDBCUpdateServlet extends HttpServlet {

  /*
   * This method is called when the servlet is first initialized.
   * Note here that both the initial lookup into the WebLogic Server JNDI
   * naming context and the location of a DataSource object from it
   * are placed here.  This ensures that the operations are only done
   * once instead of every time that the servlet is accessed.  This is
   * very important for efficiency.
   */
  public void init() {

    try {

      /* Create a connection to the WebLogic Server JNDI Naming Service:
       */
      ctx = new InitialContext();

      /* Create a new DataSource by Locating It in the Naming Service:
       */
      ds = (javax.sql.DataSource)
        ctx.lookup ("examples-dataSource-demoPool");
```

```
      } catch (Exception E) {
        /*
           Handle exception here.
        */
        System.out.println("Init Error: " + E);
      }
}

public void service(HttpServletRequest requ,
   HttpServletResponse resp)
   throws IOException
{

   Connection myConn = null;

   try  {

      PrintWriter out = resp.getWriter();

      out.println("<html>");
      out.println("<head><title>myJDBCUpdateServlet</title></head>");
      out.println("<body>");

      out.println("<h1>myJDBCUpdateServlet</h1>");

      /* Create a connection to the WebLogic Server JNDI Naming Service:
       */
      ctx = new InitialContext();

      /* Create a new DataSource by Locating It in the Naming Service:
       */
      ds = (javax.sql.DataSource)
        ctx.lookup ("examples-dataSource-demoPool");

      /* Get a new JDBC connection from the DataSource:
       */
      myConn = ds.getConnection();

      /* Create an Instance of the java.sql.Statement class and
         use the factory method called createStatement() available
         in the Connection class to create a new statement. */
      stmt = myConn.createStatement();

      /* Execute an Update to insert a new entry into the table
         named employee.  This new entry should have the name
         JOE, allocation of Louisiana, and an employee ID of 5. */
      stmt.executeUpdate
        ("INSERT INTO employee VALUES ('GARY', 'Montana'  ,5)");

      /* Use the shortcut method the available in the Statement
         class to execute our query.  We are selecting all rows
         from the EMPLOYEE table.
```

```
    */
    rs = stmt.executeQuery("SELECT * FROM EMPLOYEE ");

    /* This enumerates all of the rows in the ResultSet and
       prints out the values at the columns named ID, NAME,
       LOCATION.
    */
    while (rs.next()) {
        out.println(rs.getString("ID") + "- " +
        rs.getString("NAME") + "- " +
        rs.getString("LOCATION") + "<p>");
    }

  } catch (Exception E) {
    /*
       Handle exception here.
    */
    System.out.println("Service Error: " + E);
  } finally {
    if (rs != null) {
      try { rs.close(); } catch (Exception ignore) {};
    }
    if (stmt != null) {
      try { stmt.close(); } catch (Exception ignore) {};
    }
    if (myConn != null) {
      try { myConn.close(); } catch (Exception ignore) {};
    }
  }
}

/*
 * Local Variables
 */
Context ctx;
DataSource ds;
Statement stmt;
ResultSet rs;

}
```

Running the JDBC Update Example in WebLogic Server

This section describes deploying the JDBC Update example with the WebLogic Server running on a Microsoft Windows machine. Be sure that you have already deployed the JDBC Read example from earlier in this chapter. This is required because the JDBC Update example uses the same database table that the Read example creates.

Step 1: Deploy the Example from the CD

To deploy the JDBC Update example from the CD, locate the example code in the *examples\ch5* directory on the CD. Create a new, empty directory on your local hard disk. For example, *c:\dev6*. Copy over just the `.war` file (the archive file that contains all the files).

Using the same command shell used in the previous steps, change to the new directory. Again, make sure your environment is set correctly by running the `setExamplesEnv.cmd` (the environment settings do not persist from session to session or from command shell to command shell).

```
c:/bea/weblogic600/config/examples/setExamplesEnv.cmd
```

To run the `jar` utility, you must also set the default environment:

```
c:/bea/wlserver6.0/config/mydomain/setEnv.cmd
```

Use the `jar` utility to extract the code from the package:

```
jar xvf *.war
```

Edit the build script included to point to the proper location of your WebLogic Server deployment.

Type "build" and press Enter. The compilation, packaging, and deployment of the application should happen automatically.

Step 2: View the Example

To view the example, point a Web browser to *http://127.0.0.1:7001/myJDBCUpdateServlet /*.

You should see something that looks like Figure 5–13.

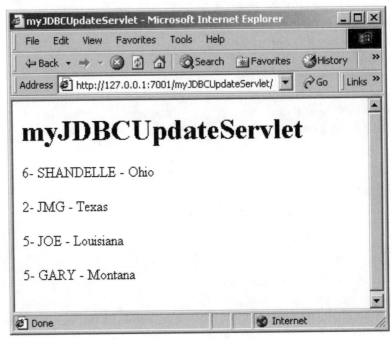

Figure 5-13 Results of the Update Servlet

If you do not see anything, be sure to check out the execution window for your Examples Server. The servlet in this example is designed to print out any problems to the console window for review.

Adding and Dropping Tables

Data administration commands such as those for adding and dropping tables can be treated just like any other SQL update. The following demonstrates this operation. First, create a table named `myTable` with two columns, `id` and `name`. These columns contain values of INTEGER type, and a variable-length string (VARCHAR) of maximum length 25, respectively.

```
try {

    /*… Load driver and create appropriate Connection here. */

            // Create the appropriate Statement object…
        Statement crstmt = myConn.createStatement();

        // Execute SQL to create a new table named myTable
        crstmt.execute("create table myTable (id INTEGER, name
VARCHAR(25)");
```

```
        crstmt.close();
    } ...
```

To remove a table:

```
/* Load driver and create appropriate Connection here. */

    try {
        // Create the appropriate Statement object...
    Statement crstmt2 = myConn.createStatement();
    crstmt2.execute("drop table myTable");
    crstmt2.close();
    }...
```

Transactions

Transactions are a means to guarantee that a series of operations against a database completes accurately. For example, the transaction framework ensures a correct result when you remove an item from inventory and simultaneously deduct money from the purchaser's account. Or, you may want to use transactions when your users want to place a bid on a given item available at auction. Transactions prevent multiple simultaneous users from winning the same auction, or from placing identical bids on a given item. Transactions represent a unit of work. Either all the work succeeds or none. It is not possible to remove items from inventory without removing money from the purchaser's account.

The transaction is not complete unless all of its operations are successful. The application server and database (working cooperatively) must ensure that transactions have the four essential properties known by the mnemonic "ACID." These properties are:

- *Atomicity*—The actions that make up the transaction must either all complete successfully, or none be executed at all.
- *Consistency*—A transaction must leave its environment and any data that it processes in a state that does not endanger integrity.
- *Isolation*—All of the actions in the transaction must result in the same values as if they were all run serially (one at a time).
- *Durability*—All results of the actions of the transaction must be persistently stored. Typically, this is on a disk.

Putting ACID into Practice

Let's look at each of these properties for a typical transaction-oriented application, such as running a small bank. If you want to transfer money from one account to another, you'll want atomicity. This ensures that it is impossible to remove money from one account without adding that money to another account. If this protection were not there, you could lose money or gain it, inexplicably.

You also want your money transfers to be consistent. The removal of money from one account should not affect any other accounts in the system. In addition, your transfer of funds operations, which simultaneously remove money from one account and give it to another, should produce the same results as if they were run sequentially. In the case of complex operations, isolation becomes very important.

Finally, you'll want your money transfer to persist over time. Typically, this means that results are written to highly available offline storage media such as a Redundant Array of Inexpensive Disks (RAID). Computer memory (RAM) is not considered to be durable because a simple power supply problem could erase the entire bank record.

Accessing Transactions via SQL

The databases you use with WebLogic Server support ACID-compliant transaction management that can be accessed via SQL.

A transaction represents a span of control over one or more SQL statements. The SQL statements can affect multiple databases. The SQL standard's transaction language includes:

- BEGIN or START, which signifies to the database that transaction should begin. All subsequent operations to the database should be part of (within the scope of) that transaction.
- PREPARE, which signifies to the database that it should prepare to commit the transaction. This is only applicable to transactions that involve multiple resources or databases. Multi-database transactions are discussed later in this chapter.
- COMMIT, which signifies to the database that it should commit the transaction. When a transaction is committed, it is written to the database disk and is final.

When to use transactions? As a general rule, transactions prove useful in applications in which atomicity is important. In other words, you either want all actions in transactions to complete, or none of them.

Simple Transactions and WebLogic Server JDBC

You may not be aware of it, but transactions in some form have already been involved in the JDBC Read and Update examples. The transactions are implicit, applied automatically to each individual SQL statement. More complex transactions are typically done in the context of the JTA driver, described later in this chapter.

By definition, `Connection` objects are responsible for handling transactions. These transactions are automatically committed. They are in *autocommit mode*.

From a usability standpoint, autocommit for JDBC is a good thing. Developers do not have to worry about inserting `begin`, `prepare`, `commit` (and so forth) commands into their applications. Unfortunately, real-world transactions require more than single SQL statements to do their work. Even something as simple as transferring money between two accounts requires a number of SQL statements.

Transaction Options in WebLogic Server

There are two different options for implementing database transactions in WebLogic Server applications. The first uses the WebLogic Server JTA driver. This is a special "wrapper" on top of JDBC that enables a transaction to be associated with multiple J2EE services, as the scope of the given user being served moves through different services. For example, a servlet could coordinate a Java Message Service (JMS) queue and an EJB in the scope of the same transaction. Or, multiple resources (databases) could participate in a single transaction, typically constructed as a *two-phase commit* operation.

The other way to use transactions is to declare them explicitly on the JDBC connection or using AutoCommit. You, as the developer explicitly use commands to tell the transaction to begin and commit. While explicitly declaring transactions is functionally easier to program, it is limited to very simple applications and can limit performance and functionality. In a serious J2EE application, which relies upon the EJB and JMS services, you should never declare transactions explicitly on the JDBC connection. The only way that a JMS destination and EJBs can participate in a transaction is through JTA. For this reason, the JTA driver is used to implement transactions in the WebAuction application, which is discussed throughout this book. Although WebLogic Server supports explicit JDBC transactions, in the context of

J2EE applications, it is a best practice to rely upon the JTA implementation in the WebLogic Server JTA driver.

In a serious J2EE application, which relies upon the EJB and JMS services, you should never declare transactions explicitly on the JDBC connection. Instead, use JTA.

Using the JTA Driver

The JTA driver enables multiple J2EE services in WebLogic Server to participate in the same transaction. These operations may involve services such as EJBs, or JMS, or direct SQL statements using standard JDBC calls. JTA is also useful when single services need transaction support, such as servlets that access the database directly. The JTA driver readily supports both transactions and connection pooling.

The JTA driver behaves differently depending on whether the transaction runs against a single database or against multiple databases. When the scope of the transaction is a single resource, WebLogic Server uses standard commands to the database to set the begin and end of a transaction across a single database connection.

Once a transaction is begun, all of the database operations for a given user share that user's connection from the same connection pool. When the transaction is committed or rolled back, the connection is returned to the pool.

WebLogic Server Multi-Database Transaction Services: JTA, XA, and 2PC

When WebLogic Server coordinates transactions across multiple resources, the more advanced features of transaction coordination in JTA come into play.

For a transaction that spans data resources, WebLogic Server uses a two-phase commit (2PC) engine. 2PC is the algorithm that is used to provide all of the ACID properties. 2PC requires that all the resources involved in the transaction implement the XA specification. In practice, 2PC is transparent to the user. You use the JTA driver in your application, acquire connections to multiple resources, specify operations on them, and so forth. As long as they are all XA-compliant resources, WebLogic Server takes care of the details of coordinating all the resources together into a single transaction that either succeeds or fails as a whole. Further details on multi-database transactions are provided later in this chapter, in the section "WebLogic Server and Distributed Transactions."

Using WebLogic Server JTA

There are seven basic steps for using WebLogic Server JTA in an application. These are:

1. Establish the transaction.
2. Start the transaction.
3. Locate a DataSource.
4. Establish a database connection.
5. Execute resource operations.
6. Close connections.
7. Complete the transaction.

Let's examine each of these steps in detail. We will now JTA-enable our JDBC examples from earlier in this chapter.

Establishing the Transaction

The first step in a WebLogic Server JTA implementation is to establish an instance of the `UserTransaction` class. The `UserTransaction` class controls the transaction on the current thread of execution. This transaction is associated with the current thread of execution for the user being served for all of the various services such as EJB, JMS, or JDBC. This class can be looked up in the JNDI. For now, we will not discuss the mechanics of JNDI, which is covered in detail in Chapter 6, *Remote Method Invocation and Distributed Naming*.

The following code is a lookup in JNDI for the `UserTransaction` object:

```
/* A Context which is used to store the user. */

Context ctx = null;
```

Locate a new initial context:

```
    ctx = new InitialContext();
```

Finally, create the `UserTransaction` object by locating it in the context object located in JNDI:

```
UserTransaction tx = (UserTransaction)
```

```
ctx.lookup("javax.transaction.UserTransaction");
```

At this point, a `UserTransaction` object is available.

Starting the Transaction

Starting the transaction is simple. Simply call the `begin` method on the `UserTransaction` object:

```
tx.begin();
```

Now, any operations that use the database are within the scope of this transaction. This includes direct JDBC calls as well as other services that rely on JDBC, including EJB or JMS.

Note that we retrieve our JDBC connection from the `TxDataSource`. You *must* get your JDBC connection from a `TxDataSource` or the Java Transaction Service (JTS) driver. A connection from the pool driver will not participate in a JTA transaction and you will not be able to include EJB or JMS services in the scope of the transaction.

> *Always get your JDBC connection for JTA transactions from a `TxDataSource` or the JTS, not from the pool driver.*

Locating a DataSource

The next step is to locate a transactional DataSource:

```
javax.sql.DataSource ds
            = (javax.sql.DataSource)
    ctx.lookup ("examples-dataSource-demoPool");
```

Establishing a Database Connection

Next, establish a database connection.

```
java.sql.Connection myConn = ds.getConnection();
```

This `Connection` object is now available for use.

Executing Resource Operations

At this point, things should look very familiar to you. We now have an instance of the `Connection` class that we can use to generate statements for the database. In contrast to the simpler examples from earlier in this chapter, it is now possible to execute multiple statements in the scope of a single transaction. All of the statements succeed and are committed in the database, or they all are rolled back, reverting the database to its original state.

For example, let's say that we want to have two different operations in a transaction. To continue our Employee Record example from earlier in the chapter, we insert two new employees using multiple SQL INSERT statements after creating a new instance of the Statement object, named stmt:

```
/* Execute an Update to insert two new entries into the
        table named employee. */
    stmt.executeUpdate (
       "INSERT INTO employee VALUES ('Benjamin', 'FRANCE' ,55)");
    stmt.executeUpdate (
       "INSERT INTO employee VALUES ('ROB', 'Illinois' ,56)");
```

Close Connections

Just as in the simple Update example earlier this chapter, the connections to the resources you created should be closed and disposed. This is done by using the close() method on each object:

```
stmt.close();
myConn.close();
```

At this time, the Connection object is held in "limbo" and not returned to the connection pool until the transaction is either committed or rolled back. This greatly affects tuning. Even when the user closes the database connection, it is not returned to the pool until the transaction commits. For this reason, you need to be sure that you either commit or roll back your transactions as soon as possible. Letting a transaction stay open until it times out is not a good idea for a scalable site. Eventually, you could exhaust all of your database connections, causing severe performance problems.

> *You need to be sure that you either commit or roll back your transactions as soon as possible. Letting a transaction stay open until it times out is not a good idea for a scalable site.*

Completing the Transaction

The final step is to complete the transaction. Before a commit or rollback, you can execute further JDBC calls by creating a new Connection object from the same connection pool. *The new connection is in the same transactional scope as those previously executed.*

Once all work is completed, the final step is to either commit the transaction or roll it back. If we commit the transaction, we assert that no error has occurred and it is now appropriate to make those changes final in the database. If things have not gone smoothly and an exception was thrown during one of the operations, the appropriate thing to do is roll back the transaction.

It is customary to bracket all of the steps in a WebLogic Server JTA–enabled transaction with a try/catch/finally block to handle any exceptions. Most applications use a `catch` block for their `rollback()` call. This looks like this:

```
try {
    …. Steps one through five here …
// Commit Transaction
tx.commit();
stmt.close();
    } catch (Exception txe) {

    // Printout the Transaction Exception
    System.out.println("Servlet error: " + txe);

    // Roll Back Transaction
    try {

      tx.rollback();

    } catch (javax.transaction.SystemException se) {}
  } finally {

    /* Close Connections */
    try {
      if (conn != null)
        if (!conn.isClosed())
          conn.close();
    } catch (SQLException sqle) {; }
  }
```

The JTA driver commits all the transactions on all `Connection` objects in the current thread and returns the connection to the pool if the transactions were committed. Or, JTA rolls back all operations involved and frees all connections and resources used.

Complete WebLogic Server JTA Example

For your reference, the following is the complete listing of the WebLogic Server JTA example covered in this section. It can be found on the CD accompanying this book in the directory *\examples\ch5\myJTAServlet.war*.

```
package com.learnweblogic.examples.ch5;

import javax.transaction.*;
import java.sql.*;
import java.util.*;
import javax.servlet.*;
import javax.servlet.http.*;
```

```
import java.io.*;
import javax.naming.Context;
import javax.naming.InitialContext;
import javax.naming.NamingException;
import javax.sql.DataSource;

public class myJTAServlet extends HttpServlet {

  /*
   * This method is called when the servlet is first initialized.
   * Note here that both the initial lookup into the WebLogic Server JNDI
   * naming context and the location of a DataSource object from it
   * are placed here.  This ensures that the operations are only done
   * once instead of every time that the servlet is accessed.  This is
   * very important for efficiency.
   */
  public void init() {

    try  {

      /* Create a connection to the WebLogic Server JNDI Naming Service:
       */
      ctx = new InitialContext();

      /* Create a new DataSource by Locating It in the Naming Service:
       */
      ds = (javax.sql.DataSource)
        ctx.lookup ("examples-dataSource-demoPool");

    } catch (Exception E) {
      /*
         Handle exception here.
      */
      System.out.println("Init Error: " + E);
    }
  }

  public void service (HttpServletRequest req,
    HttpServletResponse res)
  {

    Connection myConn = null;
    UserTransaction tx = null;

    try {

      PrintWriter out = res.getWriter();

      out.println("<html>");
      out.println("<head><title>myJTAServlet</title></head>");
      out.println("<body>");

      out.println("<h1>myJDBCJTAServlet</h1>");
```

```
/* Assign a new transaction context based:
 */
ctx = new InitialContext();

/* Create the UserTransaction object by locating it
   in the context object located in JNDI: */
tx = (UserTransaction)
  ctx.lookup("javax.transaction.UserTransaction");

/* Start the Transaction */
tx.begin();

/* Create a new DataSource by Locating It in the Naming Service:
 */
ds = (javax.sql.DataSource)
  ctx.lookup ("examples-dataSource-demoPool");

/* Get a new JDBC connection from the DataSource:
 */
myConn= ds.getConnection();

stmt = myConn.createStatement();

/* Execute an Update to insert two new entries into the
   table named employee. */
stmt.executeUpdate (
  "INSERT INTO employee VALUES ('Benjamin', 'FRANCE' ,55)");
stmt.executeUpdate (
  "INSERT INTO employee VALUES ('ROB', 'Illinois' ,56)");

// Commit Transaction
tx.commit();

out.println("Success!");

} catch (Exception E) {
  /*
     Handle exception here.
  */
  System.out.println("Service Error: " + E);
} finally {
  if (rs != null) {
    try { rs.close(); } catch (Exception ignore) {};
  }
  if (stmt != null) {
    try { stmt.close(); } catch (Exception ignore) {};
  }
  if (myConn != null) {
    try { myConn.close(); } catch (Exception ignore) {};
  }
}
}
}
```

```
/*
 * Local Variables
 */
Context ctx;
DataSource ds;
Statement stmt;
ResultSet rs;

}
```

Running the Complete WebLogic Server JTA Example

You can install and build this example using the code and script included in the accompanying CD. First, copy the file *examples**ch5**myJTAServlet.war* from the CD onto your system and follow the steps outlined earlier for examples in this chapter.

You should still have the other example applications from this chapter deployed. Use the JDBC Read example to see the status of the database before and after you execute the JTA servlet.

Be sure to clear your Internet temporary files and History before you re-run the Read servlet, so that you are seeing the current Web page version rather than a cached version.

Figure 5–14 displays the JDBC Read servlet showing information from the database before the JTA servlet is run.

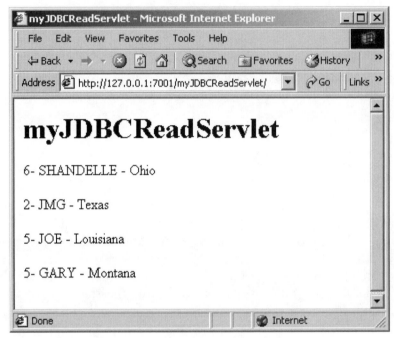

Figure 5–14   State of the Database before Running the JTA Servlet

The JTA servlet is run (see Figure 5–15).

Figure 5–15 Notification from the JTA Servlet

And you can see in Figure 5–16 that the database is updated with two new employee entries.

Figure 5-16 Results of Running the Complete JDBC/JTA Example

WebLogic Server and Distributed Transactions

Distributed transactions are those that span multiple resources such as an Oracle database, a Sybase database, and a message-oriented middleware product such as IBM MQSeries. In these combinations, a single transaction should govern all of the operations on all of the resources. As with any other transaction, either all operations succeed, or none of them do.

Distributed Transactions and Standards

A distributed transaction uses the 2PC protocol, which was defined in the late 1970s in academic research. This protocol follows standards from the X/Open Distributed Transaction consortium.

The X/Open standards specify a model called X/Open Distributed Transaction Processing (DTP). This model describes how all the different components in a distributed transaction work together. One important part of this standard is called *XA*, which is the standardized interface between a resource (such as a database) and the transaction manager (such as WebLogic Server's JTA implementation). Resources or databases that can work in distributed transactions are specified as XA-compliant resources.

Using XA-Compliant Resources and JTA

WebLogic Server can use any number of XA-compliant resources and coordinate transactions that span all resources. In practice, this works by creating *bridges* to multiple XA-compliant resources made available through a `TxDataSource`. The JTA implementation handles enlisting the underlying resources in the JTA transaction.

Within the scope of the JTA driver transaction, your application code can make SQL updates and reads to the database either directly using JDBC, or indirectly by using higher level services such as EJB or JMS. Behind the scenes, the JTA driver handles all of the details to ensure that your operations either all succeed, or all fail. From an application developer's point of view, all of this happens without your knowledge. To take advantage of distributed transactions, simply use the standard procedure for WebLogic Server JTA as described in this chapter, except extend your resource access to include more than one database or other resource.

You should understand that there is overhead for using 2PC: It should only be used when necessary. Given a choice between using 2PC and doing a one-phase commit to a single resource, you should always avoid using 2PC. Use 2PC only if you have to enlist multiple resources in a transaction.

In fact, the WebLogic Server's JTA implementation includes a one-phase optimization. If only a single resource is enlisted, no 2PC is done. WebLogic Server enables you to enlist non-XA resources in a 2PC transaction. You have to set the `EnableTwoPhase` option in your *config.xml*. This is convenient for development, but it is not recommended for deployed applications.

Transaction Isolation Levels

Transaction isolation levels specify how the database handles the "I" in ACID. If you remember from previous discussions in this chapter, this is how the database handles concurrency issues, which are conflicts that arise when two or more simultaneous operations/transactions are operating on the same data. For example, one transaction might be in the process of obtaining data in the database while another process wants to update that same data. The setting of isolation levels enables you to specify how the database behaves in those situations.

There are five levels of transaction isolation defined by the JDBC specification. These five levels are database dependent, so you should review your driver and database documentation to see what works with your specific database. The five levels are (going from least restrictive to most restrictive):

- TRANSACTION_NONE—No attempt is made to isolate the transaction and participating data from other transactions.
- TRANSACTION_READ_UNCOMMITTED—Allows what are called "dirty" reads. A dirty read is a read of another transaction's uncommitted data. For instance, transaction-1 changes your account balance from $1,000 to $500. Before transaction-1 commits, transaction-2 reads the account balance as $500. This is a dirty read since transaction-1's change has not yet been committed.
- TRANSACTION_READ_COMMITTED—Guarantees that all reads return committed data. This prevents dirty reads, but it does not guarantee repeatable reads (for instance, if transaction-1 reads the account balance as $1,000). Now before transaction-1 commits, another transaction changes the account balance to $500 and commits the change. Now, when transaction-1 reads the account balance again, it may now see the balance as $500. This is a nonrepeatable read because the same column was read twice within the transaction but different results were returned. Note that there was no dirty read because transaction-2 committed its account balance change before transaction-1 read the new value. READ_COMMITTED is the default isolation level for Oracle databases and is commonly used in practice.
- TRANSACTION_REPEATABLE_READ—Prevents dirty reads and nonrepeatable reads, but phantom reads are still possible.

A phantom read occurs because a row has been added or deleted from a table, but this transaction still sees the side effects. For instance, consider a database schema with a Voters table listing citizens and their choice of candidate A or B. There is also an auxiliary table that lists the total vote count for each candidate. Transaction-1 reads in all of the rows in the Voters table and computes its own totals for candidates A and B. It then compares these totals against the vote totals in the auxiliary table and finds they do not match! The problem is that transaction-2 has inserted a new voter into the Voters table and updated the vote count. Transaction-1 has seen a phantom read. REPEATABLE_READ isolation is rarely used in practice because it is expensive to implement, and it does not provide true serializable transactions.

- TRANSACTION_SERIALIZABLE—Prevents dirty, nonrepeatable, and phantom reads. The SERIALIZABLE isolation level offers the highest level of protection, but it also gives the lowest performance.

Choosing an isolation level is a trade-off between performance and correctness. Use the lowest possible isolation level that guarantees correct semantics in your application.

Setting Isolation Levels

Developers can set the transaction isolation level for any or all transactions. The isolation level affects all JDBC access, because even the simplest accesses are treated as transactions by the database.

Setting transaction isolation levels is particularly important when data is shared between multiple clients. Many applications use the READ_COMMITTED isolation level because it enables readers to proceed without waiting for an update to commit. This is particularly important for Web-based applications, in which most users are browsing the data and not performing updates.

The mechanics of changing transaction isolation levels is simple. A method included in the Connection class called setTransactionIsolation() enables the transaction isolation level to be set for a given connection. The isolation level can be changed at any time for a given transaction on most databases, except during a transaction. The acceptable values are defined as constants in the Connection class. These are, as stated:

- Connection.TRANSACTION_NONE
- Connection.TRANSACTION_READ_UNCOMMITTED
- Connection.TRANSACTION_READ_COMMITTED
- Connection.TRANSACTION_REPEATABLE_READ
- Connection.TRANSACTION_SERIALIZABLE

To set the transaction isolation level in a Connection myConn to Connection.TRANSACTION_READ_COMMITTED, you could use the following immediately after obtaining the database connection from the connection pool:

```
conn.setTransactionIsolation (Connec-
tion.TRANSACTION_READ_COMMITTED);
```

The setting of isolation levels often brings out idiosyncrasies of different databases. Many databases do not support all isolation levels. It is also important to realize that databases use different locking algorithms. In particular, Oracle databases use an optimistic scheme with multiple versions of data. It is important to consult your database server's documentation when choosing an isolation level.

Prepared Statements

The JDBC specification supports language for executing the same statements repeatedly while changing only the parameters in the statements. Such operations use a PreparedStatement interface that extends the Statement interface.

To use prepared statements, first create an instance of the Prepared-Statement object. You do this by calling the prepareStatement() method on your instance of the Connection object. This method takes a single parameter, a string of SQL with wild cards represented by question marks. Assuming that we have already acquired a Connection object, we can create the following PreparedStatement:

```
PreparedStatement pstmt = myConn.prepareStatement("INSERT INTO
employee VALUES (?,?,?)");
```

In the original Update example in this chapter, we used two different SQL statements to add users to our Employee table:

```
/* Execute an Update to insert two new entries into the table named
employee.  */
stmt.executeUpdate ("INSERT INTO employee VALUES ('JOE', 'Louisiana'
,5)");
stmt.executeUpdate ("INSERT INTO employee VALUES ('SHANDELLE',
'Ohio'  ,6)");
```

For each of these statements, the database and JDBC driver must map our values to those understood by the underlying database. Performance can be greatly improved by removing this step. These two updates can be consolidated in a single `PreparedStatement`:

```
// Load DataSource Instance, Get Connection, etc. here…

/* Create instance of the PreparedStatement
   class with SQL wildcards specified by ?'s */
PreparedStatement pstmt = myConn.prepareStatement(
"INSERT INTO employee VALUES (?,?,?)");

/* Execute an Update to insert two new entries
   into the table named employee using PreparedStatement.  */

/* Replace wildcards with values for each.  */
pstmt.setString(1, 'JOE');
pstmt.setString(2, 'Louisiana'
pstmt.setInt(3, 5));

/* Execute statement */
int opNum = pstmt.executeUpdate();

/* Replace wildcards with values for each.  */
pstmt.setString(1, 'SHANDELLE');
pstmt.setString(2, 'Ohio'
pstmt.setInt(3, 6));
pstmt.executeUpdate();

/* Execute statement and assign the returned integer
   to a holding variable.  Each time that the executeUpdate
   method is called the return value is either the row count for
   INSERT, UPDATE or DELETE statements; or 0 for SQL statements
    that return nothing. */
opNum = pstmt.executeUpdate();

.
.
.
```

The trick is to use methods in the `PreparedStatement` class to set values for the wild cards before executing the statement. Each `setXXX` method takes two different parameters. The first is the index of the wild cards they replace. These indexes begin with 1 and increment to the right. The second parameter is the values to be inserted. Specific `setXXX` methods exist for each type of Java object. A complete list of these methods can be found in the documentation or at the Java Web site at *http://java.sun.com/j2se/1.3/docs/api/index.html*.

All the methods that apply to standard `Statement` objects also apply to `PreparedStatements`. For example, prepared statements can return `ResultSets` when the `executeQuery()` method is called on them.

Where possible, use `PreparedStatement` as opposed to a standard statement. This enables the database to compile the SQL into a statement that can be used repeatedly with only the parameters changing. This increases speed of execution, because the database does not need to repeatedly recompile the SQL.

Error Handling and SQL Warnings

JDBC errors are thrown as exceptions. The specific class for representing these errors is `java.sql.SQLException`. As with any other exception, the appearance of an `SQLException` signifies that something has gone wrong and needs to be appropriately handled.

SQL warnings are represented by an instance of the `java.sql.SQL-Warning` class that derives from the `java.sql.SQLException` class. It provides information on database access warnings. Unlike serious exceptions, SQL warnings are silently chained to the object whose method caused it to be reported.

Handling SQLException Errors

`SQLExceptions` store three pieces of information:

- A string describing the error.
- An `SQLstate` string, which follows the X/OPEN `SQLstate` conventions. The values of the `SQLState` string are described in the X/OPEN SQL specification.
- An integer error code that is specific to each vendor. Normally this is the actual error code returned by the underlying database.

In the previous examples, a try/catch block bracketed the entire JDBC operation. In your catch block, you can handle the exception to suit the needs of your application.

```
try {
… do JDBC work here …
} catch (SQLException sqle) {

     // Print the summary message of the exception
     System.out.println("JDBC exception encountered: " + sqle);

     // Retrieve and print the SQLState for this SQLException object.
     System.out.println("SQL state string: " + sqle.getSQLState());

     // Print the database specific error code
     System.out.println("Database specific error code: " +
sqle.getErrorCode());
}
```

Handling SQL Warnings

SQL warnings arise when the DBMS wants to alert you about a possible unintended consequence of your executed SQL statements. For example, if you have received truncated data, `SQLWarning` returns a `DataTruncation` warning. SQL warnings are silently attached to the object that generates them. Any relevant JDBC class (including `Connection`, `ResultSet`, and `Statement`) can generate an SQL warning.

Accessing SQL warnings is relatively simple. Each relevant JDBC class includes a method called `getWarnings()`. Calling this method on any instance of those objects returns the last created `SQLWarning`. You should always examine any SQL warnings before closing your `Statement` objects:

```
try {
… do JDBC work here …

     /* Check for SQL Warnings */
     SQLWarning mySQLW = myStatement.getWarnings();

If (mySQLW != null) {

     // Print the summary message of the exception
     System.out.println("JDBC exception encountered: " + mySQLW);

     // Retrieve and print the SQLState for this SQLException object.
     System.out.println("SQL state string: " + mySQLW.getSQLState());

     // Print the database specific error code
     System.out.println("Database specific error code: " +
mySQLW.getErrorCode());
```

```
}
} catch (SQLException sqle) {
    ....
} finally {
    /* Close the Instance of Statement */
    myStatement.close();
}
```

Note that both SQL warnings and JDBC errors are "chained." Each exception might have other exceptions nested inside it, if it contains object references to those other exceptions. Nested exceptions can be accessed by calling the getNextWarning() method, which returns an instance of SQLException or SQLWarning, depending upon the exception from which it was called.

Metadata

Metadata is data about data. It provides information about how data is organized. In the case of JDBC, metadata includes information such as column names, number of columns, and so forth. Because you might not always know what type of information is returned by result sets, the JDBC standard includes features that let us look at the structure of the returned Result-Sets. This is called *ResultSetMetadata*, or data about the organization of ResultSets.

> Note: JDBC keeps metadata about the database schema. A DatabaseMetaData object is available in most JDBC drivers. In the majority of WebLogic Server applications, the schema of the database is already known or not relevant. For this reason, DatabaseMetaData is not discussed in depth. The procedure to use DatabaseMetaData parallels that for using ResultSetMetadata.

Using Metadata

There are three basic steps for using metadata:

1. Generate a result set by executing a query.
2. Generate an instance of the metadata object by calling the appropriate method on the ResultSet.

3. Call the appropriate methods on the metadata object to derive the appropriate information.

The next section includes an example of using the steps based on the Employee table from the previous sections of this chapter.

As you might recall from earlier in the chapter, you first generate a result set by executing a query on the database:

```
// Load DataSource, Get Connection, etc. here…
```

```
/* Create an Instance of the java.sql.Statement class and
   use the factory method called createStatement() available
   on the Connection class to create a new statement. */
Statement stmt = myConn.createStatement();
```

```
/* Use the shortcut method the available in the Statement
   class to execute our query.  We are selecting all rows
   from the EMPLOYEE table. */
ResultSet rs = stmt.executeQuery("SELECT * FROM EMPLOYEE ");
```

Next, generate an instance of the `ResultSetMetaData` object by calling the appropriate method on the `ResultSet` object:

```
/* Use the factory method getMetaData to generate
   a ResultSetMetaData object for our result set 'rs'. */
ResultSetMetaData rsmd = rs.getMetaData();
```

Finally, call the appropriate methods on the metadata object to derive the appropriate information:

```
/* Find out how many columns are in the result set. */
System.out.println("Number of Columns: " +
rsmd.getColumnCount());
```

```
/* For each of those columns, print out information: */
for (int i = 1; i <= rsmd.getColumnCount(); i++) {
```

```
System.out.println("Column Name: " + rsmd.getColumnName(i));
```

```
System.out.println("Nullable: " + rsmd.isNullable(i));
```

```
System.out.println("Precision: " + rsmd.getPrecision(i));
```

```
System.out.println("Scale: " + rsmd.getScale(i));
```

```
System.out.println("Size: " + rsmd.getColumnDisplaySize(i));
```

```
        System.out.println("Column Type: " + rsmd.getColumnType(i));
```

```
        System.out.println("Column Type Name: " + rsmd.getColumnType-
Name(i));
```

}

This last section of code first displays the number of columns in the result set. Then, for each of those columns, it prints out data on different characteristics.

The methods illustrated here are only a subset of the methods available for metadata. A complete list can be found in the generated JavaDoc available with the standard JDK or via the Web at *http://java.sun.com/j2ee/1.3/docs/api/index.html*.

Advanced Features

This section covers some of the advanced features of JDBC:

- Binary Large OBjects (BLOBs) and Character Large OBjects (CLOBs), which make moving large objects to and from the database faster and easier
- Dates and times, which are used to handle timestamps and so forth
- Batch updates, which are used to improve the efficiency of making many updates to the database at a single time

Let's look at each of these in detail.

BLOBs and CLOBs

BLOBs and CLOBs are SQL data types available for efficient storage and retrieval of large objects. BLOBs contain binary data while CLOBs contain only characters.

BLOB and CLOB data types are created to store and retrieve very large objects such as a user's pictures or very large text files. BLOBs and CLOBs offer two benefits: First, they provide a convenient way to represent a large amount of data as a single database object. In other data types, such as integers, the amount of data that can be stored is limited. Second, DBMSs have been optimized to work with these data types, which means that reading and writing large objects is efficient, and certainly much faster than if you had to break them up into multiple smaller objects.

Using BLOBs and CLOBs

Both BLOBs and CLOBs are accessed via the `ResultSet` object returned as part of an SQL query. First, create instances of BLOBs and CLOBs:

```
java.sql.Blob myBlob = null;
java.sql.Clob myClob = null;
```

Next, get a `ResultSet` that contains a column named `"blobcolumn"` of BLOBs and a column named `"clobcolumn"` of CLOBs by doing a query:

```
... query that returns ResultSet with BLOB and CLOB here ...
myBlob = rs.getBlob("blobcolumn");
myClob = rs.getClob("clobcolumn");
```

Finally, display the BLOB using an `InputStream`:

```
java.io.InputStream readis = myReadBlob.getBinaryStream();
for (int i=0 ; i < STREAM_SIZE ; i++) {
    r[i] = (byte) readis.read();
    System.out.println("output [" + i + "] = " + r[i]);
}
```

And also display the CLOB using another `InputStream`:

```
java.io.InputStream readClobis = myReadClob.getAsciiStream();
char[] c = new char[26];
for (int i=0 ; i < 26  ; i++) {
    c[i] = (char) readClobis.read();
    System.out.println("output [" + i + "] = " + c[i]);
}
```

Batch Updates

Batch updates enable you to combine a group of updates to the database into a single batch operation. All the updates can be sent inside of a single database call. So, if you have *n* updates, instead of doing *n* database calls, you only do one. This streamlines the process of doing multiple updates to the database. In single updates, the JDBC driver contains a lock on a given table and then releases it for every update. Batch updates enable updates to be optimized around a single lock and can only be used on a single table in a database.

If you remember from the earlier Update examples, multiple updates to the database are handled as follows:

```
... locate driver, create Connection Object, etc. ...

/* Execute an Update to insert two new entries into the
table named employee.
```

```
stmt.executeUpdate ("INSERT INTO employee VALUES ('JOE', 'Louisiana'
,5)");
stmt.executeUpdate ("INSERT INTO employee VALUES ('SHANDELLE',
'Ohio'   ,6)");
```

These statements could be combined into a single batch of updates:

```
… locate driver, create Connection Object, Etc. …

// create a Statement object
Statement stmt = myConn.createStatement();

// add SQL statements to the batch
stmt.addBatch("INSERT INTO employee VALUES ('JOE', 'Louisiana'
,5)");
stmt.addBatch("INSERT INTO employee VALUES ('SHANDELLE', 'Ohio'
,6)");

/* Send the statements using the executeBatch method
to the DBMS in a try/catch block to catch exceptions.  */
try {

    stmt.executeBatch();

} catch (Exception e) {
    System.out.println("Exception in batch:\n " + e);
}
```

Batch statements are executed in the order that they are received. Using batch updates with prepared statements is similar:

```
// Load Driver Instance, Get Connection, etc. here…

/* Create instance of the PreparedStatement
   class with SQL  wildcards specified by ?'s */
PreparedStatement pstmt =
   myConn.prepareStatement("INSERT INTO employee VALUES (?,?,?)");

/* Execute an Update to insert two new entries
   into the table named employee using PreparedStatement.  */

/* Replace wildcards with values for each.
pstmt.setString(1, 'JOE');
pstmt.setString(2, 'Louisiana');
pstmt.setInt(3, 5));

/* Instead of calling executeQuery() here, call a addBatch
   method to add the current batch parameter specified above.  */
pstmt.addBatch();

/* Replace wildcards with values for each for the second
```

```
    values in the batch update. */
pstmt.setString(1, 'SHANDELLE');
pstmt.setString(2, 'Ohio'
pstmt.setInt(3, 6));

/* Instead of calling executeQuery() here, call a addBatch
   method to add the current batch parameter specified above.  */
pstmt.addBatch();

/* Call executeBatch to finish it off.  This method returns an array
of integers that specify the number of updated rows for each state-
ment in the batch. */
int[] updateCounts = pstmt.executeBatch();

.
.
```

Best Practices for JDBC

There are a number of best practices that enable your JDBC-based applications to be as successful as possible:

Make Your Queries as Smart as Possible

Learning to select only the data you really want at the server side is crucial.
For many applications where performance is a problem, it is often due to
poorly written SQL. Typical problems include returning too many rows, queries that are too general, and so forth. There are many tricks for SQL that are
worth learning to optimize performance. Some are simple while some are
complicated. While SQL joins and subqueries are beyond the scope of this
book, there are simple things that you can do to improve your performance,
such as using prepared statements and accessing stored procedures.

Tune the Database

Many databases enable you to specify which tables and objects should
receive preferential treatment for being cached in memory. For applications
that have a large working set but a small number of objects that are accessed
repeatedly, an appropriate database-caching strategy can make a very large
difference. Examine your application's behavior and, for objects that are
accessed regularly and repeatedly, be sure to designate those data sets to be

cached in memory as much as possible. More broadly, you should have a DBA and use a tuned database with a tuned schema. The database is a part of the overall system that must be optimized for proper performance.

Put Initialization Code in init()

A common mistake is to cause your servlet to do more work than is necessary by placing too much in the `service()` method. Be certain to place code that is meant to be executed only once in a servlet if initialized inside of the `init()` method of your servlet. This ensures that the operations are only done once instead of every time the servlet is accessed.

Get Your JDBC Connection from a TxDataSource or the JTS Driver

To ensure the correct use of transactions, get your JDBC connection from a `TxDataSource` or the JTS driver. If you get it from the pool driver, it does not participate in the JTA transaction and you won't be able to include EJB or JMS services in the scope of the transaction. Always get your JDBC connection for JTA transactions from a `TxDataSource` or the JTS, rather than from the pool driver.

Use Batch Updates

Batch updates provide much improved performance for multiple updates. If you need to do many updates, it is not efficient to obtain a connection to the database for each update. Batch updates so that they can all be accomplished in the scope of a single command sent to the database.

Updates require the DBMS to obtain all the locks necessary on the various rows and tables; use them and release them. Each single-update lock blocks other clients from accessing this data, and substantially degrades performance.

Do In-Place Updates Where Possible

It is more efficient to update a row in-place than to remove a row and insert another. For this reason, architect your application to use UPDATEs rather than INSERTs, DELETEs, and REMOVEs.

Use the Appropriate Method to Get a JDBC Connection Object

Use the DataSource-based technique, as described in this chapter.

The older DriverManager technique for acquiring a JDBC connection is synchronized and prevents concurrent access. Because WebLogic Server is multi-threaded internally, this presents scalability problems.

Release the JDBC Resources Appropriately

Release JDBC resources as quickly as possible and as efficiently as possible by placing the `close()` calls to each resource such as `Statements`, `Connections`, and `ResultSets` in the appropriate place in the `try/catch/finally` block. At the end of your `try {...}` block, you should release `ResultSets` and then release `Statements`. In the `finally { ... }` section, you should then release your `Connection`. By placing it in the `finally` section, you ensure that this connection is always released no matter what happens in the `try/catch` block.

Use Autocommit Appropriately

As noted in this chapter, it is possible to instruct the JDBC driver to commit on every statement or to require explicit committing of transactions. If possible, use explicit commits for your database operation. This requires much less overhead from the database and streamlined communication over the network to your database instance.

Don't Hang onto JDBC Connections

One common mistake in JDBC programming is to hold onto JDBC connections instead of immediately releasing those connections. For example, you may have a servlet that relies upon a JDBC connection. An inefficient application would store the JDBC connection persistently in the servlet and keep it open. This inhibits scalability: Connections to the database are limited. If the number of simultaneous requests for the service is greater than the size of the JDBC pool, this could mean that requests must wait to acquire a new JDBC connection.

As noted in this chapter for the JDBC example for the WebAuction application, a JDBC connection is acquired for every method and released at the end of that method. This enables JDBC connections to be spread efficiently among incoming requests. To avoid this scalability trap, your application should acquire connections from the connection pool and release them as quickly as possible.

Work in the Database If You Can

If possible, find ways to execute work in the database such as database triggers or stored procedures accessed through `CallableStatements`. This enables your application to avoid making unnecessary trips to the database, increasing performance.

Commit or Roll Back Your Transactions as Soon as Possible

You need to be sure that you either commit or roll back your transactions as soon as possible. Letting a transaction stay open until it times out is not a good idea for a scalable site.

Set Your Pool Size Appropriately

WebLogic Server enables variable pool sizes to be created for database connection pools. In general, there is no magic formula to determine how large these pools should be. But, a good rule of thumb is that the maximum size of the connection pool should be equal to the number of `ExecuteThreads` in your WebLogic deployment. This basically assumes that each thread uses one transaction to service a request and therefore needs one connection.

However, this value may need to be increased if a given thread uses more than one transaction in the scope of handling a user's request. For example, the WebAuction application generates ID numbers in a separate transaction from the other work being done in the database. For this reason, it could be helpful to specify a slightly larger connection pool in the WebAuction application, or any that requires more than one transaction in the scope of a single user request.

Also, it is recommended that you set your minimum connection pool size equal to the maximum pool size. This minimizes the amount of connections that are created to fill the connection pool to react to increased load on the server. This helps minimize response time and maximize performance by creating all of the database connections at server startup. Your server should not waste time creating connection pools when it is under load.

Do Not Have Your Transactions Span User Input

Transactions consume resources in the DBMS and WebLogic Server, and should be used judiciously. Avoid instances in which you unnecessarily rely on long-running transactions. For example, if a transaction begins on the load of a browser page and only commits when the user clicks Submit, you could be asking for trouble. The open transaction consumes resources in the database and in WebLogic Server. If you need to break up a long transaction into several shorter transactions, consult Chapter 7, *Enterprise Messaging with the Java Message Service (JMS)*, for more information.

> WebLogic Server also includes some good documentation on best practices for JDBC performance available at http://www.weblogic.com/docs60/jdbc/ performance.html.

JDBC and Transactions in the WebAuction Application

JDBC is used substantially in the WebAuction application. However, it is not used explicitly during development. Instead, as in the context of a real application, the JDBC access is encapsulated in an EJB. The WebAuction application uses Container Managed Persistence (CMP), which automatically generates JDBC code to map the relational data in the database to an object form.

There is one instance in which explicit JDBC is used in the WebAuction application. It is necessary to use the database to keep a sequence for the WebAuction application to generate new ID numbers for auction items. An EJB is used to encapsulate this SQL.

REMOTE METHOD INVOCATION AND DISTRIBUTED NAMING

In this chapter:

This chapter presents a high-level overview of RMI and Java Naming and Directory Interface (JNDI) concepts, and best practices for using RMI and JNDI in distributed programming. The chapter covers:

- RMI

- Using the remote interface

- The RMI programming model

- Serialization and the `java.io.Serializable` interface

- Using RMI in distributed applications

- WebLogic RMI optimizations

Chapter 6

In the Internet age, networked applications are commonplace. From Web browsers to hand-helds, every device becomes a networked device communicating with distant servers. In this networked world, enterprise applications require communication and distribution facilities. Millions of users rely on standard protocols to access distributed programs such as Simple Mail Transfer Protocol (SMTP)—for email, and Hypertext Transfer Protocol (HTTP)—for Web traffic. Although bounced e-mail messages and slow Web sites destroy the illusion, Web browsers were designed to provide a generic interface to access the world's computers as if they were all located under your desk. Java programs also can make method calls on objects located in other processes and even on other computers. These method calls across the network rely on Java's Remote Method Invocation (RMI) service.

Remote Method Invocation

RMI is a Java-based distributed programming model. RMI objects consist of a remote interface and an implementation class. When RMI clients make method calls against the remote interface, the method calls are transported across the network to the RMI implementation. The RMI server calls the method on the RMI implementation object, and the result is sent back across the network to the RMI client.

The RMI advantage is that the Java programmer does not have to write code to package the method call, send it across the network, and receive the response. The RMI programmer provides only an implementation object and the remote interfaces. WebLogic Server's RMI implementation handles transporting the method call from the client across the network into the RMI object. Finally, the server's RMI implementation sends the return value back across the network to the client. From the client's perspective, it appears just like any local method call.

Java 2 Enterprise Edition (J2EE) services such as Enterprise JavaBeans (EJB) are built on top of RMI. While RMI objects can be programmed directly, most WebLogic applications use higher level services such as EJB. However, it is important for EJB programmers to understand RMI and the complications of distributed programming.

Using the Remote Interface

An RMI client always accesses the RMI object through the remote interface. The object implementing the remote interface on the client is referred to as the *stub*. When the client calls an RMI method, it is actually making a method call to the stub. The stub provided by the WebLogic RMI implementation converts the method parameters into a format that can be transmitted across the network. This process is known as *marshaling*. The method call and its directives are sent in network packets to the WebLogic Server. The server reads the bytes from the network and calls a server-side object known as the *skeleton*. The skeleton is responsible for unpacking the network format and recreating the Java objects that were passed as parameters to the RMI method. This process is known as *unmarshaling*.

The skeleton then makes the method call against the RMI implementation class. When the RMI implementation class returns, the skeleton marshals the return value and sends a network response to the client. Finally, the stub unmarshals the return value and returns it to the client application (see Figure 6–1).

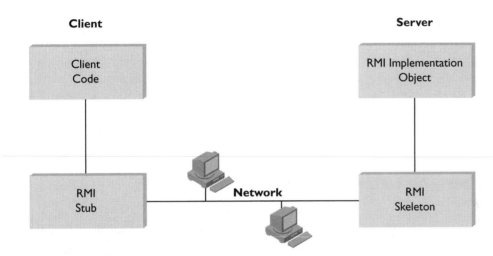

Figure 6–1   RMI Call from Client to Server

Marshaling is required because the RMI stub cannot merely write the native representation of an object to the wire. For instance, a Java object might have a reference to another object in one of its fields. Generally, an object reference is implemented by storing a memory address in the field. It is extremely unlikely that the RMI server would store the objects at the same memory addresses as the object's source. Without marshaling, a client's object reference would be unusable on the server. Marshaling also handles such low-level details as network byte ordering, so that RMI programs can work correctly if the client and server run in different environments such as UNIX and Windows. With the RMI programming model, application code does not need to consider these low-level details.

The RMI Programming Model

It is important to recognize that RMI is a programming model. It does not designate the underlying network packet format exchanged between the client and server. The actual RMI clients and implementation objects are independent of the wire format, since they interface directly only with the RMI classes. Only the lower communication levels use the RMI wire format. This is analogous to network programs communicating with TCP/IP. TCP/IP is a network protocol, but it must be transported in an interface-specific format. Like RMI clients, a TCP/IP client programs to the TCP/IP model. It does not care which Ethernet card actually transports the packets.

The WebLogic RMI implementation supports three different wire protocols: T3, T3/HTTP, and IIOP. T3 is WebLogic's optimized protocol for transporting remote method calls across network wires. T3/HTTP is the T3 protocol tunneled within HTTP packets. T3/HTTP can be used to make RMI calls across a firewall that only permits HTTP traffic. IIOP is the CORBA wire protocol. WebLogic's RMI/IIOP enables Java programs to communicate with legacy CORBA systems. Each of these protocols may also be encrypted with SSL for secure client-server communication.

Serialization

Remote method calls travel across the network wire between the client and server. Since network packets are just a series of bytes, the parameters to a remote call must be converted into a byte stream. When the network packets arrive on the server, the RMI implementation then converts the byte stream back into objects. RMI utilizes Java's serialization facilities to handle converting remote method parameters to the wire format and back into objects on the server.

Unlike local method calls where parameters can be arbitrary types, RMI parameters and return values must implement either the `java.io.Serializable` or the `java.rmi.Remote` interface.

RMI parameters must implement *`java.io.Serializable`* or *`java.rmi.Remote`*.

The Serializable Interface

Java's serialization process enables an object to be converted into a stream. When a Java program reads the stream and reconstitutes the object, the process is known as deserialization. Not every class can be serialized automatically by Java. In general, references to external resources are not serializable. For instance, a database connection or a network socket would not be serializable. An object with a database connection variable normally releases the connection before serialization and grabs the connection again after deserialization.

A Java class indicates that it supports serialization by implementing the `java.io.Serializable` interface. The `java.io.Serializable` interface does not contain any methods. It is merely a marker to indicate that the class may be serialized. A serializable class must ensure that its member variables are serializable, as well. If a member variable should not be serialized (such as a database connection), it should be declared transient. When a Java object is serialized, all transient fields are ignored.

Ensure all member variables are serializable or transient.

In addition to its member variables, a serializable class must consider its super-class. If the super-class is also serializable, then its contents are stored in the stream, as well. If the super-class is not serializable, then it must include a default, no-argument constructor. During serialization, the super-class is not stored in the stream. During deserialization, the no-argument constructor is used to create the super-class. If neither of these cases applies, a `java.io.NotSerializableException` is thrown to indicate failure during the serialization process.

Ensure that the super-class implements serializable or has a default constructor.

When a serializable object is used as an RMI parameter or return value, the object is serialized into a byte stream. The bytes are then sent across the network to the WebLogic Server. The server deserializes the bytes and receives a copy of the original object. Because this is only a copy of the RMI parameter, any changes made in the object are not visible in the client's object. This calling convention is known as *pass-by-value.*

RMI calls pass serializable objects by value.

The Remote Interface

All RMI interfaces must extend the `java.rmi.Remote` interface. Like the serializable interface, remote contains no methods and is a marker indicating that this is a RMI interface. The remote interface enables clients to make remote method calls to the RMI object. Remote interfaces can also be used as parameters or return values for remote methods. This is very common when an RMI service is a factory for creating other RMI objects. As we discuss in Chapter 8, EJB Homes are a factory for returning `EJBObjects` that are RMI objects.

Unlike serializable objects, remote interfaces are not stored by value in the stream. Instead, the remote interface is automatically replaced by a stub during the serialization process. The client receives a stub that enables it to call the remote server. For instance, the EJB Home returns an `EJBObject` that is a remote interface. When this object is returned to the client, the `EJBObject` is replaced with a stub. The client makes RMI calls through this stub to the `EJBObject` on the server.

RMI replaces `java.rmi.Remote` parameters with stubs.

Hand-Coding Serialization

For most types of applications, Java serialization is an automatic means to convert objects into a network-ready format. However, like most automatic procedures, there also are cases where hand-coding the serialization process can be advantageous. JavaSoft provides the `java.io.Externalizable` interface to enable classes to completely override their serialization process. Programmers generally implement the externalizable interface if they require precise control over their serialized representation or because the performance of Java's serialization is not sufficient. It is important to understand that an externalizable class must also handle the serialization of its super-classes. The externalizable interface contains two methods:

- `writeExternal(java.io.ObjectOutputStream)`
- `readExternal(java.io.ObjectInputStream)`

An externalizable class writes its serialized representation in the `writeExternal` method and reconstitutes itself in the `readExternal` method. Implementing externalizable gives the programmer complete control, and it can be faster than Java's standard serialization process.

However, programmers need to be aware that writing externalizable classes places the burden of serialization on the code. A bug in serialization can lead to bugs that are difficult to find in a large application. Implementing externalizable should be used with caution, but when used appropriately, it can improve the performance of marshaling and unmarshaling objects.

Implementing `java.io.Externalizable` can improve marshaling performance.

Externalizable Example

The `ThreeIntegers` example shows a simple class that provides its own serialization implementation with the externalizable interface. Notice that the class implements java.io.Externalizable, writes its fields in writeExternal, and restores its values in readExternal. Also, note that the member variables must be read and written in the same order. This is an important consideration when maintaining a class that implements the externalizable interface.

```java
public final class ThreeIntegersimplements java.io.Externaliz-
able{  private int a;   private int b;
  private int c;

  public ThreeIntegers() {}

  public ThreeIntegers(int A, int B, int C) {
    a = A;
    b = B;
    c = C;
  }

  public void writeExternal(java.io.ObjectOutputStream oos)
    throws java.io.IOException
  {
    oos.writeInt(a);
    oos.writeInt(b);
    oos.writeInt(c);
  }

  public void readExternal(java.io.ObjectInputStream ois)
    throws java.io.IOException
  {
    a = ois.readInt();
    b = ois.readInt();
    c = ois.readInt();
  }
}
```

Using RMI in Distributed Applications

By design, RMI programs closely resemble local Java applications. Programmers invoke a service on a distant networked server merely by making a method call. RMI's transparency is extremely valuable for a programmer's productivity because it makes distributing an application a relatively easy task. However, designing a scalable, reliable, and high-performance distributed application is not easy. Distributed programming brings a whole new class of potential errors.

While RMI might provide the illusion of network transparency, it is important to disregard this illusion and design RMI applications as distributed programs.

Distributed programming is a complicated task, and one chapter cannot discuss all the issues. However, we will discuss common mistakes that most programmers trip over at least once during their career.

Handling the Unreliable Network

While it seems obvious when stated in a book, many developers of distributed programs make the cardinal error of ignoring the unreliable and potentially insecure network between the client and server. Even today when nearly every Web user has learned to expect a Web site outage and refuses to enter credit card information except on a secure site, it's all too easy to overlook these issues. It's not that programmers are careless, but in many cases, it is difficult to spot all the potential failure scenarios.

Consider writing an Internet banking application, which, for simplicity, only allows customers to deposit money. Every programmer should see that the deposit needs to run in a transaction to ensure that the account update is atomic and durable. Customers will not accept balance mistakes or lost deposits. However, there are also new failure cases in a distributed application. Some of these failure cases are handled automatically by the transaction infrastructure. For instance, if the server machine or the database dies during the transaction, a rollback returns the customer's original balance. Of course, the client would see an error message. This is undesirable, but customers can try their deposit again later.

Now consider the case where the deposit completes, the transaction commits, but the network fails during the communication with the client. In this case, the client again sees an error message, but in fact, the transaction has completed and the deposit is in the account. In this case, an unsuspecting customer might try the deposit again, not realizing that the previous transaction had in fact completed.

Distributed programs must consider the potential for failure during any point in the communication path. Sometimes the only reasonable answer is to display a message asking the user or system administrator to access the transaction logs and determine the current state.

Distributed programs must consider the potential for failure at any point in the communication path.

Performance Implications of Cross-Network Method Calls

Another common distributed programming error is to neglect the performance overhead of making method calls across the network. Local method calls are a relatively cheap operation, but remote calls are usually at least 100 times slower.

Remote calls are much slower than local calls.

There are two main problems with the performance of remote method calls: network bandwidth and latency. RMI calls send method parameters across the network connection to the server. Thus, the amount of network traffic depends on the size of the method parameters. Local Java calls do not have this issue because objects are passed by reference: Only a pointer is actually passed from the caller into the method. RMI calls with large parameters might work fine on a fast local network, but on the Internet, network bandwidth becomes a real issue. Clients connecting from throughout the world across congested networks can see very poor performance if large amounts of data need to be transferred between the client and server.

Remote calls must consider the amount of data sent across networks, especially in WAN environments.

In addition to minimizing the data sent across the network connection, distributed applications must also be concerned with the frequency of remote method calls. Local method calls are relatively inexpensive, and most Java programs make thousands—if not millions—of method calls per second. Remote method calls across a network wire cannot achieve this level of performance. Programmers need to make this distinction and, where possible, minimize the number of round trips between the RMI client and server. One common pattern is to avoid calling fine-grained methods on a remote object. For instance, a customer might be a remote object. Instead of making individual remote calls to read the customer's name, address, and phone number, the distributed application should make a single remote call that returns all the required information in one network round trip.

Avoid frequent, fine-grained calls to remote objects.

WebLogic RMI Optimizations

In many cases, an RMI client and server are located on the same WebLogic Server. This is very common because all communication with EJBs is via RMI. If a servlet needs to call an EJB, it is making an RMI call although both components might run in the same WebLogic Server. Because this is a common case, the WebLogic Server includes optimizations to make these calls run nearly as fast as direct method calls. Obviously, there is no point in having the client and server communicate over a network connection so the WebLogic RMI implementation recognizes that the client and server are co-located and no network communication is required.

Take advantage of WebLogic's RMI optimizations by co-locating components.

The WebLogic Server also includes a co-location optimization where the client's call skips the RMI infrastructure and calls directly on the implementation object. This optimization makes the RMI call's performance comparable to a local method call. However, programmers should be aware that because the call is skipping marshaling and unmarshaling, the client and server are using call by reference. While this optimization is a departure from RMI's parameter passing, the semantics should be familiar to programmers. In fact, call by reference is the calling convention used by local Java method calls.

JNDI: Java's Naming Service

A *naming service* is an integral piece of distributed systems. With the explosion of the Internet, naming services have become commonplace. While computers communicate with raw IP addresses such as *198.137.241.43*, humans prefer symbolic names such as *whitehouse.gov*. Naming is not only a convenience for humans: It also adds a level of indirection. If the user always uses the *whitehouse.gov* name, the mapping of the name to a raw address can change without breaking a client.

The naming service is also *location-independent*. For instance, an email about the latest foreign policy might indicate that more information can be found on *whitehouse.gov*. The name *whitehouse.gov* is independent of the client; anyone can use the name to locate the Web page.

Like the Internet, distributed Java programs require a naming service to locate distributed objects. JavaSoft has defined the JNDI as Java's standard naming service. JNDI enables servers to host objects at specified names. Remote clients can perform a lookup in the JNDI service and receive a reference to the specified object.

The JNDI architecture consists of a common client interface and a set of JNDI providers that define the back-end naming system. JavaSoft defines an SPI interface through which new JNDI providers can be plugged into the JNDI system. Implementing a JNDI provider is not terribly difficult, but it is beyond the scope of this book. Instead, we cover the WebLogic implementation of JNDI and how a user program makes use of the JNDI system.

Using JNDI

A JNDI client interacts with the JNDI system through the classes in the `javax.naming` package. The `javax.naming.Context` interface is the fundamental JNDI object. The Context interface has methods for a client to add, remove, and look up objects in the naming service.

The `javax.naming.InitialContext` class implements the Context interface. Clients use this class to interact with the JNDI system. Clients create an `InitialContext` object with the code snippet:

```
Context ctx = new InitialContext();
```

When the `InitialContext` method is created in the WebLogic server, the caller receives an `InitialContext` that references the JNDI service on the local server. Remote clients can also create `InitialContext` references, but a client must let the JNDI client know the location of the WebLogic Server. One way to accomplish this is to explicitly pass a `Proper-ties` object to the `InitialContext` constructor:

```
java.util.Properties p = new java.util.Properties();  p.put(Con-
text.INITIAL_CONTEXT_FACTORY,            "weblogic.jndi.WLInitial-
ContextFactory");  p.put(Context.PROVIDER_URL, "t3://
revere:7001");

Context ctx = new InitialContext(p);
```

In this example, we create a `Properties` object, specify that WebLogic Server is the JNDI provider, and give the URL to the server. For example, in this case we are creating a connection to the machine named "revere" on port 7001.

It is important to note that the PROVIDER_URL *should only be set when connecting to a naming service that is not running in the local Java virtual machine (JVM).*

For instance, a client that is connecting to a WebLogic Server uses the PROVIDER_URL *to indicate which WebLogic Server or cluster to use. It is also possible for a WebLogic Server to be a client of another WebLogic Server or another JNDI provider.*

This commonly occurs when a servlet engine looks up EJBs deployed in another WebLogic Server instance. When the JNDI lookup occurs in the servlet engine, it will provide the PROVIDER_URL *of the target EJB server.*

However, the PROVIDER_URL *should not be specified when code running in the server is connecting to the local naming service. The* PROVIDER_URL *indicates that a network connection should be made. This is unnecessary when the naming service is running within the same WebLogic Server instance as the calling code. Also, server-side code such as WebLogic start-up classes run before the server has begun listening for network connections. Server-side code should use* new InitialContext () *to connect to the local naming service.*

It is also possible for clients to use the default constructor to gain InitialContexts, for example:

```
Context ctx = new InitialContext();
```

In this case, the client needs to specify the provider and URL with other methods. One option is to define the Java properties on the command line with:

```
-Djava.naming.factory.initial=weblogic.jndi.WLInitialContextFac-
tory
```

and

```
-Djava.naming.provider.url="t3://revere:7001"
```

Another possibility is to specify the factory and the URL in a jndi.properties file. This properties file is a Java resource file. For instance, our jndi.properties file would contain:

```
java.naming.factory.initial=weblogic.jndi.WLInitialContextFacto-
ryjava.naming.provider.url="t3://revere:7001"
```

In general, it is preferable to use the default *InitialContext* constructor in all cases. For stand-alone clients, the `jndi.properties` file is the preferred method to specify the attributes.

With the `InitialContext` object, the JNDI client can store objects in the naming system. Like RMI parameters, an object stored in JNDI must either implement `java.io.Serializable` or `java.rmi.Remote`. The bind method of the `InitialContext` object is used to establish a name to object mapping in the JNDI tree. For instance, this example binds a `String` object to the name `"Chapter6"`.

```
Context ctx = new InitialContext();
String s = "Test String.";
ctx.bind("Chapter6", s);
```

The bind call establishes a mapping between the name `Chapter6` and our string. Clients can now look up the name `Chapter6` in the WebLogic Server's JNDI system and receive a copy of our string. The bind call fails if an object named `"Chapter 6"` already exists in this JNDI tree.

The rebind call can be used to reassign an already existing name. If there is no current mapping for the given name, rebind behaves like bind.

```
Context ctx = new InitialContext();
String s = "New Test String.";
ctx.rebind("Chapter6", s);
```

Mappings can be deleted with the unbind method. For instance, the following code fragment removes the object we just bound:

```
ctx.unbind("Chapter6");
```

A client uses the `InitialContext`'s lookup method to get a reference to an object in the naming service. For instance, after our call to bind there is a mapping from the name `"Chapter6"` to our string. The client can get a reference to this object with:

```
Context ctx = new InitialContext();
String s = (String) ctx.lookup("Chapter6");
```

Because `java.lang.String` is a serializable object, the client receives a copy of the bound object. If this had been an RMI object, the client would have received a stub.

JNDI, Security, and Identity

In addition to providing an object naming service, JNDI also establishes a client's identity within the server. By default, `InitialContexts` are created by the guest user. When an `InitialContext` is made, the client can specify a user name and password, and the WebLogic security system authenticates the user password combination. If the password is invalid, a `javax.naming.NoPermissionException` is thrown to the client. With a valid password, the user establishes an identity with the server.

Many resources in the WebLogic Server can be protected by Access Control Lists (ACLs). These resources may only be accessed by appropriate users. Creating an `InitialContext` with a user name and password effectively switches the client identity to the user name. For instance, this example establishes the identity of `"Paul"` within the server:

```
Properties p = new Properties();      // Set WebLogic as the JNDI
Provider  p.put(Context.INITIAL_CONTEXT_FACTORY,
"weblogic.jndi.WLInitialContextFactory");

// Set the URL to machine named revere, port 7001

p.put(Context.PROVIDER_URL, "t3://revere:7001");

// Login as user Paul
p.put(Context.SECURITY_PRINCIPAL, "Paul");

// and the password
p.put(Context.SECURITY_CREDENTIALS, "Bee");

Context ctx = new InitialContext(p);
```

JNDI and Clustering

From the client's perspective, a WebLogic cluster should appear as one high-performance and fault-tolerant server. This idea carries over to the WebLogic cluster's shared JNDI naming service. The naming service is fault-tolerant because the naming service survives server failures in the cluster. As new servers join the cluster, they automatically participate in the naming service. The naming service is high-performance because each server runs the naming service in parallel, and client requests can be processed on many servers simultaneously.

Replicated Naming Service

Each WebLogic Server maintains its own copy of the cluster's naming service. The advantage of this approach is performance. Each naming service is able to locally cache the cluster's naming tree and handle any naming request out of its own memory. This approach also provides transparency. To a client, a naming service is identical regardless of which clustered server is contacted. However, any distributed caching mechanism brings with it the issue of cache coherency. Whenever a change occurs in the JNDI tree, the other servers must be notified. For instance, when a new object is bound into the JNDI tree at a given name, every naming service must be made aware of the new mapping (see Figure 6–2).

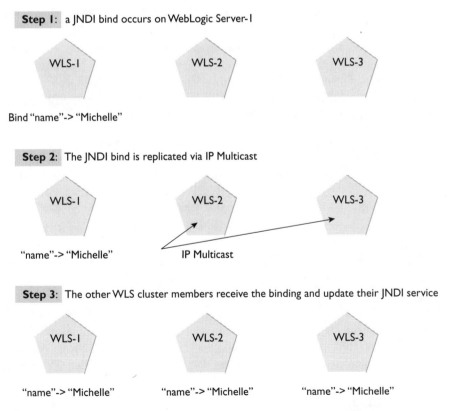

Step 1: a JNDI bind occurs on WebLogic Server-1

WLS-1   WLS-2   WLS-3

Bind "name"-> "Michelle"

Step 2: The JNDI bind is replicated via IP Multicast

WLS-1   WLS-2   WLS-3

"name"-> "Michelle"   IP Multicast

Step 3: The other WLS cluster members receive the binding and update their JNDI service

WLS-1   WLS-2   WLS-3

"name"-> "Michelle"   "name"-> "Michelle"   "name"-> "Michelle"

Figure 6–2   Cluster with Replicated Naming Service Propagating Changes

WebLogic maintains the cluster-wide service through network updates. Each clustered WebLogic server sends its JNDI updates over multicast to the other cluster members. IP multicast enables a single message to be delivered to a number of receivers, in this case all the servers in the cluster. For tightly coupled clusters, this is much more efficient because updating *n* other servers requires a single network message rather than the *n* messages required by point-to-point connections.

JNDI changes are sent to other cluster members with IP multicast.

When a clustered server receives a JNDI change from another server, it updates its local cached copy of the JNDI tree. It is possible for the update to conflict with another object in the cached copy of the JNDI tree. We discuss how this is possible, and suggest solutions, in a later section.

WebLogic Server's clustered naming service is designed for high performance and to minimize network traffic between servers. Because each server is caching the clustered naming tree, it is possible for the cache to be slightly out of date. In this case, an update has occurred on one server but has not yet reached another server's cache. In general, this is not an issue. Because JNDI is a naming service, it is used to advertise services and objects residing on particular servers. JNDI updates are only sent when a JNDI bind, rebind, or unbind occurs within the cluster. These changes in the JNDI tree are relatively rare, and network traffic and coherency are not very frequently an issue with the WebLogic Server's JNDI implementation.

Understanding Conflicts in the JNDI tree

RMI objects can be compiled as clustered RMI objects or nonclustered objects. There is no change in the RMI code. It merely determines the behavior of the RMI stub used by the RMI subsystem. A clustered RMI object must not store any client-associated state. Many of the WebLogic subsystems (including stateless session EJBs) default to clustered RMI objects.

When an object is bound into the JNDI tree on a WebLogic Server, the WebLogic JNDI service enables the user to specify whether this binding should be replicated to the other clustered servers. By default, bindings are replicated, and the WebLogic Server will send a multicast message to the cluster members. It is also possible to specify that a binding should not be replicated. We will see why this might be desirable in a moment. Nonreplicated bindings must be selected before the `InitialContext` is created.

```
Environment env = new Environment();
env.setReplicateBindings(false);
Context ctx = env.getInitialContext();
```

Clustered JNDI with Replicated Bindings

By default, the WebLogic JNDI service replicates bindings to the other servers within the cluster. The semantics of replicated bindings depends on whether the RMI object is clustered or nonclustered.

Clustered RMI objects are aggregated in the JNDI tree. When a clustered object is bound into the JNDI tree, its server is added to the list of servers offering that service. As long as every server binds in the same type, every server can offer a clustered object under a given name. This enables the WebLogic cluster to map a single JNDI name to a service offered by multiple cluster members.

Clustered objects are aggregated in the JNDI tree.

Unlike clustered RMI objects, nonclustered RMI objects do not aggregate in the JNDI tree. When replicated bindings are used, a nonclustered object may not be bound to the same name on multiple servers. This condition is known as a conflict, and will be detected by the WebLogic Servers and an error will be printed to the system log. JNDI conflicts indicate that the WebLogic Servers have been misconfigured.

With replicated bindings, only a single server may bind a nonclustered object to a given name. JNDI conflicts are configuration errors and must be resolved manually by the WebLogic Server administrator.

Clustered JNDI with Nonreplicated Bindings

When the JNDI context is created without replicated bindings, the WebLogic Server will not send a multicast update when the JNDI bind occurs. Nonreplicated bindings can be useful to avoid JNDI conflicts. For instance, an application might read configuration details into a `Properties` object and bind the `Properties` object into the JNDI tree. Because this is not a clustered RMI object, there would be a JNDI conflict if multiple servers attempted to bind their `Properties` to the same name. With nonreplicated bindings, each server binds its own copy of the `Properties` object. Since there are no multicast updates, there will be no conflict in the JNDI service.

With nonreplicated bindings, each server may bind its own copy of a nonclustered service without receiving a JNDI conflict.

JNDI Best Practices

As with any distributed program, JNDI clients need to be aware of efficiency concerns to ensure high performance and scalability. Like RMI calls, the WebLogic Server optimizes JNDI lookups from code running in the server's JVM when they are performed. A lookup within the WebLogic Server is a very efficient operation. In essence, it amounts to a direct method call and a data structure lookup. JNDI clients running within the server should not generally bother to optimize their usage of the naming service.

JNDI lookups within the WebLogic Server are highly optimized.

However, remote clients should consider optimizing (minimizing) the number of round trips between the client and server. Like any remote interaction, each naming service lookup must travel across the network connection between client and server. If lookups are performed repeatedly, this can be a performance bottleneck.

Every JNDI lookup across the network is a remote method call.

Local Caching

One alternative, where appropriate, is to locally cache the results of a lookup. For instance, JNDI might be used to store a remote object containing some runtime properties. Instead of accessing this object repeatedly to read individual configuration properties, a client could look up the object once and read in all the properties to a local object. Any further accesses would use the local object. Caching the results of JNDI lookups needs to be used judiciously. Obviously, it requires that the data not be subject to frequent change.

Consider local caching to avoid repeated JNDI lookups from remote clients.

Using JNDI Effectively to Increase Performance

While JNDI lookups within the WebLogic Server are highly optimized, there is some overhead when an `InitialContext` is created or a JNDI lookup is performed. There are a number of common JNDI usage patterns that provide better performance and scalability.

Note that, in general, servlets should not store objects in member variables. Unless the single-threaded model is chosen, multiple threads may access a servlet concurrently, and member variables could be accessed in multiple threads. Using a `DataSource` or an `InitialContext` is thread-safe and may be performed by multiple threads concurrently.

Perform as many JNDI lookups as possible during component initialization. For instance, it is much better to look up a JDBC `DataSource` in a JSP's `init()` method and store it in a member variable rather than performing a JNDI lookup on every page hit. The service method then uses the `DataSource` member variable to get its JDBC connection. EJBs can perform these lookups in the `setSessionContext`, `setEntityContext`, or `setMessageDrivenContext` methods.

Use JNDI during component initialization.

Some components may still require JNDI lookups in the service method or the EJB's business methods. For instance, a servlet might retrieve a different `DataSource` depending on which user accesses the page. Unless the number of `DataSources` is very small and static, they cannot all be stored in member variables. In this case, it is still worthwhile to store the `InitialContext` in a member variable. This does not consume any resources in the server (other than the member variable) and, within the server, creating `InitialContext` references is more expensive than performing JNDI lookups to the local naming service. With remote clients, the JNDI lookup is more expensive because each lookup must travel across the network wire to the server.

If lookups cannot be performed during initialization, cache the `InitialContext` in a member variable.

Minimizing Frequency of Updates

Another aspect of building high-performance JNDI programs is recognizing that, at its core, JNDI is merely a naming service. JNDI should be used to provide names to objects so distributed clients can access them. JNDI is not a suitable place to store arbitrary data and to make frequent updates. Remember that in WebLogic clusters, each WebLogic Server instance maintains its own instance of the cluster-wide naming tree.

Any change in the naming tree needs to be sent over multicast to the other clustered servers. It is important to recognize that this mechanism is intended for keeping the naming service coherent. For instance, it would be inappropriate to have an RMI call add information to the JNDI tree on every method call. Each JNDI update would be added to the server's periodic update message. This would quickly lead to very large JNDI updates being sent between servers.

JNDI should not be used to store out-of-band data.

Conclusion

RMI and JNDI are core services offered by the WebLogic Server to enable scalable distributed applications. While RMI and JNDI make distributed programming much easier, it is important to understand the many failure cases in networked applications. As we see in the following chapters, core J2EE services such as EJB and Java Message Service (JMS) are built on top of RMI and JNDI.

ENTERPRISE MESSAGING WITH THE JAVA MESSAGE SERVICE (JMS)

In this chapter:

- The fundamentals of JMS, describing and illustrating both point-to-point and publish-and-subscribe messaging

- JMS queuing mechanisms for point-to-point messaging, with examples

- JMS topic creation for publish-and-subscribe messaging, with examples

- Configuring JMS messages

- JMS and transactions

- How JMS works in a WebLogic Server cluster

- JMS exception handling

- Best practices for using JMS in WebLogic Server applications

Chapter 7

The Java Message Service (JMS) provides a standard enterprise messaging service for Java 2 Enterprise Edition (J2EE) applications. JMS acts as an intelligent switchboard for routing messages among application components and processes in a distributed application. JMS queues messages and can deliver them asynchronously: Messaging need not take place in real time; and messages can be sent and consumed at different times.

Benefits of JMS

There are a number of reasons to use a messaging system for interprocess communication instead of making direct method calls. A messaging system provides a clean way to connect disparate systems within an application. Messaging systems also help divide long-running work into multiple transactions for greater efficiency. When communication is asynchronous, the client need not wait for all of the processing to complete.

Messaging systems also provide reliability. JMS can optionally save a message to a persistent store. There is, however, a trade-off between reliability and performance. The messaging system runs faster if messages are not persistent, but the application must tolerate lost messages in the event of a server crash. Messaging systems also enable clients to disconnect and reconnect to the server without losing work. JMS can be configured to save messages while the client is disconnected and deliver them once the client has reconnected. Unlike method calls on a single object, JMS allows sending a single message to many recipients.

Interprocess Communication

Most large systems are divided into several separate functional units. JMS provides reliable communication between these separate processes. For instance, an e-commerce application might include a Web front-end for customer order entry. A warehouse then receives the order, packages the appropriate items, and forwards the order to the shipping department. Finally, the shipping department sends the package and updates the customer's account records.

JMS provides the communication backbone for workflow applications.

Point-to-Point Messaging

The order fulfillment application uses JMS's point-to-point (PTP) messaging model to provide reliable communication within this multi-stage application. In PTP communication, JMS delivers each message to a single message consumer. For instance, in this application, the Web front-end sends a message including the new order information. A single warehouse receives the message and processes the order. The message system guarantees that multiple warehouses do not fill the same order. This application also uses JMS's reliability guarantees. Because customer orders are important information that should be retained, the developer will request JMS to mark these messages as persistent. With persistent messages, JMS saves the message contents to a persistent storage such as a database or file store.

Publish/Subscribe Messaging

In addition to PTP communication, JMS provides a publish-and-subscribe messaging model. With publish/subscribe messaging (also known as pub/sub), a message is sent to a named *topic*. There might be multiple message listeners subscribed to each topic. The JMS subsystem delivers a copy of the message to each of the topic's subscribers. For instance, an e-commerce site might define a frequent-customer topic. When a customer makes several purchases, a message is sent to this topic. The site can then send "special deals" messages to a select group of listeners, the frequent customers. Because there might be several message listeners, each offering a separate special deal, it is appropriate to use pub/sub instead of PTP communication.

JMS Fundamentals

The JMS specification defines both PTP and pub/sub APIs. A JMS Server can implement one or both of these APIs. The WebLogic Server's JMS implementation includes both the PTP and pub/sub APIs.

The JMS APIs define a set of fundamental objects. Each object is separately defined in the PTP and pub/sub domains, but their function is nearly identical in both domains.

Connection Factories

Connection factories are created by the server administrator and bound into the Java Naming and Directory Interface (JNDI) tree. A JMS client uses JNDI to look up the `ConnectionFactory` and then uses the `ConnectionFactory` to establish a JMS connection. The PTP connection factory is `javax.jms.QueueConnectionFactory` while the pub/sub domain uses `javax.jms.TopicConnectionFactory`.

The WebLogic Server binds a standard connection factory with the name `weblogic.jms.ConnectionFactory`. It also is possible to define additional connection factories with the WebLogic Server's Administration Console. An application uses a user-defined `ConnectionFactory` if needed to impose additional security constraints on the `ConnectionFactory`.

Connections

A JMS connection represents the active connection between the JMS client and the WebLogic Server. The JMS client creates the JMS connection by calling the `createQueueConnection` or the `createTopicConnection` methods on the `ConnectionFactory`. A JMS connection is a relatively heavyweight object and normally each client uses a single JMS connection. Each JMS connection can be associated with many JMS destinations. The PTP connection is `javax.jms.QueueConnection` while the pub/sub connection is `javax.jms.TopicConnection`.

Sessions

The JMS session represents a client's conversational state with a JMS Server. A session is created from the JMS connection, and it represents a single thread of conversation between a JMS client and server. Sessions define message ordering, and JMS uses sessions for transactional messaging. The PTP model uses `javax.jms.QueueSession` while the pub/sub model uses `javax.jms.TopicSession`.

Destinations

JMS destinations are the actual messaging resource. PTP messaging defines `javax.jms.Queue` while pub/sub includes `javax.jms.Topic`. The server administrator uses the WebLogic Console to create destinations with a specified JNDI name. The JMS client then performs a JNDI lookup to locate the JMS destination.

Table 7.1 compares the terminology for PTP and pub/sub APIs.

Table 7.1 Comparing PTP and Pub/Sub APIs

	PTP	*Pub/Sub*
Connection Factory	QueueConnectionFactory	TopicConnectionFactory
Connection	QueueConnection	TopicConnection
Session	QueueSession	TopicSession
Destination	Queue	Topic

Sample JMS Queue Producer/ Consumer

This section demonstrates simple JMS PTP and pub/sub message producers and consumers.

Configuring JMS

First, create a folder to use as a JMS file store in the file system. Create a folder called *jms_store* at the root level of your WebLogic Server installation.

Then, configure the JMS file store using the WebLogic Server Administration Console. Figure 7–1 shows a JMS store named "MyJMSFileStore" that is mapped to the directory *jms_store*.

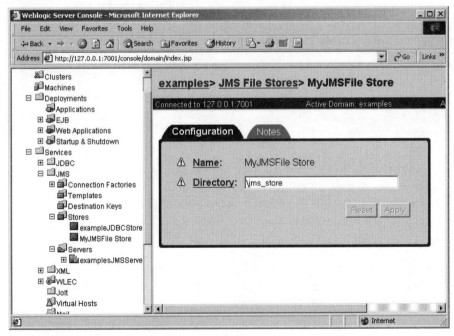

Figure 7-1   Creating the JMS Store

Creating the JMS Server

Next, the WebLogic Server administrator configures a JMS Server with the Administration Console. All JMS-administered objects such as destinations or connection factories exist within a JMS Server. Each WebLogic Server instance can include multiple JMS Server instances. Because these examples use persistent messages, the server administrator has specified a backing store, the file-based storage previously created (see Figure 7–2).

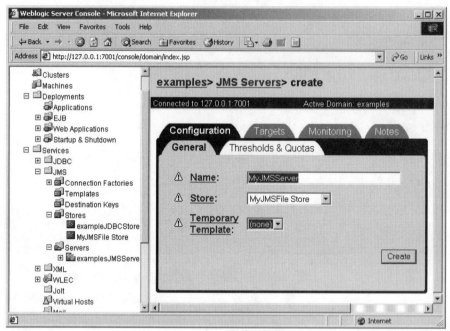

Figure 7–2   Creating the JMS Server

The server administrator can also create JMS connection factories at this time. Because these examples do not require any special configuration parameters, we can use the standard connection factories.

Administrator Creates JMS Destinations

After configuring the JMS Server, the server administrator creates the JMS destinations. These examples require a JMS queue named `MessageQueue` and a JMS topic named `MessageTopic` (see Figure 7–3).

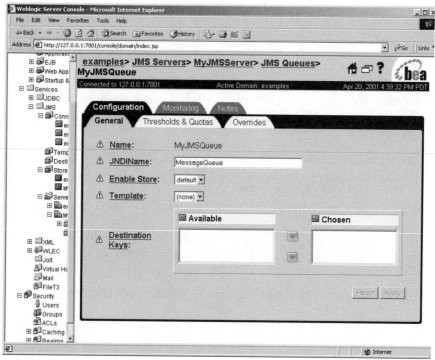

Figure 7-3   Creating a JMS Queue

Sample JMS Queue Producer/Consumer

This example demonstrates a message producer, a synchronous message consumer, and an asynchronous message consumer for a JMS queue.

Message Producer

The message producer begins by creating a JNDI `InitialContext` and looking up the JMS `QueueConnectionFactory`. Because our examples use the standard JMS connection factories, it looks up `"weblogic.jms.ConnectionFactory"`.

```
Context ctx = getInitialContext();
QueueConnectionFactory qConFactory =
      (QueueConnectionFactory)
      ctx.lookup("weblogic.jms.ConnectionFactory");
```

Now the `MessageProducer` looks up the JMS destination in JNDI. The server administrator created the JMS queue with the JNDI name "MessageQueue". The WebLogic Server binds the queue into the JNDI tree, making it available to clients.

```
Queue messageQueue = (Queue) ctx.lookup("MessageQueue");
```

The message producer now creates the QueueConnection and a QueueSession. The parameters to the createQueueSession call specify that it is nontransacted and uses automatic message acknowledgment. Using transactions with JMS and message acknowledgment are covered later in this chapter.

```
QueueConnection qCon = qConFactory.createQueueConnection();

 QueueSession session = qCon.createQueueSession(
    false, /* not a transacted session */
    Session.AUTO_ACKNOWLEDGE
 );
```

Finally, the message producer creates a sender and a JMS message. This message is a TextMessage and will include only a string.

```
sender = session.createSender(messageQueue);

msg = session.createTextMessage();
```

The message producer is now prepared to send messages. The TextMessage's setText method attaches our Hello string to the message. The QueueSender's send method sends our message to the persistent queue. When the send call returns, the message producer may send another message.

```
msg.setText("Hello");
sender.send(msg);
```

Synchronous Message Consumer

The message consumer begins with an initialization code that is nearly identical to the message producer. The QueueConnectionFactory and queue are found in JNDI. Next, a QueueConnection and QueueSession are created.

```
Context ctx = getInitialContext();

 QueueConnectionFactory qConFactory = (QueueConnectionFactory)
    ctx.lookup("weblogic.jms.ConnectionFactory");

 Queue messageQueue = (Queue) ctx.lookup("MessageQueue");

 QueueConnection qCon = qConFactory.createQueueConnection();
```

```
QueueSession session = qCon.createQueueSession(
    false, /* not a transacted session */
    Session.AUTO_ACKNOWLEDGE
);
```

The message consumer next creates a `QueueReceiver` from the `QueueSession`. Finally, the start method is called on the `QueueConnection`. Message delivery is inhibited until the start method is invoked. This allows a message consumer to finish initialization before messages become available.

```
receiver = session.createReceiver(messageQueue);

qCon.start();
```

A synchronous message consumer uses the `receive()` method to ask JMS for the next message on this destination. The receive method blocks until a message is available on this destination. This client then uses the `TextMessage`'s `getText` method to retrieve the message string and prints it to the screen.

```
msg = (TextMessage) receiver.receive();

System.err.println("Received: "+msg.getText());
```

Asynchronous Message Consumer

The asynchronous message consumer begins with the same set of initialization code as a synchronous message consumer.

```
Context ctx = getInitialContext();

    QueueConnectionFactory qConFactory = (QueueConnectionFactory)
        ctx.lookup("weblogic.jms.ConnectionFactory");

    Queue messageQueue = (Queue) ctx.lookup("MessageQueue");

    QueueConnection qCon = qConFactory.createQueueConnection();

    QueueSession session = qCon.createQueueSession(
        false, /* not a transacted session */
        Session.AUTO_ACKNOWLEDGE
    );

    receiver = session.createReceiver(messageQueue);
```

An asynchronous message consumer must use the receiver's `setMessageListener` method and pass an object that implements the `javax.jms.MessageListener` interface. Finally, the `QueueConnection`'s start method begins message delivery.

```
receiver.setMessageListener(this);
```

```
qCon.start();
```

Because this is an asynchronous consumer, the JMS implementation delivers messages by calling the `onMessage` method. This simple implementation just prints out the message's text and returns.

```
public void onMessage(Message m) {
    TextMessage msg = (TextMessage) m;

    System.err.println("Received: "+msg.getText());
}
```

Because message delivery is asynchronous, the client program is not blocked, waiting for messages to arrive. And, because our simple example program has no other work to perform, it exits before the messages can be delivered. To prevent this, we introduce an artificial wait to ensure that the program does not exit before the producer's messages are delivered.

Running the Queue Example

This example resides in the *examples/ch7/queue* directory on the accompanying CD-ROM. You can run the example from that directory.

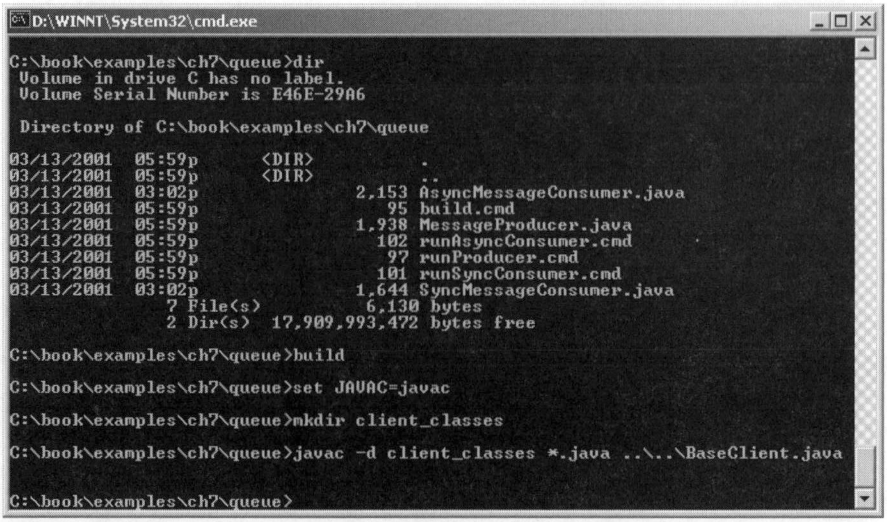

Figure 7–4 Listing of the Queue Examples Directory

Before running the queue example, the WebLogic Server's JMS implementation must be configured. This example requires a JMS Server to be created with the Administration Console. Next, a JMS queue with the JNDI name of "MessageQueue" must be created. See the preceding examples or the WebLogic Server documentation for more information on creating and configuring JMS Servers.

The example can be built with the supplied *build.cmd* script for Windows NT or Windows 2000. UNIX users will need to modify the script to fit their environment. There also are *runProducer.cmd*, *runSyncConsumer.cmd*, and *runAsyncConsumer.cmd* scripts to run the message producer, synchronous consumer, and asynchronous consumer examples.

Open a command window and execute the *runProducer.cmd* script.

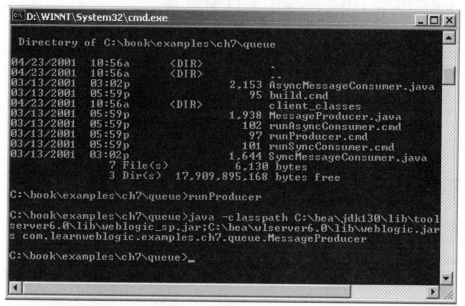

Figure 7–5 Running the runProducer Script

In another command window, run the runAsyncConsumer script. You can see in Figure 7–6 that the messages were received successfully.

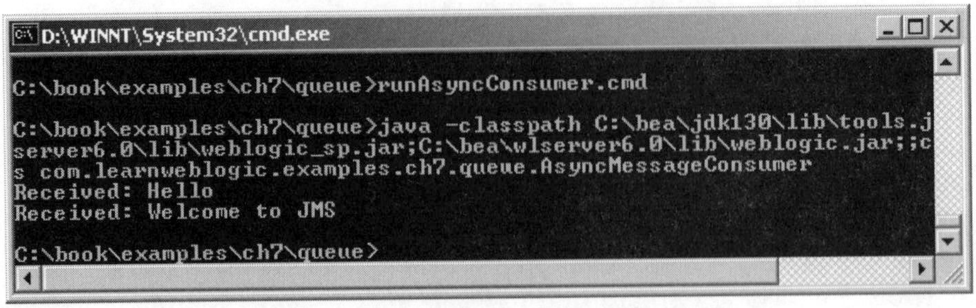

Figure 7-6 Results of Running the runAsyncConsumer Script

Sample JMS Topic Producer/ Consumer

The JMS topic example demonstrates publishing messages to a "Message-Topic" and synchronous and asynchronous message consumers. Because this is a topic, both consumers can run simultaneously and receive each message.

Message Producer

Like the JMS queue examples, the topic message producer begins by using JNDI to look up the ConnectionFactory and JMS destination. This example uses the standard JMS ConnectionFactory, so it looks up "weblogic.jms.ConnectionFactory".

```
Context ctx = getInitialContext();

TopicConnectionFactory tConFactory = (TopicConnectionFactory)
    ctx.lookup("weblogic.jms.ConnectionFactory");

Topic messageTopic = (Topic) ctx.lookup("MessageTopic");

TopicConnection tCon = tConFactory.createTopicConnection();

TopicSession session = tCon.createTopicSession(
    false, /* not a transacted session */
    Session.AUTO_ACKNOWLEDGE
);
```

A topic message producer creates a TopicPublisher instead of a QueueSender and uses this object to publish messages to the topic.

```
publisher = session.createPublisher(messageTopic);

msg = session.createTextMessage();

msg.setText("Hello");
publisher.publish(msg);
```

Synchronous Message Consumer

The topic's synchronous message consumer begins with the standard JMS initialization code.

```
Context ctx = getInitialContext();

 TopicConnectionFactory tConFactory = (TopicConnectionFactory)
     ctx.lookup("javax.jms.TopicConnectionFactory");

 Topic messageTopic = (Topic) ctx.lookup("MessageTopic");

 TopicConnection tCon = tConFactory.createTopicConnection();

 TopicSession session = tCon.createTopicSession(
     false, /* not a transacted session */
     Session.AUTO_ACKNOWLEDGE
   );
```

A topic consumer creates a `TopicSubscriber` object from the JMS session. The `TopicSubscriber` is then used to receive messages.

```
subscriber = session.createSubscriber(messageTopic);

tCon.start();

msg = (TextMessage) subscriber.receive();

System.err.println("Received: "+msg.getText());
```

Asynchronous Message Consumer

The asynchronous topic consumer begins with the standard JMS initialization code to find the `ConnectionFactory` and topic, and creates the `TopicSession` and `TopicSubscriber`. Because this is an asynchronous consumer, the client must call the subscriber's `setMessageListener` method.

```
Context ctx = getInitialContext();
```

```
TopicConnectionFactory tConFactory = (TopicConnectionFactory)
  ctx.lookup("weblogic.jms.ConnectionFactory");

Topic messageTopic = (Topic) ctx.lookup("MessageTopic");

TopicConnection tCon = tConFactory.createTopicConnection();

TopicSession session = tCon.createTopicSession(
  false, /* not a transacted session */
  Session.AUTO_ACKNOWLEDGE
);

subscriber = session.createSubscriber(messageTopic);

subscriber.setMessageListener(this);

tCon.start();
```

The JMS implementation delivers messages asynchronously to the
onMessage method. This simple client prints out the text message and
returns.

```
public void onMessage(Message m) {

    TextMessage msg = (TextMessage) m;

    System.err.println("Received: "+msg.getText());

}
```

Running the Topic Example

This example resides in the *examples/ch7/topic* directory on the accompanying CD-ROM.

Before running the topic example, the WebLogic Server's JMS implementation must be configured. This example requires a JMS Server to be created with the Administration Console. Next, a JMS topic with the JNDI name of "MessageTopic" must be created. See the preceding examples or the WebLogic Server documentation for more information on creating and configuring JMS Servers (see Figure 7–7).

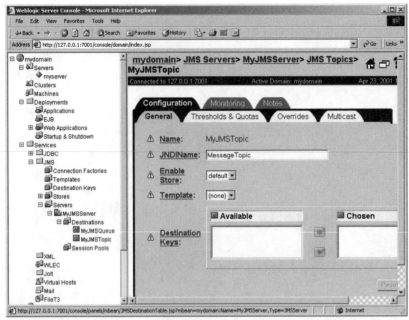

Figure 7-7 Configuring the JMS Topic

The example can be built with the supplied *build.cmd* script for Windows NT or Windows 2000. UNIX users will need to modify the script to fit their environment. There also are *runProducer.cmd*, *runSyncConsumer.cmd*, and *runAsyncConsumer.cmd* scripts to run the message producer, synchronous consumer, and asynchronous consumer examples.

In a command window, build the example and run the runProducer script (see Figure 7–8).

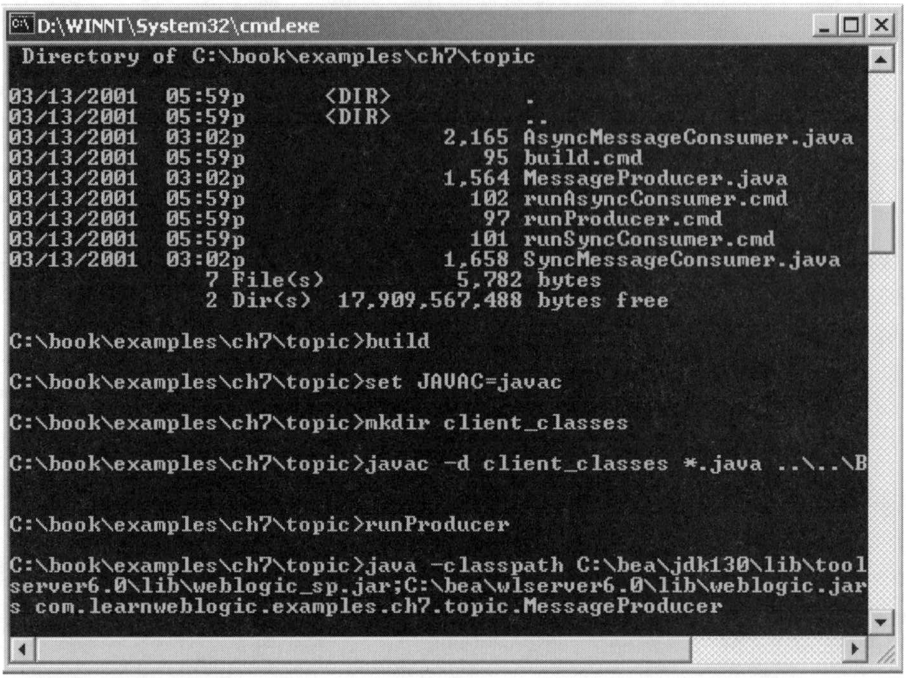

Figure 7–8   Running the runProducer Script

Open a command window and run the runSyncConsumer script. As Figure 7–9 shows, the messages were received successfully.

```
D:\WINNT\System32\cmd.exe                                    _ □ ×

C:\book\examples\ch7\topic>runSyncConsumer

C:\book\examples\ch7\topic>java -classpath C:\bea\jdk130\lib\tools.j
server6.0\lib\weblogic_sp.jar;C:\bea\wlserver6.0\lib\weblogic.jar;;c
s com.learnweblogic.examples.ch7.topic.SyncMessageConsumer
Received: Hello
Received: Welcome to JMS

C:\book\examples\ch7\topic>
```

Figure 7–9   Running the runSyncConsumer Script

JMS Messages

While our simple examples only exchange string messages, there are several possible JMS message types. Every JMS message type is a subclass of `javax.jms.Message`. The different message types merely dictate the type of the message contents.

A JMS message consists of a header, a set of properties, and the message body.

JMS Header

The JMS header includes a standard set of fields defined in the JMS specification. The `javax.jms.Message` type includes a `get` and `set` method for each of the JMS header fields. The header fields are named metadata values used by the application to provide further information about the message.

The JMS header fields provide extra information about the JMS message. Many of the fields contain basic information about the message, and these are commonly used to filter messages. This is done in JMS with selectors and is covered in detail later in this chapter.

JMS header fields also can be used by the application code. For instance, the `JMSReplyTo` can be used by the application programmer for a request/response application. The sender sets the `JMSReplyTo` header field to a response JMS destination. When the consumer receives the message, a response is sent to the `ReplyTo` destination (see Table 7.2).

Table 7.2 The JMS Header Fields

Name	*Set by*	*Description*
JMSDestination	Send Method	The JMSDestination includes the destination name where the message was sent. The WebLogic Server sets it automatically after the send() method completes.
JMSDeliveryMode	Send Method	The JMSDeliveryMode specifies whether this is a persistent or nonpersistent message. A persistent message is stored on a backing store such as a file system or database so that it survives a server crash.

Table 7.2 The JMS Header Fields (continued)

Name	*Set by*	*Description*
JMSExpiration	Send Method	The JMSExpiration defines when the message has expired and will be removed from the system. This field depends on the time-to-live (TTL) specified when the message was sent. By default, messages have a TTL of 0 and a JMSExpiration of 0, which means they will never expire.
JMSPriority	Send Method	The JMSPriority specifies the priority (0–9) of the message. Message priorities from 0–4 indicate normal priority, while priorities from 5–9 are expedited priority. The default priority is 4.
JMSMessageID	Send Method	The JMSMessageID contains a string that uniquely identifies the message. The ID starts with ID: and is generated automatically by the WebLogic Server.
JMSTimestamp	Send Method	The JMSTimestamp is a long value that represents a timestamp of when the message was accepted for delivery by WebLogic's JMS system.

Table 7.2 The JMS Header Fields (continued)

Name	Set by	Description
JMSCorrelationID	Application	The JMSCorrelationID is an arbitrary string that can be set by the application before sending the message. This can be used to correlate requests and responses by storing the JMSMessageID of the request in the JMSCorrelationID of the response. Another common use of this header field is linking several messages together in an application-specific manner. For instance, if an order consisted of multiple messages, the order number could be included in the JMSCorrelationID to allow the consumer to associate all of the messages together with a single order.
JMSReplyTo	Application	The JMSReplyTo header is a JMS destination that the consumer can use to send a response. Note that this field only passes a destination to the consumer; it does not guarantee that the consumer will actually send a response to this destination. This is the responsibility of the application code.
JMSType	Application	The JMSType enables the application to associate this message with a message type. This message type is an arbitrary java.lang.String, and it may be used if applications want to distinguish messages based on an application-specific type.

Table 7.2 The JMS Header Fields (continued)

Name	Set by	Description
JMSRedelivered	WebLogic Server	The JMSRedelivered flag is set when a JMS message is redelivered because the receiver failed to acknowledge the message or because the session is being recovered. Message acknowledgment is covered in detail later in this chapter.

Message Properties

JMS also provides message properties. A JMS message producer can set application-specific property values in the message. The properties are transmitted with the messages and may be read by JMS message consumers.

Properties are name/value pairs and are set with the setObjectProperty or the type-specific setProperty calls on javax.jms.Message. The valid property types are boolean, byte, double, float, int, long, short, and java.lang.String.

For instance, a message producer can set the property named "MyProperty" to the value 4 with:

```
msg.setIntProperty("MyProperty", 4);
```

Properties are useful for associating application-specific metadata with a message. They are generally used for message filtering with JMS selectors. JMS selectors are covered in detail later in this chapter.

Message Types

There are five standard JMS message types, and the WebLogic JMS implementation defines an additional XML message type.

JMS Message Types

Table 7.3 lists the JMS message types.

Table 7.3   JMS Message Types

Message Type	Description
StreamMessage	This message type consists of a serialized stream of objects. The objects must be read from the stream in the order they were written.
MapMessage	A message consisting of name/value pairs. Like a hash table, these are unordered, and each name must be unique within the map.
TextMessage	A message type to hold a string.
ObjectMessage	A message that holds a serialized object.
BytesMessage	A raw stream of bytes. Clients who need complete control over the raw message format use this message type.
XMLMessage	The WebLogic JMS implementation extends the TextMessage type with the XMLMessage to provide optimized delivery and selection of XML messages.

Reusing Message Objects

A JMS Message object can be reused for many messages. When a message is sent, the JMS provider copies the associated message data into an internal buffer before the send call returns control to the caller. Once the send call has returned, the sender can reuse the Message object. This enables the producer to avoid the cost of creating a Message object every time a message is sent.

The message consumer receives a Message object from the JMS Server. The JMS specification prohibits the message receiver from modifying the Message object. To the receiver, the Message object is read-only. This enables the WebLogic JMS implementation to be more efficient because it does not have to copy the message before it delivers it to the consumer.

JMS Delivery Modes

JMS allows messages to be either persistent or nonpersistent. When a persistent message is sent, the JMS implementation saves the message to a backing store such as a database or a file store. The JMS Server ensures that the send does not complete until the message has been saved. Because this message is persistent (it's stored in \jms_store\MyJMSFileStoreXXX.dat), it can survive a system crash. JMS also offers nonpersistent messages. Unlike persistent messages, JMS only keeps nonpersistent messages in memory. If a system crash occurs, all nonpersistent messages are lost.

The choice between persistent and nonpersistent messages is a trade-off between reliability and performance. Nonpersistent messages offer higher performance because no disk writes or database updates are performed. However, nonpersistent messages can be lost in a system crash. Applications that require reliability and durable messages should use persistent messages.

Choose nonpersistent messages when messages do not need to survive a server crash. Choose persistent messages when messages must be delivered at least once.

When the server administrator creates a `ConnectionFactory`, a default delivery mode may be specified. If no delivery mode is specified, the WebLogic JMS implementation defaults to persistent delivery. Any connection created from the `ConnectionFactory` will use the default delivery mode. The JMS client may override the default delivery mode when a message is sent by explicitly passing a delivery mode. For instance:

```
msg.setText("Override for this message");
sender.send(
  msg,
DeliveryMode.NON_PERSISTENT,
Message.DEFAULT_PRIORITY,
Message.DEFAULT_TIME_TO_LIVE
    );
```

Persistent messages require the WebLogic Server administrator to configure a backing store. The WebLogic JMS implementation supports either Java Database Connectivity (JDBC) or file stores. If a persistent store is not configured, only nonpersistent messages may be used. Figure 7–1 illustrates creating a backing store in the file system.

Synchronous vs. Asynchronous Receivers

JMS supports both synchronous and asynchronous message consumers. A synchronous consumer uses the `QueueReceiver`'s or `TopicReceiver`'s `receive()` method to retrieve the destination's next message. If a message is available, the JMS implementation will return it; otherwise, the client's call waits indefinitely for a message. JMS also offers two variants, `receive-`

NoWait() and receive(long timeout). The receiveNoWait()
method returns a message if one is available; otherwise, it returns null. The
receive(long timeout) method takes a timeout parameter to specify
the maximum amount of time to wait for a message. If a message is available
within the timeout, it is returned, but if the timeout expires, null is returned.

Asynchronous message consumers must implement the javax.jms.
MessageListener interface, which contains the onMessage(Message) method.

```
public class AsyncMessageConsumer
   implements javax.jms.MessageListener
{

   ...

   public void onMessage(Message m)
     throws JMSException
   {

     // process message here
   }

}
```

The asynchronous receiver calls the QueueReceiver or TopicReceiver's setMessageListener method to register itself with JMS.

```
receiver.setMessageListener(new AsyncMessageConsumer());
```

The JMS implementation delivers messages by calling the MessageListener's onMessage method and passing it the new message. The JMS
implementation will not deliver another message to this MessageListener instance until the onMessage method returns.

Most JMS applications should use asynchronous message consumers and
avoid making synchronous receive calls. A receive call consumes a server
thread while it is blocking, but an asynchronous receiver is dispatched to an
available thread only when a message is received. Threads are valuable server
resources and blocking should be minimized or avoided. If a design requires a
synchronous consumer, the receiveNoWait or receive(long timeout) methods should be used instead of blocking, possibly indefinitely, in
receive().

Use receive(long timeout) or receiveNoWait for
synchronous consumers.

Message Selectors

Many message consumers are only interested in a subset of all delivered messages. JMS provides a standard message selector facility to perform automatic message filtering for message consumers. The message filtering is performed by the JMS implementation before delivering the message to consumers.

A JMS message consumer writes a JMS expression to perform message filtering. This expression is evaluated by the JMS implementation against the JMS message headers and properties. The message filtering never considers the message body. If the JMS expression evaluates to true, the message is delivered to this consumer. When the JMS expression evaluates to false on a queue, the message is skipped, but it still remains in the queue. On a topic, a false selector will ignore the message for this subscriber. If the topic includes multiple subscribers, then the message may be delivered to other subscribers who do not filter it out.

JMS message selectors are string expressions based on SQL-92. The expression must evaluate to a boolean value using a set of standard operators and the message's header and properties. Each message consumer may use a single selector, and the selector must be specified when the consumer is created.

For instance, this selector ensures that messages will only be delivered if the priority is greater than 5.

```
receiver = session.createReceiver(messageQueue,
    "JMSPriority > 5");
```

Most JMS filtering uses the message properties. This enables the producer to set application-specific values in the message, and then the message filtering can use these properties for filtering.

Durable JMS Subscriptions

In JMS's pub/sub domain, message consumers subscribe to topics. A given topic might have many subscribers. When a message arrives, it will be delivered to all subscribers who do not filter the message. If the subscriber's process terminates or there is a network outage, the consumer will miss messages delivered to the topic. These messages will not be redelivered when the client reconnects. This behavior is desirable for many pub/sub applications. For time-sensitive information, there is no reason to retain the message, and the JMS implementation will have higher performance if it does not need to retain messages for lost clients. However, some applications might have identified clients that need to recover topic messages when they reconnect to the server. JMS provides durable topic subscriptions to allow this behavior. Note that durable subscriptions apply only to JMS topics. JMS queues cannot use durable subscriptions.

When durable topic subscriptions are used, the client must provide a unique identifier. For instance, an application could use a user's login name. This enables the server to identify when a client is reconnecting to the JMS Server so that the JMS implementation can deliver any pending messages. The client can set the ID by either creating a connection factory with an associated ID or by calling the `setClientID` method on the `Connection` object. While the JMS specification recommends the `Connection-Factory` approach, it requires the server administrator to create a `ConnectionFactory` for each durable client. This is impractical for large production systems. In reality, most applications should set the connection ID explicitly on the JMS connection. The `setClientID` method *must* be called immediately after the connection is obtained. Note that it is the client's responsibility to ensure that the client ID value is unique. In a WebLogic cluster, the JMS implementation cannot always immediately determine that there are multiple clients with a given client ID.

This example code creates the `TopicConnection` from the JMS `ConnectionFactory` and then establishes a client ID of 1.

```
connection = connectionFactory.createTopicConnection();

connection.setClientID("1");
```

The JMS consumer then uses the `createDurableSubscriber` method to create its `subscriber` object.

```
subscriber = session.createDurableSubscriber(topic, "1");
```

The subscriber will now be attached to the JMS Server with the client ID of `"1"`. Any pending messages to this topic are delivered to this client.

When a durable subscriber is not connected to the JMS Server, the JMS implementation must save any messages sent to the associated topic. This enables durable clients to return and receive their pending messages, but it also forces the JMS Server to maintain a copy of the message until all durable clients have received the message. JMS provides the unsubscribe method for durable subscribers to delete their subscription. This prevents the server from retaining messages for clients that will never return.

```
// unsubscribe the client named "1"

session.unsubscribe("1");
```

Using Temporary Destinations

JMS destinations are administered objects created from the WebLogic Server's Administration Console. Destinations are named objects that survive server restarts and may be used by many clients. However, some messaging applications require a lightweight, dynamic destination that is created for temporary use and deleted when the client finishes. JMS includes temporary destinations to address this requirement.

A JMS client creates a temporary destination with `QueueSession`'s `createTemporaryQueue()` method or `TopicSession`'s `create-TemporaryTopic()` method.

```
TemporaryQueue tempQueue = session.createTemporaryQueue();
```

The `TemporaryQueue` (and conversely `TemporaryTopic`) extend the `Queue` class and add only a `delete()` method. The `delete()` method destroys the temporary destination and frees any associated resources. This `TemporaryQueue` is a system-generated temporary queue. Temporary destinations do not survive server restarts, and clients may not create durable subscribers for temporary topics. Each temporary destination exists within a single JMS connection, and only the encompassing JMS connection creates message consumers for a temporary destination. Because temporary destinations never survive a server restart, there is no reason to persist messages. Any persistent message sent to a temporary destination will be remarked as `NON_PERSISTENT` by the WebLogic JMS implementation, and it will not survive a server restart.

One common use for temporary destinations is a reply queue. A JMS client sends messages to a JMS Server setting the `JMSReplyTo` field to the temporary destination name. The message consumer then sends a response to the temporary destination.

Temporary destinations enable JMS applications to dynamically create short-lived destinations. Because temporary destinations do not survive system failures, applications using temporary destinations must be prepared for lost messages.

JMS clients should always call the `delete()` method when they have finished with a temporary destination. Each temporary destination consumes resources within the WebLogic Server. These resources are reclaimed when the `delete()` method is called or through garbage collection.

Message Acknowledgment

The JMS Server retains each message until the consumer acknowledges the message. When messages are consumed within a transaction, the acknowledgment is made when the transaction commits. With nontransacted sessions, the receiver specifies an acknowledgment mode when the session is created. The JMS specification defines three standard acknowledgment modes, and the WebLogic JMS implementation adds two additional options.

Table 7.4 lists the JMS acknowledgment modes.

Table 7.4   JMS Acknowledgment Modes

Acknowledgment Mode	*Description*
AUTO_ACKNOWLEDGE	For synchronous receivers, the message will be automatically acknowledged when the consumer's receive method call returns without throwing an exception. With an asynchronous consumer, the message is acknowledged when the onMessage callback returns.
DUPS_OK_ACKNOWLEDGE	This acknowledgment mode enables JMS to lazily acknowledge message receipt. It is more efficient than AUTO_ACKNOWLEDGE because every message is not acknowledged, but messages may be redelivered if a system crash or network outage occurs.
CLIENT_ACKNOWLEDGE	This acknowledgment mode requires the client to use the javax.jms.Message.acknowledge() method to explicitly acknowledge messages. It is not necessary for the client to acknowledge every message. Instead, a call to acknowledge() will acknowledge the current and any previous messages.

Table 7.4   JMS Acknowledgment Modes (continued)

Acknowledgment Mode	*Description*
NO_ACKNOWLEDGE	This is a WebLogic JMS acknowledgment mode to indicate that no acknowledgment is required. The JMS implementation does not retain the message after delivering it to the consumer.
MULTICAST_NO_ACKNOWLEDGE	This is a WebLogic JMS acknowledgment mode that delivers JMS messages via IP multicast to topic subscribers. Like NO_ACKNOWLEDGE, the JMS implementation does not retain the message after delivery.

Which Acknowledgment Mode Is Right for Your Application?

NO_ACKNOWLEDGE or MULTICAST_NO_ACKNOWLEDGE should be used by applications where performance outweighs any durability or recoverability requirements. In many applications, messages are created frequently to send out updates such as the latest stock quotes. Because this information is continually being generated, performance is paramount, and if a system crash occurs, there is no reason to recover any lost stock quotes since the quote will be out of date by the time the system has recovered.

AUTO_ACKNOWLEDGE is a simple model because the container handles acknowledgment, but JMS programmers should be aware that messages can be redelivered. If there is a system outage between the time that the receive or onMessage call returns and the JMS Server acknowledges the message, the last message will be redelivered when the system recovers. Consumers who need stronger messaging guarantees should use JMS's transaction facilities, which are discussed in the next section.

DUPS_OK_ACKNOWLEDGE allows higher performance than AUTO_ACKNOWLEDGE at the cost of more redelivered messages after a system failure. If consumers can detect or tolerate redelivered messages, its performance advantages make it preferable to AUTO_ACKNOWLEDGE.

CLIENT_ACKNOWLEDGE gives the receiver complete control over the message acknowledgment. It enables the client to acknowledge a batch of messages with a single operation.

JMS and Transactions

The JMS acknowledgment modes provide varying levels of reliability for message consumers, but enterprise applications often require stronger, transactional guarantees. For instance, an application might need to dequeue a message, update some database tables, and enqueue the message on another JMS queue. If any of these operations fails or a system failure occurs, the entire operation should roll back to its original state. JMS offers two transactional options: transacted sessions and an integration with the WebLogic Server's Java Transaction API (JTA) transaction service.

Using Transacted Sessions

Transacted sessions are used when transactional behavior is required within a single JMS session. Other resources such as database or EJB operations cannot participate in a transacted session's transaction. Passing a boolean true argument when the session is created creates a transacted session. The acknowledgment mode is also specified, but it is ignored for transacted sessions.

```
Session txSession = qCon.createQueueSession(
    true, /* transacted session */
    Session.AUTO_ACKNOWLEDGE /* IGNORED for transacted session */
    );
```

Transacted sessions use the chained transaction model. A transaction is always open for each transacted session. When the transaction is committed, the JMS implementation automatically starts a new transaction. The `javax.jms.Session` object includes `commit()` and `rollback()` methods for the JMS client to explicitly commit or roll back the associated transaction.

Both message producers and message consumers may use transacted sessions. When a message producer uses a transacted session, sent messages are buffered until the transaction commits. No message consumers will receive these uncommitted messages. When the message producer calls the session's commit method, the messages are all enabled for delivery. If the transaction aborts, the JMS implementation will discard the buffered messages.

With message consumers, transacted sessions control message acknowledgment. The consumer can receive multiple messages just like the `CLIENT_ACKNOWLEDGE` mode. When the associated transaction is committed, the JMS implementation acknowledges all messages received in the associated transaction. If the transaction aborts, the JMS implementation returns the messages to the associated queue or topic.

> *Transacted sessions are used when transactional behavior is required within a single JMS session. Other resources such as database or EJB operations cannot participate in a transacted session's transaction.*

Using JTA Transactions with JMS

Transacted sessions enable a JMS producer or consumer to group messages into a single, atomic send or receive. However, a transacted session is only used within JMS. Many applications need JMS and JDBC or EJB work to participate in a single transaction. For instance, an application might dequeue a message containing a customer order and use the order information to update some inventory tables in the database. The order processing and the inventory update must be within the same transaction, so a transacted session is insufficient because it only handles JMS. The application must use a JTA `javax.transaction.UserTransaction` to wrap the JMS and JDBC work in a single transaction.

> *The JTA* `UserTransaction` *API may only be used with nontransacted sessions. A transacted session will not participate in any JTA transaction, and it will ignore any* `UserTransaction` *commits or rollbacks.*

The acknowledgment mode must be specified when creating a JMS session, but it is ignored when the `UserTransaction` API is being used.

> *Before using JTA* `UserTransactions` *with JMS, the server administrator must set the* `ConnectionFactory`'s *User Transactions Enabled checkbox in the WebLogic Server's Administration Console.*

```
QueueSession session = qCon.createQueueSession(
   false, /* not a transacted session */
   Session.AUTO_ACKNOWLEDGE
);
```

The JMS client will use JNDI to find a reference to the server's JTA implementation.

```
Context ctx = new InitialContext();

UserTransaction tx = (UserTransaction)
   ctx.lookup("javax.transaction.UserTransaction");
```

The JMS client must use the `UserTransaction`'s begin method to start a transaction. Unlike transacted sessions, the `UserTransaction` API is not a chained model, and clients must explicitly begin a transaction.

```
// start transactional work
tx.begin();
```

Now any JMS work performed in this session and JDBC or EJB operations will participate in this transaction. For instance, our message producer sends several messages within the transaction.

```
msg.setText("Transacted Message-1");
sender.send(msg);

msg.setText("Transacted Message-2");
sender.send(msg);
```

The sender might then perform some JDBC operations.

```
// We have omitted the JDBC setup code, but this shows
// executing a database insert within the same tx as our JMS
// operations

statement.executeUpdate (
    "INSERT INTO demoTable VALUES ('Hello', 'World')");
```

Finally, the transaction must be explicitly committed or rolled back.

```
// commit our JMS and JDBC work

tx.commit ();
```

When the transaction commits, any JMS messages produced within the transaction are enabled for delivery. Any received messages will be acknowledged with a commit. A transaction abort will release any sent messages while received messages will be returned to their JMS destination and redelivered.

JTA `UserTransactions` *should be preferred to transacted sessions since the transaction can enlist other resources such as JDBC or EJB access.*

Clustering JMS

Many WebLogic Server deployments use WebLogic clustering to achieve scalability and reliability. When designing JMS applications, it is important to understand JMS semantics within a WebLogic cluster. Please note that the

WebLogic Server's JMS implementation continues to improve its clustering offerings.

This section discusses the WebLogic 6 JMS implementation. It is recommended that users consult their WebLogic Server manuals for a discussion of the clustering offerings of their WebLogic Server.

WebLogic 6 introduces the concept of a JMS Server. A JMS Server includes administered JMS objects such as connection factories, connections, and destinations. Each WebLogic Server may include multiple JMS Servers, but each JMS Server is deployed on a single WebLogic Server. Each JMS Server uses an associated backing store. Deploying multiple JMS Servers within a single WebLogic Server allows multiple applications to each access a separate JMS instance (see Figure 7–10).

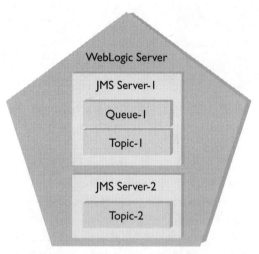

Figure 7-10   Multiple JMS Servers within a WebLogic Server Instance

JMS destinations are assigned to a single JMS Server. Because JMS Servers exist on a single WLS instance, each JMS destination exists on a single WLS instance. The server achieves scalability by distributing destinations to different WebLogic Server instances in the cluster. Because the destinations reside on different WebLogic Server instances, the JMS Server work is effectively load-balanced throughout the cluster.

Although destinations exist on a single WebLogic Server instance, the message producers and consumers for a given destination can exist anywhere in the cluster or even in client applications.

When a WebLogic Server instance fails, all JMS destinations within the failed server become unavailable. All temporary destinations and nonpersistent messages are lost during a server failure. Note that only the failed server will be affected—destinations on other servers in the cluster continue to operate. When the failed WebLogic Server is restarted, the associated JMS destinations will again become available. All persistent messages and permanent destinations are again available.

If a JMS client is connected to a failed JMS Server, its connection exception listener receives a JMSException. Any attempt to send or receive messages will also receive a JMSException. The client application must reconnect to an available JMS Server to restart JMS operations.

Exception Listeners

Many messaging applications include consumers who receive messages and perform work but never send any JMS messages. Because these clients are only active when a message is delivered, there is no means to notify them when their JMS Server has failed. JMS provides the ExceptionListener facility to deliver these out-of-band exceptions to clients.

A JMS ExceptionListener asynchronously receives connection error exceptions. ExceptionListener only receives exceptions that cannot be thrown to a method call. For instance, a send call on a broken connection will receive a JMSException, but this exception will not be transmitted to the ExceptionListener.

ExceptionListeners implement javax.jms.ExceptionListener that contains the onException(JMSException) method. When an out-of-band exception occurs, the ExceptionListener's onException method receives the raised exception. ExceptionListeners are not written to be thread-safe or reentrant. A new exception will not be delivered until the ExceptionListener's onException method has returned.

```
public class MyExceptionListener
  implements javax.jms.ExceptionListener
{
  public void onException(javax.jms.JMSException e) {

    ... //handle exception
  }
}
```

A client registers an `ExceptionListener` on the JMS connection with the `setExceptionListener(ExceptionListener)` method.

```
qConnection.setExceptionListener(new MyExceptionListener());
```

WebLogic's JMS implementation also enables the `ExceptionListener` to be registered with the entire JMS session by using `WLSession`'s `setExceptionListener(ExceptionListener)` method.

```
import weblogic.jms.extensions.WLSession;

WLSession wlSession = (WLSession) session;

wlSession.setExceptionListener(new ExceptionListener());
```

Using Multicast JMS

A messaging system is commonly used as the application's communication backbone. Messages might travel to hundreds or thousands of subscribers. Appropriate message selectors can greatly limit the number of delivered messages, but systems with thousands of clients will still spend considerable system resources delivering messages.

WebLogic's JMS implementation provides a multicast option to efficiently deliver messages to a large number of subscribers.

The WebLogic JMS implementation optionally uses IP multicast to deliver a message to a potentially large set of subscribers. A message producer sends a JMS message to the WebLogic Server using a standard JMS connection. The WebLogic Server then sends a single message via IP multicast to the message consumers. This provides greater scalability than standard PTP connections because the server needs to send a single message to reach many clients instead of sending a message per client. This multicast option also greatly reduces the network traffic between JMS clients and the WebLogic Servers.

The multicast JMS option is only available for the pub/sub model, and durable subscriptions are not supported. Because a single message consumer receives each message to a JMS queue, it does not make sense to extend the multicast option to the JMS PTP model. The multicast JMS option also only supports asynchronous message listeners. Any attempt to synchronously receive messages with multicast JMS will cause a `JMSException` to be thrown.

Because IP multicast is not a reliable protocol, message delivery is not guaranteed with the JMS multicast option. The messages are sequenced, and the WebLogic JMS implementation automatically indicates when a gap in the sequence has occurred. This gap indicates that a message has been lost or received out of order. The frequency of lost or misordered messages depends on the network topology and the message size. Small messages on a high-bandwidth LAN rarely (if ever) will be lost. Large messages across a congested network might see frequent lost or misordered messages. If a sequence gap is detected, a `weblogic.jms.extensions.Sequence-GapException` is delivered to the session's `ExceptionListener`.

Configuration Changes for Multicast JMS

The JMS destination is configured with the appropriate multicast address, port number, and TTL. Multicast addresses are in the range 224.0.0.0 to 239.255.255.255, and the port number should be an available port on the client machine. The TTL determines the Time To Live field in the IP multicast packet. Every time a multicast packet takes a network hop through a router, the TTL value in the packet is decreased. If the TTL value is 0, it is discarded. Thus, a TTL value of 1 will reach only hosts on the local network. A TTL value of 2 will reach all hosts on the local network and cross one router to reach an additional network (see Figure 7–11). If you are unsure how to set these values, please consult your network administrator for appropriate values.

You can use 237.124.35.35. Apply, and restart the WebLogic Server.

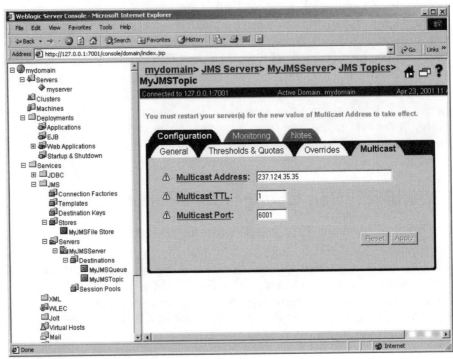

Figure 7-11   Configuring Multicast JMS

Using Multicast JMS Sessions

A message consumer uses multicast delivery by creating a `TopicSession` with the `MULTICAST_NO_ACKNOWLEDGE` acknowledgment mode.

```
multicastSession = topicConnection.createTopicSession(
  false, /* non-transacted session */
  WLSession.MULTICAST_NO_ACKNOWLEDGE
);
```

Because this is an asynchronous consumer, the `javax.jms.Message-Listener` interface must be implemented.

```
public class MulticastMessageConsumer
  implements javax.jms.MessageListener
{
  public void onMessage(Message m)
    throws JMSException
  {
    // message consumer code
    ...
  }
}
```

The message consumer must then register a `javax.jms.Message-Listener` with the `TopicSubscriber`.

```
tsubscriber.setMessageListener(new MulticastMessageConsumer());
```

Once message delivery is enabled, the consumer will asynchronously receive multicasted JMS messages.

JMS Best Practices

The following paragraphs describe some best practices for coding JMS applications.

Avoid Unneeded Features

JMS provides a powerful messaging facility with support for transactions, persistence, durable subscribers, and message selection and sorting. While these are important features of WebLogic's JMS implementation, they do affect the messaging system's performance. Selecting the correct acknowledgment mode or using nonpersistent messages where appropriate can greatly increase the throughput of a JMS application.

Avoid unnecessary features for maximum JMS performance.

Selection Performance Costs

JMS message selectors are a convenient and powerful means to filter messages from a queue or topic, but care must be taken to ensure that selection does not deter overall system performance.

Every JMS message sent to a destination must be compared against the consumers' message selectors. Message selectors that only consider message header fields will run the fastest. A selector that uses the message properties is slower, and if a selector examines the message body, it will be even slower.

Message selection is well suited to JMS topics. The WebLogic JMS implementation can efficiently evaluate the selectors and deliver the messages to the appropriate consumers. If no topic consumers select the message, it does not need to be retained.

Use selectors that only examine message header fields. A selector that examines message properties will be slower, and examining the message body produces the slowest message selectors.

However, message selection with queues can incur performance overheads if it is not used carefully. When a consumer does not select a message, it must be retained in the queue. Each selector must be compared against every undelivered message in the queue. If a message is never selected, it continues to consume resources.

Message selectors are more efficient when used with topics than queues.

Using Asynchronous Message Consumers Where Possible

JMS supports both synchronous and asynchronous message consumers. It is recommended that, where possible, asynchronous message consumers be used. Asynchronous message consumers provide better resource usage because threads are not blocked waiting for messages.

Synchronous message consumers always block a thread in the client. If the receive call is made from an external client, the WebLogic JMS implementation will not block a thread in the WebLogic Server. This is important for server scalability because the server cannot dedicate a blocking thread to each client. However, the thread in the client is blocked until the receive call returns.

If a synchronous receive call is made from within the WebLogic Server, a server thread must block until the receive call returns. Threads are valuable resources within a scalable server, and it is unacceptable to block these threads for long periods of time. Asynchronous consumers make better use of threads, especially within the server process.

Use asynchronous message consumers.

Prefer JTA Transactions to Transacted Sessions

Many JMS applications require transactional messaging. Transacted sessions provide a convenient means to use transactions within JMS, but other components such as EJBs or JDBC access cannot participate in these transactions. The JTA `UserTransaction` interface enables nontransacted sessions to participate in a transaction that can encompass other components, including JDBC or EJB. However, JMS does not provide a method to include an asynchronous consumer's message receipt in a JTA transaction. The problem is that there is no way to explicitly start a `UserTransaction` before the `onMessage()` callback. In this case, transacted sessions could be used or, as we'll see in Chapter 11, EJB's message-driven beans are asynchronous message listeners whose message receipt may optionally participate in a JTA transaction.

Use JTA `UserTransactions` *rather than transacted sessions.*

JMS Transactions and Error Handling

Large applications are often divided into multiple systems or separate processes, and JMS provides the communication between these subsystems. This workflow is PTP and is modeled with a queue. To ensure that messages are not lost, the JMS work is handled within a transaction. In production applications, it is possible that a message will contain application data that includes invalid data or errors. A transactional JMS client needs to be careful when handling invalid messages. If the transaction aborts, the message will be returned to the queue and delivered again to the consumer. Unless this error is transient, the second delivery will cause a transaction rollback, and the process continues.

One common solution is to introduce a separate error destination. When an invalid message is discovered, the message is sent to the error destination, and the JMS transaction commits. This ensures that the message is not redelivered. A message consumer on the error queue can handle the invalid messages appropriately. A simple solution is to use JavaMail to send an email to the customer or system administrator informing them of the error condition.

Send invalid messages to a separate error destination.

Another common solution separates the message acknowledgment from the JDBC or EJB transaction. This is desirable if the JDBC or EJB layer will detect that the message is invalid and abort the transaction. The message consumer needs to ensure that message is still acknowledged. The JMS consumer uses the `CLIENT_ACKNOWLEDGE` or `AUTO_ACKNOWLEDGE` modes. When a message is received, the transaction will begin; the JDBC or EJB work is performed within the transaction; and the message consumer commits or aborts the transaction.

Then, the message consumer acknowledges the message. This opens the possibility that the transaction will commit, but the system will fail before the message is acknowledged. The application can often prepare for this case by making the message actions idempotent or by detecting this situation. For instance, an e-commerce application might send a JMS message that processes new customer accounts. If each message includes a customer ID number, the message consumer can determine whether this customer has already been processed.

Conclusion

JMS provides a standard enterprise messaging system for J2EE applications. The WebLogic Server provides a robust and high-performance version of JMS and includes a number of JMS extensions. JMS is often used in conjunction with other J2EE APIs to build a complete enterprise application. The EJB 2.0 specification includes message-driven EJBs, which are an integration between JMS and EJB. Chapter 10 covers message-driven EJBs.

USING SESSION ENTERPRISE JAVABEANS

In this chapter:

- Basics of EJBs
- Programming stateless session EJBs
- Writing stateful session EJBs
- Using EJBs in transactions
- How to write secure EJBs
- Best practices for using session EJBs in WebLogic Server applications

Chapter 8

Enterprise JavaBeans Overview

JavaSoft defined the Enterprise JavaBeans (EJB) specification to give Java developers a foundation for building distributed business components. EJBs are Java components that implement business logic and follow a contract designated in the EJB specification. EJBs live inside an EJB container, which provides a set of standard services, including transactions, persistence, security, and concurrency. This means that the application programmer is freed from developing these services from scratch.

EJB also provides portability for its components. Any EJB that conforms to the EJB 1.1 or EJB 2.0 specifications works correctly in the WebLogic Server. While the WebLogic Server supports both EJB 1.1 and EJB 2.0, these chapters focus on EJB 2.0. In general, all new development should use EJB 2.0.

Basics of EJBs

In EJB 2.0, there are four types of EJBs:

- Stateless session beans provide a service without storing a conversation state between method calls.

- Stateful session beans maintain state; each instance is associated with a particular client.
- Entity beans represent an object view of persistent data, usually rows in a database. Entity beans have a primary key as a unique identifier. There are two operational styles for entity beans: *container-managed persistence* (CMP) and *bean-managed persistence* (BMP).
- Message-driven beans were added in EJB 2.0. Message-driven EJBs, the integration between JMS (Java Message Service) and EJB, are used to perform asynchronous work within the server.

Session Beans

Session beans (both stateful and stateless) represent a conversation with a client. Stateless session beans are generally used to provide a service. Because they are stateless, no conversation state is stored between method calls. For instance, you could model a bank teller as a stateless EJB with a method named withdraw. Each call to withdraw would have to include all of the information necessary to access the account.

The advantage of a stateless session bean is that a small number of instances can be used to satisfy a large number of customers. Each instance has no identity and is equivalent to any other instance.

The number of simultaneous tellers is the number of concurrent operations (similar to a real bank).

Stateful session beans also represent a conversation, but each instance is associated with a particular client. If the teller EJB were a stateful session bean, each client would create his own teller instance (perhaps passing the account number as a parameter). Now the teller stateful session bean is associated with a particular client and his or her account number.

In the stateful session bean example, the number of tellers is equal to the number of active customers. This can simplify the programming model.

Entity Beans

Entity beans represent an object view of persistent data, usually rows in a database. Entity beans have a primary key which, like a database primary key, uniquely identifies the entity. There are two main divisions of entity beans:

CMP and BMP. In a CMP entity bean, the EJB container automatically generates code to persist the entity bean to a database. In a BMP entity bean, the bean writer must write the data access code. Generally, this involves writing Java Database Connectivity (JDBC) code to insert, remove, and query the entity bean in the database.

The advantage of BMP is it offers the bean writer complete flexibility about the entity bean's persistence. Because the bean writer is writing the data access code, almost any persistent store can be used. The main advantage of CMP is that it relieves the bean writer from having to write the data access code to persist the entity bean to a relational database. Instead of writing the tedious JDBC code, CMP automates this process. In addition, EJB 2.0 CMP offers standard mapping for relationships between entity beans. This enables the container automatically to manage the interactions between business objects. Because the container has more control over data access in CMP, the performance of EJB 2.0 CMP beans is usually better than with BMP entities. We cover entity beans in detail in Chapter 9.

Message-Driven Beans

Message-driven EJBs, added in EJB 2.0, are the integration between JMS and EJB. Unlike other EJBs, clients never directly call a message-driven EJB. Instead, the client posts a message to a JMS destination. When a message arrives at the JMS destination, a `MessageDrivenBean`'s `onMessage` method is called to process the message. Message-driven EJBs generally are used to perform asynchronous work within the server.

Stateless Session EJB Example: HelloWorld

EJBs consist of three main pieces:

- The remote interface
- The home interface
- The bean class

To illustrate these components, we create a very simple Hello World stateless session EJB. This example can be found on the accompanying CD at examples/ch8/helloworld/.

The remote interface lists the business methods that are available to clients of this EJB. Because this is an interface, the EJB writer does not implement these methods. The EJB container is responsible for supplying the concrete implementation of the methods in the remote interface. The remote interface only stipulates the contract between the client and the EJB.

HelloWorld Remote Interface

We define the remote interface in a file called HelloWorld.java:

```
package com.learnweblogic.examples.ch8.helloworld;

import java.rmi.RemoteException;
import javax.ejb.EJBObject;
public interface HelloWorld extends EJBObject {
  public String helloWorld()
    throws RemoteException;

}
```

The EJB developer uses the remote interface to expose business logic to the client. In this case, the EJB offers a single `helloWorld` method.

HelloWorldHome Interface

The home interface is the EJB's factory. Clients use the home interface to create, find, and remove instances of an EJB. Like the remote interface, the EJB writer only defines the signature for the methods in the home interface.

```
package com.learnweblogic.examples.ch8.helloworld;
import java.rmi.RemoteException;
import javax.ejb.CreateException;
import javax.ejb.EJBHome;

public class HelloWorldHome extends EJBHome {
  public HelloWorld create()
    throws CreateException, RemoteException;
  }
```

The `HelloWorldHome` interface contains a single `create` method. This `create` method is a factory that produces references to the HelloWorld EJB. Notice that the return type is the `HelloWorld` interface. The return type of `create` methods is always the EJB's remote interface.

HelloWorldBean EJB Class

The bean class implements the business logic that is exposed to the client through the remote interface. For instance, the bean class must implement the `helloWorld` business method:

```
package com.learnweblogic.examples.ch8.helloworld;

import javax.ejb.SessionBean;
import javax.ejb.SessionContext;

public class HelloWorldBean implements SessionBean {

  private SessionContext ctx;

  public void setSessionContext(SessionContext c) {
    ctx = c;
  }

  public String helloWorld() {
    return "Hello World.  Welcome to EJB!";
  }

  public void ejbCreate() {}
  public void ejbRemove() {}

  public void ejbActivate() {}
  public void ejbPassivate() {}
}
```

The remaining methods in the `HelloWorldBean` class (except for `ejb-Create()`) are inherited from the `javax.ejb.SessionBean` interface. We cover these methods in detail later in this chapter.

EJB Deployment Descriptors

Before clients can use the HelloWorld EJB, we must deploy it into the WebLogic Server. First, like any other Java application, we need to use the Java compiler to produce the class files. The next step is to create the deployment descriptors. When the EJB container deploys the EJB, it reads configuration parameters and metadata from the deployment descriptor. For instance, the container uses the deployment descriptor to determine what type of EJB is being deployed, the name of the home interface, and other vital information. One of the deployment descriptors is named *ejb-jar.xml*.

The ejb-jar.xml Descriptor

The document type descriptor (DTD) for this XML document is defined by the EJB specification. This is a standard EJB 1.1 or EJB 2.0 deployment descriptor that is used by all EJB vendors.

Here is the *ejb-jar.xml* file for the HelloWorld EJB:

```
<?xml version="1.0"?>
<!DOCTYPE ejb-jar PUBLIC
'-//Sun Microsystems, Inc.//DTD Enterprise JavaBeans 2.0//EN'
'http://java.sun.com/dtd/ejb-jar_2_0.dtd'>


<ejb-jar>
  <enterprise-beans>
    <session>
      <ejb-name>HelloWorld</ejb-name>
      <home>
        com.learnweblogic.examples.ch8.helloworld.HelloWorldHome
      </home>
      <remote>
        com.learnweblogic.examples.ch8.helloworld.HelloWorld
      </remote>
      <ejb-class>
        com.learnweblogic.examples.ch8.helloworld.HelloWorldBean
      </ejb-class>
      <session-type>Stateless</session-type>
      <transaction-type>Bean</transaction-type>
    </session>
  </enterprise-beans>
</ejb-jar>
```

The deployment descriptor begins by declaring its XML document type. EJB deployment descriptors are XML documents that must use the structure defined in the standard EJB DTD. The *ejb-jar.xml* descriptor gives the WebLogic EJB container the names of the home interface, remote interface, and the ejb (bean) class. The `ejb-name` parameter is a logical name for this EJB. It is used throughout the deployment descriptor to refer to this EJB. The *ejb-jar.xml* also includes a session-type parameter. This informs the container that this deployment is a stateless session EJB. Finally, we specify that we are using bean-managed transactions. We cover the EJB transaction options later in this chapter.

The weblogic-ejb-jar.xml Descriptor

In addition to the standard deployment descriptor, the WebLogic Server also requires a WebLogic-specific deployment descriptor. This deployment descriptor enables the EJB writer to configure parameters that are specific to the WebLogic implementation. This file is named *weblogic-ejb-jar.xml*. Here is the *weblogic-ejb-jar.xml* for the HelloWorld EJB.

```
<?xml version="1.0"?>
<!DOCTYPE weblogic-ejb-jar PUBLIC
```

```
"-//BEA Systems, Inc.//DTD WebLogic 6.0.0 EJB//EN"
"http://www.bea.com/servers/wls600/dtd/weblogic-ejb-jar.dtd" >

<weblogic-ejb-jar>
  <weblogic-enterprise-bean>
    <ejb-name>HelloWorld</ejb-name>
    <jndi-name>HelloWorldEJB</jndi-name>
  </weblogic-enterprise-bean>
</weblogic-ejb-jar>
```

This simple WebLogic deployment descriptor contains only two pieces of information. First, it uses the `ejb-name` tag to specify that these parameters are for the HelloWorld EJB. This enables the container to associate these values with the parameters read from the *ejb-jar.xml* descriptor. The second tag is the Java Naming and Directory Interface (JNDI) name. When the HelloWorld EJB is deployed in the WebLogic Server, the EJB container binds the home interface into the JNDI tree using the `<jndi-name>` specified in the *weblogic-ejb-jar.xml*. Clients can then find the EJB by using JNDI to look up the name `"HelloWorldEJB"`.

Building the EJB Jar File

This example is in the *examples/ch8/helloworld/* directory on the accompanying CD-ROM. For best results, build and deploy this example from this directory, using the scripts provided.

The build script compiles the EJB components into an ejb-jar file for deployment to the WebLogic Server. The deployment descriptors should be in the META-INF directory, while the class files should be in directories that reflect their package structure.

Note that the META-INF name is case-sensitive. It must be named META-INF, not meta-inf or Meta-Inf.

The structure of the *ejb-jar* is:

```
com/learnweblogic/examples/ch8/helloworld/
com/learnweblogic/examples/ch8/helloworld/HelloWorld.class
com/learnweblogic/examples/ch8/helloworld/HelloWorldBean.class
com/learnweblogic/examples/ch8/helloworld/HelloWorldHome.class
META-INF/
META-INF/ejb-jar.xml
META-INF/weblogic-ejb-jar.xml
```

Most developers use Integrated Development Environments (IDEs) or command-line tools such as *makefiles* or *ant* to automate the process of building and assembling their EJBs. For simplicity, we use shell scripts to demonstrate the necessary steps.

A *build.cmd* script is included to demonstrate the required steps to compile and build the EJB and its client. The *deploy.cmd* script copies the ejb-jar file into the server's applications directory where it will be deployed. See Figure 8–1.

Figure 8–1   Results of Running the deploy.cmd Script

The *runClient.cmd* script may be used to run the sample EJB client. See Figure 8–2.

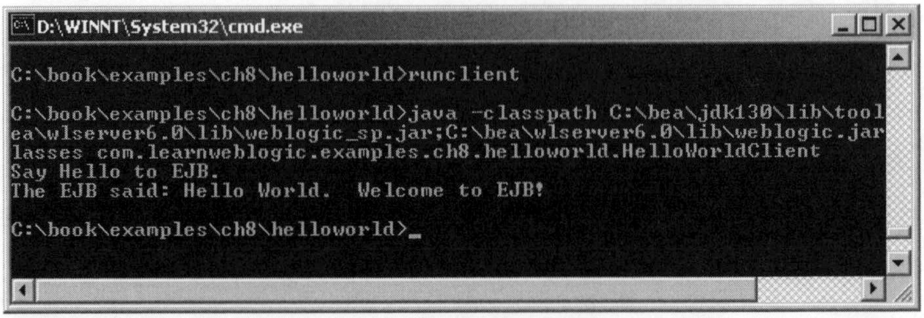

Figure 8–2   Results of Running the runClient.cmd Script

Deploying the EJB

The HelloWorld ejb-jar file can now be deployed in the WebLogic Server by copying the jar file into the server's applications directory. The WebLogic Server recognizes the new *ejb-jar* file and automatically deploys it to the local server. This is a convenient means to deploy new EJBs, especially during development.

EJBs also can be deployed through the Administration Console or through the command-line `weblogic.deploy` utility. Production systems should always deploy EJBs through the server's Administration Console.

Writing a Simple EJB Client

The HelloWorld EJB is now ready to be used by clients. In the *weblogic-ejb-jar.xml*, the deployer specified a `jndi-name` where the HelloWorld EJB is bound in the JNDI tree. A client uses the EJB by first making a JNDI lookup for this name.

```
Context ctx = new InitialContext();
Object h = ctx.lookup("HelloWorldEJB");
HelloWorldHome home = (HelloWorld)
PortableRemoteObject.narrow(h, HelloWorldHome.class);
```

First, the client creates an `InitialContext` to access the server's JNDI service. Next, the client does a JNDI lookup to find the home interface. This JNDI name (`"HelloWorldEJB"`) is the JNDI name specified previously in the *weblogic-ejb-jar.xml* file. Finally, the client uses the `PortableRemote-Object` to narrow the scope to the home interface. This is required by the EJB specification for portability reasons.

Next, the client can use the home as a factory to create an instance of the EJB.

```
HelloWorld hw = home.create();
```

The `create` method defined in the `HelloWorldHome` interface returns a new reference to the HelloWorld EJB.

The client can now call the `helloWorld` business method and print out the result.

```
String hello = hw.helloWorld();
System.out.println("My EJB said: "+hello);
```

The EJB Container

All EJBs exist inside the EJB container. The EJB container and other WebLogic Server subsystems provide the EJB writer with persistence, distributed objects, concurrency, security, and transactions. To best take advantage of the EJB container's services, it is essential to understand the relationship between an EJB and its container.

Using JNDI to Look Up the EJB Home

We now show the HelloWorld EJB example with comments on what is occurring in the EJB container underneath.

```
Context ctx = new InitialContext();
```

The client has created a standard JNDI context.

```
Object h = ctx.lookup("HelloWorldEJB");
HelloWorldHome home = (HelloWorldHome)
  PortableRemoteObject.narrow(h, HelloWorldHome.class);
```

When the EJB is deployed, the *weblogic-ejb-jar.xml* specifies `Hello-WorldEJB` as the JNDI name. At deployment time, the WebLogic Server binds an object that implements the `HelloWorldHome` interface at the name "HelloWorldEJB".

The client's lookup call travels across the network connection to the WebLogic Server. The server returns a Remote Method Interface (RMI) stub to the client.

The final step is to call `PortableRemoteObject.narrow` on the stub that is returned from the server. This step is necessary for portability reasons. Some EJB servers might not return a stub that implements the home interface. The narrow step takes the object returned from the server and produces an object that implements the home interface. The call to `PortableRemoteObject.narrow` is generally required on EJB servers that are CORBA-based.

With WebLogic's standard RMI/T3, the server returns a stub that implements the home interface. Therefore, the narrow step is optional, but your client programs should use narrow step anyway for portability reasons. If you are using RMI/T3, narrow simply returns the object that it is passed.

Creating an EJB Instance

```
HelloWorld hw = home.create();
```

Because the home object is an RMI object, the `create` call travels across the network connection to the WebLogic Server. The EJB container is responsible for providing an object that implements the home interface. The `create` RMI call arrives on the WebLogic Server and calls the `create` method on the home object that the server has provided.

At this point, the EJB is using the EJB container. The implementation of the `create` method is part of the container's responsibility. The container's `create` method first performs security checks before proceeding (we cover the EJB security model in detail later in this chapter). You can specify which users are allowed to call EJB methods. In this case, the container must check that the current caller is allowed to call the `create` method.

The EJB container also provides a transaction service to EJB writers. For instance, the *ejb-jar.xml* file can specify that the container must automatically start a transaction before it calls any method on an EJB and must commit a transaction when the method completes. We cover EJB's transaction support later in this chapter. Depending on the deployment descriptor, the container might need to start a transaction at this point.

The next portion of the container's `create` method depends on the type of EJB. We cover all four types of EJBs in detail in later chapters. For now, let's skip to the end of the container's `create` method. The container must return an object to the client that implements the EJB's remote interface. In the example, this is the `HelloWorld` interface. Because this is a remote object, the client receives an RMI stub.

Calling Business Methods

```
// call the business method
String hello = hw.helloWorld();
```

The client now has a stub to the HelloWorld interface. The `helloWorld` method call is an RMI call that travels to the WebLogic Server. Like the home interface, the EJB writer only supplies the interface for the HelloWorld interface. The EJB container provides an object that implements this interface.

Like the home interface, the container first checks security and then handles transactions for a business method call. The container's next responsibility is to get an instance of the bean class (in this case, `HelloWorldBean`) and call the `helloWorld` method on it. Remember that the EJB writer has implemented the business logic within the EJB bean class.

When the `helloWorld` method on the EJB bean class returns, the container again resumes control. Depending on the transaction settings, the EJB container might have to commit a transaction at this point.

The EJB container is also responsible for handling any exceptions that were thrown by the EJB's business logic. The exact behavior of exceptions is covered in a later chapter, but the EJB container might be required to roll back the transaction or even to destroy the EJB instance.

The EJB container takes the return value from the business method and returns it to the client. In this case, the `helloWorld` method returns a string across the wire to the client.

Obviously, the HelloWorld EJB is a very simple EJB that makes very little use of the services of an EJB container. While developing deployment descriptors and following the EJB specification's rules can be complicated, it is much easier to master these skills than to write a distributed, transactional, secure, and persistent component from scratch.

Stateless Session EJBs

In the previous sections, we developed, deployed, and used a very simple stateless session EJB. In the following sections, we cover session EJBs in-depth and explain how to take advantage of container services such as transactions and security.

Stateless session EJBs are generally considered the easiest to program. Their simplicity has a number of advantages for both the bean writer and the EJB server. As their name implies, stateless session beans follow a stateless programming model.

In a stateless programming model, the object cannot maintain any state on behalf of its caller.

For instance, imagine we are developing a bank account stateless EJB. We might develop a remote interface `Account.java` with these methods:

```
public double getBalance(int accountNumber)
     throws RemoteException;

public void deposit(int accountNumber, double amount)
     throws RemoteException;

public void withdraw(int accountNumber, double amount)
     throws RemoteException;
```

Because this is a stateless model, we do not store the `accountNumber` in the object. Each method takes the `accountNumber` as a parameter, performs the appropriate action, and then returns. Because the EJB does not contain any state, it is reasonable to use a database to store the account information. The `getBalance` method uses its account parameter to query the database and return the result.

Stateless Programming Model

The stateless programming model presents a number of advantages to the programmer. Because there is no state associated with the EJB instance, every instance of the bean class is essentially identical.

For instance, imagine the client calls the `getBalance` method on the remote interface. The container must then call the `getBalance` method on a bean class instance. Imagine that the container has two instances of the bean class in memory. Because the bean is stateless, the client does not care which of the two instances gets the `getBalance` method call. In this case, the account number is the necessary state, and it is passed as a parameter. If the EJB stored the account number (or any client-associated state) as a member variable, the stateless programming model would not be appropriate.

A stateless session bean must implement the `javax.ejb.Session-Bean` interface. This interface contains a number of callbacks that the container makes to the stateless session bean class.

Stateless Session Bean Lifecycle

It is important to understand that the container determines the lifecycle of a stateless session bean. When a client calls `create` on the home interface, the container does not necessarily create an instance of the EJB. It merely needs to return an instance of the remote interface. When method calls are made against that remote interface, the container has to find or create an instance of the bean class. The container then calls the business method on this instance. Likewise, calling remove on a stateless session bean does not necessarily remove a bean instance.

With stateless session EJBs, the container is allowed to create and destroy bean instances as it sees fit.

When the container creates a new instance, the bean class first receives a call to its default (no argument) constructor. The container then calls the `setSessionContext` method and passes in a `SessionContext` as a parameter. The `SessionContext` is an object that can be used by the EJB to communicate with the EJB container and perform a number of standard functions. We cover the `SessionContext` in a later section. Generally, the `setSessionContext` method stores this context in a member variable.

Finally, the EJB container calls the `ejbCreate()` method. A stateless session bean can only have a single, no-parameter `create` method. This restriction is necessary because `ejbCreate` is called at the discretion of the container. There is no mechanism for passing parameters. The `ejbCreate` method initializes member variables, and, depending on the EJB, may perform additional initialization. At this point, the EJB container can call business methods on this bean instance. If the EJB container ever decides that it no longer needs this instance, it calls `ejbRemove`.

About Stateless Session Bean Pooling

Within the EJB container, the WebLogic Server uses a technique called *instance pooling* to manage stateless session bean instances. An EJB server can comply with the EJB specification if it creates a new stateless bean instance every time a business method is called, but that would not perform well. Another option would be for the container to create a single instance of the bean and have method calls wait for this instance to be available. This saves the time to create an instance, but unless method calls are very short, performance suffers.

The WebLogic Server implements a better approach that keeps around a pool of ready instances. When a stateless session bean method call enters the server, the EJB container grabs an instance from the pool. After the method call completes, the bean instance is returned to the pool. Thus, the EJB container saves the time required to create new instances and is able to concurrently service a large number of clients.

Configuring Pooling

There are two parameters in the *weblogic-ejb-jar.xml* file that control the pooling behavior. The `initial-beans-in-freepool` tag specifies an initial size for the instance pool. When the EJB is deployed, the container populates the instance pool with as many instances as specified by this tag. This enables the EJB container to immediately respond to requests without having to initialize bean instances.

The deployer also can specify a `max-beans-in-freepool` value in the *weblogic-ejb-jar.xml* file. This parameter is an upper limit on the number of instances of this stateless EJB that can be used concurrently. When the EJB container asks the pool for an instance and there are none available, it is allowed to create new instances until it reaches the `max-beans-in-freepool` limit. Once this limit is reached, the container waits until an instance becomes available. If the method's transaction times out before an instance enters the pool, the container aborts the current transaction and returns to the caller. With proper configuration, this should be a very rare event.

Most users should not tune the `max-beans-in-freepool` parameter.

The default configuration does not limit the number of bean instances in the pool. In reality, the maximum number of instances is limited by the number of execute threads in the WebLogic Server. The maximum parallelism is achieved when each thread is using an instance from the pool.

Stateless Session Bean Clustering

Remember that a bean instance is returned to the instance pool when the method call returns. This means that the WebLogic Server can use a small number of bean instances to service a large number of clients. For instance, imagine that there are 10,000 clients each using the account stateless session EJB. Perhaps at any given instant, there are only 30 users simultaneously accessing their balance. Because all instances are identical, the server can use only a relatively small pool of 30 instances to service a large client base. The stateless programming model provides another clear advantage with WebLogic clusters. Because all instances of a stateless session bean are equivalent, a WebLogic cluster can not only choose from a pool of instances, but it also can consider multiple servers. For example, WebLogic can use load balancing to route stateless session bean method calls to different servers in a cluster. Stateless session beans also contribute to scalable architectures. Because WebLogic can automatically load-balance method calls on a stateless session bean, increasing capacity is as simple as adding more servers to the cluster. The clustered stateless session beans automatically use the new servers.

Handling Failure with Clustered Stateless Session EJBs

The behavior of stateless session beans during a WebLogic Server (or network failure) depends on a flag called `stateless-methods-are-`

idempotent that is set in the *weblogic-ejb-jar.xml* descriptor at deploy-time. The flag should be set to true if all of the business methods in the state-less session bean are idempotent; otherwise, it should be false.

A method is idempotent if it can be called many times and the results and effects are the same as if it were called only once.

Methods that merely do reads are usually idempotent. For instance, the helloWorld method on the HelloWorldEJB is idempotent. The caller always receives the same value, and it can be called many times without caus-ing any side effects. On the other hand, a method that is incrementing a counter is clearly not idempotent because the client gets a new value on each call.

Idempotent Stateless Session EJBs

If the stateless session bean is marked as idempotent, the "smart stub" always retries the call on another server in case one of the members in the cluster dies. For instance, imagine a WebLogic cluster of three servers named A, B, and C. When the client calls the idempotent stateless session bean, its busi-ness method is load-balanced and directed to one of the servers, A for exam-ple. If A dies before the client receives a result from the stateless session bean call, the smart stub chooses between B and C and tries the call again. Because the methods are idempotent, it is always acceptable for the stub to automatically retry the method on another server.

Nonidempotent Stateless Session EJBs

Unfortunately, stateless session beans that are not idempotent cannot always automatically failover. Consider the three-server cluster again, but now the client is invoking a deposit method. Clearly the deposit method is not idem-potent. Like the previous case, the smart stub load-balances the invocation and chooses a server in the cluster to call, B for example. If B fails there are two possible scenarios: The first case is that B died before it started on the deposit method. In this case, the smart stub automatically fails-over to another server. Because it knows that B has not done any of the work in the deposit method, there is no harm in automatically failing-over. The second case is that B fails after it has already started on the deposit method call. The smart stub has no way to tell how far the call has proceeded before the server failed. It is even possible that the method call completed and the deposit was committed, but the server failed before it could respond to the client. If the smart stub were to automatically failover, it is possible that two deposits would be committed instead of the expected one. While this situation might appeal to some bank customers, they would not be too happy if the example had a withdraw method. Now that server B is offline, the smart stub will not try server B until it reenters the cluster.

Using Member Variables with Stateless Session Beans

After understanding the stateless programming model, it is important to realize that stateless session beans can have member variables and even state! The important qualification is that the member variables cannot be associated with a particular client. For instance, a stateless session bean would not store an account number or a user name in its variable. This information is associated with a client, and it breaks when another instance is chosen to handle a method call.

However, stateless session beans can have member variables that are associated with the bean and not the client. For example, a common use of stateless session beans is to provide an object interface to a legacy system. Each instance of the stateless session bean can have a legacy system connection as a member variable. The caller does not care which connection it receives for the method call so it is fine if subsequent method calls receive different instances and hence different connections.

Using Freepool Settings to Limit Resources

In fact, stateless session beans with connections (or other resources) as member variables is the reason that the container blocks if `max-beans-in-freepool` bean instances are already in use. For example, imagine that your legacy system allows 10 simultaneous connections and each stateless session bean instance has a connection as a member variable. If the EJB container continued to allocate bean instances when there were 11 simultaneous callers, the legacy system would not allow the 11th connection. This is why the WebLogic EJB container makes the `max-beans-in-freepool` setting a hard limit. By setting `max-beans-in-freepool` to 10, the deployer is ensured that there will never be more than 10 stateless instances for the EJB concurrently in use.

Stateful Session EJBs

At first glance, stateful session beans seem very similar to stateless session beans. In theory, there are no required code changes to convert a stateless session bean to become stateful. Both EJB types must implement the `javax.ejb.SessionBean` interface and have the same basic requirements on the home and remote interface. However, in practice, stateful session beans look quite different from their stateless counterparts. Most of this differentiation is due to their stateful programming model.

The Stateful Programming Model

In the stateful session bean programming model, a client calls a `create` method on the home interface to create a new instance. Unlike stateless session beans, this causes the container to allocate a new bean instance in the server and associate it with this client. The client often passes initial conversational state as a parameter to the `create` method. For example, the bank account number could be passed when we create the teller stateful session bean.

The client receives a reference to the stateful session bean's remote interface from the `create` method. When the client calls a business method on the remote interface, the container must dispatch the call to the instance that is associated with this particular client. Unlike stateless session beans, the container does not have a pool of instances to multiplex on client calls. Each client reference to a stateful session bean refers to a specific EJB instance (see Figure 8–3).

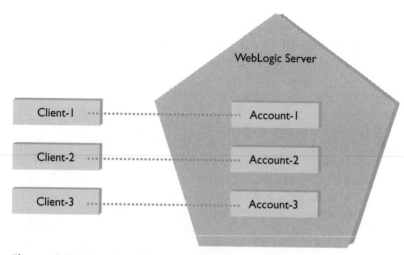

Figure 8–3   One Stateful Session EJB Instance Per Client

Most programmers are familiar and comfortable with the stateful programming model. For example, a Java program might create a list and add a string `"WebLogic"` to the list. If the program has not removed the value from the list, we assume that a search of the list finds the `"WebLogic"` string. Java uses the stateful programming model. If the list were implemented with a stateless session bean, a call could be routed to an instance that did not contain the `"WebLogic"` string.

Coding stateful session beans is often easier than their stateless counterparts.

The stateful bank teller EJB could store the account number and other account metadata during the `create` call. Any subsequent business method call would have this information at its disposal, and it would not have to be passed as a parameter. This simplifies coding and can provide better encapsulation.

Stateful Session EJB Lifecycle

Because each instance of a stateful session bean has an implicit identity, its lifecycle is quite different from a stateless session bean. When a client calls a `create` method on the stateful session's home interface, the container allocates a new instance of the bean class. This calls the default (no parameter) constructor of the bean class. The container then calls `setSessionContext` with a `SessionContext` object. The `SessionContext` can be used to call back into the EJB container from the bean class. We cover the

`SessionContext` in detail in a later section of this chapter. The container next calls the `ejbCreate` method in the stateful session bean class. The `ejbCreate` method is an opportunity to initialize the stateful session bean instance with parameters passed in the `create` method.

Creating Stateful Session EJBs

A stateful session bean can overload the `create` method in the home interface with many versions, each of which has different parameter types. Each `create` method in the home interface must have a corresponding `ejb-Create` method with the same parameters in the stateful session bean class. When a `create` method is called on the home interface, the container calls the corresponding `ejbCreate` method on the bean class.

After the `ejbCreate(...)` method has completed, the stateful session bean is in the ready state. If a business method is called on the stateful session's remote interface, the container can call the corresponding method on the bean class.

Removing Stateful Session EJBs

The `javax.ejb.EJBObject` interface defines a `remove()` method. Because all EJB remote interfaces must extend `EJBObject`, this method is available to clients of all EJBs. When a client makes a `remove` call on a stateful session bean instance, the container calls `ejbRemove` on the bean instance. This call removes the stateful session bean from the EJB container. After calling `remove`, the reference to the stateful session bean is dead. If a client attempts to call a business method after the bean has been removed, the EJB container throws a `java.rmi.NoSuchObjectException` to indicate that this stateful session bean instance no longer exists.

Passivation and Activation

The main advantage of the stateful programming model is that the object can store client-associated data within its member fields. For stateful session beans, this means that each client creates its own stateful session bean instance. For a large Internet site, however, the number of clients might be in the thousands—or even millions. It is not always feasible to store all of these instances in memory for the lifetime of a client.

In order to support large numbers of clients, the EJB container manages its working set of stateful session bean instances through mechanisms called passivation and activation.

> *Just like a virtual memory system can swap memory pages to disk, the EJB container can swap out stateful session bean instances to free up memory and other resources.*

Swapping a bean out is called *passivation*. Before a passivated bean can be used for a method call, the container must activate the instance. This process is called *activation*.

Passivation

In the WebLogic EJB container, passivation is implemented with Java serialization. When a bean is passivated, it is serialized and stored on a backing store such as a disk. Before the bean can be passivated, the container must call the stateful session bean's `ejbPassivate`. This gives the bean writer a chance to clean up and release any nonserializable resources that the bean might hold in its member variables. For instance, if a stateful session bean held a database connection, it could release the database connection in the `ejbPassivate` method. The EJB specification requires that the container cannot passivate a stateful session bean while it is in use or is participating in a transaction.

Activation

When a client calls a business method on a stateful session bean's remote interface, the EJB container needs to locate the corresponding bean class instance. If the bean is in memory, then the business method can be called, but if the bean has been passivated, the container must first activate the bean. This can involve reading the serialized bean from the disk and then deserializing the bean. The container then calls `ejbActivate()` on the bean, which gives the EJB a chance to reacquire any resources. For instance, the EJB could grab a database connection from a pool in the `ejbActivate` method.

Storing bean instances to disk and later reading them from disk is an expensive operation. In any modern computer, accessing memory is several orders of magnitude faster than reading from the disk. For this reason, the WebLogic EJB container uses a heavily optimized memory cache to store stateful session bean instances.

Configuring the EJB Cache

The WebLogic deployment descriptor contains a parameter `max-beans-in-cache`. This parameter represents the maximum number of stateful session bean instances that can be held in the in-memory cache. Most WebLogic deployments have sufficient memory, and it is not uncommon to see this parameter set to be tens of thousands of instances. In the common case, there is sufficient space in the EJB cache to store all active stateful session bean instances. The WebLogic EJB cache strives to add as little overhead to this case as possible. For example, a simple implementation might store all of the bean instances in a list ordered by the last time they were used. Whenever a new request comes in, the bean instance can be moved to the head of the list. While this is easy to implement, it does not scale well to a large server. For example, imagine a cache with a maximum size of 5,000 instances, but only 1,000 stateful session beans are currently being used. Clearly in this case, the EJB server can store all of the instances in memory. In the LRU (least recently used) implementation, the container must continually reorder the list as each method call is made. It's worse on a multi-processor system because each CPU must contend for the list's lock.

In the WebLogic cache implementation, the container does nothing until the number of instances in the cache approaches a tunable percentage (usually 85 percent). At this point, the container begins to reorder its data structures. If the number of instances continues to grow, the WebLogic container passivates instances to disk to free up resources.

Stateful Session EJBs and Clustering

Clustering stateful session beans is a much more difficult proposition than stateless session beans. Because all instances of a stateless session bean are equivalent, the container can route method calls to other servers. However, stateful session beans have an identity: Method calls are destined for a particular instance. One possible cluster implementation is to keep a copy of every stateful session bean in memory on every system in the cluster. Such an implementation quickly breaks down. In general, the problem is similar to cache coherency problems in multi-processor machines.

First of all, the cluster must propagate any changes made to the stateful session bean to every member in the cluster. For a large cluster this might be very expensive, and it is problematic if a server fails or if the cluster becomes segmented. Another problem is that scalability is greatly affected. For instance, imagine that a single WebLogic instance can support n instances of a stateful session bean. Ideally, a 50-server cluster could support $50 \times n$ instances. However, if each server must store each instance in its cache, it is overwhelmed with recording all the updates on $50n$ instances. To overcome these problems, WebLogic uses an in-memory-replication cache based on process pairs.

By default, stateful session beans are not clustered. The `create` method on the home interface is load-balanced, and stateful session bean instances are created across the cluster. However, each instance will be tied to a particular server and lost if the server terminates. When the in-memory replication is selected in the WebLogic deployment descriptor, the container supports failover in a WebLogic cluster.

Stateful Session EJB Replication

In WebLogic in-memory replication, every stateful session bean instance is stored in memory on two servers. One server is designated as the primary while the other is a secondary. The primary and secondary are determined per instance and are distributed throughout the cluster. For instance, consider a four-server cluster with servers A, B, C, and D. If a client creates a stateful session bean, the cluster might choose B to be the primary server and C to be the secondary for this instance. Another client might then create another stateful session bean instance. For this instance, the cluster chooses D as the primary and B as the secondary (see Figure 8–4).

Figure 8–4 In-Memory Replication of Stateful Session EJBs

Handling Failure with Clustered Stateful Session EJBs

Whenever a method call is made on the stateful session bean, it is routed to the primary server. If the primary server fails, the secondary server becomes the new primary, and the WebLogic cluster automatically chooses another available server as the secondary. If a secondary fails, the cluster automatically chooses a new secondary server. In the case where multiple WebLogic Servers are running on the same physical machine, the cluster attempts to locate the primary and secondary WebLogic Server instances on different machines, if possible.

Unlike a fully distributed cache, each instance is only stored in memory in two servers in the cluster. This makes updates much cheaper, and it greatly reduces the memory requirements of the WebLogic cluster. The stateful session bean instance is only lost if both the primary and secondary fail before the cluster is able to select new servers. This case is extremely rare in practice. Because stateful session beans are not persistent components, they do not contain mission-critical data such as account balances. For this reason, it is acceptable for an extremely rare occurrence to lose the instance. In practice, if the primary and secondary are both instantly lost, it indicates that there are probably major failures on the Web site.

Managing State Updates

To implement failover correctly for stateful session beans, the WebLogic cluster must correctly propagate updates from the primary server to the secondary server. Because this update occurs across a network boundary, the bean instance must first be converted to a serialized form. The EJB specification requires that the bean writer receive an `ejbPassivate` callback before the bean is serialized. Because `ejbPassivate` can never be called while the EJB is participating in a transaction, the EJB container never sends an update to the secondary until the stateful session bean method call and its associated transaction have committed. After the transaction commits, the EJB container calls `ejbPassivate` on the bean and then sends the appropriate update across the wire to the secondary server.

There is a possibility that the primary server dies after the update has committed but before the secondary server has received the update. In this case, the client might see slightly stale data when the cluster fails-over to the secondary. In general, this is acceptable with stateful session beans. Unlike entity beans (which we examine in depth in the following chapter), the state in a stateful session bean is not transactional.

Failover with Stateful Session EJBs

Like stateless session beans, a stateful session bean method call can automatically failover to its secondary. However, this automatic failover can only occur if the method call is not started on the primary. If the method call does not connect to the primary, it automatically fails-over to the secondary. If the primary starts processing the method call and then fails before returning to the client, the client has no idea of the data's state. It is possible that the transaction was rolled back, but it also is possible that the stateful session bean committed its transaction, and the container died before it was able to return the value. In this case, the stub does not automatically failover. Of course, any subsequent method calls use the new primary (see Figure 8–5).

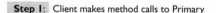

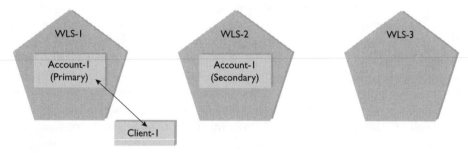

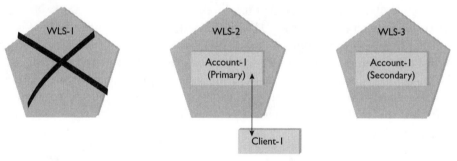

Figure 8–5   Failover with In-Memory Stateful Session EJBs

Stateful Session Beans and Concurrency

It is important to remember that stateful session beans are designed for use by a single client. The EJB specification requires that only a single method call may be active on any single stateful session bean instance at a given time. If another call arrives on the EJB server for a given instance while the instance is already in a method call, the EJB server is required to throw a RemoteException to the second caller.

> *A multi-threaded client should either serialize calls to a stateful session bean instance on the client or create a stateful session bean instance for each thread.*

Using Stateful Session EJBs in Web Applications

Unfortunately, it can be difficult to use stateful session beans correctly from a servlet or Java ServerPages (JSP) page. If a stateful session bean is used with the scope of a single request, then multiple threads do not use the instance. However, Web designers often store a reference to a stateful session bean in the servlet's session and attempt to use the stateful session bean with session scope. While this solution works for a while, it may fail if a session is ever used concurrently. This can happen, for instance, if a user clicks on Stop in a browser while a stateful session bean is processing a request. If the user then clicks on Reload, he or she enters the same session and attempts a concurrent call. If the previous call has not finished the previous invocation, the container throws a `RemoteException`.

There are two possible solutions for this scenario. One is to only use stateful session beans in the scope of a single request. While this is possible for requests that are very involved, it is a lot of overhead to create a new stateful session bean instance for every HTTP request. The other option is to enable a WebLogic-specific option `<allow-concurrent-calls>` in the WebLogic deployment descriptor. When this option is enabled, the WebLogic Server blocks any concurrent callers until the previous method call has finished with the stateful session bean instance. Once the previous method call finishes, the concurrent call gains access to the stateful session bean instance.

Using Transactions with Session Beans

The EJB container provides support for transactions as one of its primary services. The WebLogic EJB container makes use of the WebLogic Server's Java Transaction API (JTA) implementation.

In session EJBs, there are two transaction possibilities: bean-managed transactions and container-managed transactions. The `transaction-type` tag in the *ejb-jar.xml* selects the transaction type. For example, `<transaction-type>Bean</transaction-type>` would use bean-managed transactions.

Container-Managed Transactions

Container-managed transactions free the bean writer from explicitly coding calls to begin or commit a transaction. Instead, the EJB writer declares transaction attributes in the *ejb-jar.xml* deployment descriptor. The container reads these attributes and automatically starts and commits a transaction as required. This enables the EJB writer to concentrate on writing business logic. It also eliminates a class of bugs where the EJB writer does not handle transaction demarcation correctly.

The container's behavior for each of these attributes also depends on whether the caller is participating in a transaction. This can occur if the caller is another EJB that is already participating in a transaction. It is also possible for clients to explicitly start a transaction with the `UserTransaction` interface. A client starts a transaction by looking up `"javax.transaction.UserTransaction"` in JNDI and calling begin. The transaction can be committed by the commit method on the `UserTransaction` interface.

For example:

```
// Use an InitialContext for JNDI lookup
Context ctx = new InitialContext();

// get a UserTransaction reference
UserTransaction tx = (UserTransaction)
  ctx.lookup("javax.transaction.UserTransaction");

// start the transaction
tx.begin();

// call an EJB
cart.addItem(new Car());

// commit the transaction
tx.commit();
```

There are six different keywords for container-managed transactions: *Never, NotSupported, Supports, Required, RequiresNew,* and *Mandatory.* These attributes determine how and when the container should start and stop transactions. See Table 8.1 for a list of keywords for container-managed transactions.

Table 8.1 Keywords for Container-Managed Transactions

Keyword	*Definition*
Never	This EJB call should not participate in a transaction. If the bean is called within a transaction, the EJB container throws a `RemoteException`.
NotSupported	The EJB call does not participate in a transaction regardless of whether the caller is transactional.
Supports	If the caller is participating in a transaction, the EJB call participates in that transaction. Otherwise, the EJB call does not participate in a transaction.
Mandatory	If the caller has a transaction, the EJB participates in that transaction. Otherwise, the container throws a `TransactionRequiredException`.
Required	If the caller has a transaction, the EJB participates in that transaction. Otherwise, the container starts a transaction before it calls the EJB method and commits the transaction when the method call completes.
RequiresNew	The container starts a new transaction before it calls the EJB's method. It commits the transaction when the method call returns.

The transaction attribute is assigned in the *ejb-jar.xml* deployment descriptor. It can be specified on a per-bean basis, on a method name, or on a particular method signature. The transaction attribute is set using the `container-transaction` tag.

> If no transaction attribute is set, the WebLogic EJB container defaults to `Supports`.

Here is a snippet from the `ShoppingCart` stateful session bean where we define transaction attributes.

```
<container-transaction>
  <method>
    <ejb-name>ShoppingCartEJB</ejb-name>
    <method-name>*</method-name>
  </method>
  <trans-attribute>Required</trans-attribute>
```

```
</container-transaction>
```

Because the method-name is `*`, this declaration is specifying the default transaction attribute for the `ShoppingCartEJB` as `Required`. If no more specific transaction attribute is found for a method on this EJB, the container uses `Required`.

```
<container-transaction>
  <method>
    <ejb-name>ShoppingCartEJB</ejb-name>
    <method-name>getContents</method-name>
  </method>
  <trans-attribute>NotSupported</trans-attribute>
</container-transaction>
```

In this declaration, methods named `getContents` are assigned the transaction attribute of `NotSupported`. This overrides the previous declaration of `Required`.

```
<container-transaction>
  <method>
    <ejb-name>ShoppingCartEJB</ejb-name>
    <method-name>getContents</method-name>
    <method-params>
      <method-param>java.lang.Object</method-param>
    </method-params>
  </method>
  <trans-attribute>Supports</trans-attribute>
</container-transaction>
```

This declaration states that the method `getContents` (`java.lang.Object`) should get the transaction attribute of Supports. It overrides both of the previous declarations.

Using these declarations, we can see how the container assigns transaction attributes when methods are called on this EJB. For example, when the `addItem` business method is called, the container uses the transaction attribute `Required` because no rule other than the default applies. A call to `getContents()` is run as `NotSupported` because there is declaration for methods named `getContents`, but the signature does not match the `getContents(java.lang.Object)` declaration. Finally, a call to `getContents(java.lang.Object)` is run as `Supports`.

SessionSynchronization Interface

Stateful session beans with container-managed transactions can optionally implement the `javax.ejb.SessionSynchronization` interface.

This interface contains three methods: `afterBegin()`, `beforeComple-tion()`, and `afterCompletion(int)`. The container calls the `after-Begin` method when the stateful session bean enters a transaction. The `beforeCompletion` call occurs before the transaction is prepared to commit. The `afterCompletion` callback has a status Boolean as a parameter. If the container passes true to `afterCompletion`, the transaction was committed; a false value means there was a rollback.

> The *beforeCompletion* callback is often used to write cached data to the database before the transaction commits. Because *afterCompletion* is called after the transaction has completed, it is inappropriate to do transactional work in this callback. Instead, *afterCompletion* is generally used to release locks on shared resources or to update statistics on transaction commits and aborts.

Bean-Managed Transactions

Session EJBs also support bean-managed transactions. In container-managed transactions, the EJB code never made an explicit reference to the `User-Transaction` interface. All transaction demarcation was either done in the client or automatically by the EJB container. In a session bean using bean-managed transactions, the bean writer explicitly codes transaction demarcation.

> A session bean with bean-managed transactions cannot participate in the caller's transaction. If the caller is participating in a transaction and calls a session bean with bean-managed transactions, the container does not pass the caller's transaction to the bean-managed session bean.

The bean-managed transaction session bean gets a `UserTransaction` reference by calling the `getUserTransaction()` method on its `Ses-sionContext`. Remember that the container calls the `setSessionCon-text` method before it calls `ejbCreate`. Generally, the `SessionContext` is then stored in a member variable and can be used throughout the bean's lifetime.

With the `UserTransaction` reference, the session bean can use the `begin`, `commit`, and `rollback` methods to demarcate transactions. Stateless session beans with bean-managed transactions must commit or roll back their transaction before returning from a method call. A stateful session bean is allowed to return from a method without finishing the transaction. When the stateful session bean instance is called again, the container re-associates the instance with the former transaction.

EJB Security

Security is an integral component of almost every enterprise application. A secure application must examine security policies and protect resources at every level. Chapter 12 comprehensively details how to build a secure WebLogic application. This section describes the standard security features in the EJB container. A secure EJB application makes use of the EJB container security services and integrates with an application security model.

The standard EJB security model is based on declarations in the EJB deployment descriptor as well as a simple programmatic security interface. EJB security relies on the concept of the security role. A security role is a logical group that represents an application role. For instance, a payroll application might define an administrator security role. The payroll application can specify that only the administrator role can modify the payroll schedule. The EJB deployer can define method permissions for EJB methods in the home and remote interfaces.

Method permissions define one or more security roles that may call the associated method. If the calling identity is a member of one of the listed roles, the EJB container permits the method call to proceed. Otherwise, the EJB container throws a `java.rmi.RemoteException`, and the method call is not permitted. It should be noted that the calling identity must only match one of the associated roles. Assigning multiple security roles to a method permission is a Boolean OR, not a Boolean AND.

Assigning Security Roles in the EJB Deployment Descriptors

EJB security roles are declared in the EJB deployment descriptor with the `security-role` tag. The security role includes an optional description and the name of the role.

For instance, the following tag defines the administrator role:

```
<security-role>
  <description>
      Payroll Administrator. This role is permitted to change the
      payroll schedule and perform administrative functions.
```

```
  </description>
  <role-name>Administrator</role-name>
</security-role>
```

The EJB deployer also defines method access control lists in the EJB deployment descriptor with the `method-permission` tag. The `method-permission` tag contains a description, one or more role names, and one or more method declarations. The semantics of the tag are that any of the listed role names may access any one of the matching method declarations. The methods may be defined in three different ways. The first option is to specify the * wild card, which applies to all methods within a given EJB. For instance, the following declaration requires that the caller be a member of either the payroll users group or the administrators group to access the payroll EJB.

```
<method-permission>
  <role-name>PayrollUser</role-name>
  <role-name>Administrator</role-name>
  <method>
    <ejb-name>PayrollEJB</ejb-name>
    <method-name>*</method-name>
  </method>
</method-permission>
```

The method tag also can specify that any overloaded method with a given name receives this method permission. For instance, this declaration requires that any method named `getSalary` can only be called by members of the management role.

```
<method-permission>
  <role-name>Management</role-name>
  <method>
    <ejb-name>PayrollEJB</ejb-name>
    <method-name>getSalary</method-name>
  </method>
</method-permission>
```

Finally, a method tag may specify an exact method signature, which receives the associated method permissions. For instance, this declaration restricts the `setSystemPassword(java.lang.String)` method to the administrator role.

```
<method-permission>
  <role-name>Administrator</role-name>
  <method>
    <ejb-name>PayrollEJB</ejb-name>
    <method-name>setSystemPassword</method-name>
    <method-params>
```

```
<method-param>java.lang.String</method-param>
    </method-params>
  </method>
</method-permission>
```

The EJB container always applies the most specific method permission declaration. Setting a method permission on the exact signature overrides any other settings. Likewise, setting the method permission on a method named would override the * setting.

At this point, the EJB deployer has defined a security model for the payroll EJB because only users in appropriate roles can access the sensitive portions of the `PayrollEJB`. However, the EJB deployer has not yet specified how to map actual system users (principals) to the application's security roles. This is accomplished with the `security-role-assignment` tag in the WebLogic deployment descriptor. This tag includes the security role name and one or more principals that are members of the security role. The EJB deployer must map principals to all of the security roles defined in the EJB deployment descriptor. For instance, the following tag defines the users Bob and Joy in the administrator role:

```
<security-role-assignment>
  <role-name>Administrator</role-name>
  <principal-name>Bob</principal-name>
  <principal-name>Joy</principal-name>
</security-role-assignment>
```

Using declarative security has the advantage that the security policies are independent of the bean code. Security settings may be adjusted at deploy time to match the constraints of the runtime environment. However, not all security policies can be specified with declarative method permission tags. The EJB specification provides a simple programmatic interface for beans to write explicit security checks within the bean code.

Using Programmatic Security with EJBs

The EJB security API consists of only the `java.security.Principal getCallerPrincipal()` and `boolean isCallerInRole(String roleName)` on the `EJBContext`. The `isCallerInRole(String)` method is a programmatic interface to the declarative security model. It merely tests whether the current user is a member of the passed role. The `getCallerPrincipal` method returns the security principal of the method's caller. Generally, this method is used to perform explicit security checks against the principal (for instance, the payroll EJB that each user should be allowed to modify on his or her payroll account information). How-ever, user A should not be able to access or modify user B's account informa-tion. This cannot be accomplished with EJB's declarative security because the allowed principals depend on the bean instance, and it would require a secu-rity role for each user. Instead, the security is contained within the bean code. For instance, the following code shows how the bean code might maintain that the caller of the `setBillingAddress(String address)` function is a member of the users group and is also setting his or her own billing address.

```
// set in setSessionContext
private SessionContext ctx;

// user name of this Payroll account.  Set in ejbCreate.
private String userName;

public void setBillingAddress(String roleName) {

  if (! ctx.isCallerInRole("Users")) {

    throw new SecurityException("Caller is not a member of Users");
  }

  if (! userName.equals(getCallerPrincipal().getName())) {
    throw new SecurityException("Caller cannot access this account");
  }

  // business logic
  ...
}
```

When the EJB code uses the `isCallerInRole` method, it is referenc-ing a logical role name that is local to the bean instance. This logical role name must be mapped to a concrete role name in the EJB deployment descriptor. This mapping can be accomplished with the `security-role-ref` tag. This tag contains an optional description as well as a concrete role being referenced. For instance, the following declaration maps the user's log-ical role to the payroll user's role already defined in the EJB deployment descriptor.

```
<security-role-ref>
  <description>A Payroll User</description>
  <role-name>PayrollUsers</role-name>
  <role-link>Users</role-link>
</security-role-ref>
```

EJB Environment

Almost every program requires a means for users to override configuration parameter values. Standalone Java programs typically use Java system properties, and these values can be changed by specifying -D options to the Java virtual machine. Likewise, EJB components can use the EJB environment to read configuration parameters whose values may be adjusted by the deployer. The EJB environment enables the bean code to refer to the configuration parameters with logical names that can then be assigned values during deployment. Because the EJB code only refers to the logical name, the values may be changed without touching the bean classes.

Declaring Environment Variables

EJB environment values are declared in the ejb-jar.xml deployment descriptor as name-value pairs. The values may be any of the Java wrapper types: string, character, integer, boolean, double, byte, short, long, or float. User-defined types may not be used as EJB environment values. The environment value is declared with an `env-entry` tag that consists of an optional description, the logical name, the type, and a value. For instance, an EJB might use a configuration parameter named `maxWidgets`. This can be declared as an EJB environment variable and assigned the value 100783 with the following entry in the ejb-jar.xml:

```
<env-entry>
  <description>
      Maximum number of widgets that our EJB accepts
  </description>
  <env-entry-name>maxWidgets</env-entry-name>
  <env-entry-type>java.lang.Integer</env-entry-type>
  <env-entry-value>100783</env-entry-value>
</env-entry>
```

The EJB environment values declared in the EJB deployment descriptor are made available through JNDI to the EJB code. When an EJB is deployed, the container creates a JNDI context at `java:/comp/env` that includes the EJB environment values. To obtain the value associated with a logical name, the bean writer makes a JNDI lookup for `java:/comp/env/` followed by the `env-entry-name` declared in the EJB deployment descriptor. For instance, the writer of the widget bean could use the following code to find the value of `maxWidgets` at runtime:

```
Context ctx = new InitialContext();
Integer maxWidgets = (Integer)
  ctx.lookup("java:/comp/env/maxWidgets");
```

EJB environment variables are a convenient and standard method to store and retrieve configuration parameters from the bean class. It is important to note that these values are read-only. The bean code cannot use JNDI to bind in additional environment variables at runtime or modify the existing value for an environment entry. In addition, the bean writer should be aware that environment entries are local to the EJB deployment. They're not visible to other EJBs or components within the server. Also, there are no means for a client to look up these values. This is required since every EJB uses the `java:/comp/env` context to read its environment variables. In the WebLogic Server, environment variables are implemented within the EJB server by attaching the bean's `java:/comp/env` context immediately before a method on the bean class is called and removing the `java:/comp/env` context when the bean method returns.

Environment entries are read-only and local to the EJB.

EJB References

EJB components do not exist in a vacuum, and the business logic within EJBs often makes use of other EJBs deployed in the server. Normally, a client references another EJB by looking up the JNDI name where the EJB was deployed. It is undesirable to hard-code the JNDI name within the bean code because this limits the EJB's portability and reusability. One possible solution is to store the JNDI name as an EJB environment entry because this approach allows the names to be changed at deployment time without modifying the bean code. However, there is essentially no validation that can be performed on this JNDI name by the server's tools. For instance, the EJB server cannot validate that this JNDI name corresponds to an EJB of the appropriate type. The EJB specification includes EJB references as a portable way to safely reference another EJB within bean code. Unlike a simple JNDI name, an EJB reference gives the EJB server sufficient information to ensure that the EJB reference corresponds to a deployed EJB of the appropriate type.

Declaring EJB References

Like environment entries, EJB references are defined in the EJB deployment descriptor. The EJB deployer includes the ejb-ref tag to define an EJB reference. The <ejb-ref> tag consists of an optional description, the logical name, the type of the reference, the home interface class, and the remote interface class. The reference type is Session for all session EJBs and Entity for all entity EJBs. (Chapter 9 discusses entity beans in detail.) For example, the following XML tag provides an EJB reference named ejb/WidgetEJB.

```
<ejb-ref>
  <description>An EJB reference to the Widget EJB</description>
  <ejb-ref-name>ejb/WidgetEJB</ejb-ref-name>
  <ejb-ref-type>Session</ejb-ref-type>
  <home>chapter8.WidgetHome</home>
  <remote>chapter8.Widget</remote>
</ejb-ref>
```

Each EJB reference also requires an entry in the WebLogic deployment descriptor to map the ejb-ref-name to a concrete JNDI name in the server. The following example maps our ejb-ref-name, ejb/WidgetEJB, to the JNDI name DeployedWidget.

```
<ejb-reference-description>
  <ejb-ref-name>ejb/WidgetEJB</ejb-ref-name>
  <jndi-name>DeployedWidget</jndi-name>
</ejb-reference-description>
```

The bean class can now use this EJB reference to refer to the WidgetEJB without storing any concrete JNDI name. Like environment entries, EJB references are stored in JNDI under the java:/comp/env context. It is recommended that EJB references always be stored under the context java:/comp/env/ejb. As you can see in the preceding example, the EJB reference name begins with a leading ejb/ in accordance with this recommendation. The bean code can reference the widget home interface by making a JNDI lookup to java:/comp/env/ejb/WidgetEJB as in the following code:

```
Context ctx = new InitialContext();
Object h = ctx.lookup("java:/comp/env/ejb/WidgetEJB");
WidgetHome home = (WidgetHome)
   PortableRemoteObject.narrow(h, WidgetHome.class);
```

The EJB container requires that EJB references specify the concrete JNDI name for each EJB reference in the WebLogic descriptor. This approach is flexible because the EJB reference might point to an EJB in another application that has not yet been deployed.

Resource Manager References

In addition to configuration parameters and EJB references, the EJB specification also provides a portable method to reference resource manager factories from the bean class. Like the other environment references, resource manager references are logical names that can be used to reference server resources. For instance, a resource manager reference might point to a JDBC `DataSource`. Instead of hard-coding the data source name and JDBC driver information, the bean code refers to a logical name. At deployment time, the EJB deployer maps the logical name to a concrete resource factory.

Declaring Resource Manager References

Like other environment references, resource manager references are defined in the EJB deployment descriptor. Resource references use the `resource-ref` tag, which contains a description of the reference, the logical name, the resource type, and an authorization setting. The resource type depends on the underlying resource factory that is being mapped. The authorization setting may be either `Container` or `Application`. When the `Container` setting is used, the appropriate security permissions should be set in the WebLogic Server before deploying the EJB. In this case, the bean code does not contain code to sign on or authenticate itself with the resource manager. When the authorization setting is `Application`, it is the bean code's responsibility to explicitly sign on to the resource manager. The container authorization setting is generally preferred because it defers security settings to deployment time. This enables the same bean code to be used in different environments where the security settings may not be identical. The following `resource-ref` example creates a logical name `jdbc/DBPool` that maps to a JDBC data source:

```
<resource-ref>
  <description>
      This DataSource is mapped to a connection where the Widget
      EJB  store inventory information.
  </description>
  <res-ref-name>jdbc/DBPool</res-ref-name>
```

```
  <res-type>javax.sql.DataSource</res-type>
  <res-auth>Container</res-auth>
</resource-ref>
```

Like EJB references, resource manager references also require an entry in the WebLogic deployment descriptor. The `resource-description` tag includes the corresponding `res-ref-name` of the `resource-ref` and maps it to a server-wide JNDI name of a resource. Table 8.2 shows the name of the Resource Type for each Resource manager.

Table 8.2 Resource Manager Types

Resource Manager	Resource Type
JDBC DataSource	javax.sql.DataSource
JMS Connection Factories	javax.jms.QueueConnectionFactory
JavaMail Session	javax.mail.Session
URL Connection Factory	java.net.URL

For example, this entry in the *weblogic-ejb-jar.xml* maps `jdbc/DBPool` to the name `DBPool`.

```
<resource-description>
  <res-ref-name>jdbc/DBPool</res-ref-name>
  <jndi-name>DBPool</jndi-name>
</resource-description>
```

The final step in using a JDBC resource manager reference is mapping the server-wide JNDI name to an actual resource. For JDBC, this resource is a JDBC connection pool. The following *config.xml* entry maps the JNDI name `DBPool` to the connection pool named `DevelopmentPool`.

```
<JDBCTxDataSource
  Name="DBPool"
  Targets="myserver"
  JNDIName="DBPool"
  PoolName="DevelopmentPool"
/>
```

Resource Reference Advantages

At first glance, a lot of mapping and deployment descriptor elements are used to create a resource manager reference. However, this approach makes it easy for the deployer to reconfigure the application without changing the actual implementation classes. For instance, the development team might code and test the EJB in a private development environment. In this case, the JNDI name is mapped to the `DevelopmentPool` connecting to a development database. When the bean is deployed in the production system, the deployer can simply remap the `DBPool` JNDI name to the production database connection pool. No changes are required in the bean code or even the EJB deployment descriptors.

Like other environment references, the bean writer looks up resource manager references in the JNDI tree under the `java:/comp/env` context. By convention, JDBC `DataSources` are mapped under the JDBC subcontext; JMS connection factories typically use the JMS subcontext; JavaMail connection factories use mail; and URL connection factories use URL. The bean code can reference the `jdbc/DBPool` reference with the following code:

```
Context ctx = new InitialContext();
DataSource dataSource = (DataSource)
  ctx.lookup("java:/comp/env/jdbc/DBPool");
```

Handles

In some cases, an EJB client may wish to save its `EJBObject` reference to persistent storage for retrieval at a later date or more likely by another program. The EJB specification defined the concept of `Handles` as a serializable object that encapsulates sufficient information to reconstitute an `EJBObject` reference. `Handles` might be used to pass EJB references between two cooperating processes. The receiving process gets the `EJBObject` reference back again from the `Handle`. To get a `Handle`, the programmer calls the `getHandle()` method on the `EJBObject` interface. This returns the programmer an instance of `javax.ejb.Handle`. To re-create the `EJBObject` reference, the `Handle` interface contains a `getEJBObject()` method.

For instance:

```
// convert EJBObject into a Handle reference
HelloWorld hw = home.create();
javax.ejb.Handle handle = hw.getHandle();

// get the EJBObject reference back
HelloWorld backAgain = (HelloWorld)
  PortableRemoteObject.narrow(handle.getEJBObject(), HelloWorld.class);
```

HomeHandles

The EJB specification also defines the javax.ejb.HomeHandle interface. HomeHandles are similar to Handles but instead of applying to EJBObject references, they contain enough information to rebuild EJB-Home references. To get a HomeHandle reference, the programmer calls the getHomeHandle method on the EJBHome reference. This method returns an instance of the javax.ejb.HomeHandle interface. The programmer can then regain the Home reference by calling HomeHandle's getEJBHome method.

For instance:

```
// save to a HomeHandle reference
Context ctx = new InitialContext();
Object h = ctx.lookup("HelloWorldEJB");
HelloWorldHome home = (HelloWorldHome);
  PortableRemoteObject.narrow(h, HelloWorldHome.class);

HomeHandle homeHandle = home.getHomeHandle();

// rebuild the Home reference

Object nh = homeHandle.getEJBHome();

HelloWorldHome newHomeReference = (HelloWorldHome)
  PortableRemoteObject.narrow(nh, HelloWorldHome.class);
```

Advantages of Handles

The main advantage of HomeHandles and Handles is that they automatically store the information needed to rebuild the reference. For instance, a HomeHandle encapsulates the information necessary to create an InitialContext to the WebLogic Server and then looks up the correct Home object. A client that receives a HomeHandle can get the EJBHome reference without having to know the server's URL or the JNDI name of the EJBHome.

A common misconception is that HomeHandles are more efficient than explicitly building an InitialContext and performing a lookup on the JNDI name. In general, both cases perform identical steps. The HomeHandle merely stores the information that the programmer would have to provide.

It is also important to note that Handles do not store the current identity, and they may not be used as a security credential. For instance, consider a password EJB where only principals in the role of administrator may access the bean. An administrator may access the bean and store a `Handle`. Now, if another user receives the `Handle` and calls `getEJBObject`, the new user has a password reference. To call any restricted method on the password reference, the new user still needs to be authenticated as an administrator. The `Handle` does not automatically grant any permissions.

Cars Example

Real applications combine many of the concepts presented in this chapter. Our cars example demonstrates using a stateful and stateless session bean to model an automobile dealer and a prospective buyer. Of course, this example does not illustrate all of the required information and steps in purchasing a real car, but it does illustrate a typical design of a larger application.

The automobile dealer presents a purchasing service to the potential customer. Users need to be able to query the automobile dealer to look for cars in the dealer's stock that match their criteria. Then, the customer may make an offer on a particular car. If the dealer accepts the offer, the car is sold and removed from the dealer's stock.

Because the dealer stock is persistent and must survive any system crashes or outages, it is stored in a database table. The automotive dealer is modeled with a stateless session bean. The stateless session bean presents a facade to the potential customer, and the customer never directly accesses the database. This design separates the customer from the persistent representation allowing the persistent logic to be changed independently of the customer application (see Figure 8–6).

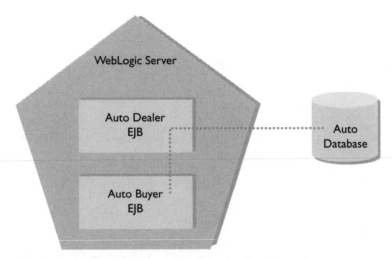

Figure 8-6 Objects and Database for the Cars Example

The potential automobile buyer is modeled with a stateful session bean. Each instance of this bean corresponds to a single auto shopper, and it maintains conversational state with its associated shopper. The client application interacts directly with the automobile buyer stateful session bean. This bean, in turn, accesses the `AutoDealer` stateless session bean. This is a common arrangement where a client application maintains a stateful conversation with a bean, which then proxies work back to a stateless service.

Running the Example

To run the Cars example, follow the procedures outlined in Chapter 5 for connecting to the default Cloudscape database, or follow your standard procedures for connecting WebLogic Server to your in-house database. In a command window, set your environment with `bea\wlserver6.0\config\mydomain\setEnv.cmd` to build the application.

In another command window, set your environment with `bea\wlserver6.0\config\examples\setExamplesEnv.cmd` to run the Cars example once it has been built. Use the Examples Server to enable the default Cloudscape database connection.

The following paragraphs explain the functions of the build and deploy scripts for the Cars example.

Before running the application, we must create the associated database table.

```
CREATE TABLE AutoStock (make varchar(25), model varchar(25), year integer,
```

```
color varchar(25), mileage integer, price float(7), vin integer);
```

Next, we manually populate the dealer's inventory with database inserts.

```
INSERT INTO AutoStock VALUES (
'Porsche', '911', 2001, 'Black', 25, 90000, 123456
);

INSERT INTO AutoStock VALUES (
'Ferrari', 'Maranello', 2001, 'Red', 15, 200000, 24601
);

INSERT INTO AutoStock VALUES (
'Lamborghini', 'Diablo', 2001, 'Yellow', 20, 275000, 80386
);

INSERT INTO AutoStock VALUES (
'Audi', 'TT', 2001, 'Gray', 25, 40000, 5000
);
```

This example requires a value object to represent a car. The code that accesses the database populates these objects and returns them to the client. The client code accesses the values in the car value object to choose a car to buy. Because this object is passed through the remote interface, it must implement `java.io.Serializable`.

```
public final class CarValueObject implements Serializable {

  private static String EOL = System.getProperty("line.separa-
tor");

  private String make;
  private String model;

  private int year;

  private String color;

  private int mileage;

  private double price;

  private int vin;  // vehicle identification number

  public CarValueObject() {}

  public CarValueObject(String make, String model, int year,
    String color, int mileage, double price, int vin) {
```

```java
      setMake(make);
      setModel(model);
      setYear(year);
      setColor(color);
      setMileage(mileage);
      setPrice(price);
      setVin(vin);

   }

   public String toString() {

      StringBuffer sb = new StringBuffer();

      sb.append(EOL);
      sb.append("Make: "+getMake());
      sb.append(" Model: "+getModel());
      sb.append(" Year: "+getYear());
      sb.append(" Color: "+getColor());
      sb.append(" Mileage: "+getMileage());
      sb.append(" Price: "+getPrice());
      sb.append(" VIN: "+getVin());

      sb.append(EOL);

      return sb.toString();
   }

   public String getMake() { return make; }
   public void setMake(String m) { make = m; }

   public String getModel() { return model; }
   public void setModel(String m) { model = m; }

   public int getYear() { return year; }
   public void setYear(int y) { year = y; }

   public String getColor() { return color; }
   public void setColor(String c) { color = c; }

   public int getMileage() { return mileage; }
   public void setMileage(int mi) { mileage = mi; }

   public double getPrice() { return price; }
   public void setPrice(double p) { price = p; }

   public int getVin() { return vin; }
   public void setVin(int v) { vin = v; }
```

```
}
```

The `AutoBuyer` EJB is the stateful session bean that acts as the client's interface to the auto dealer. The `AutoBuyerHome` exposes a single `create` method. The `AutoBuyer` bean stores the required make, model, and maximum price, and the stateful session bean uses these values when interacting with the auto dealer.

```
public interface AutoBuyerHome extends EJBHome {

  public AutoBuyer create(String make, String model, double max-
Price)
    throws CreateException, RemoteException;

}
```

It exposes three business methods in its remote interface. The `getAvailableCars` method asks the `AutoDealer` for cars matching the buyer's criteria. The `getPreviousOffers` method returns a map from vehicle ID numbers to the last bid amount on that car. This is conversational state maintained by the `AutoBuyer` bean. Finally, there is a `buyCar` method that returns true if the dealer accepts the offer. If the car is no longer available, a `NoSuchCarException` is thrown.

```
public interface AutoBuyer extends EJBObject {

  public Collection getAvailableCars()
    throws RemoteException;

  public Map getPreviousOffers()
    throws RemoteException;

  public boolean buyCar(int vin, double offer)
    throws RemoteException, NoSuchCarException;

}
```

The `AutoBuyerBean` is the EJB's bean class. It implements the business methods exposed in the remote interface.

```
public class AutoBuyerBean implements SessionBean {

  private SessionContext ctx;

  private String make;
  private String model;
  private double maxPrice;
```

```
    private AutoDealer autoDealer;

    private Map offerMap = new HashMap();

    public void setSessionContext(SessionContext c) {
      ctx = c;
    }
```

The `AutoBuyerBean` references the `AutoDealer` EJB. An EJB reference is used to avoid hard-coding the `AutoDealer`'s JNDI name into the
bean class.

```
    public void ejbCreate(String ma, String mo, double mp) {
      make     = ma;
      model    = mo;
      maxPrice = mp;

      AutoDealerHome dealerHome = null;

      try {
        Context ic = new InitialContext();

        Object h = ic.lookup("java:/comp/env/ejb/AutoDealerHome");

        dealerHome = (AutoDealerHome)
          PortableRemoteObject.narrow(h, AutoDealerHome.class);

      } catch (NamingException ne) {
        // Cannot find AutoDealerHome

        ne.printStackTrace();

        throw new EJBException(ne);
      }

      try {
        autoDealer = dealerHome.create();
      } catch (Exception e) {
        // exception during a creation of the Dealer
        e.printStackTrace();

        throw new EJBException(e);
      }

    }

    public void ejbRemove() {}
```

```
public void ejbActivate() {}
public void ejbPassivate() {}
```

The `getAvailableCars` and `buyCar` methods proxy their work to the `AutoDealer` EJB. A real application often interposes additional logic within the stateful session bean to manage additional state.

```
public Collection getAvailableCars()
  throws RemoteException
{
  return autoDealer.getAvailableCarsInPriceRange(make, model,
    maxPrice);
}


public Map getPreviousOffers() {
  return offerMap;
}

public void deletePreviousOffers() {
  offerMap.clear();
}

public boolean buyCar(int vin, double offer)
  throws RemoteException, NoSuchCarException
{

  offerMap.put(new Long(vin), new Double(offer));

  return autoDealer.buyCar(vin, offer);
}

}
```

The `AutoDealer` is modeled as a stateless session bean, and it exposes the `buyCar` and `getAvailableCarsInPriceRange` business methods. These methods access the underlying database to query or update the associated data.

The `buyCar` method is deployed with the `Required` transaction attribute. It makes database updates and must run within a transaction. The `getAvailableCarsInPriceRange` runs a query against the database. It is deployed with the `NotSupported` attribute because this application does not require the query to run within a transaction. This helps minimize the length of time locks are held in the database layer. Any data updates are through the `buyCar` method and use transactions.

```
public interface AutoDealer extends EJBObject {

  public boolean buyCar(int vin, double offer)
    throws RemoteException, NoSuchCarException;

  public Collection getAvailableCarsInPriceRange(String make,
    String model, double highPrice)
    throws RemoteException;
}
```

The `AutoDealerBean` provides the implementation of the dealer's business methods.

```
public class AutoDealerBean implements SessionBean {

  private SessionContext ctx;

  private DataSource dataSource;

  private String tableName;
```

The database table name is stored as an EJB environment name. This allows the table name to be changed without altering the EJB code. The `AutoDealerBean` keeps a `DataSource` in its member variables. Business methods use this `DataSource` to create JDBC connections. The data source is found through a resource reference. Like the table name, this enables the data source name to be changed without affecting the bean code.

```
  public void setSessionContext(SessionContext c) {
    ctx = c;

    try {
      Context ic = new InitialContext();

      tableName = (String) ic.lookup("java:/comp/env/TableName");

      dataSource = (DataSource) ic.lookup("java:/comp/env/jdbc/DBPool");

    } catch (NamingException ne) {
      ne.printStackTrace();

      throw new EJBException(ne);
    }
  }

  public void ejbCreate() {}
  public void ejbRemove() {}

  public void ejbActivate() {}
  public void ejbPassivate() {}
```

Accessing the Database

The buyCar method must determine whether the car is still available and then decide whether the offer is acceptable. This dealer uses a simple algorithm that any offer greater than 95 percent of the list price is acceptable. If the car is bought, it is removed from the database table and true is returned.

The database code is written to minimize potential deadlocks. First, a conditional delete is performed. This blind write succeeds and returns one row if the VIN exists and the offer is acceptable. In this case, true is returned. If zero rows were deleted, it is possible that the car has already been sold or the offer is not acceptable. The EJB performs a query to determine whether the VIN exists in the database table. If no car exists, a NoSuchCarException is thrown.

Note that the EJB is using rather generic SQL in this example. Real applications often incorporate database-specific SQL to enhance performance or scalability.

Finally, the buyCar method is careful to close any JDBC resources that it has used by closing the Connection, Statement, and ResultSet.

```java
public boolean buyCar(int vin, double offer)
  throws NoSuchCarException
{
  boolean accepted = false;

  // This dealer accepts an offer of 95% of the list price or
  // higher.  We use the offer price to figure out the purchas-
ing
  // power of this offer.
  double priceLimit = Math.floor(offer / 0.95);

  Connection conn = null;
  Statement st = null;
  ResultSet rs = null;

  try {
    conn = dataSource.getConnection();

    st = conn.createStatement();


    int rowCount = st.executeUpdate("delete from "+tableName+
      " WHERE vin="+vin+" AND price <="+priceLimit);

    if (rowCount == 1) {
      // car was bought
```

```
      return true;
    } else {

      // need to determine whether no rows were deleted because
      // the vin does not exist, or because the price was not
      // acceptable.

      st = conn.createStatement();

      rs = st.executeQuery("select vin from "+tableName+
        " WHERE vin="+vin);

      if (rs.next()) {
        // vin exists so price was not acceptable
        return false;
      } else {
        // vin no longer exists

        throw new NoSuchCarException("The car with vin: "+vin+
          " is no longer available.");
      }
    }
  } catch (SQLException e) {

    e.printStackTrace();

    throw new EJBException(e);

  } finally {

    // close out resources

    if (rs != null) try { rs.close(); } catch (Exception ignore)
{}
    if (st != null) try { st.close(); } catch (Exception ignore)
{}
    if (conn != null) {
      try { conn.close(); } catch (Exception ignore) {}
    }
  }
}
```

The `getAvailableCarsInPriceRange` is another example of a stateless session bean method accessing an underlying database. This method receives a `ResultSet` and iterates through the `ResultSet` populating `CarValueObjects` to return to the client.

```java
public Collection getAvailableCarsInPriceRange(String make,
  String model, double highPrice) {

  List cars = new ArrayList();

  Connection conn = null;
  Statement st   = null;
  ResultSet rs   = null;

  try {
    conn = dataSource.getConnection();

    st = conn.createStatement();

    rs = st.executeQuery("select make, model, year, color,"+
      " mileage, price, vin from "+tableName+
      " WHERE price<="+highPrice+" AND model='"+model+"' AND
make='"+
      make + "'");


    while (rs.next()) {

      int year      = rs.getInt(3);
      String color = rs.getString(4);
      int mileage  = rs.getInt(5);
      double price = rs.getDouble(6);
      int vin       = rs.getInt(7);

      cars.add(new CarValueObject(make, model, year, color,
mileage,
        price, vin));
    }

    return cars;

  } catch (SQLException e) {

    e.printStackTrace();
    throw new EJBException(e);

  } finally {

    // close out resources

    if (rs != null) try { rs.close(); } catch (Exception ignore)
{}
```

```
        if (st != null) try { st.close(); } catch (Exception ignore)
  {}
      if (conn != null) {
        try { conn.close(); } catch (Exception ignore) {}
      }
    }
  }
}
```

Client Code

The client code creates an `AutoBuyer` and then queries for the available cars matching its criteria. Finally, the `buyCar` method is called in an attempt to make an offer on the car. This simple example always offers 98 percent of the list price which, as we've seen, is accepted by the dealer. We have omitted the auxiliary client code and only demonstrate here the EJB interactions.

```
AutoBuyer buyer = home.create(make, model, price);

// finding the cars that match my criteria
Collection cars = buyer.getAvailableCars();

if (cars.isEmpty()) {
  System.out.println("Sorry there was no available "+
    make + " " + model + " for under $"+price);
} else {

  try {
    // Bid on the first car in the Collection
    CarValueObject car = (CarValueObject) cars.itera-
tor().next();

    System.out.println("Found a car: "+car);

    double bidPrice = Math.floor(car.getPrice() * 0.98);

boolean accepted = buyer.buyCar(vin, price);

  } catch (NoSuchCarException nsce) {
    System.err.println("Sorry.  This car is no longer avail-
able.");
  }
}
```

We can see the output of our sample client when it attempts to buy a Porsche 911 for less than $100,000.

```
Created a customer to find a Porsche 911.
```

```
Found a car:
Make: Porsche Model: 911 Year: 2001 Color: Black Mileage: 25
Price: 90000.0 VIN: 123456

Congratulations.  Your bid of 88200.0 was accepted.
```

We can query the database and see that indeed the Porsche no longer exists in the database table.

```
select * from AutoStock;
    make     |   model    | year | color  | mileage | price  |  vin
-------------+------------+------+--------+---------+--------+---
----
 Ferrari     | Maranello  | 2001 | Red    |      15 | 200000 |
24601
 Lamborghini | Diablo     | 2001 | Yellow |      20 | 275000 |
80386
 Audi        | TT         | 2001 | Gray   |      25 |  40000 | 5000
(3 rows)
```

If we run our client again asking for a Porsche 911 for less than $100,000, we find that none are available.

```
Created a customer to find a Porsche 911.

Sorry there was no available Porsche 911 for under $100000.0
```

Best Practices

The following are some best practices for coding stateful and stateless session EJBs.

Coding Business Interfaces

Many new EJB programmers are confused by the relationship between the remote interface and the EJB class. This arrangement is necessary for the container to intercept all method calls to the EJB. One confusing aspect is that the EJB class implements the methods defined in the remote interface, but the EJB class doesn't implement the remote interface itself. In fact, the EJB class should never implement the remote interface. While the EJB specification allows this practice, it can cause very serious but subtle bugs. The problem with having the EJB class implement the remote interface is that now the EJB class can be passed as a parameter to any method that expects the remote interface as a parameter.

Remember that the remote interface exists to allow the container to intercept method calls in order to provide necessary services such as transactions or security. If the bean class is used, the method calls arrive directly on the bean object—creating a dangerous situation in which the container cannot intercept method calls or intervene in case of error. If (as recommended) the EJB class does not implement the remote interface, this problem becomes apparent at compile time. The Java compiler will reject the attempt to pass the bean class as a parameter of the remote interface's type.

Never implement the remote interface in the EJB class.

The only advantage of implementing the remote interface in the bean class is that the Java compiler catches any method that is defined in the remote interface but not implemented in the bean class. However, this also means that the bean class has to provide dummy implementations of the remote interface's super-class (`javax.ejb.EJBObject`) to satisfy the Java compiler.

Clearly, implementing the remote interface in the bean class is not a good practice, but it is desirable to catch the bean writer's errors as early as possible. The WebLogic Server provides an EJB compliance checker to catch as many violations of the EJB specification as possible. The compliance checker analyzes an EJB and flags any specification violations with the related section in the EJB specification. The compliance checker can be run as `java weblogic.EJBComplianceChecker` on the command line or by using the graphical deployment tools. The compliance checker catches any methods that are defined in the remote interface but not implemented in the EJB class.

Another method for catching this class of errors is by using a pattern known as the business interface. In this pattern, all of the business methods are defined in a separate interface. The remote interface extends the business interface and the `javax.ejb.EJBObject` interface. The bean class can then implement the business interface. For instance:

```
public interface MyBusinessInterface {
  public void businessMethod()
    throws RemoteException;
}

public interface MyRemoteInterface
  extends MyBusinessInterface, EJBObject
{
  // empty
```

```
  }

public class MyBean
   implements SessionBean, MyBusinessInterface
{

public void businessMethod()
   throws RemoteException
{
  // provide implementation
}

// implement SessionBean methods here

}
```

By using the business interface, the compiler ensures that the bean class implements the methods in the business interface. The pattern is also safe because the bean class cannot be passed into a method expecting the remote interface. While both classes are assignable from the business interface, the remote interface is still a distinct type.

Tips for Transactions

Almost every EJB application uses transactions at some point. Transactions ensure correctness and reliability and are essential to e-commerce applications. However, misusing transactions can greatly affect performance and even produce incorrect results. It is important to understand that session beans themselves cannot be transactional.

A common misperception is that the member variables of the session bean will be rolled back when their transaction aborts. Instead, session beans merely propagate their transaction to any resource that they acquire. For instance, at the beginning of a transaction, a session bean has a member variable with a value of 0. During the transaction, the member variable is set to 2, and a row is inserted into the database. If the transaction rolls back, the member variable will not be reset to 0. However, the row will no longer be in the database. Because a database is a transactional resource, it will participate in the session bean's transaction, and a rollback will abort any associated work.

Session bean state is not transactional.

Transactions can have a huge impact on performance. Because transactions provide durability, a transaction commit is a relatively expensive operation. Many EJB applications limit their performance by making their transactions too fine-grained. Operations that are closely related and occur in a series should usually be in the same transaction. For instance, our user page may read the associated user data and write the last accessed timestamp, all within the same transaction.

User Interactions and Transaction Performance

Transactions also can cause problems if they span too many operations. In particular, a transaction should never encompass user input or user think time. Regardless of the underlying concurrency model, transactions acquire locks and resources. If a user starts a transaction and then goes to lunch or even visits another Web site, the transaction is not committed. Instead, the transaction continues to hold valuable locks and resources within the server.

In general, all transaction demarcation should occur within the server. There are a number of well-known techniques to avoid keeping long-running transactions open. When you ask a user to submit a form, break the operation up into two transactions. The Web page should read the data in a single transaction along with a version stamp. This transaction is committed before the form is returned to the user. The user can now modify the data as he or she sees fit. The form update occurs in a new transaction.

But what if another transaction has modified the data and our user has updated a form with stale data? There are several methods to handle this case: The correct approach depends on the application. One option is to write back all the data in the user's form. In this case, our user can overwrite any modifications that occurred after we read the data.

A more common approach adds an additional time or version stamp to the associated database table. When the data is read, this version stamp is read as well. When the write occurs, the update statement is conditional and commits only if the versions match. This ensures that the data is only updated if another client has not modified the underlying data. If the update fails, the correct behavior in this scenario depends on the application. For instance, the user might be alerted to the situation and shown to the latest data. Another variant on this approach is to verify that only the modified fields are consistent with the read data.

Transactions should never encompass user input or think time.

Container-Managed vs. Bean-Managed Transactions

The EJB specification allows a session bean to choose either container-managed or bean-managed transactions. In container-managed transactions, the bean writer declares transaction attributes in the deployment descriptor. The EJB container then automatically starts and commits transactions as requested. The bean writer does not have to write any code to manage transactions. In bean-managed transactions, the bean writer uses the `UserTransaction` interface to explicitly start and commit transactions. Container-managed transactions should always be the bean writer's first choice.

Transactions consume resources in both the application server and in databases, which means you should keep transactions as short as possible. Container-managed transactions encompass a set of method calls. When the outer method completes, the transaction is committed or rolled back by the container.

In bean-managed transactions, the bean writer must ensure that the transaction is committed or rolled back. While the WebLogic Server includes a transaction timeout, the bean writer should not rely on this feature, but instead release transaction resources as soon as possible. With bean-managed transactions, the bean writer needs to ensure that every exceptional path handles the transaction rollback or commit correctly. With container-managed transactions, this is handled automatically by the EJB container.

Use container-managed instead of bean-managed transactions.

Transactions and Error Handling

When an EJB encounters an error, the bean writer often needs to force a transaction rollback. The EJB container automatically rolls back a container transaction if a system exception is thrown. For a bean writer, the easiest way to force transaction rollback is by calling the `EJBContext.setRollbackOnly` method. This makes the bean code easier to maintain because it is explicit that the transaction will be rolled back.

Force transaction rollback with the `EJBContext`'s `setRollbackOnly` method.

Application Partitioning

Transactions should never span client input. As noted, a scalable application cannot start a transaction and wait for a user to complete a form or click Submit on a Web form. In fact, it is best to avoid handling transactions in the Web tier. JSPs and servlets should be concerned with presentation logic and use an interface to communicate with the business logic. Transactional business logic should be handled within the EJB layer.

Generally, a stateless session bean is a good interface between the Web tier and the EJB layer. The stateless session bean should be starting transactions, and committing or rolling back transactions, before returning to the Web tier. This ensures that transactions are short and only encompass the transactional logic.

Don't expose transactions to the Web tier or presentation layer.

The EJB deployer selects the container-managed transaction demarcation by setting the transaction attribute to `Never`, `NotSupported`, `Supports`, `Required`, `RequiresNew`, or `Mandatory` in the EJB deployment descriptor. In general, `Supports` should not be used in an enterprise application. The danger of using the `Supports` setting is that the EJBs will run in a transaction only if the caller has started a transaction. If a business component must run in a transaction, use `Required`, `RequiresNew`, or `Mandatory`. If nontransactional behavior is needed, use `Never` or `NotSupported`.

Avoid using the `Supports` transaction attribute.

When Not to Use Stateful Session Beans

Stateful session beans represent a stateful conversation between a single client and a bean instance. Stateful session beans cannot be shared between multiple users. You should not model a shared cache or any shared resource as a stateful session bean. If multiple clients need to access a single EJB instance, use an entity bean.

Stateful session beans are not shared by multiple users.

Because each client requires its own stateful session bean instance, the number of bean instances and the associated resource requirements can grow quickly. If an application can tolerate the stateless programming model, stateless session beans are easier to scale than stateful session beans.

Applications should always call `remove` after finishing with a stateful session bean instance. This enables the EJB container to release container resources as soon as possible. If the `remove` call is omitted, the EJB container will eventually passivate the bean, but this involves extra disk access.

Stateless session beans are easier to scale than stateful session beans.

Stateful session bean writers must also be careful when integrating their stateful session beans with Web applications. Stateful session beans should not allow concurrent method calls. As mentioned earlier, it is possible for multiple requests to cause concurrent calls on a stateful session bean. Unfortunately, this error usually shows up under load, so it is often missed in testing. For this reason, use stateful session beans only within the scope of a request. Use entity beans or servlet sessions for applications that need to store data between requests.

Best Practices for EJB Security

EJB provides a declarative security support as well as a simple programmatic interface for explicit security checks within the bean code. In practice, EJB security settings need to be considered within the entire application's security model. It is common for Web-based applications to handle authentication within the Web tier. In this environment, the EJB tier may contain very few security constraints. This arrangement simplifies the EJB design, and because the security checks are localized to the presentation layer, the application may modify security policies without modifying the EJB tier.

Applications with standalone programmatic clients often directly access session beans. Because there is no intermediate tier, the security access control must be handled in the EJB tier.

Declarative security control is preferred for simple applications. Since the security constraints are declared in the deployment descriptor, the bean classes' business logic is not polluted with security checks. The declarative security model is based on security roles that are declared in the deployment descriptor. Declarative security works best when the number of roles is fixed and does not depend on the number of clients. For instance, an application might include a user role and an administrator role. Because there are only two access domains, it is feasible to declare these roles in the deployment descriptor.

However, declarative security should not be used when each user requires individual security constraints. Such applications require programmatic security checks within the EJB code. It is also common to combine both security models. For instance, an account bean might use declarative security to ensure only registered users access any methods. The bean code then includes additional constraints to ensure that each user only gains access to his or her account.

Use declarative security checks when an application contains few roles. Choose programmatic security when each user needs individual security checks.

Conclusion

EJBs are server-side Java components that leverage the standard transaction, persistence, concurrency, and security services provided by the EJB container. This chapter described session beans, which represent conversations with clients. In the next chapter, we discuss entity beans. Chapter 10 completes the coverage of EJBs with a discussion of message-driven EJBs.

ENTITY EJBS

In this chapter:

- Entity beans and their lifecycle
- How to write container-managed persistence (CMP) and bean-managed persistence (BMP) entity beans
- Useful techniques, optimizations, and patterns for writing entity beans
- Best practices for developing and deploying entity beans

Chapter 9

Entity Enterprise JavaBeans (EJBs) present an object view of persistent data. The fields in entity beans correspond to underlying data in a persistent store—usually, a relational database. An entity bean's state is transactional. When a client updates fields within a transaction, the updates are only permanent if the transaction commits. When a transaction rolls back, the entity bean's state returns to its last committed state. Later in this chapter, we discuss the contract between the EJB container and the entity bean that provides these guarantees.

Rationale for Entity EJBs

In a multi-tier e-commerce application, back-end persistence is provided by one or more databases. The Web engine uses HTML for static content, and servlets and JSPs for dynamic presentation logic. EJBs provide the business logic between the Web tier and the database.

As described in Chapter 8, session beans can take advantage of container services such as transactions, security, and concurrency. Although session beans do not provide any direct persistence support, they often include Java Database Connectivity (JDBC) code that accesses persistent stores.

However, session beans cannot *directly* represent persistent data. Java is an object-oriented language, but databases store data relationally, as rows in tables. Session beans using JDBC cannot easily represent data as first-class objects. Moreover, session beans do not share some of the defining characteristics of persistent data: Multiple clients do not share them, and they do not generally survive server reboots or crashes.

The EJB specification provides *entity beans* as a persistent, transactional, and shared component, so that business data can be simultaneously used by many clients and persistently stored until it has been explicitly deleted.

Entity Bean Basics

As persistent objects, an entity bean's state must be saved to the database. Entity beans have two operational styles: They either use BMP or CMP.

With BMP, the bean writer provides the code to load and persist the entity bean to the database. This usually requires JDBC code in the bean class to read and update the entity bean's fields to the database.

With CMP, the EJB container automatically provides code to persist the entity bean to the database. No JDBC code is required. The programming model for CMP changed drastically between EJB 1.1 and EJB 2.0. The EJB 2.0 CMP model offers a number of additional features for both the bean writer and the EJB container. In this chapter, we discuss only the EJB 2.0 CMP model. While the WebLogic Server supports both EJB 1.1 and EJB 2.0 CMP entity beans, it is strongly recommended that any new development use EJB 2.0.

Entity Bean Components

Entity beans consist of a home interface, remote interface, bean class, primary key class, and deployment descriptors.

Home Interface

The home interface extends the `javax.ejb.EJBHome` interface and contains `create` methods, `remove` methods, `finder` methods, and `home` methods.

An entity bean's `create` method calls the corresponding `ejbCreate` method on the bean class. The responsibility of the `create` method is to create the persistent representation in the backing store. This is usually implemented as a database insert.

An entity bean `create` is a database insert.

The entity bean's home interface must define a `remove` method that takes a primary key as a parameter. This method removes the entity bean instance with the corresponding primary key from the persistent store. Usually this represents a database delete operation.

An entity bean `remove` is a database delete.

Primary Keys and Identities

Like stateful session beans, entity beans have identities. A business method in the remote interface must be called against a specific entity bean instance. The entity bean client receives the entity bean reference by creating, finding, or using an EJB *handle*. A bean either has *identity* (it has a unique identifier such as a primary key) or it is *anonymous* (no primary key has been attached).

The primary key identifies an entity bean instance.

Each entity bean reference is associated with a particular primary key. When calls are made against that reference, they are dispatched to a bean instance with the same primary key.

Primary Key Classes

Unlike session beans, entity beans must include a primary key class. The primary key class identifies the entity bean instance: Its value must be unique for the entity bean type. The primary key class can be either a Java primitive type such as `java.lang.String` or `java.lang.Integer`, or the user may write a custom primary key class. The primary key class maps to one or more fields in the entity bean. A primary key with multiple fields is known as a *compound primary key*.

Usually, the entity bean primary key fields are also its primary key fields in a database. The primary key class must provide suitable implementations of `public int hashCode()` and `public boolean equals (Object)`. Implementing `hash code` and `equals` can be confusing. We discuss common techniques later in this chapter.

Finder Methods

`Finder` methods enable the client to make queries and receive references to entity beans that satisfy query conditions. Every entity EJB must have a `findByPrimaryKey` method in its home interface. This special `finder` method returns an EJB reference that has the corresponding primary key. Bean writers may also define more complex `finders` that return many entity references that match the `finder`'s condition. For instance, a "U.S. citizen" entity bean might have a `finder` named `findBillionaires` that returns data on all citizens who are worth more than $1 billion.

Home Methods

Entity beans also can have `home` methods. `Home` methods are business methods that do not apply to a particular instance. Instead, the container merely chooses an available instance and calls the `home` method on it. This programming model is similar to stateless session beans. We discuss when to use entity beans versus stateless session beans later in this chapter.

The Bean Class and Bean Context

Like session beans, the entity bean's remote interface extends the `javax.ejb.EJBObject` interface and contains the signatures for business methods. The actual implementation of these methods is provided in the bean class.

The entity bean's implementation class implements the `javax.ejb.EntityBean` interface. Like the `javax.ejb.SessionBean` interface, the `EntityBean` interface contains the signatures for callbacks from the EJB container to the bean instance. The `setEntityContext` method is called immediately after the bean's constructor and passes the bean instance the `EntityContext`. The `EntityContext` is generally stored in a member variable and is used by the bean instance to make some standard calls into the EJB container. The `setEntityContext` method may be used to acquire some basic resources such as `DataSource` references that are not specific to a particular primary key.

When `setEntityContext` is called, the EJB container has not yet assigned a primary key to this bean instance. The entity bean interface also has a corresponding `unsetEntityContext` method that is called before the bean instance is destroyed. Generally, this method frees any resources acquired in `setEntityContext`.

Activation and Passivation

The entity bean interface also includes `ejbActivate` and `ejbPassivate` methods. Remember that in stateful session beans `ejbActivate` and `ejbPassivate` are used to load and save the stateful session bean's state to a backing store, usually located in the file system. While the entity bean interface uses the same names, the `ejbActivate` and `ejbPassivate` methods have a different meaning.

> In entity beans, `ejbActivate` is called when an entity bean instance is associated with a particular primary key. The `ejbPassivate` method is called when this association is removed and the entity bean instance no longer has a particular identity.

Home Methods and Business Methods

The entity bean's implementation class implements home methods and business methods from the remote interface. Home methods are called against an anonymous instance. A home method should not make use of or expect an associated primary key value.

Business methods are called on a specific instance having a primary key and identity. The remaining methods in the bean implementation class depend on whether the bean uses BMP or CMP.

CMP Entity Bean Example

Instead of writing cumbersome JDBC code, the CMP bean writer provides only the business logic and deployment descriptors. CMP can offer the developer faster development time and better performance than BMP entity beans. The CMP entity bean class is abstract. This enables the EJB container to implement persistence logic by generating a class that extends the bean class.

> Note: This section covers the EJB 2.0 CMP model. At the time of publication, the EJB 2.0 specification is not yet final. Please consult the EJB 2.0 specification and the WebLogic Server documentation for information about late changes in the specification.

Container-Managed Fields

Every container-managed entity bean has a set of container-managed fields, which are saved and loaded from the database. Generally, each container-managed field corresponds to a column in a relational database. For instance, in a Student entity bean, container-managed fields could be the `name`, `ssn` (Social Security number), and `grade`.

Writing getXXX and setXXX Methods

The bean provider cannot declare container-managed fields. Instead, the bean writer declares abstract `get` and `set` methods for each container-managed field. For instance, instead of declaring a `private String name` in the bean class, the bean provider uses `public abstract void set-Name(String name);` and `public abstract String get-Name();`. These `get` and `set` methods are public and abstract because the EJB container provides the actual implementation. While this requirement seems a bit strange at first, it allows the EJB container to detect when fields are read and written. This enables the EJB container to optimize the calls to the database. For instance, if no fields are updated within a transaction, the WebLogic Server EJB container does not write back to the database.

Declaring the Container-Managed Fields

Each container-managed field must be declared in the *ejb-jar.xml* deployment descriptor. This enables the container to match the container-managed fields with the `setXXX` and `getXXX` methods in the bean class. The bean provider then includes the database mapping in a separate CMP deployment descriptor named *weblogic-cmp-rdbms.xml*, which contains the database table name and a mapping between each container-managed field and its corresponding database column.

A CMP entity bean must set the values of the primary key fields in its `ejbCreate` method. Then the `ejbCreate` method always returns null.

The EJB container determines the primary key value by extracting the primary key fields after the `ejbCreate` has returned. The bean needs to set the primary key fields in `ejbCreate` because the container does the database insert after it calls `ejbCreate`.

The convention of returning null instead of void enables a BMP entity bean to extend a CMP entity bean (more about this later). The Java language specification does not allow you to overload a method while changing only the return type. Therefore, the bean writer could not have a BMP version in which `ejbCreate` returns the primary key type and extend that bean with a CMP version returning void.

Student CMP Example

Our first example demonstrates the simplicity of CMP. This is the `StudentBean`:

```
package com.learnweblogic.examples.ch9.cmp;

import java.util.Collection;

import javax.ejb.EntityContext;
import javax.ejb.EntityBean;

public abstract class StudentCMPBean implements EntityBean {

  private EntityContext ctx;

  // container-managed fields
  public abstract String getName();
  public abstract void setName(String n);

  public abstract Integer getSsn();
  public abstract void setSsn(Integer ssn);

  public abstract int getGrade();
  public abstract void setGrade(int gr);


  public void setEntityContext(EntityContext c) {
    ctx = c;
  }

  public void unsetEntityContext() {
    ctx = null;
  }


  public Integer ejbCreate(String name, int ssn, int grade)
  {
    setName(name);
    setSsn(new Integer(ssn));
    setGrade(grade);

    return null;
```

```
    }

    // This implementation requires no post-create initialization
    // so this required method is empty
    public void ejbPostCreate(String name, int ssn, int grade) {}


    // These methods are required by the EntityBean interface but
    // are not used in this implementation.

    public void ejbRemove() {}

    public void ejbLoad() {}

    public void ejbStore() {}

    public void ejbActivate() {}
    public void ejbPassivate() {}

}
```

The bean class contains `get` and `set` methods for the bean's three container-managed fields: `name`, `ssn`, and `grade`.

ejb-jar.xml Deployment Descriptor

The *ejb-jar.xml* deployment descriptor specifies that our bean use CMP and the EJB 2.0 model. The `<cmp-field>` elements specify all the container-managed fields in this CMP entity bean. Note the EJB-QL query element for the `findStudentsInGrade` method.

```xml
<?xml version="1.0"?>

<!DOCTYPE ejb-jar PUBLIC
"-//Sun Microsystems, Inc.//DTD Enterprise JavaBeans 2.0//EN"
"http://java.sun.com/dtd/ejb-jar_2_0.dtd">


<ejb-jar>
  <enterprise-beans>
    <entity>
      <ejb-name>StudentCMPEJB</ejb-name>
      <home>com.learnweblogic.examples.ch9.cmp.StudentHome</home>
      <remote>com.learnweblogic.examples.ch9.cmp.Student</remote>
      <ejb-class>
        com.learnweblogic.examples.ch9.cmp.StudentCMPBean
      </ejb-class>
      <persistence-type>Container</persistence-type>
```

```
        <prim-key-class>java.lang.Integer</prim-key-class>
        <reentrant>False</reentrant>
        <cmp-version>2.x</cmp-version>
       <abstract-schema-name>StudentCMPBean</abstract-schema-name>

        <cmp-field>
          <field-name>name</field-name>
        </cmp-field>
        <cmp-field>
          <field-name>ssn</field-name>
        </cmp-field>
        <cmp-field>
          <field-name>grade</field-name>
        </cmp-field>

        <primkey-field>ssn</primkey-field>

        <query>
          <description>
              finds students in a given grade
          </description>
          <query-method>
            <method-name>findStudentsInGrade</method-name>
            <method-params>
              <method-param>int</method-param>
            </method-params>
          </query-method>
          <ejb-ql>
            <![CDATA[FROM StudentCMPBean s WHERE s.grade = ?1]]>
          </ejb-ql>
        </query>

     </entity>

  </enterprise-beans>


  <assembly-descriptor>
    <container-transaction>
      <method>
        <ejb-name>StudentCMPEJB</ejb-name>
        <method-name>*</method-name>
      </method>
      <trans-attribute>Required</trans-attribute>
    </container-transaction>

  </assembly-descriptor>
</ejb-jar>
```

weblogic-ejb-jar.xml Deployment Descriptor

The CMP EJB also requires a *weblogic-ejb-jar.xml* deployment descriptor that contains WebLogic Server–specific options and settings. The persistence stanza, required for CMP entity beans, specifies that this CMP entity bean is using the WebLogic Server 6.0 CMP engine, and that the CMP deployment descriptor is located in *META-INF/weblogic-cmp-rdbms.xml*. This is required for WebLogic Server to support plug-in CMP engines from other vendors. The examples in this book assume the WebLogic Server CMP engine.

```xml
<?xml version="1.0"?>

<!DOCTYPE weblogic-ejb-jar PUBLIC
"-//BEA Systems, Inc.//DTD WebLogic 6.0.0 EJB//EN"
 "http://www.bea.com/servers/wls600/dtd/weblogic-ejb-jar.dtd" >

<weblogic-ejb-jar>
  <weblogic-enterprise-bean>
    <ejb-name>StudentCMPEJB</ejb-name>

    <entity-descriptor>
      <persistence>
        <persistence-type>
          <type-identifier>WebLogic_CMP_RDBMS</type-identifier>
          <type-version>6.0</type-version>
          <type-storage>
            META-INF/weblogic-cmp-rdbms.xml
          </type-storage>
        </persistence-type>
        <persistence-use>
          <type-identifier>WebLogic_CMP_RDBMS</type-identifier>
          <type-version>6.0</type-version>
        </persistence-use>
        </persistence>
    </entity-descriptor>

    <jndi-name>StudentCMPEJB</jndi-name>
  </weblogic-enterprise-bean>

</weblogic-ejb-jar>
```

weblogic-cmp-rdbms.xml Descriptor

The third required deployment descriptor is the CMP deployment descriptor, *weblogic-cmp-rdbms-jar.xml*. The *weblogic-cmp-rdbms-jar.xml* includes the database information necessary to map the abstract persistence schema to the physical schema in the database. Each entity bean maps to a database table, and each container-managed field maps to a database column.

```
<?xml version="1.0"?>

<!DOCTYPE weblogic-rdbms-jar PUBLIC
 '-//BEA Systems, Inc.//DTD WebLogic 6.0.0 EJB RDBMS Persistence/
/EN'
 'http://www.bea.com/servers/wls600/dtd/weblogic-rdbms20-persis-
tence-600.dtd'>
```

```
<weblogic-rdbms-jar>
  <weblogic-rdbms-bean>

    <ejb-name>StudentCMPEJB</ejb-name>
    <data-source-name>DBPool</data-source-name>
    <table-name>studentcmptable</table-name>

    <field-map>
      <cmp-field>ssn</cmp-field>
      <dbms-column>ssn</dbms-column>
    </field-map>
    <field-map>
      <cmp-field>name</cmp-field>
      <dbms-column>name</dbms-column>
    </field-map>
    <field-map>
      <cmp-field>grade</cmp-field>
      <dbms-column>grade</dbms-column>
    </field-map>

  </weblogic-rdbms-bean>

</weblogic-rdbms-jar>
```

Building and Running the Example

This example is located in the examples/ch9/cmp directory on the accompanying CD-ROM. The example includes a *build.cmd* script to build and compile the EJB and its client. The *tables.ddl* file includes the necessary schema for the database. These tables should be created before deploying the EJBs. The deploy.cmd script copies the ejb-jar into the server's applications directory for it to be deployed. The *runClient.cmd* script can be used to run the EJB client.

CMP

Entity beans that use CMP do not include JDBC code: The EJB container generates code that provides automatic persistence. The EJB container calls the ejbCreate methods before the bean has been inserted into a database. The ejbCreate method generally uses its parameters to initialize the entity bean's fields. The ejbCreate method must set primary key fields.

ejbCreate

After the ejbCreate method returns, the EJB container extracts the primary key fields from the bean instance and performs a database insert. The ejbCreate method always returns null in any CMP entity bean. While this looks strange at first, it is required to enable a BMP bean to extend a CMP bean. We'll discuss this requirement later in this chapter.

ejbRemove

A CMP entity bean's ejbRemove method is called before the EJB container deletes the entity bean from the database. The entity bean writer can include code in the ejbRemove method that is run immediately before the bean is deleted, but this is not a common practice.

ejbLoad

The EJB container calls the ejbLoad method of a CMP entity bean after loading the bean's state from the persistent store. The ejbLoad method can be used to post-process any container-managed field loaded from the database. For instance, the ejbLoad method might decompress a container-managed field extracted from the database and store the value in a transient member variable. This, again, is not a common practice.

ejbStore

The ejbStore method is called before the entity bean's state is written to the database. You can add code to perform post-processing such as decompressing transient data, but this is not commonly done.

Finders

Unlike BMP entity beans, the CMP bean writer does not implement `finder` methods within the bean class. Instead, the bean writer provides a query for each `finder`. Queries are written in the EJB-QL language and are included in the deployment descriptor. EJB-QL, which resembles the SQL query language, is discussed in detail later in this chapter.

ejbPostCreate

Entity bean classes can contain an `ejbPostCreate` method for each `ejbCreate` method. The `ejbPostCreate` method has the same parameters as its corresponding `ejbCreate` method, but the `ejbPostCreate` method returns void. Generally, `ejbPostCreate` is used to initialize container-managed relationships (CMR).

Container-Managed Entity Bean Lifecycle

Entity beans exist in a persistent store until they are deleted by either the entity bean's `remove` method or by a direct database delete. Therefore, the entity lifecycle must accommodate instances that exist before the EJB server is started and that continue to live after the EJB server is halted.

Entity bean instances exist in two states: *anonymous* and *identity*. An anonymous entity bean is similar to a stateless session bean. It has no associated identity: One anonymous instance is as good as any other. An identified bean has an associated primary key that uniquely identifies this instance. Through its lifetime, the entity bean transitions between these states in response to callbacks from the EJB container.

Anonymous Instances

When the EJB container creates a new bean instance, it first calls the bean's default constructor. Next, the EJB container calls the `setEntityContext` method passing an `EntityContext` object to the newly created bean. Note that the bean is, at this point, anonymous. The `setEntityContext` method cannot use primary key fields, nor can it use the `EntityContext`'s `getPrimaryKey` method.

The WebLogic EJB container maintains a pool of anonymous instances so that it can quickly dispatch finder, home, and business methods. The container removes instances from the anonymous state by calling the unset-EntityContext method, which frees memory and other resources within the EJB server.

When a finder method is called on the home interface, the EJB container selects an anonymous instance and uses it to run the corresponding find method. When a finder completes, the bean instance is returned to the pool. If the client calls a create method on the home interface, the container selects an anonymous instance and calls the corresponding ejbCreate and ejbPostCreate methods on the instance.

Identified Instances

At this point, the newly created instance transitions to the identity state. A business method invocation can also cause the bean to transition to the identity state. In this scenario, the EJB container selects an instance from the pool, assigns it a primary key, and then calls the ejbActivate method, which moves the bean to the identity state.

Entity beans in the identity state are ready to run business methods. The EJB container can preserve resources by returning an entity bean to the anonymous state by calling the ejbPassivate method. An ejbRemove callback also returns the bean to the anonymous state.

Reading and Writing the Database

Entity beans use the ejbLoad and ejbStore methods to synchronize their state with the database. Because entity beans are transactional components, these methods run within the business method's transaction. When business methods are called on an entity bean reference, the EJB container might need to load and store the bean's state to the database.

While there are many options to control when the EJB container calls ejbLoad and ejbStore, this section discusses the default behavior. Later in this chapter, we discuss techniques to optimize database access with ejbLoad and ejbStore. In the default behavior, the EJB container calls ejbLoad at the beginning of a transaction and runs any business methods within the transaction. When the transaction commits, the ejbStore method writes the bean's state back to a database. The bean then remains in the ready state until another business method appears, or until the bean is passivated to the pool state.

Introduction to CMRs

Objects do not exist in a vacuum: Designs specify relationships between a system's objects. For instance, the StudentBean would naturally have a relationship with a SchoolBean. With the EJB 2.0 specification, there is standard support for relationships between entity beans. In EJB 2.0, the container handles the persistence logic necessary to manage the relationship between EJB 2.0 CMP beans (see Figure 9–1).

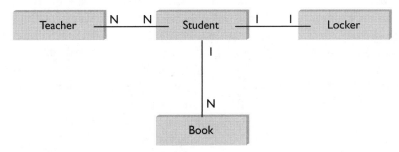

Figure 9–1   CMRs with the Student EJB

Container-managed entity beans may use one-to-one (1:1), one-to-many (1:N), or many-to-many (N:N) relationships. A StudentBean and a Locker-Bean might have a one-to-one relationship. Each Student has one corresponding Locker. Each Locker has one corresponding Student.

A StudentBean and BookBean might have a one-to-many relationship. Each Student has many Books, but a single student only uses each Book.

A StudentBean and a TeacherBean have a many-to-many relationship. Each Student has many Teachers, and each Teacher has many Students. Note that an entity bean can participate in several relationships, and each can be of a different cardinality.

Unidirectional and Bidirectional Relationships

CMRs can be either bidirectional ($\leftrightarrow$) or unidirectional ($\rightarrow$). In a bidirectional relationship, either bean may navigate to its related bean. For instance, in our Student $\leftrightarrow$ Locker example, the Student bean can get to the Locker bean, and vice versa. It is also possible to specify a unidirectional relationship, such as Student $\rightarrow$ Locker. In this case, the Student bean can navigate to the Locker bean but not vice versa. There is no performance advantage to using unidirectional relationships; in general, bidirectional relationships should be preferred.

Like container-managed fields, CMRs are exposed via abstract `get` and `set` methods in the bean class. For single object relationships, the `get` and `set` methods take the remote interface of the target bean. For instance, in our preceding Student → Locker example, the Student bean would contain a `public abstract Locker getLocker();` and `public abstract void setLocker(Locker l);` methods. If this relationship were bidirectional, the Locker bean would contain the corresponding methods to access the Student bean.

Many relationships have `get` and `set` methods that use a `java.util.Collection` or `java.util.Set` to contain the remote interface of the related beans. Unlike a `Collection`, using a `Set` guarantees there are no duplicates returned by the `get` method. For instance, in the StudentBean-to-BookBean 1:N relationship, the StudentBean would include `public abstract Collection getBooks();` and `public abstract void setBooks(Collection books)` methods. Because this is a 1:N relationship, the BookBean would have `public abstract Student getStudent();` and `public abstract void setStudent();` methods.

CMR Example

Let's see how the Student CMP bean example can be modified to support CMRs. We have included a bidirectional 1:1 relationship with a Locker CMP bean, a bidirectional 1:N relationship with the Book CMP bean, and a N:N relationship with the Teacher CMP bean.

To keep things simple, we won't show all of the code here. Instead, we'll show the changes made to support relationships: We have used ellipses in the code to show where code has been removed for brevity. We have also omitted the home and remote interfaces of the related beans from the text.

```
package com.learnweblogic.examples.ch9.cmp;

import java.util.Collection;

import javax.ejb.EntityContext;
import javax.ejb.EntityBean;

public abstract class StudentCMPBean implements EntityBean {

    private EntityContext ctx;

    public abstract String getName();
    public abstract void setName(String n);
```

```
...

public abstract Locker getLocker();
public abstract void setLocker(Locker l);

public abstract Collection getBooks();
public abstract void setBooks(Collection b);

public abstract Collection getTeachers();
public abstract void setTeachers(Collection t);

'''

public void assignLocker(Locker l) {
    setLocker(l);
}

public void assignBook(Book b) {
    Collection books = getBooks();
    books.add(b);
}

public void assignTeacher(Teacher t) {
    Collection teachers = getTeachers();
    teachers.add(t);
}
}
```

Because the Locker bean is a 1:1 relationship, the getter returns the single Locker remote interface while the 1:N relationship with Books and N:N relationship with Teachers return `Collections`.

Note the code to add an element to a relationship. An empty-many relationship returns an empty `Collection` (not null), so it is always safe to call the getter and add an item. These relationships are bidirectional; there also are `get` and `set` methods included in the related classes.

Because the Locker bean is involved in a 1:1 relationship with Student, its getters and setters return the Student remote interface:

```
package com.learnweblogic.examples.ch9.cmp;

import javax.ejb.EntityBean;
import javax.ejb.EntityContext;

public abstract class LockerCMPBean implements EntityBean {
```

```
private EntityContext ctx;

public abstract Integer getNumber();
public abstract void setNumber(Integer n);

public abstract Student getStudent();
public abstract void setStudent(Student s);

...
}
```

The Book bean is involved in a 1:N relationship with Student. Recall that Student's `getBooks` method returns a `Collection` of related Books, but because this is a 1:N relationship, the Book getters return only a single Student.

```
package com.learnweblogic.examples.ch9.cmp;

...

public abstract class BookCMPBean implements EntityBean {

    ...

    public abstract Student getStudent();
    public abstract void setStudent(Student s);

    ...
}
```

Finally, the Teacher bean is in a N:N relationship with Student. In the many-to-many case, both sides of the relationship use `Collection` or `Set` in their `get/set` methods.

```
package com.learnweblogic.examples.ch9.cmp;

...

public abstract class TeacherCMPBean implements EntityBean {

    ...

    public abstract Collection getStudents();
    public abstract void setStudents(Collection students);

    ...

}
```

Writing CMR Deployment Descriptors

All related beans are deployed in the same ejb-jar.xml deployment descriptor. This is a requirement for entity bean relations. Each relationship is described in the *ejb-jar.xml* deployment descriptor in the `<relationships>` element.

```
<relationships>
```

This first stanza describes the 1:1 relationship from Student to Locker.

```
<!-- One to One Student - Locker -->
    <ejb-relation>
        <ejb-relation-name>Student-Locker</ejb-relation-name>
```

Because this is a bidirectional relationship, there are two `<relation-ship-role>` entries. The first, `student-has-locker`, describes the Student-Locker relationship. Note that the source is the Student bean, and the field is named Locker. The EJB container expects to find `getLocker` and `setLocker` methods in the Student bean class.

```
<ejb-relationship-role>
  <ejb-relationship-role-name>
    student-has-locker
  </ejb-relationship-role-name>
  <multiplicity>one</multiplicity>
  <role-source>
    <ejb-name>StudentCMPEJB</ejb-name>
  </role-source>
  <cmr-field>
    <cmr-field-name>locker</cmr-field-name>
  </cmr-field>
</ejb-relationship-role>
```

The second `ejb-relationship-role` describes the relationship from the locker to the student. This time, the locker is the source and the cmr field is named student.

```
<ejb-relationship-role>
  <ejb-relationship-role-name>
    locker-has-student
  </ejb-relationship-role-name>
  <multiplicity>one</multiplicity>
  <role-source>
    <ejb-name>LockerCMPEJB</ejb-name>
  </role-source>
  <cmr-field>
    <cmr-field-name>student</cmr-field-name>
  </cmr-field>
</ejb-relationship-role>
</ejb-relation>
```

The next stanza describes the bidirectional 1:N relationship from Student to Books.

```
<!-- One to Many Student - Books -->
  <ejb-relation>
    <ejb-relation-name>Student-Books</ejb-relation-name>
```

This describes the Student side of the relationship. Notice that the <cmr-field-type> indicates that the relationship uses the Collection type instead of a Set, which is required when the related role is many.

The full package name, java.util.Collection, must be used. A common error is to just write "Collection." Unlike a Java program file, packages are not imported, so classes and interfaces should be specified with their full package names.

```
<ejb-relationship-role>
  <ejb-relationship-role-name>
      student-has-books
    </ejb-relationship-role-name>
    <multiplicity>one</multiplicity>
    <role-source>
        <ejb-name>StudentCMPEJB</ejb-name>
      </role-source>
    <cmr-field>
      <cmr-field-name>books</cmr-field-name>
      <cmr-field-type>java.util.Collection</cmr-field-type>
    </cmr-field>
    </ejb-relationship-role>
```

The second ejb-relationship-role is the Books-to-Student relationship. Notice that this relationship has a multiplicity of many. This indicates that many Books map into a Student.

```
  <ejb-relationship-role>
   <ejb-relationship-role-name>
     books-have-student
   </ejb-relationship-role-name>
   <multiplicity>many</multiplicity>
   <role-source>
     <ejb-name>BookCMPEJB</ejb-name>
   </role-source>
   <cmr-field>
     <cmr-field-name>student</cmr-field-name>
   </cmr-field>
  </ejb-relationship-role>
</ejb-relation>
```

Finally, there is the N:N relationship between Students and Teachers. This is similar to the preceding 1:N relationship, except that now both sides are many, and both sides specify the `<cmr-field-type>`.

```
<!-- Many to Many Student - Teacher -->
    <ejb-relation>
        <ejb-relation-name>Student-Teacher</ejb-relation-name>
        <ejb-relationship-role>
          <ejb-relationship-role-name>
          students-have-teachers
        </ejb-relationship-role-name>
        <multiplicity>many</multiplicity>
        <role-source>
            <ejb-name>StudentCMPEJB</ejb-name>
          </role-source>
        <cmr-field>
          <cmr-field-name>teachers</cmr-field-name>
          <cmr-field-type>java.util.Collection</cmr-field-type>
        </cmr-field>
        </ejb-relationship-role>
        <ejb-relationship-role>
          <ejb-relationship-role-name>
          teachers-have-students
        </ejb-relationship-role-name>
        <multiplicity>many</multiplicity>
        <role-source>
            <ejb-name>TeacherCMPEJB</ejb-name>
          </role-source>
        <cmr-field>
          <cmr-field-name>students</cmr-field-name>
          <cmr-field-type>java.util.Collection</cmr-field-type>
        </cmr-field>
        </ejb-relationship-role>
    </ejb-relation>

</relationships>
```

Like other EJBs, it is necessary to include a standard *weblogic-ejb-jar.xml* deployment descriptor. You need to make a few changes to the *weblogic-cmp-rdbms.xml* deployment descriptor for CMRs. Like CMP fields, CMRs must include their database mappings in the *weblogic-cmp-rdbms.xml* file.

The EJB container uses *foreign keys* to implement relationships in the database. A foreign key is a column in a database table that is a primary key of another table. For instance, the Student table's primary key is the Student's Social Security number. If the Locker table stored the Student's Social Security number as a foreign key, rows in the Locker table could be matched against the related rows in the Student table.

Creating the Database Tables

Before running the entity bean examples, the deployer must create database tables that support the entity beans. These database tables must include the required foreign key columns. A join table must be created for the N:N relationship.

Here, we show the data definition language (DDL) for the Student table and for the join table. The schemas for the other tables are similar to those cited for other examples.

```
create table studentcmptable (

  ssn integer primary key,
  name varchar(255),
  grade integer,
  lockerkey integer
);

create table StudentTeacherJoin (

  teacher_ssn integer,
  student_ssn integer
);
```

Note the `lockerkey` column in the `StudentCmpTable`. This is the foreign key column for the Student-Locker relationship. This database column must match the mappings given in *weblogic-cmp-rdbms.xml*.

Unlike 1:1 or 1:N relationships, N:N relationships cannot be implemented by storing a foreign key field in the bean's table. Instead, an auxiliary database table is used to store the sets of foreign keys. This extra table is often referred to as a *join table*.

The `StudentTeacherJoin` table is the join table for the N:N relationship between Students and Teachers. It stores the foreign keys described in the *weblogic-cmp-rdbms.xml* descriptor.

Mapping CMP Entity Beans to the Database

The physical mappings for CMRs depend on the cardinality of the relationship.

Mapping 1:1 Relationships

The WebLogic Server EJB container supports three different mappings for 1:1 relationships. There can be a foreign key on either side of the relationship, or foreign keys can be stored on both sides of the relationship. While it seems appealing at first to store foreign keys on both sides of the relationship, this mapping should usually be avoided. With twice as many foreign keys, there will be twice as many database updates when the relationship is changed.

Avoid storing foreign keys in both sides of a 1:1 relationship.

Here is the mapping information in the *weblogic-cmp-rdbms.xml* file for the Student-Locker example. In this mapping, we store a foreign key in the Student table. The database column named `lockerkey` maps to the number primary key field in the Locker bean.

```
<weblogic-rdbms-relation>
    <relation-name>Student-Locker</relation-name>
    <weblogic-relationship-role>
      <relationship-role-name>student-has-locker</relationship-role-name>
      <column-map>
        <foreign-key-column>lockerkey</foreign-key-column>
        <key-column>number</key-column>
      </column-map>
    </weblogic-relationship-role>
  </weblogic-rdbms-relation>
```

Mapping 1:N Relationships

The WebLogic Server EJB container supports a single physical mapping for 1:N relationships. Each bean on the many side of the relationship supports a foreign key pointing to the one bean on the other side.

In the Student→Books relationship, the Books table stores a foreign key pointing back to the Student. The `studentkey` field points to the `ssn` primary key field of the `StudentCMPBean`.

```
<weblogic-rdbms-relation>
    <relation-name>Student-Books</relation-name>
    <weblogic-relationship-role>
      <relationship-role-name>student-has-books</relationship-role-name>
      <column-map>
        <foreign-key-column>studentkey</foreign-key-column>
        <key-column>ssn</key-column>
      </column-map>
    </weblogic-relationship-role>
  </weblogic-rdbms-relation>
```

Mapping N:N Relationships

Here is the Students↔Teachers mapping. The join table named Student-TeacherJoin includes foreign keys for both sides of the relationship. The teacher_ssn column is a foreign key to the ssn primary key field for Teachers, while the student_ssn field is a foreign key to the Student's ssn field.

```
<weblogic-rdbms-relation>

    <relation-name>Student-Teacher</relation-name>

    <table-name>StudentTeacherJoin</table-name>

    <weblogic-relationship-role>

        <relationship-role-name>students-have-teachers</relationship-role-name>

        <column-map>

            <foreign-key-column>student_ssn</foreign-key-column>

            <key-column>ssn</key-column>

        </column-map>

    </weblogic-relationship-role>


    <weblogic-relationship-role>

        <relationship-role-name>teachers-have-students</relationship-role-name>

        <column-map>

            <foreign-key-column>teacher_ssn</foreign-key-column>

            <key-column>ssn</key-column>

        </column-map>

    </weblogic-relationship-role>


</weblogic-rdbms-relation>
```

Running the Example

Like any other entity bean, the client code calls the remote and home interfaces. We use the client code to update the relationships and view the changes in the database.

Again, we have simplified the client code and removed exception handling for brevity.

Before the client code executes, the database tables are empty:

```
select * from studentcmptable;
ssn | name | grade | lockerkey
-----+------+-------+-----------
(0 rows)
```

Like other EJBs, the client does a Java Naming and Directory Interface (JNDI) lookup to find the `StudentHome`. It can then create the entity bean from the home interface.

```
StudentHome studentHome =
    (StudentHome) narrow(ctx.lookup("StudentCMPEJB"),
StudentHome.class);
```

In this example, several Students are created in a loop:

```
students[i] = studentHome.create(names[i], i, 10);
```

The database now includes the Students:

```
select * from studentcmptable;
 ssn |  name   | grade | lockerkey
-----+---------+-------+-----------
   0 | Andrew  |    10 |
   1 | Evelyn  |    10 |
   2 | Joe     |    10 |
   3 | Matt    |    10 |
   4 | Jim     |    10 |
(5 rows)
```

Notice that the `lockerkey` field is empty. This field is null until we call the `setLocker` method in the `StudentBean` to initialize the relationship.

The client now goes on to create some Locker entity beans:

```
Locker [] lockers = new Locker[N];
    for (int i=0; i<N; i++) {
        // create students in the 10th grade
        lockers[i] = lockerHome.create(new Integer(i));
    }
```

The Locker beans are very simple entity beans: Only a single column is stored in the database.

```
select * from lockercmptable;
 number
--------
      0
      1
      2
      3
      4
(5 rows)
```

The client can now assign Students to Lockers. This updates the 1:1 relationship. The example client calls the `assignLocker` method on the Student remote interface. This method calls the `setLocker` method, which updates the relationship information.

```
// Assign each Student a Locker
   for (int i=0; i<students.length; i++) {
      students[i].assignLocker(lockers[i]);
   }
```

Now the database table includes the foreign key to indicate the relationship has been updated:

```
select * from studentcmptable;
 ssn |   name   | grade | lockerkey
-----+----------+-------+-----------
   0 | Andrew   |    10 |         0
   1 | Evelyn   |    10 |         1
   2 | Joe      |    10 |         2
   3 | Matt     |    10 |         3
   4 | Jim      |    10 |         4
```

(5 rows)

Using 1:N Relationships

The client also creates Book entity beans for the 1:N relationship. The bean creation code is identical to the other beans, so we do not show it again. The client can then call the `assignBook` method on the Student interface to add a Book to the 1:N relationship.

The Books array has a copy of each Book for every Student, so the client code iterates through all the Books, assigning each copy to a different Student.

```
// Assign the books out to the students
   for (int i=0; i<books.length; i++) {
      students[i % students.length].assignBook(books[i]);
   }
```

We can see the results of updating the 1:N relationship in the database by looking at the Book table. The foreign key points back to a Student.

```
select * from bookcmptable where studentkey=0;
 isbn | copynumber |    title     |   author    | studentkey
------+------------+--------------+-------------+-----------
   0  |          0 | Hamlet       | Shakespeare |          0
   1  |          0 | Moby Dick    | Melville    |          0
   2  |          0 | The Stranger | Camus       |          0
(3 rows)
```

This query shows that the Student with primary key 0 has a 1:N relationship with 3 books. The `studentkey` column is a foreign key into the Student table.

Using N:N Relationships

The client uses similar code to update the N:N relationship of Students and Teachers. In this case, the join table is updated.

```
// Assign students to teachers
   // Student 0 gets teacher 0
   // Student 1 gets teachers 0,1 etc.
   for (int i=0; i<teachers.length; i++) {
     for (int j=0; j<i; j++) {
       students[j].assignTeacher(teachers[i]);
     }
   }
```

The database contents of the join table show the updated N:N relationship:

```
select * from StudentTeacherJoin;
 teacher_ssn | student_ssn
-------------+-------------
           0 |           1
           0 |           2
           1 |           2
           0 |           3
           1 |           3
           2 |           3
(6 rows)
```

Writing EJB-QL for CMP Finders

The EJB-QL language is based on SQL-92 and should be familiar to database users. EJB-QL is used for `finders` and `ejbSelect` methods. `Finder` methods always return the entity bean's remote interface or a `Collection` containing remote interfaces.

`Select` methods are like `finder` methods, but they can return any of the container-managed fields. `Select` methods are not exposed in the remote interface and are called against an identified instance. `Finders` run against an anonymous instance. A `select` method is similar to a `data access` method on a stateless session bean. The advantage of using an `ejbSelect` method is that the query operates on the container-managed fields and relationships and is independent of the physical schema.

EJB-QL queries consist of three clauses: `SELECT`, `FROM`, and `WHERE`. The `FROM` clause is the only one that is always required.

The EJB-QL query is specified with the `<query>` tag in the ejb-jar.xml. There is an optional description element, and the `finder` method must be specified. The EJB-QL query is then specified with the `<ejb-ql>` tag. Note that it is wrapped in a `CDATA` block. This instructs the XML parser not to attempt to interpret the query as anything but raw character data.

EJB-QL queries use the `finder` method's parameters. The first parameter is referred to as `?1`. The second parameter is `?2`, and so on.

The Student CMP bean includes a `findStudentsInGrade(int grade)` in the home interface. This `finder` returns all the Students whose grade matches the parameter:

```
<query>
  <description>finds students in a given grade</description>
<query-method>
  <method-name>findStudentsInGrade</method-name>
    <method-params>
      <method-param>int</method-param>
    </method-params>
  </query-method>
  <ejb-ql>
    <![CDATA[FROM StudentCMPBean s WHERE s.grade =?1]]>
  </ejb-ql>
</query>
```

This query uses the `grade` container-managed field and compares it against the first parameter to the `finder`.

The client code accesses this code by calling the `findStudentsIn-Grade` method on the home interface. This method returns a `Collection` of Student remote interfaces. The client code must use `javax.rmi.Por-tableRemoteObject.narrow` to convert the `Collection`'s contents into the remote interface. This is required by the EJB specification for compatibility with CORBA-based EJB servers.

```
Collection c = studentHome.findStudentsInGrade(10);

     if (c.isEmpty()) {
        System.err.println("No Students were found in grade
10.");
     } else {

        Iterator it = c.iterator();
```

```
while (it.hasNext()) {
  Student s = (Student) narrow(it.next(), Student.class);

  System.err.println("Found student named: "+s.getName()+
    " in grade 10.");
}

System.err.println("");
```

We can check the results of the finder by manually running the query against the database table.

```
select * from studentcmptable where grade=10;

ssn |  name  | grade | lockerkey
----+--------+-------+-----------
  0 | Andrew |  10   |     0
  1 | Evelyn |  10   |     1
  2 | Joe    |  10   |     2
  3 | Matt   |  10   |     3
  4 | Jim    |  10   |     4
(5 rows)
```

The `finder` query returns the expected results. Running queries manually in the database is a good way to check your EJB-QL statements.

```
Found student named: Andrew in grade 10.
Found student named: Evelyn in grade 10.
Found student named: Joe in grade 10.
Found student named: Matt in grade 10.
Found student named: Jim in grade 10.
```

Let's examine some other EJB-QL examples. We will omit the XML descriptor format for readability.

```
findAllStudents:
find All of the Students
<ejb-ql>FROM StudentCMPBean</ejb-ql>

findSSNGreaterThan10:
find Students with a social security number > 10
<ejb-ql>FROM StudentCMPBean s WHERE s.ssn > 10</ejb-ql>

findStudentsBetweenGrades(int low, int high:
find Students whose grade is >= low and <= high

<ejb-ql>
FROM StudentCMPBean s WHERE s.grade BETWEEN ?1 AND ?2
</ejb-ql>
```

EJB-QL queries also can navigate CMRs. In our example beans, Student uses its Locker field to navigate the 1:1 relationship with its Locker.

`FindStudentsWithoutALocker`

```
<ejb-ql>
  FROM StudentCMPBean s WHERE s.locker IS NULL
</ejb-ql>
```

`findStudentsWithALocker`

```
<ejb-ql>FROM StudentCMPBean s WHERE s.locker IS NOT NULL</ejb-ql>
```

EJB-QL queries that are 1:N or N:N can use the `IN` operator to qualify each of the related beans. For instance, this query navigates the 1:N relationship from Student to Books. The `b` variable iterates over each book and compares its title to the passed parameter.

`findStudentsWithBooksTitled(String bookTitle)`

```
    <ejb-ql>
      FROM StudentCMPBean s, b IN s.books WHERE b.title = ?1
    </ejb-ql>
```

EJB-QL queries with 1:N and N:N relations can also use the `EMPTY` operator to determine if there are any related beans.

`findStudentsWithNoBooks()`

```
    <ejb-ql>FROM StudentCMPBean s WHERE s.books IS EMPTY</ejb-ql>
```

These examples demonstrate many of the possible EJB-QL operators. The EJB 2.0 specification includes a complete grammar for EJB-QL and its operators.

CMR Programming Restrictions

The CMP 2.0 specification enables the EJB container to optimize the database accesses required to support relationships. These optimizations can greatly improve the application's performance, but there are also programming requirements that apply to CMRs but not to simple container-managed fields. In particular, a container-managed field can be assigned in the `ejb-Create` method, but a CMR cannot be set in the `ejbCreate` method.

The CMR must not be set until the `ejbPostCreate` method.

Another CMR restriction is that `getXXX` methods cannot be exposed in the remote interface. This rule exists because the EJB container might lazily load the relationship. If the `Collection` of remote interfaces were not materialized, it could not be serialized to an external client.

Materializing Collections

The WebLogic Server EJB container takes advantage of the CMP programming restrictions to automatically optimize database access with relationships. When a "many" relationship is accessed via a `getter` method, there is no database round trip. Instead, the container returns a `Collection` that includes enough information to materialize the `Collection`. The database is accessed only when the client actually attempts to iterate on the `Collection`.

The container also optimizes data access when an element is added to the `Collection`. For instance, it is a common pattern to call the CMR `get` method to return the `Collection` and add another element to the `Collection`. With a naive implementation, the EJB container would read all the related beans from the database into memory, add one element to the `Collection`, and write back all the elements to the database. Clearly, this would make adding beans to large collections very expensive.

Instead, the WebLogic Server EJB container does not access the database on the `get` method. The `Collection` addition simply adds a single element to the memory cache. When the `Collection` is written back at the end of the transaction, only the single new element is written to the database. In the naive implementation, there are N beans read and $N+1$ beans written to the database. In the WebLogic Server EJB container, there are 0 beans read and 1 bean written.

BMP Entity Beans

The EJB specification also supports entity beans with BMP. Unlike CMP entity beans that rely on the EJB container to provide the persistence logic, BMP entity beans must write explicit code to access the persistent store. For most users, this involves writing JDBC code to access a relational database.

Writing the Student BMP Entity EJB

The following sections demonstrate the process for creating an entity bean with BMP. In this example, we model a Student as an entity bean. This entity bean could be used to model Student records and make them available to Teachers and Parents.

First, create the remote interface, which extends `javax.ejb.EJBObject` and provides the signatures for `business` methods that the Student entity bean exposes to clients. Because this is an RMI interface, all methods must include `RemoteException` in their `throws` clause.

```
package com.learnweblogic.examples.ch9.bmp;
import java.rmi.RemoteException;
import javax.ejb.EJBObject;


public interface Student extends EJBObject {
  public String getName() throws RemoteException;
  public Integer getSsn() throws RemoteException;
  public int getGrade() throws RemoteException;
  public void setGrade(int grade) throws RemoteException;

}
```

The Student remote interface outlines a few basic methods that can retrieve and update fields in the entity bean.

Next, we define the home interface for the Student BMP EJB. This interface must extend `javax.ejb.EJBHome`, and it defines the `create` and `finder` methods for the Student BMP EJB.

```
package com.learnweblogic.examples.ch9.bmp;

import java.rmi.RemoteException;
import java.util.Collection;

import javax.ejb.CreateException;
import javax.ejb.FinderException;
import javax.ejb.EJBHome;

public interface StudentHome extends EJBHome {

  // create method

  public Student create(String name, int ssn, int grade)
    throws CreateException, RemoteException;

  // finders
```

```
public Student findByPrimaryKey(Integer ssn)
  throws FinderException, RemoteException;

public Collection findStudentsInGrade(int grade)
  throws FinderException, RemoteException;

}
```

Like the remote interface, the home interface is called through RMI: All methods must throw `RemoteException`. Additionally, all `create` methods must include `CreateException`, and all `finders` must include `FinderException`.

This home interface includes two `find` methods: `findByPrimaryKey` and `findStudentsInGrade`. The `findByPrimaryKey` (required) returns the Student with the matching Social Security number if that Student exists. If a matching Social Security number is not found, the bean writer throws a `FinderException`.

The `findStudentsInGrade` is an example of a multi-object finder. In this case, the container returns an EJBObject reference for each student whose grade matches the parameter.

Note that the container is returning a `Collection` of remote interfaces and not a `Collection` of beans. The actual bean class never travels to the client. As with session beans, the client always uses the entity bean by making calls on the home or remote interfaces.

Finders return `EJBObjects`, *not the actual bean classes.*

Writing the BMP Bean Class

The next step is to create the bean implementation class, which implements the `javax.ejb.EntityBean` interface and the business logic exposed in the remote interface. Because this is a bean-managed bean, the data access code is also included in the implementation of the `create` method and the `finders`. The bean also implements the data access code for `ejbLoad`, `ejbStore`, and `ejbRemove`.

```
package com.learnweblogic.examples.ch9.bmp;

import java.rmi.RemoteException;
import java.sql.Connection;
import java.sql.PreparedStatement;
import java.sql.ResultSet;
```

```
import java.sql.SQLException;
import java.util.ArrayList;
import java.util.Collection;

import javax.ejb.DuplicateKeyException;
import javax.ejb.EntityContext;
import javax.ejb.EntityBean;
import javax.ejb.EJBException;
import javax.ejb.NoSuchEntityException;
import javax.ejb.ObjectNotFoundException;
import javax.ejb.RemoveException;
import javax.naming.Context;
import javax.naming.InitialContext;
import javax.naming.NamingException;
import javax.sql.DataSource;
```

Note that this file uses explicit imports instead of importing a `package*`. While this is a matter of personal preference, using explicit imports allows the user to quickly scan the file and learn which package contains a class.

```
public class StudentBean implements EntityBean {
```

The next three variables are instance variables that are not tied to a particular identity/primary key. These variables are set in the `setEntityContext` method before the bean has an identity and are used for the lifetime of the bean instance.

```
private EntityContext ctx;
private DataSource dataSource;
private String tableName;
```

The `name`, `ssn`, and `grade` variables are the bean's fields. They are initialized in `ejbCreate`, loaded from the database in `ejbLoad`, and stored to the database in `ejbStore`.

```
private String name;
private Integer ssn; // primary key
private int grade;
```

setEntityContext/unsetEntityContext

The `setEntityContext` method stores the `EntityContext` reference in a member variable. It also uses the EJB's environment context to look up deployment-specific parameters. When the EJB is deployed, the deployer specifies appropriate values for the `tableName` and `poolName` parameters in the *ejb-jar.xml*. This prevents these values from being hard-coded into the bean. The `setEntityContext` method also gets a `DataSource` object from the environment, which gets database connections from the connection pool.

```
public void setEntityContext(EntityContext c) {

    ctx = c;

    try {
      Context envCtx =
        (Context) new InitialContext().lookup("java:/comp/env");

      tableName = (String) envCtx.lookup("tableName");

      String poolName = (String) envCtx.lookup("poolName");

      dataSource = (DataSource) envCtx.lookup("/jdbc/"+poolName);
    } catch (NamingException ne) {
      // EJB was not deployed properly
      throw new EJBException(ne);
    }

}

public void unsetEntityContext() {
    ctx = null;
}
```

ejbCreate

The `ejbCreate` method initializes the member variables from the passed parameters and inserts the new entity bean into the database. If the insert fails, an `SQLException` is thrown. The `ejbCreate` method then uses its `ejbFindByPrimaryKey` method to determine whether the key already exists in the table. If the key is already present in the table, `ejbFindBy-PrimaryKey` returns successfully, and the `ejbCreate` method throws the `DuplicateKeyException` to inform the caller. Otherwise, an `EJBException` is thrown with the `SQLException`.

```
public Integer ejbCreate(String name, int ssn, int grade) {

    this.name     = name;
    this.ssn      = new Integer(ssn);
    this.grade    = grade;

    Connection          con = null;
    PreparedStatement   ps = null;
```

```
try {
  con = dataSource.getConnection();

  ps = con.prepareStatement("insert into "+tableName+
    " (name, ssn, grade) values (?,?,?)");

  ps.setString(1, name);
  ps.setInt(2, ssn);
  ps.setInt(3, grade);

  ps.executeUpdate();

  return this.ssn;

} catch (SQLException sqe) {
  try {
    ejbFindByPrimaryKey(this.ssn);

    throw new DuplicateKeyException("A student with social "+
      "security number: "+ssn+" already exists.");
  } catch (Exception Ignore) {}

  sqe.printStackTrace();

  throw new EJBException (sqe);

} finally {
  try {
    if (ps != null) ps.close();
    if (con != null) con.close();
  } catch (Exception ignore) {}
}


}
```

ejbPostCreate

Since this implementation requires no post-create initialization, this required method is empty:

```
public void ejbPostCreate(String name, int ssn, int grade) {}
```

ejbRemove

The ejbRemove method is responsible for deleting the instance from the database. This method uses a SQL delete to remove the instance.

```
public void ejbRemove ()
    throws RemoveException
  {

    Connection con = null;
    PreparedStatement ps = null;

    try {
      con = dataSource.getConnection();
      ps  = con.prepareStatement("delete from "+tableName+
        " where ssn=?");
      ps.setInt(1, ssn.intValue());

      if (ps.executeUpdate() < 1) {
throw new RemoveException ("Error removing Student with"+
" ssn: "+ssn);
      }
    } catch (SQLException sqe) {
      throw new EJBException (sqe);
    } finally {
      try {
        if(ps != null) ps.close();
        if(con != null) con.close();
      } catch (Exception ignore) {}
    }
  }
```

ejbLoad

`ejbLoad` reads the entity bean's current state from the database and assigns the values to its member variables. The primary key is available from the `EntityContext` member variable. If the entity bean no longer exists, `NoSuchEntityException` is thrown. This might occur if the entity bean was deleted by another client or directly from the database.

```
public void ejbLoad() {

    ssn = (Integer) ctx.getPrimaryKey();

    Connection con        = null;
    PreparedStatement ps = null;
    ResultSet rs          = null;
    try {
      con = dataSource.getConnection();
      ps  = con.prepareStatement("select name, grade from "
        +tableName+ " where ssn=?");
      ps.setInt(1, ssn.intValue());
```

```
    ps.executeQuery();
    rs = ps.getResultSet();

    if (rs.next()) {
      name  = rs.getString(1);
      grade = rs.getInt(2);

    } else {
      throw new NoSuchEntityException("Student with social "+
        "security number: "+ssn+" no longer exists.");
    }

  } catch (SQLException sqe) {
    throw new EJBException(sqe);
  } finally {
    try {
      if (rs != null) rs.close();
      if (ps != null) ps.close();
      if (con != null) con.close();
    } catch (Exception ignore) {}
  }
}
```

ejbStore

The `ejbStore` method is called to write the entity bean's state back to the database. The primary key field is not written because primary keys cannot be changed. An optimized version of this bean also can skip writing the name field, if you assume that it is never updated.

```
public void ejbStore() {

    Connection con        = null;
    PreparedStatement ps = null;

    try {
      con = dataSource.getConnection();
      ps  = con.prepareStatement("update "+tableName+
        " SET name=?, grade=? " +
        " where ssn=?");

      ps.setString(1, name);
      ps.setInt(2, grade);
      ps.setInt(3, ssn.intValue());

      ps.executeUpdate();
```

```
  } catch (SQLException sqe) {
    throw new EJBException(sqe);
  } finally {
    try {
      if (ps != null) ps.close();
      if (con != null) con.close();
    } catch (Exception ignore) {}
  }
}
```

ejbActivate/ejbPassivate

The `ejbActivate` and `ejbPassivate` methods are required even though this bean does not use these callbacks.

```
public void ejbActivate() {}
public void ejbPassivate() {}
```

ejbFindByPrimaryKey

The `ejbFindByPrimaryKey` method tests whether the passed key exists in the database. If the select returns a row, then the primary key is returned. If the key does not exist, an `ObjectNotFoundException` is thrown.

```
  public Integer ejbFindByPrimaryKey(Integer pk)
    throws ObjectNotFoundException
{

  Connection con = null;
  PreparedStatement ps = null;
  ResultSet rs = null;


  try {
    con = dataSource.getConnection();
    ps  = con.prepareStatement("select ssn from "+tableName+
      " where ssn=?");
    ps.setInt(1, pk.intValue());
    ps.executeQuery();

    rs = ps.getResultSet();

    if (rs.next()) {
      return pk;
    } else {
      throw new ObjectNotFoundException ("Student with social"+
        "security number: "+ssn+" no longer exists.");
```

```
    }
  } catch (SQLException sqe) {
    throw new EJBException (sqe);
  } finally {
    try {
      if (rs != null) rs.close();
      if(ps != null) ps.close();
      if(con != null) con.close();
    } catch (Exception ignore) {}
  }

}
```

Multi-Object Finders

The ejbFindStudentsInGrade method returns a Collection of students who match the query. The finder method returns a Collection of primary keys. The EJB container converts these into EJBObject references and returns them to the client. If no primary keys match the query, an empty Collection is returned.

```
public Collection ejbFindStudentsInGrade(int gradeValue) {

    Connection con = null;
    PreparedStatement ps = null;
    ResultSet rs = null;

    ArrayList keys = new ArrayList();

    try {
      con = dataSource.getConnection();
      ps  = con.prepareStatement("select ssn from "+tableName+
        " where grade=?");
      ps.setInt(1, gradeValue);
      ps.executeQuery();

      rs = ps.getResultSet();


      while (rs.next()) {
        keys.add(new Integer(rs.getInt(1)));
      }

      return keys;

    } catch (SQLException sqe) {
      throw new EJBException (sqe);
```

```
  } finally {
    try {
if (rs != null) rs.close();
      if(ps != null) ps.close();
      if(con != null) con.close();
    } catch (Exception ignore) {}
  }


}
```

These methods implement the `business` methods defined in the Student remote interface.

```
public String getName() { return name; }
public Integer getSsn() { return ssn; }
public int getGrade() { return grade; }
public void setGrade(int grade) { this.grade = grade; }
}
```

The ejb-jar.xml Deployment Descriptor

Finally, the bean provider writes the deployment descriptors for the BMP entity bean. Like session beans, BMP entity beans use a standard ejb-jar.xml deployment descriptor and a WebLogic Server–specific *weblogic-ejb-jar.xml* descriptor. Here is the sample *ejb-jar.xml*:

```
<?xml version="1.0"?>

<!DOCTYPE ejb-jar PUBLIC
"-//Sun Microsystems, Inc.//DTD Enterprise JavaBeans 2.0//EN"
"http://java.sun.com/dtd/ejb-jar_2_0.dtd">
<ejb-jar>
  <enterprise-beans>

    <entity>
     <ejb-name>StudentEJB</ejb-name>
     <home>com.learnweblogic.examples.ch9.bmp.StudentHome</home>
      <remote>com.learnweblogic.examples.ch9.bmp.Student</remote>
     <ejb-class>
        com.learnweblogic.examples.ch9.bmp.StudentBean
     </ejb-class>
     <persistence-type>Bean</persistence-type>
     <prim-key-class>java.lang.Integer</prim-key-class>
     <reentrant>False</reentrant>

     <primkey-field>ssn</primkey-field>
```

```
        <env-entry>
          <env-entry-name>tableName</env-entry-name>
        <env-entry-type>java.lang.String</env-entry-type>
        <env-entry-value>studenttable</env-entry-value>
        </env-entry>

        <env-entry>
          <env-entry-name>poolName</env-entry-name>
        <env-entry-type>java.lang.String</env-entry-type>
        <env-entry-value>dbpool</env-entry-value>
        </env-entry>

        <resource-ref>
          <res-ref-name>jdbc/dbpool</res-ref-name>
          <res-type>javax.sql.DataSource</res-type>
          <res-auth>Container</res-auth>
        </resource-ref>

      </entity>

    </enterprise-beans>

    <assembly-descriptor>
      <container-transaction>
        <method>
          <ejb-name>StudentEJB</ejb-name>
        <method-name>*</method-name>
        </method>

        <trans-attribute>Required</trans-attribute>
      </container-transaction>

    </assembly-descriptor>
</ejb-jar>
```

The *ejb-jar.xml* descriptor is similar to a session bean's descriptor. The main difference is that it uses the `<entity>` tag and defines a primary key class. The `<prim-key-class>` specifies the class being used as the primary key for this entity bean. If the primary key is a single field in the entity bean, the bean provider can use the field type as the primary key and specify the primary key field with the `<primkey-field>` tag. In this example, `java.lang.Integer` is the primary key class, and `ssn` is the primary key field.

It is also possible to have a compound primary key. This requires a user-defined primary key class. This class must have public data members whose names and types match the primary key fields in the bean class.

With user-defined primary key classes, the bean provider specifies the user-defined class in the `<prim-key-class>` tag but must not specify a `<primkey-field>`.

The weblogic-ejb-jar.xml Deployment Descriptor

Here's the `weblogic-ejb-jar.xml` deployment descriptor:

```xml
<?xml version="1.0"?>

<!DOCTYPE weblogic-ejb-jar PUBLIC
"-//BEA Systems, Inc.//DTD WebLogic 6.0.0 EJB//EN"
"http://www.bea.com/servers/wls600/dtd/weblogic-ejb-jar.dtd">

<weblogic-ejb-jar>
  <weblogic-enterprise-bean>
    <ejb-name>StudentEJB</ejb-name>
    <reference-descriptor>

      <resource-description>
        <res-ref-name>jdbc/dbpool</res-ref-name>
        <jndi-name>
          DBPool
        </jndi-name>
      </resource-description>

    </reference-descriptor>

    <jndi-name>StudentEJB</jndi-name>
  </weblogic-enterprise-bean>

</weblogic-ejb-jar>
```

This deployment descriptor includes only the resource information for the JDBC `DataSource` and the entity bean's JNDI name.

Building the Example

This example is located in the *examples/ch9/bmp* directory on the CD-ROM.

The example includes a *build.cmd* script to build and compile the EJB and its client. The *tables.ddl* includes the necessary schema for the database. These tables should be created before deploying the EJBs. The *deploy.cmd* script copies the *ejb-jar* into the server's applications directory for it to be deployed. The *runClient.cmd* can be used to run the EJB client.

The deployer must now put the bean classes and the deployment descriptors in a *.jar* file. The *.jar* file's contents are:

```
META-INF/ejb-jar.xml
META-INF/weblogic-ejb-jar.xml
com/learnweblogic/examples/ch9/bmp/Student.class
com/learnweblogic/examples/ch9/bmp/StudentBean.class
com/learnweblogic/examples/ch9/bmp/StudentHome.class
```

Creating the Database Table

Before the entity bean can be deployed, the database tables must be created. The exact mapping of Java types to database types depends on the database vendor, but we'll show sample DDL here:

```
create table studenttable (
  name varchar(255),
  ssn integer primary key,
  grade integer
);
```

The database primary key field(s) must match the entity bean's primary key field(s). This enables the entity bean to use the database to prevent multiple entity beans from using the same primary key. Any attempt to create an entity bean with an existing primary key will be flagged as a constraint violation by the database.

Deploying the EJB

The *ejb-jar* can now be copied into the server's applications directory. If there are any errors during deployment, they will appear in the server's output and in the log file. After deployment, the entity bean is ready to be used by clients.

Client Code

Like session beans, entity bean clients look up the home interface in JNDI. The entity bean can then be created via the home interface. Unlike a session bean, the entity bean `create` causes a database insert. You should check both the client code and the database contents as the client makes calls against the entity bean.

This client code is taken from the `StudentBMPClient.java` example. Before the client code runs, the database table is empty:

```
select * from studenttable;

name | ssn | grade
------+-----+-------
(0 rows)
```

Then the client code executes:

```
StudentHome studentHome = (StudentHome)
narrow(getInitalContext().lookup("StudentEJB"), StudentH-
ome.class);

Student s = studentHome.create("John Doe", 200, 10);
```

Now, let's look at the database contents after the `create`:

```
select * from studenttable;

  name    | ssn | grade
----------+-----+-------
 John Doe | 200 |    10
(1 row)
```

The `create` call has inserted a row into the database. The client code continues with a business method.

Now let's follow the execution of a business method: `setGrade(int)`. This business method starts a transaction. The EJB container calls the bean's `ejbLoad` method to refresh the state from the database. Next, the business method executes, and finally `ejbStore` is called to write the state back to the database.

The client calls a business method to change the `grade` field:

```
s.setGrade(4);
```

We can now see the updated database contents:

```
select * from studenttable;

  name    | ssn | grade
----------+-----+-------
 John Doe | 200 |    4
(1 row)
```

The `grade` column has been updated with the new value.

The client code then removes the bean. This causes the container to call `ejbRemove` on the bean, which deletes the row from the database.

The client code:

```
    s.remove();
```

Now the database table is empty once again:

```
select * from studenttable;
 name | ssn | grade
------+-----+-------
(0 rows)
```

Best Practices for BMP Entity EJBs

While BMP entity beans require a fair amount of JDBC code, almost every BMP bean uses similar code, and the code is not difficult to develop. However, you should make sure to include code that prints out the SQL statements that are being executed. It is very easy for typographic errors to result in cryptic database errors.

Include debugging code to print out SQL statements.

Advanced Topics for Writing Entity EJBs

Having surveyed the basic process for developing and deploying container- and bean-managed entity beans, we now turn to some advanced topics that the entity bean developer needs to know. These advanced topics include how to develop a primary key class, entity beans and inheritance, locking strategies, and other details.

How to Write a Primary Key Class

The EJB primary key class serves as its unique identifier both in the persistent store and in the EJB container. Usually, the primary key class fields map directly to the primary key fields in a database. If the primary key is only a single entity bean field that is a Java primitive class (such as `java.lang.String`), the bean writer does not have to write a custom primary key class. Instead, in the deployment descriptor, the bean writer specifies the name of the class and the name of the primary key field.

If the primary key maps to a user-defined type or to multiple fields, the bean writer must write a custom primary key class. The primary key class must implement `java.io.Serializable` and contain the primary key fields. For CMP entity beans, the field names must match the corresponding primary key field names in the bean class. This enables the EJB container to assign the appropriate CMP fields to their corresponding fields in the primary key class.

For instance, we might define an employee's primary key as a compound key using the first name, last name, and office number. Our compound key would look like this:

```
public final class EmployeePK implements java.io.Serializable {

  public String lastName;
  public String firstName;
  public int officeNumber;

  private int hash = -1;

  public EmployeePK() {}

  public int hashCode() {
    if (hash == -1) {
      hash = lastName.hashCode() ^ firstName.hashCode()
        ^ officeNumber;
    }
    return hash;
  }
  public boolean equals(Object o) {
    if (o == this) return true;

    if (o instanceof EmployeePK) {
      EmployeePK other = (EmployeePK) o;
      return other.hashCode() == hashCode() &&
             other.officeNumber == officeNumber;
             other.lastName.equals(lastName) &&
             other.firstName.equals(firstName);

    } else {
      return false;
    }
  }
}
```

The primary key class consists of the primary key fields, which must be public, and a no-argument constructor. The primary key class must also implement the `hashCode` and `equals` methods. The EJB container uses a number of data structures internally, many of which are indexed by the primary key class. It is vital that hashCode and equals be implemented correctly and efficiently in the primary key class.

Implementing hashCode

The hashCode method is implemented by returning an integer using the primary key fields. The goal of this function is to produce an integer that can be used to index tables. The hashCode for a primary key should never change. Therefore, the hashCode should only be constructed from immutable values.

A common strategy is to XOR the hashCode of the primary key elements together. OR should never be used because ORing several values will generally have most or all bits set to 1. Similarly, AND should not be used because most or all bits will converge to 0.

The hashCode method must be implemented such that two equal objects have the same hashCode. However, two objects with the same hashCode are not necessarily equal. This hashCode implementation stores the hashCode in a member variable to avoid computing it every time hashCode is called.

Implementing equals

It can also be tricky to implement equals correctly. The first line of any equals method should check the passed reference against this. This optimization simply checks whether equals has been called against itself. While this sounds strange at first, it is a common operation when the container has a primary key object and is checking to see if it already exists in a data structure.

Next, the equals method should ensure that the passed parameter is its own type. If the primary key class is final, a simple instanceof check can be used. If the primary key class is not final, the passed parameter might be a subclass of our primary key class. In this case, the equals method must use getClass().equals to ensure that the class types exactly match. It is recommended that primary key classes be final because using instanceof is cheaper than comparing classes.

Primary key classes should be final.

Finally, the equals method compares all the values in the passed object. If all of the values are identical, the objects are equal. Notice that the hashCodes are compared first. If two objects are equal, then their hashCodes

must be equal. Because our hashCode implementation precomputes the
hashCode, and integer comparisons are relatively cheap, it is usually worthwhile to perform this comparison first.

Entity Bean Inheritance and Polymorphism

Inheritance is a key advantage of object-oriented systems. Objects in a hierarchy gain functionality from their parents or superclasses. Object-oriented
systems also generally provide *polymorphism*, the capability to define common operations across distinct types. EJBs, especially entity beans, can take
advantage of inheritance and polymorphism. An EJB programmer might
define an employee entity bean with common methods such as getName
and getSalary.

The programmer could then define a manager entity bean that extends the
employee entity bean and adds manager-specific information. A method such
as getSubordinates, for example, could return the manager's employees. The advantage of using inheritance is that a manager entity bean could
also be treated as an employee. You could call a method getSalary, which
prints the total salaries of all employees, on each employee bean in the list.
Some of these beans might actually be manager beans, but to this routine,
they would all be employees (see Figure 9–2).

Figure 9–2 Employee–Manager Inheritance

Inheritance Restrictions

To design entity beans with inheritance, it is necessary to be cognizant of
restrictions in the EJB specification. While the EJB specification allows component inheritance, there are some subtle rules that limit how inherited EJBs

are designed. The EJB specification requires that the home interface's `create` method returns the remote interface type, not a sub-class or a super-class. The `ejbCreate` method on an entity bean must return the primary key type, not a sub-class or super-class. Similarly, the home interface's `findByPrimaryKey` method must take the primary key class as a parameter and return the remote interface. These requirements constrain how the bean writer may implement inheritance.

For instance, the employee home interface's `create` method returns the employee remote interface. If the programmer wants to make a management bean that extends the employee bean, a first approach might be to define a management home interface that extends the employee home interface, and a management remote interface that extends the employee remote interface. However, this approach would violate the EJB specification because the management home interface would inherit the employee `create` method, which does not return the management entity bean's remote interface. In the next section, we'll cover a number of patterns that may be used within the guidelines of the EJB specification for entity bean inheritance and polymorphism.

Design Patterns for Inheritance and Polymorphism

When designing entity beans with inheritance and polymorphism, it is important to decide which attributes will be used generically. In our employee and manager example, the programmer wants to expose the employee business methods as generics for any employee. This can be accomplished by defining a separate interface that includes only the generic employee business methods. An interface such as `GenericEmployee` would include the `getName` and `getSalary` methods. Now the employee bean has a remote interface that extends `GenericEmployee`. The manager bean's remote interface also extends `GenericEmployee` (see Figure 9–3).

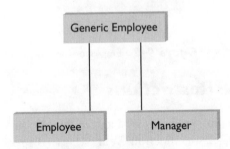

Figure 9–3   Remote Interface

Inheriting Interfaces

Because the EJBs use different remote interfaces and the `create` method must return the remote interface, our manager and employee beans must use different home interfaces. The employee home interface contains a `create` method that returns the employee remote interface. The manager home interface contains a `create` method that returns a manager remote interface. The `findByPrimaryKey` method is duplicated in each home interface. If the home interfaces contain generic methods such as home methods or `finders` returning `collection` types, these methods can be placed in a `GenericEmployeeHome` interface. In this case, the employee and manager home interfaces would extend `GenericEmployeeHome` (see Figure 9–4).

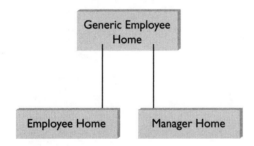

Figure 9–4   Home Interface

Inheritance can also be used when implementing the bean classes. A base class `GenericEmployeeBean` would implement the methods in `GenericEmployee` and `GenericEmployeeHome`. The employee EJB would have an employee bean class that extends the `GenericEmployee-Bean` and implements the `create` and `find` methods. Likewise, the manager EJB would have a manager bean class that implements the `create` and `find` methods, plus any manager-specific functionality.

The advantage of using the inheritance approach is that methods that treat employees polymorphically can use the `GenericEmployee` interface. In our total salary example, the method could take a `GenericEmployee` as its argument and call the `getSalary` method. Because both managers and employees implement this interface, the total salary method would work with either EJB. By using inheritance with the bean classes, the bean writer need only implement business methods once. Both beans then share this implementation.

Using Multiple Bean Implementations

Creating a base interface for the home and remote interface is not the only method for achieving polymorphism. Another common approach is to use identical home and remote interfaces, but implement them differently in the bean class. This approach is similar to using an interface that has several different implementations. The advantage is that the client does not know or care about which particular implementation is being used: The client just manipulates the interface.

For instance, an airline might model passengers as entity beans, using a remote interface with methods related to reserving seats on flights. Certain preferred or first-class seats would be available only to the airline's frequent customers. The entity bean writer could supply a different bean implementation of the passenger remote interface for frequent flyers. Ordinary customers would use a different implementation of the bean class. Any common methods could be implemented in a base class (see Figure 9–5).

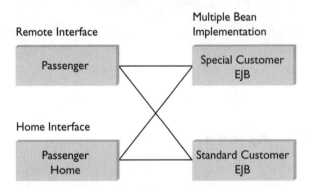

Figure 9–5   Passenger Inheritance

The advantage of this approach is that the back-end policies are independent of the client code. The bean writer could supply a new implementation of the bean class without changing any code in the client. If the airline established a new ultra customer whose benefits surpassed even the preferred customers, the bean writer would merely introduce a new bean class. The client code would be undisturbed.

Entity Beans and Locking

Entity beans are transactional, shared resources, simultaneously used by many clients. Clearly, to ensure that clients view consistent data, the EJB container and the database must enforce concurrency control. Entity EJBs are not written as re-entrant or thread-safe components. Each entity bean instance never has more than one thread of control in its object. This simplistic concurrency control is handled by the EJB container and mandated by the EJB specification. For this reason, methods in the entity bean class are not synchronized.

Database Concurrency

The database also provides concurrency control. The entity bean interacts with the database through its data access code and transactions. Generally, the database knows nothing of entity beans: It sees only transactions and JDBC or SQL commands. The database uses a combination of locking and private per-transaction copies of the data to manage concurrency. The actual locking strategy used by the database depends on the database vendor and the transaction's isolation level. Any transaction that violates the database constraints is unable to commit, and an SQLException is thrown. For instance, a database using optimistic concurrency control might detect at commit time that the associated transaction cannot serialize correctly. Generally, this exception occurs as a result of the ejbStore call.

In addition to the database, the EJB container supports concurrency control for entity beans. Because the EJB specification mandates a single entity bean instance that must not be written as thread-safe, the EJB container must serialize all container callbacks and business methods. This means, for example, that the container cannot call ejbPassivate while the business method is running.

EJB Container Concurrency

Although the EJB specification does not require a specific implementation, there are two general strategies for implementing entity bean concurrency control within the EJB container.

One approach is to activate an entity bean instance for each transaction. In this scenario, if two clients in separate transactions each call the same entity bean, the EJB container activates two instances, one instance for each transaction. Each instance calls `ejbLoad` at the beginning of the transaction to read its state. To the database, it appears as two transactions accessing the same data. This is handled by the database locking: The specific behavior depends on the database vendor and the isolation level. In most cases, because both transactions have only requested read locks, the transactions can proceed concurrently.

Another strategy is to maintain a single entity bean instance per primary key. In this scenario, only one transaction accesses the entity bean at a time. Once the previous transaction commits or rolls back, another transaction is permitted to use the entity bean instance.

Choosing a Database Concurrency Strategy

There are two concurrency control strategies: database concurrency and exclusive concurrency.

Database Concurrency

The WebLogic Server enables the entity bean deployer to choose a concurrency control strategy. By default, the WebLogic Server activates an entity bean instance for each transaction. This approach is called the database concurrency strategy because it defers the locking to the database. The database concurrency model leverages the database's deadlock detection capabilities. When the database detects a deadlock, one of the deadlocked transactions is aborted. An `SQLException` is thrown to the victim, and the EJB container processes the transaction rollback.

Exclusive Concurrency

The WebLogic Server also offers an option to activate a single instance per primary key, per WebLogic Server instance. This scenario forces the bean writer to be even more vigilant in avoiding deadlocks and concurrency conflicts. Because there is only a single instance per primary key, the EJB container implements an exclusive lock. For entity beans that are used by many clients concurrently in read-only or read-mostly situations, the exclusive lock can greatly limit parallelism. On the other hand, the exclusive lock enables data to be cached between transactions. Note that the exclusive lock is a per-server lock. In a WebLogic cluster, there can be an active instance with the same primary key in every server. The concurrency between servers is managed by the database.

Generally, entity beans should use the default database concurrency option because it places much less burden on the programmer. EJB 2.0 CMP beans can employ more advanced concurrency options because the EJB container has greater control over when data is read and written to the database.

Except in special cases, use the default database concurrency option.

Optimizing Data Access Calls

Entity bean programmers concerned about performance try to minimize the number of round trips between the EJB container and the database. By default, the WebLogic Server calls the entity bean's `ejbLoad` method at the beginning of a transaction to read the current state from the database. When the transaction commits, the EJB container calls `ejbStore` to write the entity bean's contents to the database. Note that database access occurs on transaction boundaries, not on method-call boundaries.

Programmers writing their first entity beans can incur performance problems by making their transactions too fine-grained. For instance, a Web page might need to gather 10 attributes from an entity bean to populate a page. If each method call runs in its own transaction, there are 10 database reads (`ejbLoad` calls) and 10 database writes (`ejbStore` calls). If the 10 method calls are wrapped in a single transaction, there is only one database read and one database write. For an operation such as populating a Web page, the database write is actually unnecessary because this transaction is read-only. We discuss how the WebLogic Server EJB container eliminates unnecessary database writes in a later section.

Minimizing Database Round Trips

In addition to batching multiple operations in a single transaction, there are a number of optimizations to minimize database round trips. Note that there is little opportunity to optimize `creates`. As a database insert, a `create` must write the initial values passed to the `ejbCreate` method. Because `creates` are a relatively rare event, their database access generally does not limit performance.

The EJB writer should try to optimize database reads (`ejbLoad` calls), database writes (`ejbStore` calls), and `finders` (database queries). BMP entity beans and CMP entity beans generally use different optimization strategies to minimize database round trips.

BMP Optimization

BMP entity beans that handle a great deal of data can optimize reads by writing ejbLoad so that it either reads a subset or, if appropriate, does nothing. In response to a business method call, the entity bean needs to determine whether the data has already been read in this transaction. You can achieve this by storing a bitmask in the entity bean that has one bit for each field. Then, ejbLoad sets a bit when its associated field is loaded. The remaining bits are cleared. The business method checks the bit mask to determine whether it needs to load its data.

The bitmask technique needs to be used with caution. If every attribute is brought in only on demand, the entity bean can exhibit extremely poor performance. The bitmask approach is best used when entity bean fields are very large, but seldom used. For example, an employee entity bean may have a picture stored as a binary image in the bean. Presumably, many users of the entity bean do not display the picture, so the bean limits the amount of data transferred from the database by only loading the picture when requested. If the remainder of the bean's fields are simple relational types or are frequently used, they should all be loaded in the ejbLoad call. The memory overhead of loading a few extra integers is minimal compared to the cost of extra trips to the database.

Write Optimizations

There are two main write optimizations that can be performed with BMP entity beans: omitting database writes in read-only transactions and tuned writes. Read-only transactions are common in real-world applications because entity bean data is often used to populate Web pages. Tuned writes are used to write only modified fields, instead of every field in the entity bean. Both optimizations are implemented using the same technique and are generally combined.

The entity bean keeps a bitmask with one bit per field. The bit mask is cleared in the ejbLoad callback. As with EJB 2.0 CMP beans, the bean should access its fields through get and set methods. This simplifies porting EJBs to CMP. With BMP beans, the bean writer implements the get and set methods. The get method simply returns the associated field. The set method sets the bitmask field associated with the EJB field and then assigns the value. The ejbStore implementation first checks the bit mask. If the bit mask is all zeroes, ejbStore returns immediately without writing to the database. The ejbStore method also can perform tuned writes because the bit mask shows which fields were modified in the transaction.

A common error when implementing this pattern is to clear the associated bit in the `get` method. This implementation does not work because the value may be read again after it has been written. If the bean writer clears the mask in the `get` method, the previous write is lost.

Optimizing Finder Methods

BMP entity beans also can optimize their `finder` methods, but the techniques apply only in certain situations. In general, BMP `finders` simply access the database and return the associated primary keys. As we see in the following section, CMP `finders` may be better optimized.

Implementing the `findByPrimaryKey` method is a special circumstance. The general contract for the `findByPrimaryKey` method is to ensure that the primary key exists and then return the primary key. Usually the bean implementation selects the primary key from the database, and if a row is returned, the implementation knows that the key exists. In some application-specific situations, the entity bean may already be aware that this primary key exists, and `findByPrimaryKey` can skip the data access and simply return the primary key. This optimization only applies when the primary key exists in a known domain or verification is performed at another level.

Optimizing CMP Entity Beans

CMP entity beans also can minimize the number of database round trips, but because the EJB container controls the data access code, optimizations are made in the deployment descriptor rather than in the bean code. By default, the WebLogic Server CMP implementation treats reads in the same way as standard BMP entity beans. At the beginning of the transaction, `ejbLoad` is called, and the bean's state is cleared. When the first `getXXX` method is called, the CMP engine reads the entire bean state from the database.

The standard behavior for `finders` is also identical to standard BMP behavior. Each `finder` selects the matching keys from the database. In the WebLogic Server CMP implementation, the container provides a feature called grouping to optimize `finders` and reads. The deployer must specify grouped fields in the CMP deployment descriptor. The bean writer can then assign `finders` or `business` methods to specific groups. When a `finder` or `business` method runs, it loads all the fields in its group.

For example, a U.S. citizen entity bean may have a Social Security number (as a primary key) and a name attribute. You could call `findByPrimaryKey` on a specific Social Security number, and then call a `business` method that reads the name attribute. By default, there would be one database access for the `findByPrimaryKey` call and another database access to load the name attribute. If the deployer specified a group containing the name and Social Security number fields, the `findByPrimaryKey` method and the `getName` method could use the same group. Then only one database access is required.

If the `getName` method is called again within the same transaction, it skips the data access and uses the cached name parameter. The grouping feature is effective because it does not require that every field be retrieved, which can be very expensive. Instead, the bean writer can create large entity beans that make small and efficient data access calls. One of the limitations of the BMP programming model is that it cannot match the CMP container's cooperation between `finders` and subsequent `business` methods.

Using Read-Only Entity Beans

As we've seen throughout this chapter, entity beans provide an object view of persistent and transactional data. However, not all persistent data is truly transactional. Many Web applications are dominated by reads and can even tolerate slightly stale data. The WebLogic Server offers an option called *read-only entity beans* to provide greater performance for read-intensive applications.

The advantage of read-only entity beans is that their data can be cached in memory, in many servers in the cluster. Read-only entity beans do not use expensive logic to keep the distributed caches coherent. Instead, the deployer specifies a timeout value, and the entity bean's cached state is refreshed after the timeout has expired.

Like any entity bean, the bean state is refreshed with the `ejbLoad` method call. When a method call is made on a read-only entity bean, the EJB container checks whether the associated data is older than its timeout value. If the timeout period has elapsed, `ejbLoad` is called and the bean state is refreshed. Because read-only beans do not have updates, `ejbStore` is never called. Read-only entity beans never participate in transactions, and they generally do not have `create` methods because `creates` should generally run in transactions.

Read-only entity beans are portable and follow the EJB specification. A WebLogic Server read-only entity bean is the same as a normal entity bean, except for some special deployment parameters in the WebLogic Server deployment descriptor and a different timing for calling `ejbLoad` and `ejbStore`.

Designing Read-Mostly Entity Beans

While there are many situations where data is only read, most applications have some updates. Read-only entity beans can be very effective in environments where reads dominate, but there are occasional updates. For instance, a Web site displaying sports scores might use an entity bean to model the game score. The game entity bean could store the teams playing the game, the current score of the game, and the time remaining.

Most of the requests to this entity bean are from Web pages that are reading the associated data and displaying it to the user. The Web site also has software that receives the score updates; it can then call the game entity bean and update the page with the new score and the remaining time. Viewing a score is not a transactional operation. In general, it does not matter if a user misses an instantaneous score update. In fact, this deployment could increase its performance by writing the game bean as a read-only entity bean. Because sports scores change relatively rapidly, a timeout of 30 seconds might be reasonable. To perform the updates, you can write a game update entity bean that extends the game bean. The game update bean is a traditional transactional entity bean that includes the methods to update the entity bean's state. The technique of using a read-only bean and extending it with a traditional entity bean that adds the update methods is referred to as the read-mostly pattern. It greatly increases the performance of sites that are dominated by reads but also have some updates.

Read-Mostly Example

This example demonstrates the read-mostly pattern for a Web site that displays basketball game scores and receives updates from an external process. The `BasketballScoreReader` is a read-only entity bean deployed with a read-timeout of 30 seconds. The read-timeout parameter is set in the *weblogic-ejb-jar.xml* file. The methods exposed through the `BasketballScoreReader` interface are read-only and return the cached copy of the data. The `BasketballScoreUpdater` bean is a standard, read/write entity bean. Its interface extends the reader interface with update methods. The `BasketballScoreReader` bean reads the updated data every 30 seconds. Between updates, the `BasketballScoreReader` reads cached data.

```
public BasketballScoreReader extends EJBObject {

  public String getHomeTeamName() throws RemoteException;
  public String getAwayTeamName() throws RemoteException;

  public int getHomeScore() throws RemoteException;
  public int getAwayScore() throws RemoteException;

  public int getQuarter() throws RemoteException;
  public int getTimeRemaining() throws RemoteException;

}

public BasketballScoreUpdater extends BasketballScoreReader {

  public void setHomeScore(int s) throws RemoteException;
  public void setAwayScore(int s) throws RemoteException;

  public void setQuarter(int q) throws RemoteException;
  public void setTimeRemaining(int t) throws RemoteException;

}
```

Session Beans as a Wrapper for Entity Beans

One of the main advantages of modular software is *abstraction*. An abstract implementation's components communicate through well-defined interfaces, so that any component could be replaced with an alternate module. Entity beans are not fully abstract: Although they expose remote interfaces to clients, their structure is closely tied to the fields in a particular database.

As we have shown, the Web tier uses an EJB layer to interact with the database. If the Web tier manipulates the entity beans directly, encapsulation could be violated because the database schema is exposed through the entity beans to the Web tier. A better design is to place session beans in front of entity beans. In that case, the Web tier calls the session bean, which in turn calls one or more entity beans.

The advantage of this pattern is that the session bean exposes only a business interface to the Web tier. The actual persistence layer can be implemented with (your choice): straight JDBC, one or more entity beans, or even a persistent queue. Because the persistence layer is hidden behind a layer of abstraction, the Web tier is independent of the persistent implementation. The practice of wrapping entity beans with session beans is known as the *facade pattern.*

Transaction demarcation is another advantage of using stateless session beans to wrap entity beans. If the Web tier called entity beans directly using multiple calls in a transaction, the Web tier would have to use a `User-Transaction` and explicitly demarcate each transaction. In general, it is advisable to enclose transactions with the persistence logic and keep them out of the Web tier. The Web tier should be concerned with presentation logic, not systems-level programming.

Transaction demarcation should be handled in the session bean facade. Transactions should not be exposed to the Web or presentation tier.

With a session bean facade, all of the transactions can be handled within the session bean. You can mark the session bean methods as `RequiresNew`, and the entity bean methods as `Mandatory`. In this scenario, the EJB container automatically begins a transaction before any method call on a session bean and commits the transaction when a session bean call returns. Any entity bean called from the session bean participates in its transaction. By marking the entity bean as mandatory, the bean writer asserts that the caller should be handling the transaction.

Entity beans should never be exposed to the client, or even to the Web tier.

Using Java Beans as Value Objects

Even when using the facade pattern, the EJB programmer must be careful to avoid exposing the entity beans directly to the client or Web tier. For example, a Web application displays a list of current orders for a given customer. The Web tier displays the information, and the EJB layer accesses the persistent store with an Order entity bean. With the facade pattern, the Web tier accesses a stateless session bean that finds the appropriate Order entity beans. The stateless session bean returns a `Collection` of Order entity objects to the Web tier. The Web tier can then call `getXXX` methods on the Order references and display the information to the user.

While this approach makes sense intuitively, it represents a poor use of entity beans and it does not perform well. Because entity beans are transactional components, the EJB container starts a transaction every time it calls `ejbLoad` and reads from the database. Because the Web tier should not be concerned with transactions, a single transaction cannot span the call to the stateless session bean and the presentation logic. The extra database round trips can greatly decrease performance.

A better approach is to never return the entity beans to the Web tier. Instead, the session bean can create Java bean *value objects* that encapsulate the information needed by the presentation logic. A collection of these value objects is returned to the Web tier. The presentation logic can make regular method calls to retrieve the order information from the `order` value object, without returning to the database.

Expose serializable value objects instead of entity beans to the Web or client tiers.

For example, here is an `OrderValueObject` that encapsulates the information in an order entity bean. The client receives these objects and never directly touches an entity bean. This ensures a clean separation between the persistent tier and the presentation layer.

```
public final class OrderValueObject
   implements java.io.Serializable
{
   private double price;
   private int quantity;
   private int itemNumber;

   public void setPrice(double p) { price = p; }
   public double getPrice() { return price; }

   public void setQuantity(int q) { quantity = q; }
   public int getQuantity() { return quantity; }

   public void setItemNumber(int in) { itemNumber = in; }
   public int getItemNumber() { return itemNumber; }

}
```

BMP vs. CMP

An important design decision for entity bean developers is the choice between BMP and CMP.

> *The main advantage of BMP is its flexibility. Because the bean writer explicitly codes the data access logic, he or she has complete control over the entity bean's persistence.*

While most entity beans keep a persistent representation in a database, with BMP the bean writer has the flexibility to choose any type of persistent store. For instance, BMP might be used to persist an entity bean to a legacy system.

CMP Design Advantages

> *A clear advantage of CMP is simplicity. With CMP, the EJB container automatically generates the data access code.*

This not only makes the bean simpler, but it also separates the bean code from its persistent representation. In a CMP bean, the database mappings occur at deployment time. The deployer can take a prepackaged CMP entity bean and map the persistent fields to arbitrary column and table names.

Another EJB 2.0 CMP advantage is the container's support for relationships between entity beans. In an EJB 2.0 CMP entity bean, EJB QL and the EJB container automatically handle relationships. For a BMP bean to support relationships, the bean writer must explicitly manage foreign key relationships, join tables, and join queries.

CMP Performance Advantages

Many people believe that because BMP gives the bean writer control over the data access logic, BMP should outperform container-generated code. However, this conclusion is generally not correct, especially with EJB 2.0 CMP beans. WebLogic Server's EJB 2.0 CMP container achieves high performance by minimizing the number of round trips between the EJB container and the database.

The most notable performance difference between BMP and CMP entity beans occurs with `finder` methods. In a BMP entity bean, `finder` methods return primary keys from the database. The EJB container creates a bean reference for each key and returns the references to the client. The key observation is that the BMP `finder` can only return the primary key. It is very common for clients to find a set of beans and then call `business` methods on the returned references. Each `business` method triggers an `ejbLoad` call and a round trip to the database. If `business` methods are called on each reference, the BMP `finder` returns N references using N+1 database round trips. Also, the `ejbLoad` call does not have any contextual information. For instance, the `ejbLoad` call does not know that it is immediately following the `finder`.

> A BMP `finder` that returns N objects and then accesses each object makes N+1 database round trips. A CMP `finder` can do a single `SELECT` that returns all of the necessary data.

The WebLogic Server EJB 2.0 CMP container enables the deployer to instruct the container how to optimize the situation by grouping attributes that should be loaded together. For instance, instead of loading only the primary key in the `finder`, the container could select the primary key plus attributes that are used in the following `business` method calls. In this case, there is only a single database access needed to run the `finder` and all the related `business` methods.

Another advantage of the WebLogic Server EJB 2.0 CMP implementation is that it does not require an all-or-nothing approach. The CMP implementation can load attributes in batches as they are required. For entity beans that represent a large amount of data, it is inefficient to load the entire bean from the database. The WebLogic Server EJB 2.0 CMP implementation enables the deployer to determine exactly how `finders` and methods bring data into the EJB container. The cooperation between `finders` and method invocations cannot be accomplished with a standard BMP entity bean.

Combining CMP and BMP

Choosing between CMP and BMP is not an absolute decision. In fact, it is possible to take a hybrid approach, using BMP and CMP within the same entity bean. When a CMP entity bean is deployed, the deployment descriptor specifies which of the bean's fields should be persisted by the EJB container. These are the container-managed fields. The entity bean may have other fields that are not in the container-managed list. In this case, the bean writer would explicitly manage the persistence of these fields. The BMP fields could be stored with the CMP fields, or they could be processed into a different table, a different database, or even a different persistent store.

Another option is to create both BMP and CMP versions of your entity beans. This approach is not as arduous as it sounds and does not require maintaining two completely separate code versions. First, write a CMP bean. The BMP version then extends the CMP bean class and provides the data access code. For instance, the BMP version could implement `ejbLoad` by loading the appropriate data from the persistent store and then calling `super.ejb-Load()`. The BMP version must also provide implementations of the `get` and `set` methods for the container-managed fields and relationships.

Stateless Session Beans vs. Entity EJBs

How do entity beans compare to stateless session beans using explicit JDBC code? Stateless session beans with embedded data access code give the developer direct access to the backing store. As with BMP entity beans, the developer has complete control over the data access code. This is particularly useful when accessing a legacy or non-database system that does not support entity beans.

A stateless session bean also has complete control over the objects it returns from a query. Unlike `finder` methods, JDBC queries return raw objects, and the stateless session bean writer must handle the lifecycle and caching of these objects.

The CMP engine reads data from the database when the first container-managed field is accessed in a transaction. The bean writer then modifies state with `business` methods, and the EJB container calls `ejbStore` at the end of the transaction to write back the modified state. This read-modify-write model works well for a variety of applications, but there are exceptions that are better coded with session beans and SQL.

The usual example given is a *blind update*. If you run an election over the Web in which each candidate's vote count is stored in the database and an entity bean is used, each vote reads in the current vote total, increments it, and writes back the new total. This is a simple construction that results in terrible performance and risks database deadlocks. In this case, the database read is unnecessary. The operation simply needs to increment the current vote total, which can best be done using SQL in a session bean. As in the blind update `UPDATE    votes    SET    candidate_A_count    = candidate_A_count  +  1`, this single JDBC statement performs much better than its entity bean counterpart and avoids database deadlock issues.

Entity EJBs use a read-modify-write model. When the read is unnecessary and only a modify and write are performed, JDBC outperforms the entity model.

CMP entity beans do possess a number of advantages over the stateless session bean with JDBC. In addition to freeing the programmer from having to write data access code, CMP entity beans might outperform stateless session beans because CMP beans can maintain state and cache the results of queries.

CMP entity beans can also leverage the EJB container by writing an `ejb-Home` method that uses an `ejbSelect` method to run the database query. Like stateless session beans, the EJB container selects a bean instance from the ready pool to run the `ejbHome` method. In using the `ejbSelect` method, the bean writer simply writes the EJB-QL query in the deployment descriptor, and the EJB container generates the required JDBC code. Using `ejbSelect` methods also allows the bean code to be separated from the database schema. The EJB-QL only accesses container-managed fields and relationships: It does not use physical database mapping names, which can be changed without updating the query.

Conclusion

Along with session beans, entity beans provide a powerful abstraction from Java objects to persistent, transactional business logic. CMP entity beans free the bean provider from writing tedious data access code. Business logic can be rapidly developed while leaving the infrastructure to the EJB container. With the EJB 2.0 specification and WebLogic Server 6.0, the EJB container contains optimizations to make CMP entity beans' performance very comparable to hand-coded SQL. As we've seen in this chapter, there are many cases in which the EJB container can optimize CMP entity beans to outperform BMP or hand-coded JDBC code.

USING MESSAGE-DRIVEN EJBS

In this chapter:

- Message-Driven EJB Lifecycle
- Writing Deployment Descriptors for Message-Driven Beans
- Message-Driven Beans and Concurrency
- Using Transactions with Message-Driven Beans
- Message-Driven Bean Advantages

10

Chapter

Session and entity beans use a well-defined interface for processing workflow from client requests. Enterprise JavaBeans (EJB) clients use the home and remote interfaces to make synchronous Remote Method Invocation (RMI) calls to the EJB server. The client thread making the EJB call blocks until the EJB server call returns. As discussed in Chapter 7, *Enterprise Messaging with the Java Message Service (JMS)*, messaging allows an asynchronous model. Instead of waiting for the server's response, the client sends a message to a JMS destination and returns. In addition to scalability benefits, this model enables client programs to continue without waiting for server operations to complete.

In the EJB 1.0 and 1.1 specifications, it was difficult to integrate the synchronous EJB model with messaging systems. EJBs can be used to send messages, but session and entity beans cannot be used as JMS message listeners. The problem is that session and entity beans instances live within the EJB container, and the EJB container determines their lifecycle. With the EJB 2.0 specification, there is a new EJB type that integrates EJB and JMS. This new EJB type is the message-driven EJB.

Message-Driven EJB Basics

Message-driven EJBs are the integration between EJB and the JMS. Like other EJB types, message-driven EJBs live within an EJB container and benefit from EJB container services such as transactions, security, and concurrency control. However, a message-driven EJB does not interact directly with clients. Instead, message-driven EJBs are JMS message listeners. A client publishes messages to a JMS destination. The JMS provider and the EJB container then cooperate to deliver the message to the message-driven EJB (see Figure 10–1).

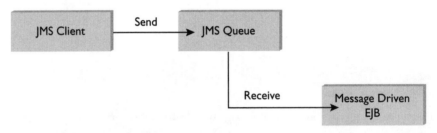

Figure 10–1   Message-Driven EJBs

Because message-driven EJBs do not have clients, they do not require home or remote interfaces. A message-driven EJB is a bean class that implements   the   `javax.ejb.MessageDrivenBean`   and   the `javax.jms.MessageListener` interfaces. The `MessageDriven-Bean` interface includes only two methods: `setMessageDrivenContext` and `ejbRemove`. The `MessageListener` interface is even simpler: It contains only a single method, `onMessage`. In addition to implementing these three methods, the bean writer provides a single `ejbCreate` method with no parameters. One of the best features of message-driven EJBs is their simplicity: This single bean class has only four methods.

Message-driven beans include a single class, which implements the `javax.ejb.MessageDrivenBean` and `javax.jms.MessageListener` interfaces.

Message-Driven EJB Lifecycle

The lifecycle of a message-driven EJB is very similar to a stateless session bean. When the container creates a new message-driven EJB instance, it first calls the bean class's default (no-parameter) constructor. While EJBs may implement a constructor, it is preferable to place initialization code in the setMessageDrivenContext or ejbCreate methods. The container next calls the setMessageDrivenContext method and passes the EJB a javax.ejb.MessageDrivenContext. This context, like the SessionContext or EntityContext, is generally saved in a member variable and can later be used to make calls into the EJB container. Finally, the EJB container calls the ejbCreate() method.

Like stateless session beans, message-driven beans only have a single, no-argument ejbCreate method. Message-driven EJB instances do not have an associated identity and, like session beans, they are created at the container's discretion. Also, like stateless session beans, message-driven bean instances should not keep any conversational state in the bean class.

When a message-driven EJB is deployed into the EJB container, the ejb-jar.xml specifies a JMS queue or topic. The EJB container registers the message-driven bean instance as a JMS listener. When a message arrives on the associated JMS destination, the EJB container retrieves a bean instance and calls the bean's onMessage method with the new message. Like stateless session beans, message-driven EJBs are pooled to minimize object creation. We discuss the WebLogic EJB container's pooling of message-driven EJBs later in this chapter.

Message-Driven EJB Example

Let's now develop a simple message-driven EJB to receive text messages from a JMS queue and print the messages to the server's stderr.

The MessageDrivenBean class includes the four required methods. The onMessage method receives the JMS message and prints the associated text. For this simple example, any error is simply printed to the server's stderr.

MessagePrinterBean Class

```
package com.learnweblogic.examples.ch10.textmessage;

import javax.ejb.MessageDrivenBean;
import javax.ejb.MessageDrivenContext;
import javax.jms.JMSException;
import javax.jms.Message;
import javax.jms.MessageListener;
import javax.jms.TextMessage;
```

```
public class MessagePrinterBean
  implements MessageDrivenBean, MessageListener
{
  private MessageDrivenContext ctx;

  public void setMessageDrivenContext(
MessageDrivenContext c)
  {
    ctx = c;
  }

  public void ejbCreate() {}
  public void ejbRemove() {}

  public void onMessage(Message m) {

    TextMessage msg = (TextMessage) m;

    try {
      System.err.println(
"Message-Driven EJB received message: "+
        msg.getText());
    } catch (JMSException e) {
      System.err.println(
"Exception receiving text from message: ");
      e.printStackTrace();
    }
  }
}
```

Writing Deployment Descriptors for Message-Driven EJBs

Like other EJBs, message-driven EJBs require an *ejb-jar.xml* deployment descriptor. This descriptor includes the name of the bean class, the transaction type, and the JMS destination. Like session beans, message-driven EJBs may use either bean or container transaction attributes. We discuss the different transaction settings later in this chapter

Sample ejb-jar.xml Descriptor

```
<!DOCTYPE ejb-jar PUBLIC
"-//Sun Microsystems, Inc.//DTD Enterprise JavaBeans 2.0//EN"
 "http://java.sun.com/dtd/ejb-jar_2_0.dtd">
```

```
<ejb-jar>
  <enterprise-beans>
    <message-driven>
      <ejb-name>MessagePrinterEJB</ejb-name>
      <ejb-class>
com.learnweblogic.examples.ch10.textmessage.MessagePrinterBean
          </ejb-class>
          <transaction-type>Container</transaction-type>
          <message-driven-destination>
            <jms-destination-type>
              javax.jms.Queue
            </jms-destination-type>
            </message-driven-destination>
          </message-driven>
        </enterprise-beans>
      </ejb-jar>
        .
```

Sample weblogic-ejb-jar.xml Descriptor

Message-driven EJBs also require a *weblogic-ejb-jar.xml* deployment descriptor. Like other EJBs, this deployment descriptor contains deployment information that is WebLogic-specific or simply not specified by the standard *ejb-jar.xml* deployment descriptor.

The only required element for a message-driven EJB is the `<destina-tion-jndi-name>`. When the EJB container deploys the message-driven EJB, it uses this Java Naming and Directory Interface (JNDI) name to look up the JMS destination. Unlike other EJB types, a `<jndi-name>` for the EJB is not required because there is no direct client interaction.

```
<?xml version="1.0"?>

<!DOCTYPE weblogic-ejb-jar PUBLIC
"-//BEA Systems, Inc.//DTD WebLogic 6.0.0 EJB//EN"
"http://www.bea.com/servers/wls600/dtd/weblogic-ejb-jar.dtd">

<weblogic-ejb-jar>

  <weblogic-enterprise-bean>
    <ejb-name>MessagePrinterEJB</ejb-name>

    <message-driven-descriptor>
      <destination-jndi-name>
        MessageQueue
      </destination-jndi-name>
    </message-driven-descriptor>
```

```
</weblogic-enterprise-bean>
</weblogic-ejb-jar>
```

Building the Example Message-Driven Bean

This example is in the *examples/ch10/textmessage/* directory on the accompanying CD-ROM. The *build.cmd* script will compile and build the `ejb` and the client classes. The *runclient.cmd* script runs the JMS client to publish messages.

The message-driven bean class may now be packaged along with the deployment descriptors in an ejb-jar file.

```
META-INF/ejb-jar.xml
META-INF/weblogic-ejb-jar.xml
com/learnweblogic/examples/ch10/textmessage/MessagePrinter-
Bean.class
```

Deploying the Example Message-Driven Bean

Before the ejb-jar file can be deployed in the WebLogic Server, the deployer must ensure that the associated JMS destination exists. In this case, the server must have a JMS queue deployed with the JNDI name `Message-Queue`.

Once the JMS destination exists, the ejb-jar is deployed by copying the file into the server's applications directory. The deploy.cmd script demonstrates this process.

An Example JMS Client

A client can now indirectly interact with the message-driven EJB by publishing JMS messages to the messages queue.

A message-driven EJB client uses standard JMS message producer code. The JMS client has no idea what consumers will receive the JMS messages—message-driven EJBs or other types of JMS consumers. For a more detailed explanation of JMS message producers, please see Chapter 7.

```
package com.learnweblogic.examples.ch10.textmessage;

public final class TextMessageSenderClient
  extends BaseClient {
  private QueueConnection queueConnection = null;
  private QueueSender queueSender         = null;
  private QueueSession queueSession       = null;
  private Queue queue                     = null;
  private TextMessage msg                 = null;
```

```
public TextMessageSenderClient(String [] argv)
  throws Exception
{
  super(argv);
  try {
    Context ctx = getInitialContext();

    QueueConnectionFactory factory =
      (QueueConnectionFactory)
      ctx.lookup(JMS_CONN_FACTORY);

    queueConnection = factory.createQueueConnection();

    // Create a non-transacted JMS Session
    queueSession =
      queueConnection.createQueueSession(false,
          Session.AUTO_ACKNOWLEDGE);

    queue = (Queue) ctx.lookup(JMS_QUEUE);

    queueSender = queueSession.createSender(queue);

    msg = queueSession.createTextMessage();

    queueConnection.start();

  } catch (Exception e) {
    System.err.println("Error while attempting to "+
     "connect to the server and look up the JMS"+
      " QueueConnectionFactory.");
    System.err.println("Please make sure that you have"+
     " deployed the JMS Queue and specified the correct"+
     " server URL.");

    e.printStackTrace();

    throw e;
  }
}

public void send(String message)
     throws JMSException
{
  try {
    msg.setText(message);
    queueSender.send(msg);
  } catch (JMSException e) {
```

```
      System.err.println("Exception raised while sending"+
       "to queue: "+ JMS_QUEUE);
      e.printStackTrace();
      throw e;
    }
  }
```

Message-Driven Beans and Concurrency

Like other EJB components, the EJB container handles concurrency for message-driven bean instances. Message-driven EJBs are not written with thread-safe code, and the EJB container never makes a re-entrant call into a bean instance. As with stateless session beans, message-driven bean instances are pooled in memory by the container. The *weblogic-ejb-jar.xml* deployment descriptor contains two parameters to control the pool size: `<initial-beans-in-freepool>` and `<max-beans-in-freepool>`. When the EJB is deployed, the container pre-allocates as many instances as specified in the `initial-beans-in-freepool` parameter. As messages arrive, this enables the server immediately to accept work without spending time creating bean instances. This parameter defaults to 0. The `max-beans-in-freepool` gives the upper bound on the number of bean instances created by the container.

The `<max-beans-in-freepool>` *determine the number of message-driven bean instances that can concurrently process messages.*

Parallel Message Dispatch

When a message arrives on the associated JMS destination, the EJB container asks the free pool for an available instance. If there is an instance in the pool, its `onMessage` method is called and the message is delivered.

If the free pool is empty and there are less than `max-beans-in-freepool` instances in use, the container allocates a new instance and uses it to deliver the message. If `max-beans-in-freepool` instances are already processing messages, the new message remains in the JMS destination until one of the message-driven bean instances returns from its `onMessage` callback.

Setting max-beans-in-freepool for Message-Driven EJBs

Most users should not need to tune the `max-beans-in-freepool` or `initial-beans-in-freepool` settings for message-driven EJBs. By default, the `initial-beans-in-freepool` parameter is 0, so beans will be created as needed. This ensures that instances are created only when needed.

The `max-beans-in-freepool` parameter is not limited by default. However, the number of concurrent instances is numbered by the amount of execute threads in the server. The maximum parallelism is achieved when each thread is concurrently using a message-driven EJB instance to process a message.

The default `max-beans-in-freepool` setting gives the maximum parallelism.

Message Ordering

The message-driven EJB concurrency model enables the EJB container to process as many messages as possible in parallel. While this maximizes throughput, programmers should be aware that messages might be processed out of order. Because the container is processing the messages in parallel threads, it is possible for a later message to be processed before an earlier message.

Applications should not make assumptions about the order in which messages are delivered to message-driven beans.

Specifying a JMS Connection Factory

The WebLogic JMS server defines standard queue and topic connection factories, and additional user-defined connection factories may be created with the Administration Console. By default, message-driven EJBs use the standard JMS connection factories, but it is possible to override this and specify a user-defined connection factory with the `<connection-factory-jndi-name>` tag in the *weblogic-ejb-jar.xml:*

```
<connection-factory-jndi-name>
  MyConnectionFactory
</connection-factory-jndi-name>
```

Using Transactions with Message-Driven Beans

Like other EJBs, message-driven beans make use of the EJB container's transaction service. Because message-driven beans never directly interact with clients, they never participate in the client's transaction.

Message-driven EJBs offer three different transaction options:

- `Required` transaction attribute
- NotSupported
- Bean-managed transactions

Required Transaction Attribute

If the `Required` attribute is specified, the EJB container automatically starts a transaction. The message receipt from the JMS queue or topic is included in this transaction. The message-driven bean's `onMessage` method is then called in the transaction context. When the `onMessage` method returns, the EJB container commits the transaction. If the transaction aborts, the JMS message remains in the JMS destination and is delivered again to the message-driven EJB.

Use the `Required` *transaction attribute to ensure that the JMS message receipt and* `onMessage` *callbacks participate in a Java Transaction API (JTA) transaction.*

NotSupported Transaction Attribute

With the `NotSupported` transaction attribute, the EJB container does not start a transaction before calling the EJB's `onMessage` callback. The message-driven EJB acts as a standard JMS consumer. It relies on JMS's message acknowledgment semantics to confirm that the message was successfully received and processed. Chapter 7 provides details on JMS message acknowledgment facilities.

---

*Use the **NotSupported** attribute when message receipt is not transactional and JMS's acknowledgment modes are sufficient.*

Bean-Managed Transactions

Finally, like session EJBs, message-driven EJBs may use bean-managed transactions. With bean-managed transactions, the bean code uses the `EJB-Context.getUserTransaction()` callback to get a reference to a `UserTransaction` object. The bean code may then explicitly begin and commit transactions.

Because the transaction demarcation is within the `onMessage` callback, the message receipt does not participate in the transaction. If the `UserTransaction` aborts, the message does not automatically get redelivered.

---

*Use bean-managed transactions when message receipt is not transactional, but the **onMessage** callback uses Java Database Connectivity (JDBC), EJB, or other resources that need to participate in a transaction.*

Error Handling with the Required Transaction Attribute

Message-driven beans with the `Required` transaction attribute need to be careful when aborting transactions. A transaction aborts either because it was explicitly marked for rollback, or because a system exception was thrown. One potential issue is known as the "Poison Message." In this scenario, a message-driven EJB receiving stock trade orders from an order queue might encounter a stock symbol that does not exist. When the message-driven EJB receives the error message, the underlying logic might be to abort the transaction because the symbol is invalid. When the JMS implementation delivers the message again in a new transaction, the process repeats. Clearly, this is not the desired behavior.

A good solution for this potential problem is to separate application errors from system errors. An application error, such as an invalid stock symbol, should be handled by sending an error message to a JMS error destination. This enables the transaction to commit, and the "Poison Message" leaves the system. A system error might be that the back-end database has failed. In this case, our transaction should roll back so that this message is still on the queue when the database recovers.

Use a separate JMS destination to handle application-level errors. This ensures that improper messages are not continually redelivered.

Message Acknowledgment

The EJB container automatically handles JMS message acknowledgment for message-driven EJBs. When a message-driven EJB is deployed with the `Required` transaction attribute, the container acknowledges the message when the transaction commits.

A message-driven EJB deployed as `NotSupported` or with bean-managed transactions uses `AUTO_ACKNOWLEDGE`. Like other asynchronous JMS message consumers, the acknowledgment is performed when the `onMessage` method returns.

Message-driven beans may also specify the `DUPS_OK_ACKNOWLEDGE` mode with the `<jms-acknowledge-mode>` tag in the *ejb-jar.xml* deployment descriptor. This acknowledgment mode enables the underlying JMS implementation to lazily acknowledge messages.

`DUPS_OK_ACKNOWLEDGE` performs better than `AUTO_ACKNOWLEDGE` because acknowledgments are less frequent, but the application must be able to tolerate duplicate messages in the case of failure.

Message-driven EJB writers should also be aware that even `AUTO_ACKNOWLEDGE` can cause a duplicate message to be delivered. This occurs if the JMS implementation fails after the `onMessage` method returns but before the acknowledgment completes. This case is covered in Chapter 7.

The WebLogic JMS implementation adds the `NO_ACKNOWLEDGE` and `MULTICAST_NO_ACKNOWLEDGE` modes that may also be selected for message-driven EJBs. `NO_ACKNOWLEDGE` provides the best performance but the worst reliability because messages leave the system as soon as they are delivered. `MULTICAST_NO_ACKNOWLEDGE` sends messages to a JMS topic over IP multicast. These acknowledgment modes are covered in detail in Chapter 7.

The acknowledgment mode is a trade-off between performance and reliability. The strongest delivery guarantee is the `Required` transaction attribute, which ensures that the message receipt participates in JTA transaction. The `NO_ACKNOWLEDGE` and `MULTICAST_NO_ACKNOWLEDGE` modes provide the highest message throughput because messages are not retained after delivery.

New Customer Example

Let's now take a look at an example that combines message-driven EJBs with stateless session and entity beans. This example demonstrates the process of entering new customer records into a database. The customer information is sent to a JMS queue named `newCustomers`. A message-driven EJB listens on this queue, unpacks the message, and calls a stateless session bean to enter the new customer record.

```
public class NewCustomerReceiverBean
  implements MessageDrivenBean, MessageListener
{
  private static final int BAD_MESSAGE_TYPE = 1;
  private static final int CUSTOMER_ALREADY_EXISTS = 2;

  private MessageDrivenContext ctx;

  private NewCustomer newCustomer;
```

The `setMessageDrivenContext` creates a reference to the New-Customer stateless session bean. This is stored in an instance variable and will be used in `onMessage` to enter new customers.

```
  public void setMessageDrivenContext(
      MessageDrivenContext c)
  {
    ctx = c;
    try {
      Context ic = new InitialContext();
      Object h =
       ic.lookup("java:/comp/env/ejb/NewCustomerHome");

      NewCustomerHome home = (NewCustomerHome)
        PortableRemoteObject.narrow(h,
            NewCustomerHome.class);
```

```
      newCustomer = home.create();

  } catch (Exception e) {
    e.printStackTrace();
    throw new EJBException(e);
  }

}

public void ejbCreate() {}
public void ejbRemove() {}
```

The onMessage method unpacks the information from the JMS message. Next, it calls the NewCustomer stateless session bean to enter the new customer record. This message-driven EJB is deployed with the Required transaction attribute, so the onMessage method runs in a transaction. A JMSException occurs if the message was incomplete. For instance, the sender might not have set one of the fields in the MapMessage. The InvalidCustomerException is thrown if the customer ID already exists. These two errors are considered application errors. The transaction still commits, but we publish an error message to allow the system administrator to correct this action. The RemoteException is considered a system exception. The message-driven EJB marks the transaction for rollback.

```
public void onMessage(Message m) {

  MapMessage msg = (MapMessage) m;

  try {
    int id               = msg.getInt("ID");
    String firstName     = msg.getString("FIRST_NAME");
    String lastName      = msg.getString("LAST_NAME");
    String emailAddress  = msg.getString("EMAIL_ADDRESS");

    newCustomer.enterNewCustomer(id, firstName, lastName,
        emailAddress);

  } catch (JMSException e) {
    // message was mal-formed

    publishError(BAD_MESSAGE_TYPE, e);

  } catch (InvalidCustomerException ice) {

    // customer id already exists

    publishError(CUSTOMER_ALREADY_EXISTS, ice);
```

```
    } catch (RemoteException re) {
      re.printStackTrace();
      ctx.setRollbackOnly();
    }
  }
}
```

The NewCustomerBean is a stateless session bean that serves as a facade to the persistence layer. The setSessionContext looks up an EJB environment reference to find the Customer entity bean.

```
package com.learnweblogic.examples.ch10.customer;

public class NewCustomerBean implements SessionBean {

  private SessionContext ctx;

  private CustomerHome customerHome;

  public void setSessionContext(SessionContext c) {
    ctx = c;

    try {
      Context ic = new InitialContext();
      Object h =
            ic.lookup("java:/comp/env/ejb/CustomerHome");

      customerHome = (CustomerHome)
        PortableRemoteObject.narrow(h, CustomerHome.class);

    } catch (NamingException ne) {
      ne.printStackTrace();
      throw new EJBException(ne);
    }
  }

  public void ejbCreate() {}
  public void ejbRemove() {}

  public void ejbActivate() {}
  public void ejbPassivate() {}
```

The enterNewCustomer method creates a new Customer entity bean with the passed customer information. An entity bean's create method throws a DuplicateKeyException if the ID already exists in the database. This exception is wrapped in an application exception and thrown back to the messaging layer.

```
public void enterNewCustomer(int id, String firstName,
  String lastName, String emailAddress)
  throws InvalidCustomerException
{
  try {
    customerHome.create(new Integer(id), firstName,
          lastName, emailAddress);

  } catch (DuplicateKeyException dke) {
    // customer already exists
    throw new InvalidCustomerException("Customer:" "+id
      + " already exists.");
  } catch (Exception e) {
    // unexpected error
    e.printStackTrace();
    throw new EJBException(e);
  }
}
```

Finally, the `Customer` entity bean models the actual persistent representation in the database. Because this is a CMP entity bean, the EJB container generates the required data access code. The CMP entity bean includes abstract `get` and `set` methods for each of the container-managed fields that are stored in the database.

```
package com.learnweblogic.examples.ch10.customer;

public abstract class CustomerBean implements EntityBean {

  // Container-managed fields

  // primary key field
  public abstract Integer getId();
  public abstract void setId(Integer id);

  public abstract String getFirstName();
  public abstract void setFirstName(String firstName);

  public abstract String getLastName();
  public abstract void setLastName(String lastName);

  public abstract String getEmailAddress();
  public abstract void setEmailAddress(String email);

  private EntityContext ctx;

  public void setEntityContext(EntityContext c) {
    ctx = c;
```

```
}

public void unsetEntityContext() {
  ctx = null;
}
public Integer ejbCreate(Integer id, String firstName,
  String lastName, String emailAddress)
{
  setId(id);
  setFirstName(firstName);
  setLastName(lastName);
  setEmailAddress(emailAddress);

  return null;
}

public void ejbPostCreate(Integer id, String firstName,
  String lastName, String emailAddress)
{
  // This bean does no ejbPostCreate initialization
}

public void ejbRemove() {}

public void ejbActivate() {}
public void ejbPassivate() {}

public void ejbLoad() {}
public void ejbStore() {}
}
```

Building and Running the Example

This example is located in the *examples/ch10/customer* directory on the accompanying CD-ROM. It includes a *build.cmd* script to compile and build the EJBs. There is a *tables.ddl* file that demonstrates the required database schema. These tables must be created before deploying the EJBs. Finally, the *runclient.cmd* script can be used to execute the sample JMS client.

Message-Driven EJB Advantages

Message-Driven EJBs provide a number of advantages over standard JMS consumers, and they should be the default choice when writing message consumers.

Using JTA Transactions with an Asynchronous Consumer

The WebLogic JMS implementation provides a powerful integration with the JTA transaction manager. This allows JMS message producers and consumers to participate in JTA transactions and enlist other resources such as EJBs or JDBC code in these transactions.

A standard JMS consumer enlists a JTA transaction by explicitly using a `UserTransaction` reference to begin and commit transactions. The message consumer can begin a `UserTransaction` and then call its receive method to consume a JMS message within that transaction. This approach works fine for synchronous receive calls, but it is not possible with asynchronous message consumers.

There is no means in the JMS specification to register an asynchronous `MessageListener` (such as a message-driven EJB) and ask the JMS implementation to start a JTA transaction before delivering the message.

With message-driven EJBs using the `Required` transaction attribute, the EJB and WebLogic JMS implementations cooperate to start JTA transactions before the `onMessage` callback. This ensures that the message receipt is part of the transaction.

A message-driven EJB is the only way for an asynchronous consumer to include its message receipt in a JTA transaction. This is not possible with standard JMS consumers.

Parallel Message Processing

Many JMS applications need to maximize throughput by processing as many messages as possible in parallel. This can be accomplished with the JMS specification using the `ServerSessionPool` extensions, but it requires the application programmer to include additional logic to support parallel messaging processing.

Message-driven EJBs automatically support parallel message processing with the EJB container's deployment descriptors. The *weblogic-ejb-jar.xml* includes a `max-beans-in-freepool` parameter to configure the number of message-driven bean instances that may be used in parallel. By default, the EJB container configures the message-driven EJB to process as many messages as possible in parallel.

> The EJB and JMS containers automatically handle parallel message processing with message-driven EJBs.

Simple and Standards-Based

Message-driven EJBs require a single implementation class, which implements two small interfaces. They are simple to develop and portable to other Java 2 Enterprise Edition (J2EE) implementations.

> With their simplicity and standard J2EE architecture, message-driven EJBs should be the default choice for JMS consumers.

Conclusion

Message-driven EJBs provide an easy and effective means to integrate messaging into a J2EE application. They are commonly used to perform back-end work asynchronously. Message-driven beans can take advantage of the EJB container's concurrency, security, and transaction support. This allows the bean writer to concentrate on writing the business logic without needing to develop the infrastructure code for a JMS listener.

INTERFACING WITH INTERNET MAIL USING WEBLOGIC SERVER JAVAMAIL

In this chapter:

This chapter discusses Internet mail (email) protocols, including the Simple Mail Transport Protocol (SMTP), and the Post Office Protocol Version 3 (POP3) and Internet Mail Access Protocol (IMAP) mail retrieval protocols. JavaMail is the Java 2 Enterprise Edition (J2EE) implementation of a mail service. This chapter includes:

- The JavaMail API, which supports the `Session`, `Message`, and `Transport` classes
- Using Java to send simple email
- Adding email capability to the WebAuction application

11

Chapter

Up to this point, user interactions with WebLogic Server applications have taken place either through a Web browser or through application clients. Web applications also typically interact with users through email, for operations such as confirming that a user's bid has been accepted, or verifying a newly registered user's email address. These connections to email use WebLogic Server's implementation of the *JavaMail* functionality for integrating email into Web applications.

About Email

Email is the Internet standard for exchanging messages between users or applications. Email messages can contain plain text or more complicated data types such as multimedia files. Every email message includes information about the origination of the message, the address to which it is being sent, and other routing information in the email header. This header is a text representation of all the details of the sender and the receiver of the message, as well as all intermediate servers dealing with the message.

About Simple Mail Transport Protocol (SMTP)

When a user sends an email message, the message first visits what is called a *mail server*. This server receives the message transmitted over SMTP, which is the Internet standard for communication between mail clients and mail servers. SMTP also is used when two mail servers want to exchange email messages. In most cases, mail servers are standard PC servers that run one of the mail server application packages. Leading mail server packages include Sendmail and qmail on UNIX systems, and Microsoft Exchange for the Windows platform.

Mail Retrieval Protocols (POP3, IMAP)

There are two commonly used mail retrieval protocols that are defined by the Internet standards. POP3 stores mail for the user on the server. The user's mail client connects to the mail server and retrieves messages on behalf of the user. In most cases, enterprises using POP3 expect users to download their messages and then delete them from the mail server.

In contrast, IMAP enables users to access their mail from the mail server, but without expectations that they immediately delete those messages. Using IMAP, the user's mail is stored on the mail server and is displayed by an IMAP email client, such as Netscape Communicator or Microsoft Outlook. Because IMAP does not store messages on the user's local machine, individuals using IMAP can move from client machine to client machine, with uninterrupted access to new and archived messages.

About JavaMail

JavaMail is the J2EE standard set of APIs for interfacing with email systems. JavaMail specifies a plug-and-play architecture that supports various email protocol implementations including POP3, SMTP, and others. The WebLogic Server implementation of JavaMail includes implementations of SMTP and IMAP. WebLogic Server JavaMail is available as a standard part of the WebLogic Server environment.

WebLogic Server Version 6.0 does not include a native POP3 provider. To use JavaMail to access POP3 mail, download the POP3 provider available on the Java Web site at *http://java.sun.com/products/javamail/*.

The JavaMail API for WebLogic Server applications has four major components, which we cover in the following sections.

The Session Class

The Session class defines the global and per-user mail-related properties that define how the clients and server interact. An application locates an instance of the Session class to use as a basis for creating new mail messages and for locating information about the remote mail server.

Java mail sessions are configured through the WebLogic Server console. When an application needs to locate a mail session, it locates it in the Java Naming and Directory Interface (JNDI) using the following code:

```
Session mailSession;
String sessionJNDIName = "myMailSession";

try {
    Context ctx = new InitialContext();
    mailSession = (Session) ctx.lookup(sessionJNDIName);
catch (NamingException ne) { … }
```

In the preceding code, the mail session is located by doing a lookup into WebLogic Server JNDI. If the mail session was configured using the WebLogic Server console, the appropriately configured mail session is included in the mailSession instance of the Session class.

The Message Class

The Message class included in the JavaMail package represents a single mail message. It contains attributes that contain the addressing information and define the structure of the contents, including its type. A number of useful methods are included in the Message class (see Table 11.1).

Table 11.1 Methods of the Message Class

`abstract "C:\WINNT\Profiles\michaelg\javax\mail\Address.html" []`	`"C:\WINNT\Profiles\michaelg\javax\mail\Message.html" \1 "getFrom()" ()` Returns the From attribute.
`abstract java.lang.String`	`"C:\WINNT\Profiles\michaelg\javax\mail\Message.html" \1 "getSubject()" ()` Gets the subject of this message.
`abstract "C:\WINNT\Profiles\michaelg\javax\mail\Message.html"`	`"C:\WINNT\Profiles\michaelg\javax\mail\Message.html" \1 "reply(boolean)" (boolean replyToAll)` Gets a new Message suitable for a reply to this message.
`abstract void`	`"C:\WINNT\Profiles\michaelg\javax\mail\Message.html" \1 "setFrom()" ()` Sets the From attribute in this message.
`abstract void`	`"C:\WINNT\Profiles\michaelg\javax\mail\Message.html" \1 "setFrom(javax.mail.Address)" ("C:\WINNT\Profiles\michaelg\javax\mail\Address.html" address)` Sets the From attribute in this message.

Table 11.1 Methods of the Message Class (continued)

```
void        "C:\WINNT\Profiles\michaelg\javax\mail\Message.html" \
            1 "setRecipient(javax.mail.Message.RecipientType, javax.mail.Address)"
            ("C:\WINNT\Profiles\michaelg\javax\mail\Message.RecipientType.html" type,
            "C:\WINNT\Profiles\michaelg\javax\mail\Address.html" address)
            Sets the recipient address.

abstract void   "C:\WINNT\Profiles\michaelg\javax\mail\Message.html" \
            1 "setRecipients(javax.mail.Message.RecipientType, javax.mail.Address[])"
            ("C:\WINNT\Profiles\michaelg\javax\mail\Message.RecipientType.html" type,
            "C:\WINNT\Profiles\michaelg\javax\mail\Address.html" [] addresses)
            Sets the recipient addresses.

void        "C:\WINNT\Profiles\michaelg\javax\mail\Message.html"
            ("C:\WINNT\Profiles\michaelg\javax\mail\Address.html" [] addresses)
            Sets the addresses to which replies should be directed.

abstract void   "C:\WINNT\Profiles\michaelg\javax\mail\Message.html" \
            1 "setSentDate(java.util.Date)" (java.util.Date date)
            Sets the sent date of this message.

abstract void   "C:\WINNT\Profiles\michaelg\javax\mail\Message.html" \
            1 "setSubject(java.lang.String (java.lang.String subject)
            Sets the subject of this message.
```

To construct a new instance of a `Message`, you can use its constructor, which takes a single parameter, the current mail session. For example:

```
Message msg = new Message (mySession);
```

The preceding code fragment creates a new `Message` that has the appropriate settings for use with the mail session. This new `Message` class is empty. To insert the appropriate data into it, you can use a number of the methods previously specified:

```
// Sets the subject of the message:
msg.setSubject("I missed you!");

// Set the recipient of the message in the TO: field:
msg.setRecipient(Message.RecipientType.TO,
                "skywalker@someaddress.com");

InternetAddress dest = new InternetAddress("someone@mine.com");
// Set the recipient of the message in the CC: field:

msg.setRecipient(Message.RecipientType.CC,
                dest);

// Set the contents of the message to be "foo bar baz":
msg.setContent("foo bar baz", "text/plain");
```

The Transport Class

Each implementation of a mail protocol such as POP3 and IMAP includes its own implementation of the `Transport` interface, which is used for both inbound and outbound mail. This class has a single method of importance for WebLogic Server applications:

```
Message msg = new Message (mySession);
Transport.send(msg);
```

The `send()` method takes an instance of the JavaMail `Message` class. It then routes the message appropriately, according to the settings in the `Message` object itself.

Mapping to Internet Addresses

When sending and receiving standard Internet email, JavaMail enables users to specify addresses according to the Internet standards. The class that allows this is a subclass of the JavaMail `Address` class, `InternetAddress`. To create an instance of an Internet address from an email address, use the following code:

```
// Create New Internet Address for Destination
InternetAddress dest = new InternetAddress("some-
one@mine.com");
```

This creates a new instance of an Internet Address class called dest. This new Internet address is set equal to someone@mine.com. This Internet address is used to construct a Message object. The following sets the destination address (that is, the "To:" in the email) to the address specified in the destination object dest:

```
msg.setRecipient(Message.RecipientType.TO, dest);
```

Using JavaMail to Send Simple Email

In this section, we use WebLogic Server JavaMail to construct a Java Server-Page (JSP) Web page that generates an email based on the data included in the form (see Figure 11–1).

Figure 11-1   Form for Sending Email

The user inputs an Internet address for both the recipient and the sender, and requests that the message be sent. The recipient of this message would see something like Figure 11–2.

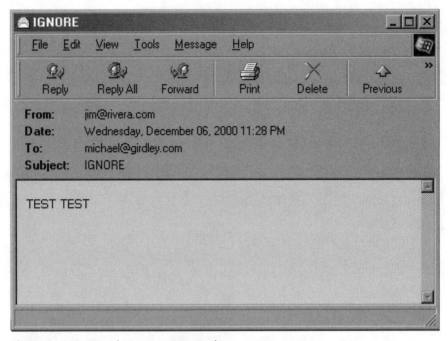

Figure 11–2 Email Message Received

Note that the message subject is IGNORE. As you'll see, this is because our demonstration JSP sets it to that value.

To create a JSP page, we first import the necessary classes and declare the HTML page:

```
<%@ page import= "java.util.*,
            javax.mail.Message,
            javax.mail.Session,
            javax.mail.Transport,
            javax.mail.internet.MimeMessage,
            javax.mail.internet.InternetAddress,
            javax.naming.Context,
            javax.naming.InitialContext,
            javax.naming.NamingException"
%>

<!doctype html public "-//w3c/dtd HTML 4.0//en">
<html>
<head>
```

```
<title>Mail Sender JSP</title>
</head>
<body>
```

Because this JSP page both displays the form and processes the results, we need to check to see what the request method is. If it is an HTTP POST, then the JSP page knows that it is to process a form submission:

```
<%

if ("POST".equals(request.getMethod())) {

try {

    String to = request.getParameterValues("to")[0];
    String from = request.getParameterValues("from")[0];
    String message = request.getParameterValues("message")[0];
```

Now that we have parsed the HTTP POST input that is part of the HTTP request, we can do the work with JavaMail:

```
    // Get the Naming context
    Context ctx = new InitialContext();

    // Lookup Mail Session
    Session mailSession = (Session) ctx.lookup("MailSession");

    // Create New Internet Message Object
    Message msg = new MimeMessage(mailSession);

    // Create New Internet Address for Destination
    InternetAddress dest = new InternetAddress(to);

    // Set Parameters for Message:
    msg.setFrom(new InternetAddress(from));
    msg.setSubject("IGNORE");
    msg.setRecipient(Message.RecipientType.TO, dest);
    msg.setContent(message, "text/plain");

    // Send the Message:
    Transport.send(msg);

    out.println("<h2>Your message to " + to + " was sent successfully!<h2>");

  }
  catch (Exception e) {

    out.println(e);

  }
} else {
%>
```

In the rest of this JSP, we display the HTML form:

```
<h1>Send Email!</h1>
<form method="post" name="mail" action="mail.jsp">


To :<input type="text" name="to" size=16><p>


From :<input type="text" name="from" size=16><p>


Message :<input type="text" name="message" size=16>
<p>
<font face="Helvetica"><input type="submit"
  value="Submit" name="Command">


<%
}
%>
</body>
</html>
```

> For the sake of example, the JNDI `InitialContext ()` is generated in
> the JSP page body here. This means that it will be re-created every time the
> page is accessed. For performance reasons, as noted in Chapter 3, you
> always want to put `InitialContext ()`, and any lookups that do not
> need to change, in the `init ()` method of your servlet or JSP page.

Deploying MailSender.jsp

The complete source code for the MailSender JSP sample is included in the
CD accompanying this book, in the directory \examples\ch11\.

Step 0: Configure WebLogic Server Mail Session

To deploy this JSP page, first configure a mail session inside of WebLogic
Server. To do this, start your default server using the link from the WebLogic
Server Start menu. In the WebLogic Server console, navigate to the Mail
option in the left-hand navigation panel. Click on this option (see Figure 11–3).

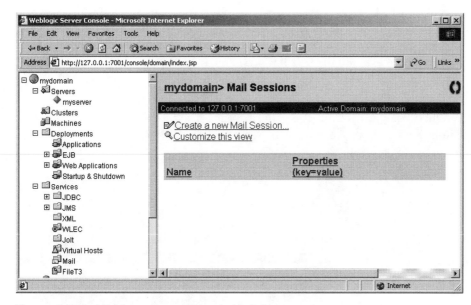

Figure 11-3 WebLogic Server Console Mail Option

Next, follow the steps to create a new mail session. You are prompted for a JNDI name and data about the server to be used to send mail (see Figure 11–4).

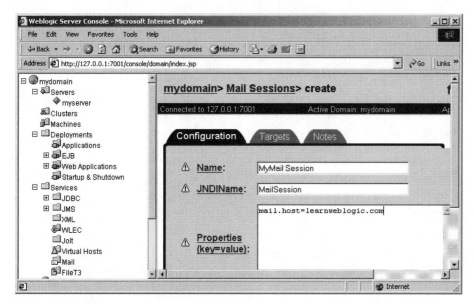

Figure 11-4 Creating a New Mail Session

For the JNDIName, enter "MailSession". This is the name that the JSP page uses to locate the mail session object. Finally, specify a mail server that accepts mail from you. Do *not* use *somemailserver.com*. You need to set this value to be the name of the mail server or Internet service provider for your organization. This value is typically the same as the mail server configured for your email client, such as Microsoft Outlook or Netscape Navigator.

Once you have entered the appropriate values, click the Create button. Then, *manually* deploy the mail session on your server instance. Click the Targets tab (see Figure 11–5).

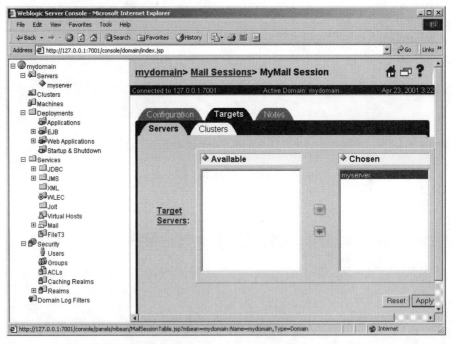

Figure 11–5   Selecting the Target Servers

Select the server "myserver" and move that into the Chosen panel using the Red Arrow button. Click to apply the changes.

Step 1: Deploy and Visit JSP Page

Copy the JSP page from the CD into the *applications\DefaultWebApp_ myserver* directory. This is the root of your WebLogic Server instance. Locate a Web browser and visit *http://127.0.0.1:7001/mailsender.jsp*.

You should see a form. Complete the form, and then click Submit (see Figure 11–6).

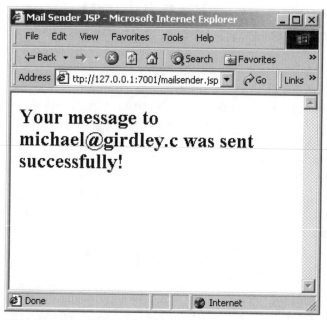

Figure 11-6 Testing the MailSender JSP

Note: Problems with this sample are usually caused by the inability to reach a mail server that allows you to send messages through it. Unfortunately, because of the proliferation of unsolicited commercial email ("Spam"), most mail servers (including *somemailserver.com*) have restricted access to their mail services to registered users only. If you have questions, contact your mail system administrator.

Adding Email Capability to the WebAuction Application

The WebAuction application includes email notification. When a user submits a bid, he or she receives a confirmation by email that the bid was successfully entered.

Notifying users via email is not done synchronously in the WebAuction application. The JSP page and tag libraries do not call the JavaMail API as demonstrated in the previous example JSP page. That mail paradigm is not scalable, especially when a WebLogic Server application is servicing many thousands of simultaneous requests. It is easy for a mail server to become overloaded and negatively affect the application performance.

Where to Find More Information on JavaMail and Internet Mail

Note that WebLogic Server applications primarily make use of sending email. For this reason, the details on how to *receive* email messages through JavaMail are beyond the scope of this book. For more information on how to create a standalone Java application that is a consumer of email messages, you can visit the JavaMail Web site, located at Sun Microsystems, at *http://java.sun.com/products/javamail/*.

In addition, this chapter has only introduced the concepts surrounding Internet Mail SMTP, POP3, and IMAP. For more information, consult the following links on the Internet:

Internet Mail: *http://www.w3.org/Protocols/rfc822/*

IMAP: *http://www.imap.org/*

SMTP: *http://info.broker.isi.edu/in-notes/rfc/files/rfc821.txt*

POP3: *http://info.broker.isi.edu/in-notes/rfc/files/rfc2449.txt*

JavaMail Best Practices

Here are some best practices you can follow when using JavaMail in your WebLogic Server applications:

Using JavaMail to Confirm Email Addresses

When a user registers for your site, your application probably asks for the user's correct email address. Use JavaMail to send an email from your system to validate the email address. To have users confirm that they have correctly received the email, have them revisit your site using a URL that you provide in the body of the mail.

The URL that the user clicks in the email you send should be unique for that user. You can encapsulate a unique value into that URL by including it as an HTTP POST: *http://myhost.com/validate?token=someuniquevalue*

Once the user revisits your site with this unique value, you can locate that value in the database and validate his or her account accordingly.

DEVELOPING SECURITY WITH WEBLOGIC SERVER JNDI AND JAAS

In this chapter:

In this chapter, we survey security technologies and show you how to incorporate security realms and JAAS into your WebLogic Server applications. Specifically, this chapter includes:

- Information on security technologies and concepts
- Details on the Java 2 Enterprise Edition (J2EE) security model, WebLogic realms, and the WebLogic Server JAAS implementation
- How to create secure application and Web clients
- Securing the WebAuction application
- Security best practices for WebLogic Server applications

Chapter

The WebLogic Server platform supports several different security technologies for applications, including:

- Security realms that coordinate user and group access to WebLogic Server resources

- Authentication of clients by user name/password or X.509 digital certificate identity

- Authorization of clients via Java Naming and Directory Interface (JNDI) using Access Control Lists (ACLs)

- `LoginContext` authentication and subject authorization through the Java Authentication and Authorization Service (JAAS) API

The WebLogic Server platform provides tools for user management, security for connectivity, and runtime support for security development and deployment. WebLogic Server enables developers to build applications without knowing the underlying security infrastructure. There also are tools to make an underlying security infrastructure *plug and play* with multiple different security options.

Security Technology Overview

WebLogic Server relies on a number of standards-based technologies for its security services. The following sections discuss each technology and its place in the WebLogic Server security infrastructure.

Users and Groups

Users and groups are required in a security system for authentication (who are you?) and authorization (what are you allowed to do?). A *user* is the application end user's account name. WebLogic Server represents each user with a user name, such as "John Doe," and some information (sometimes called *proof material*) for verifying the user's identity during the login process. The verification information is usually a password, but other authentication methods such as digital certificates are described later.

A *group* is a named collection of zero or more users. Typically, a group represents a set of application users who have similar permissions to access system resources. For example, you might have an "employees" group, which contains every single one of the users in the company. The "managers" group is a subset of the employees group that has greater access to privileged information such as employees' salaries. In this context, the job of WebLogic Server's security system is to verify that only members of the managers group can access sensitive salary data.

Roles and Principals

A *role* is an abstract, logical grouping of users that is defined by the application developer. For example, in WebAuction, we define a group of users named *auction_user*. Every site visitor who is a valid user is a member of the *auction_user* role. The WebAuction application maps this role into a WebLogic Server group. Roles refer to a group of users who all have similar permissions to access resources. Roles are mapped to security identities, such as principals (users or groups), in the runtime environment.

Roles are often confused with "groups" in WebLogic Server, which contains the notion of grouping of one or more users or groups. Instead, roles are used by the application code. At deployment time, the roles are then mapped to actual groups in the WebLogic Server. This allows the security settings to be changed without altering the application code.

When a user logs into an application, WebLogic Server associates a *principal* with that user. A principal is the identity assigned to a user as a result of authentication. WebLogic Server enforces security for a principal according to the security attributes of that calling principal. A given user can map to a different principal depending upon the security context and resource being accessed. WebLogic Server does not discriminate among different principals for a given user, but a user can have multiple principals when accessing external resources.

What exactly happens with the user and principal depends on the security programming model that is being used in the WebLogic Server application: either *programmatic* or *declarative* security.

J2EE Security Programming Models

J2EE defines two security programming models. The first is called *declarative security*, which expresses an application's security structure, including roles, access control, and authentication requirements, in a form that can be changed without modifying the application. The external security configuration is typically stored in the deployment descriptor files (*web.xml* and *weblogic.xml*).

The second model is called *programmatic security*. Programmatic security is just adding explicit security checks within the application's code. Declarative security is preferred where possible because there is a better separation between the application code and the security constraints. Programmatic security is used by security-aware applications when declarative security alone is not sufficient. For example, if you have an Enterprise JavaBean (EJB) that accesses user accounts based on permissions, you cannot code an EJB for every single user account in order to restrict access to certain types of data. Therefore, the application itself needs to be aware of security and make dynamic decisions based on user requests and permissions. Programmatic security consists of adding security knowledge to the application so that the application can make security decisions based on a user's identity.

This chapter includes examples of both programmatic and declarative security.

Authentication

Authentication is the process of verifying a user's identity, with a user name/password combination or stronger forms of authentication. It is assumed that only the "real" user knows the secret password.

Alternatives to password-based authentication are:

- Form-based authentication
- Digital certificate/HTTPS authentication

The following sections describe each authentication paradigm in detail.

Password-Based Authentication

In an application client deployment, the application GUI itself typically requests the user name and password from the user at login time (see Figure 12–1).

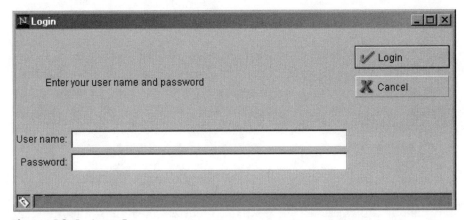

Figure 12–1   Login Form

The user enters a user name and password, which is only transmitted to the WebLogic Server deployment and verified when the user accesses a server-side resource.

In a Web browser application deployment, the Web browser presents the user with a login dialog for entering the user name and password (see Figure 12-2).

Figure 12–2 Web Browser Login Dialog

This dialog is not part of the browser window itself. It is a new window spawned from the browser window.

If the user's authentication information or proof material is valid, the access is allowed. If not, a message is displayed (Web deployment) or an exception is thrown to the client application (application deployment).

Form-Based Authentication

Form-based authentication is a refinement on the Web browser login mechanism. A Web form is presented for the user to enter a user name and password. This information is then submitted by an HTTP POST and received by WebLogic Server. If the information entered is correct, WebLogic Server automatically logs in the user. If the information entered is incorrect, WebLogic Server returns an error message and optionally lets the user try again. The logic of the form-based authentication method can extend to remembering the user's proof of identity based on the user's email address, and other features.

Form-based authentication, the method used in the WebAuction application, enables you to create your own login page with your own help options and layout instead of the standard browser dialog box (see Figure 12–3).

Figure 12–3   Custom Login Dialog

Secure Sockets Layer (SSL)

A higher level of security for authentication in Web and application deployments is provided by SSL, which is part of the WebLogic Server J2EE model. SSL is a protocol that ensures privacy of data by encrypting it in transit. It also is used to authenticate clients and users. The SSL service is based on a technology called *cryptography*. This technology encrypts human-readable "plain text" into "cipher text," which cannot easily be read.

WebLogic Server's implementation of the SSL technology follows the Internet standard for security between two hosts connected on an insecure network. More information on the details behind SSL is included later in this chapter.

Authorization

So far, this chapter has discussed how WebLogic Server authenticates users and protects user information in transit. Authorization is another area of security: When you have different users who have different levels of access, how do you decide who should be permitted to do which actions? This problem is solved by WebLogic Server's *authorization services*.

Authorization is when power is granted to do a certain act, such as when a client is permitted to access a specific EJB. In the J2EE model, the application server provides the authorization for clients to access resources.

Access Control Lists (ACLs) and Permissions

WebLogic Server manages user and group permissions with ACLs. An ACL records the business rules that ensure only an authorized client can access a given resource. ACL authorizations can be defined as either granting or denying access to a resource. ACLs are used whenever a client attempts a resource access. As we discuss later in this chapter, how the WebLogic Server handles situations in which the client does not have permission depends both on the client type and the server's configuration.

WebLogic Server Security Realms

A *security realm* is a logical grouping of users, groups, and ACLs. A WebLogic Server resource is protected under only one security realm and by a single ACL in that security realm. A user must be defined in a security realm in order to access any resources belonging to that realm. When a user attempts to access a particular WebLogic Server resource, WebLogic Server tries to authenticate and authorize the user by checking the ACL and permissions assigned the user in the relevant realm.

WebLogic Server security realms group the data and policies associated with the various WebLogic Server authentication and authorization services. You can use the default security realm, which uses the local disk for storage, or one of a set of alternative security realms that enable you to use Windows NT, UNIX, and LDAP. WebLogic Server also supports custom-developed security realms.

During startup, WebLogic Server sets up a realm that it uses to authenticate and authorize WebLogic Server users. This realm contains the ACLs and assorted authorization information used to permit users access to resources according to their group membership.

Using Realms in WebLogic Server

The WebLogic Server configuration files specify the usage of security realms. Except in the case of EJB and Web applications, all configuration of access control for WebLogic Server application components and services is handled in the WebLogic Server console. At any one time, only one realm is used in a WebLogic Server deployment except in the case of the *caching realm*, which enables you to include other realms underneath it. The caching realm enables you to specify one or more additional realms and cache results of queries to those realms. The cache is configurable based on time, size, or other parameters that you choose.

The RDBMS Realm

The Relational Database Management System (RDBMS) security realm is shipped as source code with WebLogic Server. It maps security information from the realm into a relational database. Very large sites and Web applications use the RDBMS realm to store user security information. Sample configurations for several databases are included in the WebLogic Server package, with instructions. This chapter covers the deployment of a Web application using the RDBMS realm.

The File Realm

By default, WebLogic Server uses the security realm called the *file realm*. This security realm is intended for prototyping and small deployments of WebLogic Server. Typically, the file realm is used for deployments of fewer than 1,000 users, for which security information does not need to be stored in a database.

The WebLogic Server file realm stores security policies, users, groups, and credentials (passwords) on the file system in encrypted text. This file is typically located in the directory corresponding to your configuration name under the *config/* directory in your installation. For the standard mydomain server installation (the default server), this file might be located at

c:\bea\wlserver6.0\config\mydomain\fileRealm.properties.

Creating Secure Web Applications

To review, authentication for a Web application can be done as:

- Form-based authentication, which uses Web forms to authenticate users into WebLogic Server
- Browser-based authentication, which incorporates HTTP authentication methods to log in users to WebLogic Server

Declarative Security in Web Applications

Declarative security for Web applications uses deployment descriptors (*web.xml* and *weblogic.xml*) to express an application's security structure, including roles, access control, and authentication requirements. The information in the deployment descriptors maps the application's logical security requirements to its runtime representation. At runtime, the servlet container uses the security policy to enforce authentication.

Implementing Declarative Security in Web Applications

The following deployment descriptor fragments define and map the role web-users in a Web application to the principal (group or user name) that is stored in WebLogic Server. The following is part of a *web.xml* deployment descriptor:

```
<security-role>
  <role-name>web-users</role-name>
</security-role>

<security-constraint>
  <web-resource-collection>
    <web-resource-name>Success</web-resource-name>
    <url-pattern>/welcome.jsp</url-pattern>
    <http-method>GET</http-method>
    <http-method>POST</http-method>
  </web-resource-collection>
  <auth-constraint>
    <role-name>web-users</role-name>
  </auth-constraint>
</security-constraint>
```

The next section of the deployment descriptor sets a constraint on a resource in the Web application. In this case, a restriction on two types of HTTP access methods, GET and POST, is placed on the Java ServerPage (JSP) page */welcome.jsp*, which is located at the root of the Web application.

This security role is mapped to a corresponding role in WebLogic Server. A principal can be mapped to either a WebLogic Server user or a WebLogic Server group in the declarative security entry in the deployment descriptor.

Declarative Security Scenarios

There are two possible scenarios for what happens in a Web application when a user attempts to access a restricted resource. Remember, the server handles the login and security checking automatically. The following processes happen behind the scenes:

1. Group match: If you have mapped a security role in your Web application to a WebLogic Server group, WebLogic Server checks the group of the calling principal. If the principal's group matches the group in the security role, the principal is allowed access.

2. Principal match: If you have mapped a security role in your Web application to a single user in WebLogic Server, WebLogic Server checks the user name of the calling principal. If there is a match with the user name in the security role, the calling principal is allowed access.

The next section illustrates how to use declarative security for form-based authentication in a Web application.

Developing Form-Based Authentication

In form-based authentication, the user name and password submitted are automatically logged into WebLogic Server security. Say the user is named Benjamin. All subsequent calls to resources in the WebLogic Server environment are done using the principal Benjamin. Consequently, if the servlet that Benjamin invokes calls an EJB, that access is done with the user and group permissions associated with Benjamin.

Internally, WebLogic Server manages security by associating a security context with a given thread of execution inside of WebLogic Server. As this thread executes (for example, beginning with servlets, into JavaBeans, to EJBs, etc.), every piece of code is executed on behalf of the user. This allows the security context to flow with a user and security checks to be made at each step in serving the request. With form-based authentication, this allows a single point of login for all of the WebLogic Server services that execute on behalf of a user.

How to Implement Form-Based Authentication

Form-based authentication requires modifications both to the application deployment configuration information and to the application itself. There are five steps to create form-based authentication for a Web application:

1. Create the login form: a servlet or JSP page that has a Web form.
2. Create the welcome page: a servlet or JSP page that is the initial start page for the Web application.
3. Create the logout page: a servlet or JSP page that makes calls to log out the user.
4. Create the failed login page: a basic HTML page telling users they have entered an incorrect set of credentials.
5. Edit the Web application configuration information: Modify the Web application configuration files *web.xml* and *weblogic.xml*.

Form-Based Authentication Example

This section illustrates the steps described with a simple application that uses a suite of JSP pages in a single Web application. These pages enable a user to attempt to log in by providing a user name and password. If the login succeeds, the welcome page is displayed. If the user name and password are not valid, the failed login page is displayed.

Creating the Login Form: login.jsp

First, create a JSP page that displays the login form to visitors. This is simply a basic HTML form as described in Chapter 4:

```
<html>
  <head>
    <title>Form Based Authentication Example Login Page</title>
  </head>

  <blockquote>
  <h2>Please enter your username and password:</h2>
  <p>
  <form method="POST" name="Login" action="j_security_check">
  <table border=1>
    <tr>
      <td>Username:</td>
      <td><input type="text" name="j_username"></td>
```

```
    </tr>
    <tr>
      <td>Password:</td>
      <td><input type="password" name="j_password"></td>
    </tr>
    <tr>
      <td colspan=2 align=right>
<input type="submit" value="Login" name="Submit"></td>
    </tr>
  </table>
  </form>

  </blockquote>
  </body>
</html>
```

Note that this form is a standard Web form. The page begins with the standard <HTML> header tags. The next section includes a Web form specified by the <form> HTML tag. This form is defined to POST the data from the form to the action j_security_check. This action and the j_username and j_password names are defined in the servlet specification. When this form arrives at the server, it is validated against the internal WebLogic Server realm.

Creating the Welcome Page: welcome.jsp

The welcome page is the page that users see once they are authenticated. In the WebAuction application, the welcome page is the page that visitors see when they first visit the WebAuction application.

Create a separate JSP for the welcome page:

```
<html>
  <head>
    <title>Form Based Authentication Example Welcome Page</title>
  </head>

  <h1> Form Based Authentication Example Welcome Page </h1>

  <p> Welcome <%= request.getRemoteUser() %>!

  <p> Click here to <a href="logout.jsp">logout</a>.

  </blockquote>
  </body>

</html>
```

WebLogic Server calls this page when the user has been properly authenticated. Note that the implicit JSP object request is queried to print out what the remote user name is. Also included is a link to the logout page.

If you attempt to visit *login.jsp* directly in the preceding form authentication example, you receive an error (see Figure 12–4).

Figure 12–4 Form-Based Authentication Failure

This is especially problematic if you would like to include a link for users to log in without visiting a restricted page. To work around this limitation, create a second login page that includes access constraints in the *web.xml* deployment descriptor. This second login page simply sends an HTTP redirect back to the client browser, forwarding it to your main Web application page. For example:

```
<%
    response.sendRedirect("/formauth/welcome.jsp");
%>
<html>
</html>
```

To create a link in your site that enables users to log themselves in, use the URL to this second login page. You must also change the information in the deployment descriptor before using this in order to restrict access to this login page.

For your convenience, in the form authentication example on the CD that accompanies this book, this file is already created and registered in the example as *login2.jsp*.

Creating the Logout Page: logout.jsp

A user who wants to log out navigates to a logout page. This logout page is typically a JSP page:

```
<html>
  <head>
    <title>Form Based Authentication Logout Page</title>
  </head>

  <blockquote>

  <h1> Goodbye <%= request.getRemoteUser() %>! </h1>

  <% session.invalidate(); %>

  <p> You are now logged out.

  <p> Click here to <a href=<%=
"\""+request.getContextPath()+"\""%>>revisit
  the site</a>.

  </blockquote>
  </body>

</html>
```

To log out a user, your JSP page should simply call the `invalidate()` method on the implicit `session` object in the following manner:

```
<% session.invalidate(); %>
```

How does this work? WebLogic Server associates the user's login information with that particular user and session. A Web application developer uses the HTTP `session` object to track values about users; WebLogic Server uses the `session` to track users that have logged in using form-based authentication. Invalidating the `session` logs out the user from WebLogic Server security.

Creating the Failed Login Page: login_failure.jsp

If a user provides invalid information, such as an invalid user name or an incorrect password, the form-based authentication mechanism allows you to specify a failed login page that is called by WebLogic Server. First, create the failed login page:

```
<html>
  <head>
    <title>Form Based Authentication Login Failure</title>
  </head>

  <blockquote>
  <h2>Sorry, your username and password were not recognized.</h2>
  <p><b>
  <a href="welcome.jsp">Return to welcome page</a> or
  </b>
  </blockquote>
  </body>
</html>
```

This page redirects users to the welcome page, where they can try again to log in.

Creating the WebLogic Server Application Deployment Descriptor: web.xml

As you recall from Chapter 3, the configuration for every Web application is contained in the *web.xml* deployment descriptor included in the Web application package. To configure the Web application to use form-based authentication, change some fields in the *web.xml* file.

First, include the XML document type descriptor. The following defines that this XML document should use the document type descriptor defined by the Servlet 2.2 specification:

```
<!DOCTYPE web-app PUBLIC
"-//Sun Microsystems, Inc.//DTD Web Application 2.2//EN"
"http://java.sun.com/j2ee/dtds/web-app_2_2.dtd">
```

Next, the following tag defines the Web application:

```
<web-app>
```

Then, define the file to use as the initial welcome page for the Web application. In this case, it is the file named *welcome.jsp*:

```
<welcome-file-list>
    <welcome-file>welcome.jsp</welcome-file>
</welcome-file-list>
```

Specify that some of the application should be protected by form-based authentication. The form login page should be *login.jsp*, and login failures should result in *login_failure.jsp* being displayed:

```
<login-config>
  <auth-method>FORM</auth-method>
  <form-login-config>
      <form-login-page>/login.jsp</form-login-page>
      <form-error-page>/login_failure.jsp</form-error-page>
  </form-login-config>
</login-config>
```

Specify the security role (i.e., which users) are allowed to access resources in the site:

```
<security-role>
      <role-name>web-user</role-name>
  </security-role>
```

Finally, specify the security constraints for each resource to be protected in *welcome.jsp* and *login2.jsp*:

```
<security-constraint>
  <web-resource-collection>
    <web-resource-name>Success</web-resource-name>
    <url-pattern>/welcome.jsp</url-pattern>
    <http-method>GET</http-method>
    <http-method>POST</http-method>
  </web-resource-collection>
  <auth-constraint>
    <role-name>web-user</role-name>
  </auth-constraint>
</security-constraint>

<security-constraint>
  <web-resource-collection>
    <web-resource-name>Login</web-resource-name>
    <url-pattern>/login2.jsp</url-pattern>
    <http-method>GET</http-method>
    <http-method>POST</http-method>
  </web-resource-collection>
  <auth-constraint>
    <role-name>web-user</role-name>
  </auth-constraint>
</security-constraint>

</web-app>
```

The complete form-based authentication *web.xml* deployment descriptor is:

```
<!DOCTYPE web-app PUBLIC
"-//Sun Microsystems, Inc.//DTD Web Application 2.2//EN"
"http://java.sun.com/j2ee/dtds/web-app_2_2.dtd">

<web-app>

    <welcome-file-list>
        <welcome-file>welcome.jsp</welcome-file>
    </welcome-file-list>

    <login-config>
        <auth-method>FORM</auth-method>
        <realm-name>default</realm-name>
        <form-login-config>
         <form-login-page>/login.jsp</form-login-page>
         <form-error-page>/login_failure.jsp</form-error-page>
    </form-login-config>
    </login-config>

    <security-role>
        <role-name>web-user</role-name>
    </security-role>

    <security-constraint>
      <web-resource-collection>
        <web-resource-name>Success</web-resource-name>
        <url-pattern>/welcome.jsp</url-pattern>
        <http-method>GET</http-method>
        <http-method>POST</http-method>
      </web-resource-collection>
      <auth-constraint>
        <role-name>web-user</role-name>
      </auth-constraint>
    </security-constraint>

    <security-constraint>
      <web-resource-collection>
        <web-resource-name>Login</web-resource-name>
        <url-pattern>/login2.jsp</url-pattern>
        <http-method>GET</http-method>
        <http-method>POST</http-method>
      </web-resource-collection>
      <auth-constraint>
        <role-name>web-user</role-name>
      </auth-constraint>
```

```
</security-constraint>

</web-app>
```

Note that you also can specify URL patterns that include wild cards, for example,

```
<url-pattern>/someURLpattern/*</url-pattern>.
```

Creating the WebLogic Server–Specific Deployment Descriptor: weblogic.xml

Every Web application also has a configuration file specific to the application server, such as *weblogic.xml*. For form-based authentication, use *weblogic.xml* to map a security role (such as `web-user`) to the appropriate WebLogic Server group or user.

In this application, we want to configure the deployment descriptor so that any user is part of the group named `myGroup` in the WebLogic Server realm. The *weblogic.xml* file first declares its XML version and the DTD:

```
<?xml version="1.0"?>
<!DOCTYPE weblogic-web-app PUBLIC
"-//BEA Systems, Inc.//DTD Web Application 6.0//EN"
 "http://www.bea.com/servers/wlserver6.0/dtd/weblogic-web-
jar.dtd">
```

Next, declare this to be a WebLogic Server Web application, and specify the role assignment for security:

```
<weblogic-web-app>

  <security-role-assignment>
    <role-name>web-user</role-name>
    <principal-name>myGroup</principal-name>
  </security-role-assignment>

</weblogic-web-app>
```

The preceding tells WebLogic Server that you are mapping the role named `web-user` to the principal named `myGroup`.

In the next section, we deploy this example using the WebLogic Server file realm.

Deploying the Form-Based Authentication Example Using the File Realm

To deploy the form-based authentication example, use the example deployment process that applies to every example in this chapter. First, navigate to the example code for the basic servlet, *formauth.war*, from the subdirectory */code/ch12* on the CD accompanying this book.

Step 1: Set Up the Development Environment

Create a new, empty directory on your local hard disk. We used *c:\dev14*.

To set your environment variables correctly so that you can access WebLogic Server Java services, open a command shell and execute the environment script for the server in mydomain:

```
c:\bea\wlserver6.0\config\mydomain\setEnv.cmd
```

The path differs if you have installed WebLogic Server in a different directory.

Next, change to your development directory using the cd command.

Step 2: Copy and Unpack the Example

Now, copy over the example code from the CD-ROM into your development directory, for example:

```
copy E:\examples\ch12\formauth.war c:\dev14\
```

Check that the file has arrived correctly by listing the directory.

Then, unpack the package using the *jar* utility:

```
jar xvf *.war
```

You should see something like Figure 12–5.

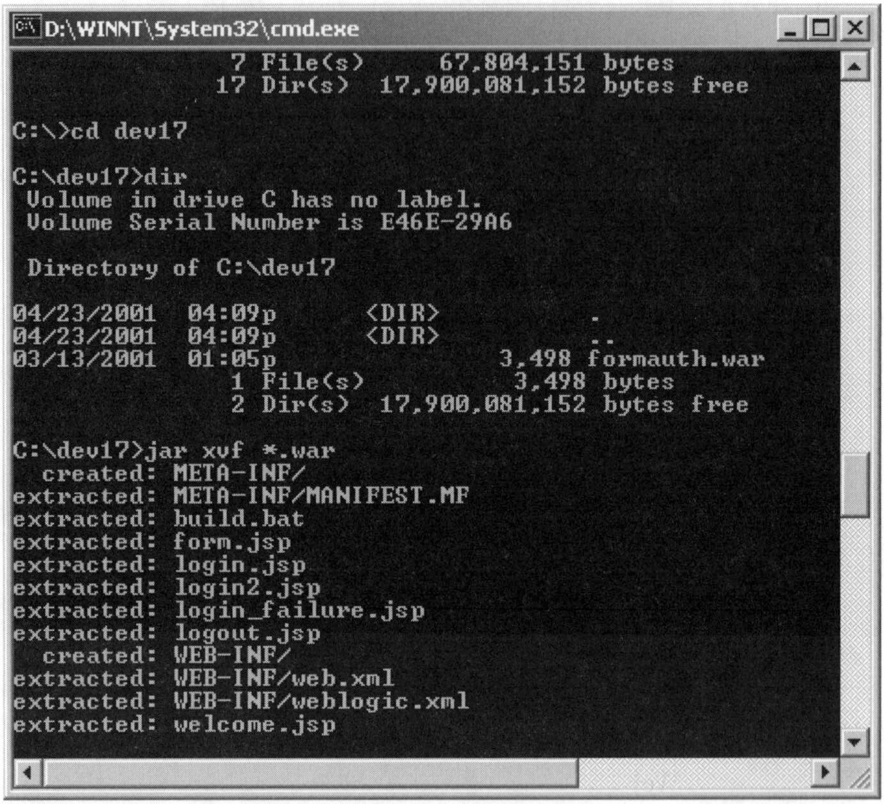

```
D:\WINNT\System32\cmd.exe                                    _ □ ×
             7 File(s)        67,804,151 bytes
            17 Dir(s)  17,900,081,152 bytes free

C:\>cd dev17

C:\dev17>dir
 Volume in drive C has no label.
 Volume Serial Number is E46E-29A6

 Directory of C:\dev17

04/23/2001  04:09p      <DIR>          .
04/23/2001  04:09p      <DIR>          ..
03/13/2001  01:05p               3,498 formauth.war
             1 File(s)           3,498 bytes
             2 Dir(s)  17,900,081,152 bytes free

C:\dev17>jar xvf *.war
   created: META-INF/
 extracted: META-INF/MANIFEST.MF
 extracted: build.bat
 extracted: form.jsp
 extracted: login.jsp
 extracted: login2.jsp
 extracted: login_failure.jsp
 extracted: logout.jsp
   created: WEB-INF/
 extracted: WEB-INF/web.xml
 extracted: WEB-INF/weblogic.xml
 extracted: welcome.jsp
```

Figure 12–5   Unpacking the Contents of formauth.war

Step 3: Build and Deploy the Example

A script for compiling the example under Microsoft Windows is included. This script can easily be tailored to work for other platforms. Be sure to edit the build script to point to the location of your WebLogic Server deployment if you did not install WebLogic Server in the standard location on the C: drive.

Type "build" and press Enter. The compilation, packaging, and deployment of the application should happen automatically (see Figure 12–6).

Figure 12-6   Building the Form Authentication Example

Step 4: View the Example

To view the example, point a Web browser to *http://127.0.0.1:7001/formauth/* after starting the WebLogic Server default server using the link on your Windows Start menu.

You should be automatically redirected to the login JSP (see Figure 12-7).

Figure 12-7   Running the Form Authentication Example

Now, try to log in. Enter a user name of "Griffith" and a password of "abc" and click "Login:" (see Figure 12–8).

Figure 12–8   Form Authentication Failure

Your user name and password will not be recognized! We have not yet created the groups and users in the WebLogic Server file realm.

Step 5: Create Security Settings

Open the WebLogic Server console in your Web browser by starting a new browser and typing in "http://127.0.0.1:7001/console".

Or, use the link from the Windows Start menu. Once the console has started, use the navigation panel on the left side of the browser to load the Users configuration option under the Security category (see Figure 12–9).

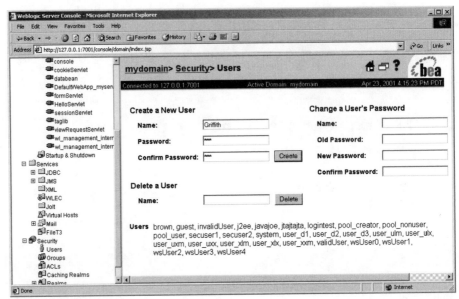

Figure 12–9   Users

Create a new user named "Griffith" with the password "abc". Be sure that you get the capitalization correct. Click the Create button. You'll see a message across the top of the console that says the user has been created, but the changes have not yet been saved to the realm implementation. Don't save now: we will save all changes after we create a group and add the user to it.

Now click on the Groups option in the left-hand panel of the console. You should see Figure 12–10 displaying all of the groups in the WebLogic Server realm.

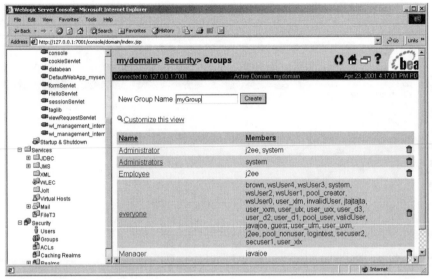

Figure 12–10 Groups

Fill in the box next to the New Group Name label with the name, "myGroup". Click Create. You are presented with an option to add users or other groups to your new group (see Figure 12–11).

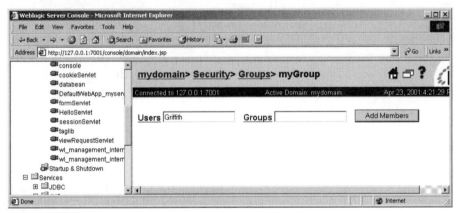

Figure 12–11 Adding a Group

Then, you should see Figure 12–12.

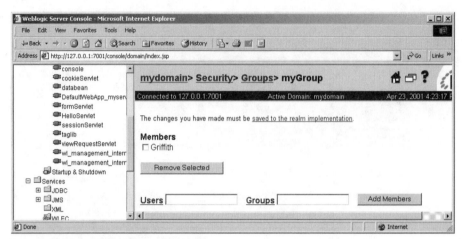

Figure 12–12 Saving Security Settings

Click on the hyperlink to "saved to the realm implementation". This saves your changes to the underlying file realm. You have now created a new user and group for use with your form-based authentication example.

Step 6: View the Example (Again)

To view the example, point a Web browser to *http://127.0.0.1:7001/formauth/*.

Or, click on the "return to the welcome page" link at the failure page displayed in Step 4. Enter the user name and password ("Griffith" and "abc") again. Make sure that you get the capitalization correct (see Figure 12–13).

Figure 12–13 Form-Based Authentication Success

Click on the link to log out. Note: The logout page includes a link to *login2.jsp*, which allows a "click here to login" link on your application. This process is also used in the WebAuction application.

Programming to the Caching Realm in Web Applications

You might need to access the caching realm in order to modify the security realm, for operations such as adding users to your Web application. You also might want to allow users to register *themselves* and automatically log into the system. So far, we have only described how to add users through the WebLogic Server console.

In this section, we expand the form-based authorization example to include programmatic access to the caching realm. We then configure and deploy the expanded example using the RDBMS and the caching realm together.

The Realm API

The WebLogic Server realm API can be accessed from your Web application code. First, your application acquires an instance of the current caching realm. Remember, the caching realm is the "umbrella" realm in WebLogic Server. It encloses other realms. This provides a single API and allows developers to switch in other realms underneath the caching realm, without changing their application.

In most cases, you will not necessarily need to access the realm API directly. For example, logging in users through form-based authentication transparently affects the underlying realm. However, there are many administrative tasks that require you to directly access the realm, such as programmatically creating a new user or group. There also are rare occasions when you are required to directly access the realm to augment services such as form-based authentication. In the WebAuction application, for example, it is desirable to automatically log in users after they create a new account. The only way to accomplish this is to directly call the realm to log in the user after he or she creates the account.

The full API for the caching realm is included in the online Java documentation for WebLogic Server at *http://www.weblogic.com/docs51/classdocs/javadocs/weblogic/security/acl/CachingRealm.html*.

Getting an Instance of the Realm

To acquire an instance of the realm, use the `weblogic.security.acl.CachingRealm` object. Create a new instance of the `CachingRealm` and then call `getRealm()`:

```
weblogic.security.acl.CachingRealm realm =
(weblogic.security.acl.CachingRealm)
weblogic.security.acl.Security.getRealm();
```

Your instance of the caching realm is then available for use.

Adding and Retrieving Users in the Realm

Use the `weblogic.security.acl.User` object to represent a user in the caching realm. The following code creates a new user object, which acquires its value from the `newUser` method. This method takes the user name and password as strings:

```
weblogic.security.acl.User u = realm.newUser(userName, password, null);
```

To acquire an existing user, use the `getUser()` method:

```
weblogic.security.acl.User u = realm.getUser(userName);
```

To acquire all the users as an Enumeration, use the `getUsers()` method on the realm:

```
Enumeration allOfTheUsersInRealm = realm.getUsers()
```

Adding a User to a Group

A user added to the realm can be assigned to one or more groups. You also can assign groups to other groups. To acquire an instance of the realm, again use the `weblogic.security.acl.User` object. The following code creates a new user object into the group named "`foo`":

```
weblogic.security.acl.User u;
java.security.acl.Group g = realm.getGroup("foo")
g.addMember(u);
```

Adding and Removing Groups

You can add and remove groups from the realm. To add a new group, with the name "`foo`", use the following code:

```
java.security.acl.Group g = realm.newGroup("foo");
```

To remove that same group, use the `deleteGroup()` method:

```
realm.deleteGroup(g).
```

NewUser.jsp Example

This example builds a JSP page that implements programmatic access to the WebLogic Server realm. This JSP page includes a Web form that has three text fields and three submit buttons (see Figure 12–14).

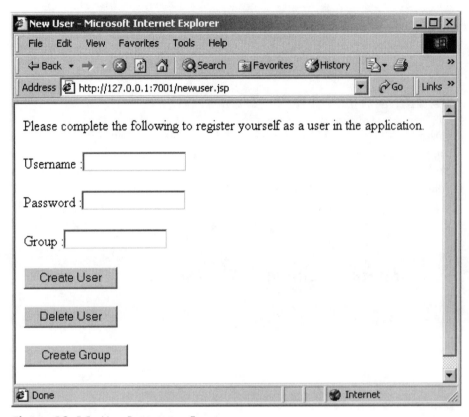

Figure 12-14   User Registration Form

The JSP page processes the submitted values. If all three spaces are filled in, and the Create User button is clicked, then a new user is created and logged into the system. The Create Group button enables the user to create a new group in the caching realm. Finally, the Delete User button deletes the account of the user whose name is entered in the Username field.

To begin creating this page, we define the Web form to be processed:

```
<html>
<head>
   <title>New User</title>
</head>
<body text="#000000" bgcolor="#FFFFFF">

<p>Please complete the following to register yourself as a user
in the
   application.</font>
```

```
<p>
<form method="post" name="NewUser" action="newuser.jsp">

Username :<input type="text" name="userName" size=16><p>

Password :<input type="password" name="password" size=16><p>

Group :<input type="text" name="groupName" size=16><p>

<font face="Helvetica"><input type="submit"
  value="Create User" name="Command">
<p>
<font face="Helvetica"><input type="submit"
  value="Delete User" name="Command">
<p>

<font face="Helvetica"><input type="submit"
  value="Create Group" name="Command">
<p>
```

The standard HTML form uses a POST that is directed back to the same JSP page. Three buttons are defined for submit, each with a different value for the "Command" parameter name.

Now, we put Java code into the JSP page to demonstrate access to the realm API.

```
<%

  // We will encapsulate everything in a try/catch block to catch
  // exceptions.  Because this is an example, it does not include
  // complete error checking:

  try {

    // Next check to see if the request method is a POST of
    // information from the form:

    if ("POST".equals(request.getMethod())) {

    weblogic.security.acl.CachingRealm realm =
    (weblogic.security.acl.CachingRealm)
weblogic.security.acl.Security.getRealm();

    // Define variables to be used internally:

    weblogic.security.acl.User u;
    java.security.acl.Group g;

    String userName;
    String groupName;
    String password;
```

```
// Get the command that has been received with the POST:
String command = request.getParameterValues("Command")[0];

if (command.equals("Create User")) {

  userName = request.getParameterValues("userName")[0];
  password = request.getParameterValues("password")[0];
  groupName = request.getParameterValues("groupName")[0];

  //  Add a new user to the realm with the appropriate username
  //  and password.  Then, add that user to the appropriate group:
  u = realm.newUser(userName, password, null);
  realm.getGroup(groupName).addMember(u);

  out.println("New user "+ userName + " created!");

  // This piece of code allows applications to register a new
  // user & automatically log them into the WebLogic realm:
  int ret = weblogic.servlet.security.ServletAuthentication.weak
    (userName, password, session);

  out.println("<br>New user created, added to group " + groupName
    + " and logged in!");

  out.println("<br>Now that you are logged in, go " +
    "<a href=\"welcome.jsp\">visit welcome.jsp</a>.");

} else if (command.equals("Delete User")) {

  userName = request.getParameterValues("userName")[0];

  //  Locate a User object with the appropriate username and
  //  delete it.
  u = realm.getUser(userName);
  realm.deleteUser(u);
  out.println("User " + userName+ " created and logged in!");

} else if (command.equals("Create Group")) {

  groupName = request.getParameterValues("groupName")[0];
  g = realm.newGroup(groupName);
  out.println("New group " + groupName + " created.");

}

}
}
catch (Exception e) {
  out.println(e);
}


%>

</body>
```

```
</html>
```

Deploying a Realm API Authentication Example Using the RDBMS Realm

To practice using the RDBMS security realm, we can modify the form-based authentication example from the previous section. The RDBMS realm example is contained in the *rdbmsauth.war* file in the */code/ch12* directory on the CD-ROM. Use the Cloudscape database (installed with WebLogic Server) as the RDBMS, and use the Examples Server version of WebLogic Server (rather than the default).

Step 0: Set Up the RDBMS Realm in the Examples Server

First, configure the Examples Server to use the Cloudscape RDBMS realm instead of the default file store. Start the Examples Server using the shortcut on the Windows Start menu. Then, launch a Web browser and visit the Examples Server console. Use the following URL:

http://127.0.0.1:7001/console/.

The database connectivity to Cloudscape, the caching realm, and the RDBMS realm have been pre-configured for the Examples Server, as you can see from the console's security settings in the left-hand navigation panel of the Security section.

To enable the RDBMS realm with Cloudscape, simply instruct WebLogic Server to use its currently defined caching realm instead of the file realm.

Navigate to the Security section in the left-hand navigation panel (see Figure 12–15).

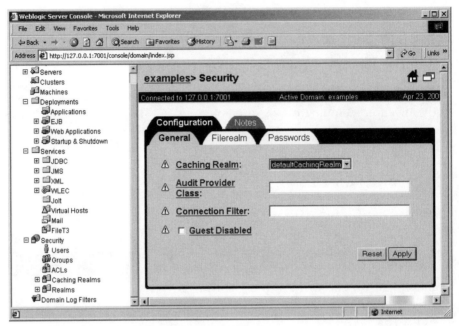

Figure 12–15 Setting Up a Realm in the Console

Under the option for configuring your caching realm, choose to use defaultCachingRealm. Click the Apply button. You will be prompted to restart the Examples Server. Do that now either through the console or by closing the window where the server started.

The RDBMS realm can also be connected to other databases. You can connect to Oracle, Sybase, Informix, and so forth simply by switching in a new RDBMS realm configuration. The Examples Server configuration contains several database configurations in the Realms section under Security. After you prototype using the Cloudscape RDBMS realm, you can deploy your production Web application using your standard database as the RDBMS security realm.

Step 1: Set Up the Development Environment

Create a new, empty directory on your local hard disk. For this example, the directory *c:\dev15* will be used. To set your environment variables correctly to access Java services, execute the configuration script for the *Examples Server* environment:

```
c:\bea\weblogic600\config\examples\setExamplesEnv.cmd
```

The preceding path will differ if you have installed WebLogic Server in a different directory.

Next, navigate to your new directory.

Step 2: Copy and Unpack the Example

Copy the example code from the CD-ROM into this directory. If your CD-ROM is the E: drive, you can use the following command:

```
copy E:\examples\ch12\dbmsauth.war c:\dev15\
```

Double check that the file has arrived correctly by doing a directory listing.

Unpack the package using the *jar* utility:

```
jar xvf *.war
```

Step 3: Build and Deploy the Example

Use the build script (*build.bat*) to compile the example for Microsoft Windows. Edit this script to reflect the correct location of your WebLogic Server installation. The build script also can be modified to work for other platforms. Then, type "build" and press Enter. The compilation, packaging, and deployment of the application should proceed automatically (see Figure 12–16).

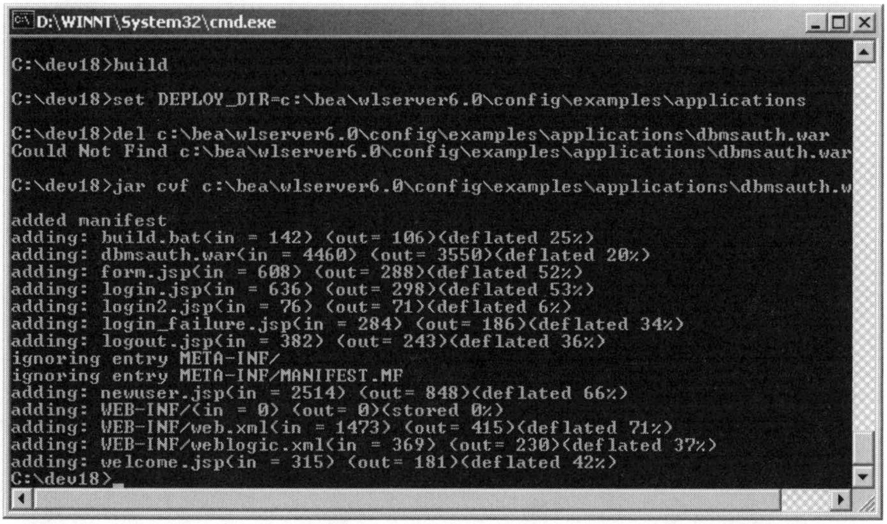

Figure 12–16 Building the RDBMS Authentication Example

Step 4: View the Example

To view the example, point a Web browser to *http://127.0.0.1:7001/dbms-auth/* after starting the WebLogic Server *default server* (the example runs on the default server even though it had to be built on the Examples Server).

You should automatically be redirected to *login.jsp* and see something that looks exactly like the form-based authentication example from the previous section. You should attempt to log in. Enter a user name of "ruslan" and a password of "sporty" and click Login (see Figure 12–17).

Figure 12–17   RDBMS Authentication Failure

Your user name and password will not be recognized! We have not yet created groups and users in the WebLogic Server realm.

Step 5: Create User and Group

In the form-based authentication example, we used the WebLogic Server console to manage users and groups. In this example, we can use the JSP that we previously created to manipulate the RDBMS realm underlying the caching realm. To visit this JSP page, launch a Web browser and type in "http://127.0.0.1:7001/dbmsauth/newuser.jsp".

Create a new group to match the group defined in *weblogic.xml*. Because the principal named myGroup has been defined to match the web-user role in *web.xml*, type "myGroup" into the field labeled Group (see Figure 12–18).

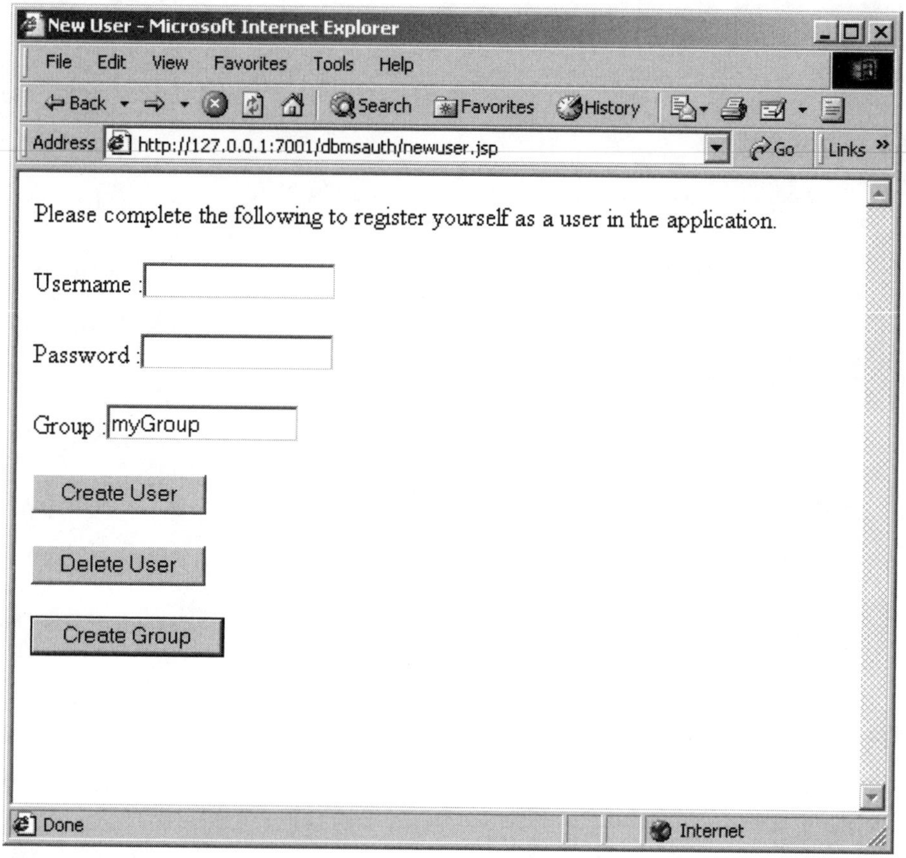

Figure 12–18 Self-Registration

Click on the Create Group button. You should receive a message stating that the group was successfully created.

Next, add the user name and password ("ruslan" and "sporty") to the fields in the form (see Figure 12–19).

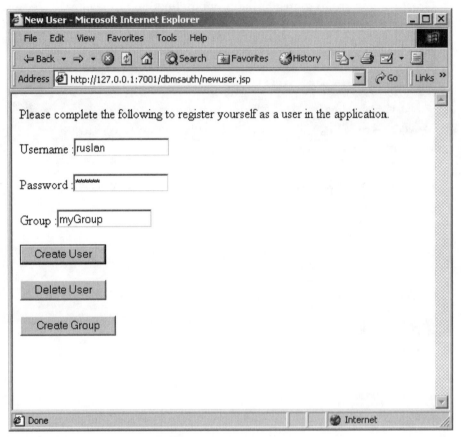

Figure 12-19 Creating a Group

Click Create User. You should receive a message stating that your user has been successfully created and logged into the system (see Figure 12–20).

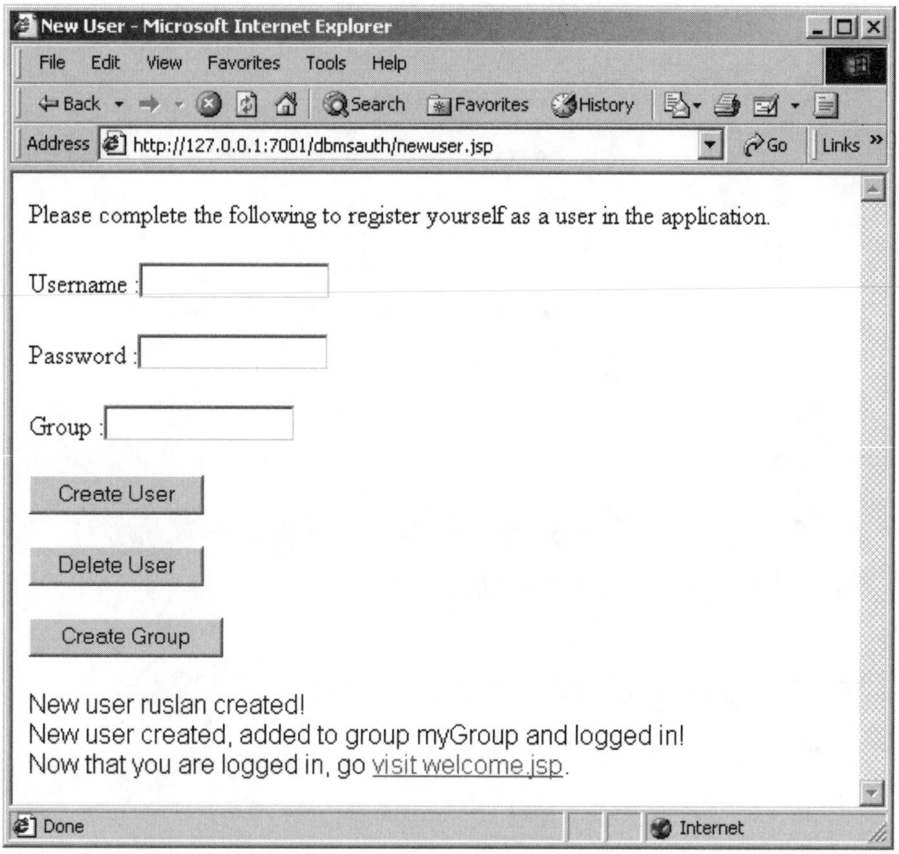

Figure 12–20 Self-Registration Success

You can now go directly to the welcome page. Check the WebLogic Server console to make sure the new user is in the RDBMS realm (see Figure 12–21).

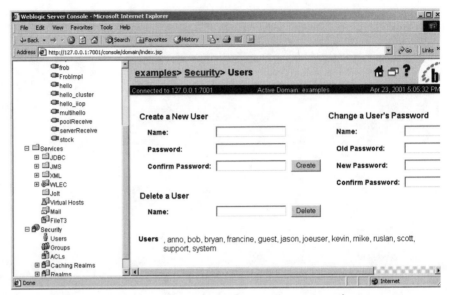

Figure 12-21   Checking Results in the WebLogic Server Console

Developing Browser-Based Authentication

To change the login method to use browser-based authentication, simply modify the deployment descriptor, *web.xml*. Browser-based authentication is defined completely in the deployment descriptor and nowhere else.

Specifying Deployment Descriptor Web Authorization Methods

The `<login-config>` XML tag is used to encapsulate a new authorization method (`<auth-method>`). There are three options for the `<auth-method>`:

- `BASIC`, in which the Web browser displays a user name/ password dialog box. This user name and password is authenticated against the realm.
- `FORM`, which is the HTML form-based authentication used in the form-based example.

- CLIENT-CERT, which requires SSL and a client-side certificate. This option is discussed later in this chapter.

Browser-Based Authentication Deployment Descriptor Example

A deployment descriptor file for browser-based authentication might look like the following:

```
<!DOCTYPE web-app PUBLIC
"-//Sun Microsystems, Inc.//DTD Web Application 2.2//EN"
"http://java.sun.com/j2ee/dtds/web-app_2_2.dtd">

<web-app>

    <welcome-file-list>
        <welcome-file>welcome.jsp</welcome-file>
    </welcome-file-list>

    <login-config>
        <auth-method>BASIC</auth-method>
        <realm-name>default</realm-name>
    </login-config>

    <security-role>
        <role-name>web-user</role-name>
    </security-role>

    <security-constraint>
      <web-resource-collection>
        <web-resource-name>Success</web-resource-name>
        <url-pattern>/welcome.jsp</url-pattern>
        <http-method>GET</http-method>
        <http-method>POST</http-method>
      </web-resource-collection>
      <auth-constraint>
        <role-name>web-user</role-name>
      </auth-constraint>
    </security-constraint>

</web-app>
```

This deployment descriptor is identical to the form-based authentication deployment descriptor, except the login configuration method has been changed to BASIC. In the final section, we have added a security constraint on the Web resource named Success with a URL pattern of *welcome.jsp*.

The basicauth.war Example

A complete browser authentication example (*basicauth.war*) is included on the CD-ROM in the directory named *examples\ch12*. Install this Web application as you have the others in this chapter.   Create a new development directory at the root level, and unpack the example with the jar command. The *.war* file also includes a build script. Open a command window and set your environment with `bea\wlserver6.0\config\mydomain\setEnv.cmd` before running the script.

To view the example, start the Default Server and point your Web browser to *http://127.0.0.1:7001/basicauth/welcome.jsp*.

You should be presented with a login window from your browser (see Figure 12–22).

Figure 12–22   Basic Browser-Based Authentication

After pressing OK, you'll notice that your credentials are not authenticated. This is because you have not yet added the myGroup group and added the user George to it. Use the WebLogic console to add this group and user to your file realm, as discussed in the previous examples. Upon success, you'll see something like Figure 12–23.

Figure 12–23   Browser-Based Authentication Welcome Page

Programmatic Security in Web Applications

Programmatic security is used by security-aware applications when declarative security alone is not sufficient to express the security model of the application. Programmatic security permits dynamic enforcement of security policies. For example, say you have a Web client that allows you to access arbitrary data. You want your application to recognize the user requesting the access and check to see whether that user is authorized to access that data. User Joe should only be allowed to access his own account information and not that of Vanessa. Programmatic security is also useful if the role and security information is highly data-dependent, as when you can only determine the appropriate role at runtime.

Programmatic Security API

The servlet specification has APIs that enable servlets to make business logic decisions based on the logical role of the remote user. The `HttpServ-`

letRequest interface implements the servlet `request` object available in JSP pages or through the `service()` method in servlets:

- `getRemoteUser` returns the login of the user making this request, if the user has been authenticated, or `null` if the user has not been authenticated. Whether the user name is sent with each subsequent request depends on the browser and type of authentication.
- `isUserInRole` queries the underlying security mechanism of the container to determine if a particular user is in a given security role. For example, you can ask if Joe is part of the Administrator role before allowing him to access another user's account.
- `getUserPrincipal` returns a `java.security.Principal` object containing the name of the current authenticated user. If the user has not been authenticated, the method returns `null`.

Programmatic Security Example

Let's say that you have a servlet that accesses data from your database. Only users in the Administrator group/role should be able to update data. To verify the group can execute and update data, add the following method to your servlet:

```
public void onlyAdministrators() {

  out.println("onlyAdministrators was called by: "+
    request.getUserPrincipal());

  if (request.isUserInRole("Administrator")) {

    out.println("Only admins are allowed in this method.");

    // Do privileged work here.

  } else {

    out.println("User: "+ request.getUserPrincipal()+
      " was not in the Administrator role.");


  }
}
```

This method displays the principal that is accessing the servlet. Then, it checks to see whether the requesting user is in the Administrator role. If so, the privileged code is executed. Otherwise, a message printing out that the requester does not have the appropriate permissions is displayed.

Developing Secure Application Clients

The two security paradigms implemented in WebLogic Server Version 6.0, JNDI security and JAAS, provide APIs for applications to access the security realm. For example, a security realm might contain access control information for a Java Message Service (JMS) destination. An application client requesting access to that JMS destination must make a number of API calls to authenticate itself to WebLogic. This section describes how to program to each security service API in order to access the underlying security realm data.

Why Two Security Services?

WebLogic Server implemented JNDI-based security (as did other vendors) before the J2EE standards for application-level authorization and authentication of users were in place. In 1999, the Java specifications introduced the JAAS standard APIs and services for security. JAAS is currently one of the enterprise standards scheduled to be part of J2EE Version 1.3. The complete specification for JAAS can be found at *http://java.sun.com/products/jaas*. As of WebLogic Server Version 6.0, WebLogic Server has implemented JAAS only for *authentication services*. JAAS authorization services are to be implemented in a later release. For authorization services, the WebLogic Server developer must use JNDI-based security.

In practice, WebLogic Server JAAS is not commonly used because WebLogic Server does not yet support the full JAAS specification. Use WebLogic Server's proprietary JNDI security for applications that require complete authorization and authentication functionality. However, JAAS will become the security standard for J2EE in the future. To maximize portability, you should begin to use JAAS services for authentication.

WebLogic Server JAAS Authentication

WebLogic Server's JAAS authentication determines who is currently executing Java code in WebLogic Server. WebLogic Server JAAS is built on top of the standard Java platform security available in the Java Development Kit (JDK). The JAAS 1.0 authentication framework is, in turn, based on Pluggable Authentication Modules (PAM), which is a standard for plug-and-play security in a UNIX environment. It enables system administrators to plug in and configure the appropriate authentication service(s) to meet their specific security requirements without requiring component modification. More information on PAM can be found at *http://java.sun.com/security/jaas/doc/pam.html*.

Using JAAS for Application Client Security

When you use JAAS to secure a client in an application or mixed deployment of WebLogic Server, the client:

- Logs into WebLogic Server
- Is verified by the appropriate JAAS module
- Accesses resources inside of WebLogic Server

JAAS authentication requires adding a chunk of code to each application client.

Writing JAAS Authentication Code

The *subject* is a key concept in JAAS authentication services. The subject is the source of a request to WebLogic Server. The subject can have more than one *identity* associated with it. You can have an identity represented both by your full name (e.g., "John Greene") and by your Social Security number (e.g., "420-420-1999"). The different identities are called *principals* by the JAAS standard.

Each subject typically has one or more identity representations. These identity representations are mapped to WebLogic Server user names. For example, a subject could have the identities "Administrator" as well as "Bob".

JAAS Modules

JAAS modules are the components that map the JAAS API to the security store. During the authentication process, JAAS modules evaluate subjects.

For example, a module might map a JAAS login to the Windows NT domain security. When you log into a client application, the module provided by the vendor handles that subject's login. Modules exist for all the security stores that WebLogic Server supports, including:

- LDAP directories
- Native WebLogic Server file realm
- Windows NT domain security
- The RDBMS security realm

JAAS LoginContext

The JAAS `LoginContext` class is very similar to the JNDI `InitialContext` that is used for EJB access. When your application logs in a user, this class generates the initial context surrounding the login. The `LoginContext` class includes the basic methods used to authenticate subjects, and provides a way to develop an application independent of the underlying authentication technology. Your WebLogic Server configuration specifies what modules are used to authenticate subjects.

JAAS Callback

To generate an initial `LoginContext`, define a class to receive method calls from the JAAS module handling the authentication. These method calls implement the `CallbackHandler` interface. `CallbackHandler` enables the JAAS module to interact with the application to retrieve specific authentication data, such as user names and passwords, or to display error and warning messages.

Method invocations on the `CallbackHandler` include implementations of the `Callback` class. These implementations provide the means to pass requests or messages to applications, and for applications, if appropriate, to return requested information to the underlying security services.

Using WebLogic Server JAAS Authentication

Step 1: Instantiate LoginContext

An application first instantiates a `LoginContext`. This is an instance of `javax.security.auth.login.LoginContext`, which takes a number of different constructors, depending on the login situation. At minimum, the LoginContext requires one parameter, which specifies the configuration to be used for the authentication.

For example, if your application were attempting to instantiate a new LoginContext using password-based authentication:

```
LoginContext lc = new LoginContext("password");
```

Step 2: Invoke LoginContext.login

The application invokes the LoginContext's login method. Calling this login method causes the LoginContext to invoke all of the loaded LoginModules. Each LoginModule attempts to authenticate the subject. The application calls the LoginContext created previously:

```
        lc.login();
```

Step 3: Retrieve Authentication Status

The LoginContext returns the authentication status to the application by throwing one of the exceptions associated with JAAS. The attempt to log in to WebLogic Server must therefore include a try/catch block for exceptions. The login can throw a number of exceptions, all of which are extensions of *../../../../javax/security/auth/login/LoginException.html*:

- Public class AccountExpiredException extends LoginException, which signals that a user account has expired for example, if a user account that was valid for a given time is no longer valid).
- Public class CredentialExpiredException extends LoginException, which signals that a credential has expired (for example, if a password is no longer valid because it has expired).
- Public class FailedLoginException extends LoginException, which signals that user authentication has failed (for example, a LoginModule throws this exception if the user entered an incorrect password).

If the login failed for some reason other than those previously stated, a message is generated and an instance of LoginException is thrown that encapsulates that message.

Step 4: Retrieve Authenticated Subject

If authentication succeeds, the application retrieves the authenticated subject from the LoginContext. This subject is used to access resources using the `Subject.doAs()` method. This method allows application code to be executed under the permissions of a particular user.

Step 5: Log Out User

Once work has been completed on behalf of the particular user, the user should be logged out:

```
lc.logout();
```

Now we can put all of the steps together to create a complete application using the JAAS login.

JAAS-Secured Application Client: Implementation Notes

The following application client accesses a WebLogic Server deployment located at the URL contained in the environment property `"weblogic.security.jaas.ServerURL"`. The application logs in the user, displays the verified user information, and logs out.

First, we import the necessary classes for JAAS and WebLogic Server:

```
import java.io.*;
import java.util.*;
import javax.security.auth.Subject;
import javax.security.auth.callback.Callback;
import javax.security.auth.callback.CallbackHandler;
import javax.security.auth.callback.TextOutputCallback;
import javax.security.auth.callback.NameCallback;
import javax.security.auth.callback.PasswordCallback;
import javax.security.auth.callback.UnsupportedCallbackExcep-
tion;
import javax.security.auth.login.LoginContext;
import javax.security.auth.login.LoginException;
import javax.security.auth.login.FailedLoginException;
import javax.security.auth.login.AccountExpiredException;
import javax.security.auth.login.CredentialExpiredException;
```

Next, define the class signature and main method:

```
public class SampleSecure {

public static void main(String[] args) {
```

Generate the new `LoginContext`:

```
LoginContext lc = new LoginContext("password");
```

Subsequent operations might all throw exceptions that need to be handled. So, encapsulate the login into a `try/catch` block and call the `login` method first. If no exception is thrown, then we know that the login succeeded:

```
try {
                   // authenticate the Subject
        lc.login();
        System.out.println("Authentication Succeeded.");
```

Next, retrieve the subject that was authenticated and use the doAs() method to accomplish an operation on that user's behalf. This action, called SampleAction, is defined in another class. It encapsulates the operations that we want to do against WebLogic Server resources:

```
        Subject subject = lc.getSubject();

    //Attempt to execute the SampleAction as the authenticated Subject
Subject.doAs(lc.getSubject(), new SampleAction());
```

Finally, log out the user and include code to catch any exceptions:

```
        lc.logout();

    } catch (AccountExpiredException aee) {
        System.out.println("Your account has expired.   " +
                    "Please notify your administrator.");
    } catch (CredentialExpiredException cee) {
                    System.out.println("Your credentials have
expired.");
    } catch (FailedLoginException fle) {
                    System.out.println("Authentication Failed");
    } catch (LoginException le) {
System.out.println("authenticnsuccessful"+le.printStackTrace());

    }
}
```

Now for the construction of the access. The preceding application defined a class called SampleAction that is passed to the doAs() method. To define this class, we first define the classes to be imported in the class signature.

```
import java.security.PrivilegedAction;

public class SampleAction implements PrivilegedAction {

    public Object run() {

        // Do whatever privileged actions we would like to do here.
```

```
    return null;
  }
}
```

Note that actions must always implement `PrivilegedAction`. When the `doAs()` method is called on the subject, an instance of this class is passed as a parameter. The subject class works with the underlying security mechanisms to allow this code inside of the `run()` method to be executed. This is where you would put things such as EJB access and so forth for your application clients.

More on WebLogic Server JAAS for Application Security

A complete example, including JAAS login modules and all of the associated supporting classes that go with JAAS, is included in the standard example set provided with BEA WebLogic Server 6.0. The JAAS example is located in the samples directory in your WebLogic Server installation.

Using WebLogic Server JNDI for Application Client Security

WebLogic Server implements JNDI security for both authentication and authorization. As you recall from Chapter 6, the JNDI naming tree is replicated across the entire cluster of WebLogic Server instances. This makes it ideal as a security-context tracking mechanism. Virtually every service in WebLogic Server is registered in the JNDI naming tree. ACLs are defined in the WebLogic Server console and stored in the WebLogic Server realm. These ACLs determine what principals (users or groups) are allowed access to given resources.

JNDI authentication and authorization in WebLogic Server security realms works by allowing application clients to do lookups into the JNDI tree to find objects to be accessed. These lookups are permission-based, so those clients that are not permitted to access objects do not receive references to them. The JNDI lookup with the security information is done when the client is attempting to locate an `InitialContext`, as described in Chapter 6.

WebLogic Server JNDI-Based Authentication

WebLogic Server JNDI-based authentication uses WebLogic Server JNDI as the access point for resources. An application client wanting to access a JMS destination does a lookup into the naming tree in JNDI to gain an initial context for the application. The user provides security information during the initial context lookup. WebLogic Server JNDI security validates that information and provides an initial context with the correct security settings.

Using Password-Based Authentication with the WebLogic Server Realm

Previous chapters discussed resource access using EJB and JMS. For example, Chapter 8's Hello World EJB included the following code as part of the client access to the EJB:

```
Context ctx = new InitialContext();
     HelloWorldHome home = (HelloWorld)
          PortableRemoteObject.narrow(
ctx.lookup("HelloWorldEJB", HelloWorld.class));
```

In this code, the first call generates a new `Context` object using the JNDI initial context. Because no user or environment is specified as a parameter to `InitialContext`, the current user name is used for security checks. Most real-world Web applications handle all security at the Web application layer. If a user has not logged in to a Web application, the subsequent code relying upon EJB or other resources is executed on security as the "guest" user. If the user has logged in, the subsequent code relying upon EJB and other resources is executed on behalf of that user.

In real-world application client deployments, there is no Web layer for authentication. So, you would need to do a lookup into JNDI securely. To add security to a JNDI lookup, you must change the properties when generating the `InitialContext`. Pass these parameters as a `HashTable` object to the constructor for the `Context` object.

Initial Context Properties

Five properties can be changed when generating an initial context. The following summarizes these properties and their possible values:

- `INITIAL_CONTEXT_FACTORY`, which provides an entry point into the WebLogic Server environment. The `weblogic.jndi.WLInitialContextFactory` class provides the JNDI services for WebLogic Server.

- PROVIDER_URL, which specifies the host and post of WebLogic Server. For example: *t3://my.weblogic.com.7001.*

As noted in previous chapters, it is recommended that the
INITIAL_CONTEXT_FACTORY and PROVIDER_URL for JNDI
lookups be set using a jndi.properties file, which enables you to change your
provider without modifying your application.

- SECURITY_AUTHENTICATION, which indicates the types of authentication to be used. The valid values for the property are as follows:

  - None indicates that no authentication is performed.

  - Simple indicates that password authentication is performed.

  - Strong indicates that digital certificate authentication is performed.

- SECURITY_PRINCIPAL, which specifies the identity of the principal used when authenticating the caller to the WebLogic Server realm.

- SECURITY_CREDENTIALS, which specifies the credentials of the principal when authenticating the caller to the WebLogic Server realm.

  - For password authentication enabled via SECURITY_AUTHENTICATION="simple", it specifies a string that is the user's password or an arbitrary object User used by WebLogic Server to verify the credentials of the principal.

  - For certificate authentication enabled via SECURITY_AUTHENTICATION="strong", it specifies the name of the X509 object that contains the digital certificate and private key for the WebLogic Server. Subsequent sections discuss the use of digital certificate–based authentication.

Using Initial Context Properties for Login

The following code generates an initial context that uses properties for the initial context login instead of the guest user:

```
Hashtable env = new Hashtable();

env.put(Context.INITIAL_CONTEXT_FACTORY,
    "weblogic.jndi.WLInitialContextFactory");
    env.put(WLContext.PROVIDER_URL, "t3://
my.weblogic.com:7001");
    env.put(WLContext.SECURITY_AUTHENTICATION "simple");
    env.put(Context.SECURITY_PRINCIPAL, "myusername");
    env.put(Context.SECURITY_CREDENTIALS, "mypassword");

    ctx = new InitialContext(env);
```

This replaces the following:

```
ctx = new InitialContext();
```

Instead of attempting to log in using the guest user name, the application attempts to log in with a user name and password in the WebLogic Server realm. It gets that initial context from the server deployment located at *my.weblogic.com* on port 7001.

After using these properties for login, all subsequent actions using the initial context object `ctx` are accomplished under the user `myusername` with all the permissions associated with it as configured in the WebLogic Server console.

Example: Secure Application Client Using EJB

In this section, we create a sample stateless session EJB that uses JNDI security and programmatic security. In this EJB, programmatic security is demonstrated as well as declarative security. This EJB is called `SecureBean`.

To implement declarative security in EJB, use the same techniques as used in securing Web applications. All access is restricted by configuration information in the EJB deployment descriptor. First, create the EJB deployment descriptor, *ejb-jar.xml*:

```
<?xml version="1.0"?>

<!DOCTYPE ejb-jar PUBLIC "-//Sun Microsystems, Inc.//DTD Enter-
prise JavaBeans 2.0//EN" "http://java.sun.com/dtd/ejb-
jar_2_0.dtd">
```

```
<ejb-jar>
  <enterprise-beans>
    <session>
      <ejb-name>SecureEJB</ejb-name>
      <home>chapter12.SecureHome</home>
      <remote>chapter12.Secure</remote>
      <ejb-class>chapter12.SecureBean</ejb-class>
      <session-type>Stateful</session-type>
      <transaction-type>Container</transaction-type>

      <security-role-ref>
        <description>Administrator role</description>
      <role-name>Administrator</role-name>
      </security-role-ref>

    </session>

  </enterprise-beans>

  <assembly-descriptor>

    <security-role>
      <description>
        Administrator role used to demonstrate EJB security.
      </description>
      <role-name>Administrator</role-name>
    </security-role>

    <method-permission>
      <role-name>Administrator</role-name>
      <method>
        <ejb-name>SecureEJB</ejb-name>
      <method-name>onlyAdministrators</method-name>
      </method>
    </method-permission>

  </assembly-descriptor>

</ejb-jar>
```

Note that this EJB deployment descriptor has a new section not discussed in the previous EJB chapters. It includes an `<assembly-descriptor>` tag, which has nested inside it a definition of a security role called Administrator. Next, permissions on the EJB method named `onlyAdministrators` are set for users in the role of Administrator.

weblogic-ejb-jar.xml

As with Web applications, we still need to define a WebLogic Server–specific deployment descriptor that maps the role defined for this EJB to the principal in the WebLogic Server realm (the user or the group). The following *weblogic-ejb-jar.xml* file defines a principal named Bob, who matches the Administrator role defined for the EJB:

```
<?xml version="1.0"?>

<!DOCTYPE weblogic-ejb-jar PUBLIC
"-//BEA Systems, Inc.//DTD WebLogic 6.0.0 EJB//EN"
"http://www.bea.com/servers/wlserver6.0/dtd/weblogic-ejb-
jar.dtd" >

<weblogic-ejb-jar>
  <weblogic-enterprise-bean>
    <ejb-name>SecureEJB</ejb-name>

    <jndi-name>secureHome</jndi-name>
  </weblogic-enterprise-bean>

  <security-role-assignment>
    <role-name>Administrator</role-name>
    <principal-name>Bob</principal-name>
  </security-role-assignment>

</weblogic-ejb-jar>
```

SecureBean.java

In the EJB implementation, the protected method is defined:

```
private SessionContext ctx;

public void onlyAdministrators() {

    System.err.println("onlyAdministrators was called by:
"+ctx.getCallerPrincipal());

    if (ctx.isCallerInRole("Administrator")) {
      System.err.println("Only admins are allowed in this
method.");
    } else {
      System.err.println("User: "+ctx.getCallerPrincipal()+
        " was not in the Administrator role.");
```

```
    System.err.println("This indicates the security con-
straints"
        + " are not correct in the ejb-jar.xml.");
    }
  }
```

Note that the EJB includes a set of programmatic security APIs similar to those for Web application security. These APIs refer to the `SessionContext` instead of the HTTP `request` object:

- `getCallerPrincipal` obtains `java.security.Principal` and returns the `Principal` object that identifies the caller. This method never returns null.
- `Boolean isCallerInRole(java.lang.String roleName)` tests whether the caller has a given security role. The role must be one of the security roles that is defined in the deployment descriptor (true if the caller has the specified role).

Notice that there is no method to acquire the user name in programmatic EJB security. It is not required because there is no notion of explicitly defined users as in the Web application model.

In the second part of the `SecureBean`, a method is added that demonstrates the usefulness of programmatic security. In this case, it is not possible to recognize the owner of an EJB instance in advance: The owner can only be determined dynamically, at runtime. So you develop a method that can only be called by the user, who owns the EJB instance:

```
public void onlyUser() throws RemoteException {

    Principal caller = ctx.getCallerPrincipal();

    System.err.println("onlyUser was called by: "+ caller);

    if (! caller.getName().equals(userName)) {
        String notAllowedMsg = "User : "+caller.getName() +
          " cannot call the onlyUser method on " +
          userName + "'s Secure bean.";

        System.err.println(notAllowedMsg);

        throw new RemoteException(notAllowedMsg);
    }
```

Deploying the Secured EJB Client

The Secured EJB Client Example resides in the directory named *examples\ch12*, in the file named *SecureBean.jar*.

1. Copy this file onto a temporary directory on your local hard disk.
2. Set your environment correctly using the environment script for the standard, default server:
   c:\bea\wlserver6.0\config\mydomain\set-Env.cmd
3. Use the *jar* utility to unpack the jar as demonstrated in previous examples.

You should see something like this Figure 12–24.

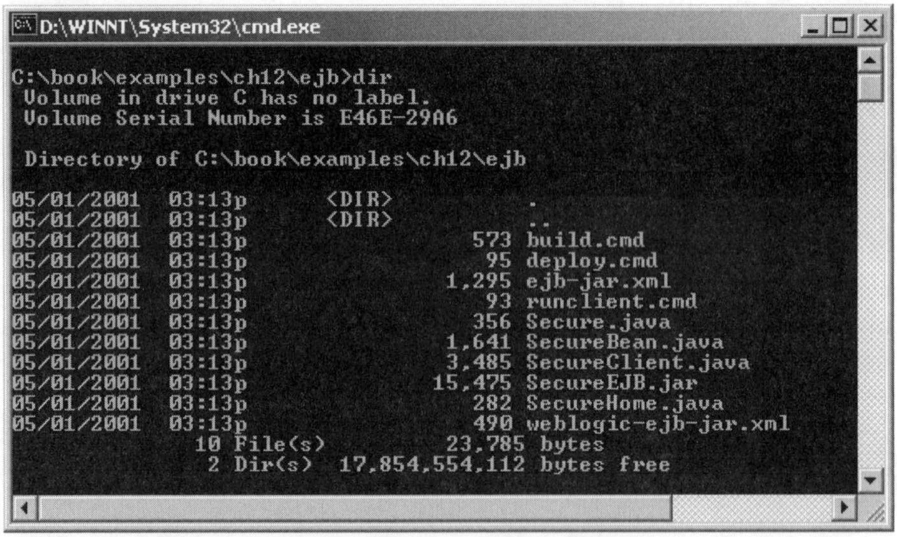

Figure 12–24   Listing of the Secure Bean Example Directory

4. If necessary, edit the build and deploy script, *build.bat*, to reflect the directory of your default server installation. Run the build script (see Figure 12–25), then run the *deploy.cmd* script.

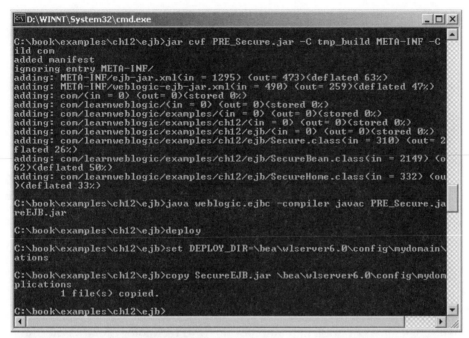

Figure 12–25 Building the SecureBean Example

5. Next, load the WebLogic Server console. Create two users: "Bob" with the password "SAMPLE_PASSWORD" and "Michelle" with the same password. Make sure that you have the capitalization correct. In addition, add Bob to the group named Administrators. If the group does not exist, create it first. Save the changes to the security store ("refresh the security realm").

6. Run the client with the *runclient.cmd* script, or by typing in the following in the same window:

```
"java -classpath Secure.jar;%CLASSPATH%chapter12.SecureClient
t3://127.0.0.1:7001".
```

The last entry is the host name and port number for your WebLogic Server instance. After the client runs, you should see that Bob and Michelle were able to access resources inside of the EJB (see Figure 12–26).

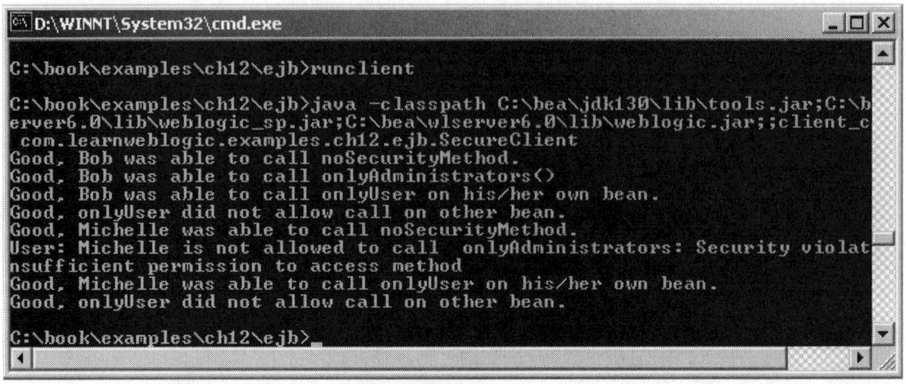

Figure 12–26 Running the SecureBean Example

About WebLogic SSL

WebLogic Server's implementation of the SSL technology follows the Internet standard for security between two hosts connected on an insecure network. Use SSL in WebLogic Server whenever you want to protect data by authenticating users. The SSL protocol uses *public key encryption*. Public key encryption is a more secure form of standard encryption, also known as *symmetric key encryption*.

Symmetric Key Encryption

Most people are familiar with standard encryption, in which there is a *shared* secret between two parties. For example, Andrew and Bob could share a secret, called a *key*, which would then be used as part of the algorithm for encrypting their messages to each other.

Standard encryption uses a number of different algorithms. Some are secure and use industry and government standard encryption algorithms. Some are not secure, such as the key to a secret decoder ring that came in a cereal box. However, all standard encryption schemes share the concept that both sides know the same secret. As you can imagine, the distribution of the encryption keys can be a problem. How does Andrew secretly get a message to Bob before they have shared a secret key? What if Bob and Andrew are in separate countries? Will they need to meet in person before they can exchange encrypted messages? Public key encryption provides a way out of these dilemmas.

Public Key Encryption

Public key encryption technology was developed in the late 1970s by (among other scientists) MIT Professors Rivest, Shamir, and Adleman, who gave their names to the *RSA algorithm*. Over time, the RSA algorithm has become a widely used and respected encryption algorithm. The RSA public key encryption algorithm enables anyone to encrypt a message for Andrew, but only Andrew can decode it.

To use public key encryption, Andrew has two keys: a public key and a private key. Andrew provides his public key to anyone and everyone. Anyone who wants to send a message to Andrew uses this public key to encrypt the message. Once encrypted, the private key is required to decrypt it. As long as Andrew keeps his private key to himself, security is ensured.

RSA encryption works in both directions. If Andrew encrypts something with his private key, then anyone can use Andrew's public key to decrypt that message. This process is called a *digital signature*, because only Andrew can encrypt a message that can be decrypted by his public key.

However, how do you know that the public key you have for Andrew is really *Andrew's* public key? In practice, this problem is solved by a technology called *digital certificates*.

Digital Certificates

Digital certificates contain information that enables people to associate a given public key with a given user. If you receive Andrew's public key, you can use his digital certificate to prove that it is really Andrew's public key and not an impersonator's. A digital certificate typically contains the following information, at a minimum:

- Information regarding the keyholder's identity, such as name, organization, and so forth
- The keyholder's public key
- A digital signature on the information contained in the digital certificate, via an entity called a *certificate authority*

Certificate Authorities

A certificate authority certifies that a given public key corresponds to a given user. For example, a certificate authority might grant a digital certificate to a user who receives mail at a given email address. The certificate authority verifies that the user definitely owns that email address through a series of email exchanges with the user. Certificate authorities sometimes require stronger proof material, such as a valid driver's license number.

How Certificate Authorities Work

Certificate authorities provide a number of well-known public keys that match highly protected private keys maintained by the certificate authority. These public keys also are included in digital certificates that can be found in all commercially available Web browsers.

A certificate authority uses its private key to sign certificates for the users that it validates. In a sense, it is vouching for every single one of those user's identities. Because the public keys of the certificate authorities are both well known and embedded in many applications, you can use them to verify the signature on the digital certificate.

Certificate Authorities and WebLogic Server

In the WebLogic Server, digital certificates and certificate authorities are used in conjunction with the SSL protocol. The SSL protocol relies on digital certificates for authenticating clients and servers.

Because each digital certificate maps to only one private key, each WebLogic Server instance has its own digital certificate. Clients connecting to WebLogic Server securely over the SSL protocol need to verify that they are connecting to the correct host. The host name entered on the digital certificate enables clients to verify that they are connecting to the intended machine.

This level of verification is required for sensitive online transactions, when customers want to do things like:

- Manage their bank accounts
- Make credit card purchases
- Manage their 401(k) program

Digital certificates help give customers peace of mind.

Commercial Certificate Authorities

Vendors such as VeriSign and Entrust are commercial certificate authorities. For a public deployment, such as an Internet e-commerce site, you must obtain a digital certificate for each WebLogic Server instance. BEA's documentation includes specific details on how to acquire digital certificates for your WebLogic Server deployment.

WebLogic Server deployers and developers should take the time to understand how digital certificates work in the context of a secure application deployment. It is not a good idea to deploy your production application using the demonstration digital certificates that are provided for development purposes. The sample certificates are not secure for production deployments. Best practice: Do not use the demonstration digital certificates included with the WebLogic Server in your production deployment.

Notes on SSL Encryption

The SSL protocol aggregates several encryption technologies, including digital certificates, standard symmetric encryption, and public key encryption. For example, an SSL-protected data transfer connection uses all three technologies, as follows:

- First, the client requests the server's public key from the server's digital certificate.

- The client then uses that public key to encrypt a message for the server. The message contains the client information and bootstrap information for the SSL connection.

- Ultimately, the server and the client use each other's public keys to agree on a *symmetric key*, which they subsequently use to encrypt all the data they share.

SSL uses symmetric encryption once a secure connection has been verified because it is much more efficient from a computational standpoint. Public key encryption is very expensive in terms of CPU utilization. If you were to try to implement "bullet proof" security using public key encryption exclusively, your systems could grind to a halt while maintaining only a few simultaneous connections.

WebLogic Server SSL Usage Scenarios

WebLogic Server uses SSL in three ways:

1. To protect communication with browser clients who are accessing Web resources such as JSP pages, servlets, or any other component in a Web application
2. To secure communication with Java clients that are using SSL and making Remote Method Invocation (RMI) calls
3. To secure communication with the WebLogic Server administration infrastructure, which uses SSL to protect the RMI calls it uses to access the WebLogic Server management APIs

One-Way and Two-Way Authentication

SSL uses digital certificates to authenticate both the client and the server. This mode is called *two-way authentication*. For two-way authentication, both the server and the client have a digital certificate from a certificate authority that both parties recognize. The server verifies the client's digital certificate while the client verifies the server's digital certificate. This provides mutual assurance that both the client and the server are whom they claim.

There is another option in the standard: The client can remain anonymous while the server is authenticated. This option is often called *one-way authentication* or server authentication. One-way authentication is the common mode for Internet deployments of WebLogic Server, where large-scale distribution of digital certificates is not practical. For example, imagine a bank trying to provide digital certificates to all of its customers. Most Internet deployments settle for password authentication of users in conjunction with digital certificates to authenticate servers to users.

In most real-world Web applications, only password-based authentication is used for the servers to authenticate a given user's identity. On the other hand, consumers want to be assured that they are sending their credit card numbers and personal information to a secure site. So, digital certificates are used to authenticate servers to users when servers are handling sensitive information.

In one-way authentication, a digital certificate provided by a certificate authority authenticates the server. The certificate authority (such as VeriSign) has its public key embedded in a digital certificate in the Web browser.

Web Clients: Using SSL Security

Using SSL with Web applications requires only a change to the deployment descriptor *web.xml*. Add a new field to every `<security-constraint>` entry, which defines security properties for individual Web resources. For example:

```
<user-data-constraint>
    <transport-guarantee>
      CONFIDENTIAL
    </transport-guarantee>
</user-data-constraint>
```

The keyword `CONFIDENTIAL` specifies to WebLogic Server that the SSL protocol needs to be used. There are three options in total:

- `NONE` means that the application does not require any transport guarantees.
- `INTEGRAL` means that the application requires that the data sent between the client and server be sent in such a way that it can't be changed in transit.
- `CONFIDENTIAL` means that the application requires that the data be transmitted in a fashion that prevents other entities from observing the contents of the transmission.

In the case of WebLogic Server, the presence of the `INTEGRAL` or `CON-FIDENTIAL` flag indicates that the use of SSL is required.

SSL Security Example

To show how to use SSL security, we use a simple Web application with a single servlet. We protect the servlet by defining some security constraints:

```
<!DOCTYPE web-app PUBLIC
"-//Sun Microsystems, Inc.//DTD Web Application 2.2//EN"
"http://java.sun.com/j2ee/dtds/web-app_2_2.dtd">

<web-app>

  <servlet>
    <servlet-name>HelloServlet</servlet-name>
    <servlet-class>book.ch12.HelloServlet</servlet-class>
  </servlet>
```

```
<welcome-file-list>
  <welcome-file>/HelloServlet</welcome-file>
</welcome-file-list>

<servlet-mapping>
  <servlet-name>HelloServlet</servlet-name>
  <url-pattern>/</url-pattern>
</servlet-mapping>

  <security-role>
      <role-name>web-user</role-name>
  </security-role>

  <security-constraint>
    <web-resource-collection>
      <web-resource-name>Success</web-resource-name>
      <url-pattern>/HelloServlet</url-pattern>
      <http-method>GET</http-method>
      <http-method>POST</http-method>
    </web-resource-collection>
    <auth-constraint>
    <role-name>web-user</role-name>
    </auth-constraint>
    <user-data-constraint>
        <transport-guarantee>
        CONFIDENTIAL
        </transport-guarantee>
    </user-data-constraint>
  </security-constraint>
```

```
</web-app>
```

Note that this *web.xml* is virtually identical to the browser-based authentication example used earlier. In addition, the above security constraints only apply to the path */HelloServlet* in the Web application. All other URL requests are handled without SSL being required.

Deploying the SSL Security Example

The complete SSL Security Example resides in the directory *examples\ch12* in the file *sslServlet.war*. Set your environment, unpack the example, edit the appropriate *build.bat* script, and deploy the application as usual.

Visit the application by loading the following URL in your browser: *http://127.0.0.1:7001/sslServlet/*.

You can view the servlet output. Remember, only the following path is protected by SSL: *http://127.0.0.1:7001/sslServlet/HelloServlet* (see Figure 12–27).

Figure 12–27 SSL Required

The WebLogic Server listens for responses to requests on a different port from incoming requests, typically 7002. To view a response, you must use this port number and HTTPS, which is SSL-enabled HTTP: *https://127.0.0.1:7002/sslServlet/HelloServlet*.

You will be confronted by a strange window and a security alert. If you are using Netscape, it will look like Figure 12–28.

Figure 12–28   New Site Certificate

Remember, your Web browser needs to have the certificate authority information in order to validate a certificate. The demonstration certificates included with WebLogic Server are not signed by a certificate authority, which means they are not recognized by your Web browser. For development, this is fine. For production, you must acquire a digital certificate from a certificate authority such as VeriSign.

You should be able to click to a browser-based security window where you can enter a user name and password to log in and view the servlet. The user name and password (for example, "George" and a password) must be previously defined in the WebLogic Server console and valid in the principal (i.e., the WebLogic Server group) that is defined in the Web application's *weblogic.xml* deployment descriptor. Enter the username "system" and the password you use to start the default server (see Figure 12-29).

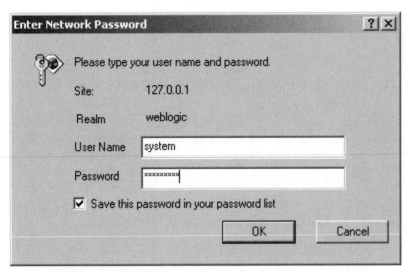

Figure 12-29   Logging in as the system User

Upon success, you'll see the output of the Hello World servlet (see Figure 12-30).

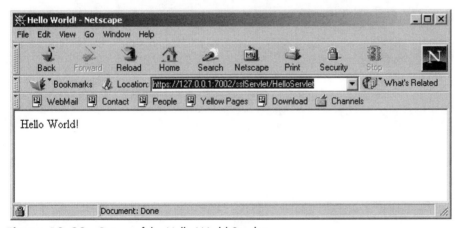

Figure 12-30   Output of the Hello World Servlet

Application Clients: Using SSL Security

To enable one-way authentication using digital certificates with application clients, the only change to be made in the application involves the *initial context properties*. The following hash table specifies that the login requires both SSL and certificate-based authentication of the WebLogic server:

```
Hashtable env = new Hashtable();
env.put(Context.INITIAL_CONTEXT_FACTORY,
"weblogic.jndi.WLInitialContextFactory");
env.put(WLContext.PROVIDER_URL, "t3s://weblogic:7443");
env.put(WLContext.SECURITY_AUTHENTICATION "simple");
env.put(Context.SECURITY_PRINCIPAL, "myusername");
env.put(Context.SECURITY_CREDENTIALS, "mypassword");
ctx = new InitialContext(env);
```

Note that only one field differs from the standard hash table listed for unencrypted, password-based authentication. Changing the protocol type to t3s instead of t3 creates an initial context that is encrypted using SSL. Note also that the port number reflects the SSL listen port for the WebLogic Server deployment. In this case, the port is 7443. The principal of myusername and credentials of mypassword specify the use of password-based authentication of the user.

A number of advanced security services are available in WebLogic Server, which are not discussed as part of this book. The services are available for advanced situations that require specialized security.

Checking Security by Auditing

Auditing is the process of keeping track of all accesses to a system, for later review. For example, you might want to keep a log for accesses to your payroll information. You could then review this information to ensure that permissions have been set correctly, that only authorized users are accessing the system. You also can use an audit trail to see if a given user is behaving abnormally.

WebLogic Server's auditing capabilities require some custom programming. You must write your own audit handler and plug it into WebLogic Server. For more information, review the following in the WebLogic Server documentation:

http://e-docs.bea.com/wls/docs60/security/prog.html#1028328.

Connection Filtering

WebLogic Server offers a programmatic way to dynamically filter out undesirable connections from your WebLogic Server deployment. This process is called *connection filtering*. For example, you can create a connection filter that refuses any connection to administrative resources that does not come from an authorized IP address or domain name. You could, for example, ensure that only administrators located on your internal network could access your configuration information. For more information on how to create a connection filter, see the following WebLogic Server documentation: *http://e-docs.bea.com/wls/docs60/security/prog.html#1031452.*

WebLogic Server Security Best Practices

Follow these best practices to ensure a successful deployment of your security configuration and application.

Review the Documentation for Securing Your WebLogic Server Deployment

The WebLogic Server documentation includes a section entitled "Securing Your WebLogic Server Deployment." This helpful document steps through all of the considerations for creating a secure deployment of WebLogic Server. The best practice is to consult it and follow instructions there before deployment.

Have Your Deployment and Code Reviewed

It is very helpful to have reviews of both deployment architecture and application code for security holes. For large enterprises, it might be beneficial to engage an outside firm to do a security audit of both your deployment and application design. For institutions that do not have as many resources, peer reviews can be helpful as well. In these reviews, another developer reviews the application code and deployment configuration for possible security vulnerabilities.

Study Encryption and Digital Certificates

Deployers and developers of WebLogic Server should take the time to understand how digital certificates work in the context of a secure WebLogic Server deployment. For example, one of the greatest mistakes made is using the demonstration digital certificates that are used only for development and are not secure for production deployments. A best practice is to not use the demonstration digital certificates included with WebLogic Server in your production deployment.

Putting It All Together

In a typical WebLogic Server application, all of these technologies fit together to create a secure deployment:

- *A WebLogic Server realm is used to store all of the security information for an application*. It includes a given set of resources, rules to protect resources (ACLs), users, and groups.
- *Form-based authentication is used to secure a Web application*. This Web application has roles that are mapped in *weblogic.xml* to the deployed WebLogic Server caching realm instance that is deployed.
- *Resources in the Web application are designated to have different security attributes in the* web.xml *deployment descriptor file*. This designates that certain pages should be sent unencrypted while others should be protected with encryption. Those pages that are designated to be protected with encryption use SSL to encrypt the data between client and server. SSL also uses a digital certificate for the client Web browser to authenticate the Web server.
- *When a user logs into the application, the security realm authenticates that user and authorizes him or her to use the resource*. If the security realm is configured to use an external security store, such as an LDAP server for the RDBMS realm, the WebLogic Server security service will access that store to perform an authentication. If the caching realm has been defined, the server may not directly access the LDAP server but use the cache instead.

Figure 12–31 shows all of these components working together in a single WebLogic Server application deployment.

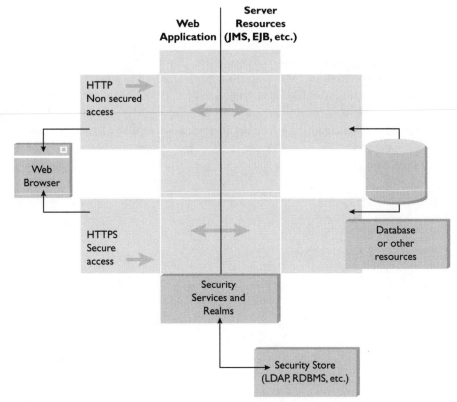

Figure 12–31   WebLogic Server Security Technologies

Securing the WebAuction Application

You should review the WebAuction Web code at this time. You'll notice that many of the techniques used in this chapter have been implemented in the WebAuction application. Most notable and applicable are the form-based authentication functionality, and the use of the RDBMS and the caching realm. Every time a user logs into the site or registers, WebAuction uses form-based authentication. In order to process the form for registration, a JavaBean is used. The Java code in the JSP pages makes calls into the WebLogic Server realm.

DESIGNING THE PRODUCTION DEPLOYMENT

In this chapter:

This chapter details sample configurations and best practices for properly designing a WebLogic deployment for an e-commerce application such as our WebAuction example.

This chapter describes and illustrates:

- A variety of WebLogic deployment scenarios
- A sample WebLogic deployment configuration for each deployment scenario
- Best practices for deploying WebLogic Server applications

13

Chapter

As you move from development and testing of a new WebLogic Server application to production deployment on one or more WebLogic Servers, you create a *design for deployment*. WebLogic Server applications can be deployed in a variety of environments. The WebLogic Server product suite runs on many different platforms and supports many types of clients: Web browsers, C++ applications, and Java applications. For each type of client, the WebLogic Server container provides a complete set of standard services such as messaging, transactions, and dynamic Web page generation. Both front-end and back-end components can be clustered to help assure performance, scalability, and reliability.

Using WebLogic Server's Java 2 Enterprise Edition (J2EE) implementation and extensions, WebLogic Server developers can build customized solutions for their unique mix of platforms and clients. However, WebLogic Server's support of mix-and-match platform and client deployments adds to the challenge of designing a scalable and robust deployment. This means that developers must follow good design principles.

Rather than detailing the specific "how to's" for deploying the WebAuction application (we do that in Chapter 14), this chapter gives the developer a general picture of how to plan for a successful WebLogic Server deployment, and illustrates standard deployments with case studies.

Designing for Deployment

The successful deployment of an application should be one of the first design considerations, not the last. Once you know the basic functionality of an application, you should create a separate architecture sketch for the application as deployed into your customer base.

Deployment architecture specification details should include:

- Types of clients
- Types of server hardware and OS platforms
- Available Database Management Systems (DBMSs)
- Network configuration
- Expected number of users
- Expected volume of transactions
- Security requirements

Planning for deployment is not an idle exercise. Before your application "goes live" before a worldwide audience of thousands, you need to know that your application will continue to perform well as loads increase. You may code, configure, and test a prototype in a single-user high-performance development environment; then you need to assess the real-world requirements of the deployed application.

The following scenarios may suggest some areas for investigation.

WebLogic Deployment Scenarios: Case Studies

WebLogic deployment architectures can be differentiated according to:

- What types of client software connect to WebLogic Server
- The degree of clustering of WebLogic Server instances
- Whether servlets/Java ServerPages (JSPs) are used with Enterprise JavaBeans (EJBs) in the same cluster
- Whether servlets/JSPs are used with EJBs in separate clusters
- Whether you use WebLogic Server's native Web services as the front-end to the Internet

- Whether you use a third-party Web server such as Netscape/ Apache/Microsoft Internet Information Server (IIS) with WebLogic Server

We discuss these deployment possibilities in the following sections.

Types of Client Software

Clients in a WebLogic Server deployment can be:

- Web deployments (clients are Web browsers)
- Application deployments (clients are applications)
- Mixed deployments (clients are both Web browsers and applications)

Web and mixed deployments are the most common scenario. The WebAuction application is a mixed deployment.

Web Deployments: A Standard Configuration

A Web deployment of WebLogic Server is one in which the client software accesses WebLogic Server on the Internet using the protocols (such as HTTP and HTTPS) of the World Wide Web. In most cases, a Web browser is used for the presentation of HTML-encoded information on the end user's machine.

Web deployments are the preferred deployment style when you do not have control over the client machine(s). The beauty of the Web is that the ubiquitous Web browser enables you to build systems that do not require client code on every machine that accesses your site. Yet, you can still have rich presentation in user interfaces using an open Internet standard such as HTML.

The basic Web deployment architecture begins with the connection to the Internet. In most cases, this is a direct feed from an Internet service provider (ISP). This connection typically terminates to a router that has Ethernet capability. Client connections (typically, HTTP requests) are routed through this hardware to servers at your location.

You have a deployment decision to make: whether to use a commercial Web server, or use WebLogic Server as the Web server.

Web Deployment Scenario #1: Commercial Web Server

WebLogic Server provides customers with the option to integrate with standard Internet Web servers such as Apache, Netscape Enterprise Server, or Microsoft IIS. WebLogic Server is distributed with modules that can plug in to these different Web servers. The plug-in is configured so that when requests are received that have a relative path that includes WebLogic Server, those requests are forwarded to a remote WebLogic Server instance. The plug-ins can also work by file extension or content type. For example, you can set the plug-in to forward all JSPs to WebLogic Server while the third-party Web server handles everything else.

The WebLogic Server Web service plug-ins fully support the proxy capability in the `HttpClusterServlet` described later in the section, "Using WebLogic Server Clustering in a Web Deployment." Figure 13–1 shows a cluster of WebLogic Servers residing behind a Web server instance that contains a WebLogic Server plug-in.

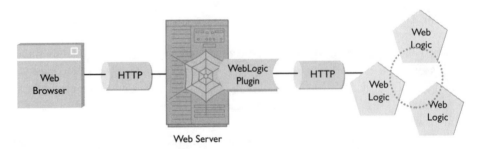

Figure 13–1 A Cluster of WebLogic Servers Residing Behind a Web Server

Requests made to the Web server are forwarded to WebLogic Server if appropriate. Other requests can be handled directly by the Web server.

No matter what components you choose for your deployment configuration, WebLogic Server provides a means of integration. In the case of Netscape, WebLogic Server can share the same store of users and groups in an Light Directory Access Protocol (LDAP) repository. WebLogic Server also can integrate with the NT user domains in Windows environments so that security information need not be duplicated in multiple stores (see Figure 13–2).

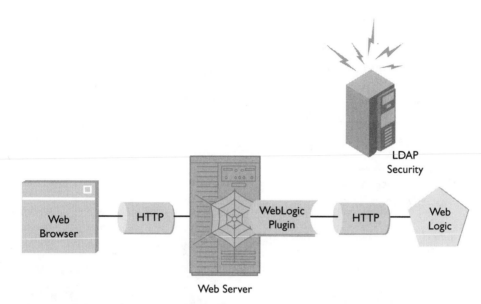

Figure 13-2 WebLogic Server Residing Behind a Web Server with a Shared Security Store

Scenario #2: Using WebLogic Server as the Web Server

Although BEA WebLogic Server integrates well with commercial Web servers, you also can use WebLogic Server itself as the HTTP server for enterprise deployments. Features of WebLogic Server that support this include:

- *Native code acceleration for WebLogic Server file serving.*
  Version 6.0 of WebLogic Server takes advantage of native operating system calls to optimize file serving. In virtually all cases, WebLogic Server is equivalent to a commercial Web server in static file-serving performance for a single user. WebLogic Server also is generally more scalable because it takes advantage of Java's threading architecture.
- *Advanced Web server features in WebLogic Server, such as virtual hosting, LDAP integration, and more.* Virtual hosting is the ability to host multiple domains on a single instance of a Web server. Therefore, a single Web server can host *www.domain2.com* and *www.domain1.com* without having to have a separate Web server for each domain name. Other Web

server features supported by BEA WebLogic Server include LDAP integration and cryptographic acceleration for Secure Sockets Layer (SSL) communication.

- *Integration with a number of the Web routers used for very large Web deployments.* It is possible to deploy a cluster of WebLogic Servers and take advantage of all advanced functionality without needing to use one of the WebLogic Server proxy plug-ins.

Best practice: Integrating with a third party Web server should be considered when a legacy Web server deployment already exists in an enterprise. Otherwise, using WebLogic Server as the Web server allows for the simplest and easiest-to-maintain deployments.

Using a DMZ and Firewalls in a Web Deployment

Most secure Web deployments involve the use of a demilitarized zone (DMZ) for greater security. A DMZ is an isolated and protected network that is separate from the corporate network.

A DMZ-based Web architecture is the preferred structure for a Web deployment of WebLogic Server. Figure 13–3 shows the components of this architecture.

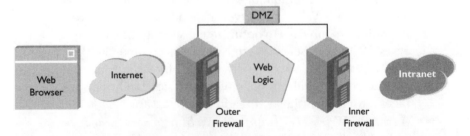

Figure 13–3   A DMZ Deployment of WebLogic Server

Client requests arrive from the Internet and are routed through firewall No. 1. This firewall is configured to support only HTTP connections originating from the Internet. WebLogic Server receives requests, processes them, and then responds directly. All of these components are connected via a standard LAN.

Best practice: A DMZ should be considered for every secure WebLogic Server installation.

A Web architecture with a DMZ is suitable for basic e-commerce deployments of WebLogic Server. A more complex architecture using WebLogic Server clustering, firewalls, and other features is required for deployments that need greater scalability and reliability. See "Hardware Specifics for Clustering," later in this chapter.

Firewalls

A firewall helps guarantee Internet security. If you are not familiar with the mechanisms by which a firewall protects Internet resources, you should visit the Web sites of some of the leading vendors of firewall software and hardware including Checkpoint, Axent, and Cisco.

Firewalls should be used to protect *both* the DMZ and your internal network. The DMZ is protected against non-HTTP traffic such as Telnet or other Internet protocols. Figure 13–4 shows how firewalls fit into the typical WebLogic Server security picture.

Best practice: Firewalls should be as restrictive as possible. Be sure to disallow access for any protocol type or client type that is not required for your application. For example, firewalls can allow HTTP but disallow SMTP, FTP, and other Internet protocols.

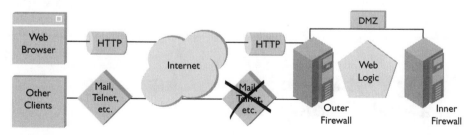

Figure 13–4 Firewalls Protecting a DMZ and Internal Network with WebLogic Server

Internet traffic crosses the DMZ firewall to access a WebLogic Server residing in the DMZ. The corporate network is protected by another firewall.

Integrating Web Deployments with Data Stores

Most applications using WebLogic Server will necessarily include a data store, usually a Relational Database Management System (RDBMS) such as those from Oracle, IBM, Sybase, or Informix. DBMSs provide deployments with the capability to execute transactions and persistently store data in a highly scalable and reliable manner. More information on how to configure WebLogic Server to use a database is included in the WebLogic Server documentation.

In a Web deployment, it is important not to expose your data store to the outside world. Typically, this is accomplished by placing the database server on the network behind the internal firewall. Figure 13–5 shows a WebLogic Server deployment that includes a data store.

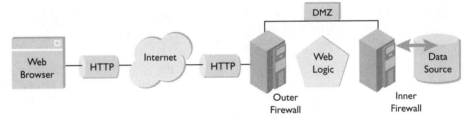

Figure 13–5   Deploying Your Data Store with WebLogic Server in a Web Deployment

Requests from the Internet are placed to WebLogic Server. WebLogic Server relies on the data store that is located behind the internal firewall for transactional support and data storage.

Best practice: Protect your database server as much as possible by placing it behind an inner firewall.

Using WebLogic Server Clustering in a Web Deployment

For WebLogic Server's most common application type—a Java-based e-commerce application running on the Web—you must build for scalability, availability, and performance from the outset. WebLogic Server's *software clustering* functionality is a critical success factor in an enterprise-scale deployment of an e-commerce application. A WebLogic Server cluster features multiple instances of WebLogic Server connected by a local area network (LAN). Software clustering lets a number of WebLogic Servers share a network name so they can function cooperatively. Clustering is the mechanism that supports production services, including:

- *Load balancing*—Distributing work among WebLogic Servers in a cluster to maintain throughput
- *Failover*—Transparently switching to the next WebLogic Server in a cluster when a server becomes unavailable

The WebLogic Server instances, or *nodes*, work together to share common information and balance the application-processing load among themselves. High availability is provided through the capability of the cluster to automatically recognize a failure of a node and route traffic around it. Scalability is provided by the capability to easily add servers to the cluster.

First, requests come in to the front-line WebLogic server(s). The server then uses WebLogic Server's `HttpClusterServlet` to distribute requests among all the nodes in the cluster.

The WebLogic Server `HttpClusterServlet` acts as the front-line handler for Web requests and proxy requests, for a cluster of WebLogic Server servers. For information on how to configure `HttpClusterServlet`, see the WebLogic Server documentation at *http://e-docs.bea.com/wls/docs60/adminguide/config_web_app.html*.

The deployment of a WebLogic Server cluster is key to any Web site that wants to provide the ultimate in scalability and reliability. Sites that expect very high traffic volumes should plan to use a WebLogic Server cluster.

Best practice: No high-end Web deployment should be built without WebLogic Server clustering.

Configuring Hardware for a Clustered Web Deployment

WebLogic Server instances are deployed one per CPU, on multiple hardware servers. As mentioned previously, these instances can communicate in order to share information about client data and enable load balancing and redundancy. When a WebLogic Server cluster uses multiple independent hardware servers, it is resilient against failures of one or more hardware components.

WebLogic Server nodes in a cluster communicate via *multicast*, which is a style of network communication that's like standing up in a crowded room and screaming (or "broadcasting") your message to everyone. This highly efficient protocol enables nodes in the WebLogic Server cluster to send messages addressed to all of the other nodes with updates on recent events.

Multicast uses IP (the Internet Protocol that is the part of TCP/IP) on a LAN to efficiently communicate between nodes of the cluster. Multicast does not incur the overhead that is required by TCP. To use TCP to update remote information in a cluster of n servers, a given server would have to make $n-1$ connections to the other servers: one connection for each other server in the cluster. As you can imagine, this architecture does not scale because every request causes dozens or hundreds of connections to be created and removed.

When your clients go from client/server or from server/server for Remote Method Invocation (RMI) or EJB access, their traffic always flows over TCP/IP, never multicast—except in the case of Java Message Service (JMS) multicast transport, described in Chapter 7.

Multicast Security

Because intracluster messages are circulated on a LAN, routers and bridges typically do not forward them. This makes a WebLogic Server cluster something that can exist securely inside of the DMZ (see Figure 13–6).

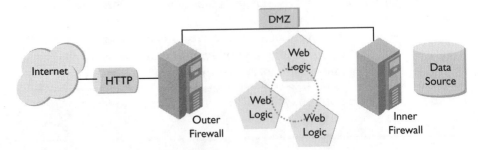

Figure 13–6 Cluster Traffic Staying in the DMZ

Choosing the Right Network Architecture

The LAN connecting the hardware servers for the WebLogic Server cluster typically supports TCP/IP. WebLogic Server clustering relies on Internet-style addressing, including IP addresses. You should follow the instructions included in the WebLogic Server documentation for the specifics on configuring your LAN for a WebLogic Server cluster.

It is strongly recommended that you employ a high-speed network of at least 100Mbps or greater to connect the nodes in your WebLogic Server cluster.

Best practice: A higher speed network for the cluster helps to improve response times.

Clustering on a Multi-CPU Server

You can place multiple instances of WebLogic Server on a single hardware server (one per CPU) if you are deploying WebLogic Server on a large multi-CPU server. This optimizes communication and management of WebLogic Servers. For example, if you are deploying WebLogic Server on a 4-CPU server, you can have one instance of WebLogic Server on each CPU.

Clustering several WebLogic Server instances on a single machine improves the performance of the Java virtual machine (JVM). Java's automatic "garbage collection," or the restoration of unused memory to the free memory space for the applications, can interrupt processing of application code. The larger your JVM memory setting, called a "heap," the longer your application server must wait to service more requests.

Therefore, it is more efficient to have multiple instances of WebLogic Server on a single hardware server, using the minimum heap size that you can get away with. In most cases, this is 128 to 256MB. There are also cases in which a larger heap size is desirable. For example, if you have a large amount of user data that you are handling at a given time, you want to ensure that you have more memory in the typical deployment. In these cases, it does not cause problems to expand the size to 384MB or even 512MB.

Placing a cluster on a single piece of hardware also reduces network overhead. If you put a 10-node cluster on 10 individual machines connected by a network, each cluster operation would require WebLogic Server to access the network. Co-located WebLogic Server instances can communicate directly without incurring the overhead of traveling across the wire to other boxes.

A good general rule is that you should have one instance of WebLogic Server per one or two CPUs, and cluster on a single server where possible (see Figure 13–7).

Best practice: Cluster WebLogic Servers on multi-CPU servers.

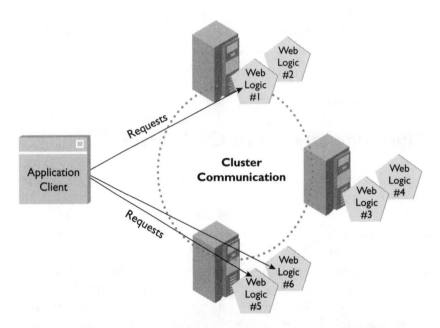

Figure 13-7   A Cluster of Six WebLogic Servers on Three 2-CPU Servers

Hardware Specifics for Clustering

So far, this chapter has not discussed how other components of the network fit together with WebLogic Server in the hardware environment. Choosing these components is an important area, and one in which mistakes often are made. However, the good news is that choosing hardware for a WebLogic Server deployment and configuring it correctly is not difficult once all of the components are identified.

There are a number of components that fit together in a complete WebLogic Server deployment for the Internet:

- Internet connectivity via an Internet router
- Firewall software or hardware
- A Web router or internal Domain Name Service (DNS)
- Internal LAN infrastructure

The following sections discuss each of these components in detail.

Internet Connectivity

The ISP provides the connectivity to the Internet. In many enterprises, this connectivity already exists and goes straight to the network center for the enterprise. When the enterprise maintains the hardware and Internet connection itself, this is typically referred to as an *on-site deployment* of WebLogic Server.

It is also possible to deploy WebLogic Server in what is called the *co-hosted* or *co-located* scenario. Vendors such as Exodus Communications, Level 3, and LoudCloud provide solutions that enable WebLogic Server deployers to place the entire deployment at a facility maintained by the co-location host. Depending upon the services offered by the vendor, the co-location agreement might even extend to having the vendor monitor and administer the WebLogic Server deployment.

In all of these cases, an ISP provides Internet connectivity. Typically, this connectivity takes the form of a physical connection to the Internet that is terminated at the location of the deployment. This connection typically terminates in an Internet router. This Internet router is in charge of taking traffic that comes from the Internet and running it into the appropriate hosts inside of the deployment. It also is responsible for routing the responses back to clients.

The ISP usually takes care of registering and administering the host names that you require for your deployment. When clients across the Internet access your WebLogic Server deployment, they use the DNS to locate the IP addresses of your deployment.

Firewalling Internet Traffic

Firewalls are used to filter out inappropriate traffic based on a set of rules. In a WebLogic Server deployment, the first line of firewalls protects the Web servers and the load-balancing mechanisms against unwanted requests. In a typical deployment, these firewalls act as gateways to the Internet and only accept Web requests on designated ports. The methods for configuring firewalls are specific to the vendors (for example, Checkpoint, Axent) who supply firewalls.

In Figure 13–7, the firewalls had IP addresses that were visible to the Internet. The firewalls are then intelligent enough to route requests and distribute them amongst the load-balancing mechanisms. Whether this is possible or not depends upon the firewall that you choose. Whatever your architecture, the firewalls should filter out unwanted traffic and then hand off those requests to your load-balancing mechanism.

Most deployments also take advantage of another set of firewalls to protect the enterprise network. If this is an on-site deployment, the second set of firewalls typically protects traffic going from the WebLogic Server deployments to back-end resources such as the DBMS or another legacy system. In the case of a co-located deployment, this firewall may be used to access a virtual private network (VPN) that connects back to the corporate network and its legacy systems for a shared database system.

Distributing Web Traffic

After traffic passes through the firewall, the *load-balancing mechanism* for Web requests handles the distribution of Web traffic. There are four common ways to distribute load:

- *Load-balancing software integrated into the firewall.* Vendors such as CheckPoint (*http://www.checkpoint.com*) offer software solutions that can be used with their firewalls to load balance traffic to WebLogic Server Web servers. In most cases, this type of load balancing is only suitable for very small deployments because it does not contain the advanced functionality provided by other load-balancing solutions. If you are making a small deployment of WebLogic Server, using an integrated load-balancing solution may be appropriate.
- *Hardware load balancing.* This solution is the one most commonly used by very large-scale Web deployments. Vendors such as Alteon Websystems (*http://www.alteonwebsystems. com*), Cisco (*http://www.cisco.com*), and others offer hardware boxes that receive Web requests and distribute those among a cluster of Web servers, such as WebLogic Server. These boxes typically work by having a link directly to the Internet gateway and multiple links to the Web servers in the back end. With WebLogic Server Version 6.0, functionality such as automatic failover and load balancing is integrated directly with these machines.
- *Software load balancing not integrated in the firewall.* This solution takes advantage of TCP/IP manipulation in order to create automated load balancing and failover. It provides the same functionality as hardware load balancing, but in a software-only package. The current leading vendor in this space is Resonate (*http://www.resonate.com*), which provides a product called Local Dispatch.

- *DNS round robin.* This is the oldest of all load-balancing techniques. A local DNS server contains a list of Web servers. Every time a request is made, the DNS server is configured to get a Web server at a different IP address. Unfortunately, there are a number of limitations to DNS round robin; therefore, it is typically not used for serious e-commerce sites. The problems with DNS round robin are:
  - *The load balancing is very simple.* There is no random or parameterized load-balancing algorithms possible.
  - *DNS is difficult to administer.*
  - *You do not really get failover.* If you look up *www.foo.com* and get w.x.y.z and that server goes down, then the client code will not necessarily re-look it up to failover.

The configuration of the WebLogic Server deployment depends upon which load-balancing solution is used. Because every load-balancing solution is slightly different, configuration details depend on the features of the solution that you choose.

LAN Infrastructure Components

A TCP/IP network provides the LAN infrastructure for a WebLogic Server deployment. In the vast majority of deployments, Ethernet is the preferred protocol for the LAN. There are a number of components involved in creating an Ethernet LAN:

- Network Interface Cards (NICs), which are placed in each individual server to connect it to the rest of the network
- An Ethernet switch, which acts as a central hub for all of the TCP/IP communications
- A DNS infrastructure on the internal network that is used to locate other hosts both internally and externally. Install this if you need to resolve names of clients, or if you will use DNS round robin.

Web Application Deployment Details

Web application deployments are the most common types of deployments for WebLogic Server. For your consideration, we present three architectures that we recommend for Web application deployments.

- The first co-locates the WebLogic Server servlet and JSP services with the WebLogic Server EJB services.

- The second groups together the servlet and JSP services with the Web server tier.

- The third uses WebLogic Server as the Web server.

Co-located Front- and Back-End Services

In this architecture, Web browsers communicate across the firewall to a Web server proxy that includes the WebLogic Server Web server plug-in. This plug-in then redirects requests to WebLogic Server instances in a cluster, which in turn rely upon the database (see Figure 13–8).

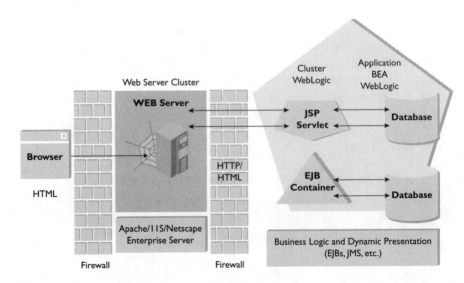

Figure 13–8   Co-located Front- and Back-End Services

Web Services in the DMZ; EJB Outside

In this architecture, the Web services in WebLogic Server are placed inside of the DMZ, with the Web servers. When a request requires that the Web services rely upon EJB services, RMI calls are made through the firewall to the EJB container, which in turn relies upon the database (see Figure 13–9).

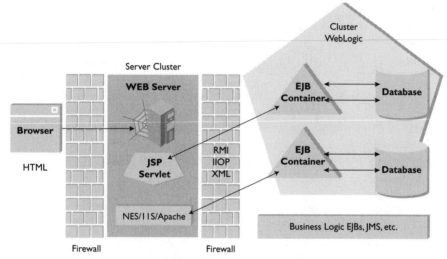

Figure 13–9   Scenario with Web Services in the DMZ and EJB Outside

Using WebLogic Server as the Web Server

In this architecture, the Web services in WebLogic Server function as the Web Server and are placed inside of the DMZ. When a request for an HTML page or a static resource such as an image or multimedia document is made, WebLogic Server responds. When a request requires that the Web services (JSP, servlet) rely upon EJB services, RMI calls are made through the firewall to the EJB container, which in turn relies upon the database (see Figure 13–10).

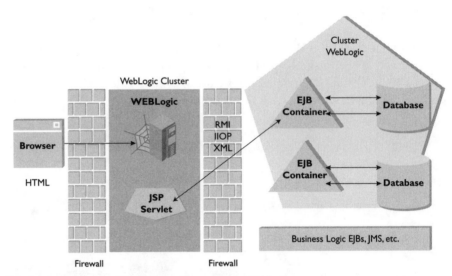

Figure 13-10   Using WebLogic Server as the Web Server

Application Deployments

Application deployments are the simplest to architect for WebLogic Server. In application deployments, the only clients that access WebLogic Server are applications. These communicate via the Java standards for RMI.

Typical Application Deployment Architecture

The typical deployment architecture for an application deployment involves two types of components: client-side applications and WebLogic Server instances. The clients communicate over a network to make requests to the WebLogic Server instances (see Figure 13–11).

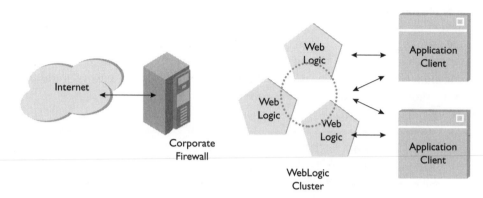

Figure 13–11   Application Clients Connect Directly to WebLogic Server

Code on the client side directs the request to WebLogic Server, which responds to the user.

Security Considerations in an Application Deployment

Security is important for application deployments. Fortunately, most application deployments exist behind the corporate firewall. This means that the communication between WebLogic Server and the clients travels over a relatively secure network. Figure 13–12 shows a WebLogic Server deployment behind the corporate firewall.

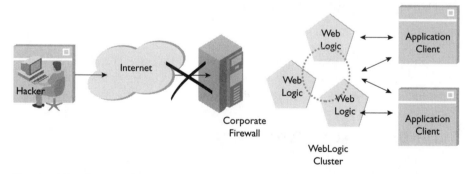

Figure 13–12   A WebLogic Server Application Deployment Behind a Corporate Firewall

If WebLogic Server network traffic will pass over an insecure network or the corporate network is not secured, you can secure the application with SSL technology.

Security does not come without a cost because the server and client must perform resource-intensive encryption operations. WebLogic Server includes optimizations that make this SSL support have less of an impact. In most cases, a server that is not using SSL can serve 25 to 35 percent more clients than a server that is using SSL. However, this depends very much on application details, such as how often clients create new sessions with a server and similar factors.

Best practice: Always enable SSL for WebLogic Server application clients if there is any risk of prying eyes seeing your data in transit.

Recommended Application Deployment Architecture

One recommended application deployment architecture for WebLogic Server consists of a cluster of servers located on a secure network. Application clients connect to the WebLogic Server cluster and automatically handle load balancing and recovery from failure. The preceding figure (Figure 13–12) shows the recommended application deployment architecture.

Using this architecture provides the best in scalability, reliability, and recovery from failure.

Mixed Deployments

Mixed deployments are the most complex WebLogic Server configurations. These are deployments that serve both application clients and Web clients. Care must be taken to ensure security and scalability of the deployment.

Simple Mixed Deployment Architectures

The simple mixed deployment architecture consists of WebLogic Server existing inside of the corporate firewall. External clients typically access WebLogic Server via the Web interfaces across the Internet or another network. Application clients typically exist on the corporate intranet to access WebLogic Server services. Figure 13–13 shows the simple mixed deployment architecture.

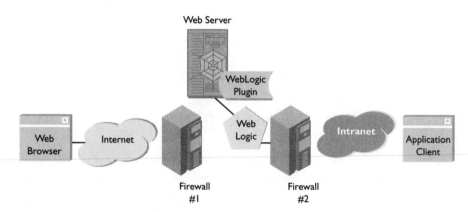

Figure 13-13 Simple Mixed Deployment Architecture

Note that the application clients access WebLogic Server via the corporate intranet, while external clients access WebLogic Server from the Internet. Internet clients access a Web server such as WebLogic Server, Apache, or Microsoft IIS in the DMZ. This Web server then forwards Web requests to WebLogic Server behind the internal firewall.

Using WebLogic Server Clustering in a Mixed Deployment

As in the application and Web deployments, WebLogic Server clustering is key for any scalable and reliable mixed deployment. WebLogic Server offers both Web and application services clustering with similar architecture.

Integrating with Web Services

As mentioned previously in the simple deployment architecture, integrating Web services is key to any mixed deployments of WebLogic Server. Because it is desirable to have WebLogic Server behind the corporate firewall, a Web service should be enabled to forward requests that enter the Web DMZ.

Security Considerations in a Mixed Deployment

Security considerations for a mixed deployment should be a composite of the considerations used for application deployments and Web deployments. You should protect your information using SSL. You also should protect your information from access using restrictive firewalls.

Best practice: Security for a WebLogic Server mixed deployment should include all of the security measures used for both Web and application deployments.

Recommended Mixed Deployment Architecture

The recommended mixed deployment architecture is the combination of the recommended WebLogic Server application deployment with the recommended WebLogic Server Web deployment. All of the components that make a recommended Web component, including a DMZ, firewalls, and integration with Web services, should combine with the components for the application deployment. Figure 13–14 shows these two architectures combined to create a recommended mixed deployment.

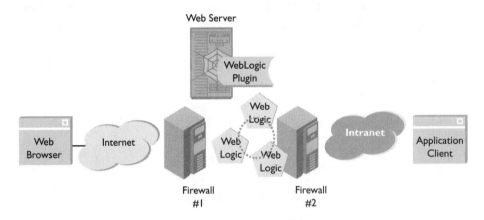

Figure 13-14 A Recommended Mixed Deployment Architecture

Clients from the Internet access the Web services existing in the DMZ. The firewalls protect the resources existing in the DMZ. Valid Web requests are sent through the internal firewall to the cluster of WebLogic Server servers deployed there.

Application clients access the WebLogic Server cluster directly over the corporate intranet. The WebLogic Server cluster handles those requests in response directly to the client applications. No special configuration is required to enable this mixed deployment.

Application Deployment Process

This section discusses the infrastructure and process that enterprise developers should use in deploying WebLogic Server applications to the production environment.

Infrastructure Components in Application Deployment

Application developers need a few very important infrastructure tools—a versioning system, load testing, and quality assurance tools—to ensure the success of WebLogic Server deployments.

Versioning Systems

Versioning systems enable an enterprise to manage multiple versions of application components. The systems are built to accommodate any file type—an image, source code, compiled application code, and so forth. These files are kept in a single, centralized repository. Typically, this repository resides on a server that acts as the master for the entire repository.

To use the system, WebLogic Server developers check in and check out components. Because the versioning system also tracks changes to those files and components, developers can revert to earlier versions. This enables a development group to quickly revert back to the last known version of an application that performed correctly.

Versioning systems also allow for the storage of multiple versions under different names, for example, "version100" for the first version of your system, and "version200" for the second. In many WebLogic Server deployments, a production version of the application is frozen, and forward development proceeds on the next generation of the application. Maintenance work can be performed on the production version while forward development is done on the development version.

Choosing a Versioning System

A number of versioning systems are available on the marketplace today. Some are free, and some are commercially available:

- Perforce (*http://www.perforce.com*) is the versioning system used by BEA to develop the WebLogic Server. It is supported on many platforms and has numerous features that help manage multiple concurrent releases.
- Microsoft Visual SourceSafe (*http://www.Microsoft.com*) is a Windows-based versioning system used by many organizations focused on Windows development.
- Concurrent Versions System (*http://www.cvshome.org*) is an open source versioning system that is available for free.

A number of other versioning systems are available, many of which will suit the needs of a WebLogic Server application deployment.

Load-Testing and Quality Assurance Tools

WebLogic Server does not include tools for load testing and quality assurance as part of its product suite. You will need to use third-party tools to test for capacity and to ensure quality.

Load-testing tools test the application under stress. These tools typically fire up simultaneous sessions to simulate many concurrent users accessing the WebLogic Server–based application. These tools are programmed to follow a typical user's path through the application. For example, a banking application built on WebLogic Server might use a load-testing tool to simulate 10,000 users checking their balance at the same time.

Quality assurance tools for WebLogic Server applications are often used in conjunction with or as part of the load-testing tool. Quality assurance tools are similar to load-testing tools because they simulate users' paths through the application. However, unlike load-testing tools, quality assurance tools enable the developer to verify the responses from the application to ensure that they are correct.

These tools typically work by coordinating one or more machines to simulate virtual clients. These virtual clients follow scripted interactions with the WebLogic Server application. A quality assurance tool also can check the response coming from the WebLogic Server application to ensure that it is correct.

Choosing Load-Testing and Quality Assurance Tools

A number of solutions for testing and quality assurance for applications are available:

- Mercury Interactive (*http://www.mercuryinteractive.com/*) offers a number of products that incorporate both load testing and quality assurance into a single suite of tools. They also offer services to load test your real application remotely from machines that they operate.
- Segue Software (*http://www.segue.com*) offers a suite of products similar to Mercury Interactive. Their products are similarly targeted at high-end deployments.
- Apache JMeter (*http://java.apache.org/*) is a simple Java-based tool that can be used to generate loads for Web applications. It is available for free and suitable for low-end applications. It offers no coordination between the testing client machines and no support for quality assurance.
- Microsoft Web Application Stress Tool (*http://homer.rte.microsoft.com/*), which is the testing tool we use in Chapter 14 with the WebAuction application. This is a free and easy-to-use tool available for Microsoft Windows.

Stages in Application Deployment

The deployment of a WebLogic Server application should go through a number of stages. These stages ensure that the application performs as expected and meets requirements. Figure 13–15 summarizes the stages in a WebLogic Server application deployment:

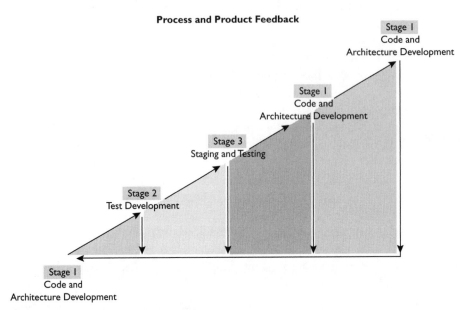

Figure 13-15   Stages in Application Development

While there are distinct stages during application development and deployment process, note that each stage results in feedback that is redirected to the process itself. At all times, information from the production operation, test development, test execution, and staging processes is funneled back to the development and architecture process. In this way, you create a process that results in continual improvement.

Stage 1: Architecture Development and Process Planning

In this stage, the architecture is developed or modified for a version of a WebLogic Server application. Code is then developed to implement that architecture. The application can be a first version developed from scratch, or a new release that modifies the original application source code.

The code is kept in the central versioning system. The versioning system includes the notion of multiple *versioning lines*. It is useful to create new code lines for new development and maintain older lines going forward, especially if those older lines are currently deployed in production.

In the typical WebLogic Server application development process, each developer has a development workstation. This workstation has a client to the versioning system and each developer uses that client to synchronize the local copy of the source code. The developer makes changes to the relevant source files.

Before submitting those changes, the developer typically deploys the changes on a local copy of WebLogic Server and executes tests against those changes. Once the developer is satisfied with the changes, the developer then changes the source code as necessary and submits those changes into the versioning system.

In addition, it is at this first stage that the entire process for rolling out the WebLogic Server application is developed. This is where plans should be developed around testing, and staging any eventual production of the application. If this is not the initial generation of the application, it is likely that feedback from previous steps through the process will be used to improve both the functional aspects of the application as well as the rollout process itself.

Stage 2: Test Development

Complex applications require quality assurance tests. The exact methodology to develop these tests is beyond the scope of this book. Many tests simulate the user experience. For example, a bank application should test the creation of new accounts and the subsequent viewing of balances. Tests should be developed for all new functionality developed for a release.

The tests themselves are also checked into the versioning system, because they are specific to the application version. More advanced enterprises should create automated testing based on the application code, and include tests included for each version of the application. Many enterprises deploy and test the application on a nightly basis, providing constant feedback for developers.

Develop and execute tests for your WebLogic Server application to streamline the quality process and to ensure the expected execution.

Stage 3: Staging and Testing

Before any WebLogic Server application is deployed in production, it should be *staged*. A staged application is one that is deployed in a separate environment that is nearly identical to the production environment. The staging environment should reflect the production environment, down to every detail, including:

- Operating system version and patches
- Operating system configuration and parameters
- JVM version and patches
- JVM configuration and parameters
- WebLogic Server version with appropriate service packs
- WebLogic Server configuration
- Application version (the exact code to be deployed in production—no different)
- Network configuration (DNS configuration, TCP/IP configuration, etc.)
- Hardware configuration

Most successful WebLogic Server deployments configure the staging area as a scale model representation of the production area. Ideally, an exact replica of the production environments can be used as a staging environment. If the budget is available, this is definitely preferred. At minimum, a general guideline is that the staging area should be 1/3 to 1/2 scale to the production area for small deployments, using 8 to 12 CPUs. Larger configurations, such as those of 15 or more CPUs, often can successfully use a staging area that is 1/4 the production configuration size.

Under the staging area environment, tests are executed to ensure that the application will perform properly. In the staging area, two types of tests should be executed:

- *Functional testing*—These tests usually are run using either manual or automatic quality assurance tools. They ensure that the application functionality is complete and performs as expected.
- *Stress testing*—These tests are run using the stress testing tools in order to ensure that the application scales appropriately to handle the load for which it is designed.

Both functional and stress testing should be completed before deploying the application. Chapter 14 contains substantial information on the testing process for WebLogic Server applications, including functional and stress testing.

Never deploy an application in production without stress and functional testing it first.

Stage 4: Production

After the application has successfully completed functional testing and stress testing in the staging area, it is ready for production. The application code and configuration used in the staging area should be migrated exactly into the production area for deployment. This is most often accomplished by copying both the application code and configuration. They are then placed directly onto the production machines.

Best Practices for Deploying WebLogic Server

Over the history of WebLogic Server, customer experience has revealed a number of best practices for deployment. This section covers some of the best practices that you should keep in mind when designing your own WebLogic Server deployment.

Design for Security

It is very important that the architecture of a WebLogic Server deployment be designed with security in mind. Firewalls and other components mentioned in this chapter are all essential to secure WebLogic Server or any other server. In addition, definitely make use of a Web DMZ to isolate any breaches that might occur in your system.

Securing Your Platform

While many architects for WebLogic Server design their deployment for security, they oftentimes forget to secure their deployment platform. Do not forget to review the available documentation for your deployment platform OS for techniques to secure the operating system and hardware platform on which you will run WebLogic Server.

Also, do not forget to follow all of the steps in the WebLogic Server documentation regarding securing your WebLogic Server deployment. A bad configuration can result in open security holes that attackers can exploit.

Do not deploy your WebLogic Server without securing the underlying platform.

Test and Stage Your Application

In today's Web world, fast and easy development should not be taken as an excuse for not thoroughly testing your WebLogic Server application. One of the biggest mistakes that WebLogic Server developers make is rushing too quickly to deployment.

It is a best practice to develop a test plan that covers testing and quality assurance for your WebLogic Server application. In addition, consider creating a staging environment for your application. If possible, this environment should be identical to your real production environment. Test your application in a staging area to be sure that you will see the performance and quality that you desire.

Deploy your WebLogic Server application only after thoroughly assuring its quality through testing. If possible, write your tests before you write your code. It will assist in locating bugs and also help in solidifying requirements.

Load Testing Your Application

Capacity planning information for WebLogic Server is included as Chapter 15 in this book. We strongly recommend that you work with this guide to develop the appropriate hardware for your system. But, even with the best capacity planning efforts, you cannot be sure that you will have enough hardware and the proper configuration to support the client load that you expect.

One of the greatest mistakes made in application deployment is the failure to test against high loads. Therefore, you should estimate how many clients you will want to service as a maximum. Use one of the available load-testing tools such as WebBench (*http://www.webbench.com/*), Mercury Interactive LoadRunner (*http://www.mercuryinteractive.com/*), or any of the other available Web load-testing tools to test the Web components in your application. For application clients, you probably will need to create your own load-testing applications.

Absolutely do not deploy your application without testing it for handling high loads.

Don't Get Too Creative

This best practice applies to any enterprise software purchase: Do not get creative. Ask your software vendor what configurations they test. How often do they test those configurations? What is their hardware configuration? What type of network do they use? What type of JVM do they use? Get that information and replicate one of the regularly tested configurations in your own deployment.

WebLogic Server is certified to work under a given set of configurations and platforms. It is a best practice to review the documentation for WebLogic Server as to what configurations are tested. Do not stray from those configurations in order to prevent the risk of failure. Similarly, WebLogic Server is tested in the recommended configurations described in this chapter. Plan these configurations in order to minimize the possibility of malfunction or poor performance due to configuration or architecture issues.

Avoid creative architectures in your WebLogic Server deployment. With so many moving parts, go with the herd to ensure your success.

Minimize the Number of Moving Parts

A number of options exist for WebLogic Server deployments. The most simple of these involves WebLogic Server being placed behind a Web routing solution. Currently a number of these products, both hardware and software, integrate directly with WebLogic Server out-of-the-box. An off-the-shelf configuration should be considered strongly because it minimizes the number of moving parts in a deployment. Minimizing the number of moving parts means that there are fewer things that can break.

THE
WEBAUCTION
APPLICATION

In this chapter:

- The complete architecture and design for the WebAuction application
- Application component assembly
- Instructions for deploying the WebAuction application
- Performance and functional testing of the WebAuction application

14

Chapter

Chapters 3 through 13 covered WebLogic Server Java 2 Enterprise Edition (J2EE) services and suggested best practices for developing to those services. The earlier chapters outlined the J2EE technologies and illustrated each technology with simple examples.

You are now at a point to develop and deploy a more complex application. This chapter includes step-by-step instructions for packaging, deploying, and testing the WebAuction application. The instructions for the WebAuction application should aid you with your own application development and deployment.

Application Architecture and Design: WebAuction

WebAuction is a Web-based auction system built with the WebLogic Server and J2EE. Like a real auction, it includes bidding, categorized items, and user accounts. The source code for WebAuction is included on the accompanying CD-ROM. The application and its source code can be accessed online at *http://learnWebLogic.com*.

WebAuction Design Goals

The WebAuction application is an e-commerce application that uses nearly all of the J2EE APIs: It uses Java ServerPages (JSP), Java Database Connectivity (JDBC), Java Message Service (JMS), Java Naming and Directory Interface (JNDI), Enterprise JavaBeans (EJB), and JavaMail. Going beyond "hello world" examples, WebAuction demonstrates how these APIs are used together in production applications. Learning APIs is a necessary first step, but developing production-quality applications requires the ability to combine the J2EE APIs effectively.

The WebAuction application is designed to take advantage of the performance and scalability of the WebLogic Server and its clustering capabilities. Because Web applications must accommodate an ever-growing user base, it is important to consider scalability throughout the development cycle.

While WebAuction demonstrates the design and components of a production application, there are several simplifications in the application that would not appear in the real world. Since this is a sample application, we demonstrate important design choices and J2EE features without creating an overly complex application.

Every element of the WebAuction software is a design pattern, a J2EE service, or a WebLogic Server feature. We have chosen to omit auction site features that did not fit these criteria or whose implementation was similar to other components. The interested reader can easily enhance the WebAuction application framework to build a production-quality auction.

In addition to making the application easier to understand, simplicity enables the reader to build and deploy WebAuction on his or her own machine. Although the application is available on our Web site, building and running the application locally provides valuable practice in WebLogic Server administration. Configuring WebLogic Server to handle a real application is a necessary skill for WebLogic Server developers as well as administrators.

WebAuction Subsystems

Like many e-commerce applications, WebAuction has two layers: a presentation layer and a business logic layer (see Figure 14-1). Clients use Web browsers to interact with the presentation layer. The presentation layer (also known as the Web tier) is responsible for relaying client requests to the business logic layer and rendering the business logic's responses into HTML.

The business logic layer handles the application's logic and communication with back-end systems such as databases. The database, which provides a persistent repository for the application's data, usually resides on a separate server.   As you would expect, the presentation layer is implemented with Web components including JSP pages and tag libraries. WebAuction implements the business logic layer with EJB components, JMS, JavaMail, and JDBC. Because WebAuction's entity beans use container-managed persistence (CMP), the EJB container handles the data access code.

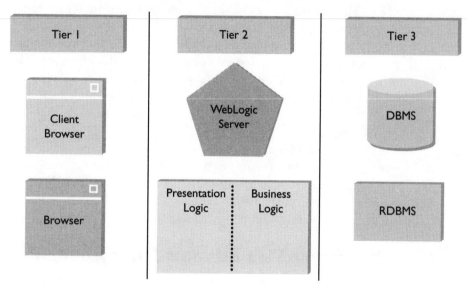

Figure 14–1   Multi-tier Architecture

WebAuction Interfaces

Designing good interfaces between components is an important but challenging piece of software development. When software is properly decoupled into modules, implementations become easier and cleaner. Interfaces promote *information hiding*, which enables software components to minimize the exposure of internal information to other areas of the system. This minimizes dependencies: Components may be redesigned or re-implemented without affecting other parts of the system.

For instance, the business logic could be changed from using database-stored procedures to using EJBs, without changing the presentation logic. Without good interfaces, it is easy to have subtle design assumptions creep into the source code. Unfortunately, designing clean interfaces is not trivial. A prototype implementation is usually required to reveal design flaws or false assumptions. The WebAuction implementation should help serve as a demonstration of successful design patterns for your own applications.

Separating the Web and Business Logic Tiers

A clear separation between the presentation layer and the business logic tier is important. The design goals of the presentation layer's user interface are clean and clear Web pages, and providing a user-friendly and satisfying Web site experience. The presentation layer also handles issues such as internationalization and tracking a user's identity between Web pages.

Many e-commerce applications also include security in the presentation layer. All privileged access must first access a form-based login page. This enables the application to change security policies without modifying the back-end logic. However, this arrangement is not always possible, especially if the back-end logic is used directly by another presentation layer, such as a standalone client application.

Separating the presentation and business logic allows for parallel development. In many environments, separate groups or even separate companies develop each application tier. The presentation layer team includes Web page designers and Web experts, while the business logic developers mainly deal with database, messaging, and transaction issues.

Accessing Server-Side Business Logic from JSP Pages

The WebAuction application uses JSP to access its presentation logic. Because JSP pages can include Java code, it is possible to access business logic directly from the JSP page. However, this design should be rejected: Instead, it is recommended that JSP pages contain little—if any—Java code. JSP pages should use tag libraries, JavaBeans, or servlets to access the business logic layer. This means that JSP pages are essentially HTML pages with extra tags to access tag libraries, or small snippets of code to access JavaBeans or servlets. Because there is little code in these pages, the Web page layout can be altered by graphic designers without affecting the remainder of the system. This design also facilitates internationalizing the Web site, because the display output is cleanly separated from the logic needed to generate the Web pages.

The WebAuction JSP pages use tag libraries to make requests to the business logic tier. One advantage of tag libraries is their syntax resembles other HTML documents. This is beneficial for Web page designers who are more familiar with HTML than Java code. Another advantage of using tag libraries is that a library structure facilitates reusing the tags in other application components. While servlets and JavaBeans may also be reused, reusability requires more effort because they were not designed as libraries.

JavaBeans in the Presentation Layer

In addition to tag libraries, WebAuction's presentation layer uses JavaBeans as value objects when interfacing with the business logic. JavaBeans are simple objects with `get` and `set` methods for each field. The value objects pass information such as the new account profile to the business logic layer. The business logic layer also uses JavaBeans to return information to the Web tier. The Web tier renders pages by retrieving the information held in the value objects.

The disadvantage to this approach is that extra objects must be created to encapsulate information that already exists within the business object layer. For instance, when the JSP page needs to show the current items available for bid, the WebAuction application must find the appropriate items and then create a value object holding the information for each item. While this creates additional objects, the advantages of this approach is that the presentation layer sees only the value objects, so the persistence layer can be changed without affecting the JSP pages or the tag libraries (see Figure 14–2).

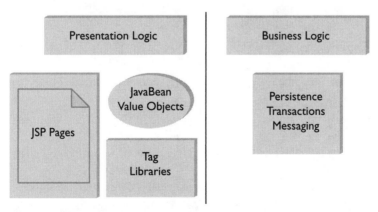

Figure 14–2 Separating Presentation Logic and Business Logic

The Tag Library-to-Business Logic Interface

To avoid mixing the Web page presentation with Java code, WebAuction's control logic is encapsulated in tag libraries. Information is passed between the presentation layer and the business logic layer by means of JavaBean value objects. The tag libraries contain Java code to access the business logic layer. To decouple persistence, transactions, and messaging from the presentation layer, it is important to minimize the entry points into the business logic layer. In WebAuction, the tag libraries must use either the bids JMS queue or the WebAuction stateless session bean to communicate with the business logic layer.

When a WebAuction customer submits a bid, the bid information is encapsulated in a JMS message and sent to a JMS queue. Once the information is on the queue, the JSP page displays a message stating the bid has been received by the system. This is an asynchronous design: The bidder need not wait for the system to process the bid. It is only necessary to wait for the bid's information to be entered in the persistent queue. A JMS listener handles the actual bid processing in the background.

It might be possible to use a synchronous design where the bidder waits until the bid processing completes. However, bids must be validated, and the WebAuction application updates several database tables when a bid is entered.

The asynchronous approach aids scalability because a WebLogic Server cluster can listen on the queue and do all of the processing in parallel.

The user's bids are entered into the system from *bid.jsp* with the `enter-Bid` tag:

```
<webauction:enterBid itemId="<%= bidId %>"
   userName="<%= request.getRemoteUser() %>"
   bidamount="<%= amount %>"
/>
```

The `EnterBid`. Java tag library sends a message to the JMS queue with the values passed in the tag's parameters:

```
        bidMsg.setInt("Item_ID", itemId);
        bidMsg.setString("User_Name", userName);
        bidMsg.setDouble("Amount", bidAmount);

        qsender.send(bidMsg);
```

In addition to the bids JMS queue, WebAuction's business logic layer exports a synchronous interface to the presentation layer with the WebAuction stateless session bean. Because the WebAuction bean is stateless, the tag libraries create a reference when they are initialized and make all business method calls against the reference. Remember that holding a stateless session bean reference does not tie up resources in the server. Whenever a call is made against the WebAuction remote interface, the EJB container selects a pooled bean instance to handle the call. If a stateful session or entity bean were used, the tag library would have to include more lifecycle code to manage the EJB state.

Utility Methods

The WebAuction bean's remote interface exposes utility methods that are used by the tag libraries. Notice that these methods return the `BidValue-Holder` or the `ItemValueHolder` JavaBeans.

```
public interface WebAuction extends EJBObject {

  BidValueHolder [] getBidsForUser(String userName)
    throws NoSuchUserException, RemoteException;

  ItemValueHolder getItemWithId(int id)
    throws NoSuchItemException, RemoteException;

  ItemValueHolder [] getItemsInCategory(String category)
    throws RemoteException;

}
```

The `GetBidsForUser` tag library keeps a reference to the WebAuction stateless session bean in the WebAuction member variable. The `getBids-ForUser` method call returns an array of `BidValueHolder` objects, which are then assigned to the `bids` variable in the JSP page.

```
      BidValueHolder [] bids = webAuction.getBidsForUser(user-
Name);

      pageContext.setAttribute("bids", bids);
```

The *currentbid.jsp* page uses the `GetBidsForUser` tag library to receive the array of `BidValueHolder` objects:

```
<webauction:getBidsForUser id="bids"
userName="<%= request.getRemoteUser() %>"
/>
```

Finally, the *currentbid.jsp* page renders the bids into the HTML page. We have simplified the HTML here, but each bid is shown as a row in a table. Note the use of the `wl:repeat` tag. This is a standard tag included in the WebLogic Server's tag library. It iterates through the elements of an array or `java.util.Collection` and applies the tag body to each element. In this case, it iterates through the `bids` array and assigns each value in the array to the `bid` variable. Within the tag body, the *currentbid.jsp* page includes a table row for each bid.

```
<table>

  <tr>
    <td>Item</td>
    <td>Bid Price</td>
  </tr>

  <wl:repeat id="bid" set="<%= bids %>" type="webauction.jsp.BidValueHolder" >

    <tr>
      <td><%= bid.getItemDescription() %></td>
      <td><%= bid.getBidAmount() %> </td>
    </tr>

  </wl:repeat>
</table>
```

WebAuction Security

Like most e-commerce applications, WebAuction requires security constraints. The WebAuction security model is based on user accounts. Users register with the WebAuction site and create user accounts with passwords and an associated email address.

Not every page in WebAuction needs to be protected. In particular, Web site visitors should be allowed to browse the auction without creating a user account. This enables new users to visit the auction site without requiring them to enter user information. Also, it helps minimize resource usage on the server because no session data is kept until the user logs in. A user must log into WebAuction before providing a new auction item or entering a bid on an existing item.

WebAuction's business logic layer does not include any security checking. It assumes that the presentation layer has satisfied all security constraints. This is acceptable for most Web-based designs, and it simplifies the business logic layer. In addition, security checks can affect performance, so avoiding unnecessary access constraints helps scalability. However, more stringent security requirements might require multiple access checks at different levels in the application.

Security Constraints in the Deployment Descriptor

The *web.xml* deployment descriptor specifies the security constraints that restrict access to a protected page. If a user has not already logged into the system, the WebLogic Server redirects the browser to the login page before accepting the request.

For example, this security constraint restricts the *newitem.jsp* page to users in the `auction_user` role.

```
<security-constraint>
  <web-resource-collection>
    <web-resource-name>New Item</web-resource-name>
    <url-pattern>/newitem.jsp</url-pattern>
    <http-method>GET</http-method>
    <http-method>POST</http-method>
  </web-resource-collection>
  <auth-constraint>
    <role-name>auction_user</role-name>
  </auth-constraint>
</security-constraint>
```

The *web.xml* file also declares the abstract role named `auction_user`:

```
<security-role>
  <role-name>auction_user</role-name>
</security-role>
```

Finally, *weblogic.xml* maps the `auction_user` role name to the `user` principal.

```
<security-role-assignment>
  <role-name>auction_user</role-name>
  <principal-name>user</principal-name>
</security-role-assignment>
```

Every WebAuction user is a member of the group named `user` and can access the *newuser.jsp* page.

Authenticating Users

The WebAuction application uses the Servlet 2.2 specification's form-based authentication to verify user names and passwords. The *login.jsp* page includes a form with the `j_security_check` as the action. The user name is passed as `j_username` and the password is `j_password`. The password field uses the input type of `password` to prevent the password characters from being echoed to the screen. The *login.jsp* page is served through HTTPS to ensure that the password is encrypted on the network.

We have simplified the HTML in the form element to demonstrate it here:

```
<form method="post" name="Login" action="j_security_check">

<input type="text" name="j_username">
<input type="password" name="j_password">

</form>
```

Creating New User Accounts

New user accounts are created with the *newuser.jsp* Web page. This page includes a FORM element that contains all of the required account information. WebAuction requires that all fields in the new user form be completed, by including a JavaScript onSubmit element that instructs the browser to run validateNewUserForm before accepting the submission. The JavaScript code simply ensures that every field has a value.

```
<form method="post" name="NewUser" action="newuser.jsp"
      onSubmit="return validateNewUserForm()">

<SCRIPT LANGUAGE="JavaScript">
  <!-- Hide code from non-javascript
  function validateNewUserForm() {
    newUserForm = document.NewUser;

    if ((newUserForm.userName.value == "") ||
        (newUserForm.password.value == "") ||
        (newUserForm.firstName.value == "") ||
        (newUserForm.lastName.value == "") ||
        (newUserForm.streetAddress.value == "") ||
        (newUserForm.city.value == "") ||
        (newUserForm.zipCode.value == "") ||
        (newUserForm.email.value == "")) {

        alert("You must fill out all fields to create a WebAuction account.");
        return false;
    } else {
        return true;
    }
 }
 // end hiding -->
</SCRIPT>
```

Business Logic Design

The business logic layer implements the application logic as well as maintaining the transactional integrity and persistence of the application data. The presentation layer contains no code for managing transactions or accessing the database. In fact, transactions should never become the responsibility of the presentation layer because this would violate modularity and limit scalability. Transactions are important resources, but their lifetimes should be as short as possible. By manipulating transactions only within the business logic layer, WebAuction can maintain tight control over when transactions begin and commit.

The business logic layer is entered either via the bids JMS queue or via the WebAuction stateless session bean. The `BidReceiverBean` is a message-driven bean that listens on the bids JMS queue. When a new bid arrives, `BidReceiverBean` receives the message and updates the persistent representation. Both the `BidReceiverBean` and the WebAuction stateless session bean must update the persistent state in the database. WebAuction stores its persistent state in three entity beans: the `UserBean`, `BidBean`, and `ItemBean` (see Figure 14–3).

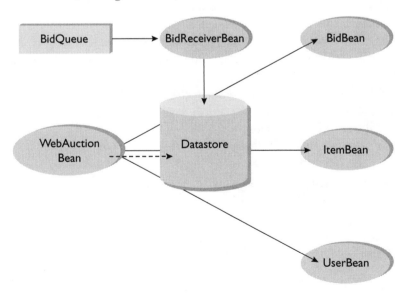

Figure 14–3 Business Logic Design Using EJBs

The `UserBean` stores account information that is entered when the account is created. This information should exist until the account is removed from the system. This persistent information is stored in the database and modeled with an entity bean.

The `ItemBean` represents a WebAuction item that is available for auction. The item information is populated when the item is entered into the auction, and it must be persistent.

The `BidBean` is the persistent representation of a user's bid. When the `BidReceiverBean` dequeues the bid message, it validates the message and creates a new `BidBean` entity bean with the corresponding bid information.

WebAuction Stateless Session Bean

The WebAuction stateless session bean is the synchronous interface into the business logic layer for the entity beans and their persistent data. The WebAuction bean is responsible for reading the persistent information and populating the value objects. As discussed in the previous section, the presentation layer always receives value objects. Another possible design is to return the entity beans to the presentation layer. This design is rejected because it exposes the persistent layer to the presentation layer. Once the entity beans are exposed, it becomes increasingly difficult to make changes as the application grows. Creating value objects also helps performance. Remember that entity beans are transactional objects, and their state is refreshed from the database on transaction boundaries. If the presentation layer accessed the returned entity beans in another transaction, it would cause another round of database hits to refresh the returned information. It is strongly recommended that WebLogic Server applications follow the WebAuction model and minimize the exposure of the persistence layer.

For instance, the `WebAuctionBean`'s `getBidsForUser` method returns all the bids for a given user name. This method uses the `BidBean`'s `finder` method to return the appropriate bid references. It then iterates through each bid and creates a matching `BidValueHolder`.

```
public BidValueHolder [] getBidsForUser(String userName)
   throws NoSuchUserException
{

  try {
    User user = userHome.findByPrimaryKey(userName);

    Collection bids = bidHome.findBidsForUser(user);

    int size = bids.size();

    if(size == 0) {
      // no bids for this user
```

```
        return null;
      } else {
        // build an array of java bean value objects

        Iterator it = bids.iterator();
        BidValueHolder [] bidValues = new BidValueHolder[size];

        for (int i=0; i<size; i++) {

          Bid b = (Bid) narrow(it.next(), Bid.class);

          bidValues[i] = new
            BidValueHolder(b.getItem().getDescription(), b.getAmount());
        }

        return bidValues;
      }

    } catch (FinderException fe) {
      throw new NoSuchUserException("User with name: "+userName+
        " does not exist or could not be loaded.");
    } catch (Exception e) {
      throw new EJBException("Error looking for bids for user:"
        +userName+ ".  The error was: "+e);
    }
}
```

Transaction Flow

All transaction demarcation in the WebAuction application is handled in the business logic layer, in container-demarcated transactions of the EJBs. The WebAuction stateless session bean is deployed with the `Required` transaction attribute to ensure that the container starts a transaction before running the business methods.

In our `getBidsForUser` example, the CMP engine does a single database query to retrieve the associated bids. The calls to the `BidBeans` do not incur database hits because the CMP engine has already prefetched the associated data in this transaction. If these methods ran in a separate transaction, each `bid.getAmount()` call would be another trip to the database.

The `BidReceiver` message-driven bean also demarcates transactions when it receives a message from the bids queue. The `BidReceiverBean` is deployed with the `Required` transaction attribute. The transaction starts with the JMS message receipt, and it flows into the entity beans called by `BidReceiverBean` to process the new bean. If the transaction aborts, any entity bean updates are rolled back, and the message is returned to the JMS queue. This ensures that each bid message is processed and committed (at most) once. If the server dies while processing a new bid, the bid is not lost.

Entity Bean Relationships

The WebAuction application maintains relationships among its persistent data. There is a 1:N relationship between a user and his bids; a 1:N relationship between a user and his items; and a 1:N relationship between an item and its bids (see Figure 14–4).

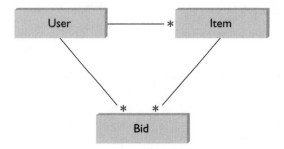

Figure 14–4 Entity Bean Relationships

Because these are EJB 2.0 CMP entity beans, WebAuction takes advantage of the container's relationship support. The application does not include any code to update the persistent relationship state. The CMP engine handles all of this.

Relationships are a natural and powerful addition to the persistence layer. With relationship support, the application can access all of a user's bids, or in more complex situations, access a user's items and then the related bids for each item.

Changes Required for a Production Application

WebAuction is designed as a sample application. While it possesses the main components of a real-world production environment, it includes some simplifications.

Limiting Query Results

The WebAuction application uses simple entity bean `finder` methods to query the database. While these simple finders are acceptable in a prototype, they need refinement for a real application. For instance, the `ItemBean` includes a finder that returns all the items in a given category. On a real auction site, this could return hundreds—if not thousands—of rows. Obviously, a thousand items is too many to display on a Web page, and it is expensive to return this many items in a result set from the database.

A production application must limit the number of results returned by a finder. One common method is to include an additional condition in the `finder` clause that limits the query to a range of IDs. For instance, our finder could return all items in a given category with an ID between 100 and 200. The Web page would have a Next button to enable the user to ask for more results. The next page could run the query again, this time asking for IDs between 200 and 300.

Unique ID Generation

Many common business objects, including WebAuction's `Items` and `Bids`, have no natural "primary key" that would uniquely identify them in the database. Instead, a new primary key value is generated for every new item and bid. The only requirement is that primary key values be unique within the items or bids. WebAuction uses a separate `IDGenerator` stateless session bean to produce these unique IDs. Before an item or bid is created, the caller uses the `IDGenerator`'s `getNextValue()` method to receive a new ID. The item or bid is then created with the generated ID.

The advantage of using a stateless session bean for unique ID generation is that the algorithm can be modified without affecting other code. WebAuction uses a database sequence value to generate unique IDs. While this scheme takes advantage of the database's existing ID generation support, it does involve an extra database round trip on each create to read the next sequence value. This is only acceptable if creates are relatively infrequent, but a successful production auction site will have frequent bidding.

There are several methods to increase the performance of the `IDGeneratorBean` and all evolve around limiting the number of trips to the database. A key point to note is that the `Item` and `Bid` objects require unique IDs, but there is no requirement that these keys be sequential.

A higher performance `IDGeneratorBean` could initially read the database sequence value to receive a new integer, but then hand out 1000 IDs based on that integer without returning to the database. For instance, the `IDGeneratorBean` might read the number "3" from the database sequence, and return the IDs 3000–3999 without returning to the database. Once the `IDGeneratorBean` has handed out ID 3999, it returns to the database sequence to get a new value. This scheme can support multiple concurrent `IDGeneratorBean` instances, each with its own 1000 ID range. This algorithm limits database access and improves performance.

Internationalizing WebAuction

Production Web sites must support multiple languages. While WebAuction includes only English language output, there is nothing to preclude internationalization. WebAuction facilitates internationalization by separating the presentation JSP pages from the presentation logic in JSP tag libraries. The WebAuction application could be internationalized by moving the printed messages from the JSP pages into separate message catalogs for each language. A user entering the internationalized WebAuction site could select a language, and the preference would be noted in the servlet session. The JSP pages would be reformatted to check the session for a language preference and access the appropriate message catalog.

Database Tuning

Nearly every e-commerce application uses a database for persistent data storage. One important aspect of improving e-commerce application performance is database tuning. WebAuction uses a simple database schema and queries. The database schema uses simple and portable data types, and tables are simple enough not to require database administration skills to understand.

However, production applications often require a database expert's skills. The database physical schema can be tuned to increase performance, for example, creating indexes to speed queries. A production application should also take advantage of the database's query optimizer and how it creates execution plans for the application's main operations. Sometimes a knowledgeable database administrator can make changes in the schema or queries that allow the optimizer to greatly improve performance. While database tuning is out of this book's scope, it should not be discounted when developing production sites.

Assembling the Application Components: WebAuction

This section covers how to assemble your application components, including Web applications and EJB jars, into an *enterprise archive*, or *.ear* file. Enterprise archives are the J2EE standard for packaging application components and deployment information into a single package, which can then be deployed on WebLogic Server or any other application server supporting J2EE.

About Enterprise Archives

Enterprise archives make it easier to archive, package, and distribute your application code because everything is in a single file. Enterprise archive filenames have the extension *.ear*. An enterprise archive includes *everything* required to deploy the application code on an application server.

Like a Web archive, an enterprise archive is a type of *.jar* file, created with the `jar` utility. The archive also includes a J2EE *application deployment descriptor* that describes how the enterprise application is to be deployed. Finally, an enterprise archive may also include *libraries* referenced by J2EE modules, Help files, and documentation.

The XML-formatted package deployment descriptor (*application.xml*) represents the top-level view of an enterprise archive's contents. The J2EE application deployment descriptor uses the special XML document type definition (DTD) specified by the J2EE standards.

Enterprise Archive Organization

Enterprise archive organization is arbitrary. However, the *application.xml* deployment descriptor must be located in a subdirectory named *META-INF* under the root directory of the enterprise archive. So, an enterprise archive that includes one EJB jar and two Web archives would have a directory hierarchy like this:

```
/my_ejb.jar
/one_web.war
/two_web.war
/META-INF/application.xml
```

Another file called the *manifest* is located in the *META-INF* directory. This file lists all the components that are in the *.jar* file so that the `jar` utility can recognize the components that it must unpack when extracting components from the *.jar* file.

Writing application.xml

The *application.xml* file is the central registry for all the components in the enterprise archive. The application server looks at each entry to configure the application deployment correctly. Here is a simple *application.xml* file, which is the deployment descriptor used for the WebAuction application:

```
<?xml version="1.0"  encoding="UTF-8"?>
<!DOCTYPE application PUBLIC
'-//Sun Microsystems, Inc.//DTD J2EE Application 1.2//EN'
'http://java.sun.com/j2ee/dtds/application_1_2.dtd'>

<application>
  <display-name>WebAuction</display-name>
  <description>WebLogic Server WebAuction</description>
  <module>
    <web>
      <web-url>auction_web.war</web-url>
      <context-root>auction</context-root>
    </web>
  </module>
  <module>
    <ejb>auction_ejb.jar</ejb>
  </module>
</application>
```

Notice that we have first defined this as an XML document and indicated the DTD, which specifies the format and contents of the XML document.

The `<application>` tag signifies that we are describing an entire application configuration. Next comes a display name and a description of the application. Then, two modules are defined using the `<module>` tag. The first is a Web module, located in the file *auction_web.war*. For this Web application, the root of the URL where it would be deployed is included using the `<context-root>` tag. In this case, the Web archive is deployed in the auction subdirectory of the application server. The URL to access the application from a Web browser would be *http://server name:portnumber/ auction/*.

The second `<module>` tag names an EJB module, *auction_ejb.jar*. Nothing need be done to link modules. Remember, the Web application descriptor includes information on the EJB resources on which it relies.

Be careful with capitalization when building your deployment descriptor, application.xml. XML is case-sensitive.

Packaging the Enterprise Archive (.ear)

In this section we cover how to create an *.ear* file using WebLogic Server. If you want to practice creating an archive, use the following steps. Otherwise, skip to the next section, "Quick Deployment of the WebAuction Application."

Step 0: Configure the Working Environment

Assuming you've performed a standard installation of BEA WebLogic Server, you'll find that you frequently need to set or check your environment variables. Environment variable settings do not carry over from one session to another, or from one command shell to another.

To configure your environment to run the WebLogic Server tools correctly for a database-connected application such as WebAuction, execute the *setExamplesEnv.cmd* script included in the *examples* directory:

```
c:\bea\wlserver6.0\config\examples\setExamplesEnv.cmd
```

You should see something like Figure 14–5.

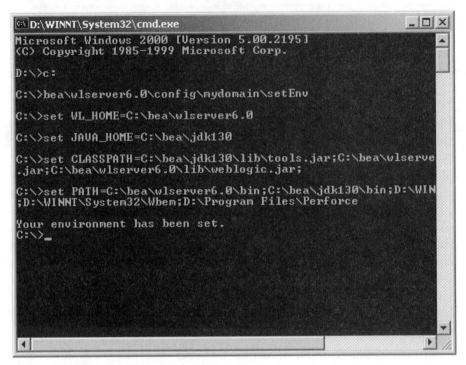

Figure 14–5 Setting the Examples Environment

In Figure 14–5, WebLogic Server is installed on the C: drive. Your installation location might differ.

Step 1: Create Directory and Copy Application Components

Create an empty directory on your file system. This example uses the directory *c:\e-archive*.

Copy the application components into this directory: *application.xml*, *auction_ejb.jar*, and *auction_web.war*. Remember to put *application.xml* in the subdirectory named *META-INF*. You should have a directory structure like Figure 14–6.

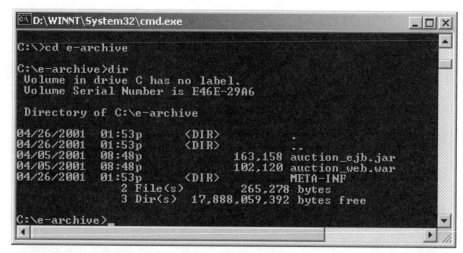

Figure 14–6 Copying the Components for the Archive

Step 2: Create the New Enterprise Archive

Use the `jar` utility to create a new enterprise archive named *auction.ear*. If the jar utility is not recognized, re-run the default `setEnv.cmd` script with:

```
bea\wlserver6.0\config\mydomain\setEnv.cmd
```

The following command creates a new archive from all the contents of the current directory:

```
jar cvf auction.ear *
```

You should see something like Figure 14–7 in your command shell.

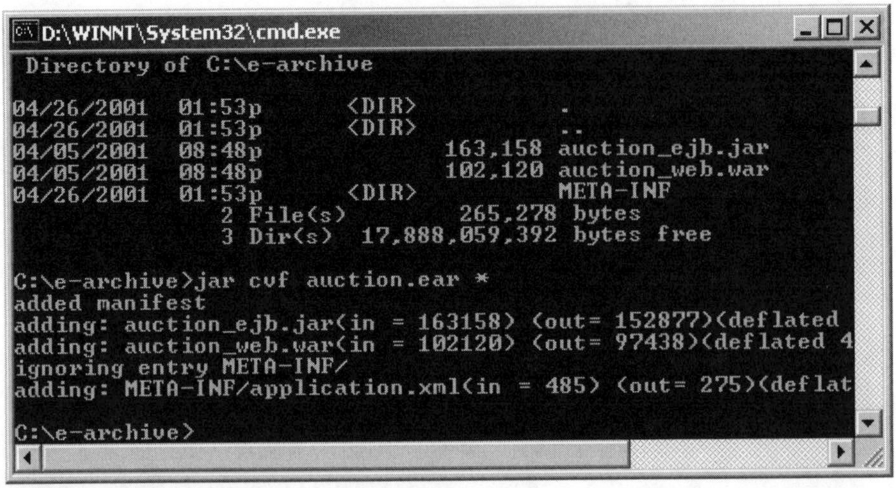

Figure 14-7 Creating the Enterprise Archive

You now have an enterprise archive that can be placed into WebLogic Server's applications directory and automatically deployed.

The process used to create the enterprise archive described here is included in the scripts supplied with the WebAuction application build and deployment, covered in the next section.

Quick Deployment of the WebAuction Application

You can quickly deploy the WebAuction application if you install it in the default directory *C:\bea\wlserver6.0*.

Be sure that you have installed the EJB 2.0 Upgrade if you're using WebLogic Server Version 6.0. WebLogic Server Version 6.0 and the EJB 2.0 Upgrade are included on the CD-ROM that accompanies this book. Copy the EJB 2.0 upgrade file into the *bea\wlserver6.0\lib* directory. Complete instructions for installing the Server, the Service Pack, and the EJB upgrade are on the accompanying CD-ROM. The WebLogic Server documentation is on-line at *http://e-docs.bea.com/wls/docs60/*.

First, copy the *WebAuction.zip* file from the directory *book\webauction*. Put it in a new directory named *c:\webauction*.

Make sure to name the quick deployment directory "webauction", all lowercase. Case is significant to the build script.

In a new command shell, set your environment by running the following in a command line:

```
C:\bea\wlserver6.0\config\mydomain\setEnv.cmd
```

Use the `jar` utility to unpack the WebAuction application:

```
jar xvf *.zip
```

Now, run the quick deploy script *quick-deploy.bat* in the directory *c: webauction* you created. This script sets your environment, populates the database correctly, copies modified XML configuration files to the examples server, and builds the WebAuction application enterprise archive (*.ear* file):

```
quick-deploy.bat
```

Visit the following URL with your Web browser after the server starts (watch the Console window to see when the server starts): *http:// 127.0.0.1:7001/auction/*.

Note that the name of the application in the URL is "auction".

The WebAuction application should then compile, and display the following (see Figure 14–8).

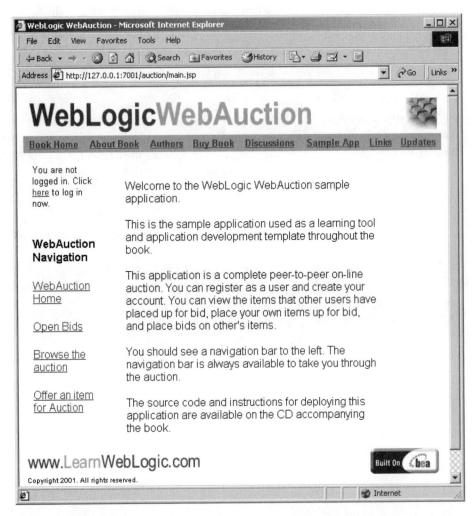

Figure 14–8   WebAuction Home Page

Why does the compilation take so long? Our experience indicates that the Sun Microsystems native compiler included with the WebLogic Server Java Development Kit (JDK) for Windows and other platforms is less efficient than it might be. You should consider replacing the Java compiler. Some options include:

- sj, which is the Symantec Java compiler available with WebGain Studio as part of their Java development environment (*http://www.webgain.com*).

- `jikes`, which is available for free from IBM. This is one of the fastest and most efficient compilers around. It also adheres more strictly to the Java language specifications (*http://oss.software. ibm.com/developerworks/opensource/jikes/project/*)

Deploying the WebAuction Application: In Detail

In the previous deployment example, a prebuilt configuration file was automatically copied into your examples directory, and the existing configuration file was archived. In a real-world situation, you would need to configure your server through the WebLogic Server console. Full details of the steps required are included in this section.

To begin, shut down the Examples Server and open a command shell.

Step 0: Configure the Environment

To configure your environment to run the tools correctly, open a Windows command shell and execute the *setEnv.cmd* script as you did before.

```
C:\bea\wlserver6.0\config\mydomain\setEnv.cmd
```

You should see something like Figure 14–9.

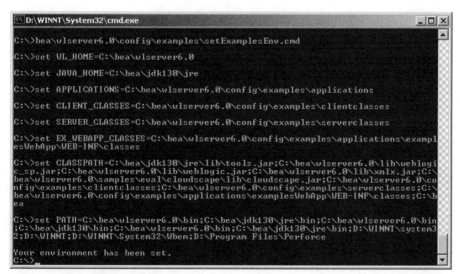

Figure 14–9   Setting the Environment

In Figure 14–9, WebLogic Server is installed on the C: drive. Your installation location may differ.

Step 1: Install WebLogic Server and WebAuction Code

If you have not done so already, install WebLogic Server 6.0, and the EJB 2.0 Upgrade from the CD-ROM accompanying this book. Use the installation wizards, entering information as prompted.

Next, copy the WebAuction code from the file *WebAuction.zip* into an empty directory named, for example, *c:\webauction*.

Navigate to the WebAuction directory (see Figure 14–10).

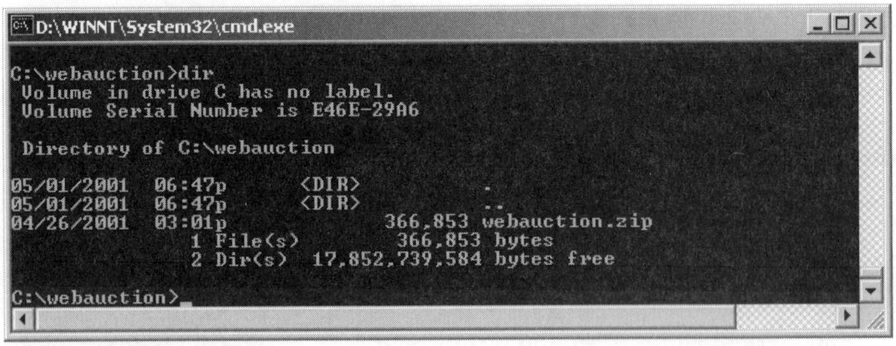

```
D:\WINNT\System32\cmd.exe

C:\webauction>dir
 Volume in drive C has no label.
 Volume Serial Number is E46E-29A6

 Directory of C:\webauction

05/01/2001  06:47p       <DIR>          .
05/01/2001  06:47p       <DIR>          ..
04/26/2001  03:01p               366,853 webauction.zip
               1 File(s)         366,853 bytes
               2 Dir(s)   17,852,739,584 bytes free

C:\webauction>
```

Figure 14–10   Listing of the WebAuction Directory

As you did for the quick deploy, use the `jar` utility to unpack the application (see Figure 14–11).

```
jar xvf *.zip
```

You should see a complete listing of the contents of the *.zip* file.

Figure 14–11   Extracting the WebAuction Application Components

As noted, it is essential that you use a directory named webauction for this deployment.

Step 2: Configure Cloudscape

In this step, configure the Cloudscape database (included) and insert the database tables required for the WebAuction application. We need to accomplish four basic tasks:

2a. Configure the environment correctly.

2b. Configure and populate Cloudscape data.

2c. Configure the JDBC connection pool.

2d. Configure a DataSource based on the JDBC pool created in step 1b (following), which will be used by the WebAuction EJBs.

Note: Steps 2a and 2b can be automated: Run the script named cloudscape-tables.bat from the WebAuction directory that you created in the previous steps. If you use this automated command script, which is recommended, review steps 2a and 2b (following) to understand what is going on.

Step 2a: Configure the Cloudscape Environment

To configure the Cloudscape tables and data, use the command-line `ij` utility included with Cloudscape. Run this utility from a command shell.

Since you're dealing with the database, set your environment with

```
bea\wlserver6.0\config\examples\setExamplesenv.cmd
```

The `ij` utility included with Cloudscape enables you to use a command-line interface to modify the contents of an instance of Cloudscape. To start the `ij` utility and affect the correct data store, you must first change your working directory to the location of the Cloudscape data. If you installed WebLogic Server on your C: drive, this directory would be:

```
C:\bea\wlserver6.0\samples\eval\cloudscape\data>
```

You should see something like Figure 14–12 if you do a directory listing.

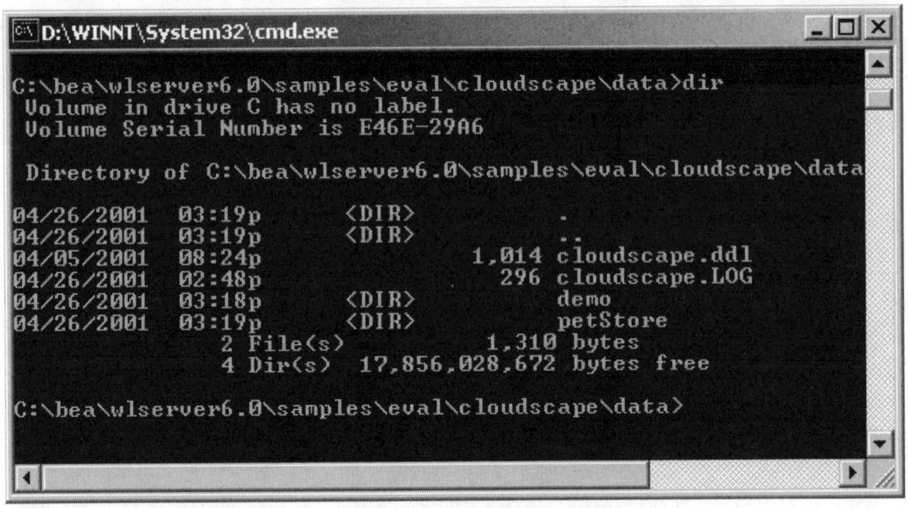

Figure 14–12   Listing of the Cloudscape Data Directory

Next, type the following (all on one line) and press Enter to run the `ij` utility:

```
"java -classpath %CLASSPATH%;..\lib\tools.jar COM.cloud-
scape.tools.ij"
```

The –`classpath` setting makes the `ij` utility known to the Java interpreter. After entering this command, you should see Figure 14–13.

Figure 14–13 Launching the Cloudscape ij Tool

The Cloudscape `ij` tool is now ready for use.

As a shortcut to launching the `ij` tool, run *cloudscape-ij.bat*.

Step 2b: Run the Database Population Commands

In Chapter 5, *Using Databases and Transactions with JDBC and JTA*, we used the command-line interface for Cloudscape to create the database instance and populate it with data. For the WebAuction application, the appropriate Cloudscape SQL commands are included in a file as part of the WebAuction package.

We need to create a number of tables and remove any existing tables. The complete set of commands is located in the file *cloudscape-tables.bat*, which should be located in the directory where you unpacked the WebAuction components.

The commands in this script are executed sequentially by the `ij` tool. First, the script instructs Cloudscape to drop (remove) all existing tables that share the same names as those to be used by WebAuction:

```
DROP TABLE usertable;
DROP TABLE itemtable_seq;
DROP TABLE itemtable;
DROP TABLE bidtable;
DROP TABLE aclentries;
DROP TABLE groupmembers;
DROP TABLE users;
```

After dropping tables, we reconstruct them using CREATE SQL commands:

```
CREATE TABLE usertable (username varchar(40) primary key, first-
name varchar(40), lastname varchar(40), street varchar(40), city
varchar(40), zipcode varchar(40), email varchar(40));

CREATE TABLE itemtable_seq (seqNo integer);

CREATE table itemtable (id integer primary key, description
varchar(128), category varchar(128), userkey varchar(128), end-
date date, topbidamount float);
```

```
CREATE table bidtable (id integer primary key, itemkey integer,
userkey varchar(128), amount float);

CREATE TABLE aclentries (A_NAME varchar(255), A_PRINCIPAL var-
char(255), A_PERMISSION varchar(255));

CREATE TABLE groupmembers (GM_GROUP varchar(255), GM_MEMBER var-
char(255));

CREATE TABLE users (U_NAME varchar(255), U_PASSWORD var-
char(255));
```

Because Cloudscape does not support the SEQUENCE datatype, which is supported by other databases, WebAuction must emulate it. To begin, initialize the table to be used for the sequence with a starting value of 1:

```
INSERT INTO itemtable_seq VALUES (1);
```

Then, run ij and instruct it to execute the following set of commands contained in the *cloudscape.ij* file:

```
copy ejb\cloudscape.ddl c:\bea\wlserver6.0\samples\eval\cloud-
scape\data

cd c:\bea\wlserver6.0\samples\eval\cloudscape\data

java -Dij.connection.toursDB=jdbc:cloudscape:webauction;cre-
ate=true -classpath %CLASSPATH%;..\lib\tools.jar COM.cloud-
scape.tools.ij cloudscape.ddl
```

For your convenience, these commands are included in the script *cloudscape-tables.bat* in the root directory of the WebAuction package. To run the script, exit from the ij tool with Control-C, start the Examples Server (from the Windows Start menu or equivalent), and run *cloudscape-tables.bat* in a command shell. When the script executes, you should see the results in Figure 14–14.

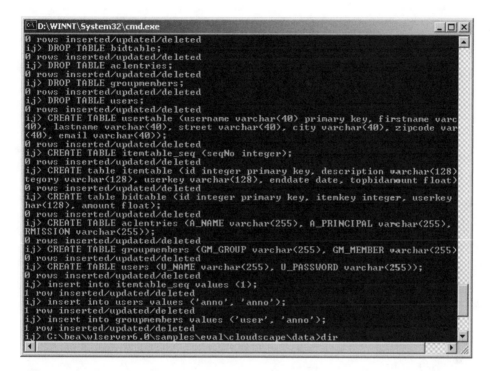

Figure 14–14   Populating the Database

Congratulations. Your database instance is now properly configured for the WebAuction application.

Step 2c: Configure the Database Connection Pool in WebLogic Server

Use the Examples Server and the default console to configure the database connection pool. If necessary, start the WebLogic Server using the Start Examples Server option on the Windows Start menu. It's under the Examples menu item.

Examples Server: Connection Pool is Preconfigured

The Examples Server already has the Cloudscape connection configured. You can view this by starting the WebLogic Server console and clicking on the Start Default Console option in the Windows Start menu. A Web browser should appear with the console in it. Click on the Connection Pools option underneath the JDBC menu item (see Figure 14–15).

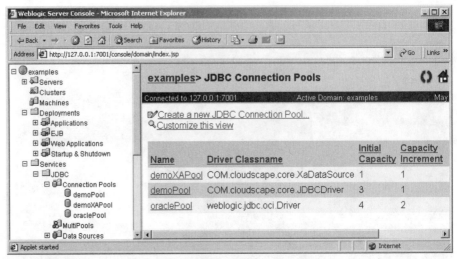

Figure 14–15   Viewing the Pre-Configure Cloudscape Connection Pool

You can see that three database connection pools are already configured. We are going to use the pool named demoPool, the JDBC pool we use to create a JDBC DataSource in the next section. Click on the link for more information. You should see Figure 14-16, which contains all of the configuration options for the database connection pool.

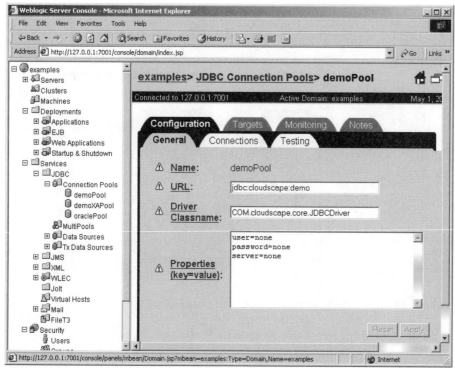

Figure 14–16 JDBC Connection Pools

You also can click on the Connections tab and change the number of connections to the database if you desire. In this case, the number of database connections has been modified to 3. If you modify the number of connections, you will need to restart the server (see Figure 14–17).

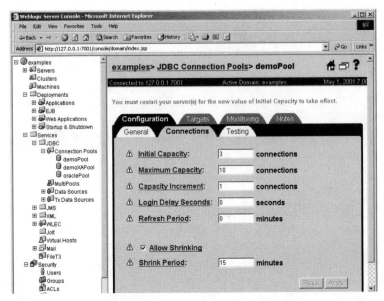

Figure 14–17   Modifying the Capacity of a Connection Pool

Step 2d: Configure DataSource in WebLogic Server

The WebAuction application uses a JDBC `DataSource` abstraction. As specified in the EJB deployment descriptors (*weblogic-ejb-jar.xml* and *weblogic-cmp-rdbms.xml*), the `DataSource` to be used is the `examples-dataSource-demoPool`. This `DataSource` is specified multiple times for the CMP EJBs specified in *weblogic-cmp-rdbms.xml*. Here's a subsection of the *weblogic-cmp-rdbms.xml* deployment descriptor:

```
<?xml version="1.0"?>

<!DOCTYPE weblogic-rdbms-jar PUBLIC
 '-//BEA Systems, Inc.//DTD WebLogic Server 6.0.0 EJB RDBMS Per-
sistence//EN'
 'http://www.bea.com/servers/wls600/dtd/weblogic-rdbms20-persis-
tence-600.dtd'>

<weblogic-rdbms-jar>
  <weblogic-rdbms-bean>
    <ejb-name>UserEJB</ejb-name>
    <data-source-name>examples-dataSource-demoPool</data-source-
name>
    <table-name>usertable</table-name>

    <field-map>
```

```
      <cmp-field>userName</cmp-field>
      <dbms-column>username</dbms-column>
    </field-map>
    <field-map>
      <cmp-field>firstName</cmp-field>
      <dbms-column>firstname</dbms-column>
    </field-map>
    <field-map>
      <cmp-field>lastName</cmp-field>
      <dbms-column>lastname</dbms-column>
    </field-map>
    <field-map>
      <cmp-field>streetAddress</cmp-field>
      <dbms-column>street</dbms-column>
    </field-map>
    <field-map>
      <cmp-field>city</cmp-field>
      <dbms-column>city</dbms-column>
    </field-map>
    <field-map>
      <cmp-field>zipCode</cmp-field>
      <dbms-column>zipcode</dbms-column>
    </field-map>
    <field-map>
      <cmp-field>email</cmp-field>
      <dbms-column>email</dbms-column>
    </field-map>

  </weblogic-rdbms-bean>

  <weblogic-rdbms-bean>
    <ejb-name>BidEJB</ejb-name>
    <data-source-name>examples-dataSource-demoPool</data-source-
name>
    <table-name>bidtable</table-name>
      .
      .
      .
```

To view the DataSource settings, click the Data Sources item in the left-hand navigation panel of your WebLogic Server console (see Figure 14–18).

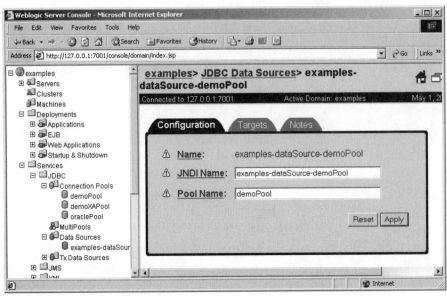

Figure 14–18   DataSource Settings

To deploy this application against a different database, you must change both the JDBC Connection Pool settings and the `DataSource` settings, using the WebLogic Server console.

Step 3: Configure JavaMail

If necessary, re-start the Examples Server. As you recall, WebAuction uses JavaMail to send emails to confirm the acceptance of bids into the system. JavaMail requires that a mail session be created and stored in JNDI. Whenever JavaMail needs to send an email, it locates the appropriate mail session. WebAuction requires the JavaMail session to be bound to the name `Mail-Session`, which is specified in the `BidReceiverBean.java` and the other components that use the `MailSender` utility class included in the WebAuction.

To view the mail session entries for WebLogic Server, find the "mail" entry in the console navigation panel (see Figure 14–19).

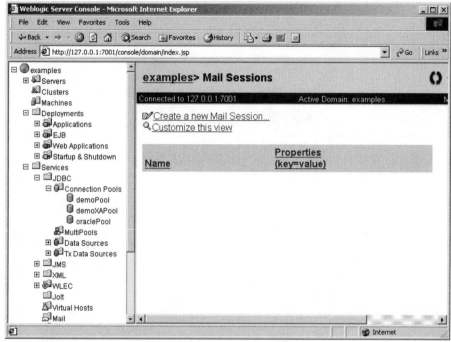

Figure 14–19 Mail Sessions

You should see that no mail sessions are configured in the server. You need to create a mail session by clicking on Create a New Mail Session (see Figure 14–20).

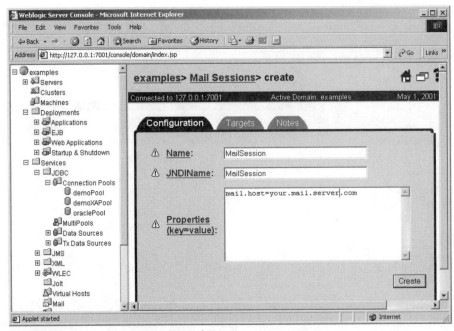

Figure 14-20   Creating a New Mail Session

The new mail session must have identical names (Name, JNDIName) to those specified in the WebAuction application `BidReceiverBean`. This code looks in JNDI to find the object under the name `MailSession`. In addition to specifying `MailSession` for both the mail session name and the JNDI name, you need to specify the properties for your mail server, for example:

```
mail.host=learnweblogic.com
```

Replace the value `your.mail.server.com` with the host name of your mail server.

After entering these values, click the Create button.

Now that the mail session is created, you need to make sure that it is deployed on your server. To do that, click on the Targets tab (see Figure 14–21).

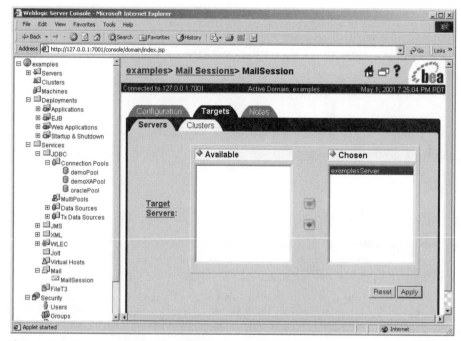

Figure 14–21 Moving the Examples Server to the Chosen Target

Move the Examples server to the Chosen Servers panel. Click Apply.
You now have configured a JavaMail session.

Step 4: Configure JMS

In this step, you configure JMS. We need to accomplish four basic tasks:

4a. Create JMS connection factories.

4b. Create JMS message templates.

4c. Create a JMS server.

4d. Create JMS queues.

The WebAuction application requires JMS for a number of its services
including processing incoming bids and outgoing e-mails. This is all defined
in the *ejb-jar.xml* deployment descriptor. We need to configure WebLogic
Server to offer the services specified in this deployment descriptor.

The following subsection of this file defines the message-driven EJBs and
the JMS destination to which they are attached. Note also that this deployment descriptor specifies the JNDI names to be used for the different
resources available using the `<resource-ref>` tag:

```
<message-driven>
    <ejb-name>BidReceiverEJB</ejb-name>
```

```
<ejb-class>webauction.ejb.BidReceiverBean</ejb-class>
<transaction-type>Container</transaction-type>
<message-driven-destination>
   <jms-destination-type>javax.jms.Queue</jms-destination-
type>
   </message-driven-destination>
```
.
.

The value specified by the `<resource-env-ref-name>` tag is the JNDI name under which the resource will be available to the application. As we create the configuration for WebLogic Server and these JMS destinations, those are the names that will be used for JNDI.

Step 4a: Create JMS File Store

You need to configure WebLogic Server to store your JMS messages. In this case, use the JMS file store (be sure to create its directory first, in the file system). You could also use a database.

To create a new JMS file store, open the WebLogic Server console and click on the Stores option in the left-hand navigation panel. In the right-hand panel, you should see the option to create a new JMS file store. Click on it. In the new window, choose the directory for your file store (see Figure 14–22).

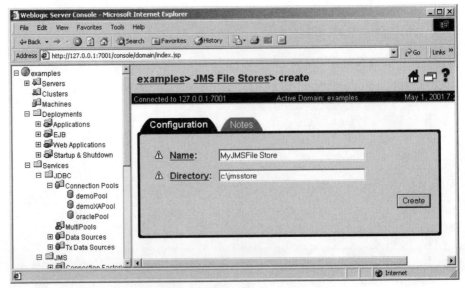

Figure 14–22   Creating the JMS File Store

This directory can be named anything that you wish, for example *jmsstore*. Note that WebLogic Server does not create this directory automatically.

To create the directory, use either a command shell or Windows Explorer to create a new folder.

Step 4b: Create JMS Server

We need to create a JMS server type that can be deployed on either a local or remote server. Let's deploy this one on the server running on your machine.

To create a new JMS server type, click on the Servers option under the JMS section in the navigation panel. For both the Store and Temporary Template options, choose the file store and templates that you created in the previous steps. Click Apply and wait for "document done" (see Figure 14–23).

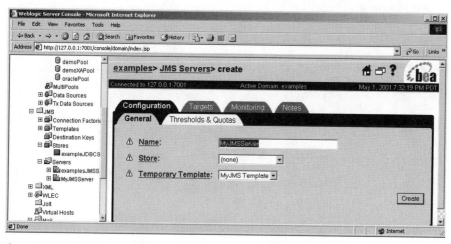

Figure 14-23   Creating the JMS Server

Do not restart your server yet. First, deploy the JMS server you just created. Choose the Targets option at the top of the right-hand panel to make the Examples Server the target of the JMS Server you just created (see Figure 14–24).

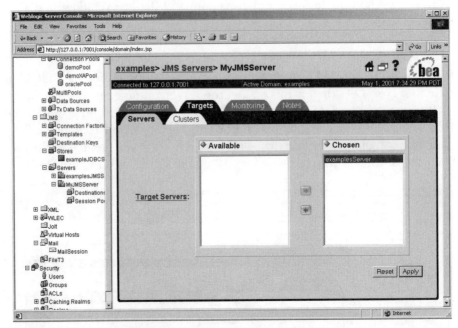

Figure 14–24 Mapping the JMS Server to the Examples Server

After moving the Examples server to the Chosen Servers panel, click Apply. If all goes well, you should see the results in Figure 14–25.

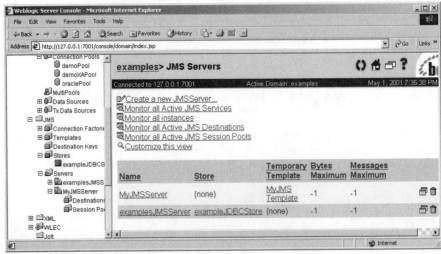

Figure 14–25 Viewing MyJMSServer in the List

You have now created a new JMS server. Finally, add the two *JMS queues*, "Bids" and "OutGoingMailQueue", that are required for the application.

Step 4c: Create JMS Queues

Now that the JMS server instance has been configured, create the queues required by the WebAuction application in the server. To do this, click on Destinations underneath the name of the server that you created in the previous step. Click on Create a New JMS Queue (see Figure 14–26).

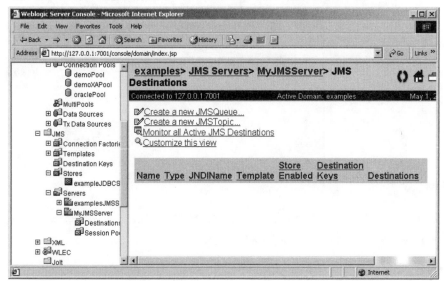

Figure 14–26   Creating JMS Queues

You should be presented with a form enabling you to enter the name and JNDI name for the queue. Assign the JNDI name "Bids". The queue name only represents how the queue will appear in the console (see Figure 14–27). Repeat this process to create "OutgoingMailQueue".

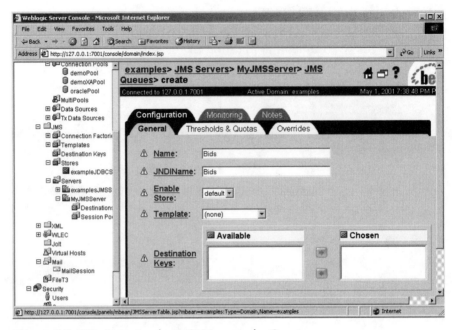

Figure 14–27 Assigning the JNDI Name to the Queue

Step 5: Configure Security

The WebAuction application uses the *Relational Database Management System (RDBMS) realm* to store security information. In addition, the WebLogic Server caching realm is used on top of the RDBMS realm. This enables a configurable security cache to exist.

In this step, you configure the security settings for the WebAuction application on the Examples server. We need to accomplish three basic tasks:

5a. Create the RDBMS instance.

5b. Create the caching realm instance.

5c. Instruct WebLogic Server to use the caching realm.

Step 5a: Create the RDBMS Realm Instance

A number of RDBMS realm instances are already created in the Examples server configuration. Because the RDBMS realm for Cloudscape is already instantiated and chosen, you should use Cloudscape as the database for this example. To view the Cloudscape configuration, choose the Realms option under the Security option in the left-hand navigation panel (see Figure 14–28).

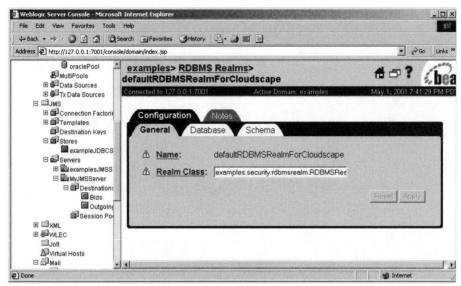

Figure 14–28   Creating the RDBMS Realm Instance

You can choose the different tabs in the right-hand panel of the console to view the database options and schema for the RDBMS realm using Cloudscape. In addition, different realm configurations are supplied for databases other than Cloudscape. In a real-world situation, you would copy the configuration for these realms into an empty server.

Step 5b: Configure the Caching Realm

We need to specify that WebLogic Server's caching realm should use the RDBMS realm. To do this, choose the Caching Realm option in the left-hand navigation panel under security. You can see that the RDBMS is already chosen as the underlying realm for the caching realm. In a real-world situation, you would use the RDBMS realm that you created in step 5a here, and assign it to the caching realm. Nothing needs to be changed in the Example server to link these together (see Figure 14–29).

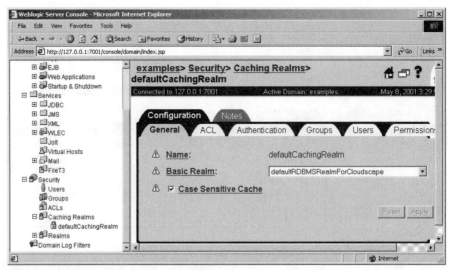

Figure 14–29   Configuring the Caching Realm

Step 5c: Instruct WebLogic Server to Use the Caching Realm

Finally, we need to instruct WebLogic Server to use the caching realm configuration we have defined as its default realm. Click on the main Security menu item in the left-hand navigation panel. You can see an option for the Caching Realm. Choose the caching realm that we just specified, the `defaultCachingRealm` (see Figure 14–30).

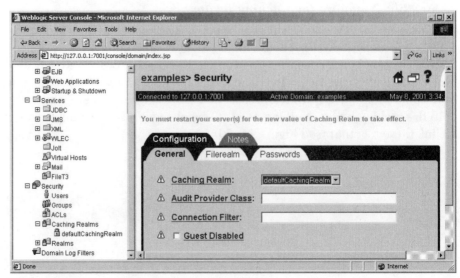

Figure 14–30   Choosing the Caching Realm

At this point, your server is properly configured and ready for the WebAuction code to be deployed.

Now, stop and then restart your server in order to apply all the changes that have been made to the configuration.

Step 6: Build and Deploy the WebAuction Application

The WebAuction application directory includes a build and deployment script. Change back to the directory that you created in Step 1 for the WebAuction source code and configuration files, *c:\webauction*. (If you open another command shell, re-run the *bea\wlserver6.0\config\mydomain\set-Env.cmd* script just to make sure that your environment is still configured correctly. When you run a script to set the environment, it only applies to your currently running shell.)

Next, stop the WebLogic Server.

Then, run the build script from *c:\webauction* by typing "build.bat".

When you restart the WebLogic Server, you'll see that the WebAuction application has been automatically deployed. You can visit it by opening *http://127.0.0.1:7001/auction/* in your Web browser. Note that the application name in the URL is "auction".

You should see the WebAuction application in your browser window.

Deploying the WebAuction on Another Database

To deploy the WebAuction application on a database other than Cloudscape, you must make three changes from the process previously described. In this section, we will configure WebAuction for Oracle Version 8 running on Windows 2000.

Step 1: Run the Database Population Commands

Instead of using Cloudscape's i j utility, you need to use the utility specific to your database. For Oracle, this is the SQL*Plus utility. Consult your database documentation for more information.

When populating your database, use the table creation commands specific to your database. With the WebAuction application, the SQL required to set up the correct database schema is included for Oracle, Postgres, and Cloud-scape. These scripts are located in the EJB subdirectory.

After the installation of Oracle has been completed, use SQL*Plus to enter the commands to populate the database. The simplest way to do this is to load the *oracle.ddl* database commands into the Windows Clipboard by opening the file in a text editor and copying it. Then, paste these commands into the SQL*Plus client using the Paste command in the Edit menu (see Figure 14–31).

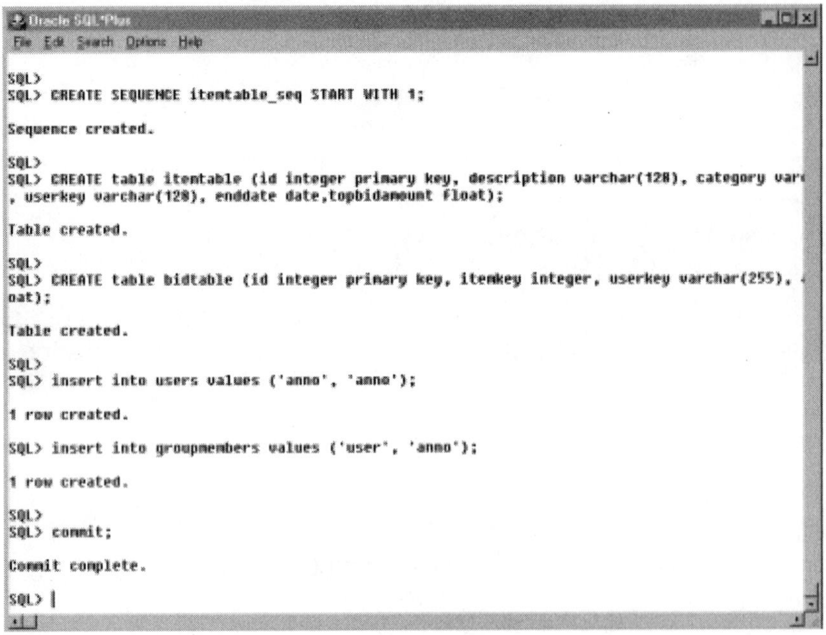

Figure 14–31 Populating the Oracle Database

After pasting in the database population commands, you can see that each command has entered correctly. Oracle also supports using a text file as input.

Step 2: Configure the Database Connection Pool in WebLogic Server

In the WebLogic Server console, configure the database connection pool to point to your Oracle database instance. Examples and instructions on how to configure the database instance connectivity are included with the WebLogic Server console documentation, in the configuration examples.

To configure WebLogic Server to use its Type 4 JDBC driver to connect to Oracle, open the WebLogic Server console and select JDBC connection pools in the navigation panel. Select the option to create a new `connec-tionPool`. You should see a form to enter new values for the connection pool (see Figure 14–32).

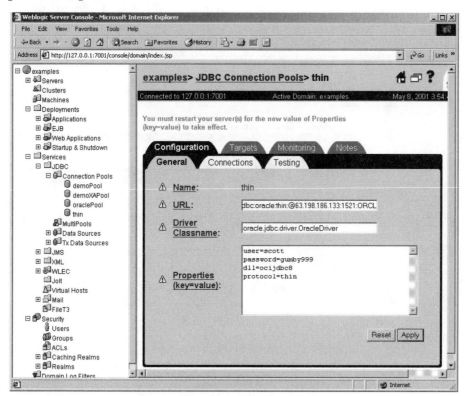

Figure 14–32 Configuring the Database Connection Pool

In Figure 14–32, we created a new JDBC pool named "thin". For the URL, enter "jdbc:oracle:thin:@63.198.186.133:1521:ORCL".

The first part of the URL specifies that we are using the Oracle `thin` driver, which is included and installed with WebLogic Server. The values after the @ symbol specify the IP address of the database server, the port on which it is listening, and the database instance that we are accessing. In this case, we are accessing a server at IP address 63.198.186.133, port 1521, with an instance name of ORCL. Enter the Driver classname and the properties, as shown. Restart the Server.

Step 3: Create the RDBMS Realm Instance

For the RDBMS realm, select and enter the database of your choice. Examples of how to configure the RDBMS realm for databases such as

Cloudscape, Oracle, and Microsoft SQL Server are included in the Examples server console.

To configure the RDBMS realm for Oracle, it is easiest to copy the configuration out of the Examples server installation distributed with WebLogic Server (see Figure 14–33).

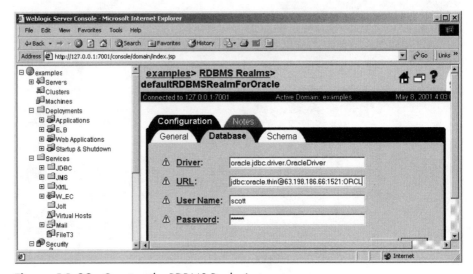

Figure 14–33   Creating the RDBMS Realm Instance

Copy the configuration from the Examples Server ("scott", "gumby999", etc.). Replace the values for the driver entry and correctly configure the URL, user name, and password. After doing this, make sure that the caching realm that you are using points to this RDBMS realm.

Testing the WebAuction Application

When developing and deploying a WebLogic Server application, you want to make sure that the application performs as expected. It should present a user interface that functions as expected. When many requests come in simultaneously, your deployment should scale to meet the needs of your users.

The testing process assures that the application will perform as expected when it is deployed. In most organizations, this process is called quality assurance (QA). The QA group designs, implements, and runs tests for each new release to ensure that the application continues to meet defined quality standards.

Every organization will have different requirements and different styles for testing their WebLogic Server applications. There is no universal testing methodology that addresses the needs of every environment. However, it is important you understand that QA is a key component of the Web application development process. It is unlikely that the procedures used in this section will apply exactly to your deployment. However, you should model the thought processes described in the following sections as you define your own QA process, suitable to your environment.

In this section, we discuss two types of application testing:

- *Functional testing*, which ensures that the application functions as expected
- *Stress and performance testing*, which ensures that the application performs as expected under heavy load and real-world conditions

We cover the methodology for implementing both of these types of testing, and illustrate the testing process through the use of third-party tools.

Functional Testing

Functional testing ensures that the application performs as expected. For example, if someone enters a bid, then that bid should appear in the auction system. You implement functional testing in order to isolate any bugs in the application. You should design your tests to be repeatable, so that they can be applied to new versions of your application as they are developed.

Functional Testing Methodology

There are three major steps in the functional testing of WebLogic Server Web applications:

1. *Define scope of testing*. Define the areas and features of your application that should be tested. These areas should be listed in a document or otherwise captured, so that everyone involved in the project is aware of the goals of your functional testing. Tests for the WebAuction application include features such as:
   - Can a user create a new account?
   - Is a user who creates a new account automatically logged in?

- Can a user submit a bid that is less than $0?
- Can two users have the same user name?
- And so forth.

2. *Design tests.* After you define the scope of your testing, design tests that will address all the features to be tested. For WebAuction, create tests to assess the functional questions previously listed:

  - Allow a user to create a new account; then verify the account exists.
  - Allow a user to create a new account; then verify the user has been automatically logged in.
  - Simulate a user entering a bid that is less than $0, and verify that this bid is rejected.
  - Attempt to create two users with the same user name, and verify that the second attempt is rejected.
  - And so on, for all of the functional areas.

3. *Implement and execute tests.* Later in this chapter, we will demonstrate creating and executing a single test case using a Web testing tool on the WebAuction application.

4. *Review results and repeat.* After the tests have been executed, both before your application goes into production and after, you should develop a feedback process that gathers results from testing as well as defects that are found in the real-world deployment. The data that you gain from both testing and defects not located by testing can be used to refine your testing scope and process.

Infrastructure Requirements for Functional Testing

In many organizations, individuals are designated to specialize in QA and testing for applications. These individuals are in charge of developing a test plan, and implementing and executing the test. They're responsible for assuring that the product meets the quality requirements defined by the organization.

Very large organizations might have dozens or even hundreds of QA specialists. In very small organizations, the developers of the product themselves often perform both QA and development roles for the product. Depending on your situation, you should balance your organization's quality requirements with the resources available to meet those requirements.

Most functional testing can be done in a scaled-down manner. Because functional testing is meant to verify that subsets of the application's functionality perform as expected, QA specialists often can perform testing on a single PC, as was the case with the WebAuction functional testing described in this chapter.

Functional Testing Example with the WebAuction Application

In the majority of cases, it makes sense to use third-party, specialized Web testing tools on your applications. Many WebLogic Server developers attempt to write custom test frameworks for their applications. Most discover that off-the-shelf testing tools provide superior functionality and improved efficiency over home-grown tools.

This section shows how to apply functional testing methodology on a single feature of the WebAuction application, and test it using a third-party tool.

Define Scope of Testing

In a real-world testing situation, you would specify the complete scope of testing all the features of the WebAuction application. In this case, we will limit the scope, for the sake of the example, to a single feature.

Here's the feature: WebAuction should reject a user name that's already registered.

Design Tests

Design a test that attempts to create two users with the same user name and verifies that the second attempt is rejected.

Implement and Execute Tests

To implement this test, use the Astra QuickTest product available from Mercury Interactive (*http://www.mercuryinteractive.com/*). A free seven-day evaluation version of this product is available for download. Several other Web application–testing tools perform in much the same way as Astra QuickTest.

The QuickTest product enables you to record user interactions in a Web application, directly from the Web browser. We can record the actions required to create a new user.

First, start the QuickTest product and choose the option for Record. You will be prompted to enter your Web browser preference. Your Web browser will start at the URL you specify (*http://127.0.0.1/auction/*).

Start the WebAuction application and click the link to create a new account. After this is successful, log out of the application and attempt to create another new user with the identical user name and password (see Figure 14–34).

Figure 14–34   WebAuction Rejects a Previously Registered User Name

At this point, you can instruct QuickTest to stop recording your behavior in the browser. The QuickTest application should reappear, now containing all of the steps used in the recording you just created in the left-hand panel (see Figure 14–35).

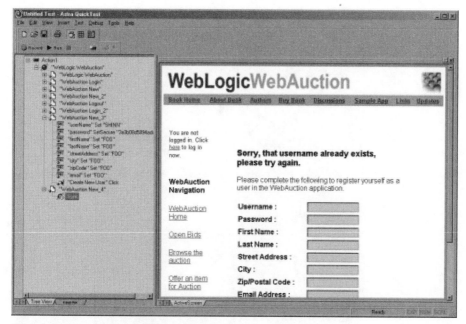

Figure 14–35 QuickTest Record of Application Behavior

To finish the test, instruct QuickTest to verify that we did indeed receive notice that the user name we just attempted already exists. To do this, add in a *checkpoint* that verifies the message "user name already exists" is displayed in the final page of the recording.

To add the checkpoint, click on the final page, which will likely be WebAuctionNew_4 in the left-hand navigation panel of QuickTest. Use the menu bar to instruct QuickTest to insert a new text checkpoint (see Figure 14–36).

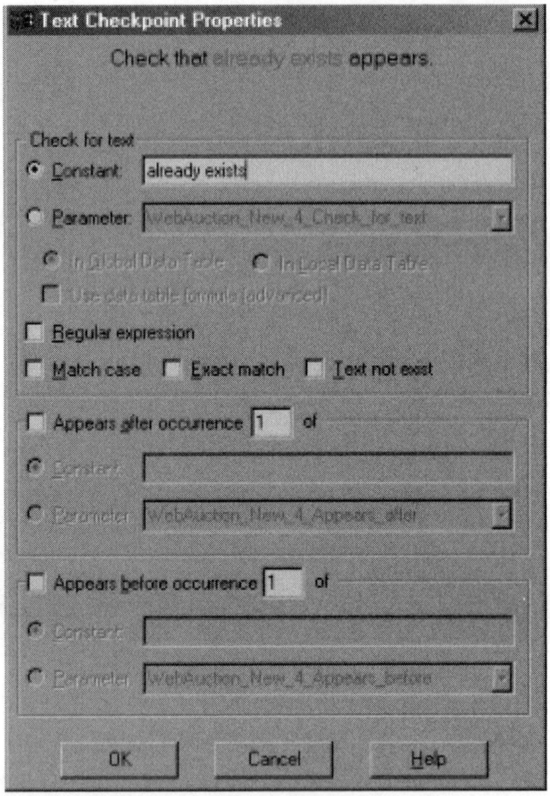

Figure 14–36 Adding a CheckPoint

To execute this test, you should first empty your database of users. You can do this by dropping and then re-adding the database tables. Then, click the Run button at the top of the QuickTest application. You should see a simulated browser run through your entire application, mimicking the steps that you recorded earlier.

Finally, you should see the results of your tests displayed in a report window (see Figure 14–37).

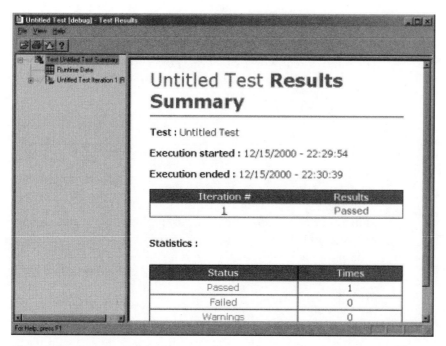

Figure 14-37 Test Results Summary

In this example, we have successfully tested that the application performs as expected when you attempt to create a user whose name already exists. In a real-world situation, you would extend this process to all of the major features of your application.

Stress and Performance Testing

In the previous section, functional testing was used to assure that the WebAuction application performed as expected. It also is important to make sure that your applications perform as expected in high-stress situations. As many users connect to your site simultaneously, your deployment must scale to handle the increased demand. To verify that your application will scale to meet the needs, stress and performance testing attempts to replicate the load that will be placed on your application when it is put into production.

Stress and Performance Testing Methodology

There are four major steps in stress and performance testing with WebLogic Server Web applications:

1. *Define scope of testing.* You must define how you expect users to interact with your application. The purpose of this step is to develop an estimation of how your users will interact with your application in a real-world situation. For example, a simplified interaction model for the WebAuction application could be:
    *   Ninety-five percent of all interactions will either involve no database access (using only *main.jsp*) or simply will browse the items up for auction.
    *   Five percent of all interactions will involve updates to the database (using *newuser.jsp*).
2. *Design tests.* After you define the scope of your testing, you should design tests that represent the interaction model you developed in the previous step. For example, in WebAuction, tests should address the features listed previously:
    *   Simulate many users browsing items simultaneously.
    *   Simulate many users registering for the site simultaneously.
    *   Simulate both user interactions by performing both reads and updates in a single test run.
3. *Implement and execute tests.* The execution parameters of the test should be designed to locate possible bottlenecks or limitations in the architecture of the application and deployment.

For example, tests should be executed and monitored to determine whether an application wastes CPU cycles, requires special WebLogic Server tuning parameters, requires database tuning, and so forth. Limiting factors, such as CPU usage and so forth should be isolated one at a time in testing your application.

Typically, the order that works well in performance testing is to first, attempt to maximize the usage of each resource, and then attempt to make changes to further optimize their use:

*   CPU utilization
*   Memory utilization
*   WebLogic Server `ExecuteThreads`
*   Database utilization and connectivity

Later in this chapter, we will demonstrate creating and executing a single test case using a Web load-testing tool on the WebAuction application.

4. *Review results and repeat.* After the tests have been executed, both before your application goes into production and after, you should develop a feedback process that builds on results from

the tests that you run. In the previous step, tests located possible bottlenecks or limitations in the architecture. In this step, the limitations that you recognize should be analyzed in order to improve the performance of your application. This data also can be used to revise your planning scope, and also to revise your application architecture and implementation as necessary.

In a real-world application, your interaction model could be much more complicated. In the case of the WebAuction application, the interaction model is actually more complex than that previously described. Nonetheless, it is beneficial to make the interaction model for testing as simple as possible, so long as it is not radically different than what will occur during deployment.

For example, the preceding model grouped interactions involving only database reads, and those involving no database access, into a single group. If you tested the capacity of your system to browse items up for auction only, with no testing of the non-database pages, you can be assured that the results will be no worse than testing *main.jsp* by itself. You can then discover what the minimum capacity is of your application.

Infrastructure Requirements for Performance and Stress Testing

The infrastructure requirements for performance and stress testing are much greater than for functional testing. Because you are attempting to simulate how the application will perform under very heavy load, you must create an operating environment that represents your real deployment environment. In most cases, this involves substantial network and hardware infrastructure.

To test performance and stress on the WebAuction application, we used a combination of four 4-CPU Windows NT 4.0 Server machines with 1GB of memory each. Each machine contained four network interface cards (NIC), which connected it to a 32 Port 100Mb Ethernet switch. Standard hardware, including SCSI disks and Intel Pentium II 500Mhz Xeon processors, powered each machine.

In terms of software, an Oracle database instance was installed on one of the machines. This instance was the standard untuned Oracle installation. Two of the machines acted as clients to a third machine, which ran the WebLogic Server deployment (see Figure 14–38).

SYSTEM CONFIGURATION FOR TESTING

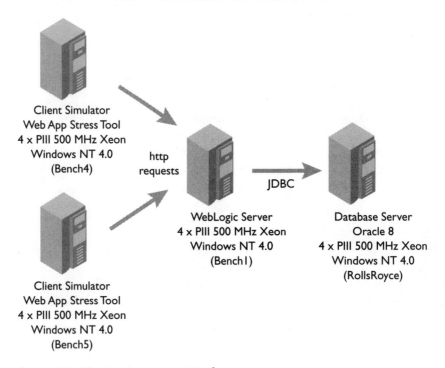

Figure 14–38 Test Environment Configuration

The client machines each ran a load-testing tool available for free from Microsoft, which is called the Microsoft Web Application Stress Tool (WAST). It is a fully functional Web application load-generation tool, which includes the capability to record user interactions through a Web browser, much like Astra QuickTest. In addition, it enables you to simulate many different users, each with a different login and password.

The Microsoft WAST can be downloaded from the Microsoft Web site at *http://homer.rte.microsoft.com*.

Stress and Performance Testing Example with the WebAuction Application

To demonstrate stress and performance testing methodology with the WebAuction application, we follow the steps defined previously.

We will implement, execute, and review the results for each of these tests.

Simulating Browsing

In each client machine, use the recording feature available in the Microsoft WAST to create a script that represents a single user browsing a single category. In this case, every simulated user would make a request for the items available in the books category in the WebAuction.

This test includes visiting a single URL repeatedly to display the items in the books category: *http://bench1:7001/auction/browseitems?cat=books*.

We ran 60-second simulations in which the client machines put heavy load on the server machine. We initially began with 8 client threads each opening 25 sockets to the server. It became apparent that this was not enough load to stress the server CPUs sufficiently. Thus began an iterative process to attempt to locate bottlenecks in the application deployment (see Table 14.1):

Table 14.1 Stress and Performance Test Results

Run	Client Threads	Client Sockets per Thread	WebLogic Server Execute Thread Count	Server Heap Size	WebLogic Server Database Connection Pool Size	Pages per Second	Server CPU Utilization
1	8	25	15 (default)	64MB	15	210	80%
2	24	25	15 (default)	64MB	15	251	83%
3	36	25	15	64MB	15	310	87%
4	48	25	15	64MB	15	320	90%
5	64	25	15	64MB	15	312	93%

After the second run, it became apparent that we were making full utilization of the CPU for the WebLogic Server server instance by looking at the Windows NT processor monitor (see Figure 14–39).

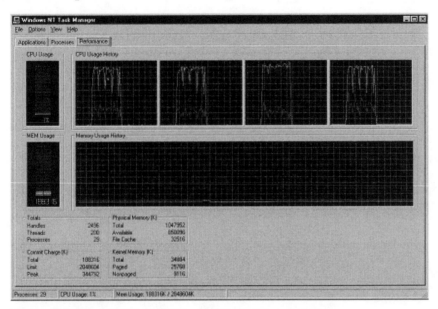

Figure 14–39 CPU Usage for the WebLogic Server Instance

Next, we tested to see if memory utilization was a limiting factor. To test this, we hypothesized that the memory heap size might have been too low. We ran the same test again, but with a greater memory size. We increased the memory to 256MB in the WebLogic Server heap, which is a parameter set in the command line starting WebLogic Server:

```
java -hotspot -Xms64m -Xmx256m -classpath
```

You can edit this value by changing the start scripts used for your WebLogic Server installation. These are found in the \bea\wlserver6.0\config\<servername> directory and are the scripts that are called from the Windows Start menu (see Table 14.2).

Table 14.2 Running the Tests Again with a Greater Heap Size

Run	Client Threads	Client Sockets per Thread	WebLogic Server Execute Thread Count	Server Heap Size	WebLogic Server Database Connection Pool Size	Pages per Second	Server CPU Utilization
6	64	25	15 (default)	256MB	15	254	92%

Because the CPU utilization and the throughput did not change, we can conclude that the application is limited by the CPU in this case and changing the memory size will not likely affect performance greatly. In more complex applications, it is likely that larger heap sizes will be required. The WebAuction application is relatively simple and requires less memory. As you performance test your own applications, modify the heap size to determine how changes affect performance. You can use this data to figure out the appropriate heap sizes for optimum performance.

Next, we modified the number of WebLogic Server *execute threads* inside of WebLogic Server to see if there was *contention* around connections to the database. Contention is a phenomenon that occurs when more than one thread or process of execution attempts to access a resource at the same time. In the case of database connections, disk access, or memory access, only a single Java entity can access that resource at a time. If multiple threads attempt access simultaneously, one will block (sit idle) while waiting for that resource to become available.

Understanding ExecuteThreads

In order to understand the tuning of execute threads, it is helpful to understand the internal architecture of WebLogic Server. At the heart of WebLogic Server is a set of queues, called ExecuteQueues. Each of these queues contains all of the work currently slated for WebLogic Server. This includes work such as creating a new database connection, executing a servlet on behalf of a user, and so forth. Work enters the WebLogic Server system through one of many ways. It can arrive through a request to the servlet engine over HTTP, and a request to the T3/IIOP subsystem for RMI access to objects like EJB, among others.

A pool of Java threads is maintained that does all of the work inside of WebLogic Server and allows for parallel execution of work tasks. These Java threads are called execute threads and their number is determined by the size of the ExecuteThread count in the WebLogic Server configuration. As work arrives and is placed into the execute queue, ExecuteThreads become free and perform the work tasks. When a response to a client is required, the response is handed off to other special threads whose job is to deal with the input and output to the server. The number of those threads is not regularly changed.

Figure 14–40 graphically depicts this process.

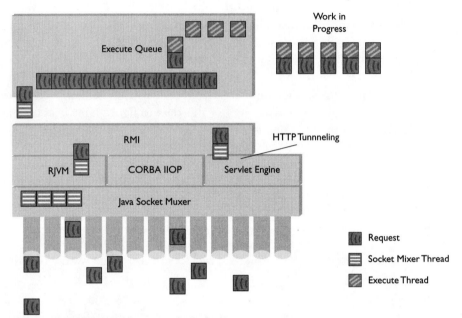

Figure 14–40 Mutiplexing with Threads

Changing the size of the ExecuteThread pool enables you to modify the amount of parallelism possible in your WebLogic Server deployment. But, as is mentioned in the WebLogic Server tuning guide, greater parallelism has a greater cost in terms of thread context switching and memory usage. For this reason, WebLogic Server permits a maximum of 400 execute threads, though virtually all applications will require much less than this.

In most deployments, the default value for the count of ExecuteThreads is sufficient though this parameter should be manipulated slightly during your load-testing process to see if changes can enhance performance of your particular application.

You want your application to avoid contention for resources as much as possible. In WebLogic Server, execute threads are the Java threads that do work on behalf of clients. When work enters WebLogic Server in the form of a request from a user, that work is put on a queue maintained by WebLogic Server. This queue is different than the JMS queues discussed previously: It is not visible to applications or developers.

WebLogic Server maintains a pool of threads, the size of which is configurable by the administrator through the WebLogic Server console. WebLogic Server removes work from the work queue, and execute threads perform those work items. When those work items result in contention for resources, threads will sit idle and the CPU utilization will go down. If you notice that your CPU utilization is very low under heavy load, increasing the execute thread count through the WebLogic Server console is an option. You can modify this value in your console (on a per-server basis) under the Configuration Tuning tab in your individual server (see Figure 14–41).

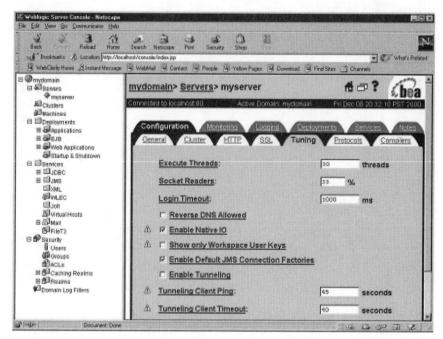

Figure 14–41   Changing the Number of Execute Threads

To determine if increasing execute threads in WebLogic Server would help ease contention (and maximize CPU utilization at 100 percent), another test was run with 30 execute threads (see Table 14.3).

Notice that the size of the WebLogic Server database connection pool to the Oracle instance was also increased. As stated in the WebLogic Server tuning guide, the number of database connections that you have should never be greater than the number of execute threads. Preferably, the number of database connections should be about equal to the number of execute threads.

In Run No. 4, the server utilization and throughput of the application actually went down relative to Run No. 3. It is likely that the addition of new threads and connections to the database resulted in increased *context switching* inside of WebLogic Server. Context switching occurs anytime the Java virtual machine (JVM) must switch between two threads of execution. During this switching time, work cannot be done, resulting in lower performance.

Table 14.3 Performance with an Increased Number of Execute Threads

Run	Client Threads	Client Sockets per Thread	WebLogic Server Execute Thread Count	Server Heap Size	WebLogic Server Database Connection Pool Size	Pages per Second	Server CPU Utilization
7	64	25	30	64MB	30	342	94%

At this point, we made use of an application profiler tool called OptimizeIt, which is one of the many Java profiling tools available today. These tools enable you to monitor the execution of a Java application and take snapshots of the performance of the application at any given point. You can see the internal workings of every thread operating inside of the JVM to determine where your application bottlenecks might lie. For example, you might see that every thread inside of WebLogic Server is blocked as it waits on a resource, such as a database connection. Or, you might see that all of the application code that you have built on top of WebLogic Server is blocked and waiting for access to a single resource, such as a static variable or a connection to a legacy system.

In the case of the WebAuction application, using the Java profiler validated that our architecture had no issues surrounding contention or lack of resources.

If you recall, the fourth step in application performance and stress testing is to review and analyze the results. It was at this point we noticed that the WebAuction application repeatedly reads the same data.

For this type of read-mostly application, we should make use of one helpful feature of WebLogic Server: *caching tags for JSP*. Therefore, we improved the *browseitems.jsp* page to specify that the output from the JSP page that includes the data items should be cached for 10 minutes, using the following code:

```
<wl:cache key="application.cat" timeout="10m" >


// JSP and HTML print out all of the items in the current category


</wl:cache>
```

More information on how to use the WebLogic Server caching tags can be found in the WebLogic Server documentation.

With the caching tags added to the application, the same tests were executed again resulting in a substantial performance increase of over 10 percent (see Table 14.4).

Table 14.4 Increased Throughput Using Caching Tags

Run	Client Threads	Client Sockets per Thread	WebLogic Server Execute Thread Count	Server Heap Size	WebLogic Server Database Connection Pool Size	Pages per Second	Server CPU Utilization
8	64	25	15	64MB	15	342	87%

Table 14.5 Testing New User Creation

Run	Client Threads	Client Sockets per Thread	WebLogic Server Execute Thread Count	Server Heap Size	WebLogic Server Database Connection Pool Size	Pages per Second	Server CPU Utilization	Database CPU Utilization
9	1	25	15	64MB	15	26	50%	12–15%

At 342 pages per second, the WebAuction application could theoretically provide nearly 30 million page views in a single day:

```
342 pages/s * 60s/minute * 60 minutes/hour * 24 hours/1 day =
29,548,800 pages/day
```

Bandwidth

What about bandwidth? A request for the *browseitems.jsp* page retrieves all of the following HTML and images:

```
2,797 browseitems.jsp
2,435 built_bea_web.gif
  317 footer.jsp
  152 header.jsp
1,402 header2.jsp
1,293 logo.gif
1,993 lwl.gif
3,427 title.gif
-------
13,816 bytes = 13KB per page
```

At 342 pages per second, each at 13 KB, this constitutes 4442 KB per second. Or, about 35Mbps, which is enough to saturate most high-end Internet connections. Chapter 15, "Capacity Planning for the WebLogic Server," covers how server output relates to Internet connection speeds.

In addition, another test run, not included here, compared the results of our performance testing efforts when multiple network interfaces were used. In that case, even though connections were spread across two different network connections, the throughput rate of pages per second did not change noticeably.

Simulating New Users

The Microsoft WAST has limited capabilities to simulate user behavior that is dependent upon the user name. The tool enables you to create thousands of virtual users, with each one interacting differently with this site. To simulate new users, we created 20,000 virtual users inside of WAST on each of the two client machines. Unfortunately, the WAST had difficulty generating large amounts of load and is only able to be single-threaded for virtual user tests.

We ran a single test with new user creations using the same server configuration previously determined optimal (see Table 14.5).

At this point, we would have attempted to continue increasing load upon the server if the tool had provided sufficient functionality. In this case, we deemed 26 new users per second to be an acceptable throughput. This would result in the capability for the configuration to add about 2.25 million users to the site per day.

Note also that the database CPU utilization became a factor in doing updates to the user table. Previously, the database utilization had been negligible for read operations because of the data caching functionality in WebLogic Server. For applications that are heavily oriented toward updating the database, make sure to pay attention to the database usage by your application. In many cases, database updates can cause the most substantial bottleneck for the application.

Simulating a Complete User Interaction

The goal of the final test was to simulate a complete and realistic user interaction with the application. To create this final test, a data read was added to the new user creation test completed in Run No. 9. In this test, a user first visits the main page for the site. The virtual user then creates a new account and enters an item for bid. The virtual user then browses the items before logging out (see Table 14.6).

This test represented a realistic user case and also stressed multiple parts of the application inside a single user account creation and logout from the system. With this data, it is very likely that the WebAuction application will perform extremely well in production situations from a performance standpoint.

Table 14.6 Testing Simulated User Interactions

Run	Client Threads	Client Sockets per Thread	WebLogic Server Execute Thread Count	Server Heap Size	WebLogic Server Database Connection Pool Size	Pages per Second	Server CPU Utilization	Database CPU Utilization
10	1	25	15	64MB	15	178	73%	12–15%

CAPACITY PLANNING FOR THE WEBLOGIC SERVER

In this chapter:

- Analysis—What factors to consider for capacity planning
- Metrics—A "baseline" set of capacity-planning numbers derived from an existing application (we'll use our sample application, WebAuction) you can use in determining the infrastructure required to meet your deployment requirements
- Capacity planning best practices

15

Chapter

After designing your WebLogic Server deployment and building the application, the next step is to test your deployment to see whether it meets your intended performance criteria. How many registered users should your system support? How many requests per second should it be able to handle? What sort of network and hardware infrastructure is required to meet your deployment goals? This chapter covers the methodology and information required to answer these questions for your application.

Analysis of Capacity Planning

The art of determining requirements for a WebLogic Server deployment and planning an infrastructure that will support those requirements is collectively referred to as *capacity planning*. Capacity planning is an attempt to determine the resources, such as CPUs, Internet connection size, or LAN infrastructure, required to support performance. Capacity planning answers the question, "What hardware infrastructure and network configuration will enable my WebLogic deployment to fulfill specified performance requirements?"

Capacity planning is an inexact science because there are so many factors that influence the capacity of a given application deployment. These factors include:

- How database intensive is the application?
- How large are the pages that Java ServerPages (JSPs) display?
- What is the typical usage pattern for a user?
- How do users access the system?
- How fast is the underlying hardware?

In fact, so many factors influence capacity planning that it borders on being an art form. Nonetheless, it is possible to take some of the guesswork out of the process of capacity planning. In reality, the hardware capacity to support your application will greatly depend on the application specifics. For this reason, this chapter aims only to provide information that will assist your own capacity testing and application design efforts. Creating "a one size fits all" formula to compute the amount of hardware required for a given application is a futile effort.

Factors Affecting Capacity

There are three major areas for focusing capacity-planning efforts for a WebLogic deployment:

- *Server hardware*—Obviously, the capacity of the servers where WebLogic runs directly affects the capacity of the WebLogic deployment. For example, every JSP request from a client requires both memory and CPU time to generate a response from WebLogic. You need to assess the number and power of CPUs, RAM size, Java virtual machine (JVM) efficiency, and other factors relating to the server hardware platform: How much capacity is required from your server platforms?
- *LAN infrastructure*—As noted in previous chapters, a WebLogic cluster relies on a LAN for communication between cluster nodes. Depending upon the application, the requirements for a LAN can vary. For example, a very large cluster that is doing *in-memory replication* for either Enterprise JavaBeans (EJB) or servlet session replication requires a higher bandwidth network than a small cluster. In addition, the size of session data, the size of a cluster, and the power of the server machines affect the requirements for the LAN infrastructure.

You need to assess cluster network hardware performance: How much capacity is required from the LAN between the nodes of the WebLogic cluster?

- *External network connectivity*—The WebLogic deployment communicates to other resources such as databases or legacy systems, or externally to systems such as the Internet. You must assess the frequency of connections to external systems and the size of data being transferred: How much capacity is required from the network that connects the WebLogic cluster, the clients, and back-end resources?

This chapter focuses on each of these three areas independently. Capacity planning should be applied across *all* the components of a WebLogic deployment, not just the servers that run WebLogic. All the components in the deployment affect the capacity of a WebLogic deployment.

Methodology and Metrics for Capacity Planning

Capacity planning focuses on how the WebLogic deployment deals with *maximum performance requirements*. What is the peak load that your deployment will be able to handle? In other words, what is its maximum capacity for handling requests? Capacity-planning methodology focuses on the worst-case scenario, such as when your company's advertisement appears on the Super Bowl and your deployment suddenly receives a flood of millions of new requests. The underlying assumption of planning for the worst case is that your WebLogic Servers and the infrastructure should be able to scale up to that peak load.

In order to quantify the worst cases, *set goals* or *measurable objectives* for capacity, such as "the WebLogic deployment should be able to handle 10,000 open user sessions at a given time."

The application deployment should have distinct capacity goals that quantify the maximum capacity required for the deployment.

Setting Capacity Goals

The first step in capacity planning is to *set goals for the deployment*. These goals should be quantified as maximums:

- *User interactions per second with WebLogic.* This value represents the total number of user interactions that should be handled per second by a WebLogic deployment. User interactions are typically accesses to JSP pages or servlets, for Web deployments. For application deployments, user interactions are accesses to EJBs.

- *Total number of concurrent user sessions.* This value represents the total number of user sessions that WebLogic should handle at a given time. Concurrent user sessions are mostly an issue for Web deployments, when WebLogic is maintaining HTTP session objects around for each user. However, concurrency measures are also important when application deployments access stateful session EJBs.

- *Storage capacity for user information.* This value represents the capacity required to store user information. In the simplest case, this value is the disk and memory required to store security information for each user. User-related storage is not covered in this chapter because it is either trivial or because it directly depends on external systems such as databases. In the trivial case where the WebLogic-based security realm or the database is used for storage of user information, simply multiply the size of each user's information by the total number of users. If each user requires 1MB of storage, then 20 registered users require 20MB; 1000 users require 1GB, and so on.

To illustrate how capacity planning works for these three basic deployment characteristics, let's come up with some requirements for deploying the WebAuction application. The capacity goal for the WebAuction application will be 800 user requests per second or 69,120,000 requests per day. Note that goals are stated in terms of maximums, the worst-case possibility for capacity.

Server Hardware Capacity Planning

Many usage-related factors affect the capacity of a deployed application:

- Client protocol
- Security profile
- Degree of platform optimization for running Java and WebLogic

This section covers each of these factors, detailing how each factor affects the overall capacity of the WebLogic deployment.

Client Protocol

The client protocol is directly related to the type of WebLogic deployment. Application deployments and mixed deployments of WebLogic generally rely heavily on the Remote Method Invocation (RMI) programming model to access WebLogic services.

RMI can rely on the native WebLogic T3 protocol or can use HTTP tunneling to allow the RMI calls to pass through a firewall. Performance of RMI tunneled over HTTP is typically worse than that of nontunneled T3.

Application clients can use HTTP by directly making HTTP POSTs and GETs to access servlets. In these cases, the application client should be treated as a Web browser client generating HTTP requests.

Security Profile

The level of security that is put in place between clients and WebLogic is a factor in determining the capacity of the deployment. WebLogic supports SSL (Secure Sockets Layer) as the security mechanism to ensure privacy and to authenticate users. SSL protects JSP pages for credit card purchases and bank statements, ensuring that attackers cannot view sensitive information.

SSL is a very intensive computing operation. The overhead of SSL cryptography means that WebLogic Server can handle fewer simultaneous connections than in a system without SSL.

You should note the total number of SSL connections required, over time, for your average client load. Typically, the server can handle three non-SSL connections for every one SSL connection. Given that users need not use an SSL connection for every request, SSL reduces the capacity of the server substantially. The amount of overhead incurred from SSL is directly related to how many client interactions use it.

Clustering Profile

The clustering profile affects the capacity of the WebLogic deployment. Two factors in clustering affect capacity:

1. Cluster size
2. Usage pattern of in-memory replication

Cluster Size and In-Memory Replication

The cluster size directly influences how much network traffic is required to support the cluster. Various categories of traffic flow over the LAN that connects the WebLogic nodes in the cluster. The nodes in the cluster can coordinate some of this traffic, but a larger cluster requires a higher power network to communicate efficiently.

In-memory replication of session information is usually the largest consumer of LAN network bandwidth in a WebLogic cluster. As you recall from previous chapters, both servlets and session EJBs can replicate their session information across the cluster. This provides a hot backup in the case of failure of a given node in the cluster.

To keep the hot backup current with the latest information, the LAN propagates changes to sessions among nodes in the cluster. The use of in-memory replication most directly affects the LAN infrastructure required to support the cluster. See step 3 of the capacity-planning methodology, later in this chapter.

Application Profile

The application profile is a summary of all of the tasks that the WebLogic application must perform in response to client requests. These include serving Web pages, handling client requests, processing forms, dealing with user sessions, opening database connections, managing connection pools, and so forth.

Applications can be simple or they can be very complex. The WebAuction application is moderately complex, involving a number of different components, including JMS and clustering for its deployment. Clearly, it is possible to create an even more complex application with even more business logic and more complex code paths. Unfortunately, there's not a good metric for how the application profile can affect capacity. However, the reliance upon back-end systems, such as databases, can help us estimate the complexity of applications using WebLogic.

Dependence on Legacy/Back-End Systems

Most WebLogic deployments rely upon back-end systems such as databases or messaging systems on mainframes. Typically, a WebLogic application uses a database to generate Web content, such as looking up an employee's record. However, as demonstrated in the WebAuction application, requests are made that do not rely upon a back-end system to be served. For example, the welcome page *index.jsp* in the WebAuction application makes no calls to the database or back-end systems.

Obviously, the more reliance there is on back-end systems, the more resources are consumed to meet requests. Each client request for which WebLogic acts as an intermediary to a back-end system consumes hardware and external connectivity resources. In the WebAuction application, the vast majority of requests incur the overhead of accessing the database system.

If your application has a higher ratio of legacy system access or accesses more than one legacy system to fill client requests, you should consider your application more complex than the WebAuction application.

Session-Based Information

The amount of session-based information that the WebLogic deployment has to handle also directly affects capacity. The WebLogic deployment must track session objects in memory, for each session. This memory is either directly available in RAM or is obtained by swapping out to disk.

The hardware must have enough RAM to hold all the session objects. As session objects per user become larger or more users' sessions must be held simultaneously, more RAM is required. This RAM is accessible to Java via the Java heap, which is where the Java environment stores all objects and application data.

A Baseline Capacity Profile

This section includes baseline numbers for capacity planning using the WebAuction application on standard server hardware in a configuration that simulates a real-world deployment.

The Baseline Capacity-Planning Profile for the WebAuction Application

The same testing configuration used in Chapter 13, *Designing the Production Deployment*, was used (see Figure 15–1).

SYSTEM CONFIGURATION FOR TESTING

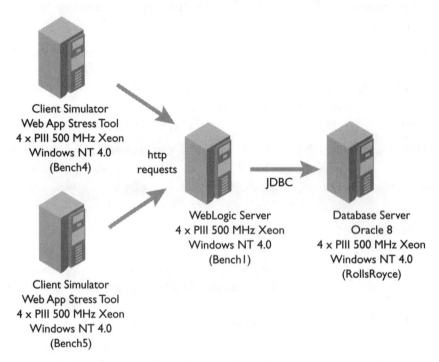

Figure 15–1   Testing Configuration

Two client machines generated load onto a single server running the WebAuction application. Oracle 8, running on another identical server, acted as the database. The entire configuration was connected by a 100Mb Ethernet. The WebLogic Server used the Java Development Kit (JDK) 1.3 for Windows NT included in the WebLogic distribution with a 256MB heap size, a size 15 `connectionPool` to the database, and 15 execute threads.

To generate baseline numbers, a scenario was developed to provide the absolute worst performance possible. By choosing a usage case by a user that demanded the most of the application, we can be sure that any other use will result in better performance, making it a safe bet for capacity planning. Remember, the idea is to measure the amount of hardware required to support your application, and the capacity-planning effort determines the low bar for application performance.

As was determined in Chapter 13, when testing the WebAuction application, updates to the database to add new users were the most expensive operations both in terms of database and application server resources. For this reason, a scenario was created with the following user action flow for one of the client machines:

1. Visit the welcome page (*main.jsp*).
2. Create a new user account (*newuser.jsp*).
3. Browse items in the books category (*browseitems.jsp*).
4. Bid on an item (*bid.jsp*).
5. Browse the user's bids (*currentbid.jsp*).
6. Log out (*logout.jsp*).

Notice that the preceding scenario creates a new user for each iteration. The second client machine focused on doing read operations to simulate that users would be viewing items in the categories:

1. Visit the welcome page (*main.jsp*).
2. Browse items in the books category (*browseitems.jsp*).

Together, these two machines were simultaneously directed at the WebAuction application. The results represent what kind of performance can be expected in a real-world deployment (see Table 15.1):

Table 15.1 Results of Performance Testing with Two Machines

CPUs	New Users per Second	New Users per Day	Http Requests Served per Second	Http Requests Served per Day	Server CPU Utilization
4	3.97	342,720	312	26,956,800	87%
3	2.72	234,720	238	20,563,200	86%
2	2.10	181,440	168	14,515,200	90%
1	1.08	93,600	90	7,776,000	89%

These numbers provide a basis for comparison for other applications. By simple multiplication, we can get an idea of what sort of hardware is required to support larger configurations of WebLogic. Next, we need to see how your particular application differs from the WebAuction application.

To illustrate this process of comparing your application to the baseline capacity profile for the WebAuction application, we detail capacity planning for WebAuction in the next section, on capacity planning for the LAN infrastructure and for external connectivity.

LAN Infrastructure Capacity Planning

Now that the server hardware has been determined, we can proceed to plan the capacity of the LAN infrastructure. Fortunately, capacity planning for the LAN infrastructure is simpler than capacity planning for the server hardware. This is mainly due to the fact that only one factor heavily affects the requirements on the LAN infrastructure: *in-memory replication* of session information for servlets and stateful session EJBs.

In-memory replication of session information is the largest consumer of LAN network bandwidth in a WebLogic cluster. As you recall from previous chapters, both servlets and session EJBs can have their session information replicated across the cluster. This provides a hot backup in the case of failure of a given node in the cluster.

To keep the hot backup current with the latest information, the LAN is used to transmit session changes to nodes in the cluster. Typically, the recommended session size is 5 to 15 KB in size. Larger sessions require higher network bandwidth to support efficient operation.

The following chart summarizes the network requirements for both cluster size and in-memory replication details. Where "switched" is noted, the LAN infrastructure should be based on a switch rather than a hub, which reduces the saturation of the network under load (see Figure 15.2).

Table 15.2 Network Requirements

CPUs Running WebLogic Instances in Cluster	*In-Memory Replication Session Size (in KB)*	*Approximate LAN Capacity Minimum (in MB/s)*
2-8	0	100
2-8	<15	100

Table 15.2 Network Requirements (continued)

CPUs Running WebLogic Instances in Cluster	In-Memory Replication Session Size (in KB)	Approximate LAN Capacity Minimum (in MB/s)
2-8	>15	Switched 100
8-16	0	Switched 100
8-16	<15	Switched 100
8-16	>15	Switched 1 Gbps
16+	0	Switched 100
16+	<15	Switched 100
16+	>15	Switched 100

As the cluster size grows, the infrastructure requirements grow greatly.

External Connectivity Capacity Planning

Connectivity to external clients and resources is also a factor in capacity planning. The amount of traffic to an external resource such as a database is, of course, application-specific. This section looks at connectivity requirements for clients to WebLogic, as well as connectivity requirements to legacy/back-end systems.

Client Connectivity Requirements

A network connection is required to connect WebLogic to its clients on the Web. This network connection may be over the Internet or across the corporate network. In the case of the corporate network, bandwidth is typically very high and capacity planning is not required. However, when connections to WebLogic clients are made over the Internet, it is necessary to make sure that the bandwidth across the Internet is appropriate.

In most cases, simple calculations can be made to estimate the amount of bandwidth required to support Web users. This begins with determining the size of responses that will be sent to clients. To determine the size of these responses, you should look at your application and determine the average size of the responses. Your calculation should include both the HTML code as well as any static images that you're serving such as JPEG. After determining the average size of the transmission to the requesters, we can create a weighted average based on *how often* the various pages are served.

Let's do this calculation for the WebAuction application. We have the following JSP pages that respond to requests (see Table 15.3):

Table 15.3 Responses per JSP Page

JSP Page	*Total Size (with Images) in Kb*	*Estimated Percent of Total Responses*
login.jsp	25	48%
trade.jsp	20	48%
error.jsp	15	4%

The weighted average of these pages is (see Table 15.4).

Table 15.4 Weighted Average of Responses per Page

JSP Page	*Weighted Total Size (with Images) Based on the Percent of the Responses*
login.jsp	12Kb (=25 Kb × 0.48)
trade.jsp	9.6Kb (= 20 Kb × 0.48)
error.jsp	0.6Kb (=15 Kb × 0.04)
Weighted Average:	22.2Kb (= 12 Kb + 9.6 Kb + 0.6 Kb)

As you can see, only 4 percent of the total requests come from the *error.jsp* JSP page. The `login` and `trade` JSP pages account for 48 percent of the responses. In weighting these responses, we can estimate that the average response to each client request will be 22.2KB.

We can take this average response size of 22.2KB and look at how many requests per second could possibly be handled by different, standard Internet connectivity and network connectivity links (see Table 15.5).

Table 15.5 Theoretical Maximum Number of Responses

Network Connectivity Speed	Theoretical Maximum Responses Served per Second	Theoretical Maximum Responses Served per Day
56.6Kbit modem @ 7.075Kb per second[a]	0.32 / s	27,648 / day
Digital Subscriber Line (DSL) @ 128Kbit/16Kb per second	0.72 / s	62,208 / day
T-1/OC-1 Line @ 1.544Mbps/193Kb per second	8.69 / s	750,816 / day
T3/OC-3 Line @ 44.736Mbps/5,592Kb per second	251.89 / s	21,763,296 / day
OC-4 Line @ 274.176Mbps/34,272Kb per second	1543.73 / s	133,378,222 / day

a. 56.6k modems are measured in terms of bits per second.

This chart only represents the theoretical maximum because it does not take into account the bandwidth consumed by subsequent requests. For more information on the different capacities of digital lines, check with your local Internet service provider.

In reality, the bandwidth provided by these connections is about 50 to 75 percent of the theoretical maximum. So, a T3 line in practice can transmit 10 to 15 million 22KB pages per day. The numbers here only mean to provide a rough estimate for what one would expect in a WebLogic deployment with a typical response size. It is highly recommended that you consult your Internet service provider for the appropriate level of bandwidth for your application.

> *Several resources are available regarding Web capacity planning:*
> *Capacity Planning for Web Performance: Metrics, Models, and Methods.*
> *Prentice Hall, 1998, ISBN 0-13-693822-1 (http://www.cs.gmu.edu/*
> *~menasce/webbook/index.html) and Scaling for E-Business: Technologies,*
> *Models, Performance, and Capacity Planning.*
> *In addition, there is a capacity-planning Web portal that has a number of*
> *useful pieces of information: (http://www.capacityplanning.com/). This Web*
> *site is completely focused on capacity-planning issues for enterprise*
> *application deployments.*

Back-End Resource Connectivity Requirements

Many factors affect connectivity requirements to resources, including how much data is transferred, how often it is transferred, and what the capacity is of the back-end resource. All of these factors vary from application to application. By default, connectivity to back-end resources is viewed in the traditional client/server model, in which WebLogic is the client and the back-end resource is the server.

In the case of most legacy resources that connect to WebLogic, such as a database or a mainframe data store, the systems are mature enough to already offer recommendations for capacity planning and connectivity. For example, in the case of Oracle databases, capacity-planning information is available that includes both network connectivity and hardware server requirements. However, much of this capacity-planning information for legacy systems is based on the traditional client/server model, in which application clients connect directly to the database and therefore are not applicable.

Because WebLogic introduces a third tier to the application, in which connections are made from the client to the application server and then translated into requests for the legacy application, you must often use abstractions for capacity planning to back-end resources with WebLogic. In this abstraction, you should view the WebLogic application as a *proxy* for the client requests as it executes work for each individual user. So, if your WebLogic deployment is to service 5,000 requests per second that translate into database access, then you should plan the capacity of your database connectivity and database hardware to be able to handle 5,000 requests per second.

Fortunately, as the 3-tier model for applications becomes more common, the database vendors also are beginning to offer capacity-planning information that is tailored to application servers. The requirement that you need to abstract WebLogic as a client to the database is only temporary until the database vendors catch up.

Capacity Planning Best Practices

There exist a number of best practices that should be followed when capacity planning for a WebLogic deployment:

Be conservative with your capacity estimates. The steps detailed in this chapter are able to provide a high-level estimate of the configuration required to meet your deployment goals. Capacity planning for WebLogic is not an exact science. For this reason, it is a best practice to err on the side of caution in terms of estimates. Many successful deployments take server hardware capacity-planning estimates and increase them by 50 percent in order to be absolutely sure that they will have adequate capacity. For deployments where absolute reliability is preferable over cost savings, this is a common practice.

Load test your application. There are a great number of things that can go wrong in terms of an application's capacity that can never be identified until the application is deployed in practice. For this reason, you should plan to load test your application either in a prototype form or using the hardware that you plan to deploy upon.

Optimize your application. The application built on top of WebLogic is often the most limiting factor to capacity. For this reason, you should plan to optimize your application during the testing process. There are a number of tools that provide you with insight as to hot spots and inefficiencies in your application based on WebLogic:

- jProbe from the KL Group (*http://www.klgroup.com/*) and OptimizeIT from Intuitive Systems, Inc. (*http://www.optimizeit.com*) can be used at development time to find bottlenecks in the code.
- Introscope from Wily Technology (*http://www.wilytech.com*) is a Java product that allows for runtime performance monitoring of any Java component in WebLogic. This tool is designed for monitoring production systems and not for tuning during development.

Plan for growth. One of the major benefits of WebLogic is that it is easily extensible. Growing a cluster is as simple as adding another server machine.

Most WebLogic deployments start small, but grow substantially over time as more clients and services come online. For this reason, it is a good practice to plan your WebLogic deployment for growth. You may want to choose a LAN infrastructure that is larger than your current deployment so that it is ready when you want to grow.

In terms of external connectivity to other resources such as the Internet or legacy systems, the bandwidth and hardware resources should be extensible. Many ISPs offer instant upgrades to Internet connections for higher bandwidth.

Index

A

Access Control Lists (ACLs), 250, 473
ACID
    transaction, 205
ACLs, 250, 473
Action
    JSP tags, 129
    types, 129–130
Activate
    EJB
        BMP entity beans, 401
Activation
    EJB container, 321
    entity bean interface, 367
Add Header, 51
AddIntHeader, 51
Age, 73
Anonymous instances
    EJB container, 375
Apache JMeter, 567
Applet
    example, 133–134

Application
    building, 38
    deployed, 38
        viewing, 39–40
    test and stage, 572
Application clients
    developing secure, 511
    SSL security, 536–537
Application client security
    JAAS, 512
    WebLogic Server JNDI, 517–526
Application deployment, 560–562
    capacity goals, 651
    descriptors, 42
    infrastructure components, 565
    process, 565–571
    recommended, 562
    security, 561–562
    stages, 567–571
Application directory
    JavaBean building, 147
Application partitioning
    EJB, 359

Application profile
    capacity planning, 654–655
Application server
    developing applications, 5
Application.xml
    writing, 592
Architecture development
    production development, 568
Archive
    creating, 88
Astra QuickTest product, 627
Asynchronous consumer
    JTA transactions, 448
Asynchronous message consumer, 296
    JMS, 267
    JMS initialization code, 271–272
Asynchronous processing paradigm, 21
Atomicity
    transaction, 205
Attribute, 63
Attribute Names method, 64, 97
Auditing
    checking security, 536
Authenticated subject
    retrieve, 514–515
Authenticating users
    WebAuction, 583–584
Authentication, 469–471
Authentication status
    retrieve, 514
Authorization, 472–473
Authorization services, 472–473
AUTO_ACKNOWLEDGE, 285
Auto commit
    JDBC, 233
Automatic deployment, 163

B

Back-end resource connectivity
    capacity planning, 662–663
Back-end systems
    capacity planning, 655
Bandwidth, 645
Baseline capacity profile
    capacity planning, 655–658
        WebAuction application, 656–658
Batch updates
    JDBC, 229–231, 232
Bean class
    entity EJB, 366
Bean clustering
    handling failure, 315–316
    stateless session, 315–317
Bean context
    entity EJB, 366
Bean EJB class, 304–305
Bean finder method, 586
Bean-managed persistence (BMP), 302

vs. CMP, 424–428
    combining CMP, 426–427
    entity EJBS, 364
    optimization, 418
    writing bean class, 395
    writing entity EJB, 394–395
Bean-managed persistence (BMP) entity beans,
    393–408
    optimize finder methods, 419
Bean-managed persistence (BMP) entity EJBs
    best practices, 408
Bean-managed transactions, 330–331
    message-driven beans, 441
Bean pooling
    stateless session, 314
Beanuser.jsp page, 139–141
BEA WebLogic Server
    description, 1–2
    supported platforms, 9
    versions, 10
    web site, 9
BidBean's finder method, 586
BidReceiver message-driven bean, 587–588
Bids For User method, 581, 586
BidValueHolder, 586
Binary large Objects (BLOBs), 228
Bind call
    JNDI, 249
Blind update, 427
BLOBs, 228
BMP. *See* Bean-managed persistence (BMP)
Browseitems.jsp, 165–167
Browser-based authentication
    deployment descriptor example, 507
    developing, 506–509
Browsing
    WebAuction code, 170
Buffer
    JSP page, 124
    size, 125
        HTTP response, 118
Build.bat script, 41
Build script, 38
Business logic design, 585–588
Business logic tiers
    separating
        presentation layer, 578
Business methods
    entity bean's implementation, 367
Bytes Message
    JMS message types, 279

C

Caching
    programming
        Web applications, 493–495
Caching realm instance
    create

WebAuction application, 619
Caching tags for JSP, 643
CallerInRole method, 334
Caller Principal, 333, 523
Calling business methods, 311–312
Capacity planning
 analysis, 649–651
 back-end resource connectivity, 662–663
 be conservative, 663
 best practices, 663–664
 client connectivity, 659–662
 definition, 649
 external connectivity, 659–663
 factors affecting, 650–651
 LAN infrastructure, 658–659
 methodology and metrics, 651–663
 server hardware, 653–655
 setting goals, 652
Capitalization
 care, 163
Case
 significance, 150
Case-sensitive
 DTC, 307
Central registry
 of naming and directory services, 18
Certificate authority, 527–529
 commercial, 529
 WebLogic Server, 527
Character Large Objects (CLOBs), 228
Classes directory
 JavaBean building, 147
Clear buffer, 124
CLIENT_ACKNOWLEDGE, 285
Client code

 BMP, 406–407
Client connectivity
 capacity planning, 659–662
Client protocol
 capacity planning, 653
Client software
 types, 545
CLOBs, 228
Close method
 release, 185
Cloudscape
 configure
  WebAuction application, 601
Cloudscape environment
 configure
  WebAuction application, 602
Clustering, 4, 5
 bean, 315–317
 hardware specifics, 554–557
 JMS, 289
 JNDI, 250–253
  nonreplicated bindings, 253

 replicates bindings, 253
 multi-CPU server, 553
 profile
  capacity planning, 654
 stateful session EJB, 322–325
 stateful session EJBs
  handling failure, 323
 stateless session EJBs
  handling failure, 315–316
 Web deployment
  configuring hardware, 551–553
 WebLogic Server
  mixed deployment, 563
  servlets, 101–103
  Web deployment, 550–557
Cluster-wide naming tree, 255
CMP. *See* Container-managed persistence (CMP)
CMRs, 377–389
 example, 378–389
  running, 386–389
 programming restrictions, 392–393
 unidirectional and bidirectional relationships,
  377–378
 writing deployment descriptors, 381–384
Code
 copying and unpacking, 36–37
Coding business interfaces
 EJB, 354–356
Collection
 CMR, 393
Co-located back-end services, 558
Co-located front-end services, 558
Comments
 cookies, 73
 JSP, 160
Commercial certificate authorities, 529
Compile script
 building and deploying, 37
Compound primary key
 entity bean, 365
Concurrency
 message-driven beans, 438
 stateful beans, 325
Concurrent Versions System, 566
Configuring
 pooling, 314–315
Connection factories
 JNDI, 261
Connection failed error, 40
Connection filtering, 537
Connection object
 JDBC, 233
Connection pools, 177–178
 configuring, 178
Connections
 close
  JTA transaction, 211
 JDBC, 232, 233

JMS, 261
release, 185
Consistency
transaction, 205
Container-managed entity bean lifecycle, 375–376
Container-managed fields
declaring, 368
entity EJBs, 368–369
Container-managed persistence (CMP), 302–303
vs. BMP, 424–428
combining BMP, 426–427
design advantages, 425
entity EJBs, 364
create, 374
finders, 375
load, 374
postCreate, 375
remove, 374
store, 374
performance advantages, 425–426
Container-managed persistence (CMP) engine
transaction demarcation, 587–588
Container-managed persistence (CMP) entity bean
example, 367–373
building and running, 373
optimizing, 419–420
Container-managed persistence (CMP) finders
writing EJB-QL, 389–393
Container-managed transactions
keywords, 327–328
Contains Header method, 50–51
Content Length, 45
Content Type, 45
Context attributes
ServletContext, 96–97
CONTEXT_FACTORY
JNDI, 518
Context switching, 641
Controller
MVC components, 161
Cookies
creating, 72–74
defined, 60
description, 71
getting, 73
methods for dealing with, 73
vs. servlet sessions, 71–72
temporary, 61
CookieServlet
deploying, 81–84
display, 83
example, 78–81
visiting, 82–83
Create method, 374
EJB
BMP, 397–398
Creation Time, 65
Cross-network method calls

performance implications, 245
Current bid, 581
Custom actions
JSP, 130
Custom tag libraries, 152–159, 164
building, 154
JavaBeans, 110
JSP, 109, 153–158
packaging, 158–159

D

Data access calls
optimizing, 417
Database
establishing connections, 180–181, 198–199
executing statements, 199–200
JDBC, 231, 234
by JDBC and JTA, 16–18
mapping CMP entity beans
CMR, 384–386
reading and writing
entity beans, 376
releasing connections, 200
sending query, 181–182
Database concurrency
choosing, 416
entity bean, 415
Database connection
JTA transactions, 210
Database connection pool, 177–178
configure
WebAuction application, 605–607, 622–623
Database management system (DBMS), 19–20, 177
Database persistence, 103
Database population commands
WebAuction, 621–622
WebAuction application
run, 603–604
Database round trips
minimizing, 417–418
Database tables
creating
CMR, 384
creating BMP, 406
Database tuning
WebAuction, 590
Database updates
types, 199
Databean.war
example components, 143
Data definition language (DDL), 384
DataSource
configure
WebAuction application, 608–610
JTA transactions, 210
Data stores
integrating Web deployments, 550

DBMS, 19–20, 177
DDL, 384
Debugging information, 142
Debugging JSPs, 163–164
Debugging messages, 164
Declaration
    scripting elements, 123, 127–128
Declarative security
    definition, 469
    form-based authentication
        Web application, 476–484
    scenarios, 476
    web applications, 475–476
Default methods
    to handle web forms, 51–60
Deployment
    applications, 38
        viewing, 39–40
    designing, 544
    directory, 38
    EJB, 309, 406
    MailSender, 460
    mixed, 562–564
    process, 41
    WebLogic Server
        best practices, 571
Deployment descriptors, 42, 89
    BMP entity beans, 403–405
    entity EJBs, 370
    generic, 89
    JSP, 160–161
    security constraints, 583
    Web authorization methods, 506–509
Description element, 95
Descriptive meta information, 85
Destinations
    JMS, 262
Destroy method
    servlet, 43–44
Developing JSPs, 163–164
Development environment
    set up, 500
Digital certificates, 527
    study and review, 538
Directives
    JSP, 115–116
Directory
    changing, 35–36
    creating, 35
    deployments, 38
    structure
        creating, 86
Display-name element, 95
Distributed transactions
    standards, 219
    WebLogic server, 218–224
Distributing Web traffic, 556
DMZ

Web deployment, 548–550
Web services, 559
DNS round robin, 557
Document type description (DTD), 90
    EJB, 305–306
DoDelete, 52
DoGet, 51
DoGet method
    cookie, 76–77
DoPost, 51
DoPut, 52
Driver manager method, 181
DTD, 90, 305–306
DUPS_OK_ACKNOWLEDGE, 285
Durability
    transaction, 205

E

EJB, 1, 4, 301–361
    basics, 301–312
    business logic design, 585–588
    deploying, 309
    document type descriptor, 305–306
    example, 303–305
    interface, 431
    programmatic security, 333–334
    types, 19
EJB Activate
    BMP entity beans, 401
EJB cache
    configuring, 321–322
EJB container, 310
    concurrency, 415
EJB Create method, 374
    BMP, 397–398
EJB deployment descriptors, 305
    security roles, 331–334
EJB environment
    variables, 335–336
EJB FindByPrimarykey method
    BMP entity beans, 401–402
EJB Home, 241
    JNDI, 310
    Look Up, 310
EJB instance
    creating, 310–311
EJB Jar, 305–306
EJB jar file
    building, 307–309
EJB Load method, 374
    BMP, 399
EJB Objects, 241
EJB Passivate
    BMP entity beans, 401
EJB PostCreate, 375
    BMP, 398
EJB references, 336–337
    declaring, 337

EJB Remove method, 374
    BMP, 398
EJB security, 331
    best practices, 360–361
EJB Store method, 374
    BMP, 400
E-mail. *See* Internet mail
EncodeRedirectURL, 75
Encode URL, 75
Encryption
    study and review, 538
End of service
    JSP, 115
    servlet, 43–44
EnterBid, 580
Entering user name
    form, 139
EnterItem method, 168
Enterprise archives
    organization, 591–592
    packaging, 593–596
Enterprise JavaBeans (EJB). *See* EJB
Entity bean, 302–303
    basics, 364–367
    classes, 365
    components, 364–366
    create, 365
    identities, 365
    interface, 431
    keys, 365
    locking, 415–420
    remove, 365
    vs. stateless session beans, 427–428
    using read-only, 420–421
Entity bean inheritance
    design patterns, 412–414
Entity bean polymorphisms
    design patterns, 412–414
    restrictions, 411–412
Entity bean relationships, 588
Entity EJBs, 19–20, 363–428
    rationale, 363–364
    writing, 408–411
Entrust, 529
Enumeration, 125
    of all names, 54–55
Environment
    configure
        WebAuction application, 599
    setting, 87
    variables
        setting, 35
Equals
    implementing
        entity EJBs, 410
Error handling
    JMS transactions, 297–298
    page

JSP, 119
    required transaction attribute, 441–442
    SQL warning, 224–226
    transactions
        EJB, 358
Error logging
    enabling, 142
Error message
    send, 50
Error page, 159–160
    JSP, 118
Exception
    implicit object, 126
Exception listeners, 291–292
Exclusive concurrency, 416
Execute method
    SQL queries, 182
Execute threads
    pool
        changing size, 640
        understanding, 639–647
Executing SQL, 182
Expressions
    JSP, 129
    scripting elements, 123
External connectivity
    capacity planning, 659–663
        network, 651
Externalizable interface, 242
    example, 242–243

F

Facade patterns
    EJB, 423
Failed login page
    creating, 481
Failover, 4
    WebLogic Server, 551
File realm, 474
Find By Primary key method
    EJB
        BMP entity beans, 401–402
Finder methods
    BMP entity beans, 375
    CMP bean writer, 375
    EJB-QL, 389–393
    entity EJB, 366
    optimizing, 419
Finders
    BMP, 402–403
Firewalling Internet traffic, 555
Firewalls
    Web deployment, 548–550
Flush method, 125, 131
Foo declarations, 128
Form-based authentication, 471, 538
    deploying
        example, 485–493

developing, 476–484
example, 477–484
failures, 479
implement, 477
FormServlet, 54
deploying, 60
Forward action, 132
Forward method, 100
Freepool settings, 317
Functional testing
production deployment, 570
WebAuction application, 625–631
with example, 627–631
infrastructure requirements, 626–627
methodology, 625–626

G

Generic deployment descriptor, 89
Generic servlets, 29
Get, 51, 52
single class, 56
GetAttribute, 63
GetAttributeNames method, 64, 97
GetBidsForUser method, 581, 586
GetBufferSize, 125
GetCallerPrincipal, 333, 523
GetComment
cookies, 73
GetContentLength, 45
GetContentType, 45
GetCreationTime, 65
GetId, 65
GetLastAccessedTime, 65
GetMaxAge, 73
GetMaxInactiveInterval, 65
Get methods
writing, 368
GetParameterNames method, 54–55, 125
GetParameterValues, 125
GetPathInfo, 45
GetPathTransalted, 45
GetProperty tag, 148–149
GetProtocol, 45
GetQueryString, 45
GetRemaining, 125
GetRemoteADdr, 45
GetRemoteHost, 45
GetRemoteUser, 45
GetResource, 98–99
GetResourceAsStream, 98–99
GetResultSetType, 182
GetScheme, 46
GetSecure
cookies, 74
GetServerName, 45
GetServerPort, 45
GetServletPath, 45
GetValue

cookies, 74
Grouping multiple requests, 60
Groups
adding and removing, 495
adding user, 495
definition, 468

H

Handles
advantages, 341–342
EJB, 340–342
home, 341
Hard-coding serialization, 242
HashCode
implementing
entity EJBs, 410
Header, 51
Helper methods, 117
Hidden fields, 60
Hidden form field
defined, 60
Home finder methods
entity EJB, 366
HomeHandles, 341
Home interface
EJB, 304
EJB entity, 364–365
Home methods
entity bean's implementation, 367
HTML
vs. JSP, 108
HTML page
compose, 46
HTTP, 60, 237
HTTP requests, 15
WebLogic Server servlets, 28
HTTP Response, 15
HTTP servlet
core features, 15
use of, 29
HTTP Servlet Request object
sampling of available methods, 46
HTTP Session, 15
HTTP Session objects, 64
Hypertext transfer protocol (HTTP). See HTTP

I

IBM VisualAge
TLD, 155
Icon element, 94
Id, 65
Idempotent stateless session EJBs, 316
Identified instances
EJB container, 376
Identity
JNDI, 250
ID generation
unique, 589

IJ utility, 190
IMAP, 452
    web site, 464
Implementation
    of guaranteed messaging service, 22
Implicit objects
    JSP, 122–127
Inactive Interval, 65
inc declarations, 128
Include directives
    definition, 116
    description, 122
    JSP page, 121–122
Include method, 101
Include standard action, 130–132
Infrastructure components
    application deployment, 565
Initial-beans-in-free pool tag, 314–315
Initial Context
    JNDI, 247–251
Initial context properties
    JNDI, 518
    login, 520
    SSL security, 536–537
Initialization
    JSP, 114
    servlet, 43
Initialization code
    JDBC, 232
Initial method
    servlet, 189
In-memory replication, 102, 103
    capacity planning, 654
    stateful session EJBs, 323–324
Instance
    realm, 494
Instantiation, 43
    JSP, 114
Instruct WebLogic Server
    WebAuction application, 620–621
Interactions
    transaction
        EJB, 357
Interactive Java (IJ) utility, 190
Internal method declaration, 128
Internet addresses
    mapping, 456–457
Internet connectivity, 555
Internet mail, 451
    web site, 464
Internet mail Access Protocol (IMAP). *See* IMAP
Interprocess communication, 260
IntHeader, 51
IsCallerInRole, 523
IsNew method, 62–63
Isolation
    transaction, 205
ItemBean JavaBean, 167–169

J

JAAS, 22
    authentication code
        writing, 512–513
    callback, 513
    Login Context, 513
    modules, 512–513
    secured application client
        implementation notes, 515–517
Jar command
    JavaBean building, 147
Jar tool, 37
Jar utility, 37, 41
    running, 87–88
Java
    web site, 224
Java application server, 1
Java Authentication and Authorization Service
(JAAS). *See* JAAS
JavaBean, 16
    building
        WebLogic server, 144–148
    building into JSP, 136–140
    creating, 137
    vs. custom tag libraries, 110
    encapsulate, 164
    HTTP session, 137
    and JSP, 109
    presentation layer, 579
    properties, 148–152
        building, 149–150
        populating, 150–152
    running
        WebLogic server, 141
Java Beans
    JSP, 134–152
        vs. Enterprise Java Beans, 134
    value objects, 423–424
Java code
    and JSP, 108–110
Java compiler, 41
Java Database Connectivity (JDBC). *See* JDBC
JavaDoc
    web site, 228
Java files
    compiling, 41
JavaMail, 22, 452–453
    best practices, 464
    configure
        WebAuction application, 610–612
    message class, 453–456
    send simple e-mail, 457–463
    session class, 453
    web site, 464
Java Message Service (JMS). *See* JMS
Java naming and directory interface (JNDI). *See*
JNDI

Java 2 Platform Enterprise Edition (J2EE). *See*
J2EE
JavaServer Pages (JSPs). *See* JSP
Java servlets, 14–15
Java transaction API (JTA). *See* JTA
Java Web site, 119
JDBC, 173–235
advanced features, 228–231
best practices, 231–235
code, 363
designing and coding database access, 173–235
to read data, 180
update database, 198–205
JDBC DataSource, 180
JDBC drivers, 174
choosing, 176
configuring and installing, 177
types, 174–176
web site, 177
JDBC read
basic steps, 180–181
example, 186–188
running
WebLogic server, 189–198
JDBC specification
prepared statements, 222–224
JDBC update
example, 200–202
running
WebLogic server, 202–204
JDBC URLs, 179–180
J2EE, 1
J2EE security model, 22
programming
definition, 469
J2EE server-based programming, 4
J2EE service
purpose, 14
JMS, 21–22, 259
benefits, 259–261
clustering, 289–291
configuring, 263–265
connections, 261
destinations, 262
fundamentals, 261–262
JTA transactions, 288–289
multicast, 292–293
sessions, 262
transactions, 287–289
JMS acknowledgment modes, 285–286
JMS client
example, 436–437
que model, 21
JMS connection factory
create
WebAuction application, 613–617
specifying, 439–440
JMS CorrelationID, 277

JMS DeliveryMode, 275
JMS delivery modes, 279–280
JMS Destination, 275–278
JMS destinations, 264, 284
configuration changes, 293–295
JMS Expiration, 276
JMS file server
create
WebAuction application, 614
JMS header fields, 275–278
JMS initialization code
asynchronous message consumer, 271–272
synchronous message consumer, 271
JMS message, 274–278
header, 275–278
JMS MessageID, 276
JMS message object
reused, 279
JMS message properties, 278
JMS message selectors, 295
JMS message templates
create
WebAuction application, 613–617
JMS message types, 278–279
JMS Priority, 276
JMS PTP
message producers and consumers, 263
JMS pub/sub
message producers and consumers, 263
JMS queue
create
WebAuction application, 613–617
JMS queue producer/consumer
sample, 265–270
running, 268–270
JMS Redelivered, 278
JMS ReplyTo, 277
JMS server
create
WebAuction application, 613–617
creating, 263–264
JMS store
creating, 263–264
JMS subscriptions, 282–283
JMS Timestamp, 276
JMS topic producer/consumer, 270–274
running, 272–274
JMS transactions
error handling, 297–298
JMS Type, 277
JNDI, 18, 246–256
authentication, 517
authorization, 517
bind call, 249
clustering, 250–253
connection factories, 261
EJB home, 310
identity, 250

lookup, 254
rebind, 252
security, 250
tree
  understanding conflicts, 252
unbind method, 249
updates, 252
using, 247–248
using effectively, 254–255
JSP, 3, 15, 27, 29–31, 107–108
anatomy, 111
best practices, 164–165
example, 111–112
integrating Java code, 108–110
Java Beans, 134–152
lifecycle, 113–115
or servlets, 30–31
servlets, 161
use Bean tag, 148
WebAuction application, 165
JSP basics, 110
JSP comments, 160
JSP deployment descriptor options, 160–161
JSP error pages, 159–160, 165
JSP form page, 138
JSP page elements, 115–134
JSP tags
for using beans, 135–136
JTA
driver
  using, 208–224
running
  WebLogic server, 215–217
support, 17–18
transactions, 209–212
  asynchronous consumer, 448
  JMS, 288–289
  vs. transacted sessions, 296–297

K

Keep-Alive, 33–34, 49

L

Language name, 116
LAN infrastructure
capacity planning, 650, 658–659
components, 557
Last Accessed Time, 65
Load
EJB
  BMP, 399
Load balancing, 4, 551
hardware, 556
software, 556
Loading, 43
JSP, 114
Load method
EJB, 374

Load test, 566–567
application, 572
  capacity planning, 663
Local caching
JNDI, 254
LocalizedMessage, 126
Location-independent, 247
Locking
entity beans, 415–420
Log in
initial context properties, 520
Log in Context
instantiation, 513–514
invoke, 514
Log in form, 470
creating, 477–478
Log out page
creating, 480
Log out user, 515
Look Up
EJB home, 310

M

Macromedia Dreamweaver, 15
MailSender JSP, 460
Mail server, 452
Mandatory
definition, 328
Map Message
JMS message types, 279
Mapping
CMR example, 385–386
Internet addresses, 456–457
Marshaling, 238
Materializing collections
CMR, 393
Max Age, 73
Max-beans-in-freepool, 438, 439
Max-beans-in-freepool value, 314–315
Max Inactive Interval, 65
MaxWidgets, 335
MDBs. *See* Message-driven beans (MDBs)
Member variables
stateless session beans, 317
Memory utilization
WebAuction application, 637
Mercury Interactive, 567, 627
Message acknowledgment, 285–286
EJB container, 442
Message class
JavaMail, 453–456
methods, 454–455
Message consumer
asynchronous, 267, 271–272, 296
Message delivery
JMS, 265–268
Message-driven beans (MDBs), 21, 303–304
BidReceiver, 587–588

building
  example, 436
concurrency, 438
deploying
  example, 436
transactions, 440–442
Message-driven EJB
  advantages, 448–449
  basics, 432–438
  combined with
    stateless session and entity beans, 443–447
  example, 433–438, 443–447
  lifecycle, 432–433
  writing deployment descriptors, 434–438
Message filtering, 22, 126
Message objects
  reusing, 279
Message ordering
  message-driven EJB, 439
MessagePrinterBean class
  EJB, 433
Message producer
  JMS, 265–266
  JMS queue, 270–271
Message selectors, 282
Messaging services, 21–22
Metadata, 226–228
  steps for using, 226–227
Meta-inf
  directory, 89
Microsoft Visual SourceSafe, 566
Microsoft WAST, 645
Microsoft Web Application Stress Tool, 567
MimeType
  JSP, 119
Mixed deployments, 562–564
  recommended architecture, 564
  security, 563
Model
  MVC components, 161
Model View Controller (MVC)
  applicability, 162
  component pattern, 161
  paradigm, 27
  Web applications, 162
Multicast
  JMS, 292–293
Multicast addresses, 293–295
Multicast JMS sessions, 294–295
MULTICAST_NO_ACKNOWELDGE, 286
Multicast security, 552
Multi-CPU server
  clustering, 553
Multiple meta documents, 89
Multiplexing
  threads, 640
Multi-tier architecture
  WebAuction, 577

MVC. *See* Model View Controller (MVC)

N

Naming service
  JNDI, 246–256
  replicated, 251
Netscape Navigator's preferences dialog, 82
Network architecture
  choosing, 552
Never
  definition, 328
New mail sessions
  creating, 461
New method, 62–63
New site certificate, 534
New user accounts
  creating, 584
  WebAuction application, 584
NO_ACKNOWLEDGE, 286
Nonidempotent stateless session EJBs, 316–317
Nonpersistent
  JMS message, 279–280
Nonreplicated bindings
  clustered JNDI, 253
NotSupported
  definition, 328
NotSupported transaction attribute, 440–441

O

ObjectMessage
  JMS message types, 279
Object registry, 18–19
Object-relational mapping technology, 19–20
ODBC, 174
One way authentication, 530
On Message method
  message-driven EJBs, 444
Open Database Connectivity (ODBC), 174
Optimizations
  writing, 418
Optimize test
  application
    capacity planning, 663
Oracle Sybase, 174
Out
  implicit object, 123–125
Output buffer
  cleared, 124–125
Output Items In Category method, 168
Output stream, 49–51
  closed/flushed, 49–51
Override default methods
  overriding default methods, 51–60

P

Packages
  building and deploying, 37–38

class, 116
JavaBeans, 135
unpacking, 37
Packaging process, 41
Page directives, 116–122
example, 119–121
Parallel message dispatch
message-driven EJBs, 439
Parallel message processing
message-driven EJB, 448–449
Parameter action, 133
Parameter Names method, 54–55, 125
Parameter Values, 125
Pass-by-value, 241
Passivation
EJB
BMP entity beans, 401
EJB container, 321
entity bean interface, 367
Password-based authentication, 470–471
WebLogic Server realm, 518
Path Info, 45
Path Translated, 45
Pentagon, 2
Perforce, 566
Performance and stress testing
infrastructure requirements
WebAuction application, 633–634
Performance implications
cross-network method calls, 245
Permissions, 473
Persistent
JMS message, 279–280
Plan for growth
capacity planning, 663
Platform security, 571
Plugin action
example, 133
Point-to-point messaging (PTP)
JMS, 260
vs. Pub/Sub APIs, 262
Pooling
bean
stateless session, 314
configuring, 314–315
database connection, 177–178
Pool size
JDBC, 234
POP3
web site, 452, 464
Post Create
EJB, 375
BMP, 398
Post Office Protocol Version 3 (POP3)
web site, 452, 464
POSTs, 51, 52
on form side, 52–54
on servlet side, 54–55

single class, 56
Prepared statements
JDBC specification, 222–224
Presentation layer, 578
JavaBeans, 579
Presentation logic, 14–16, 27
tasks handled by, 27
with WebLogic Server servlets, 27–105
Primary key class, 408–409
Principal
definition, 469
PrintStackTrace, 126
Processing paradigm
asynchronous, 21
Process planning
production development, 568
Production application
changes required, 588–590
Production deployment
designing, 544
Programmatic security
definition, 469
EJB, 333
example, 510–511
Web applications, 509–511
Programmatic security API, 509–510
Properties
JSP, 148
Properties file
JNDI, 248
Property tag, 148–149
Protection
choosing level, 103
Protocol, 45
PROVIDER_URL, 248
JNDI, 519
PTP, 260, 262
JMS, 260
vs. Pub/Sub APIs, 262
Public key encryption, 526, 527
Publish-and-subscribe messaging model
JMS, 260, 262
Pub/Sub APIs
vs. PTP, 260, 262

Q

Quality assurance tools, 566–567
Que model
JMS clients, 21
Queries
JDBC, 231
Query results
limiting, 589
Query String, 45
Queue example
running, 268–270
QueueReceiver's, 280
QuickTest product, 627

R

RAID, 206
RDBMS. *See* Relational Database management System (RDBMS)
Read-modify-write model
    entity EJBs, 427
Read-mostly entity beans
    designing, 421
        example, 421–422
Read-only entity beans, 420–421
Realm
    adding and retrieving users, 494–495
    setting up, 500
    WebLogic Server, 473–474
Realm API, 494
    authentication deploying
        example, 499–500
Rebind
    JNDI, 252
Receiver message-driven bean, 587–588
Redundant Array of Inexpensive Disks (RAID), 206
Refresh, 69
Relational Database management System (RDBMS)
    realm creation
        WebAuction application, 618–619, 623–624
    realm deploying
        example, 499–500
    security realm, 474
Release resources
    JDBC, 233
Releasing connections, 185
Remaining, 125
Remote Addr, 45
Remote calls
    vs. local calls, 245
Remote database operations, 102
Remote Host, 45
Remote interface
    EJB, 304
    serialization, 241
    using, 238–239
Remote method invocation (RMI), 18–20, 237–238
    distributed applications, 243–246
    interface, 431
    object
        clustered or nonclustered, 253
    programming model, 239–340
Remote User, 45
Remove Attribute method, 64, 97, 98
Remove method
    EJB, 374
        BMP, 398
Replicated bindings
    JNDI and clustering, 253
Replicated naming service, 251

Request Dispatcher, 99–101
Request handling
    JSP lifecycle, 114
    servlet, 43
Request methods
    complete list, 46
    grouping, 60
    implicit object, 125
Request object, 28, 44–49
    code
        obtaining, 46
Request response model, 15
Required
    definition, 328
Required transaction attribute
    error handling, 441–442
    transactions, 440
RequiresNew
    definition, 328
Resource, 98–99
Resource As Stream, 98–99
Resource manager references, 338–340
    advantages, 339–340
    declaring, 338
Resource operations
    JTA transactions, 210
Response content type
    setting, 49–51
Response methods
    send Error, 50
Response object, 28
Result sets, 182–183
    handling, 183–184
    Metadata, 226
    type, 182
RMI. *See* Remote method invocation (RMI)
Role
    definition, 468

S

Scalability, 105
Scheme, 46
Scripting elements
    JSP, 122–123, 127–129
Scriptlets
    JSP page, 128
    scripting elements, 123
Scripts
    create, 163
Secure
    cookies, 74
    logins, 55
    web applications
        creating, 474–493
    WebAuction application, 540
Secure application client
    EJB
        example, 520–523

SecureBean.java, 522
Secured EJB client
    deploying, 524–525
Secure sockets layer (SSL). *See* SSL
Security, 22
    application deployment, 561–562
    choosing level, 103
    configure
        WebAuction application, 618
    design
        WebLogic Server deployment, 571
    JNDI, 250
    realm, 473–474
    services
        how many, 511
Security authentication
    JNDI, 519
Security credentials
    JNDI, 519
Security principal
    JNDI, 519
Security profile
    capacity planning, 653–654
Segue Software, 567
Selection performance
    JMS, 295
Select methods
    EJB-QL, 389–393
Send Error
    response methods, 50
SendRedirect method, 50, 81
Serializable interface, 137, 240–241
Serialization, 240–243
Server hardware
    capacity planning, 650, 653–655
Server Name, 45
Server Port, 45
Server-side business logic
    accessing, 578–579
Service method
    servlet, 43, 44–49, 189
Servlet/JSP
    URL encoding methods, 76
Servlets, 14–15, 27
    anatomy, 31–32
    API, 70
    basic, 32–40
        example, 32–33
    best practices, 104–105
    building
        to use sessions, 66–68
    class
        importing and declaring, 56
    compiling, 38
    Context, 95–98
        example, 96–97
        setting and getting attributes, 96–97
    creating, 46

default methods, 51
deploying
    in WebLogic Server, 34–40
description, 28
developing, 31–84
end of service, 43–44
execution
    output, 48
extending, 56–60
HTTP
    core features, 15
    use of, 29
initialization, 43
Java, 14–15
JSP, 30–31, 161
lifecycle, 42–44
loading and instantiating, 43
options when building, 43
output, 69
overriding default methods, 51–60
PAI, 29
Path, 45
request handling, 43
request object
    accessing data, 44
requests
    handling, 44–49
response
    generating, 49–51
sessions
    vs. cookies, 71–72
    deploying, 70
single-threaded, 43
specification, 61–64
use of, 29
WebLogic Server, 15, 28
    clustering, 101–103
Session
    implicit object, 126
    inactivity and time, 65
    interface, 431
    invalidating, 65
    JMS, 262
    recognizing, 62–63
    scope, 64–66
    and servlets example, 66–70
Session based information
    capacity planning, 655
Session beans, 20
    stateful and stateless, 302
    transactions, 326–331
Session class
    Java mail, 453
Session data
    storing and accessing, 63
Session enterprise JavaBeans
    cars example, 342–354
Session identification, 61–64

Session information
    options, 101–102
Session object
    accessing, 62
    information stores, 62
Session protection
    choosing level, 103
Session protection performance implications, 102–103
Session servlet
    deploying, 70
Session state handling, 102
Session Synchronization interface, 329
Session tag
    JSP, 118
Session tracking
    methods, 60
SetAttribute, 64, 98
SetBillingAddress, 334
SetComment
    cookies, 73
Set date header, 50
SetEntityContext method
    BMP, 396–397
Set Header, 51
SetIntHeader, 51
SetMaxAge, 73
SetMaxInactiveInterval, 66
SetSecure
    cookies, 74
SetValue
    cookies, 74
Simple Mail Transfer Protocol (SMTP), 237, 451
    web site, 464
Single-threaded JSPs, 114
Single-threaded servlets, 43
SingleThreadModel, 43
Single thread model, 105
Skeleton, 238
SMTP, 237, 451, 464
Sockets, 50
    ways to close, 34
Spacing
    care, 163
SQL. See Structured query language (SQL)
SSL, 472
SSL encryption, 529
SSL protocol aggregates
    encryption technologies, 529
SSL security
    application clients, 536–537
    example, 531–535
        deploying, 532–533
    Web clients, 531
Stack trace
    error, 126
Staging
    application deployment process, 569–570

Standard actions, 130
Standard encryption, 526
Stateful beans, 20
    concurrency, 325
Stateful programming model, 318
Stateful session beans
    avoidance, 359–360
    updates, 324
Stateful session EJB, 318–326
    activation, 320
    clustering, 322–325
    creating, 320
    failover, 324–325
    lifecycle, 319–322
    passivation, 320
    removing, 320
    replication, 323
    web applications, 326
Stateless beans, 20
Stateless programming model, 312, 313–315
Stateless protocol, 60
Stateless session
    bean
        clustering, 315–317
        vs. entity beans, 427–428
        lifecycle, 313–314
        member variables, 317
    EJB, 312–317
        example, 303–305
Statement class, 182
Statements
    release, 185
Store method
    EJB, 374
        BMP, 400
StreamMessage
    JMS message types, 279
Stress and performance testing
    WebAuction application, 631–635
        with example, 634–635
        methodology, 631–633
        results, 636
Stress testing
    production deployment, 570
Structured query language (SQL), 17
    designing and coding database access, 173–235
    error handling, 224–226
    errors handling, 224–226
    handling, 225–226
    transactions, 206
Stub, 238
Sun Microsystems' J2EE. See J2EE
Supports
    definition, 328
Symantec Java compiler, 598
Symmetric key encryption, 526
    SSL, 529
Synchronous

vs. asynchronous receivers, 280–281
Synchronous message consumer
    JMS, 266–267
    JMS initialization code, 271

T

Tables
    adding and dropping, 204–205
Tag libraries, 16, 130
    to business logic interface, 579–581
    Descriptor, 16
    handler
        example, 157–158
        requirements, 155–156
        simplified lifecycle, 156–158
    running
        WebLogic server, 159
Templates, 163
Temporary cookies, 61
Temporary destinations, 284
TemporaryQueue, 284
TemporaryTopic, 284
Test development
    application deployment process, 569
Testing. *See also* Functional testing; Load test
    application deployment process, 569–570
    capacity planning
        configuration, 656
        optimize, 663
    stress
        production deployment, 570
    URL rewriting, 75
    WebAuction application, 624–629
        performance and stress, 631–635
TextMessage
    JMS message types, 279
Threads
    multiplexing, 640
Threadsafe
    JSP page, 118
Timeout interval
    for sessions, 64–66
TLD, 154–155
    description, 154
Topic-based model
    JMS, 21
TopicReceiver's, 280
Transacted sessions
    vs. JTA transactions, 296–297
Transactions, 205–208
    demarcation
        CMP engine, 587–588
    EJB, 356–359
        container-managed *vs.* bean managed, 358
        error handling, 358
    establishing
        starting, 209–210
        WebLogic Server JTA, 209–210

flow
    WebAuction applications, 587–588
isolation levels, 220–221
JDBC, 234
JMS, 287–289
message-driven beans, 440–442
session beans, 326–331
setting isolation levels, 221–222
span
    JDBC, 235
SQL, 206
support
    by JDBC and JTA, 16–18
WebAuction
    JDBC, 235
WebLogic server JDBC, 207–208
Transport class
    mail protocol, 456
Two-phase commit engine, 18
    WebLogic server, 208
Two-phase commit protocol
    distributed transactions, 219
Two-way authentication, 530

U

Unbind method
    JNDI, 249
Uniform resource locator (URL). *See* URL
Unmarshaling, 238
Unreliable network
    handling, 244
Updates
    JDBC, 232
URL, 28
URL encoding methods
    Servlet/JSP, 76
URL rewriting
    activate and use, 164
    in applications, 75
    defined, 60
    testing, 75
UseBean tag, 135
    attributes, 135–136
User
    definition, 468
    registration form, 496
    tracking, 72
Utility methods
    WebAuction beans, 581

V

Value
    cookies, 74
ValueBound, 70
ValueHolder, 586
Value objects
    Java Beans, 423–424
ValueUnBound, 70

VeriSign, 529, 530
Versioning lines, 568
Versioning systems
    application deployment, 565–566
View
    MVC components, 161
View request servlet
    deploying, 49
Void absolute, 184
Void flush
    cleared, 124–125

W

WAP devices, 61
Web application, 41–42
    creating secure, 474–493
    declarative security, 475–476
    deployment
        details, 558–559
    description, 84–85
    MVC, 162
    package, 84
    programmatic security, 509–511
    resources, 98–99
Web archive organization, 85
WebAuction, 23–24
    application architecture and design, 575
    assembling application components, 591–596
    deploying
        another database, 621–624
    design goals, 576
    interfaces, 578–579
    internationalizing, 590
    security, 582–583
    subsystems, 576–577
WebAuction application, 5, 27, 575–647
    adding e-mail capability, 463–464
    build and deploy, 621
    deploying, 599–621
    JSP, 165
    quick deployment, 596–599
    securing, 540
    technology requirements, 23–24
    testing, 624–629
WebAuction beans
    utility methods, 581
WebAuction business logic layer, 580
WebAuction code, 600
    browsing, 170
WebAuction Home page, 598
WebAuction stateless session bean, 586–587
Web authorization methods
    deployment descriptor, 506–509
Web browser login dialog, 471
Web clients
    SSL security, 531
Web deployment
    commercial Web server, 546

DMZ, 548–550
firewalls, 548–550
standard configuration, 545
WebLogic Server, 545
WebLogic Server clustering, 550–557
Web form
    building, 52–53
Web-Gain studio
    TLD, 155
WEB-INF directory, 42
Web input form, 54
WebLogic deployment scenarios, 544–548
WebLogic RMI optimizations, 246
WebLogic Server, 27
    application deployment descriptors
        creating, 481–484
    certificate authority, 527
    clustering
        mixed deployment, 563
        servlets, 101–103
        Web deployment, 550–557
    configuration, 2
    console mail option, 461
    container, 2, 3
    distributed deployment support, 22–23
    distributed transactions, 218–224
    ejb-jar.xml, 522
    Entity EJBs, 19–20
    install, 600
    JAAS authentication, 512, 513–515
    JavaBeans, 16
    JDBC, 16–17, 173–208
        application functionality, 17
        transactions, 207–208
    J2EE
        implementation and extension, 543
    JNDI
        application client security, 517–526
        based authentication, 518
    JSP, 29–31, 107–108
    JTA
        example, 212–215
        using, 209–212
    message-driven beans, 21
    platform
        description, 3
    realm, 538
        new user example, 495–506
        password-based authentication, 518
    security
        best practices, 537
        realms, 473–474
        technologies, 539
    servlets, 15, 28
        presentation logic, 27–105
    Session EJBs, 20
    SSL, 525, 530
    strengths, 4

WebAuction application, 600

as Web server, 559

xml, 42

Web services

DMZ, 559

Web sessions, 60–70

Web tier

EJB, 422

Web.xml, 42, 89–95

deployment descriptor, 86, 143

samples, 90–94

Welcome page

creating, 478–480

Widget bean, 335

Widgets, 335

Wireless devices, 61

Wrapper

session beans

entity beans, 422–423

Writing deployment descriptors

message-driven EJBs, 434–438

Writing get methods, 368

Writing set methods, 368

WYSIWYG

vs. JSP, 108

X

XA-compliant resources

JTA, 219

XA specification, 208

XML

application

writing, 592

files, 42

Message

JMS message types, 279

Web, 42, 89–95, 143

WebLogic Server, 42, 522

Web site, 42

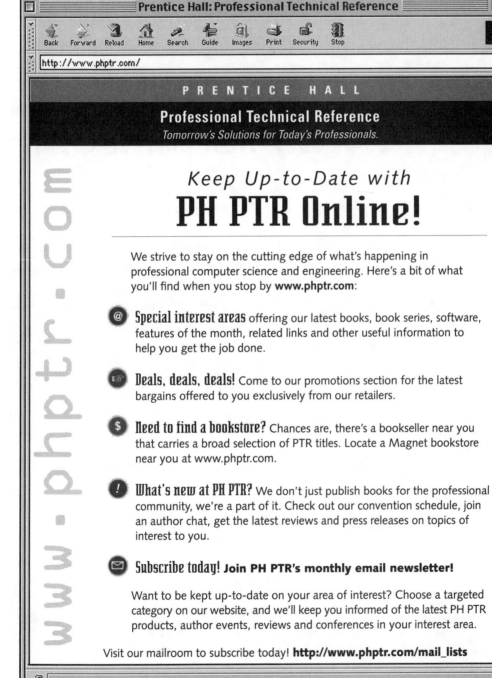

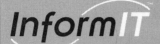

About the CD

Installation Information:

Important information about installing the evaluation copy of BEA WebLogic Server 6.0

In order to install BEA WebLogic Server 6.0, you must REGISTER on the BEA Website to obtain your 30-day evaluation software license keys.

Once you've registered, you will immediately be sent an email with the relevant instructions.

Use the following URL to register: http://www.bea.com/eval/j2eeapps/

After you register, you will be sent a password to use in the BEA Developers Center. This password gives you access to documentation and technical support for your use during the evaluation period.

INSTALLING BEA WebLogic Server

(1) Install BEA WebLogic Server ("WLS") by double-clicking on the executable /weblogic/weblogic600_win.exe. When the installation wizard appears, accept the default choices.

You MUST install WebLogic Server on a root directory named "wlserver6.0" in order to use the code samples and scripts for the book.

(2) After WebLogic Server is installed, install the EJB2.0 upgrade by copying the ejb2.0.jar archive (supplied) to the wlserver6.0/lib directory. Further information about this upgrade appears in the file "README-EJB20.html".

Contents of the CD

Each chapter contains pointers to the relevant sample code and scripts for the examples in that chapter.

Chapter 14 describes, step by step, how to build the WebAuction sample application.

IMPORTANT NOTE on the examples: after copying over example files, you must CHANGE THE PERMISSIONS from read-only to full permissions, for all files and folders. In Windows 2000, you can change permissions for all files and folders by modifying the Properties of a top-level folder.

Directories in the CD:

/examples --> book examples

/webauction --> webauction sample application

/webauction/webauction.zip --> complete webauction package

/weblogic --> BEA WebLogic Server 6.0 software

/weblogic/ejb20.jar --> EJB 2.0 Upgrade for WLS

/weblogic/weblogic600_win.exe --> WLS 6.0

System Requirements

Platforms: Windows 95/98/NT/2000

See the platform support page, which is kept up to date with all the system requirements and can be found at:

http://edocs.bea.com/wls/platforms/index.html

Use of the *J2EE Applications and BEA WebLogic Server* CD-ROM is subject to the terms of the License Agreement following the index of this book.

Technical Support

Prentice Hall does not offer technical support for this software. If there is a problem with the CD, however, you may obtain a replacement CD by emailing a description of the problem. Send your email to:

`disc_exchange@prenhall.com`